A Manual of Budhism, in Its Modern Development

Robert Spence Hardy

Nabu Public Domain Reprints:

You are holding a reproduction of an original work published before 1923 that is in the public domain in the United States of America, and possibly other countries. You may freely copy and distribute this work as no entity (individual or corporate) has a copyright on the body of the work. This book may contain prior copyright references, and library stamps (as most of these works were scanned from library copies). These have been scanned and retained as part of the historical artifact.

This book may have occasional imperfections such as missing or blurred pages, poor pictures, errant marks, etc. that were either part of the original artifact, or were introduced by the scanning process. We believe this work is culturally important, and despite the imperfections, have elected to bring it back into print as part of our continuing commitment to the preservation of printed works worldwide. We appreciate your understanding of the imperfections in the preservation process, and hope you enjoy this valuable book.

A MANUAL OF BUDHISM.

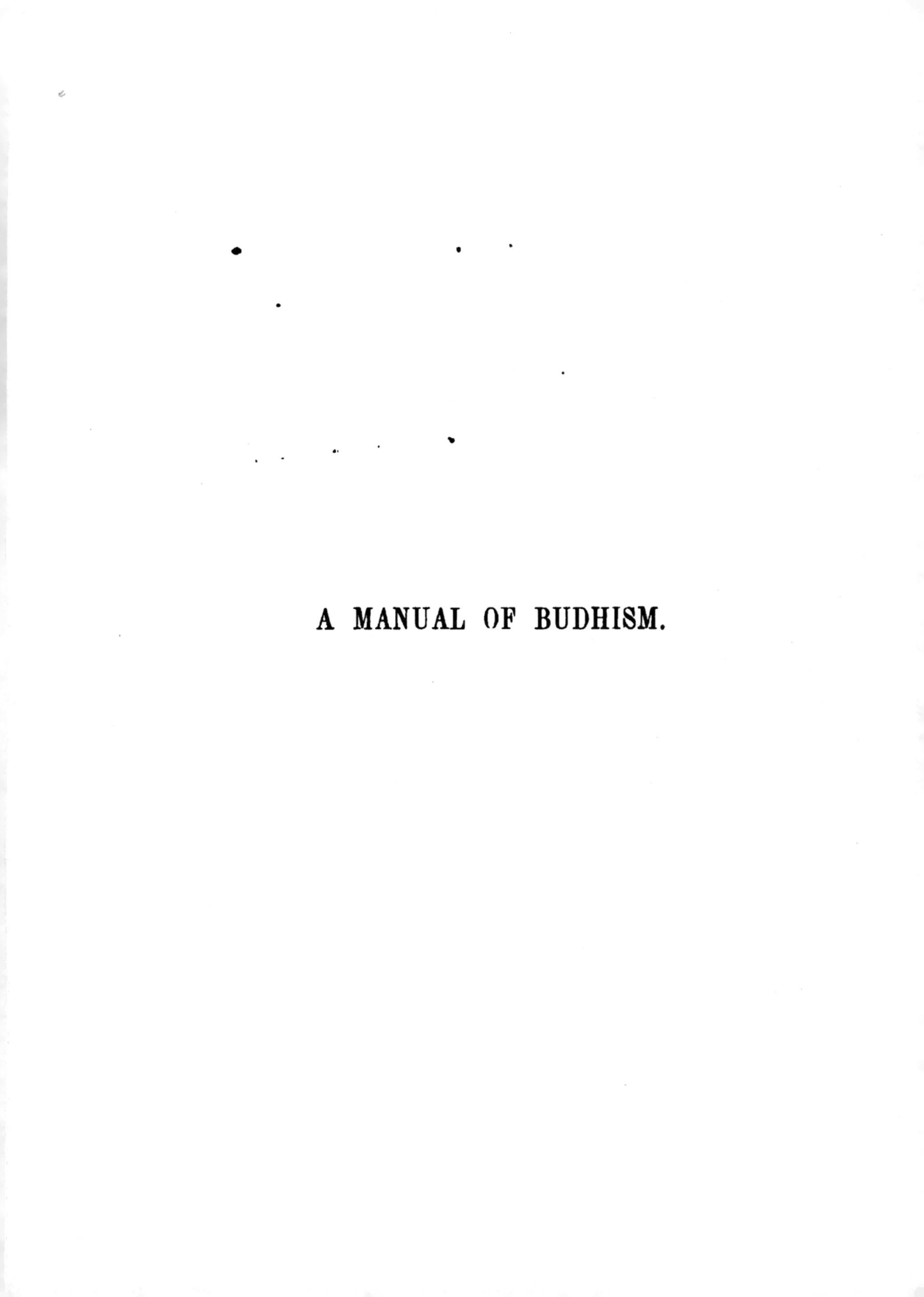

A

MANUAL OF BUDHISM,

IN ITS MODERN DEVELOPMENT;

TRANSLATED FROM SINGHALESE MSS.

BY R. SPENCE HARDY,
AUTHOR OF "EASTERN MONACHISM," "DEWA-DHARMA-DARPANAYA," ETC.

SECOND EDITION.

WILLIAMS AND NORGATE,
14, HENRIETTA STREET, COVENT GARDEN, LONDON:
AND 20, SOUTH FREDERICK STREET, EDINBURGH.
1880.

PUBLISHERS' NOTICE.

THE present volume having been out of print for some time, the demand for it, however, still being so great that copies have been sold in public sales for several pounds, the publishers have been induced to reprint a small edition of the work. They have taken the opportunity of correcting a few errors, and adding a much more complete Index, which has been kindly compiled by Dr. Frankfurter of Berlin, who is pursuing Pali studies in London. In every other respect the present is an exact reproduction of the first edition.

March, 1880.

PREFACE.

In the preparation of the present Manual, I have kept one object steadily in view. It has been my simple aim, to answer the question, "What is Budhism, as it is now professed by its myriads of votaries?" A deep interest in the subject; intense application; honesty of purpose; a long residence in a country where the system is professed; a daily use of the language from which I have principally translated; and constancy of intercourse with the sramana priests; have been my personal advantages to aid me in the undertaking. In nearly all other respects, the circumstances in which I have been placed have been unfavourable. Throughout the whole course of my investigations, I have had to exercise a laborious ministry; with the exception of one brief interval, I have been at a distance from any public library; I have received no assistance from any society, literary or religious, though that assistance has not been unasked; my acquaintance with the lore of Europe is limited; and I have had little or no access to recent publications on subjects of Asiatic literature. I have been charged by my friends, with great temerity in risking, unaided, the publication of the present work; but the same spirit that animated me to pursue my task, year after year, in the solitude of an eastern village, has urged me onward, to complete my undertaking, in the issue of the Manual now sent forth, from a more privileged residence in my native land.

My previous work, on Eastern Monachism, describes the discipline, rites, and present circumstances of the Budhist priesthood. All the reviewers who have noticed it, have spoken of it in favourable terms; and I am sincerely grateful for the encouragement that, from this source, I have received. To avoid a seeming egotism, in quoting from myself, I have restricted to the Index all reference to its pages. Inadvertently, a few sentences that have appeared in it, are inserted in the Manual. By a perusal of both these works, the student will be prepared to understand the general outline of the system; as, although its literature is elaborate, its elementary principles are few.

The native authors are not studious of method; and it is a formidable task to reduce their materials to order. The arrangement I have adopted may be open to objection; but it must be remembered, that this is the first attempt to form an analysis of the deeds and doctrines attributed to Gótama. In the first two chapters I have described the various worlds of the universe; their cycles of decay and renovation; their terrene continents; their abodes celestial; their places of torment; and the men, the divinities, the demons, and the other orders of being, by whom they are severally inhabited. It is necessary to understand these matters, or the sequel will be an impenetrable mystery. The third chapter is devoted to an account of the origin of the present race of men, with a more extended description of the teachings of Gótama and his disciples on the subject of caste. He was preceded by other Budhas, in "numbers without number," some of whose acts are detailed in the fourth chapter. Gótama became a Bódhisat, or a candidate for the Budhaship, myriads of ages before his birth as a prince in Magadha; and in the fifth chapter we have his history during some of these previous states of existence. This is followed by a notice of his ancestors, tracing his lineage, by the race of the sun, from the first king. In the legends of his life, we learn the circumstances of his birth; the promise of his youth, his marriage, and his subsequent abandonment of the world; his contest with the powers of evil; the attainment of the Budhaship, by which he received the supremacy of the universe, with unlimited power to do or to know; his first converts; his principal disciples; the most celebrated of his acts during a ministry of forty-five years; the distribution of his relics; and a detail of his dignities, virtues, and powers. The concluding chapters present a compendium of the ontology and ethics of Budhism, as they are understood by the modern priesthood, and now taught to the people.

In confining myself, almost exclusively, to translation, I have chosen the humblest form in which to reappear as an author. I might have written an extended essay upon the system, as it presents a rich mine, comparatively unexplored; or have attempted to make the subject popular, by leaving out its extravagances, and weaving its more interesting portions into a continued narrative; but neither of these modes would have fulfilled my intention. They would have enabled me only to give expression to an opinion; when I wish to present an authority. I have generally refrained from comment; but in order thereto, have had to lay aside matter that has cost me much thought in its preparation.

The attentive reader will observe numerous discrepancies. These occur, in some instances, between one author and another; and in others between one statement and another of the same author. I am not aware that I have omitted any great feature of the system; unless it be, that I have not given sufficient prominence to the statements of my authorities on the anatomy of the body, and to their reflections on the offensive accompaniments of death. It is probable that a careful review of insulated portions of the work will discover errors in my translation; as in much of my labour I have had no predecessor; but I have never wilfully perverted any statement, and have taken all practicable methods to secure the utmost accuracy. In the ontological terms I have usually adopted the nomenclature of the Rev. D. J. Gogerly, of the Wesleyan Mission in Ceylon. It is greatly to be regretted that the writings of that gentleman are so limited; as they are an invaluable treasure to the student of Budhism.

Not without some emotion, and with sincere humility on account of the imperfections of my work, I now conclude my oriental researches. They were commenced in my youth; more than a quarter of a century has rolled over during their progress; and they have been constantly carried on, with more or less earnestness, until the present moment. By the messengers of the cross, who may succeed me in the field in which it was once my privilege to labour, this Manual will be received, I doubt not, as a boon; as it will enable them more readily to understand the system they are endeavouring to supersede, by the establishment of the Truth. I see before me, looming in the distance, a glorious vision, in which the lands of the east are presented in majesty; happy, holy, and free. I may not; I dare not, attempt to describe it; but it is the joy of my existence to have been an instrument, in a degree however feeble, to bring about this grand consummation. And now, my book, we part; but it shall not be without a fervent prayer that God may speed thee.

CONTENTS.

	PAGE
PREFACE	vi

CHAPTER I.
THE SYSTEM OF THE UNIVERSE 1

CHAPTER II.
THE VARIOUS ORDERS OF SENTIENT EXISTENCE 37

CHAPTER III.
THE PRIMITIVE INHABITANTS OF THE EARTH; THEIR FALL FROM PURITY; AND THEIR DIVISION INTO FOUR CASTES   64

CHAPTER IV.
THE BUDHAS WHO PRECEDED GÓTAMA 88

CHAPTER V.
GÓTAMA BÓDHISAT; HIS VIRTUES AND STATES OF BEING . 100

CHAPTER VI.
THE ANCESTORS OF GÓTAMA BUDHA 128

CHAPTER VII.

The Legendary Life of Gótama Budha 141

CHAPTER VIII.

The Dignity, Virtues, and Powers of Budha 372

CHAPTER IX.

The Ontology of Budhism 402

CHAPTER X.

The Ethics of Budhism 477

A MANUAL OF BUDHISM.

I. THE SYSTEM OF THE UNIVERSE.

I. THE NUMBER CALLED AN ASANKYA, AND THE VARIOUS KINDS OF CYCLES CALLED KALPAS.—II. THE CLUSTERS OF WORLDS CALLED SAKWALAS.—III. THE WORLDS, MOUNTAINS, SEAS, AND CONTINENTS, CONNECTED WITH THE EARTH.—IV. THE SUN, MOON, AND PLANETS.—V. THE DÉWA-LÓKAS, BRAHMA-LÓKAS, AND PLACES OF SUFFERING.—VI. THE PERIODICAL DESTRUCTION AND RENOVATION OF THE UNIVERSE.

I. THE cycles of chronology are reckoned by asankyas (1); a word that conveys the idea of innumerable, incalculable, from *a*, negative, and *sankya*, number, that of which the sum or quantity can be determined.

The number of the years to which the life of man is extended never remains at one stay. It is always on the increase or undergoing a gradual diminution; but it never exceeds an asankya in length, and never diminishes to less than ten years; and the progress of the change is so slow as to be imperceptible, except after long intervals of time. A decrease in the age of man is attended by a correspondent deterioration in his stature, intellect, and morals.

From the time that man's age increases from ten years to an asankya, and again decreases from an asankya to ten years, is an antah-kalpa (2). Eighty antah-kalpas make a mahakalpa. There is a species of cloth, fabricated at Benares, of the cotton that is unequalled in the delicacy of its fibre. Its worth, previous to being used, is unspeakable; after it has been used, it is worth 30,000 níla-karshas (of the value of 20 or 30 small silver coins); and even when old, it is worth 12,000 karshas. Were a man to take a piece of cloth of this most delicate texture, and therewith to touch, in the slightest possible manner, once in a hundred years, a solid rock, free from earth, sixteen miles high, and as many broad, the time would come when it would be worn down, by this imperceptible trituration, to the size of a mung, or undu seed. This period would be immense in its duration; but it has been declared by Budha that it would not be equal to a maha-kalpa.

II. There are innumerable systems of worlds; each system having its own earth, sun, moon, &c. (3). The space to which the light of one sun or moon extends is called a sakwala. Each sakwala includes an earth, with its continents, islands, and oceans, and a mountain in the centre called Maha Méru; as well as a series of hells and heavens, the latter being divided into déwa-lókas and brahma-lókas. The sakwalas are scattered throughout space, in sections of three and three. All the sakwalas in one section touch each other, and in the space between the three is the Lókántarika hell. Each sakwala is surrounded by a circular wall of rock, called the sakwala-gala.

Were a high wall to be erected around the space occupied by a hundred thousand kelas of sakwalas (each kela being ten millions), reaching to the highest of the heavens, and the whole space filled with mustard seeds, a rishi might take these seeds, and looking towards any of the cardinal points, throw a single seed towards each sakwala, until the whole of the seeds were exhausted; but though there would be no more seeds, there would still be more sakwalas, in the same direction, to which no seed had been thrown, without reckoning the sakwalas in the three other points.

The sakwala systems are divided into three classes:—1. Wisayak-sétra, the systems that appear to Budha. 2. Agnyá-sétra, the systems, a hundred thousand kelas in number, that receive the ordinances of Budha, or to which the exercise of his authority extends. 3. Jammak-sétra, the systems, ten thousand in number, in which a Budha may be born (between the birth in which he becomes a claimant for the Budhaship, or a Bódhisat, and the birth in which he attains the supremacy), or in which the appearance of a Budha is known, and to which the power of pirit, or priestly exorcism, extends.

There are three other sections into which each sakwala is divided:—1. Arúpawachara, the lókas, or worlds, in which there is no perceptible form. 2. Rúpawachara, the worlds in which there is form, but no sensual enjoyment. 3. Kámáwachara, the worlds in which there is form, with sensual enjoyment.

Every part of each sakwala is included in one or other of the following divisions:—1. Satwa-lóka; the world of sentient being. 2. Awakása-lóka; the world of space, the empty void, the far-extended vacuum. 3. Sanskára-lóka, the material world, including trees, rocks, &c.

III. At the base of each sakwala is the vacuum called Ajatákása, above which is the Wá-polowa, or world of wind, or air, 960 yojanas in thickness; the world of air supports the Jala-polowa, or world of water, 480,000 yojanas in thickness; and immediately above the world of water is the Maha-polowa, or the great earth, 240,000 yojanas in thickness, which is composed of two superior strata, viz., the Sala, or Gal-polowa, consisting of hard rock, and the Pas-polowa, consisting of soft mould, each of which is 120,000 yojanas in thickness. The under surface of the earth is composed of a nutritious substance like virgin honey. In the centre of the earth is the mountain called Maha Méru (4), which, from its base to its summit, is 168,000 yojanas in height. On its top is the déwa-loka called Tawutisá, of which Sekra is the regent, or chief. Between Maha Méru and the rocks at the extreme circumference of the earth are seven concentric circles of rocks (5), each circle diminishing in height as it increases in extent. Between the different circles of rocks there are seas (6), the waters of which gradually decrease in depth, from Maha Méru to the outermost circle, near which they are only one inch. In the waters of these seas there are various species of fish, some of which are many thousands of miles in size.

In each earth there are four dwípas, or continents, the inhabitants of which have faces of the same shape as the continent in which they are born. 1. Uturukurudiwayina (7), in shape like a square seat, and 8,000 yojanas in extent, on the north of Maha Méru. 2. Púrwawidésa, in shape like a half-moon, and 7,000 yojanas in extent, on the east of Maha Méru. 3. Aparagódána, in shape like a round mirror, and 7,000 yojanas in extent, on the west of Maha Méru. 4. Jambudwípa, three-sided, or angular, and 10,000 yojanas in extent, on the south of Maha Méru. Of these 10,000 yojanas, 4,000 are covered by the ocean, 3,000 by the forest (8), of Himála (the range of the Himalayan mountains), and 3,000 are inhabited by men.

The sakwala in which Gótama appeared is called magul, festive, or joyous, because it is the only one in which a supreme Budha is ever born; and for the same reason, the most sacred continent in this sakwala is Jambudwípa. In the centre of this continent is the circle called Bódhi-mandala, which is, as it were, its navel; and this circle is so called because it contains the bódha, or bó-tree, under which Gótama became a Budha.

In the earlier ages, there were 199,000 kingdoms in Jambudwípa; in the middle ages, at one time, 84,000, and at another, 63,000; and in more recent ages about a hundred. In the time of Gótama Budha this continent contained 9,600,000 towns, 9,900,000 seaports, and 56 treasure cities.

IV. The sun and moon continually move through the heavens in three paths, accompanied by the stars that are in the same division of the sky (9). The sun gives light to the whole of the four continents, but not at the same time. Thus, when it rises in Jambudwípa, it is in the zenith to the inhabitants of Púrwawidésa, whilst at the same time it is setting in Uturukuru, and it is midnight in Aparagódána. Again, when the sun rises in Aparagódána, it is mid-day in Jambudwípa, sunset in Púrwawidésa, and midnight in Uturukuru. When the sun, moon, and stars go to the other side of the circle of rocks nearest to Maha Méru, called Yugandhara, they appear to set to the inhabitants of Jambudwípa. The sun and moon are at regular intervals seized by the asúrs Ráhu and Kétu; and these periods are called grahanas, or seizures (eclipses). The declination of the sun is caused by its gradually passing once in each year, from Maha Méru to the extreme circumference of the sakwala, and from the extreme circumference to Maha Méru.

V. There are six déwa-lókas (worlds in which there is the enjoyment of happiness), and sixteen brahma-lókas (in which the enjoyment is of a more intellectual character, gradually verging towards supreme tranquillity and utter unconsciousness) (10). Under the rock Maha Méru is the residence of the asúrs. The principal narakas (places of suffering) are eight in number (11).

VI. The earth, inhabited by men, with the various continents, lókas, and sakwalas connected with it, is subject alternately to destruction and renovation, in a series of revolutions, to which no beginning, no end, can be discovered. Thus it ever was; thus it will be, ever.

There are three modes of destruction. The sakwalas are destroyed seven times by fire, and the eighth time by water. Every sixty-fourth destruction is by wind.

When the destruction is by the agency of fire, from the period at which the fire begins to burn to the time when the destruction is complete, and the fire entirely burnt out, there are 20 antah-kalpas. This period is called a sangwartta-asankya-kalpa.

From the period at which the fire ceases to burn to the falling of the great rain (12) by which the future world is to be formed, there are 20 antah-kalpas. This period is called a sangwarttastáyi-asankya-kalpa.

From the first falling of the seminal rain to the formation of the sun, moon, rocks, oceans, &c., there are 20 antah-kalpas. This period is called a wiwartta-asankya-kalpa.

After the elapse of 20 antah-kalpas more, a great rain begins to fall; and this period is called a wiwarttastáyi-asankya-kalpa.

Thus there are four great cycles of mundane revolution: —1. Of destruction (as the names given to the four asankya-kalpas respectively signify). 2. Of the continuance of destruction. 3. Of formation. 4. Of the continuance of formation. These four asankya-kalpas make a maha-kalpa.

---

1. *An Asankya.*

Were all the mould of which the Great Earth is composed to be counted in molecules the size of the seed called tibbatu; or all the water of the four great oceans, in portions diminutive as the raindrop; the result would be a number of vast extent; but even this great accumulation would be utterly inadequate to set forth the years in an asankya. All the matter in all worlds would fail as a medium by which to exhibit its greatness, and the most skilful arithmeticians are unable rightly to comprehend it; but some idea of its magnitude may be gained from the following scale of numeration.*

10 decenniums . . make . .	1 hundred.
10 hundreds	1 thousand.
100 thousands	1 laksha.
100 lakshas	1 kóti, or kela.
100 lahshas of kótis.	1 prakóti.
1 kóti of prakótis.	1 kótiprakóti
1 ,, kótiprakótis	1 nahuta.
1 ,, nahutas	1 ninnahuta.
1 ,, ninnahutas	1 hutanahuta.
1 ,, hutanahutas	1 khamba.
1 ,, khambas	1 wiskhamba.
1 ,, wiskhambas	1 ababa.
1 ,, ababas	1 attata.
1 ,, attatas	1 ahaha.

* Every sentence that appears in the smaller type is translated from some Singhalese MS.; but as the native works abound with repetitions from each other, in the same paragraph I have sometimes culled a portion from several different authors. I have not thought it necessary, in many instances, to insert the name of my authority. To have done so would have been to crowd my pages with names that to the mass of my readers would be of no benefit, as they are not able to refer to them to test the truthfulness of my renderings. It must be understood that where no authority is given the statement appears in different works.

I. THE SYSTEM OF THE UNIVERSE.

1 kóti of ahahas	. . make	. .	1 kumuda.
1 „	kumudas	. . . .	1 gandhika.
1 „	gandhikas	. . . .	1 utpala.
1 „	utpalas	. . . .	1 pundaríka.
1 „	pundaríkas	. . . .	1 paduma.
1 „	padumas	. . . .	1 katha.
1 „	kathas	. . . .	1 maha katha.
1 „	maha kathas	. . . .	1 asankya.*

2. *The Kalpas.*

From the time that the age of man increases from ten years[†] to an asankya, and decreases from an asankya to ten years, is an antah-kalpa. Were the surface of the earth to increase in elevation at the rate of one inch in a thousand years, and the process to continue in the same proportion, the elevation would extend to twenty-eight miles before the antah-kalpa would be concluded.

Twenty antah-kalpas make an asankya-kalpa.

Four asankya-kalpas make a maha-kalpa.

To one antah-kalpa there are eight yugas, four of which are called utsarppani and four arppani. The four utsarppani yugas are progressive, and are therefore called úrdhamukha; but the four arppani are retrograde, and are therefore called adhómukha. From the period in which men live ten years, to that in which they live an asankya, is an úrdhamukha yuga; and from the period in which they live an asankya, to that in which they live ten years, is an adhómukha yuga. The four utsarppani yugas are called kali, dwápara, tréta and krita, respectively; and the four arppani yugas, krita, tréta, dwápara, and kali. Were the krita yuga divided into four parts, the whole four would be good; were the tréta divided in the same way, three would be good; were the dwápara thus divided, two would be good; and were the kali thus divided, only

---

* In other lists that I have seen, the numbers are differently arranged, and in some instances are expressed by different terms; but the numerical power of the result is always the same. "If for three years it should rain incessantly over the whole surface of this earth (or sakwala), the number of drops of rain falling in such a space and time, although far exceeding human conception, would only equal the number of years in an asankya."—Buchanan, Asiatic Researches, vi. The asankya is a unit with 140 cyphers.—Csoma Körösi, As. Res. xx. The brahmans have a number called a parárddha, which is represented by 15 (and sometimes 18) places of figures.

† "In the Kali age a man will be grey when he is twelve; and no one will exceed twenty years of life."—Wilson's Vishnu Purána.

one would be good.* It would be as great a miracle for a supreme Budha to be born in a kali yuga, as for a beautiful and sweet-scented lotus to blow amidst the flames of hell.

There are súnya and asúnya kalpas. It is only in the asúnya kalpas that the Budhas appear; they are distinguished by the names of sára, manda, wara, sáramanda, and bhadra kalpas. When one Budha is born in a kalpa, it is called sára; when two, it is called manda; when three, wara; when four, sáramanda; and when five, bhadra. It is only after very long intervals that the bhadra kalpa occurs.†

3. *The Sakwalas.*

One thousand sakwalas are called sahasrí-lókadhátu. Ten lacs of sakwalas are called madyama-lókadhátu. One hundred kelas of sakwalas are called maha-sahasrí-lókadhátu.

That space is infinite; that the beings inhabiting it are infinite: and that the sakwalas are infinite,‡ is known to Budha, and by him alone is it perceived.§

* These periods correspond with the yugs of the Brahmans, of which the satya yug comprehends 1,728,000 years; the tréta, 1,296,000 years; the dwapar, 164,000 years; and the kali, 432,000 years. The year 1852 is the 4936th year of the kali yug, and the 3,892,936th year of the kalpa. But though the two systems agree as to the order and character of the yugs, there is an essential difference in their duration. It has been remarked that these yugs correspond, in number, succession, and character, with the golden, silver, brazen, and iron ages of the Greek and Roman mythologists.

† The brahmanical kalpa, equal to the whole period of the four yugs, consists of four thousand three hundred and twenty millions of solar years, which is a day of Brahma; and his night has the same duration. Three hundred and sixty of these days and nights compose a year of Brahma, and a hundred of these years constitute his life, which therefore exceeds in length three hundred billions of solar years. This system originates in the descending arithmetical progression of 4, 3, 2, and 1, according to the notion of diminishing virtue in the several ages, applied to a circle of 12,000 divine years, each of which is equal to 360 years of mortals; and 12,000 multiplied by 360 is equal to 4,320,000.—Professor H. H. Wilson. The chronology of Manetho appears to have been constructed upon similar principles, as his dynasties are so arranged as to fill up an exact number of Sothaic circles, or per ods of the star Sirius, each comprehending 1460 Julian, or 1461 Egyptian years.—Boeckh's Manetho: Grote's History of Greece, iii. 448.

‡ The doctrine of an infinity of worlds was taught in Greece by Anaximander and Xenophanes, contemporaries of Gótama Budha, and afterwards by Diogenes Apolloniates, B.C. 428, and by Democritus, B.C. 361. They taught that there is at all times an infinity of co-existent worlds (world-islands) throughout endless and unbounded space; and that it is as absurd to think there should be only one world in space, as that in an extensive field properly cultivated, there should grow up no more than one single blade of corn. It was the opinion of Democritus that some of these worlds resemble each other, whilst others are entirely dissimilar.

§ There are four things which cannot be comprehended by any one that is not a Budha. 1. Karma-wisaya, how it is that effects are produced by the

On a certain occasion, when Gótama Budha delivered the discourse called the Arunawatí-sútra, he said that Abhibhu, a priest who existed in the time of the Budha called Sikhi, caused the rays from his body, whenever he said bana, to disperse the darkness of a thousand sakwalas. Ananda, the personal attendant of Gótama, on hearing this, respectfully enquired how many sakwalas are enlightened by the rays of a supreme Budha, when he says bana. Gótama replied, "What is it that you ask, Ananda? The powers and virtues of the Budhas are without limit. A little mould taken in the finger nail may be compared to the whole earth; but the glory of the disciple cannot in any way be compared to that of the supreme Budha. The virtue and power of the disciple are one; those of Budha are another. No one but Budha can perceive the whole of the sakwalas. The sakwalas are without end, infinite; but when Budha is situated in any place for the purpose of saying bana, all the sakwalas are seen by him as clearly as if they were close at hand; and to the beings who are in any of the sakwalas he can say bana, in such a manner that they can hear it, and receive instruction." To this Ananda replied, "All the sakwalas are not alike. The sun of one sakwala rises, whilst that of another is setting; in one it is noon, whilst in another it is midnight; in one the inhabitants are sowing, whilst in another they are reaping: in one they are amusing themselves, and in another at rest; some are in doubt, and others in certainty; therefore, when Budha says bana, how can it be equally heard by all?" The answer of Gótama was to this effect: "When Budha commences the delivery of a discourse, the sun that was about to set appears to rise, through the influence of his power, which is exercised for the producing of this result; the sun that was about to rise, appears to set; and in the sakwalas where it is midnight it appears to be noon. The people of the different sakwalas are thereby led to exclaim, 'A moment ago the sun was setting, but it is now rising; a moment ago it was midnight, but it is now noon.' They then enquire, 'How has this been caused? Is it by a rishi, or a demon, or a déwa?' In the midst of their surprise, the glory of Budha is seen in the sky, which disperses the darkness of all

---

instrumentality of karma. 2. Irdhi-wisaya, how it was that Budha could go in the snapping of a finger from the world of men to the brahma-lókas. 3. Lóka-wisaya, the size of the universe, or how it was first brought into existence. 4. Budha-wisaya, the power and wisdom of Budha.

the sakwalas; infinite though the sakwalas be, they all receive at that time the same degree of light; and all this may be caused by a single ray from the sacred person, no larger than a seed of sesamum. Were a rishi to make a lamp as large as a sakwala, and pour into it as much oil as there is water in the four oceans, with a wick as large as Maha Méru; the flame of such a lamp would appear to only one other sakwala, and to that only as the light emitted from a firefly; but one ray from the person of Budha extends to, and enlightens, all the sakwalas that exist. Were a rishi to make a drum the size of the sakwala-gala, and to extend upon it a skin as large as the earth, and to strike this drum with an instrument as large as Maha Méru, the sound would be heard distinctly in only one other sakwala; but when Budha says bana, it may be heard by all beings, in all sakwalas, as clearly as if it was spoken in their immediate presence." (*Sadharmmarat-nakáré.*)

By the practice of the rite called kasina, to see to the verge of the rocks that bound the sakwala, and then to conclude that the world is finite, i. e. that beyond these rocks there are no other worlds, is the error called antawáda. By the practice of the same rite, to see many other sakwalas, and then conclude that the world is infinite, is the error called anantawáda. To conclude that the world is finite vertically, but infinite horizontally, is the error called anantánantawáda. To conclude that the world is neither finite nor infinite, is the error called náwantánanantawáda. These errors are enumerated by Gótama Budha in the Brahma-jála-sútra, as being professed by some of the heretics included in the sixty-two sects that existed in his day.

4. *Maha Méru.*

Maha Méru,[*] at the summit and at the base, is 10,000 yojanas in diameter, and in circumference 31,428 yojanas, 2 gows, 22

---

[*] This mountain, which appears to be an exaggeration of the Himalayan range, was known to the Greeks by the name of Meros, and was regarded by them as connected with the legend of Dionysius, who was concealed in the thigh, μηρος, of Zeus. "Two truncated cones. united at their bases, may give an idea of the figure of this mountain."--Sangermanó's Burmese Empire. The Vishnu Purána says, that it is in the centre of Jambudwípa, its height being 84,000 yojanas, and its depth below the surface of the earth 16,000. There seems to be some uncertainty among the Pauránics as to its shape. In the sacredness of its character it resembles the Olympus of the Greeks. Both mountains were in the same direction, Olympus being at the northern extremity of Greece, and the highest mountain of the country, the summit appearing to reach the heavens. They were alike the residences of

isubus, 18 yashtis or staves, and 1 cubit; leaving out the upper part, at the distance of 42,000 yojanas* from the summit, on a level with the rocks called Yugandhara, it is 30,000 yojanas in diameter, and in circumference 94,285 yojanas, 2 gows, 68 isubus, 11 yashtis, and 3 cubits; and in the centre it is 50,000 yojanas in diameter, and in circumference 157,142 yojanas, 3 gows, 34 isubus, 5 yashtis, and 5 cubits. From the base to the summit its entire height is 168,000 yojanas, one half of this measurement being under the water of the great ocean, and the other half rising into the air. Were a stone to fall from the summit, it would be four months and fifteen days in reaching the earth.† The summit is the abode of Sekra, the regent or chief of the déwa-lóka called Tawutisá; and around it are four mansions, 5000 yojanas in size, inhabited by nágas, garundas, khumbandas, and yakás. At the four points, and the four half-points, Maha Méru is of a different colour, and the same colours are severally imparted to the seas, rocks, and other places in each direction. On the east, it is of a silver colour; on the south, sapphire; on the west, coral; on the north, gold; on the north-east, virgin gold; on the south-east, pale blue; on the south-west, blue, and on the north-west, red gold. Its base rests upon a rock with three peaks called the Trikúta-parwata, 30,000 yojanas in height.

the deities of their respective mythologies. It was upon Olympus that the gods were assembled in council by Zeus; and when the kings and consuls among the Romans were inaugurated, they looked towards the south, as if endowed with a portion of divinity.

* The length of the yojana is a disputed point. By the Singhalese it is regarded as about 16 miles in length, but by the Hindus of the continent as much shorter. "The yojana is a measure of distance, equal to four krósas, which at 8000 cubits or 4000 yards to the krósa or kós, will be exactly 9 miles. Other computations make the yojana but about 5 miles, or even no more than 4¼ miles."—Wilson's Sanscrit Dictionary. "The Markandeya states that 10 paramánus = 1 parasúkshma; 10 parasúkshmas = 1 trasarenu; 10 trasarenus = 1 particle of dust; 10 particles of dust = 1 hair's point; 10 hairs' points = 1 likhya; 10 likhyas = 1 yuka; 10 yukas = 1 heart of barley; 10 hearts of barley = 1 grain of barley of middle size; 10 grains of barley = 1 finger, or inch; 6 fingers = 1 páda, or foot (the breadth of it); 2 feet = 1 span; 2 spans = 1 cubit; 4 cubits = 1 staff; 2000 staves = 1 gavyúti; 4 gavyútis = 1 yojana."—Wilson's Vishnu Purána. The Singhalese say that 7 inches = 1 span; 9 spans = 1 bow; 500 bows = 1 hetekma; 4 hetekmas = 1 gowa (gavyuti); 4 gows = 1 yoduna (yojana). The word hetekma is said to be derived from ek, one, and husma, breath; meaning the distance to which a cooley can carry the native yoke at one breath, or without putting down the burden.

† "A brazen anvil, falling from the sky,
Through thrice three days would toss in airy whirl,
Nor touch the earth till the tenth sun arose."
Elton's Hesiod, Theog. 893.

5. *The Rocky Circles.*

Between Maha Méru and the circular wall of rock* bounding the Great Earth, called the sakwala-gala, are seven† concentric circles of rocks: Yugandhara, Isadhara, Karawíka, Sudarsana, Némendhara, Winataka, and Aswakarnna. The Yugandhara rocks are 84,000 yojanas high, half of this measurement being under water; the Isadhara rocks are, in the same way, 42,000 yojanas high, each circle diminishing one half in height, as it approaches the sakwala-gala; the outer circle, or Aswakarnna rocks, being 1312 yojanas, 2 gows, high. The circumference of the entire sakwala is 3,610,350 yojanas.

6. *The Oceans.*

Between the different circles of rocks there are seas,‡ the water of which gradually decreases in depth from Maha Méru, near which it is 84,000 yojanas deep, to the sakwala-gala near which

---

* The Mahomedans believe that there is a stony girdle surrounding the world, which they call Koh Kaf.

† The idea of the seven concentric circles around Méru, like that of the seven strings of the lyre of Orpheus, or the seven steps of the ladder of Zoroaster, was probably suggested by the previous idea of the orbit of the seven planets, which it is not unreasonable to suppose had its origin in the number of the days of the week, as appointed in the beginning by God. The city of Ecbatana (the Achmetha of Ezra vi. 2, and the Ecbatana of the Apocrypha, supposed to be the present Hamadan) as described by Herodotus, i. 98, might have been erected as the model of sakwala. The Brahmans teach that there are seven great insular continents, surrounded severally by great seas. According to the Bhágavata, Priyavrata drove his chariot seven times round the earth, and the ruts left by the wheels became the beds of the oceans, separating it into seven dwípas.

‡ Nearly all the ancient nations supposed that beneath and around the earth there is a fathomless sea, below which is a profound abyss, the abode of the wicked, who there undergo the punishment of their crimes. The great rivers of whose source they were ignorant, such as the Nile, were supposed to have their origin from this ocean; and it was thought that regions in opposite directions might communicate by this means. Thales held the opinion that the earth floats on the ocean, like a great ship; but this was denied by Democritus, who taught that the earth rests upon the air, after the manner of an immense bird, with its wings outspread. The opinion of the Budhists, that the earth is supported by a world of air, is more scientific than that of those Hindus who believe that it is borne upon a tortoise. When Milinda, king of Ságal, said to Nágaséna that he could not believe that the earth is supported by the world of water, and this by a world of air, the priest took a syringe, and pointed out to him that the water within the instrument was prevented from coming out by the exterior air; by which the king was convinced that the water under the earth may be supported by the Ajatákása. "The supreme being placed the earth on the summit of the ocean, where it floats like a mighty vessel, and from its expansive surface does not sink beneath the waters."—Wilson's Vishnu Purána.

it is only one inch deep.* From the Aswakarnna rocks to the sakwala-gala is 248,150 yojanas, and 1 gow, in which space is the ocean that appears to men. In the deep waters of these great seas are the fish called Timi, Timingala, Timiripingala, Ananda, Timanda, Ajháróha, and Maha Timi, some of which are two hundred yojanas in size, and others a thousand.† There are also beings in the form of men, with large claws, khura, that sport in the sea, among the rocks, like fishes, on which account it is called Khuramali. As it abounds with gold, shining like a flame of fire, or the orb of the sun, it is called Agnimali. From the emeralds that it contains, in colour like the sacrificial grass, kusa, it is called Kusamali; from its silver, white as milk, dadhi, it is called Dadhimali; from its many gems, in colour like the bamboo, nala, it is called Nalamali; and from its coral, prawála, it is called Prawála Nalamali. There are waves that rise 60 yojanas, called Mahinda; others that are 50 yojanas high, called Ganga: and others 40 yojanas, called Róhana. When a storm arises, the waves are thrown to an immense height, after which they roll with a fearful noise towards Maha Méru, on the one side, or the sakwala-gala on the other, leaving a pool or hollow in the trough of the sea, called Walabhámukha. In a former age, when Gótama Budha was the Bódhisat Suppáraka, he entered a ship with 700 other merchants; but when they had set sail, they passed the 500 islands connected with the southern continent, Jambudwípa, and still went on, until they knew not in what place they were. For the space of four months they continued their course, but they did not meet with land. They then came to the sea of the seven gems, and filled their ship with the treasures that were presented; but afterwards arrived at a part of the sea that is agitated by the flames proceeding from hell. The other merchants called out in fear, but Bódhisat, by the power of a charm with which he was acquainted, caused the ship to go,‡ in one day, to Bharukacha, Jambudwípa, at which place they

* "The waters are transparent and clear as crystal, and so very light, that the feather of the smallest bird, if thrown into them, will sink to the bottom."—Sangermanó's Burm. Emp.

† "We were once carried," says a rabbin, "in a great ship, and the ship went three days and three nights between the two fins of one fish. But perhaps the ship sailed very slowly? The rabbi Dimi says, A rider shot an arrow, and the ship flew faster than the arrow; and yet it took so long time to pass between the two fins of this fish."—The Talmud.

‡ The mariners of Phœacia, according to Homer, had ships endowed with consciousness, that required no steersman.

landed, and were within 8 isubus of their own village. The waters of the sea are not increased in the rainy season, nor are they at all dried up by the severest drought; they are ever the same. As they are composed of equal portions of salt and water, the sea is called samudra. This saltness is caused by their being acted upon by a submarine fire proceeding from one of the hells, which changes their natural sweetness, and by constant agitation they become throughout of one consistency and flavour. (*Súryódgamana-sútrasanné.*)

7. *Uturukurudiwayina.*

The square-faced* inhabitants of Uturukurudiwayina, on the north† of Maha Méru, are never sick,‡ and are not subject to any accident; and both the males and the females always retain the appearance of persons about sixteen years§ of age. They do not perform any kind of work, as they receive all they want, whether as to ornaments, clothes, or food, from a tree called kalpa-wurksha.‖ This tree is 100 yojanas high, and when the people require anything, it is not necessary that they should go to it to receive it, as the tree extends its branches, and gives

---

* It is supposed that the legends respecting square-faced or square-headed animals (Herod. iv. 109), have had their origin in the appearance of the sea-dogs (phocæ vitulinæ) that inhabit the lakes of Siberia.

† In speaking of the four points, the people of India, like the Hebrews, suppose themselves to be looking towards the rising sun. Hence the same word, both in Sanscrit and Hebrew, signifies alike the front, the eastern quarter, and aforetime.

‡ There is a resemblance, in position and general character, between the inhabitants of Uturukuru and the Hyperboreans. This happy people, dwelling beyond the influence of Boreas, never felt the cold north wind. Their females were delivered without the sense of pain. The songs and dances at their festivals were accompanied by innumerable flocks of swans. They lived to the age of a thousand years, and yet without any of the usual accompaniments of senility. "Neither disease nor old age is the lot of this sacred race, while they live apart from toil and battles, undisturbed by the revengeful Nemesis."—Pind. Pyth. x. When tired of their long existence, they leapt, crowned with garlands, from a rock into the sea. This custom of leaping from high rocks occurs, in precisely the same manner, in Scandinavian legends.—Müller's Dorians. The reader will remember, in connexion with this rite, the annual festival at the promontory of Leukate, where a criminal was cast down, with birds of all kinds attached to his person, to break his fall. The opinion that the northern regions of the earth were formerly warm and pleasant, has been confirmed by the investigations and discoveries of geologists.

§ According to Zoroaster, in the reign of Jemshid, the ancient sovereign of Iran, men appeared until death to retain the age of fifteen.

‖ The horn of Amaltheia, given by Zeus to the daughters of Melisseus, was endowed with such power, that whenever the possessor wished, it instantaneously became filled with whatever was desired.

whatever is desired. When they wish to eat, food is at that instant presented; and when they wish to lie down, couches at once appear. There is no relationship, as of father, mother, or brother. The females are more beautiful than the déwas. There is no rain, and no houses are required. In the whole region there is no low place or valley. It is like a wilderness of pearls; and always free from all impurities, like the court of a temple or a wall of crystal. The inhabitants live to be a thousand years old; and all this time they enjoy themselves like the déwas, by means of their own merit and with the assistance of the kalpa tree. When they die they are wrapped in a fine kind of cloth, procured from the tree, far more exquisite in its fabric than anything ever made by man. As there is no wood of which to form a pyre, they are taken to the cemetery and there left. There are birds, more powerful than elephants, which convey the bodies to the Yugandhara rocks; and as they sometimes let them fall when flying over Jambudwípa, these precious cloths are occasionally found by men. When the people of this region pass away, they are always born as déwas or as men, and never in any of the four hells.* (*Pújáwaliya.*)

8. *The Great Forest.*

The great forest is in the northern part of Jambudwípa,† which, from the southern extremity, gradually increases in height,‡ until it attains an elevation of 500 yojanas, in the mountains of Gandhamádana, Kailása,§ Chitrakúta, and others, there being in all 84,000.|| These mountains are inhabited by an infinite number

* On the erection of the great thúpa at Anurádhapura, B.C. 157, two sámanéra priests repaired to Uturukuru, whence they brought six beautiful cloud-coloured stones, in length and breadth 80 cubits, of the tint of the ganthi flower, without flaw, and resplendent like the sun.—Turnour's Mahawanso, cap. xxx. During a period of famine, Mugalan, one of the principal priests of Gótama Budha, proposed to invert the earth, and requested permission to take the whole of the priests meanwhile to Uturukuru.—Gogerly, Essay on Budhism, No. 2, Journ. Ceylon Branch Royal As. Soc.

† The whole diameter of Jambu-dwípa has been said to be 100,000 yojanas.—Wilson's Vishnu Puràna.

‡ The most northern parts of the earth are always regarded by the natives of India as the highest. This was also the opinion of the Hebrews, and of the ancients generally. Hence the expression to go down, or descend, is frequently used of going to the south.—1 Sam. xxv. 1; xxx. 15.

§ The source of the principal stream of the Indus is said to be at the north of this mountain.

|| In other places it is said that the principal mountain in the forest of Himála is Swéta. By modern geographers Dhawulagiri is reckoned as the highest mountain in this range. Both swéta and dhawala signify white, and

of déwas and yakás, and are beautified by 500 rivers, filled with the most delicious water, and by the seven great lakes, among which is the Anótatta-wila.* This lake is 800 miles long, and as many broad and deep; and there are four places in it in which the Budhas, Pasé-Budhas, rahats, and rishis are accustomed to bathe; and six other places where the déwas from the six inferior heavens bathe. The bath of the supreme Budhas is adorned with gems, and is exceedingly splendid; and to the other places the beings that have been named resort for refreshment and pleasure. There are mountains of gold on each of the four sides, 800 miles high; and the water is overshadowed by the mountain Sudarsana, in shape like the bill of a crow, so that the rays of the sun never fall upon it. On the other three sides are Chitrakúta, enriched with all kinds of gems; Kálakúta, of the colour of antimony; and Gandhamádana, of a red colour. In the last-named mountain there is a golden cave, and there are two others of silver and gems, provided with seats, which the Budhas and others frequently visit. Near the entrance to the cave of gems, about a yojana high, is the tree called manjusaka, upon which are found all the flowers that grow, whether in water or on land. When the Pasé-Budhas approach it, a breeze springs up to purify it, and another arises to strew it with sand like the dust of gems, whilst a third sprinkles it with water from the Anótatta-wila, and a fourth scatters around all kinds of sweet-scented flowers. The Pasé-Budhas here perform the rite of abstract meditation called dhyána. On the four sides of Anótatta are four mouths or doors, whence proceed as many rivers;† they are, the lion-mouth, the elephant, the horse, and the bull. The banks of these rivers abound with the animals from which they take their name. The rivers that pass to the north-east and west flow three times round the lake without touching each other, and after passing through countries not inhabited by man, fall into the sea. The river that runs to the south also passes three times

we might take it for granted that both names refer to the same eminence, were it not that all the peaks in this region are white, from their crown of everlasting snow.

* This lake is called in Tibetan Ma-dros, and is identified as the great lake Manassarovára.

† By Csoma Körösi these rivers are called the Ganga, Sindhu, Pakshu, and Sita. They are said by the Brahmans to encircle the city of Brahma, upon the summit of Méru, and are the Síta, Alakanandá, Chakshu, and Bhadrá, flowing from the Ganges as their source. Mr. Faber, in his Pagan Idolatry, thinks that they represent the four rivers of Eden.

round the lake, then rushes from the midst of a rock, and flows in a straight line 60 yojanas. It then strikes against another rock, and rises into the sky, like a mount of gems 12 miles in size, flows through the sky for the space of 60 yojanas, and strikes against the rock Tiyaggalá. This rock it has broken by its immense force; and after this it violently rushes on a further space of 50 yojanas, after which it flows on an inclined plane, strikes and breaks the ponderous Pánsu-parwata or Five Mountains, and again passes on 60 yojanas. It then flows 60 yojanas further, through a cave, strikes the four-sided rock Wijja, and is lastly divided into five streams, like five fingers, that are the five great rivers (Ganga, Yamuna, Achirawati, Sarabhu, and Mahí), which, after watering Jambudwípa, fall into the sea. During its course round the lake, until it turns off towards the south, it is called Awarttha; from that place, until it begins to ascend into the sky, it is called Kanhá; in its passage through the sky it is called Akása-ganga; for the next 50 yojanas it is called Tiyaggalá, and afterwards Bahala; and during its passage underground it is called Ummaga-ganga. Its whole course, from the place in which it turns towards the south, to the place where it flows against the rock Wijja, is 4540 miles. (*Súryódgamana-sútra-sanné.*)

The seven great lakes are Anótatta, Karnamunda, Rathakára, Chaddanta, Kunála, Sihapratápa, and Mandakini. In the centre of the Chaddanta lake, 12 yojanas in extent, is water as clear as a mirror. Next to this water there is a space, one yojana in breadth, covered with white water lilies, called Kalhára, around which there are other spaces, and in each of them flourishes a different kind of flower. Further still there is a space covered by a particular kind of rice, called rat-hel, so plenteous that all the people in Jambudwípa would be insufficient to exhaust it; adjoining this space there is a garden in which are all kinds of small and delicate flowers; then spaces covered with mung, gourds, &c.; and afterwards a space in which the sugar-cane flourishes in rich luxuriance. In all there are 24 spaces, each of which is a yojana in breadth, surrounding each other, in concentric circles. In like manner, around Mandakini, each half a yojana in breadth, are 12 different spaces or floral belts.

In the forest of Himála are lions, tigers, elephants, horses, bulls, buffaloes, yaks, bears, panthers, deer, hansas,* peafowl, kokilas,

* This is regarded as the king of birds, and by Europeans is generally

kinduras, golden eagles, and many other kinds of animals and birds; but the lions and kokilas are the most abundant. There are four different species, or castes, of lions, called trina, kála, pándu, and késara. The first is dove-coloured, and eats grass. The second is like a black bull, and this also eats grass. The third is like a brown bull, and eats flesh. The késara lion,* which also eats flesh, has its mouth, tail, and the soles of its feet, of a red colour, like a wagon laden with red dye. From the top of the head proceed three lines, two of which turn towards the sides, and the third runs along the centre of the back and tail. The neck is covered with a mane, like a rough mantle worth a thousand pieces of gold.† The rest of the body is white, like a piece of pure lime. When he issues forth from his golden cave, and ascends a rock, he places his paws towards the east, breathes through his nostrils with a noise like the thunder, shakes himself like a young calf at its gambols, that he may free his body from dust, and then roars out amain. His voice may be heard for the space of three yojanas around. All the sentient beings that hear it, whether they be apods, bipeds, or quadrupeds, become alarmed, and hasten to their separate places of retreat. He can leap upwards, in a straight line, four or eight isubus, each of 140 cubits; upon level ground he can leap 15 or 20 isubus; from a rock, 60 or 80. When the kokila begins to sing all the beasts of the forest are beside themselves. The deer does not finish the portion of grass it has taken into its mouth, but remains listening. The tiger that is pursuing the deer remains at once perfectly still, like a painted statue, its uplifted foot not put down, and the foot on the ground not uplifted. The deer thus pursued forgets its terror. The wing of the flying bird remains expanded in the air, and the fin of the fish becomes motionless. Prákrama Báhu, who reigned at Polonnaruwa, in

supposed to be the golden-winged swan. It is said the Nile-Ibis (Ibis religiosa) is still called Abu Hansa by the Arabs of Egypt. I have sometimes thought that there may be some connexion between the hansa of the Hindus and the ιυγξ of the Greeks. Iynx was the daughter of Pan, or of Echo, metamorphosed by Hera, out of revenge, into the bird called iynx (iynx torquilla).

* It has been supposed that the word Cæsar is derived from the Sanskrit késa, hair, and that the future emperor was so called because he had much hair on his head when he was born.

† It is said by Ctesias that "there is an animal in India, of prodigious strength, surpassing in size the largest lion, of a colour red as vermillion, with a thick coat of hair like a dog."

Ceylon, from hearing of the fame of this great forest, wished to see it; and at his death, in consequence of the merit he had acquired, he was born there as a bhúmátu-déwatá, or terrestrial deity, and he will, in the same place, see the next Budha who will appear, Maitrí.

In the same forest there is a damba tree, one hundred yojanas high, which has four branches; and the whole space that the tree covers is 300 yojanas in circumference.* From the trunk and the four branches large rivers continually flow. During the whole of the kalpa in which the world is renovated, it bears an inmortal fruit resembling gold, as large as the water-vessel called mahakala (said to be sixteen times larger than the kalas used in Ceylon, which hold about 4 gallons each). This fruit falls into the rivers, and from its seeds are produced grains of gold, that are carried to the sea, and are sometimes found on the shore.† This gold is of immense value, as there is no other equal to it in the world. From this damba, or jambu, tree, Dambadiwa or Jambudwípa, derives its name.‡ (*Súryódgamana-sútra-sanné.*)

* This fable may have had its origin in an exaggerated account of the deodar or Himalayan cedar, cedrus deodara. "Its botanical range extends from 7000 to 12,000 feet above the level of the sea, and in its most congenial locality it attains a great height and a circumference of 30 feet. When young it closely resembles the real cedar, but never sends forth spreading branches. The cone resembles that of the cedar, and is preceded by a catkin of a bright yellow colour, so that the tree when in full blossom appears covered with a rich mantle of gold. These catkins are loaded with a golden dust, which the wind shakes from the branches in such quantity that the ground for a considerable distance, about the tree, becomes as it were sheeted with gold." —Thornton's Gazetteer. "Several Indian trees have been enumerated as likely to be the almug of the Scriptures. . . . If one of the pine tribe be required, none is more deserving of selection than the deodar (deo, god, dar, wood)"—Dr. J. F. Royle.

† Gold is found in some of the mountain streams of the Himalayas, but the natives forbear to gather it, as they suppose that it belongs to certain demons, who would be displeased if they were to attempt to take it away, and inflict on them some punishment.—Thornton's Gazetteer. Philostratus, in his Life of Apollonius, mentions griffins as among the fabulous animals that guarded the gold of India.

‡ In the native authorities there usually follows, after the above statements, a list of the names of the principal places in Jambudwípa, which with slight variations is frequently repeated; but it is evidently a modern compilation, and must have been made by some one who had not visited the continent of India. There are several countries known to the Singhalese that are not mentioned; but they have great difficulty in distinguishing the character of places, though with the names they may be familiar; they call the same place at one time a city and at another a county, and seldom remember to what particular class any given place belongs. Their rahats could fly through the air, and visit at will any part of the world; but they have given us no information relative to any region beyond India, or the countries adjacent, exclusive of their accounts of Méru and the continents

9. *The Sun, Moon, and Planets.*

The disk of the sun is 50 yojanas in diameter, and 150 in circumference; within, it is composed of coral, and its surface is of gold; so that both its surface and inner material are extremely hot.

The disk of the moon is 40 yojanas in diameter, and 147 in circumference; within it is composed of crystal, and its surface is of silver; so that both its surface and inner material are extremely cold.* The path in which it moves is about a yojana lower than that of the sun.†

Extending from the summit of the Yugandhara rocks to the sakwala-gala is the lóka called Chaturmaharájika, in which there are three paths adorned with all kinds of beautiful mansions and gardens, and with kalpa-trees; they are severally called the Aja, or Goat-path; the Nága, or Serpent-path; and the Go, or Bull-path. In these paths, accompanied by the stars that are in the

---

that no man can now visit. But the confusion in the native accounts is scarcely to be wondered at, when we remember that so recently as 1545, there was published at Antwerp the Cosmography of Peter Aspianus, expurgated from all faults by Gemma Frisius, a physician and mathematician of Louvain, in which correct and expurgated work Scotland is an island, of which York is one of the chief cities.—*Fosbroke's Monachism.*

* The Singhalese universally regard the moon-beam as diffusing cold. This was also the opinion of Anaxagoras; and modern science has proved that there is a real connection between the clearness of the atmosphere and the cold produced at night by the radiation of heat from the earth's surface, which is impeded by the presence of clouds. As the moon-beam is of course brighter when the atmosphere is clear, it has been supposed that this is the cause of the greater degree of cold, instead of its being a correlative effect. "It is certain," says the Rev. Dr. Macvicar, "the sky is very cold. This fact, taken in connexion with the tendency of heat universally to diffuse itself, brings it about that the heat accumulated on the earth's surface is constantly streaming away into space; and if the sky be open and clear, and the air be still, the cold produced in this way during the night is often very great. On the 2nd of January, 1841, a register thermometer left by me on a tuft of grass in the Marandahn cinnamon garden, near Colombo, showed in the morning that it had been down to $52°$, and that although the surface of the ground when exposed to the sun had been heated twelve hours before to about $140°$. . . . Here is a variation in the temperature of the soil of $80°$ in the course of twenty-four hours; and when the nights are clear and still, similar results may always be expected."—*Meteorology in Ceylon, Ceylon Miscellany, July, 1843.*

† It was in the age of Gótama that Anaximander taught that the sun is 28 times as large as the earth, having a hole in one part of it, like the hole of a flute, whence fire proceeds; and that the moon is 19 times as large as the earth, having a similar aperture, which at certain times being shut causes what is called an eclipse. But not long afterward Anaxagoras taught that the moon is an opaque body receiving its light from the sun. Respecting the stars, there were various opinions among the Greeks, as, that they were like metal plates or spheres, or the visible summits of something that itself is hidden, or nails fixed in the sky. Xenophanes supposed that there are as many suns and moons as there are different climates and zones in the world.

same division of the sky, the sun and moon continually move. In one day the sun travels 2,700,000 yojanas; in one hour 45,000 yojanas; and in one breath 125 yojanas. Its rays extend 900,000 yojanas. Thus the sun gives light to the whole of the four continents.

From the month Asala (July) in each year, it gradually passes further from Méru and nearer to the sakwala-gala; then from the Pusa nekata in the month Durutu (January) in the same way, for the space of six months it passes gradually further from the sakwala-gala, and nearer to Méru.

When the sun and moon are in the Goat-path, there is no rain in Jambudwípa;* when they are in the Serpent-path there is much rain; and when in the Bull-path, there is a moderate quantity of both rain and heat.

The rays of the sun are always powerful, though they appear at some seasons to be more fierce, and at others more mild. This difference arises from what may be called the four diseases to which the regent of the sun is subject: that is to say, from clouds that act like a screen; from mists, that arise out of the ground; from the asur Ráhu; and from all these causes united.

From the day of the full moon in the Keti nekata, in the Il masa, though it be the hémanta, or winter season, the rays of the sun are powerful, whilst from the day of the full moon in the Utrapalguna nekata, in the month Medindina, though it be the gimhána, or summer season, its rays are mild. But this anomaly may be thus accounted for. In the hot season the dust is raised up, and floats in the air, when it is agitated by the wind; the clouds are numerous; and there are gales and hurricanes. In this way, by the dust, clouds, and wind, the sun is obscured, and its rays are less powerful. In the cold season, the face of the earth is calm; rain begins to fall; the dust is allayed; only a fine kind of dust, and certain watery particles, not perceptible to the senses, float in the air; the clouds are low; and there is little

---

* "When the sun is in the path of the Goat, the gnats who preside over showers do not choose to leave their houses, on account of the great heat, whence there is no rain. For this reason the inhabitants of the Burman empire in times of drought are wont to assemble in great numbers, with drums and a long cable. Dividing themselves into two parties, with a vast shouting and noise, they drag the cable contrary ways, the one party endeavouring to get the better of the other; and they think, by this means, to invite the gnats to come out from their houses, and to sport in the air."—Buchanan, As. Res. vi.

wind. By this dust, the watery particles, clouds, and gentle wind, the rays of the sun are purified; and then, released from all obstructions, they shine with great power.

In one day the moon travels 2,610,000 yojanas; in one hour 43,500 yojanas; in one minute 750 yojanas; and in one breath 120 yojanas, 26 isubus, 13 yashtis, 1 span, 4 inches. It has 27 nekatas, or mansions, 108 pádas (each being the fourth part of a nekata), and 10 grahanas, seizures (or eclipses). It moves in a path called Mégha, which is 2,250,000 yojanas in circumference. It is accompanied by the déwas of rain, called Abra; the déwas of dew, called Mahika; the déwas of mist, called Dhúma; the déwas of dust, or motes, called Raja; and the asur Ráhu. The regent of the moon descended to take refuge in Gótama Budha, when attacked by Ráhu.

When the course of the moon is straight, it moves more slowly; when it is cross-wise, it passes along more swiftly. When the dark póya, or day of the new moon, has come, the sun moves in one day the distance of 100,000 yojanas from the moon; on the second day, the moon appears like a line, at which time the sun is distant from it 200,000 yojanas; from this time it daily becomes larger, until on the atawaka, or first quarter, it appears like the segment of a circle, the upper part not being seen, because it is hidden or overpowered by the sun's rays. On the paholawaka, or day of the full moon, the sun being at a distance of 1,500,000 yojanas from the moon, the solar rays are not able to overpower the lunar brightness, and therefore the entire circle of the moon is seen. On the day after the full moon it approaches 100,000 yojanas nearer to the sun, on which account a line or small portion of its circle is overpowered by the sun's rays, and does not appear; on the second day it approaches 200,000 yojanas nearer to the sun; thus going on from day to day, until on the 15th day it is in conjunction with the sun; on which account, as it is directly under the sun, its light is entirely obscured, and it does not appear at all.* (*Milinda Prasna.*)

* Nearly all the astronomical works possessed by the Singhalese are translations from the Sanskrit; but many of the statements that are incidentally made upon this subject in their own books differ materially from the systems now considered to be the most popular upon the continent of India. 1. The Jainas maintain that Méru is in the centre of the earth, around which lies Jambudwípa; that the earth is without support, and is continually falling in space (which may have some relation to the fact that "the sun, with his planets, is rapidly darting towards a point in the constellation Hercules," as

When the heavenly bodies go to the other side of the Yugandhara rocks, they appear to set to the inhabitants of Jambudwípa. The sun and moon are at regular intervals seized by the asúrs Ráhu and Kétu;* and these periods are called grahanas or seizures (eclipses).

There are twelve rásis, or collections (signs of the zodiac): 1. Mésha, a red ram. 2. Wrashaba, a white bull. 3. Mithuna, a woman and man, of a blue colour, holding an iron rod and a lute. 4. Karkkataka, a red crab. 5. Singha, a lion, of a red colour. 6. Kanyá, a virgin, of a dark colour, in a ship, holding a handful of ears of rice and a lamp. 7. Tulá, a white man, with a pair of scales in his hand. 8. Wraschika, a black elk. 9. Dhanu, a figure of a golden colour, half man and half horse, with a bow in his hand. 10. Makara, a marine monster. 11. Kumbha, a white man, holding a water-jar. 12. Mína, two fishes, looking opposite ways.

In one year there are 365 days, 15 hours, 31 minutes, 15 seconds; or 21,915 hours, 31 minutes, 15 seconds; or 1,314,931 minutes, 15 seconds; or, 78,895,875 seconds. The twelve months of the year are divided in the following manner:—

Months.	days.	hours.	min.	Months.	days.	hours.	min.
1. Bak has	30	55	32	7. Wap has	29	54	7
2. Wesak	31	24	12	8. Il	29	30	24
3. Poson	31	36	38	9. Unduwap	29	30	53
4. Æsala	31	28	12	10. Durutu	29	27	24
5. Nikini	31	2	10	11. Nawan	29	30	24
6. Binara	30	27	22	12. Medin-dina	30	20	21

taught by modern astronomers); and that the moon is 80 yojanas above the sun, beyond which are the planets, at a still greater distance. 2. The Puránas teach that Méru is in the centre of the earth, around which is Jambudwípa; that the earth is supported by some animal; that there is one sun and one moon, which, as well as the stars, move horizontally over the plane of the earth, appearing to set when they go behind Méru; that the moon is twice as far from the earth as the sun; and that eclipses are caused by the monsters Ráhu and Kétu, who then lay hold of the sun and moon. 3. The Jyotishis, or followers of the Siddhantas, teach the true size and figure of the earth, but place it in the centre of the universe, around which the sun, moon, and planets move in epicycles, as was taught by Ptolemy. The authors of the Siddhantas spare no pains to ridicule the systems of the Jainas and Puránas.—Wilkinson, Journal Ben. As. Soc. 1834.

* As the belief that eclipses are caused by Ráhu is founded in explicit and positive declarations contained in the Vedas and Puránas, that are considered to be of divine authority, the native astronomers have cautiously explained such passages in those writings as disagree with the principles of their own science; and where reconciliation is impossible, have apologised, as well as

The twenty-seven nekatas, or lunar mansions (that appear to have been invented for the purpose of marking the position of the moon, and answering the same purpose for the moon that the twelve rásis do for the sun) are named thus:—1. Assuda. 2. Berana. 3. Kœti. 4. Rehena. 5. Muwasirisa. 6. Ada. 7. Punáwasa. 8. Pusa. 9. Aslisa. 10. Mánekata. 11. Puwapal. 12. Utrapal. 13. Hata. 14. Sita. 15. Sá. 16. Wisá. 17. Anura. 18. Deta. 19. Mula. 20. Puwasala. 21. Utrasala. 22. Suwana. 23. Denata. 24. Siyáwasa. 26. Puwaputupá. 16. Utraputupá. 27. Rewati.*

There are nine grahas or planets:—1. Rawi, the sun. 2. Sukra, Venus. 3. Kuja, Mars. 4. Ráhu, the asúr. 5. Sœni, Saturn. 6. Chandra, the moon. 7. Budha, Mercury. 8. Guru, Jupiter. 9. Kétu, the asúr.

10. *The Déwa-Lókas and Brahma-Lókas.*

The dówa-lóka called Cháturmaharájika extends from the summit of the Yugandhara rocks to the sakwala-gala, at an elevation of 42,000 yojanas above the surface of the earth. In this world, adorned with the seven gems, are numberless dwellings of the déwas. The four guardian déwas, Dhratarástra, Wirúdha, Wirúpaksha, and Waisráwana, have palaces on the summit of the Yugandhara rocks. The palace of Dhratarástra is on the east. His attendants are the gandhárwas, a kela-laksha in number, who have white garments, adorned with white ornaments, hold a sword and shield of crystal, and are mounted on white horses. The déwa is arrayed and mounted in a similar manner, and shining like a kela-laksha of silver lamps, keeps guard over the possessions of Sekra in the eastern division of the sakwala. The palace of Wirúdha is on the south. His attendants are the kumbhándas, a kela laksha in number, who have blue garments, hold a sword and shield of sapphire, and

they can, by observing that certain things, "as stated in the Sastras, might have been so formerly, and may be so still; but for astronomical purposes, astronomical rules must be followed!"—Sam. Davis, As. Res. ii.

* The Arabians have a similar division of the zodiac, and by them the lunar mansions are called manzils. It was thought by Sir William Jones, that the Indian and Arabian divisions had not a common origin; but Colebrooke inclined to a different opinion, and thought that it was the Arabs who adopted (with slight variations) a division of the zodiac familiar to the Hindus.—Colebrooke, Essays, ii. 322. One of Galen's chief sources of prognosis was derived from the critical days, which he believed were influenced by the moon, as did most of the ancient authorities.

are mounted on blue horses. The déwa is arrayed and mounted in a similar manner, and shining like a kela-laksha of lamps composed of gems, keeps guard over the southern division of the sakwala. The palace of Wirúpaksha is on the west. His attendants are the nágas, a kela-laksha in number, who have red garments, hold a sword and shield of coral, and are mounted on red horses. The déwa is arrayed and mounted in a similar manner, and shining like a kela-laksha of torches, keeps guard over the western division of the sakwala. The palace of Waisráwana is on the north. His attendants are the yakás, a kela-laksha in number, who have garments adorned with gold, and are mounted on horses shining like gold. The déwa is arrayed and mounted in a similar manner, and shining like a kela-laksha of golden lamps, keeps guard over the northern division of the sakwala.

There are in all six* déwa-lókas:—1. Cháturmaharájika, in which one day is equal to 50 of the years of men; 30 of these days make a month, and 12 of these months a year; and as the déwas live 500 of these years, their age is equal to nine millions of the years of men. 2. Tawutisá,† the déwa-lóka of Sekra, or Indra, on the summit of Maha Méru, in which one day is equal to 100 of the years of men; and as they live 1000 of these years, their age is equal to 36,000,000 of the years of men. 3. Yama, in which one day is equal to 200 years; and as they live 2000 of these years, their age is equal to 144,000,000 of the years of men. 4. Tusita, in which one day is equal to 400 years; and as they live 4000 of these years, their age is equal to 576,000,000 of the years of men.‡ 5. Nimmánarati, in which one day is equal to

---

* The Puránas teach that there are seven lókas, or spheres, above the earth. 1. Prájápatya, or Pitri lóka. 2. Indra lóka, or Swerga. 3. Marut lóka, or Diva lóka, heaven. 4. Gandharba lóka, the region of celestial spirits; also called Maharlóka. 5. Janalóka, or the sphere of saints. 6. Tapaslóka, the world of the seven sages. 7. Brahma lóka, or Satya lóka, the world of infinite wisdom and truth. There is a sectarial division of an eighth world, called Vaikuntha, or Goloka, the high world of Vishnu.—Wilson's Vishnu Purána.

† In former ages there were four individuals who went to Tawutisá with human bodies, viz., the famous musician Guttila, and the kings Sádhína, Nimi, and Maha Mandhátu.

‡ When the monarch Dutthagámini was near death, the assembled priesthood chaunted a hymn, and from the six déwa-lókas, as many déwas came in six chariots, each entreating him to repair to his own lóka; but the king silenced their entreaty by a signal of his hand, which implied that they were to wait so long as he was listening to the bana. That his meaning might not be mistaken by those around, he threw wreaths of flowers into the air, that

800 years; and as they live 8000 of these years, their age is equal to 2,304,000,000 of the years of men. 6. Paranirmita Wasawartti, in which one day is equal to 1,600 years; and as they live 16,000 of these years, their age is equal to 9,216,000,000 of the years of men.

The rúpa-brahma-lókas are 16 in number,* rising above each other in the following order, the figures denoting the number of maha kalpas in the age of the brahmas inhabiting the several lókas.

Maha kalpas.		Maha kalpas.
1. Brahma Parisadya one-third	9. Subhakírnnaka . .	64
2. Brahma Purohita . one-half	10. Wéhappala . . .	500
3. Maha Brahma . . 1	11. Asanyasatya† . .	500
4. Parittábha 2	12. Awiha	1000
5. Apramána 4	13. Atappa.	2000
6. Abhassara . . . 8	14. Sudassa	4000
7. Parittasubha . . . 16	15. Sudassi	8000
8. Appramánasubha . . 32	16. Akanishtaka . . .	16,000

The arúpa-brahma-lókas‡ are four in number, and the inhabitants live according to the number of maha kalpas here enumerated:—

	Maha kalpas.
1. Akásánancháyatana	20,000
2. Winyánancháyatana. . . .	40,000
3. Akinchannyáyatana	60,000
4. Néwásannyanásannyáyatana .	80,000§

Thus if the ages in the six déwa-lókas and twenty brahma-lókas be added together, it will give a total of 231,628 maha kalpas, 12,285,000,000 years.

attached themselves to the chariots and remained pendent. He then said to a priest, " Lord, which is the most delightful déwa-lóka ? " The priest replied, " It has been held by the wise that Tusitapura is a delightful déwa-lóka. The all-compassionate Bodhisat, Maitrí, tarries in Tusita, awaiting his advent to the Budhaship."—Turnour's Mahawanso, cap. xxxiv.

* In the rúpa-brahma-lókas there are no sensual pleasures, and there is no pain, the enjoyments being intellectual, although there is bodily form, resembling in some measure that which St. Paul may mean by " a spiritual body."—Gogerly, Essay on Budhism ; Journ. Ceylon Branch Royal As. Soc.

† The inhabitants of this world remain during the full period of their existence in the lóka in a state of unconscious existence.—Gogerly, Journ. Ceylon Branch Royal As. Soc.

‡ The inhabitants of these worlds have no rúpa, no bodily form.

§ The inhabitants of this world are in a state neither fully conscious nor yet altogether unconscious. It is the last of the spiritual worlds, and the nearest approximation to nirwána. Gogerly, ib.

11. *The Narakas.*

There are eight principal narakas, or places of torment:—1. Sanjíwa. 2. Kálasútra. 3. Sanghata. 4. Rowrawa. 5. Maha Rowrawa. 6. Tápa. 7. Pratápa. 8. Awíchi. They are each 10,000 yojanas in length, breadth, and height. The walls are nine yojanas in thickness, and of so dazzling a brightness that they burst the eyes of those who look at them, even from the distance of a hundred yojanas. Each hell is so enclosed that there is no possibility of escape from it. There are in all 136 narakas, and the whole are situated in the interior of the earth.*

Under the great bó-tree, at the depth of 100 yojanas,† is the roof of Awíchi, the flames from which burst forth beyond the walls, and rise to the height of 100 yojanas. There are 16 narakas called Osupat, exterior to Awíchi, four on each side. The distance from the centre of Awíchi, to the outermost part of the Osupat narakas is 19,400 gows, and at this part they verge upon the great sea. By the power of the beings who suffer in Awíchi, the doors of the Osupat narakas are continually opening and shutting. The flames proceeding through the doors, when they are thus thrown open, burst upon the waters of the sea, to the distance of many yojanas, and thus cause a vacuum. Towards this vacuum the water of the sea is continually drawn, in a powerful manner, and with great noise and tumult, so that any ship coming near would be undoubtedly destroyed.‡ This naraka is

---

* The names by which the place of punishment for the wicked is most frequently designated, are in themselves evidence that the locality to which they refer was supposed to be situated within the earth, or in some place concealed; as, sheol, hades, infernum, hell. Among the Celtic Druids the abyss whence the waters burst forth at the deluge of Gwyn, and the abode of the evil principle, was called annwn, the deep. And it was in "bottomless perdition" that Milton's place of doom was situated, where

"Hope never comes
That comes to all: but torture without end
Still urges, and a fiery deluge, fed
With ever-burning sulphur unconsumed."

† Homer makes the seat of hell as far beneath the deepest pit of earth as the heaven is above the earth, Il. viii. 16. Virgil makes it twice as far, Æn. vi. 577; and Milton thrice as far, Par. Lost, i. 73.—Bishop Newton's Milton.

‡ The position of these hells, and the effect produced by their flames, remind us of the molten sea that is regarded by geologists as existing in the interior of the globe. The flames issuing forth from a volcanic crater, with irregular intermissions, bear some resemblance to the rise and rolling, in unequal masses, of the great billows of the ocean. The earlier Budhists were familiar with caves; but these excavations were probably not sufficiently deep to have enabled them to observe the increase of temperature in proportion as we recede from the surface of the earth; and indeed, when referring

called Awíchi, from *a*, negative, and *wíchi*, refuge, because it affords no way of escape; it allows of no intermission to its misery.

There is also the hell called Lókántarika, which is the intervening space between every three sakwalas. In this world, there is above neither sun, moon, nor light; and below there is water, extremely cold. The darkness is incessant, except in the time of a supreme Budha, when occasionally the rays proceeding from his person, and filling the whole of the 10,000 sakwalas, are seen; but this appearance is only for a moment, like the lightning, no sooner seen than gone.

The inhabitants of Sanjíwa live 500 years, each year being the same length as a year in Cháturmahárajika, so that their age is 160,000 kelas of the years of men. In Kálasútra, the age is 1,296,000 kelas of years. In Sanghata it is one prakóti and 368,000 kelas. In Rowrawa, it is eight prakótis and 2,944,000 kelas. In Maha Rowrawa, it is sixty-four prakótis and 3,568,000 kelas. In Tápa, it is 530 prakótis and 8,416,000 kelas. In Awíchi it is an entire antah-kalpa.

12. *The Periodical Destruction and Renovation of the Universe.*

The rain that falls at the commencement of a kalpa is called sampattikara-maha-mégha. It is formed through the united merit of all beings (who live in the upper brahma-lókas and outer sakwalas). The drops are at first small as the gentle dew; then gradually become larger, until they are the size of a palm-tree. The whole of the space that was previously occupied by the kelalaksha of worlds destroyed by fire is filled with fresh water, and then the rain ceases. A wind then arises that agitates the water until it is dried up.* After a long period, the mansion of

to their thermal character, they represent them as places comparatively cool. There are similar speculations in the geognosy of the Greeks. " Within this earth, all around, there are greater and smaller caverns. There water flows in abundance; and also much fire, great fire-streams, and streams of wet mud. Periphlegethon flows into an extensive district burning with fierce fire; where it forms a lake larger than our own sea, boiling with water and mud. From hence it moves in circles round the earth, turbid and muddy."—Plato's Phædo. This periphlegethon was supposed to be universally prevalent in the interior of the globe. " Volcanic scoriæ and lava streams were portions of periphlegethon itself, portions of the subterranean melted and ever-moving mass."—Humbolt's Kosmos.

* " By what means is it that so great a body of water acquires the properties of solidity? By making apertures in various places, access to that body of water is afforded to the wind. Thus by the effect of the wind it becomes further concentrated, and acquires further consistency. It then begins to evaporate, and gradually subsides."—Commentary on the Patisambhidan.

Sekra appears, which is the first formation. Then the lower brahma-lókas and the déwa-lókas are formed in the place of those destroyed; and some of the brahmas from the upper lókas, either on account of the inferiority of their merit, or because their period of residence in those lókas is complete, appear in the brahma-lókas now formed, whilst others appear in the four superior déwa-lókas. The water gradually diminishes, until it reaches the place of the former earth, when a great wind arises, and by its influence completes the evaporation of the water. The earth is at first formed of a mould that in taste is like the food of the déwas, or like the honey that is distilled in the cup of the lotus. The whole surface of the earth is of a golden colour, like the kinichiri flower, a delightful fragrance arising therefrom; whilst a liquid like the drink of the déwas is exuded. The part where the sacred tree of Budha is to appear is the first spot of earth that is formed, as it is the last spot destroyed at the end of a kalpa. To point out this place, a lotus appears; and if a Budha is to be born in that kalpa a flower will be expanded: but if there is to be no Budha there will be no flower. If more Budhas than one are to appear, this will be revealed by the number of flowers that are seen; and near each flower there appears a complete set of pirikaras (the requisites of the priesthood) that are to be used by the Budha for whom they have been formed. The ruler of the brahma-lóka called Awiha descends to the earth in order that he may see whether a Budha will be born in that kalpa or not; in a moment he disperses the darkness of the world, and if he finds that there are any sets of pirikaras, he takes them with him on his return. Some of the brahmas from the lóka called Abhassara are then born here by the apparitional birth, with shining bodies, able to pass through the air, and their age is an asankya. When rice is boiled, a number of bubbles are formed at once upon the surface of the water, and there are some parts of that surface that are high, some depressed, and some level;* in like manner, at the formation of the earth, inequalities are apparent, forming hills, valleys, and plains.

It is on this wise that the destruction of the earth is effected,

---

* The true figure of the earth stands in the same relation to a regular figure "as the uneven surface of ruffled stands to the even surface of unruffled water."—Humbolt's Kosmos.

when fire is the agent. For the space of a hundred, a thousand, and a hundred thousand years, there is no rain. All plants that bear spices; all medicinal herbs; all palms and banyans; all trees of the five kinds, whether produced from the root, trunk, fruit, leaf, or seed; are entirely destroyed, so as never to spring up again.

A hundred thousand years previous to the commencement of this destruction, one of the déwas from a Kámáwachara déwalóka,* pitying the condition of the world, appears with disordered hair, eyes streaming with tears, and a form of woe. Arrayed in garments of a red colour, he proceeds throughout the whole of the sakwalas that are to be destroyed, crying out as he passes on, "In a hundred thousand years the kalpa will come to an end; a kelalaksha of worlds will be destroyed by fire; and as many earths, sakwala rocks, Himála forests, rocks encircling Méru, heavens, suns, and moons, will be involved in this destruction, which will extend to the brahma-lókas; whosoever would escape from this calamity, let him assist his parents, respect his superiors, avoid the five sins, and observe the five obligations."† The beings in the world, in great fear, approach the déwa, and ask him whether he has learnt this by his own wisdom, or has been taught it by another; when he replies, that he was sent by Maha Brahma, the déwa of many ages.‡ On hearing this declaration, the men and déwas of the earth regard each other with affection, from the fear that comes upon them, by which merit is produced, and they are born in a brahma-lóka.

When the hundred thousand years have elapsed, rain begins to fall at the same time in each of the sakwalas, at the appearance of which men rejoice, and the husbandmen begin to cultivate their fields; but when the grain has risen so high as that cattle might nibble it, no more rain will descend. The clouds entirely disappear; there is no more rain for a hundred thousand years; all

* All the worlds under the brahma-lókas are called kámáwachara.
† This warning is called kappa-kóláhala. There are in all five warnings, or presentiments.—1. Kappa-kóláhala; previous to the destruction of the world. 2. Chakrawartti; a hundred years previous to the birth of a universal monarch. 3. Budha; a thousand years previous to the birth of a Budha. 4. Mangala; twelve years before Budha preaches the Mangala-sútra. 5. Moneyya; seven years before Budha explains the Moneyya-piliwet, or ordinances of the rahats.
‡ This mission of the déwa bears some resemblance to that of Noah, the preacher of righteousness, during the respite of 120 years previous to the deluge. Gen. vi. 3; 1 Pet. iii. 20; 2 Pet. ii. 5.

forests are parched up; men suffer much from hunger and thirst, and then die; the déwas who reside in flowers and fruits, the yakás, garundas, nágas, and other beings of a similar description, after the endurance of much suffering, pass away, and are born in the déwa-lókas, and afterwards in the brahma-lókas; and the beings that have no merit are born in the hells of some outer sakwala.

After a long period, a second sun appears suddenly in the sky, and by its rays the 11,575 rivers, and the smaller ponds, tanks, and other places, are dried up, and white sand is formed.

After another long period a third sun appears, that burns up the five great rivers. Of these three suns, one traverses the sky, one is behind the mountain Hastagiri, and the other remains continually in the centre of the sky, causing its rays to fall without ceasing upon the whole of the four great continents. The déwa of the previously existing sun, terrified by the greatness of the heat, is born in a brahma-lóka, through the power of dhyána. The sun still remains in the sky, but there is no living existence connected with it. Sekra, and the rest of the déwas, through the power of the rite called wáyokasina, are born in the Parittasubha and other brahma-lókas.

After another long interval, a fourth sun is produced. By this the waters of the Anotatta and other great lakes are dried up; they boil as if agitated by a great fire, and then entirely disappear. Thus all the elements, from the Awíchi-naraka below to the Maha Brahmalóka above, are entirely destroyed.

In due time, a fifth sun appears. By means of this sun the waters of the great ocean are dried up to the depth of 100 yojanas, then of 200 yojanas, and gradually on to 1000 yojanas. They are afterwards dried up to the depth of 10,000 yojanas, and the diminution of the water proceeds until it has extended to the depth of 80,000 yojanas; and thus there will be only 4000 yojanas of water left. But the decrease goes on until there is only 1000 yojanas, then only 100 yojanas; and the process continues until the water is reduced to the depth of seven talas (or palm-trees each 80 cubits long). Thus all the water in the great oceans, from the Aswakarna to the sakwala rocks, is entirely evaporated. There is at last about the depth of one tala, then of seven porisas (the height of a man when his hand is held up over his head, or five cubits); gradually it diminishes to the height of a man, to the loins, the knee, and the ancle, to as much as would fill the feet-marks of cattle, just as the rain does on the surface of the earth in April or October; and finally, out of all the water of the lakes, seas, and oceans, not so much is left as would moisten the end of the finger.

After another long interval, a sixth sun is formed, when the earth and Méru send forth smoke; and there is thicker smoke, and still thicker, in succession. As when a fire is kindled by the potter to bake his clay, there is at first a little smoke, then more, until it rises in a great body; so from the lowest sakwala rock to the mansion of Sekra, all that exists, including the earth and Méru, sends forth one unbroken volume of smoke, which becomes thicker and blacker, the longer it continues to rise.

There is then the appearance of a seventh sun. The earth and Méru are burnt up. The flame reaches to the brahma-lókas. Pieces of rock, from 100 to 500 yojanas in size, are split from Méru, fly into the air, and are there consumed. Thus the earth and Méru are entirely destroyed, so as to be no more seen. Not even any ashes are visible. As when ghee or sesamum oil is burnt, the whole is consumed, so the whole earth, and all that is connected with it, is entirely destroyed; there are no remains of it whatever. Yet after the seventh sun has been produced, the sakwalas continue to burn through many hundreds of thousands of years, during which all the elements of confusion and ruin exert their power; whirling, roaring, bursting, blasting, thundering, until the work of destruction is perfect. From Awíchi to the brahma-lóka called Abhassara, the whole space becomes a dark void. The brahmas, dewas, men, animals, all beings of every degree, disappear, and the space once occupied by a kela-laksha of sakwalas becomes a dark abyss. This destruction is called Téjo-sangwartta.

A hundred thousand years previous to the destruction of the earth by water, a déwa appears to warn all the beings concerned of the event, as when it is destroyed by fire. A cloud forms at the same time in a kela-laksha of sakwalas, and after raining for a short time disappears. After an immense interval another cloud appears, and the rain called Khárodaka begins to fall; at first in small drops, but gradually increasing in size until they are as large as a palm-tree. This rain is so acrid that it dissolves entirely the earth and all things connected with it, after which the body of water thus produced mingles with the water of the Jala-polowa, upon which the earth had previously rested; but it is said by some, that though these waters are mingled together in one mass, there is still in that mass a separation of the two kinds of water, so that the one can be distinguished from the other. The rain goes on until the whole space between Ajatákása and the brahma-lóka called Parittasubha* is destroyed, and the void pervaded by a thick darkness. All the beings in a hundred thousand sakwalas disappear. This destruction is called Apo-sangwartta.

When the earth is destroyed by wind, there is a rain as when it is destroyed by fire or water; and after the elapse of an immense interval, a wind arises, that stirs up the fine dust, and then the gravel; and it then goes on to tear up stones, rocks, and trees, taking them into the air without letting them fall, grinding them, making a fearful noise, and reducing them to powder by the concussion, so that they entirely disappear. The wind called Prachanda arises from beneath the earth, and tears up rocks that are 500 yojanas in size, hurling them into the air, and destroying them. It next dashes earth against earth, Himála against Himála, Méru against Méru, sakwala-gala against sakwala-gala déwa-lóka against déwa-lóka, until the whole are destroyed. This destruction includes all places between the world of men and the ninth brahma-lóka, called Subhakírnnaka, which is 10,123,400 yojanas above the earth. The jala-polowa is blown into the air, and entirely disappears. Finally, from the world of men to the tenth brahma-lóka, called Wéhappala, is 13,320,600 yojanas; and the whole space between Ajatákása and the tenth brahma-lóka disappears; it is abandoned by all beings, and becomes dark and void. The déwas are born, through the exercise of the meditative rite called bháwaná, in the brahma-lókas that survive the destruction. The beings in the narakas, through the power obtained from their karma, or moral action, are born in the naraka of some other sakwala; or in an ákása, or aerial abode, formed by the same power. There are other beings that by the power of the rite called wáyokasina are born in the brahma-lókas; or if still under the power of demerit, the merit

* The Commentary on the sacred text says, "Whenever the kappo is destroyed by water, it perishes by the water below Subhakinno."—Turnour's Annals, No. 3.

they have received in births long previous exercises its power, and prevents them from going to a place of pain.* The destruction produced by the agency of wind is called Wáyo-sangwartta. (*Súryódgamana-sútra-sanné.*)

Previous to the destruction by water, cruelty, or violence, prevails in the world; previous to that by fire, licentiousness; and previous to that by wind, ignorance. When licentiousness has prevailed, men are cut off by disease; when enmity, by turning their weapons against each other; and when ignorance, by famine.

In every instance, so complete is the destruction, that no remains whatever of the sakwalas are to be found, not even anything answering to the ashes of wood that has been consumed by fire; the air above the earth, and that below, mingle together, as there is nothing to separate the one from the other.† Whether

* At the end of the day of Brahma, a dissolution of the universe occurs, when all the three worlds, earth, and the regions of space, are consumed with fire. The dwellers of Maharloka (the region inhabited by the saints who survive the world) distressed by the heat, repair then to Janaloka (the region of holy men after their decease).—Wilson's Vishnu Purána.

† According to the system of the Brahmans, the ten lower worlds are partially destroyed at the close of every kalpa, equal to a day of Brahma, and renovated at the end of each succeeding night; so that there are 36,000 revolutions of the world during one cycle of its existence. But at the dissolution of Brahma there is a maha pralaya, or complete destruction of the whole universe; all things being utterly annihilated and reduced to entire nothingness; or, if we adopt another idea, all things being merged in the deity, until Brahm shall awake and a new world be manifested. "That immutable power, Brahma, by waking and reposing alternately, re-vivifies and destroys in eternal succession, the whole assemblage of locomotive and immoveable creatures."—Manu. Inst. i. 57. "The Brahma-mimánsa (or Védánta) endeavours to reconcile the existence of moral evil under the government of an all-wise, all-powerful, and benevolent providence, with the absence of freewill, by assuming the past eternity of the universe, and the infinite renewal of worlds, into which every individual being has brought the predispositions contracted by him in earlier states, and so retrospectively without beginning or limit."—Colebrooke, Miscellaneous Essays, i. 377.

It is said to have been taught by Hermes, that the Governor of the world, "always resisting vice, and restoring things from their degeneracy, will either wash away the malignity of the world by water, or consume it by fire, and restore it to its ancient form again." The Egyptians supposed the world would be destroyed, partly by inundation, and partly by conflagration. Cudworth's Intellectual system. This idea was entertained by Pythagoras, and may have been received either during his residence in Egypt, or in his travels in Asia. It was the opinion of Anaximander, that worlds are continually in the course of formation, and that they are as constantly re-dissolved into the infinity, το άπειρον, whence they are derived. Empedocles and Heraclitus, and afterwards the Stoics, supposed that the world is generated, and then corrupted; and that this is done again and again in revolutions infinite. This phrase of Heraclitus had great celebrity, "All is, and is not; for though in truth it does come into being, yet it forthwith ceases to be." — Lewes, Biograph. Hist. Phil. i. 111. Plutarch says, that the shaking of the

the medium of destruction be fire, water, or wind, it is equally complete. But it is not to be supposed that these effects are produced by any innate power of their own. As the world is at

four bars within the circular apsis of the sistrum represented the agitation of the four elements within the compass of the world, by which all things are continually destroyed and reproduced. The Gnostics of the Alexandrian school taught that as the Godhead can never have been unemployed, an endless series of worlds must have preceded the present, and an endless series of words will follow it.—Giesler, Text-Book of Eccles. Hist. Similar opinions were entertained by the Druids and Mexicans.—Faber's Origin of Pagan Idolatry, vol. i. cap. ii: "Concerning the Pagan Doctrine of a Succession of similar Worlds." But by the Peripatetics and others a different doctrine was taught. They were of opinion that the world had never been created and could never be destroyed; as they could trace in the universe no seminal principles, they believed it to be "fatherless and eternal, destitute of origin, and beyond the influence of fate." "Violent corruptions and mutations take place in the parts of the earth; at one time, indeed, the sea overflowing into another part of the earth; but at another, the earth itself becoming dilated and divulsed, through wind or water latently entering into it. But an entire corruption of an arrangement of the whole earth never did happen, nor ever will."—Taylor's Ocellus Lucanus.

It was the doctrine of Budha, that there are not only alternate destructions and renovations of the world, but that each successive world is homogeneous in its constituent parts, having the four continents of the same size, with the same cities, under different names; but though the general features are the same, and in many instances the same individual actors are introduced, this resemblance does not extend to an identity of events, as was taught by some of the Greeks. It was affirmed by many of the Stoics that from the beginning to the end of the world, all things are dispensed by a regular law, so that not only as to the successive conflagrations and inundations, but also as to all other occurrences, there is a repetition of the same events; that which now takes place has taken place in previous ages, times innumerable, and will again take place times infinite. About the time of the commencement of Christianity this idea appears to have been very generally prevalent, and to have produced the most pernicious consequences. It was thought to be unnecessary to address the Divinity in prayer, inasmuch as "everything revolves with unchanging laws in one eternal circle."

As all the worlds below the tenth brahma-lóka are occasionally destroyed, the totality of the destruction being expressed in the strongest terms, it is not right to say, as has sometimes been assumed, that the eternity of matter is one of the dogmas of Budha. Relative to the superior worlds that are beyond the reach of all the revolutions that affect the earth, I have seen no positive statement, their existence may be eternal; but the general principles of Budhism by no means agree with the doctrine of Empedocles, and others of the same school, that "all existences are but a mingling, and then a separation of the mingled."

The opinion that the destruction of the world is at one time accomplished by the agency of fire, and at another time by that of water, agrees, to some extent, with sacred writ. Heraclitus taught that as fire is the first principle of all things, all things shall at last be redissolved into this element; Epicurus supposed that as fire is the most active of the elements, it will in the end overcome the others, and destroy them; and it was the doctrine of Zeno that the world will perish by fire, a principle everywhere diffused, which will in time resolve all things into itself, and will afterwards, as it is the seed of all things, diffuse itself again through the vacuity it has caused, thus producing a new world.

first produced by the power of the united merit, punya-bala, of all the various orders of being in existence, so its destruction is caused by the power of their demerit, pápa-bala.

The notions entertained by Gótama that there are innumerable worlds, that the earth has nothing beneath it but the circumambient air; that the interior of the earth is incandescent; and that the world will be destroyed by the agency of fire; may so far be correct;—and a small portion of his other cosmical speculations may agree with ancient philosophy or modern science;—but they are mixed up with so many other statements which have no foundation whatever in truth, that they seem like the meteors of the morass, a dim light where there are dangers numberless, or like insulated rocks that are no protection to the mariner, as they are covered by every wave that rushes near them in the storm. The whole of his cosmogony, and of his astronomical revelations, is erroneous; and there are statements in nearly every deliverance attributed to him upon these subjects which prove that his mind was beclouded by like ignorances with other men; consequently, he cannot be, as he is designated by his disciples, "a sure guide to the city of peace."

II. THE VARIOUS ORDERS OF SENTIENT EXISTENCE.

I. THE PASÉ-BUDHAS.—II. THE RAHATS.—III. THE DÉWAS.—IV. THE BRAHMAS.—V. THE GANDHARWAS.—VI. THE GARUNDAS.—VII. THE NÁGAS.—VIII. THE YAKÁS.—IX. THE KHUMBÁNDAS.—X. THE ASURS.—XI. THE RÁKSHAS.—XII. THE PRÉTAS.—XIII. THE INHABITANTS OF THE NARAKAS, OR PLACES OF SUFFERING.

As all the systems of worlds are homogeneous, so are the orders of being by whom they are inhabited; the various distinctions that are now presented being only of temporary duration. With the exception of those beings who have entered into one of the four paths leading to nirwána, there may be an interchange of condition between the highest and lowest. He who is now the most degraded of the demons, may one day rule the highest of the heavens; he who is at present seated upon the most honourable of the celestial thrones may one day writhe amidst the agonies of a place of torment; and the worm that we crush under our feet may, in the course of ages, become a supreme Budha. When any of the four paths are entered, there is the certainty that in a definite period, more or less remote, nirwána will be obtained; and they who have entered into the paths are regarded as the noblest of all the intelligences in the universe. Hence our earth, in the time of a supreme Budha, or when the sacred dharmma is rightly understood and faithfully observed, is the most favoured of all worlds; the priests, or those who observe the precepts, assume a higher rank than any other order of being whatever; and there is an immeasurable distance between even the most exalted of the déwas or brahmas and "the teacher of the three worlds," who is supreme.

Exclusive of the supreme Budhas, the various orders of intelligence include—1. Pasé-Budhas. 2. Rahats. 3. Déwas. 4. Brahmas. 5. Gandhárwas. 6. Garundas. 7. Nágas. 8. Yakás. 9. Khumbandas. 10. Asúrs. 11. Rákshas. 12. Prétas, and other monsters. 13. The inhabitants of the Narakas: in addition to the beasts of the field, the fowls of the air, the fish of the waters, and beings engendered from filth and excrement. The three superior classes are déwas, brahmas, and men. Among men appear sidhas, who can perform wonders by the aid of herbs and other medicinal substances and preparations; widyádharas, who can exercise the same powers by the aid of mantras, or charms; and rishis, who can exercise the same powers through the practice of certain rites and austerities. These orders are divided into five gati, or conditions:—1. Déwa, divine. 2. Manusya, human. 3. Préta, monstrous. 4. Tirisan, brute. 5. Niraya, infernal.

I. The Pasé-Budhas are sages of wondrous power, who never appear at the same time as a supreme Budha; yet in the kalpa in which there is no supreme Budha there is no Pasé-Budha (1). They attain to their high state of privilege by their own unaided powers. Their knowledge is limited; but they never fall into any error that would involve the transgression of the precepts. In the five gradations of being enumerated by Nágaséna, the Pasé-Budhas are placed between the rahat and the supreme Budha. Their relative dignity may be learnt from the announcement, that when alms were given to them it produces greater merit by a hundred times than when given to the rahats; and that when given to the supreme Budhas it produces greater merit by sixteen times sixteen than when given to them. The supreme Budhas reveal the paths leading to nirwána to all beings; but the Pasé-Budhas can only obtain nirwána for themselves. They cannot release any other being from the miseries of successive existence. They cannot preach the perfect bana, even as the dumb man, though he may have seen a remarkable dream, cannot explain it to others; or as the savage, who enters a city and is sumptuously fed by some respectable citizen who meets with him, is unable, on his return to the forest, to give his fellow-savages an idea of the taste of the food he has eaten, because they are not accustomed to food of the same kind, but although they cannot teach others, they may themselves attain to a perfect acquaintance with the four pratisambhidás, or modes of supernatural illumination. They can give precepts so as to lessen the power of the sensuous principle; but they cannot entirely destroy it. It is a rule of the priests in Ceylon who belong to the sect of the Amarapuras, not to follow the observances of the Pasé-Budhas, unless they have received the sanction of Gótama.

II. The fourth of the paths leading to nirwána is called arya, or aryahat. The ascetic who has entered this path is called a Rahat. He is free from all cleaving to sensuous objects. Evil desire has become extinct within him, even as the principle of fructification has become extinct in the tree that has been cut down by the root, or the principle of life in the seed that has been exposed to the influence of fire. The mind of the rahat is incapable of error upon any subject connected with religious truth; though he may make mistakes upon common subjects, or from allowing the faculty of observation to remain in abeyance. There are five great powers that the rahat possesses:—1. Irdhi, or the power of working miracles; he can rise into the air, overturn the earth, or arrest the course of the sun. 2. The power to hear all sounds, from whatever being proceeding. 3. The power to know the thoughts of other beings. 4. The power of knowing what births were received in former ages. 5. The power of knowing what births will be received by any being in future ages. But all rahats do not possess these powers in an equal degree of perfection. The rahat is subject to bodily pain; nevertheless, his mind is free from the usual accompaniments of pain, such as agitation, sorrow, or unsubmissiveness; as the trunk of the tree remains unmoved in the storm, though the branches may be subject to violent oscillations. This high state of privilege was sometimes received in an instant; as when the ascetic Nigródha became a rahat whilst his hair was being cut off to prepare him for the reception of the priesthood. But in other cases it required a long and laborious exercise of discipline; the facility of acquirement being ruled by the amount of merit received in former births. In the earlier ages of Budhism, the rahatship was attained by females. At his death, the rahat invariably enters nirwána, or ceases to exist. As the cause of re-production, karma, is destroyed, it is not possible for him to enter upon any other mode of existence; the concretive power that binds together the elements of existence is now wanting; the effect ceases, from the evanishment of the cause. To make a false profession of the attainment of rahatship is one of the four crimes that involve permanent exclusion from the priesthood.

III. The moment that man loses the aid of induction, and enters into the unseen world, his littleness becomes manifest; and yet in no department of investigation has he pursued his course with more complacency, or allowed his imagination a revelry more unrestrained. But the bolder the flight he has taken, the less has he brought conviction to the minds of those who have listened to his reveries; as all his creations are only a repetition of what any one may see in the every-day world; or they are airy nothings; or they are an unnatural jumble of things that have no affinity, and can never be really conjoined. New arrangements he can form; and when he has accomplished this simple task, he beguiles himself into the belief that he has emanated a new existence. There is, therefore, no part of heathenism that is less interesting than its description of other worlds; and in no light does it appear so absurd as in its accounts of the creatures by which they are inhabited. The Pasé-Budhas and rahats are equally partakers of humanity; but we must now pass on to the consideration of the unearthly and the monstrous.

The déwas of Budhism do not inhabit the déwa lókas exclusively, as in the world of men there are also déwas of trees, rocks, and the elements. They resemble the saints of the Romanists, or the kindred dii minores of a more ancient faith, as they are beings who were once men but are now reaping the reward of their prowess or virtue. They reside in a place of happiness; but do not possess the higher attributes of divinity. They receive birth by the apparitional form, are subject to various passions, and in size are more than colossal (2). Their number must be incalculable by the numeration of mortals; as many myriads of myriads are represented as being present when Gótama delivered the discourse called Maha Samaya, in the hall of Kútágára, near his native city of Kapilawastu. When the acquisition of merit in previous births has been small, the déwas become subject to fear as they approach the period in which they are to pass into some other mode of existence. Thus Sekra himself, the ruler of Tawutisá, previous to the occasion upon which he heard the sacred bana from the lips of Gótama (by which he received merit, and thereby a prolongation of the period of his reign), became greatly sorrowful when he reflected that he was about to leave the pleasures he had so long enjoyed. But the déwas who possess a greater share of merit are free from fear, as they know that when they are re-born it will be in some superior state of existence.

The functions of the déwas are of varied character, and in some instances inconsistent with the powers attributed to "the three gems." They endeavour to prevent the acquirement of merit by those whom they fear will supplant them in the possession of the various pleasures and dignities they respectively enjoy (3). They take cognizance of the actions of men, as we learn from the legend of the guardian deities (4). They sympathize with those who act aright, as in the case of the nobleman Wisàkha (5); and punish those by whom they themselves are injured (6), or those who insult and persecute the faithful (7).

The grand principles of Budhism would be complete without the existence of any other orders of being beside those that inhabit our earth, and are perceptible to the senses; and it would agree better with the genius of the system propounded by Gótama, to suppose that, like other sceptics, he believed in neither angel nor demon, than to imagine that the accounts of the déwas and other supernatural beings we meet with in works called Budhistical were known at its first promulgation. All the accounts of his interviews with déwas and brahmas, as well as those which represent these agencies as listening to his words and doing him homage, must, it is unnecessary to say, have been the product of a more recent age. It is possible that he may have enunciated the mundane system now attributed to him, and have spoken of other worlds, which his disciples peopled with imaginary beings, in deference to vulgar prejudice or from pride of office, making them ancillary to the exaltation of the sage in whose glory they so largely participated. There is the greater reason to believe that this class of legends has been grafted upon Budhism from a foreign source; as nearly the whole of them may be traced to opinions that are common to almost every school that arose among the Hindus in the period that succeeded the age of Gótama. We have a similar process in the hagiology of all the ancient churches of Christendom; and in the traditions of the Jews and Mussulmans, which came not from the founders of the systems, but from the perverted imaginations of their followers in after days.

In some instances the names of the déwas and brahmas are the same as those we meet with among the records of Brahmanism; but we are not on that account to confound the religion of the Pitakas with that of the Puránas. Budhism knows nothing of an infinite nihility like Brahm; nor of Brahma, the creator, Vishnu, the preserver, or Siva, the destroyer. Maha Brahma is simply the ruler of a brahma-lóka. Sekra is the déwa most frequently introduced into the tales and legends with which Budhistical works abound; but he is represented rather as being the servant of the faithful, than as receiving their adoration or as the object of their prayers. The honour that the Budhists who best understand their religion pay to the déwas is extremely small. The priests believe themselves to be higher than the most exalted of these celestial agencies. There are déwálas (places of worship dedicated to the déwas) in nearly every village in the Singhalese provinces of Ceylon; but there are few instances, if any, in which a temple is dedicated to any déwa who is prominently mentioned in the sacred books of the Budhists; which is an additional proof that the whole system is an unauthorised adjunct, being either engrafted upon Budhism from the practices of the Brahmans, or brought down from the times preceding the introduction of the bana into Ceylon. The further we go back, and the more respectable our authority, the less we find of the déwas; and in many instances their introduction is so clumsily brought about, and their design so apparent, as not to deceive any but the most unreflective mind.

There is little to excite the affection of men for the déwas, beyond the sympathy that one intelligence feels for another. The gods of the Greeks and Romans were brought before them as possessing mighty and mysterious powers; or as exercising a genial influence in some particular department of human economy; or as the inventors of some art, science, or instrument that ministers to the general comfort. But the Budhist regards the world as being under the governance of an authority over which the déwas have no control; and the native of India would despise rather than reverence the being who is in any way connected with manual exercises, even in their most pleasing or beneficial form. The déwas are feared rather than loved; and if their aid is asked, it is in sullenness or with ill-concealed contempt.

In many of the accounts that are given us of the attempts of the déwas to prevent the rishis and others from attaining the high rank that their merit would ensure if permitted to go on to its full development, we have a parallel to the envy with which the gods of the Greeks looked upon the advancement of man in those branches of knowledge that they regarded as being exclusively their own heritage. The story of Prometheus was of most terrible import to all who wished to pass beyond the bounds of common mortality; and the lesson it teaches is heard, with more or less distinctness, in almost every tradition of the mythic age.

IV. The inhabitants of the brahma-lókas have attained to a more exalted state than the déwas. In the worlds in which they have sensuous enjoyment, they are brighter and larger than the déwas, have a larger retinue, more extensive riches, and live to a greater age. The rúpa (the aggregate of the elements that constitute the body) of the Brahmas differs from that of men, and is one peculiar to themselves. They are insensible to heat and cold, and are entirely free from sexual passion. They have attained their present state of exaltation by the exercise of the rite called dhyána; and when the age allotted to them has passed away, they may be born as men, as animals, or in any other world. In some of the worlds they are self-resplendent, traverse the atmosphere, and have purely intellectual pleasure. In the arúpa worlds, four in number, they have no bodily form. In all the worlds, except one, they have a conscious state of being; in one, they are unconscious; and in another, they are in a state " not fully conscious, nor yet altogether unconscious."

The chief of the brahma-lókas, Sampati Maha Brahma (8) continually exercises the four following volitions: 1. Of friendship; thus wishing, May all beings, having received the same merit as myself, enjoy an equal reward. 2. Of compassion; thus wishing, May all beings be released from the four hells, and become happy. 3. Of tenderness; thus wishing, May all who are born in the brahma-lókas retain their happiness throughout a long period. 4. Of equity; thus wishing, May all beings receive the reward of their own proper merit. But by far higher than the Maha Brahma who exercises these volitions is the lord of the three worlds, Budha.

V. The Gandhárwas reside in the lóka called Chaturmaharájika. Their bodies are sixteen yojanas high. They are choristers and musicians, and when sent for they can go to any lóka that they may minister to the amusement of the déwas.

VI. The Garundas have the shape of immense birds, and are represented as being great enemies to the nágas.

VII. The Nágas reside in the lóka under the Trikuta rocks that support Méru, and in the waters of the world of men. They have the shape of the spectacle-snake, with the extended hood (coluber nága); but many actions are attributed to them that can only be done by one possessing the human form. They are demi-gods, and have many enjoyments; and they are usually represented as being favourable to Budha and his adherents; but when their wrath is roused, their opposition is of a formidable character. If their name be derived from the root nága, a mountain, it may have reference to the place of their abode, under Méru. There is a race of people called Nágas residing upon the elevated region between Assam and Manipur, who are said to be universally dreaded for the devastations they commit upon the inhabitants of the plains; and it is possible that the mythological nágas may have had their origin in the fears produced by the ravages of the ancient mountaineers. Another name by which they are known, nayás, bears a considerable resemblance to that of the νηιδες, naiades of the Greeks, who also resided in rivers, lakes, and streams. "As vigilant as a nayá who guards a hidden treasure," is a common expression, giving to these beings the same office that is borne by the genii of the Arabs. Even in England there is a current opinion that near abbeys and other old places there are treasures watched over by snakes.

VII. The Yakás are not to be classed with devils, though this is their popular designation. They are beings whose karma has placed them in the situation they now occupy in the scale of existence; but many of their acts might be attributed to the déwas, as many of the acts of the déwas might be attributed to them, without any appearance of impropriety (9). The Singhalese have a great dread of their power, and in times of distress the yakadurá, or devil-dancer, is almost invariably called upon to overcome their malignity by his chaunts and charms; but these practices receive no sanction from Gótama, and in some instances are condemned, especially when the life of any animal is offered in sacrifice. Though some of them are malignant, and reject the authority of their ruler, " even as in the kingdom of Magadha the thieves rebel against the king and his ministers," their enmity is to be overcome by exorcism not by sacrifice. The dwelling-place of the yakás is not in the narakas; so that they are not spirits condemned to ceaseless torments like the devils of revelation; they are found in the earth, and in the waters, and form one section of the guards round the mansion of Sekra. They marry, and delight in dances, songs, and other amusements; their strength is great; and some of them are represented as possessing splendour and dignity. There are instances in which they have entered the paths that lead to nirwána; and in one birth, after he became a candidate for the Budhaship, Gótama was himself a yaká. After his reception of the Budhaship, there came to him one night, when his residence was on the eagle-peak near Rajagaha, the guardian deities of the four quarters, attended by a large retinue. "Some of the yakás worshipped him and sat down; others sat down after having had pleasing conversation with him; others merely bowed themselves with elevated clasped hands and sat down; some announced their names and race; and others sat down in silence. When they were seated, their great king, Wessawano, thus addressed Budha: There are, my lord, some demons of great power who are opposed to Budha, and others who are attached to him; there are some demons of the middle order who are opposed to Budha, and some who are attached to him; there are some demons of the lowest order who are opposed to Budha, and some who are attached to him. What is the reason, my lord, that many demons are opposed to Budha? Budha, my lord, has preached abstinence from destroying life, from theft, from lewdness, from lying, and from intoxicating drinks, which cause irreligion. Many demons, my lord, do not abstain from destroying life, from theft, from lewdness, from lying, and from intoxicating drinks which cause irreligion, and they are dissatisfied and displeased with these doctrines. My lord, there are disciples of Budha who reside in solitary parts of forests, free from noise and tumult, in quiet and retirement, remote from men. In those retired places demons of great power reside, who are opposed to the doctrines of Budha. Therefore, my lord, to placate them, learn the átánátiya defence, or pirit, by which the priests and priestesses, the male and female (lay) disciples, may be preserved, defended, kept free from harm, and live in peace. Budha silently consented to his request. Then the great king, Wessawano, perceiving that Budha silently consented, spake the átánátiya defence." After it had been recited, the demon king declared, that "if any priest or priestess, male or female disciple, fully and perfectly learn this defence, none of the amanusa (not-men), no male or female yaká, &c., will approach him with an evil design, whether walking, standing, sitting, or reclining."—Rev. D. J. Gogerly, Ceylon Friend, iii, 21.

IX. The Khumbandas, who guard the palace of Sekra on the south, are monsters of immense size and disgusting form.

X. The Asurs reside under Méru (10). There were formerly contests carried on between them and the déwas of Tawutisá, but when Manamánawakayá became Sekra, they were finally defeated, and from that time have been kept in subjection. The four guardian deities of that lóka, with their attendants, are appointed to their respective offices that they may ward off the attacks of the asurs.

There are many allusions, even in the most sacred of the Páli writings, to the seizure of the sun and moon by the asurs Ráhu and Kétu. In the performance of the pirit exorcism, the following extract, entitled Chanda Pirit, or the Moon's Protection, is read from the Pitakas:—" Thus I heard. Budha resided in the garden of Anathapindika, in Jatawany, near Sawatti. At that time the god Chanda (the moon), was seized by the asur Ráhu (i.e., the moon was eclipsed). Then the god Chanda remembering Budha, at that moment spake this stanza: O conquering Budha, I adore thee! thou art perfectly free from evil; I am in distress; be thou my refuge! Then Budha spake this stanza to the asur Ráhu on behalf of the god Chánda: Ráhu! Chanda has taken refuge in the holy Tatágata. Release Chanda! Budha compassionates the world. Then the asur Ráhu released the god Chanda, and immediately fled to Wepachitti (the chief of the asurs) and stood trembling and affrighted by his side; when Wepachitti addressed Ráhu in the following stanza: Ráhu, why did you suddenly release Chanda? why have you come trembling and stand here affrighted? My head (replied Ráhu) would have been split into seven pieces; I should have had no comfort in my life; I have been spoken to by Budha in a stanza; otherwise I would not have released Chanda."—Gogerly; Ceylon Friend, ii, 228. There is a similar narrative, entitled Suriya Pirit, or the Sun's Protection.

The asurs have been compared to the Titans and Giants of the Greeks, as in stature they are immensely greater than any other order of being; and as they are connected with eclipses and made war with the déwas, there appears to be some ground for the comparison; it being generally agreed that the giants were personifications of the elements, and that their wars with the gods refer to the throes of the world in its state of chaos.

XI. The Rákshas resemble the yakás; but they have not, like them, the power to assume any shape that they choose. When appearing to men, they must assume their own proper form. They live principally in the forest of Himála, and feed on the flesh of the dead, whether of beasts or of men.

XII. The Prétas inhabit the Lókántarika naraka (11). In appearance they are extremely attenuated, like a dry leaf. There are some prétas that haunt the places near which they had formerly lived as men; they are also found in the suburbs of cities, and in places where four ways meet.

XIII. The inhabitants of the Narakas endure intense misery; and it was declared by Gótama that those who transgress the precepts will be born in these worlds (12). To tell the fearfulness of their affliction is difficult; it is like the joining together of all evil things; it is not possible rightly to declare it. A priest having asked Gótama to explain it by comparison, the sage proceeded thus:—" A man who has committed some great offence is brought into the presence of the king, who commands that early in the morning he shall be pierced by a hundred spears. This is done; but at noon the monarch is told that the criminal still lives; he is astonished to hear it, but commands that he be pierced by a hundred more. In the evening he is told that he is not yet dead, and he commands that the punishment be repeated. Thus the criminal is pierced by 300 spears. Can that which he endures therefrom be understood?" The priest replied, "The pain produced by one single spear would be exceedingly severe; how, then, is it possible for any one to understand the pain that would be produced by the piercing of 300 spears?" After receiving this reply, Budha took up a handful of small pebbles from the ground, and said we might affirm that the great Himála is ten, twenty, or a thousand times larger than those stones; but that it would not be an adequate comparison. "In like manner," he continued, "as this handful of stones is inadequate to show forth the extent of the great Himála, so is the pain produced by the piercing of 300 spears inadequate to show forth the greatness of the misery of the narakas."

The other beings that are introduced as living in different regions and worlds are mere deformities; and are presented before us in all their repulsiveness, without any equivalent to the covering with which the Greeks, in their more cultivated ages, invested beings who in their original shape were equally monstrous. The fallen spirits that lead men captive at their will have seized upon that creative power which, when the offspring of a hope founded on the word of God, was intended to impart the power to man to build unto himself a heaven worthy of his residence when his intellect shall become mighty as that of the seraph; and they have made it frame, out of the disjecta membra of things visible and creatures existent, regions and races of being that cannot possibly have an antitype in any world. These wild fantasies are to the spirits that have drawn them forth as the laughter-moving comedy in the great drama of man; but to the thoughtful mind they tell of the degradation of our species, and fastly-flowing tears are their proper accompaniment.

1. *The Pasé Budhas.*

Before this privilege can be obtained, there must have been the practice of the páramitás, or prescribed virtues, during two asankyakap-lakshas; as in no other way can it be acquired.* There are five things necessary to its reception. He who receives it must be a male, and not a person in whom the two sexes are conjoined; he must have seen a supreme Budha (in some previous birth), a Pasé-Budha, or a rahat; he must have exercised faith in the exalted personage thus seen; and he must have desired the same office. It is equally necessary that he be born of one of the three superior castes, as he can belong to no other; and that he appear at the period when the age of man is of the same length as is requisite for the birth of a supreme Budha. The Pasé-Budha can visit the golden cave in the forest of Himála, and can keep the póya festivals at the manjusa tree in the same forest.

2. *The Déwas.*

The inhabitants of the déwa-lókas are all twelve miles in height. When Bódhisat was in Tusita, he had a crown four miles high; he had also sixty wagon-loads of gems and jewels, all other kinds of treasures, and a kela of beautiful attendants.

* The word pachchéko, derived from pati-ékan, by permutation of letters contracted into pachchéko and pachché (in Singhalese, pasé) signifies, severed from unity (with supreme Budhahood): and is a term applied to an inferior being or saint, who is never co-existent with a supreme Budha, as he is only manifested during the period intervening between the nibbána of one and the advent of the succeeding supreme Budha, and attains nibbána without rising to supreme Budhahood.—Turnour's Mahawanso.

II. ORDERS OF SENTIENT EXISTENCE. 51

In one of our years the déwas breathe 216 times, which is 18 times in one of our months, and once in 100 hours. In one hundred of our years they eat once.

3. *The Legend of Lomasa Kásyapa.*

There was a rishi called Lomasa Kásyapa who kept the precepts so perfectly that the throne of Sekra became warm (which was an indication that his exalted office was in danger). When the déwa looked to see what was the reason of this occurrence, and discovered it, he resolved that he would try to set aside the merit of the rishi. For this purpose he went to the palace of the king of Benares, and appeared to the monarch as he was reclining upon a couch, saying, "I am Sekra; if you would become lord of the whole earth you must entreat the rishi Kásyapa, now living in the forest of Himála, to offer a sacrifice of all kinds of animals, from the elephant downwards." The king accordingly, by the beating of the city drum, found out a hunter who knew the way to the dwelling of the rishi, with whom he sent the noble Saiha. On arriving at the place, he requested in the king's name that he would offer the sacrifice; but Lomasa Kásyapa replied that he would not thus relinquish the merit he had gained by the observance of the precepts, for all the wealth of the world. After this Sekra again appeared to the king, and recommended him to send his daughter Chandrawati-déwi to make the same request. In consequence of this advice, the princess was arrayed in the most beautiful manner, and sent to the forest under the care of the same noble, who said to the rishi that the king would give him the hand of his daughter and the half of his kingdom, if he would offer the sacrifice. At the sight of the princess the rishi forgot the obligations by which he was bound, and was willing to accompany her to the city. On their arrival, the animals were all assembled in the place of sacrifice; but when he lifted up the knife to slay the elephant, the affrighted beast cried out, and all the rest joined in the lamentation. This brought the rishi to his senses; and throwing down the knife, he fled at once to the forest, where he accomplished the requisite amount of merit, and was afterwards born in a brahma-lóka. This rishi was the Bódhisat who afterwards became Gótama Budha; but as he was under the influence of a temporary madness when he thus resolved upon taking life, it is not contrary to the declaration that in every birth he received as a human being, he was kind to all sentient existence.

4. *The four Guardian Déwas.*

When Sekra is seated upon his throne, called Dharmma, in the hall of Suddharmma, on the atawaka (the eighth day after the new and full moon) the scribes of the four guardian déwas; on the day of the new moon, the sons of the four déwas; and on the day of the full moon, the déwas themselves; coming to the earth, observe in all places the following circumstances: "To-day so many men have observed the póya (or sacred day); so many women have attended to the ordinances; by so many persons the threefold protective formulary has been repeated; so many assist their parents; so many render the due honours to the chiefs of their clan; so many offer flowers and lamps in their places of worship; so many say bana, hear bana, or invite others to hear it; so many make offerings to the dágobas, the sacred trees, and the images of Budha; so many perform righteous acts with the body, the speech, and the mind; and so many perform the ten virtues." These things being written in the golden books with vermilion, the books are delivered to the children of the four guardian deities; the children give them to Wésamuna (the master of the revels), who hands them over to Panchasikha (the vizier or prime minister of Sekra, who has five heads, or faces); and by him they are presented to Mátali (the charioteer of Sekra), who gives them to Sekra. If the persons upon earth who acquire merit are few, the books of record are small in size; if many, they are large. When the books are small, all the déwas observe the circumstance and exclaim, in sorrow, "The beings upon earth who acquire merit are few; the narakas will be filled, and the déwa-lokas will not be replenished."

When the books are large, they exclaim, "The beings upon earth pass their time in the observance of the precepts, and procure an abundance of merit; the narakas will be depopulated, and our celestial worlds will be filled." The illustrious déwas who have acquired merit upon earth during the appearance of a Budha, exclaim in rapture, "We shall have joy." Then Sekra, ascending his throne of flowers, sixteen miles high, takes the books into his hands, and reads. If he reads in a low tone, the déwas can hear it to the distance of twelve yojanas; if in a high tone, it is heard by all the déwas in Tawutisá to the distance of 10,000 yojanas. In this manner, when Sekra has assembled the déwas, and seated himself in the hall of Suddharmma, these are the principal acts of the four guardian deities; they come to the earth, observe the merit acquired by men, and having recorded it in the golden books, present them in the manner now declared to Sekra; they are an assistance to the world, and perform many other acts of a similar character.

5. *The Faithful Priest.*

There was a nobleman in Pelalup, called Wisákha, who having heard of the fame of Ceylon, and of the privileges there enjoyed, gave all he possessed, though his wealth was immense, to his family, except one single piece of gold, which he tied in the corner of his garment, and went to the sea-side that he might embark for the island. But as he had to wait a whole month before he found a ship going in that direction, he began to trade with his money; and at the time of embarking, through his great skill as a merchant, he had gained a thousand pieces of gold. With this sum he arrived at Tambraparnna (Ceylon), and afterwards went to the city of Anurádhapura, where he solicited admission into the priesthood, from the inmates of the principal wihára. But when they perceived the wealth he had brought, they told him that as the priests could not make use of money he had better dispose of it previous to admission. Upon hearing this he threw it down into the midst of the court. He was then admitted to the noviciate, and five years afterwards to the order of upasampadá. After this he went from one wihára to another, remaining four months at each place, and exercising the form of meditation called maitrí-bháwaná. One day, after performing this exercise, he said aloud in the forest, "I have perfectly kept the obligations since I became a priest, and therefore a great reward awaits me." Afterwards he went towards the wihára of Kitulpaw; but on coming to a place where four ways met, he was in perplexity as to which was the right path, until the déwa of a neighbouring rock stretched forth a hand, and said, "In this direction." Having remained at the wihára four months, he thought of departing on the following morning. But in the night, as he was walking in the hall of ambulation, he saw a déwa near the steps at the entrance, weeping. On asking who he was, he said that he was the déwa who resided in the tree midháta, near that place. The priest then enquired why he wept, and he said, "Whilst you have remained here, the priests have been at peace with each other; but when you depart, they will again begin to quarrel; therefore I weep." The priest, listening to the complaint of the déwa, resolved not to leave the wihára, and abode there until he attained nirwána.

6. *The Unfortunate Priest.*

There was formerly in Ceylon, in the province of Ruhuna, a wihára, or temple, called Kshíranága, in which a number of priests resided, one of whom was indifferent, and absent in mind. Unknown to the rest of the association, this negligent priest, to suit his own purpose, cut down a ná-tree, that grew within the sacred enclosure, which was the residence of a déwa. The déwa resolved upon revenge, but knew that he could only accomplish it by practising some artifice. He therefore caused the priest to dream that something very fortunate was about to happen to him. Not long after, the déwa appeared to him in his own shape, and in seeming grief said to him, "In seven days a great calamity will happen to you." The priest enquired what it was; and he said, "In seven days your great benefactor, the king of the city, will die; and you are required to announce the event to the people." The citizens, on receiving this intelligence, as the priest without hesitation obeyed the command he had received, began to lament greatly, which attracted the attention of the king, and he enquired the cause. Upon being informed, he said that if the priest had declared the truth, the citizens must reward him accordingly; but that if the announcement was false, he would himself know how to deal with the traitor. The seventh day arrived, and passed away, without any misfortune happening to the king; and he therefore gave orders, on the eighth day, that the priest should be taken out of the city, and deprived of his arms and legs. By this means the priest died, and his next birth was in a place of misery. (*Sadharmmaratnakáré.*)

7. *The Legends of Kisawacha and Nalikéra.*

At the time that Sarabhanga Bódhisat was the chief of a company of ascetics, one of his followers, Kisawacha, left the Giwulu forest, near the river Gódáwari, where the fraternity resided, and took up his abode in a grove belonging to Dandakí, who reigned in the city of Khumbáwatí, in Kálinga. It happened in the course of time, that 500 courtezans passed through the city, in gay procession; and the people flocked in such numbers to see them, that the street of the city was completely filled. The crowd was observed by the king from the upper story of his palace, and when he learnt that it was caused by the beauties of the city, he was offended that they should thus seek to captivate the people, and commanded that they should be dismissed from their office. One day, when the same courtezans were walking in the royal garden, they saw the ascetic, Kisawacha, his face covered with hair, and his beard flowing over his breast; and as if they had been polluted by the sight of this miserable object, they called for water to wash their eyes, and spat upon the ascetic's body. Soon afterwards they were restored to their office, and concluded that this good fortune had happened to them in consequence of their having spat upon Kisawacha. About the same time the puróhita, or vizier, lost his office; but he went to the courtezans and asked them by what means they had regained the king's favour; and when they told him that it was through nothing else but their having spat upon a miserable ascetic, he went to the garden, and did the same. The king then remembered that he had dismissed the brahman without having properly enquired into his case, and commanded him to be restored; so he concluded that he also had been assisted through the insult he had shown to the ascetic. By and bye some of the provinces rebelled against the king, who collected an army to quell them. The brahman went to him, and said that if he wished to conquer his enemies, he must spit upon an ascetic who was in his garden, as it was by this means he and the courtezans had been restored to favour. The king took this advice, and went to the garden, accompanied by his courtezans, all of whom spat upon the ascetic; and an order was given to the warders that no one should be admitted to the palace who had not previously done the same. A noble who heard of the indignity went to Kisawacha, cleansed his body from the filth, and gave him other garments; after which he enquired what would be the punishment of the king, in consequence of the crime that had been committed. To this enquiry he replied, that the déwas were divided in opinion upon the subject; some were determined that the king alone should suffer; others that the king and the people should be punished in common; whilst others were resolved upon the entire destruction of the country. But he also informed the noble, that if the king would come and ask his forgiveness, the threatened calamities would be averted. The noble therefore went to the king and made known to him what was taking place; but as he refused to listen to his advice, he resigned his office; after which he again went to the ascetic, who recommended him to take all he had and go to some place at the distance of seven days' journey from the city, as it would most assuredly be destroyed. The king fought his enemies, and conquered them; and on the day on which he returned to the city it began to rain, so that the people were led to remark that he had been fortunate from the time he spat upon the ascetic. The déwas then rained flowers, money, and golden ornaments, at which the people were still more pleased; but this was succeeded by a shower of weapons that cut their flesh; then by showers of white burning charcoal, that emitted neither smoke nor flame, which was succeeded by a fall of stones, and then by sand so fine that it could not be taken up in the hand, which continued to fall until it covered the whole country to the depth of 87 cubits. The ascetic, the noble, and a certain merchant who received merit through the assistance he rendered to his mother, were the only persons saved. (*Amáwatura*).

In a former age, Nálikéra reigned in Kálinga, and at the same time 500 brahmanical ascetics took up their abode in the forest of Himála, where they lived upon fruits, and dressed themselves in the bark of trees; but they had occasionally to visit the villages, in order to procure salt and condiments; and in the course of their wanderings they came to Kálinga. The people of the city gave them what they required, in return for which they said bana; and the citizens were so much captivated with what they heard, that they requested them to remain, and say bana in the royal garden. The king observing a great crowd, enquired if they were going to some theatrical exhibition; but he was informed that they were going to hear bana, upon which he resolved that he also would be present. When the brahmans heard that the king had arrived, they appointed one of their cleverest speakers to officiate. The bana was on the subject of the five sins, and the consequences of committing them were set forth; such as birth in the form of worms, beasts, or asúrs, or in hell, where the misery will have to be endured during many hundreds of thousands of years. These things were like an iron piercing the ears of the king, and he resolved that he would have his revenge. At the conclusion he invited the brahmans to a repast at the palace; but before their arrival he commanded his servants to fill a number of vessels with filth, and cover them with plantain leaves. The brahmans, on their way to the place of refection, said among themselves that as they were about to receive food at the palace, it would be necessary for them to be very circumspect in their behaviour. When all were ready, the leaves were taken from the vessels at the king's command and the stench was most offensive; but he further insulted the brahmans by saying, "As much as you please you may eat, and as much as you like you can take home, as it is all provided for you alone. You derided me before the people, and this is your reward." So saying, he ordered his ruffians to take them by the shoulders, and hurl them down the stairs, that had previously been smeared with honey and the gum of the kumbuck tree, so that they speedily slid to the bottom, where they were attacked by fierce dogs.

A few attempted to make their escape, but they fell into pits that had been dug to entrap them, or were devoured by the dogs. Thus perished the whole of the 500 brahmans; but for this crime the déwas destroyed the country by causing the nine kinds of showers to fall, until a space of 60 yojanas was covered with sand to the depth of 87 cubits. (*Amáwatura*).

8. *Sampati Maha Brahma.*

The ruler of the brahma-lókas is 192 miles high; his foot is 30 miles long; from his elbow to the tip of his finger is 48 miles; his span is 24 miles; his robes are 256 miles in length; and he can illumine 10,000 sakwalas at once, by the stretching forth of his finger.

9. *The Yakás.*

There are Yakás in the world of men as well as those which reside upon Méru. They die here, and passing away from the state of a yaká, receive some other birth; but their dead bodies are never seen, nor is any stench from them ever perceived. The reason is, that they assume the appearance of dead chamelions, worms, ants, grasshoppers, serpents, scorpions, centipedes, or some bird or beast.

In the time of Gótama Budha there resided a merchant at Snáparanta, who was called Punna; but he embraced the priesthood, and become a rahat. After his attainment of this high state, 300 of his former associates embarked on a distant voyage, with his younger brother at their head, who had previously taken upon himself the five obligations. But the merchants were overtaken by a storm, and were carried along until they arrived at a certain island. In the morning they set about preparing their food, but could find no kind of fuel except red sandal-wood, as there were no other trees in the forest. One of them, when this was discovered, said to his companions, "We may go further, but can find nothing more valuable than red sandal-wood; so it will be well for us to heave our present cargo overboard, and load our ship with this timber, four inches of which are worth a lac of treasure." The others were willing to follow this advice, and many trees were cut down. But there were yakás in that island, who became angry with the merchants for destroying their habitations, as they thus invaded their rights. They would have killed the intruders at once, but for the stench that was to be apprehended from their dead bodies; and they therefore resolved upon punishing them after they had re-embarked. For this purpose they raised a violent storm, and appeared to the mariners in frightful shapes, so that they became greatly afraid, and each one cried to his déwas; but the younger brother called for the assistance of Punna, the rahat. This was perceived by Punna, who went to their assistance through the air; and when the yakás saw him coming, they became afraid in their turn, and fled away. After encouraging the mariners, he asked them to what port they were going, and when they said their own, he directed the head of the vessel towards it, and conveyed them thither by his supernatural power. When their families were informed of what had occurred, they all received the five obligations from Punna. They were desirous to present a portion of the sandal-wood to the rahat, but he told them to erect therewith a residence for Budha. After its completion, the teacher of the three worlds visited the place, and there remained several days, preaching to the people.* (*Amáwatura.*)

10. *The Asurs.*

The asurs, who reside under Maha Méru,† are of immense size. Ráhu is 76,800 miles high; 19,200 miles broad across the shoulders; his head is 14,500 miles round; his forehead is 4,800 miles broad; from eye-brow to eye-brow measures 800 miles; his mouth is 3,200 miles in size, and 4,800 miles deep; the palm of his hand is 5,600 miles in size; the joints of his fingers, 800 miles; the sole of his foot, 12,000 miles; from his elbow to the tip of his finger is 19,200 miles; and with one finger he can cover the sun or moon, so as to obscure their light.

11. *The Prétas.*

The inhabitants of the Lókántarika naraka are prétas. Their bodies are twelve miles high, and they have very large nails. On the top of the head there is a mouth, about the size of a needle's eye.

In the world of men there is a préta birth called Nijhámátanhá. The bodies of these prétas always burn. They continually wander about, never remaining in any one place a

---

* Brahma put forth in darkness beings emaciate with hunger, of hideous aspects, and with long beards. Those beings hastened to the deity. Such of them as exclaimed, Oh preserve us! were thence called rákshawas (from ráksha, to preserve): others, who cried out, Let us eat, were denominated from that expression yakshas (from yaksha, to eat).—Wilson's Vishnu Puråna. The word yaksha may have some affinity to the Hebrew יקש, to lay snares.

† "The (Tamul) nations of Ceylon believe that in the earliest wars of the gods, three of the peaks of Maha Méru were thrown down and driven to different parts of the world: one of them is Koníswara-parwatiya, or Trincomalee, which thenceforth became, equally with Kailasa, the abode of Siva." —Forbes' Ceylon. The Hindu tradition is of a somewhat different character. "At the marriage of Shivu and Parvutee all the gods were present, and the heavens were left empty. Seizing this opportunity Puvunu, the god of the winds, flew to Sumeru, broke the summit of the mountain, and hurled it into the sea, when it became the island of Lanká (Ceylon)."—Ward's Hindoos.

longer period than the snapping of a finger. They live thus an entire kalpa. They never receive food or water, and weep without intermission. All beings except the Bódhisats receive this birth, at some period or other of their existence.

In this world there is also the préta birth called Khuppipása. These prétas have heads 144 miles in size, tongues that are 80 miles long, and their bodies are thin, but extremely tall. For the space of a Budhántara they do not receive food or water. Were they to attempt to drink of the water of the ocean, it would disappear to them, as if it were dried up. Were a rishi to try to pour all the water of the five great rivers into their mouths, before they could taste a drop of it, it would be dried up, by the heat proceeding from their bodies. All beings except the Bódhisats are subject to the miseries of this birth.

There is the préta birth called Kálakanjaka. These prétas continually chase and maim each other with fire and shining weapons; and this birth is received by all beings except the Bódhisats.

The prétas may receive food and drink from their relatives; who can further benefit them by performing acts of merit in their name, such as the giving of food, alms-bowls, &c., to the priests. But there are many prétas who have so much demerit that they cannot in this way be assisted; still, though the act be of no benefit to the prétas, it is to the person who performs it. The prétas derive no benefit from the weeping and lamentation of their relatives, and it is no advantage to them when their merits are proclaimed.

A préti, who had two sons, one day left them near the gate of the city of Anurádhapura, whilst she roamed through the streets to seek food. The sons, seeing a priest about to enter the city to receive alms, requested that if he met with their mother he would inform her that they were very hungry. The priest asked how he was to know their mother, when they described her to him, and gave him a certain root,* by which he would acquire the power of seeing the prétas. On entering the city he saw many thousands of these beings, so that his progress through the city was greatly impeded, as he had to step on one

---

* The roots of certain trees are generally regarded as having great power over demons. The root baaras was supposed by the Jews to drive them away from the sick.—Josephus, De Bell. Jud. vii. 6.

side continually to let the prétas pass him. At last he met the mother, who was seeking offal in the street of the butchers, and he delivered to her the message from her sons. On hearing it, she enquired how he could see her, when he informed her of the root; but out of compassion she snatched it from his hand, as she knew that by its influence he would see so many prétas as to be prevented from seeking alms, and thus have to return home without food.

12. *The Inhabitants of the Narakas.*

The beings who seize upon the damned have bodies twelve miles in size; they take a flame in their right hand, and strike their victim, after which they lash him with an equal flame, held in the left hand. If he has taken life in a former birth, or committed any other great crime, he must remain in the naraka until he has received the entire punishment that is due. The tormentors throw him down on the iron floor, and cleave him with an axe. They fasten him with his feet upwards and head downwards to a chariot of fire, and urge him onward with a red-hot goad. He ascends in the flame, and is then cast down; he is enclosed in the Lohokumba hell; he is covered all over with foam, like a grain of rice in the oven; he is now up, now down, and now on one side; and he dies not until the punishment he must receive for his demerit is complete. (*Bála-pandhita-sútra-sanné.*)

It was declared by Budha, that if any one were to attempt to describe all the misery of all the narakas, more than a hundred, or even a hundred thousand years, would be required for the recital.

The beings in the narakas endure much sorrow; they suffer much pain; every member of the body, throughout all its parts, is exposed to an intense fire; they weep, and send forth a doleful lamentation; their mouths and faces are covered with saliva; they are crushed by an insupportable affliction; they have no help; their misery is incessant; and they live in the midst of a fire that is fiercer than the sun-beam, raging continually, casting forth flames above, below, and on the four sides, to the distance of 100 yojanas.

Yet even these miserable beings are afraid of death, although this fear arises from no love they have to the place of torment; from this they wish to be released. In what way, is it asked? A man is exposed to danger from a snake, an elephant, or a lion, or some punishment awarded by the king; from this he wishes to be released, and yet at the same time he fears death. Again, a man has a dangerous tumour, which the surgeon is prepared to remove by the application of caustic or the use of some sharp instrument; this man wishes to be relieved from the pain of the tumour, but still dreads the operation. Again, a poor man in prison is sent for by some great ruler, and is ushered into his presence that he may be set at liberty; this man wishes for liberty, but trembles when entering a place of so much splendour. Again, a man is bitten by a poisonous serpent; he falls to the ground, and tosses himself violently from side to side; another man who sees his danger pronounces over him a charm, that the force of the poison may be overcome; when coming to himself, and on the point of being cured, he is afraid, and trembles; nevertheless he wishes that the cure may be effected. In like manner the beings in the narakas, though they have no satisfaction in the situation in which they are placed, like all other beings, fear death. (*Milinda Prasna*).

Upon one occasion Milinda said to Nágaséna, "You affirm that the fire of the narakas is intensely more powerful than the natural fire of this world; if a small stone be here cast into the fire, it will remain a whole day without being consumed; but if a rock as large as a house be cast into the fire of a naraka, you say it will be consumed in a moment: this I cannot believe. You say again, that if a being is cast into a naraka, he will remain there many ages without coming to destruction: this also I cannot believe." Nágaséna replied, "How so? There is the sword-fish, the alligator, the tortoise, the peacock, and the pigeon; these all eat stones and gravel; but by the power of the digestive fire within the body these hard substances are decomposed; but if the females of any of these reptiles or birds become pregnant, is the embryo destroyed from the same cause?" Milinda: "No." Nágaséna: "Why?" Milinda: "By means of their individual karma they are preserved." Milinda: "So also, the beings in the narakas are preserved by their individual karma during many ages; they are there born, arrive at maturity, and die. Budha has said, Priests, so long as the karma of a being in a naraka continues to exist, that being must exist."

There were five persons who lived in the time of Gótama Budha, of whom it is recorded that they went to a naraka:—1. The noble Bhagineyya, who violated the chastity of the priestess, Upulwan. 2. The brahman Mágandhi, who reviled Budha during seven days. 3. Chinchi, the female who was instigated by the tirttakas to bring a false accusation against Budha, in the presence of the four orders of the priesthood. 4. Supra Budha, the father-in-law of Budha. 5. Déwadatta, the son of Supra Budha, who tempted some of the followers of Budha to forsake him, and fell into heresy.

III. THE PRIMITIVE INHABITANTS OF THE EARTH; THEIR FALL FROM PURITY; AND THEIR DIVISION INTO FOUR CASTES.

THE BRAHMAS COME TO INHABIT THE EARTH.—THEIR SPLENDOUR.—ITS LOSS.—THE FORMATION OF THE SUN AND MOON.—THE DEGENERACY OF THE BRAHMAS.—THE ORIGIN OF THE FOUR CASTES.

NEARLY all the ancient nations of the world, of whom we have any record, carry back their origin to a period immensely remote; nor is this to be wondered at, when we consider that the traditions of the diluvian age must then have been fresh in the memories of men. Noah lived three hundred and fifty years, and Shem five hundred years after the flood. Nimrod, from whom was "the beginning of the kingdom of Babel," was the great grandson of Noah; and the kingdom of Egypt is supposed to have had its origin from Mizraim, the son of Ham. The founders of these kingdoms, therefore, conversed with men who had seen the flood, and who had been witnesses of the most fearful mundane convulsion that had taken place since the formation of our species. Who, in the days of his childhood, when the mind yearns after information relative to the past, and the strangest fiction is received as sober truth, has ever listened to the tales that none are so ready to tell as the aged, whether grandsire or gammer, without the receiving of impressions which the experience of future years can never entirely obliterate? It is then that the spirit leaves the narrow bound that in infancy was its world, and breaks away into other regions: where it sees that which was before invisible, and hears that which was before inaudible, and enters upon a new existence. But the wildest romance ever heard in our day, from lips all garrulous, must be poor and spiritless when compared with the wondrous revelations that the members of the Noachic family could impart; and when the children to whom they told them grew up into manhood, and wandered into the lands where they founded dynasties and established kingdoms, all these tales and traditions would be cherished in the memory, increasing in extravagance as they went on, until some superior mind would arise, and reduce them to order. Thus, from that which in its origin was the simple truth, would arise the legend, the myth, and the chronological cycle almost limitless, of the times succeeding the deluge. The traditions of the Budhists are in unison with this order of development.

In the ages previous to the present Maha Bhadra kalpa, a kela-laksha of worlds was destroyed by fire, in which destruction the Great Earth was included, and all the worlds in each sakwala from the Ajatákása to the sixth brahma-lóka, Abhassara; so that the whole space was void, like the inside of a drum. But by the united merit of all sentient existence, the rain called Samartthakara, (or Sampattikara)* Mégha, began to fall. The drops were at first in size like a grain of rice, then gradually increasing in magnitude they became large as a needle, an arrow, a bamboo, an areca, a palm, four miles, and eight miles, until as much space as is occupied by a kela-laksha of worlds was entirely inundated. Then, by the same power, a wind was brought into existence, which agitated this mighty ocean, until the whole was evaporated, with the exception of that which composes the seas of the earth and the world of waters under the earth. At this time the whole space was enveloped in darkness. The monarchs of the brahma-lókas, coming to see whether the lotus was formed that indicates whether a supreme Budha will appear in the same kalpa or not, dispersed the darkness in an instant; when they beheld five flowers, with five sets of priestly requisites near them; by which they knew that the kalpa would be honoured by the presence of five Budhas. Then taking the five robes, alms-bowls, &c., they returned to their respective lókas.

* "Janárddano, in the person of Rudra, having consumed the whole world, breathes forth heavy clouds; and those called Samvartta, resembling vast elephants in bulk, overspread the sky, roaring and darting lightnings."—Wilson's Vishnu Puránа.

On the destruction of the previous worlds, the beings that inhabited them, and were in the possession of merit, received birth in the Abhassara brahma-lóka; and when their proper age was expired, or their merit was insufficient to preserve them any longer in a superior world, they again came to inhabit the earth. It was by the apparitional birth they were produced; and their bodies still retained many of the attributes of the world from which they had come, as they subsisted without food, and could soar through the air at will; and the glory proceeding from their persons was so great that there was no necessity for a sun or a moon. Thus, no change of seasons was known; there was no difference between night and day; and there was no diversity of sex. Throughout many ages did the brahmas thus live, in all happiness, and in mutual peace.* There was afterwards the formation, upon the surface of the earth, of a peculiar substance like the scum that arises upon the surface of boiled milk; but it was free from all impurity, as the virgin honey in the cell of the bee. This attracted the attention of one of the brahmas, who took up a little of the substance with his finger, and applied it to his mouth; but as its taste was most delightful, it excited the wish for more; and a principle of evil was now first manifested among the beings of the earth, who had hitherto kept themselves pure. The other brahmas soon began to follow this example; by which the glory proceeding from their persons was extinguished, and it became necessary that a sun and moon, and other shining bodies, should be brought into existence.

The whole of the brahmas assembled together; and after expressing to each other their regret for the loss of the privileges they had once enjoyed, they determined upon forming a sun. By the power of their united karma this was effected; and the shining body thus produced was called súrya, from sura, might, and wírya, energy. The name of Sun-day was given to the day upon which this luminary was formed. Before the assembly had dispersed, the sun went down, leaving the brahmas again in

* "The beings who were created by Brahmá, of the four castes, were at first endowed with righteousness and perfect faith; they abode wherever they pleased, unchecked by any impediment; their hearts were free from guile; they were pure, made free from soil, by observance of sacred institutes. In their sanctified minds Hari dwelt; and they were filled with perfect wisdom, by which they contemplated the glory of Vishnu."—Wilson's Vishnu Puráṇa.

darkness, which led them to resolve that another light should be formed. By their united karma the moon was then produced; and they called it chanda, from channa, thought or determination, because they had determined upon forming it, when the sun went down. To this day they gave the name of Monday. Upon the five subsequent days, they caused the five planets to appear in order, viz., Kuja, Budha, Guru, Sekra, and Sæni; and to these days respectively they gave the names of the planets thus formed.

When the brahmas had been long accustomed to eat the terrene production, their skins became coarse; and the complexion of one was light, whilst that of another was dark. This produced pride and contention, by which the substance was deprived of its delicious flavour, and in time entirely disappeared. But in its stead there arose a kind of fungus, in taste like cream mingled with butter, by subsisting upon which the difference in their complexions was increased, in proportion as the brahmas partook of it with more or less avidity. In process of time, the fungus also disappeared, and was followed by a climbing plant called badalátá, after which rice of a superior kind was produced. It was pure as a pearl, and had no outward pellicle. As much as sufficed for the day was formed in the morning; and at night, when the evening meal was wanted, it was again renewed. By subsisting upon the rice, the apertures of the body were produced, and the generative powers were developed; which led to passion and sexual intercourse.* But those who had preserved their purity reproached those who had indulged their passion, and drove them from the community; by which the banished brahmas were led to build houses as places of concealment and privacy. They then became too indolent to fetch each meal as it was wanted, and accordingly at one journey brought away as much rice as sufficed for many days. By degrees an outer integument was formed upon the grain, then a coarse husk, and at last, when it had been cut down it was not renewed. This loss occasioned the necessity of setting limits to

* Bardesanes in the second century taught, that the inhabitants of the world came out of the forming hand of God pure and incorrupt, endued with subtil, ethereal bodies and spirits of a celestial nature. But when in process of time, the prince of darkness had enticed men to sin, then the Supreme God permitted them to fall into sluggish and gross bodies, formed of corrupt matter by the evil principle.—Mosheim, Eccles. Hist.

the places where it grew, that each one might know his own portion. But some of the brahmas became discontented with what they received as their share; and coveting the property of others, they began to make aggressions, and commit theft. Thus arose the want of some administration, by which the lawless could be restrained; as some of the brahmas pelted the purloiners with sticks, whilst others beat them with clubs.

Then the brahmas once more assembled, and said to one of their number, "From this time forth thou shalt be the terror of the wrong-doer, that evil may be eradicated; and we will give thee a portion of our grain for support." By the suffrages of all present this individual was elected to be the supreme ruler; on which account he was called Sammata (the appointed, or the elect). From the power he exercised over the cultivated lands, khettáni, he was called a khattiyo, or kshatriyá,* and his descendants retained the same appellation. Thus the royal race, or the caste of warriors, was produced.

Among the brahmas there were some who, on observing the acts of insubordination that were committed by the wicked, thought within themselves that it would be proper to suppress their impious proceedings; on which account they were called brahmaná, suppressors.

There were others again who built habitations, and became skilful in the arts, by which wealth is acquired, on which account they were called wessá; and from them originated the waisyás, or caste of merchants.

Again, there were other brahmas who became addicted to hunting; whence they were called ludda, or sudda, and from them came the sudras.

Thus arose the four great castes; but all the brahmas were originally of one race, and were all equally illustrious. From each of the four castes, certain individuals repaired to the wilderness, and became recluses, on which account they were called sumano, or sramanas, ascetics.

No single institution, unless that of slavery is to be excepted, has exercised a greater influence upon the interests

* A. J. Pott supposes that Xerxes is a compound of the Zend ksathra, king (with the loss of the *t*), and ksahya, also meaning king, the original form of shah.

of our species than that of caste. It is found in the earliest ages; it was then almost universal; and more than one hundred and fifty millions of people are at the present moment subject to its power. Whenever we thus meet with the ancient and the universal, we are led to seek its origin in the oldest record we possess; and it is seldom that we are disappointed in our search. Upon the important subject now under review we meet with less information than the mere historian would wish; but if I mistake not, it will be found that the Bible is not entirely silent respecting it. We have evidence that before the flood there were hereditary distinctions among mankind, founded upon the same causes whence caste is represented by the Budhists to have had its origin. There was, first, a distinction moral and religious: "the sons of God," on the one side; and "the daughters of men," the children of an evil generation, on the other. There was, secondly, a professional distinction. It is said that Abel was "a keeper of sheep," and that Cain was a "tiller of the ground," so that in the first human family there was a division of labour; but we have no reason to conclude that this distinction was hereditary in the respective households of the children of Adam and Eve, nor do we know that at the beginning each branch of the family confined itself to its own productions and possessions, as the product of their labour may have been brought into one common stock. It would appear that after "Cain went out from the presence of the Lord," his former occupation was continued, as God said unto him, "When thou tillest the ground, it shall not henceforth yield unto thee her strength."—Gen. iv. 12. This may have been the reason why Cain, when he saw that the ground he attempted to cultivate was accursed, abandoned the labour of tillage, and "builded a city." It is said of Jabal, who was of the race of Cain, that he was "the father of such as dwell in tents, and such as have cattle," which would seem to intimate that there was a return, on the part of certain families, to the occupations that were abandoned by the rest of their race. Another individual, of the same race, Jubal, is said to be "the father of all such as handle the harp and organ." The word father is here supposed to mean progenitor, which would lead us to suppose that the profession was continued in the same family; but it is possible that it may mean only originator, teacher, or exemplar. It is to be remarked that all these inventions are attributed to the descendants of Cain. The restless spirit of these sons of men sought out new sources of pleasure and amusement, whilst the sons of God rested content with the peaceful occupations of their ancestors. The antediluvian record is brief, especially in that which relates to social existence; but we learn from it that in the primitive ages there were among the families of men:—1. Agriculturists, Gen. iv. 2. 2. Shepherds, Gen. iv. 2. 3. Citizens, Gen. iv. 17. 4. Nomads, Gen. iv. 20. 5. Herdsmen, Gen. iv. 20. 6. Musicians, Gen. iv. 21. 7. Artificers, Gen. iv. 22. We might draw a great number of inferences from these premises, if such a course were here admissible. There must necessarily have been other occupations in addition to those that are here enumerated, and some kind of commerce; as the artificers could not clothe themselves with their metals, nor could the musicians subsist upon the mere melody of their instruments; and we may conclude that there was also a servile class, working for hire, or Noah would not have been able to build a vessel of so large a capacity as the ark. We have thus the certainty that Noah was familiar with social distinctions of an important character; and it is probable that some of them were hereditary.

The most ancient documents that speak decisively of caste are to be found among the Hindus. "That the human race might be multiplied, the supreme ruler caused the Brahman, the Kshatriya, the Vaisya, and the Sudra, (so named from the scripture, protection, wealth, and labour), to proceed from his mouth, his arm, his thigh, and his foot." In the Játimálá, or Garland of Classes, the subject is entered into more at length. "In the first creation, by Brahma, Bráhmanas proceeded, with the Véda, from the mouth of Brahma. From his arms, Kshatriyas sprung; so from his thigh, Vaisyas; from his foot Sudras were produced: all with their females. The lord of creation, viewing them, said, 'What shall be your occupations?' They replied, 'We are not our own masters, oh God! command us what to undertake.' Viewing and comparing their labours, he made the first tribe superior to the rest. As the first had inclination for the divine sciences (bráhma véda) therefore he was Bráhmana. The protector from ill (kshayate) was Kshatriya. He whose profession (vésa) consists in commerce; which promotes the success of wars, for the protection of himself and of mankind; and in husbandry and attendance upon cattle, he called Vaisya. The other should voluntarily serve the three tribes, and therefore he became a Sudra; he should humble himself at their feet."* There was caste also among the Egyptians, Colchians, Iberians, Medes, Persians, and Etrureans; and in the new world it was found among the Peruvians and Mexicans.† "Whatever tribes are mentioned," says Niebuhr, "in ancient history, before an irresistible change of circumstances led to democratical institutions, there, so far as anything can be discovered of their nature, a difference either of caste or of national descent, is clearly apparent. The former existed indisputably among the earliest Attic tribes, which must be conceived to have been anterior to the Ionian emigration, the nobles, peasants, and craftsmen: it is less clear in the four Ionic tribes." Among the Spartans this system is most frequently to be noticed. Almost all their trades and occupations were hereditary, as those of cooking, baking, mixing wine, flute-playing, &c.‡ The kings were supposed to derive their lineage from a divine paternity, and nothing but a divine revelation could induce them to step out of the genuine lineage of Eurysthenes and Prokles. The denominations of the four Attic or Ionian tribes are supposed to have referred originally to the occupation of those who bore

---

* Colebrooke, Miscellaneous Essays, ii. 178.
† Mill's History of British India; Wilkinson's Ancient Egyptians.
‡ Müller's Dorians.

them.* Throughout the Hellenic world there were hereditary customs, tending to isolate those who observe them, especially in reference to religion, some of which were confined to single families, and others to some particular gens or tribe.† The number of the Egyptian castes is variously estimated, but in every enumeration the priests are named first, and next to them the military. Yet if it be true that when a king was elected who was not of the sacerdotal tribe, he was formally adopted into it, the caste of Egypt must have been essentially different to that of India; where, among the Hindus, a change of caste is as impossible as for the quadruped to become a fish, or the crawling serpent to take unto itself wings and soar towards the sun as an eagle. That the Egyptians had the power to change their caste is further confirmed by the statement of Herodotus, that the other castes despised the swineherds so much as never to intermarry with them; whence we may conclude that alliances were possible among the other castes. The three classes of society that existed among the Saxons were so strongly divided by the laws of caste that no marriage could take place between persons in the different ranks.‡ The severest penalties prohibited intrusion into another rank.

The establishment of caste could not be the work of a moment. For a length of time after the principle began to be manifested, its power would be comparatively trifling and

---

* Grote's History of Greece.
† "In the ancient world citizenship, unless specially conferred as a favour by some definite law or charter, was derivable only from race. The descendants of a foreigner remained foreigners to the end of time; the circumstance of their being born and bred in the country, was held to make no change in their condition; community of place could no more convert aliens into citizens than it could convert domestic animals into men. . . . Citizenship was derived from race; but distinctions of race were not of that odious and fantastic character which they have borne in modern times; they implied real differences, often of the most important kind, religious and moral. Particular races worshipped particular gods, and in a particular manner. But different gods had different attributes, and the moral aspect thus presented to the contemplation and veneration of the people, could not but produce some effect on the national character. . . . Again, particular races had particular customs which affected the relations of domestic life and of public."
—Arnold's Thucydides.
‡ Smith's Religion of Ancient Britain.

its restrictions few. It would be regarded rather as tending to mutual advantage in the social economy, than as necessary or essential. But in India there must have been peculiar circumstances that favoured its development; and when the wearing of the chain had become familiar, the Brahmans rivetted its links most firmly by declaring that its origin was divine, its existence coeval with man, and its character immutable. In other countries there arose institutions that acted as an antagonist to this principle; so that its influence was never paramount, and in time it ceased to exist.

The Brahmans and the Budhists agree as to their estimate of the number of the castes.* In the antediluvian age we have nothing that answers to this fourfold division; but it is possible that the distinction may have arisen from a perverted account of the solemn prophecy delivered by Noah relative to the destinies of his children. In this light Noah, who in the earlier ages must have been regarded by all mankind with profound reverence, would be represented as adumbrating the Kshatriyas, or the race of the kings; Shem, whose "God was blessed," would be made to represent the Brahmans, or the race of the priests; Japhet, "dwelling in the tents of Shem," would be made to represent the Vaisyas, or the race of the merchants, wandering from place to place, as was their primitive custom, and taking up their abode in other lands for the purposes of traffic; and Ham, the father of Canaan, "cursed," and "the servant of servants unto his brethren," would be prominently exhibited as the exemplar of the Sudras, the servile race.

When we name the Brahmans as the sacerdotal tribe, we must not regard them as directing their attention to religious duties alone. In the first ages we have no instance of such a restriction. The first priest of whom we read, Melchisedec, was a king regnant. Of the second, Potipherah, we know only his name, title, and place of residence; and though he

---

* In Persia there was a similar division of the human race. "The whole system of Zoroaster reposed on a fourfold division of castes: that of the priests, the warriors, the agriculturists, and the artificers of whatever denomination."—Zendavesta, i. 141.

is called a priest, the Chaldee translator renders the word by רבא, prince. On his appointment as first minister of the king, Joseph was probably admitted into the sacerdotal tribe. Among the Jews, previous to the time of David, the high-priests were generally considered as the rulers of the people, under God as the supreme monarch of Israel; and the Levites appear to have exercised an inferior authority in the provincial towns. There are also instances in after times wherein the king's ministers, those who were " at his hand," are called priests. 2 Sam. viii. 18; xx. 23; 1 Kings iv. 2; 1 Chron. xviii. 17. The priestly office was hereditary after the time of Aaron. Even in countries where other offices were not hereditary, there appears to have been something like caste among those who occupied this position in the state; and in all countries where caste existed, it was the most notable among the sages and priests. The high priests of Hephaestos professed to have registers that proved their dignity to have been transmitted through 341 generations, and they had colossal statues of this number of individuals.* The priests among the Chaldaeans, the great masters of astronomical science, received their privileges by birthright. In many families of seers among the Greeks, a knowledge of the future was considered to be hereditary. And even in our own times, especially among less cultivated tribes, such gifts as second sight are supposed to be transmitted from father to child. In the ancient legends of the Budhists, in which Brahmans are frequently introduced, they are represented as being prime ministers, privy councillors, philosophers, soothsayers, conjurors, astrologers, fortune-tellers, physicians, and ascetics.† It was acknowledged by Gótama that in some ages the Brahmans are superior to the Kshatriyas; and if a supreme Budha then appears, he is born of the brahmanical caste. It is said in the Janawansa, " The Brahmans applied themselves to study, and became priests; or they assumed

---

* Herod. ii. 82.

† The priests of Egypt resembled, in many respects, the character given of the ancient Brahmans, inasmuch as they were judges, physicians, and astrologers.

the office of preceptors; and some of them maintained themselves by the offering of sacrifices and oblations, by the practice of medicine, or the consulting of the planets. They were thus the professors of the various branches of science said to have been revealed by the chief Brahma, from whom all the sciences are supposed to be derived, such as astrology, magic, astronomy, &c." In the Dasa-brahma-játaka, Gótama is represented as relating the history of a certain noble, Widhúra, who in a former age informed Korawya, king of the city of Indupat, in Kuru, that there were ten kinds of Brahmans. "1. There are Brahmans," said he, " who tie up a quantity of medicines in a bundle, and put them in a bag, and go from place to place, proclaiming, "This medicine is good for such a disease, and this for another. They also carry about with them different kinds of oils, and proclaim, If this be poured into the nose it is good for such a disease, and this for another. They also profess to drive out devils by mantras. 2. There are others who leave the regular ordinances of Brahminism; and because they have no other mode of obtaining a livelihood, they go to the palaces of kings and the mansions of the nobility, where they play upon cymbals and sing songs for the amusement of the great. At times they only employ others to perform the same services. 3. There are others who take some kind of vessel, with which they approach the courts of kings; they then say, I must have such or such a gift, or I will not depart hence; they thus force from the kings whatever they desire. 4. There are others who go about from door to door to beg, appearing like a tree that has been burnt in the field cleared for cultivation; with long hair, dirty teeth, immense nails, heads covered with dust, and filthy bodies. 5. There are others who go about as merchants, to sell different kinds of fruits, honey, &c. 6. There are others who practise agriculture, rear cattle, poultry, and slaves; who give much wealth as the portion of their daughters, and receive much when their sons are married. 7. There are others who tell the nekatas, or lucky hours; kill animals, and sell their flesh; and follow other practices of a similar kind. 8. There are others who carry about different kinds of bowls and other utensils to sell; they also remain near places to which persons are accustomed to resort for trade, and obtain from them five hundred or a thousand pieces of money, for escorting them through wild places; thus they gain their livelihood after the manner of men who break into houses to steal. 9. There are others who live like the savages of the wilderness, killing and eating the flesh of hares, guanas, deer, and things that live in the water, as tortoises, &c. 10. There are others who profess to be released from evil desire, and to be ready to release others also. On account of their wish to gain abundance, they recommend to kings to present the sacrifice called yága; and if a king can be found willing, they place him upon a golden couch, and anoint his head with holy water, saying, that this will take away the consequences of his sins; then the couch, and the carpet upon which he has sat, his robes and ornaments, all fall to the share of the Brahmans who have conducted the ceremony." These are the words of an adversary, or they would lead us to conclude that the ancient Brahmans were something like the Gipsies of Spain and other countries in our days.

By the Budhists, the Vaisyas are regarded as merchants; and even by the Brahmans, who derive the name from a word which signifies "to enter" (as fields, &c.), they are called "the agricultural and mercantile tribe." This would intimate that the distinction was not made until the social polity had been in existence some time, and become compacted; for although there must have been commerce, in the shape of barter, during the earliest ages, a considerable period would elapse before the merchant had gained sufficient wealth to cause his occupation to be looked upon as respectable. In the time of Gótama Budha the merchants are represented as being a very influential class. They traded to great distances in caravans,* and had to exercise much dis-

* The remark of Heeren (Hist. Res. Asiatic Nations, ii. 279) is not correct, that "the conveyance of merchandise by means of a caravan, as in

cretion and brave many dangers, by which they acquired a strength of mind that caused them to be looked upon with respect, and gained them the third rank in the order of castes. It is under the character of a wanderer that the ancient merchant is generally represented; he has not only to superintend the sale of his wares, but to accompany them in their transit. Thus in Hebrew, the name of the merchant is derived from a root that signifies " to go about, to wander;" in Greek, from ἐν πορος, transitus; and our own word merchant has a similar signification in the Gothic mergan, " to spread." In India, it is not alone the man who trades to foreign countries that has to wander, as much of the retail trade is carried on by persons who pass from village to village, like the bag-men or hawkers of our own land. By the Singhalese the third caste is generally regarded as being exclusively mercantile, whilst the cultivators form the first class of the Sudras. It is said in one of their legends that the first merchant was called Wessama, who, having discovered the properties of certain medical productions, afterwards disposed of them for gain.

It is the more usual course for the cultivators of the soil to be regarded as forming the noblest class of the people, next to those who hold rank as hereditary princes; they are the eupatrids; they form the timocracy; and it is from them the rulers of the state are chosen; as delegates of the king, when the government is monarchical, or as temporary chiefs, when it is an aristocracy. The circumstances of those who reside in the country, whether as proprietors or as labourers, are favourable to the maintenance of respectability of character, as they are exposed to fewer temptations than the merchant, who has necessarily to live in the midst of the luxuries that produce vice. The higher classes among the Greeks were averse to any profession except arms, agriculture, and musical exercises; and the Spartans carried their disdain of all manual occupations so far as to leave even

other countries of the East, continued always foreign to the practice of India."

agriculture to the Helots.* The philosophers themselves were not exempt from these prejudices; they supposed that as mechanical arts rendered the body languid, whereby the mind loses its energy, the man who exercises them is unable to fulfil the duties required of him in a free state. "The ancients," says Niebuhr, "with one mind esteemed agriculture to be the proper business of the freeman, as well as the school of the soldier. Cato says, the countryman has the fewest evil thoughts. In him the whole stock of the nation is preserved; it changes in cities where foreign merchants and tradesmen are wont to settle, even as those who are natives remove whithersoever they are lured by gain. In every country where slavery prevails the freedman seeks his maintenance by occupations of this kind, in which he not unfrequently grows wealthy; thus among the ancients, as in after times, such trades were mostly in the hands of this class, and were therefore thought disreputable to a citizen; hence the opinion, that the admitting the artisans to full civic rights is hazardous, and would transform the character of a nation." It therefore appears to be contrary to the analogy presented in other nations, when we see the tribe of merchants in India holding so high a rank;† but it is to be accounted for by the peculiar circumstances of the country, the products of which were carried to the most distant parts of the world, causing its people to become rich, and placing those who were the means of the acquirement of this wealth in the position of princes. We may also learn from the same fact than an

* The Thracian chiefs also held it disgraceful to cultivate the earth; war and robbery were with them the only paths to honour. On the other hand, the earlier Romans were eminently an agricultural people.

† "Traffic and money-lending are satyántrita; even by them, when he is deeply distressed, may the Brahman support life."—Manu. Inst. iv. 6. But to the Persians, buying and selling appeared to be a mean practice, as they thought it impossible to carry it on without falsehood and cheating; and when Cyrus heard that the Lacedæmonians had a regular market at Sparta, he expressed great contempt for the nation.—Herod. i. 153. When the Lydians revolted against Cyrus, he was advised by Crœsus to enforce upon them the wearing of effeminate clothing, the practice of music, and shopkeeping, as by this means they would become women instead of men.—Ib. i. 155. Kleon, the tanner, the Hyperbolus, the lamp-maker, are greatly derided by Aristophanes for presuming to engage in politics.

extensive commerce must have been carried on in these productions, at an early period after the deluge.

The earliest cause of dissension among the primitive brahmas is said to have arisen from the difference in the colour of their skin. When two descendants of an illustrious Brahman became converts to Budhism, Gótama enquired if their change of profession had excited the displeasure of the other Brahmans; and in reply they said it was alleged by their kinsmen, that the Brahmans ate "the sons of Brahma, sprung from his mouth, pure and fair, while the other castes and sects are sprung from his feet, black and impure." This statement is in favour of the supposition that the Brahmans at first confined themselves to some region not far from the place whence the first dispersion of mankind commenced, by which the fairness of their complexion was preserved; whilst the other tribes of the Hindus went on towards the south, spreading themselves throughout the entire extent of the peninsula, and penetrating even to Ceylon; by which their complexions would be gradually rendered darker, from their residence under a vertical sun. It has been asserted by those who have had the opportunity of forming a correct opinion upon the subject, that the Brahmans are even now, at least in the north of India, a fairer race than the other tribes; hence the proverb, "Never trust a black Brahman, nor a white Pariah."

The Budhist legends agree with revelation in teaching that all men were originally of one race; but with this truth they have mixed up the error that the aborigines of mankind were many. There is also an agreement with the Scriptures, in the statement that men were originally pure, and that they fell from eating a product of the earth.

There appears to be an intimate connexion between the institution of caste and the doctrine of the transmigration of souls. Almost in every place where the former has existed, we can trace the presence of the latter. Indeed, the custom of caste is so contrary to right reason, that its establishment seems to be impossible without calling in the aid of some supernatural power to assist in its confirmation. In this respect there is consistency in the teachings of Gótama; as he rejects caste, and his doctrine on the origin of the intellectual powers, and their extinction at death, is not transmigration. There is caste among the Budhists of Ceylon, but this is contrary to the tenets of the founder of their religion; and their notions on the subject of that which constitutes the ego, the individual man, have been modified in a similar manner; the custom on the one part, and the popular notion on the other, being homogeneous deviations from primitive Budhism.

By Professor Mill, Gótama has been designated "a philosophical opponent of popular superstition and brahmanical caste." The future sage having enumerated the qualities he would require in the woman who aspired to be his wife, his royal father directed his principal minister to go into the great city of Kapilawastu, and to enquire there in every house after a woman possessed of these good qualities, shewing at the same time the prince's enumeration of the necessary virtues, and uttering two stanzas, of the following meaning: "Bring hither the maiden that has the required qualities, whether she be of the royal tribe, or the brahman caste; of the respectable, or of the plebeian class. My son regardeth not tribe, nor family extraction: his delight is in good qualities, in truth, and in virtue alone."

With the Brahmans, caste is primeval, essential, immutable and of divine appointment. But according to the Budhists there was at first no distinction of caste; all the inhabitants of the earth were of one and the same race. When the distinction arose, it was accidental; or it was embraced by the progenitors of the race of their own free will; or, as in the case of the first king, it arose from the suffrages of a general assembly. At the commencement of Budhism, persons of all castes were admitted into the priesthood; and when so admitted, the lowest Sudra held equal rank and received equal honours, with the Brahman or the Kshatriya. That which gives to caste its real importance, and by which it is exhibited in its most repulsive aspect, is, however, held as firmly by the Budhists as the Brahmans; inasmuch as they teach that the present position of all men is the result of the merit or demerit of former births; a doctrine which, if true, would make the scorn with which the outcast is regarded a natural feeling, as he would be in reality a comdemned criminal, undergoing the sentence that has been pronounced against him by a tribunal that cannot err in its decrees. By the Brahman, the Sudra is represented as an object of contempt, because he at first proceeded from the feet of Brahma; but for this statement to have any power, it must be proved that the Sudra was in every previous birth, from the beginning of the kalpa, a Sudra; and if the Brahman be honourable on account of having proceeded from the mouth of Brahma, it must be proved that he has never been any other than a Brahman in all previous generations. Yet it is said by Manu, (Inst. ii. 168):—" A twice-born man, who not having studied the Véda, applies diligent attention to a different and worldly study, soon falls, even when living, to the condition of a Sudra and his descendants after him." From this inconsistency the doctrines of Gótama are free.

The existence of the four great tribes is recognised continually in the Játakas; and inferiority of caste is represented as giving rise to the same usages, and as being attended with the same degradation, as in the works of the Brahmans. In the Sambhúta Játaka there is an account of two low-caste youths who attempted to acquire learning; but for this they were attacked by people of the higher castes, and left for dead. They then went to a distant city, assumed a different dress, that their design might not be frustrated, and passed for Brahmans. One of them completed his education, but whilst the other was yet at school, a stranger, who was detained all night at the same place on account of a storm, had some hot food placed before him; when, as he seized it too eagerly, his mouth was burnt, and he cried out from pain. The scholar called out to him to put it away quickly; but in so doing he used a low-caste word from forgetfulness, by which his caste was discovered. In the same

Játaka, the Sadol, or Chandála, is represented as one who is born in the open air, his parents not being possessed of the smallest hut, where, as he lies among the pots when his mother goes to cut firewood, he is suckled by the bitch along with her own pups. But it was uniformly declared by Gótama that there is no essential difference between the four tribes.* It having been said that alms given to the more honourable castes, punya-kshétrayo, would have a greater reward than when given to the man of mean birth, he combated the assertion, and said, that as in wet weather the husbandman sows on the hills, and during the dry weather in the valleys, and at all times in the ground that at any season can be irrigated; so the man who wishes to be blessed in both worlds will give alms to all; as he alone is not to be regarded as honourable who can only boast of his birth and worldly eminence. At another time he declared that when the man of low caste attains nirwána, his reward is the same as that of the man of high caste; thus, when the festive hall is looked at, the colours of the different flowers by which it is adorned can be distinguished, but in the shadows proceeding from the same flowers, no difference of colour can be perceived.

The immediate disciples of Gótama propounded similar doctrines upon the subject of caste. The Madhura-sútra† was spoken by Maha Kacháno, son of the Brahman próhita of the king of Ujein, soon after the death of Gótama Budha; and forms part of the Majjhima-nikáyo. According to this

---

* In the Agganna-suttán, addressed by Budha to two descendants of an illustrious Brahman, Wásettho, there is this sentence. "Descendants of Wásettho! even a Khattiyo, who has sinned, in deed, word, or thought, and become a heretic; on account of that heresy, on the dismemberment of his frame at his death, he is born in the tormenting, everlasting, and unendurable hell. Such is also the fate of the Bráhmo, the Wesso, and the Suddo, as well as of the Sumano, or ascetic. But if a Khattiyo lead a righteous life, in deed, word, and thought; and be of the true or supreme faith; by the merit of that faith, on the dismemberment of his body at death, he is reproduced in the felicitous suggalóka heavens."—Turnour, Journ. As. Soc. Aug. 1838.

† The whole of this sútra appears in the Colombo Observer, March 11, 1844, translated from the Pali by Mr. Louis de Zoyza, then a student in the native institution at Cotta, under the care of the Church Missionaries, and afterwards principal translator to the government of Ceylon.

sútra, the king of Awanti having heard of the fame of Maha Kacháno, went to visit him, and addressed the sage in the following manner: "The Brahmans say that they alone are the high caste, that others are of low caste; that they are of the white caste, others of the black caste; that the Brahmans are pure, those who are not Brahmans impure; that the Brahmans alone are the sons of Brahma, the legitimate offspring of Brahma; that they are formed by Brahma, sprung from Brahma, and are inheritors of the patrimony of Brahma." The priest replied that this declaration was a sound, and nothing but a sound; for that when a Kshatriya, a Brahman, a Vaisya, or a Sudra, abounds in wealth, members of all the four castes rise before him in the morning, and minister to his wants; go not to sleep until he has retired to rest; wait for his commands; behave themselves according to his pleasure; and use soft words to administer to his gratification; "so that the four castes are equal to each other; there is no difference to be perceived between them." Again, when a Kshatriya, a Brahman, a Vaisya, or a Sudra, takes life, and commits other sins, at the dissolution of the body, one as well as the other, falls into the wretched place of torment. Again, when a Kshatriya, a Brahman, a Vaisya, or a Sudra, observes the precepts that forbid the taking of life, as well as the other precepts, at the dissolution of the body, one as well as the other, goes to the region of the blessed. Again, when a criminal is brought before the king, whether he be a Kshatriya, a Brahman, a Vaisya, or a Sudra, he is either put to death,[*] or disgraced, or some other punishment is appointed; no difference is made on account of his caste. From all these facts, Maha Kacháno concluded that there is no real difference between the members of the four castes; the difference is only in name. The king further declared that if any one, whether he be a Kshatriya, a Brahman, a Vaisya, or a Sudra, shaving his head and beard, putting on yellow robes, &c., shall become a priest, he himself will rise

---

[*] The custom followed in the native states, to exempt all members of the caste of the Brahmans from capital punishment, must be of modern origin.

from his royal seat out of respect to that priest, present him with gifts, and protect him; "for his former appellation has disappeared; he is no longer a Kshatriya, a Brahman, a Vaisya, or a Sudra; he is become a sramana priest." "What think you, then, great king," demanded Maha Kacháno, "if this be the case, are not these four castes equal to each other; or what is your opinion on this point?" "Assuredly," said the monarch, "this being the case, they are all equal; I do not, my lord, perceive any difference between the four castes."

There is the same uncertainty relative to the number and order of the castes in Ceylon, that there is with respect to those in ancient Egypt. No two natives will give the same classification of the inferior castes; though all will agree that among the Singhalese there are no Brahmans, Kshatriyas, or Vaisyas; and all will admit that the first class among them is the Goy-wansa, or Wellála. This uncertainty in the enumeration of the castes arises, in part, from the number of subdivisions into which some of them have been ramified. There are more than 100 classes of the Brahmanical caste, each of which has a different name. There appears to be a greater leaning towards caste in Ceylon than in any other Budhistical country, which in part may have arisen from the circumstance that their recent monarchs were of Malabar extraction. These kings confined the privilege of upasampadá ordination to the Wellála priests. In Nepál, where Budhism is yet professed, the original inhabitants were all of one caste, or had no caste; but their descendants, in the course of time, became divided into many castes, according to the trades or professions that they followed; but even now we are told that in Nepal caste is merely a popular usage, without the sanction of religion, and altogether a very different thing from caste, properly so called. In Tibet and Burma, both of which are Budhistical countries, caste is unknown. In China there are clans, resembling those of the Scottish Highlanders; but this institution differs from caste, and has many features that are peculiar to this singular race.

Under almost every aspect in which caste can be viewed, its influence is most pernicious. Its restraints extend to nearly every act of social intercourse, and its existence is eternal. No power of intellect, no ingenuity, no wealth, no official rank, no personal merit of any description whatever, can break through the formidable barrier it has established. It is a deadly incubus, exerting its power every moment, throughout century after century, upon the minds of a great proportion of the people. It defies all government; it robs the state of the best energies of many of its most able subjects; it scowls at all innovation; there can be no change, no improvement, wherever it ensconces in its strength; no power can coerce it; and were it possible for a universal monarch again to reign, with all the influence that the legends give him, even this mightiest of rulers would be unable to change the caste, or in any important particular alter the social position, of one single individual among the countless millions of his subjects. Yet if a numerous population be any evidence of a nation's power, it must be apparent, that when the state is prevented from employing the intelligence of any part of its people for its own advantage, there is a proportionate loss to the well-being of the whole community, besides the injustice that is done to a class who may possibly be the most efficient of its citizens.

It is said by the apologists for caste, that those who are under its power to the fullest extent, are beings so rude, degraded, and licentious, that they deserve all the insults they receive, as their vices place them without the pale of humanity; and that they do not in reality feel their degradation, as all but the very lowest, (and even the very lowest has something upon which he prides himself), are as tenacious of their rights as the proudest of the twice-born Brahmans. But can anything be a stronger argument in favour of the abolition of this baneful institution? Unless it can be proved that these wretched beings have an inherent depravity more malignant in its nature than that which is possessed by other men, it is evident that the meanness or immorality with which they are charged must be the result of hereditary wrong, and that under other circumstances their character would have been changed. And is it not a glorious privilege we possess, in being enabled to tell these outcasts that by the great Ruler of all they are watched with the same care, and regarded with the same affection, as the rest of mankind?

At an early period after the establishment of Christianity in India by Europeans, it was deemed necessary to institute rules for the guidance of native converts in relation to caste. At the synod of Diamper, in 1599, it was declared that " it would rejoice the synod to see the superstitious and absurd customs of the heathen Malabars of the better sort not mixing with the lower, and having no correspondence or communication with those that have but touched any of them, totally abolished among the Christians of this bishopric;" but as many of the Christians resided under heathen princes, it was considered that in these circumstances the customs might be observed lawfully, and without scruple. Where these impediments did not exist, as " there is no distinction of persons with God, who is Lord of all," "the synod doth command that all that shall be guilty of forbearing to touch such, or having touched them shall wash themselves, to be severely punished as superstitious followers of the heathen customs, and commands the preachers and confessors to admonish them thereof in their sermons and confessions."[*]

The entire spirit of Christianity is opposed to the system of caste. The revelations that are made in the sacred Scriptures relative to the oneness of mankind are most emphatic; and their immense value can only be understood by those who have seen the slave of the west or the outcaste of the east, in the fulness of his degradation. The apostle Paul declared on Mars' hill, that God " hath made of one blood all nations of men for to dwell on all the face of the earth;" and wherever the love of God is felt in its power and purity, there will be an effort to raise every individual within the

[*] Hough's History of Christianity in India.

sphere of its influence to the highest pinnacle of moral and social dignity he can possibly attain. Were it known and acknowledged, according to the word of the Lord, that Jesus Christ, " by the grace of God, tasted death for every man ;" that in the communion of the gospel " there is neither Greek nor Jew, circumcision nor uncircumcision, barbarian, Scythian, bond, nor free, but Christ is all and in all ;" that " in lowliness of mind each is to esteem another better than himself ;" and that " whatsoever we would that men should do unto us, we are to do unto them ;" as a necessary consequence, there would be one holy brotherhood throughout the world, whilst cruelty, oppression, and bondage would be things unknown. We have all proceeded from one progenitor ; we have all one common nature ; we are all redeemed by the same precious blood ; we have all the same Father in heaven ; and unto all, upon equal terms, mercy is offered, as we are all transgressors of the law.* The meanest outcaste, by an individual recumbency upon the atonement, may receive the testimony that his iniquities are forgiven ; and may know, by the Spirit's witness, that he is joined in a mystical union with Christ, " the brightness of God's glory ;" and when his mortal shall put on immortality he will be welcomed to heaven with angelic symphonies more sweet than ever yet were thrown from harp or lute by minstrel's hand, when even kings with their guerdons have listened, not again to descend to some lower position after the lapse of mighty ages, but to live for ever and for ever full, unutterably full, of all that is glorious and good.

* All this was beautifully set forth by one of the Mosaic Institutions. "The rich shall not give more, and the poor shall not give less than half a shekel, when they give an offering unto the Lord, to make an atonement for your souls." Exod. xxx. 15. See also, Job xxxiv. 19; Prov. xxii. 2; Eph. vi. 9; Col. ii. 25.

IV. THE BUDHAS WHO PRECEDED GÓTAMA.

GÓTAMA BÓDHISAT RESOLVES UPON BECOMING A BUDHA: RECEIVES VARIOUS BIRTHS, EXPRESSES THE WISH HE HAD FORMED.—MANY THOUSANDS OF BUDHAS APPEAR.—GÓTAMA BÓHISAT RECEIVES THE ASSURANCE THAT HE WILL BECOME BUDHA.—THE TWENTY-FOUR BUDHAS WHO IMMEDIATELY PRECEDED GÓTAMA.—THE FIVE BUDHAS OF THE PRESENT KALPA: KAKUSANDA, KÓNAGAMANA, KÁSYAPA, GÓTAMA, AND MAITRÍ.

THE Budhas appear after intervals regularly recurring, in a series that knows neither beginning nor end. It is supposed by the Singhalese that all traces of the Budhas previous to Gótama have been lost, with the exception of such particulars as were revealed respecting them by the great teacher or his inspired disciples; and they maintain that the acts they performed, and the doctrines they taught, can be learnt from no other source. But it is thought by many orientalists, that Gótama was only the reviver of a system that had been previously taught by more ancient sages. In the inscription upon the great bell at Rangoon, it is stated that along with the eight hairs of Gótama enshrined in the dágoba of the temple to which it is attached, there are "the three divine relics of the three deities" who were his immediate predecessors. Fa Hian mentions a great town in Oude, in the neighbourhood of Ráma's celebrated city, Ayodhya, which contained "the entire bones" of Kásyapa, or "the relics of his entire body." This agrees with the Singhalese statement relative to the same Budha, that after his cremation the bones of his body still presented an unbroken skeleton; and the coincidence is the more remarkable, as the same circumstance is not related concerning any other Budha. The Chinese traveller also mentions certain sectaries, some of whom worshipped the whole of the four Budhas, and others who worshipped the three preceding Budhas, but paid no respect to Gótama. On the Budhist temple at Sanchi there are images of the four Budhas in niches; and in an inscription it is said that a female devotee, to prevent begging, caused an alms-house to be erected, and money was given for the lamps of the four Budhas. It may have been with the intention of placing themselves at as great a distance as possible from the sectaries, that the followers of Gótama asserted that he was αὐτοδίδακτος, teaching the same truths as the former Budhas, but deriving his knowledge from the intuitive power he received when he became Budha, and not from either reason or tradition.

It is said in the Milinda Prasna: "The dharmma of all the Budhas is the same, but there are four things in which they differ. 1. Some are born as brahmans and others as kings.* 2. Some are born when men live to the age of a hundred years, and others when they live to a thousand. 3. The age of the Budhas when they attain nirwána is regulated by the age of men; on which account some Budhas disappear before they are one hundred years old, and others live to the age of many hundreds of thousands of years. 4. The Budhas differ in the size of their persons, some being much taller than others." There are other differences, but none of them are of very great importance, as it is the uniform testimony of the Singhalese authors that in doctrine the Budhas are one. This, indeed, follows as a matter of course, if they possess the power of knowing all things, as truth changes not with the revolutions of time.

The date of the appearance of the three Budhas who preceded Gótama has been calculated by Major Forbes (Journ. As. Soc. June, 1836). According to this theory, Kakusanda became a Budha, B.C. 3101; Kónágamana, B.C. 2099; and Kásyapa, B.C. 1014. The first of these dates is founded principally upon the supposition that Kakusanda appeared at the commencement of the present kalpa, and that the

---

* The whole of the twenty-four Budhas who preceded Gótama were Kshatriyas, with the exception of the three last, who were Brahmans.

Maha Bhadra kalpa of the Budhists is the same as the Kali yug of the Brahmans; but neither of these ideas can be made to agree with the system as it is received in Ceylon. It may be, that Gótama presented himself to the world as the successor of men whose claims to supreme authority were then acknowledged; but I have not yet met with any well-authenticated data of their doctrines or deeds.

The beings who will in due course become Budhas are called Bódhisat. They are numberless; but the name, in common usage, is almost exclusively confined to those who have become avowed candidates for the high office. When many ages have elapsed without the appearance of a Budha, there are no beings to supply the continued diminution of the numbers in the brahma-lókas. This excites the attention of some compassionate brahma, who, when he has discovered the cause and the remedy, looks out to see in what world the Bódhisat exists who will next become an aspirant for the Budhaship; and when he has discovered the Bódhisat in question, he inspires him with the resolution that enables him to form the wish to become the teacher of the three worlds, that he may release sentient beings from the evils of existence. The ages that succeed this period are divided into three eras; in each of which we have legends of Gótama. 1. The era of resolution (1). 2. The era of expression (2). 3. The era of nomination (3).

We have little information of the innumerable Budhas who have appeared in past ages, until we come to the twenty-four who immediately preceded Gótama; and even their history consists of little more than names and correlative incidents.

In Hodgson's "Illustrations of the Literature and Religion of the Buddhists (Serampore, 1841)," the names of 143 Budhas are given, compiled from the Lalita Vistára, Kriya Sangraha, and Rakshá Bhagavati. The names in this list do not agree with those of the Budhas who are known in Ceylon. "In the Samadhi Raja," it is stated in the same work "Sárvarthasiddha (Sákya, before he became a Budha) is

IV. THE BUDHAS WHO PRECEDED GÓTAMA.

asked by Maitreya and Vajra Pani how he acquired Samadhi Jnyán. In reply, he begins by naming 120 Tathágatas, who instructed him therein in his former births; and at the conclusion of his enumeration of Budhas, Sárvarthasiddha observes, 'he has given so many names exempli gratia, but that his instructors were really no less in number than 80 crores.' There is a verse in the Aparanita Dharani (to be found in many other, and higher authorities), purporting that 'the Buddhas who have been, are, and will be, are more numerous than the grains of sand on the banks of the Ganges.' . . . . These are evident nonentities, in regard to chronology and history, yet it is often difficult to distinguish them from their more substantial compeers."

1. *The Era of Resolution.*

The kalpa in which we now live is called Maha Bhadra. In the ages that were concluded twenty asankya-kap-lakshas previous to this kalpa, there was not, for the space of a kap-asankya, any supreme Budha; so that there was no acquirement of merit, nor any attainment of a higher order of existence, except by the beings who in the kalpas previous to these un-propitious ages had entered the anágámi and sakradágámi paths, and were thus enabled, in process of time, to attain nirwána. Those beings who had only entered the path sowán, passed in order, by the ascending and descending scale, through the various degrees of men, déwas, and brahmas; and then, by the exercise of dhyána, entered the superior paths and became rahats. Among these rahats was a brahma, who, observing that the beings who entered the brahma-lókas were few, enquired what was the reason, when he discovered that it was because no supreme Budha had appeared for the space of a kapasankya. Again, looking to see whether there was any one in the world who had the necessary qualifications to become a candidate for the Budhaship, he beheld many thousands of Bódhisats existent, like so many lotus buds awaiting the influence of the sunbeam that they might be expanded. Having made this discovery, he looked once more to see which of these candidates was the nearest to the attainment of the great object they all had in view, when he saw that it was the Bódhisat who was afterwards to become Gótama Budha.*

At this time Gótama Bódhisat supported himself and his aged mother, who was a widow, by trade. To increase his wealth, he engaged with some mariners to take him to Swarnna Bhúma; but as he was sailing to this place, accompanied by his mother, a great storm arose, and the ship in which he sailed was wrecked. They were in danger of perishing, as the waves rose like mountains to the sky; but Bódhisat, regardless of his own life, and seeking only to save that of his parent, took his mother upon his back, and swam towards the shore, in the midst of sharks, sword-fish, and other monsters of the deep. When the brahma saw the resolution of Bódhisat he was assured that he possessed the requisite qualifications, and therefore bent his mind in the direction of the Budhaship, by means of which Bódhisat thought thus within himself, "I will hereafter become a Budha, that I may save the world." Animated by this resolution, and assisted by the brahma, he succeeded in gaining the land; where he continued, in the foreign country in which he now dwelt, to support his mother, until in due time he died, and was re-born in a brahma-lóka.

After enjoying the blessedness of the brahma-lóka during the accustomed age, he was born as the son of the king of Benares, at that time called Sirimati, and succeeded his father in the kingdom. On receiving the crown, he took the name of Sestratápa, and was famous for subduing wild elephants and bringing them under the yoke. At one time he overcame a very beautiful wild elephant, of which he had heard from one of his foresters; not long after which a herd of elephants broke into the royal gardens at night, and destroyed a great number of the trees, by knocking them down and trampling them under their feet. On hearing of the damage that they had done, the king mounted the elephant he had recently caught, and pursued them; but when the animal upon which he rode scented the females, it went after them with so much eagerness that the king was carried far away into the forest, until he was at so

* This statement does not agree with that which is afterwards declared; as it will be seen that there were many Bódhisats who became Budha, in the time that elapsed between this period and the appearance of Gótama.

great a distance from his attendants, that he became alarmed; and thinking that he would be in danger if a battle were to ensue between his own elephant and the wild ones, he seized the bending branches of a tree that he passed, and escaped from the elephant's back. The attendants followed the footsteps of the elephant, calling out as they proceeded, until they came near the tree; when the king heard their voices, was released, and returned with them to the city. On reaching the palace, he sent for the chief of the elephant keepers, and enquired if he had intended to take his life, by putting him on so unruly an animal; and though the keeper informed the king of the reason of its refractoriness, arising from the presence of the females, he was told that unless it returned from the forest within the space of seven days he must die. But on the seventh day, the elephant returned to the royal stable; and when the keeper informed the king, his majesty went to see it; and perceiving that it was now quite tame, he enquired how it was that the animal appeared to be thus docile, when a little time before he had been unable to restrain it, even by the application of the hook. The keeper replied, "Oh king! the passion of the sexes is sharper than the hook; it is hotter than the burning flame; it is like an arrow piercing the mind; like a thief that steals away the virtuous disposition that would be obedient to the precepts; like an asur to swallow the moon-resembling knowledge; like a fire to burn up the forest-resembling continence. The elephant's passion is over, and he has therefore returned quietly to his stall." The keeper then gave the king a proof of the elephant's obedience to his commands, produced by the power of a mantra; when the king said, "Passion is mischievous, cruel, brutal, and unruly; it is the cause of all danger and distress." After this the king looked to see in what way the evils connected with existence may be overcome; and when he saw that the dharmma of a Budha can alone produce this effect, he thought within himself, "May I become a Budha!" This resolution, or wish, is called manópranidhána. Then retiring from the kingdom, he became an ascetic in the forest of Himála, and at his death was re-born in one of the déwa-lókas.

The next birth received by Bódhisat was as a Brahman, in the village of Dáliddi; and on account of the great beauty of his person he was called Brahma. At sixteen years of age he had read the three Védas, Irju, Yaju, and Sáma, and was acquainted with all the sciences. Near the rock Eraka, but then called Munda, he became an ascetic, and had 500 followers, of whom the Bódhisat who will one day become Maitrí Budha was the chief. One day, when his disciple and Brahma were wandering about the forest to gather fruits for their sustenance, they saw near the rock a tigress that had some time before brought forth, and was then suffering from hunger. Brahma, on seeing this, reflected again on the evils of existence, and sent his disciple into the forest to see if he could find any bones or offal that they could give to the tigress to appease its hunger. During his absence, Brahma remembered that it was only by the birth of a Budha that these evils could be removed; and calling to mind the resolution he had previously formed, he reflected that in order to the attainment of this great object it would be necessary for him to give in alms, many times, his own heads, eyes, wives, and children. Then exclaiming, "May I by this become a Budha!" he placed himself in the way of the tigress, that by giving his flesh he might preserve its life and that of its little ones. When the animal perceived him, it bounded from the rock to the place where he stood, seized him, and tore him in pieces. By the power of the merit arising from this act, he was born in a déwa-lóka.

In process of time Purána Dípankara Budha was born as the son of the monarch of Kappawatí. After remaining in the state of a laic 10,000 years, he became an ascetic, and subsequently a supreme Budha. From this Budha the Bódhisat who afterwards became Dípankara Budha, then a Brahman, received the assurance that he would become a Budha. In the same age Gótama Bódhisat was a prince; and one day, when sitting in his palace, having seen Dípankara Bódhisat carrying the alms-bowl, he sent an attendant to enquire what was his business, when he was informed that he was seeking oil. On hearing this the prince called him to the palace, and filling a golden vessel with oil of white mustard-seed, sidhárttha, put it upon his head, saying at the same time, "By virtue of this act may I hereafter become a Budha; and as this is sidhárttha oil, may my name in that birth be Sidhárttha." This oil was presented by Dípankara Bódhisat to Purána Dípankara Budha, who declared that the prince would in an after age become a supreme Budha.

In the seven asankya-kap-lakshas that elapsed after Gótama Bódhisat formed the wish to become a Budha, 125,000 Budhas appeared; and during this period he was born many hundreds of times, either as a déwa or as a man. 1. In the Nanda asankya, there were 5,000 Budhas. 2. In the Sunanda asankya, 9,000. 3. In the Prathuwí asankya, 10,000. 4. In the Manda asankya, 11,000. 5. In the Dharatí asankya, 20,000. 6. In the Ságara asankya, 30,000. 7. In the Pundaríka asankya, 40,000. Throughout the whole of these ages, in what birth soever he appeared, Gótama Bódhisat continually exercised manópranidhána, the wish to become a supreme Budha.

2. *The Era of Expression.*

In the first Sarwa Bhadra kalpa of the thirteenth asankya-kap-laksha previous to the present Maha Bhadra kalpa, Gótama Bódhisat was born as the son of the monarch of Dhannya. In the course of time he succeeded to the kingdom, and became a chakrawartti. One day his magical chariot having descended to the earth from its appointed place in the sky, he was alarmed by the portent, and enquired from one of his nobles what could be its cause. The noble replied, "This sign betokens either the near approach of the death of the chakrawartti, or that the chakrawartti will become an ascetic, or that a supreme Budha has appeared in the world; but as your majesty has yet many years to live, it cannot portend your death; and it must therefore have been caused by Sákya, the Budha who at present is blessing the world." When the king heard that a Budha was in existence, he went to the wihára in which Sákya resided, and offered him all his treasures, expressing at the same time his earnest expectation that when the necessary qualifications were received, he should himself become a Budha. After this he was re-born in a brahma-lóka.

1. In the same Sarwa-bhadra asankya, 50,000 Budhas appeared. 2. In the Sarwa-phulla asankya, 80,000. 3. In the Sarwa-ratna asankya, 90,000. 4. In the Usabhakkhanda asankya, 70,000. 5. In the Manibhadda asankya, 60,000. 6. In the Puduma asankya, 20,000. 7. In the second Usabhakkhanda

asankya, 10,000. 8. In the Khandatwa asankya, 5,000. 9. In the Sarwa-séla asankya, 2,000. During the whole of these ages, in which 387,000 Budhas appeared, Gótama Bódhisat expressed his wish to become a Budha. This was the period called wák-pranidhána.

3. *The Era of Nomination; including the History of the Budhas who preceded Gótama.*

In the fourth asankya-kap-laksha previous to the present Maha Bhadra kalpa, was the Sáramanda kalpa, in which appeared the four Budhas, Tanhankara, Médhankara, Saranankara, and Dípankara.

In the time of Tanhankara, Gótama Bódhisat was born as the son of Sunanda, king of the city of Puspawatí. From Tanhankara he received aniyata-wiwarana, or an indefinite assurance that he would become Budha. From Dípankara, and the succeeding twenty-three Budhas, he received niyata-wiwarana, or a definite assurance.

Dípankara was born in the city of Rammawatí: his father was the king Sudéwa; his mother, Sumédhá; he reigned 10,000 years before he became an ascetic; his queen was called Paduma; his son, Usabhakkhanda; he exercised asceticism, previous to the reception of the Budhaship, ten months; the kusa grass was given by Sunanda; the sacred tree under which he became Budha was the pulila; his principal male disciples, degasaw, were Mangala and Tissa; his personal attendant, upastháyaha, was Sagara; he lived 100,000 years; he was eighty cubits high; he had a retinue of 400,000 rahats; and the name of Gótama Bódhisat was at this time Sumédha-bráhmana.*

In the third asankya-kap-laksha previous to the present kalpa, Kondannya was Budha. His birth-place was Rammawatí; his father, Sunanda; his mother, Sujáta; his reign, 10,000 years;

---

* Relative to each of the twenty-four Budhas we have:—His name; his birthplace; the names of his father and mother; the length of his reign; the names of his queen and son; his period of asceticism; the names of the persons who gave him the rice-cakes and the sacred grass; his sacred tree; the names of the two principal disciples, and of his personal attendant; his age, stature, and the number of his retinue; and the name of Gótama Bódhisat. Some of these allusions cannot be understood until the legend of the life of Gótama Budha has been read. In the greater number of instances, I have not copied these names from my MS., as their insertion would be of no possible use.

IV. THE BUDHAS WHO PRECEDED GÓTAMA.

his queen, Suruchi; his son, Wijiténa; his period of asceticism, ten months; the person who gave him cakes, Yasódhará; the grass giver, Sunanda; his sacred tree, the sal; his principal disciples, Bhadra and Subhadra: his attendant, Anurudha; his age 100,000 years; his height, 88 cubits; his retinue, a kela-laksha; and the name of Gótama Bódhisat was Wijitáwi-chakrawartti.

In the succeeding asankya-kap-laksha, in the Sárananda kalpa, four Budhas appeared; Mangala, Sumana, Réwata, and Sóbhita. In the time of the first of these Budhas, the name of Gótama Bódhisat was Suruchi-bráhmana; in that of the second, Atulanśgarája; in that of the third, Atidéwa-bráhmana; and in that of the fourth, Sujáta-bráhmana.

One asankya-kap-laksha previous to the present kalpa, in the Wara kalpa, three Budhas appeared; Anomadarshí, Paduma, and Nárada; in whose ages respectively, Gótama Bódhisat was Mahésákya-yaksha-sénápati, a késara lion, and an ascetic.

In the Sára-kalpa, 100,000 kalpas previous to the Maha Bhadra kalpa, there was one Budha, Piyumaturá; and the name of Gótama Bódhisat was Jatilaráshtrika.

In the Manda-kalpa, 30,000 kalpas previous to the present kalpa, there were two Budhas; Sumédha and Sujáta. In the age of the first, the name of Gótama Bódhisat was Uttara, and in that of the second he was a chakrawartti.

In the Wara-kalpa, 118 kalpas previous to the present, there were three Budhas; Piyadarshi, Arthadarshi, and Dharmmadarshi; in whose ages the names of Gótama Bódhisat were Kásyapa-brahmana, Susíma-tápasa, and Sekradewéndra.

In the Manda-kalpa, 96 kalpas previous to the present, there was one Budha, Sidhártha; and the name of Gótama Bódhisat was Mangala-bráhmana.

In the Manda-kalpa, 93 kalpas previous to the present, there were two Budhas, Tissa and Phussa; and Gótama Bódhisat was called Sujátá-tápasa and Wijitáwi-chakrawartti.

In the Sáramanda-kalpa, 91 kalpas previous to the present, there was one Budha, Wipassí, and the name of Gótama Bódhisat was Atula-nága-rája.

In the Manda-kalpa, 31 kalpas previous to the present, there were two Budhas, Sikhí and Wessabhu; and the names of Gótama Bódhisat were Arindama-rája and Sudarshana-rája.

After the dissolution of Wessabhu there were 29 kalpas in which no supreme Budha appeared.

This long period of remediless ignorance was succeeded by the Maha-bhadra* kalpa, in which five Budhas are to appear; Kakusanda, Kónágamana, Kásyapa, Gótama, and Maitrí†. The first four have already appeared; and Maitrí will be the next Budha who will arise to bless the world.

The birth-place of Kakusanda was Mékhalá; his father, Aggidatta, and his mother, Wisakhá. The father of Kakusanda was próhita to the monarch of Kshéma. He remained a laic for the space of 4000 years, and had an establishment of 30,000 females, but Rochaní was his principal queen. At the birth of his son Uttara he left the palace in a chariot drawn by six horses, and after performing the necessary rites of asceticism for the space of eight months, he received the rice-cakes from Wajiréndrayá, and the kusa-grass from Gunasubhadra; and at the root of the tree called sirisa, or márá, he attained the power of a supreme Budha. Near the city of Benares, he proclaimed the bana to 40,000 disciples. The king Kshéma was the Bódhisat who afterwards became Gótama Budha; on hearing the discourses of Kakusanda he resigned his kingdom and embraced the priesthood. The principal disciples of Kakusanda were Wadhúra and Sanjawí; his attendant, Budhajána; his principal female disciples, Sama and Upasama; his stature 40 cubits; the rays from his body extended to the distance of 10 yojanas; and his age was 40,000 years.

The name of Kónágamana was received from the circumstance that at the instant of his birth there was a golden shower (kanakawassán) throughout Jambudwípa. His birth-place was Sódhawati; his father, Sanyadatta; and his mother, Uttará. He remained as a laic for the space of 3000 years, and had 16,000 females in his palace, but Ruchigátrá was his principal queen. At the birth of his son Swárthiwahana he left the palace on his

* Pali, bhadda, from bhaddi, excellence.—Turnour's Annals.

† "There are at Varánasi (Benares), according to the dreams of the Budhists, 1000 (spiritual) thrones for the 1000 Budhas of this happy age, Bhadrakalpa, four of whom have appeared, and the rest are to come hereafter. Shákya, after becoming Budha, when he visited Varánasi, paid respect to the thrones of his three predecessors by circumambulating each of them, and then he sat down on the fourth throne. These 1000 Budhas are described in the first volume of the Do class of the Kagyur. Some wealthy Tibetans delight to keep the images of these 1000 Budhas, made in silver or other metal, and to pay respect to them."—Csoma Körösi.

state elephant, with 30,000 followers, all of whom embraced the priesthood. After performing the asetic usages for the space of four months, he received the rice-cakes from Aggiséna, and the kusa-grass from Chinduka; and at the root of the tree called udumbura, or dimbul, he attained the object of his great exertion. Gótama Bódhisat was at this time the monarch Parwata, who made an offering to Kónágamana, and heard him repeat the prediction, "In the present kalpa this individual will become a supreme Budha." The principal disciples of Kónágamana were Sambahula and Uttara; his attendant, Sortthijana; his principal female disciples, Sámuddá and Uttará; his stature 30 cubits; and he was 30,000 years of age when he attained nirwána.

The birth-place of Kásyapa was Benares; his father, Brahmadatta; his mother, Dhammawati; the period during which he remained a laic, 2000 years; his queen, Sunanda; his son Wijitasena; his period of asceticism, seven days; the cake-giver, Emasunanda; the grass-giver, Somanassa; and his sacred tree was the nuga, or banian. His principal disciples were Tissa and Bháraddwaja, his attendant, Sarwachitra; and his principal female disciples, Uruwelá and Urulá. At this time Gótama Bódhisat was the brahman Jótipála. His stature was 20 cubits; he had a retinue of 20,000 disciples; and lived in all 20,000 years. After his body was burnt, the bones still remained in their usual position, presenting the appearance of a perfect skeleton; and the whole of the inhabitants of Jambudwípa assembling together, erected a dágoba over his relics, one yojana in height. (*Sadharmmaratnakáré*).

V. GÓTAMA BÓDHISAT: HIS VIRTUES AND STATES OF BEING.

THE TEN PÁRAMITÁS.—THE QUALIFICATIONS AND ADVANTAGES OF THE BÓDHISAT.—THE FIVE HUNDRED AND FIFTY BIRTHS.—THE SUJÁTA JÁTAKA.—THE APPANNAKA JÁTAKA.—THE MUNIKA JÁTAKA.—THE MAKASA JÁTAKA.—THE GUNA JÁTAKA.—THE TINDUKA JÁTAKA.—THE ASADRISA JÁTAKA.—THE WESSANTARA JÁTAKA.

A GREAT part of the respect paid to Gótama Budha arises from the supposition that he voluntarily endured, throughout myriads of ages, and in numberless births, the most severe deprivations and afflictions, that he might thereby gain the power to free sentient beings from the misery to which they are exposed under every possible form of existence. It is thought that myriads of ages previous to his reception of the Budhaship, he might have become a rahat, and therefore ceased to exist; but that of his own free will, he forewent the privilege, and threw himself into the stream of successive existence, for the benefit of the three worlds. There is a class of virtues, called the ten páramitás, one or other of which is pre-eminently exercised during the whole period in which the Bódhisat prepares himself for the supreme Budhaship (1).

In the discourses that were delivered by Gótama, he occasionally referred to the 24 Budhas who immediately preceded him, on which occasions he related the circumstances of his own life at each of these periods. The history of these Budhas has been briefly recorded in the preceding chapter. It was also the custom of Gótama, when any event of importance occurred, to refer to some similar event that had taken place in previous ages, in which the same persons were actors. dwelling more particularly upon the part he himself had taken in the several transactions. From these relations the work called by the Singhalese Pansiya-panas-játaka-pota, or the Book of the Five Hundred and Fifty Births, was compiled. "The work known by this title," says the Rev. D. J. Gogerly (Ceylon Friend, Aug. 1838), "is a Pali commentary on one of the fifteen books belonging to the fifth section of the Sútra Pitaka, or Discourses of Budha, and forms no part therefore of the sacred code; but according to a decision that the comments are of equal authority with the text, it is regarded as of indisputable authority. There is a Singhalese translation of the greater part of it, which is exceedingly popular, not on account of the peculiar doctrines of Budhism contained in it, for these are but incidentally referred to, but from its being a collection of amusing stories which they believe to be unquestionably true. The copy of the Pali comment now before me is written on olas 29 inches long, having 9 lines on a page, and occupies 1000 leaves or 2000 pages. The text itself is very scarce; my copy was made from one in the possession of the late chief priest of the Matura district, Bówilla; it contains 340 pages of 9 lines each, written on olas 23 inches long. It is named Játaka Gáthá, or Birth Stanzas, although a large proportion of them has no reference (independent of the comment) to any birth, being general maxims or miscellaneous observations. Each of the first one hundred Játakas consists of a single verse of four lines; but some of the remainder, being histories, are much longer, the last one, or history of king Wessantara, occupying 40 pages. The comment comprises—1. The occasion upon which the verse was spoken. 2. A story illustrating it, affirmed to have been related at the time by Budha, detailing circumstances which occurred to him and the parties respecting whom the verse was spoken, in a previous birth. 3. A philological explanation of the words and sense of the stanza, the verse or verses being mostly inserted at length. This last is not translated into Singhalese, except partially in the first Játaka, as being unintelligible to the mere Singhalese reader."

The Singhalese translation, so far as it extends, appears to be a correct and literal rendering of the Pali original. I have read the greater part of it, and brought a copy to England, intending to read the whole, but have not yet found leisure to accomplish the task. Reckoning a page to contain 9 lines, with about 100 letters in each line, it extends to 2400 pages. I have not made much use of it beyond the present chapter. At my request, my native pundit made an analysis of the number of times in which Gótama Bódhisat appeared in particular states of existence, as recorded in the Játakas, and the following is the result. An ascetic 83 times; a monarch 58; the déwa of a tree 43; a religious teacher 26; a courtier 24; a próhita brahman 24; a prince 24; a nobleman 23; a learned man 22; the déwa Sekra 20; an ape 18; a merchant 13; a man of wealth 12; a deer 10; a lion 10; the bird hansa 8; a snipe 6; an elephant 6; a fowl 5; a slave 5; a golden eagle 5; a horse 4; a bull 4; the brahma Maha Brahma 4; a peacock 4; a serpent 4; a potter 3; an outcaste 3; a guana 3; twice each a fish, an elephant driver, a rat, a jackal, a crow, a woodpecker, a thief, and a pig; and once each a dog, a curer of snake-bites, a gambler, a mason, a smith, a devil dancer, a scholar, a silversmith, a carpenter, a water-fowl, a frog, a hare, a cock, a kite, a jungle-fowl, and a kindurá. It is evident, however, that this list is imperfect.

Not a few of the fables that pass under the name of Æsop are here to be found; and the schoolboy is little aware, as he reads of the wit of the fox or the cunning of the monkey, that these animals become, in the course of ages, the teacher of the three worlds, Budha. Each Játaka begins with the formula, "yata-giya-dawasa," which is an exact equivalent to our own, "in days of yore." The Hindu collection of fables, called the Hitópadésa, is well known. As the scene of these fables is laid in the comparatively modern city of Pátaliputra, whilst that of the Játaka, is almost invariably connected with a Brahmadatta, king of Benares, we may infer therefrom the superior antiquity of the Pali collection. The Játaka-pota bears a considerable resemblance to those parts of the Talmud that are described as consisting of "aphorisms and moral sentiments, illustrated by similes and parables, and also by narratives, sometimes real and sometimes fictitious." These legends are interesting, as throwing light upon the manners and customs, and upon the modes of thought, that were prevalent when this compilation was made, or in the ages immediately previous; as there is a boundary of verisimilitude beyond which the wildest imagination cannot pass. One tale, after the usual manner of eastern compositions, presents the opportunity for the introduction of several other stories that are only slightly dependent upon the principal narrative. The Singhalese will listen the night through to recitations from this work, without any apparent weariness; and a great number of the Játakas are familiar even to the women.

The Játakas here transcribed are the Sujáta (2), Apannaka (3), Munika (4), Makasa (5), Guna (6), Tinduka (7), Asadrisa (8), and Wessantara (9). In this selection I have had in view the interest of the legend as a tale; the convenience of its length; or its importance as illustrating some feature of Budhism. The Sujáta Játaka is here translated in full, with its introduction; but in the other Játakas the introduction is omitted, and the narrative much abridged. The first Játaka recorded in the original text is the Apannaka; and the last, the Wessantara.

1. *The Virtues and Privileges of the Bódhisat.*

There are ten primary virtues, called páramitás, that are continually exercised by the Bódhisats; and as each virtue is divided into three degrees; ordinary; upa, superior; and paramártha, pre-eminent; there are in all thirty páramitás.

For the space of twenty asankya-kap-lakshas, that is to say, from the time that the manópranidhána, or resolution to become a Budha, was first exercised, the thirty páramitás were practised by Gótama Bódhisat. 1. He gave in alms, or as charity, his eyes, head, flesh, blood, children, wife, and substance, whether personal or otherwise, as in the Khadirangara birth. In this way he fulfilled the three kinds of dána, viz., dána-páramitá, dána-upa-páramitá, and dána-paramartha-páramitá. 2. In the Bhusidatta birth, and in others of a similar description, he practised the síla-páramitá, or observance of the precepts, in the three degrees. 3. In the Chulla Suttasóma, and other similar births, he abandoned vast treasures of gold and silver, and numberless slaves, cattle, buffaloes, and other sources of wealth, and thus fulfilled the naiskrama-páramitá, which requires retirement from the world. 4. In the Sattubhatta, and other births, he revealed to others that which he saw with his divine eyes, and thus fulfilled the pragnyá-páramitá, or the virtue proceeding from wisdom. 5. In the Maha-janaka, and other births, he performed things exceedingly difficult to be done, thus fulfilling the wírya-páramitá, or the virtue proceeding from determined courage. 6. In the Kshántiwáda, and other births, he endured with an equal mind the opposition of unjust men, regarding it as if it were the prattle of a beloved child, thus observing the kshánti-páramitá, or virtue proceeding from forbearance. 7. In the Maha Suttasóma, and other births, he spoke the words of truth, thus exercising the satta-páramitá, or virtue proceeding from truth. 8. In the Temé, and other births, he set his mind to that which is excellent, in the most resolute manner, never giving way to evil in the least possible degree; thus fulfilling the adishtána-páramitá, or the virtue proceeding from unalterable resolution. 9. In the Nigrodhaniga, and other births, he gave away that which he enjoyed to aid the necessities of others, and took upon himself the sorrows of others; thus observing the maitrí-páramitá, or the virtue proceeding from kindness and affection. 10. In the Sara, and other births, he regarded with an equal mind those who exercised upon him the most severe cruelties, and those who assisted him and were kind; thus fulfilling the upéksha-páramitá, or virtue proceeding from equanimity.

All the páramitás were exercised in the three degrees; and the differences in question may be learnt from that which is said respecting dána. The giving of eyes, flesh, and blood, or that which belongs to the body, is the ordinary dána. The giving of children, wife, horses, slaves, cattle, buffaloes, lands, pearls, jewels, gold, and silver, or that which may be regarded as a possession, is the superior dána. And the giving of that which involves the loss of life, as the head upon which the royal crown has been placed, or the body, to feed lions, tigers, yakás, and rakshas, is the pre-eminent dána.

The period required for the exercise of a páramitá is called bhúmi. Were a Bódhisat to shed one single drop of blood in a thousand births, he would shed more blood than there is water in a thousand oceans in the space of one páramitá-bhúmi. Were he, in the same number of births, to give a portion of his flesh only the size of the undu flower, he would, in one bhúmi, give more flesh than there is earth in a thousand worlds like our own. Were he, in as many births, once to give his head, he would, in one bhúmi, give as many heads as would form a heap higher than Méru. Were he, on a similar scale, once to give an eye, he would, in one bhúmi, give more eyes than there are stars in a thousand sakwalas. Were he to give one son bound by a withe, the whole of the withes would form a heap higher than Méru. Were any being to live successively through the age enjoyed in each of the déwa and brahma-lókas, though this period would amount to many millions of years, and more than two hundred thousand maha-kalpas, it would not be a longer space of time than is required for the fulfilling of a páramitá. The páramitá-bhúmi must therefore be a period inconceivably long.

The Bódhisat is never born in any world above the Asanyasatya-lóka. He avoids the déwa and brahma-lókas, because in these worlds he cannot further the accomplishment of his design; he never prolongs his stay in places of this description, but seeks continually for opportunities to carry his design into effect; and it is for this reason that of his own free will he passes away from these lókas, and is born in the world of men. Because of his merit, he might always be born in a déwa or brahma-lóka, but as in these places he cannot further the purposes of his great intention, he prefers being born in the world of men. Other beings must remain the appointed time in these worlds, there being no dangers or accidents by which their departure can be hastened; but as the Bódhisat cannot there perform the páramitás, he has the power to depart at his pleasure. For this purpose he lies down upon a couch, and resolves upon being born in this world; when his death takes place, and he receives birth in the place and manner upon which he had previously resolved. This kind of death is called adhimukti; and the power is possessed by none but those who are to become supreme Budhas.

There are some Bódhisats who practise the páramitás during four, and others during eight, or sixteen, asankya-kap-lakshas. There are some who excel in purity, and in them wisdom is less evident; others who excel in wisdom, and in them purity is less evident; and others who excel in determined courage, and in them purity and wisdom are less apparent. The three kinds of Bódhisats are distinguished by the names of ugghatitagnya, or "he who attains quickly;" wipachitagnya, or "he who attains less quickly: and gneyya, or "he who attains least quickly." The Bódhisats who belong to the first division may attain rahatship on hearing four stanzas from a supreme Budha, and repeating them; and on the same day they might enter nirwána. Those of the second class must hear four stanzas from a supreme Budha, and ask their meaning, before they can have the power to attain rahatship; but on the same day they might enter nirwána. Those of the third class must hear four stanzas and hear them explained at length, before they can have the power to attain the rahatship; but on the same day they might enter nirwána. If there be any Bódhisat, any being looking forward to the reception of the supreme Budhaship, he must make no use of his power to become a rahat, but must continue to exercise the páramitás, that he may impart unto others the happiness of nirwána. After the assurance of the Budhaship has been received, were the Bódhisat to give the most valuable alms every day during many ages to hasten its reception, no effect of this kind would be produced. For this reason. When there is rice that is accustomed to ripen in three, four, or five months, no labour of the husbandman can accelerate the period of the harvest, however often he may water it, or whatever pains he may take; in like manner, the time for receiving the Budhaship cannot be hastened, whatever alms might be given for the purpose.

There are eight qualifications that must be possessed by the being who receives the assurance of becoming a Budha. 1. He must be a man, and not a déwa. It is therefore requisite that the Bódhisat continually keep the ten precepts, that he may have the merit to be born as a man. 2. He must be a male, and not a female; and therefore the Bódhisat must avoid all sins that would cause him to be born as a woman. 3. He must have the merit that would enable him to become a rahat; all evil desire must be destroyed. 4. There must be the opportunity of offering to a supreme Budha, in whom also firm faith must be exercised. 5. There must be the abandonment of the world, and the Bódhisat must become an ascetic. 6. He must possess the virtue derived from the practice of dhyána and other similar exercises, nor can the assurance be received by one that is unjust or wicked. 7. He must firmly believe that the Budha with whom he communicates is free from sorrow, and that he himself will possess the same power; and he must enquire at what period he will receive the Budhaship. 8. He must exercise a firm determination to become a Budha; and were he even told that in order to obtain its exalted rank he must endure the pains of hell during four asankya-kap-lakshas, he must be willing to suffer all this for its sake.

In the time of Dípankara Budha, Gótama Bódhisat might have attained nirwána, but that he might save countless beings from the woes of repeated birth, he voluntarily chose to continue in existence during the period that would elapse before he could become a Budha, the design he had formed being constantly kept in view, until the whole of the páramitás were fulfilled. There is nothing in all existence to which the páramitás that he accomplished can be compared. When any of these four things are taken, the earth, the ocean, the stars, or Méru, it is like saying that the king of the garundas is larger than a snipe; now the king is 150 yojanas in height.

There are some persons who, on hearing of the afflictions of the Bódhisat, might suppose that his sufferings are excessive; but in reality his enjoyment preponderates. Were a kalpa to be divided into eight parts, to other beings there is enjoyment in seven parts, and in one part suffering; but to the Bódhisat there is enjoyment throughout the whole of the eight parts. The attainment of the Budhaship is like the ascent of a man to the top of a tree, in order that he may gather of its fruit; the choice of the fruit is before him, and he can take that which is ripest and best.

There are thirteen advantages that the Bódhisat enjoys: 1. He is never born in any of the eight great hells; all other beings receive this birth, but the Bódhisats never. 2. He is never born in the Lókántarika hell. 3. He is never born in the Nijhámatanhá préta world. 4. He never receives the Khuppipása préta birth, though all other beings endure it. 5. He never receives the Kálahanjanaka préta birth, though all other beings are subject to it. 6. He is never born as any kind of vermin; he is never a louse, bug, ant, or worm; all other beings receive these births, but the Bódhisat is never born less than a snipe; nor is he ever born as a serpent or as any other animal of a similar species. 7. He is never born blind, dumb, deaf, a cripple, or leprous. 8. He is never born as a female. 9. He is never born as one of doubtful sex. 10. He never commits any of the five great sins. 11. He is never born in an arúpa world, as in those states there is no acquisition of merit. 12. There are other states of existence in which he is not born, as the prince never defiles his caste by entering the dwellings of common men. 13. He is never a sceptic. These advantages are enjoyed by the Bódhisats from the time that they resolve upon the exercise of the páramitás. Though the giving of their heads and of their children are in themselves sacrifices most painful, the pain is overpowered by the joy which is felt when looking forward to the greatness of the reward.

From the time when Gótama Bódhisat received the assurance that he would become a Budha, throughout the whole of his various births, his mind was ever inclined towards merit and averse to demerit. When thoughts of demerit arose, his mind was agitated, like a feather thrown into the fire; but towards merit his mind was enlarged, like a broad canopy of cloth or like pure sesamum oil spread out on the surface of a placid lake. He was never indolent or fearful, but at all times exercised the most determined resolution; no other being, whether it be Maha Brahma, Vishnu, Iswara, or any other déwa, had the power to exhibit an equal courage. We will record an instance. At a certain time Gótama Bódhisat was born as a squirrel,* on account of some demerit of a former age. In the forest he was attentive to his young ones, providing for them all that was necessary; but a fearful storm arose, and the rivers overflowed their banks, so that the tree in which he had built

* It is said (Journ. Bengal As. Soc. 1835), that in the island of Rambree, near the coast of Arrakan, there are the remains of Budhist temples, in which are relics of Gótama, such as the hair, feathers, bones, &c., of the several creatures whose form he assumed previous to his becoming a man; but according to the Singhalese authors these relics must have perished many hundred of thousands of years ago.

his nest was thrown down by the current, and the little ones were carried along with it far out to sea. But Bódhisat determined that he would release them; and for this purpose he dipped his tail in the waves, and sprinkling the water on the land, he thought in this manner to dry up the ocean.* After he had persevered seven days, he was noticed by Sekra, who came to him and asked what he was doing. On being told, he said, "Good squirrel! you are only an ignorant animal, and therefore you have commenced this undertaking; the sea is 84,000 yojanas in depth; how then can you dry it up? Even a thousand or a hundred thousand men, would be unable to accomplish it, unless they were rishis." The squirrel replied, "Most courageous of men! if the men were all like you, it would be just as you say, as you have let the extent of your courage be known by the declaration; but I have no time just now to spend with such imbeciles as you, so you may be gone as soon as you please." Then Sekra caused the young squirrels to be brought to the land, as he was struck with the indomitable courage of the parent. Thus was fulfilled the wírya-páramitá. The whole of the ten virtues were fulfilled with equal ability. (*Pujáwaliya; Sadharmmaratnakáré*).

2. *The Sujáta Játaka.*

It came to pass that whilst Gótama Budha resided in the wihára called Jetawana, near the city of Sewet, he related the following Játaka, on account of an ascetic who had lost his father. In what way? Budha having perceived that an ascetic who had lost his father endured great affliction in consequence, and knowing by what means he could point out the way of relief, took with him a large retinue of priests, and proceeded to the dwelling of the ascetic. Being honourably seated, he enquired, "Why are you thus sorrowful, ascetic?" to which the bereaved son replied, "I am thus sorrowful on account of the death of my father." On hearing this, Budha said, "It is to no purpose to weep for the dead; a word of advice is given to those who weep for the thing that is past and gone." In what manner? That which follows is the relation.

* The inhabitants of Lavinium had a legend that the forest in which their city was afterwards built took fire of its own accord, when a fox tried to extinguish it by dipping its tail in water.

In a former age, when Brahmadatta was king of Benares, Bódhisat was born of a wealthy family, and was called Sujáta. The grandfather of Sujáta sickened and died, at which his father was exceedingly sorrowful; indeed his sorrow was so great, that he removed the bones from their burial-place, and deposited them in a place covered with earth near his own house, whither he went thrice a day to weep. The sorrow almost overcame him; he ate not, neither did he drink. Bódhisat thought within himself, that it was proper to attempt the assuaging of his father's grief; and therefore, going to the spot where there was a dead buffalo, he put grass and water to its mouth and cried out, "Oh, buffalo, eat and drink!" The people perceived his folly, and said, "What is this, Sujáta? Can a dead buffalo eat grass or drink water?" But without paying any attention to their interference, he still cried out, "Oh, buffalo, eat and drink!" The people concluded that he was out of his mind, and went to inform his father; who, forgetting his parent from his affection for his son, went to the place where he was, and enquired the reason of his conduct. Sujáta replied, "There are the feet and the tail, and all the interior parts of the buffalo, entire; if it be foolish in me to give grass and water to a buffalo, dead, but not decayed, why do you, father, weep for my grandfather, when there is no part of him whatever to be seen?" The father then said, "True, my son, what you say is like the throwing of a vessel of water upon fire; it has extinguished my sorrow;" and thus saying he returned many thanks to Sujáta.

This Sujáta Játaka is finished. I, Budha, am the person who was then born as the youth Sujáta.

3. *The Apannaka Játaka.*

In a former age, when Brahmadatta was a king of Benares, in the country called Kasi, Gótama Bódhisat was a merchant, who traded to different places, with a train of 500 wagons. There was a time when he went from the east to the west, and from the west to the east. In the same city there was another merchant, unwise, foolish, unskilful in expedients. Bódhisat filled his 500 wagons with the most valuable goods, and was ready to take his departure. The other merchant was in a similar position. Bódhisat reflected thus: If this other merchant accompanies me, there will be a thousand wagons, for which the road will be insufficient; fuel and water will be wanted for the men, and grass for the oxen; it will be better that one should precede the other." He then called the unwise merchant, and said to him, "It will not be possible for us both to go together. What will you do? Will you go the first, or shall I?" The unwise merchant thought, "If I go first, I shall derive many advantages therefrom; the road will be free from ruts; the oxen that draw the wagon will have fresh grass to eat, and the men will have vegetables that have not previously been culled by any one else; there will be excellent water; I can put what price I choose upon my goods, and still sell them." So he said, "Friend, I will go first." But Bódhisat saw that there would be many advantages from going last; and thus reflected: "Those who go first will make the rough places in the road even; the oxen will eat the coarse grass, whilst mine will crop that which is newly grown and tender; my men will pluck the tender vegetables that will spring up in the place of the former ones; those who go first will dig wells in places where there is no water, and we can drink therefrom; it is like putting one's life in danger to fix a price upon goods, but if I go last, I can sell my wares at the price already fixed." So he said, "Friend, you may go first." The unwise merchant, saying, "It is all right, Friend," prepared his wagons, and commenced his journey. But he soon came to a region uninhabited and wild. Then filling his water vessels, he entered the desert, sixty yojanas in extent. When they had come to the centre of the desert, a yaká who dwelt there thought that if he could persuade them to throw away their water, they would become weak, and he could then devour them. In order to effect this purpose, he caused a magnificent chariot to appear, drawn by two oxen, white, and in every respect beautiful, near which was a retinue of ten or twelve demons (literally, not men), armed with bows and other weapons. Seated in the chariot, he himself appeared like a respectable man, adorned with flowers and garlands, his head and clothes all wet, and the wheels of his chariot covered with mud. His attendants, both before and behind, were adorned in a similar manner, with red and white lotus flowers in their hands, and were eating the roots of the nelumbium and other water plants, whilst drops of water and mud were sprinkled around. When the yaká saw the merchant approaching, he caused his own chariot to go a little out of the way, and enquired about his welfare. The merchant also caused his carriage to leave the road, that the wagons might be able to pass on, and said to the yaká, "We have come from Benares; but where have you come from, adorned with flowers, eating the roots of water plants, and your bodies streaming with water? Have you had rain on the road, and met with ponds covered with plants?" The yaká replied, "What is it you say, Friend? The verge of the green forest appears in the distance like a line; from thence the whole forest abounds with water; the rains are constant; the ripple plays upon the entire surface of the water-course; and ponds, covered with lotus flowers and water plants, appear here and there. But where are you going in such order with your train of wagons?" The merchant said, "I am going to such a region." The yaká asked, "What have you in these wagons and in these?" and was answered, "Such and such goods." "The last wagons," said the yaká, "appear to come on very heavily; with what goods are they laden?" and when the merchant replied that they carried water, he said that he had done well to bring water thus far, but that thenceforward there would be no benefit in conveying it, as he would meet with abundance, so that it would be better to break his water vessels, and spill the water, by which means the wagons would be able to get on more easily. Then saying that he must not delay any longer, he went a little distance, and disappearing returned to his demon-city. The unwise merchant listened to the words of the yaká, and breaking his water vessels so that not a particle of water was left, he drove on. But they did not meet with anything like the appearance of water; the men became exhausted from thirst; and when evening came, they untied the wagons and placed them in a circle, fastening the oxen to the wheels; there was no water for the oxen to drink or for the men to prepare their rice; exhausted, they threw themselves down here and there, and fell asleep. When the night was about half over, the demons came from their city, slew the oxen and men, and devoured them, leaving at their departure nothing but their bones. Thus, through the folly of the merchant, all these beings came to destruction; their bones were scattered abroad; and the 500 wagons were left in the path, full of goods.

About a month and a half after the departure of the unwise merchant, Bódhisat commenced his journey, after lading his 500 wagons with goods, and by degrees came to the beginning of the desert. Here he filled his large jars with water, and when the people were encamped, he called them together by beat of drum, and said, "No one is allowed to touch even a drop of water without permission from me; there are poisonous trees in this desert; therefore let no one eat any leaf, fruit or flower that he has not been accustomed to before, without my consent." After giving this advice, he entered the desert, along with his wagons. When he had arrived at about the middle, the yáka, in the same manner as in the former instance, appeared in the path; but Bódhisat knew him, and reflected, "There is no water in this desert; it is on this account that it has received its name of waterless; this person has fearless, red eyes; his shadow does not appear; without doubt, the unwise merchant who preceded me has thrown away his water, so that the men have become exhausted, and then been devoured; this demon knows not my superior wisdom, nor my readiness in expedients." Then he said to the yáka, "You may all be off, out of the way; we shall not throw away our water until we meet with more; when we come to other water, we will then throw away the water we have brought, and thus lighten our wagons." Upon hearing this, the yáka went to a little distance, vanished, and returned to his demon city. After his departure, the attendants of Bódhisat came to him, and said, "My lord, these people say that the verge of a green forest appears in the distance; from thence the rains are constant; they are adorned with lotus flowers, and carry red and white water flowers in their hands; they are eating the roots of water plants; and their garments are dripping with wet; it will be better, therefore, to throw away our water, that we may lighten our wagons, and proceed more quickly. But Bódhisat no sooner heard these words, than he commanded the people to stop, and assembling them together, he enquired, "Did you ever hear from any one that there is either lake or pond in this desert?" They replied, "We never heard of any such thing; is it not called the Waterless Desert?" Bódhisat: "The men we saw told us that the verge of a green forest, where the rains are constant, appears in the distance; now to what distance does the rainy wind extend?" The attendants: "It blows about a yojana." Bódhisat: "Well, has any one of you all felt this wind?" The attendants: "No, sir." Bódhisat: "How far may the rain-cloud be seen?" The attendants: "About a yojana." Bódhisat: "Has any one of you all seen it?" The attendants: "No, sir." Bódhisat: "To what distance does the lightning appear?" The attendants: "About a yojana." Bódhisat: "Has any one of you all seen its flash?" The attendants: "No, sir." Bódhisat: "How far can the sound of the thunder be heard?" The attendants: "About a yojana." Bódhisat: "Has any one of you all heard it?" The attendants: "We have not heard it, sir." Bódhisat: "Good people, these are not men; they are demons; they wish us to throw away our water, that when we are exhausted they may devour us; the unwise merchant who preceded us, will have thrown away his water and been destroyed: the 500 wagons will be left in the road, full of goods, and we shall find them; do not throw away a single drop of water, but drive on with all haste." They soon afterwards found the 500 wagons, full of goods, with the scattered bones of the men and oxen. Then untying their oxen, they put their wagons in the form of an encampment, and when the oxen had eaten grass, and the men been refreshed, they placed the cattle in a circle, and the men around them, the stoutest of whom kept guard during the three watches, until the dawn, with swords in their hands. The next day, early in the morning, when the men and oxen had again been refreshed, they put away their weak wagons and took strong ones, and exchanged their inferior goods for those that were valuable. On their arrival at the place of merchandise, Bódhisat sold his goods at a high price, and the whole company returned in safety to their own city.

At the conclusion of this discourse, Budha said to the nobleman, Anépidu (for whose sake it was spoken), "The followers of the reasoner (whose perception of truth is limited) came to a great destruction; whilst the followers of the non-reasoner (who has an intuitive perception of the truth) were preserved from the demon, went in safety to the place at which they wished to arrive, and then with great satisfaction returned in safety to the city whence they came. Joining the history of Anépidu and the Játaka together, Budha delivered the following stanza:

"Apannakanthánameke,
Dutiyan áhutakkiká.
Etadannyáyamedháwi,
Tanganheyadapannakan."*

4. *The Munika Játaka.*

In this birth, Bódhisat was a bull. He had a younger brother, who one day complained to him that they did all the work and lived only on grass, whilst a boar, their master had purchased, was fed on all kinds of dainties, and did nothing. But Bódhisat told him not to envy the lot of the boar, as it would soon have the worst of it. And thus it fell out, as the boar was killed for food at a feast that was celebrated in honour of the marriage of their master's daughter.†

5. *The Makasa Játaka.*

In this birth, Bódhisat was a tradesman, who went from village to village to dispose of his wares. One day, when at the house of a carpenter, whose head was bald, like a copper porringer, a musquito alighted thereon; and the carpenter called to his son, who was near, to drive it away. The son, taking a sharp axe for this purpose, aimed a blow at the insect, but split his father's head in two, and killed him. On seeing what was done, Bódhisat said that an enemy was better than a foolish relative or friend.

6. *The Guna Játaka.*

In this birth, Bódhisat was a lion, and lived upon a rock, near a small lake, surrounded by mud. Upon the pasturage which the mud afforded, deer and other animals of a similar species were accustomed to graze. One day Bódhisat being hungry, ascended to the top of the rock, and looking around, he espied a deer feeding on the borders of the lake. Approaching the spot, he roared aloud, and sprang forward to seize the deer; but the animal being affrighted by the noise, bounded away. The lion, therefore, fell into the mud, and as he sank so deep that his four feet were held fast, he was unable to get away. Seven days

---

* The stanza is thus translated by Mr. Gogerly: "Some declare unmixed truths: reasoners speak diversely. The wise man, knowing this, takes that which is unmixed."—Friend, ii. 20.

† This legend bears a considerable resemblance to the fable of "the wanton calf."

there he remained, without a morsel of food, when a jackal came near; and though he was at first afraid, yet as the lion informed him of his situation, and requested his assistance, he assumed courage, and making a channel for the water to come from the lake to the feet of the lion, he thus softened the mud, and released the prisoner from his confinement. The lion and jackal, with their families, afterwards lived together for some time, in the same cave, in great harmony.

7. *The Tinduka Játaka.*

In this birth, Bódhisat was the king of 80,000 monkeys. The tribe lived in the forest of Himála, near a village, in which was a timbery tree laden with fruit. The monkeys requested permission of their king to go and seize the fruit; but his majesty forbade them, when he learnt that the village was inhabited. They, however, ascended the tree in the middle of the night, and were busy at work, when one of the villagers having occasion to rise, saw what they were about, and gave the alarm. The tree was soon surrounded by people, armed with sticks, who were resolved to wait until the dawn, and then kill the monkeys. Information was conveyed to the king that his tribe were in this predicament; so he immediately went to the village, and set fire to the house of an old woman. The people, of course, ran to extinguish the flames, and thus the monkeys escaped.

8. *The Asadrisa Játaka.*

In this birth, Bódhisat was the son of Brahmadatta, king of Benares, and was called Asadrisa. He had a younger brother, Brahmadatta. On arriving at a proper age, he received all necessary instructions from a learned preceptor; and the king at his death commanded that the kingdom should be given to Asadrisa, and the viziership to his brother. The nobles were willing that the royal command should be obeyed; but as Bódhisat positively refused the kingdom, it was given to his younger brother, and he became vizier, or inferior king. A certain noble afterwards insinuated to the king, that Asadrisa was plotting against his life; on hearing which he became enraged, and commanded that the traitor should be apprehended. But Bódhisat received warning of the danger in which he was placed, and fled to the city of king Sámánya. On arriving at the gate of the city, he sent to inform the king that a famous archer had arrived in his dominions. The king gave orders that he should be admitted into the royal presence, and asked what wages he would require; and when he was answered that a thousand masurans would be a reasonable salary, he gave his promise that this sum should be allowed. The king's former archers were naturally envious that a mere stranger should receive an allowance so much superior to their own. One day, the king having entered the royal garden, commanded that a couch should be placed, and a cloth spread, at the foot of a mango tree. When seated, he espied a mango fruit at the very uppermost part of the tree; and as it was impossible that any one could get to it by climbing, he intimated that the archers should be called, who were to bring it down by an arrow. The archers of course gave way to the man of the thousand masurans; and the king repeated his command to Asadrisa, who requested that the royal couch might be removed from under the tree. The archers perceiving that Bódhisat had neither bow nor arrow in his hand, resolved among themselves, that if he were to request their assistance, they would refuse him the use of their weapons. Bódhisat then laid aside his usual garment, arrayed himself in a splendid robe, girt his sword by his side, and his quiver upon his shoulder; and putting together a bow that was made of separate pieces, jointed, with a coral necklace as the bow-string, he approached the king, and enquired whether the fruit was to be felled by the arrow as it went or as it returned. The king replied that it would be the greater wonder if the fruit were brought down by the returning arrow. Bódhisat gave notice that as the arrow would proceed right into the firmament, it would be necessary to wait for its return with a little patience. An arrow was then shot, which cleft a small portion from the mango, then went to the other world, and was seized by the déwas. Another arrow was shot, and after some time, there was a noise in the air,—thrum, thrum, thrum; at which the people were afraid. Bódhisat told them it was the sound of the arrow; and they were then more fearful, as each one thought it might fall upon his own body. The arrow, as it returned, divided the mango from the tree; and Bódhisat going to the place, caught the fruit in one hand and the arrow in the other. At the sight of this, the people a thousand times shouted in triumph, a thousand times clapped their hands, and a thousand times waved their kerchiefs round their heads and danced; and the king gave Asadrisa countless treasures.

At this time seven kings, having heard that Asadrisa was dead, surrounded the city of Benares, and gave the king his choice, either to fight or to deliver up his kingdom. Brahmadatta sighed for the assistance of his elder brother, and having received information of his place of retreat, sent a noble to invite him to return. Asadrisa at once took leave of Sámánya, and on arriving near Benares, he ascended a scaffold, from which he shot an arrow, with an epistle attached to the following effect: "This is the first arrow from the hand of Asadrisa; if the second should be sent, you will all be slain." The arrow fell upon a dish from which the seven kings were eating rice,* and as they thought within themselves that the threat would certainly be accomplished, they fled to their own cities. Thus Bódhisat conquered the seven kings, without the shedding of a single drop of blood. Brahmadatta now offered to resign the kingdom, but Bódhisat again refused it, and going to the forest of Himála, by strict asceticism, he gained supernatural power, and afterwards passed away to the highest of the celestial regions.

9. *The Wessantara Játaka.*

In the Jambudwípa of a former age, the principal city of Siwi was called Jayaturá, in which reigned the king Sanda, or Sanja; and his principal consort was Phusatí, who was previously one of the queens of the déwa Sekra, and during four asankyas and a kaplaksha had exercised the wish to become the mother of a Budha. In due time they had a son, who was called Wessantara, from the street in which his mother was passing at the time of his birth. This son was the Bódhisat who in the next birth but one became Gótama Budha. From the moment he was born, for he could speak thus early, he gave proof that his disposition was most charitable. When arrived at the proper age, he re-

---

* The native authors, when mentioning a meal or feast, always describe it as the eating of rice, this grain being the principal article of food in India. In the same way. fish being one of the most favourite kinds of food in use among the Greeks, the word οψον became applied to all things that were eaten with bread. Our own word "meal," as used in the sense of a repast, may have been derived from the period when that article was in common use among our ancestors.

ceived in marriage Madrídewí, the beautiful daughter of the king of Chétiya; and Sanda delivered to them the kingdom. They had a son, Jáliya, and a daughter, Krishnájiná, and lived together in the greatest happiness and prosperity. The country of Chétiya and the city of Jayaturá became as one. At this time there was a famine in Kálinga, from the want of rain; but the king thereof having heard that Wessantara had a white elephant that had the power to cause rain, sent eight of his brahmans to request it. When the messengers arrived at Jayaturá, it was the póya day, when the prince, mounted on his white elephant, went to the public alms-hall to distribute the royal bounty. The brahmans were seen by the prince, who asked them why they had come: and when they told him their errand, he expressed his regret that they had not asked his eyes or his flesh, as he would have been equally ready to give them, and at once delivered to them the elephant, though its trappings alone were worth twenty-four lacs of treasure, saying at the same time, "May I by this become Budha!" When the citizens saw that the elephant from which they derived so much assistance was taken away, they went to the prince's father, and with many tears informed him of what had occurred. On hearing their complaints, Sanda promised to inflict upon the prince any punishment they might mention; but their anger being now somewhat appeased, they said that they desired no other punishment but that he should be banished without delay from the kingdom to the rock Wankagiri. When the citizens were gone, the king sent the noble Kattá to his son, to inform him of their demand, and to tell him that on the morrow he must leave the city. This intelligence caused no sorrow to Wessantara; and he told the noble to inform the king that on the morrow he would make an alms-offering, and the next day retire to the forest. Having commanded slaves, elephants, horses, and chariots, 700 of each, to be prepared, he went to Madrídewí, and requested her to collect together all the wealth she had brought from her parents; but she (supposing it was with the intention of giving it away in alms), said that he had not spoken to her when on previous occasions he had distributed his bounty, and asked why he did so now; and after further conversation, in which Wessantara set forth the benefit of alms-giving, she informed him that in his charitable deeds he had ever acted in accordance with her own wishes. The prince then made known to her the determination of the citizens, but requested that she would continue in the enjoyment of her present advantages, and be the guardian of their children. Upon hearing this, she said that she had rather go with him to death than live without him. The queen mother entreated the king not to let his son go; and to allay her grief, he promised that after he had remained some time in the forest, he should be recalled.

The next day the principal noble of Wessantara having informed him that the treasures were collected, 700 of each, he commanded the mendicants to be assembled, and made an offering to them of the whole collection, consisting of elephants, horses, bulls, buffaloes, cows, virgins, youths, boys and girls, with gold and silver, and all kinds of gems and pearls. When the doors of the treasury were opened, the mendicants poured upon the offering with all eagerness, like so many bees flying to a forest covered with lotus flowers newly blown; some taking silks, garlands, robes, or chaplets, and others ornaments for various parts of the body, rings or crowns. After this Madrídéwí, in the same way, presented her own robes, jewels, and other articles of value. When they went to take leave of their parents, the queen mother again endeavoured to persuade Madrídéwí to remain with her, as there were so many hardships to be endured in the forest; but she replied, that she had rather live with her lord in the wilderness, than without him in the city. The prince himself made known to her the dangers arising from wild beasts and serpents, but she said that she was prepared to endure all these trials; and when he wished her to leave the children, as instead of having rich couches they must sleep upon the bare rock; instead of being fanned by costly chámaras, they must be exposed to the sun and winds; instead of having delicate food, they must subsist on fruits; she replied, that she must have her children with her as well as her lord. The courtezans and others wept aloud in unison, like a forest of sal trees struck by an impetuous wind. The nobles then brought a chariot, and Madrídéwí, taking her daughter in her arms, and her son by her hand, entered it.

Wessantara having worshipped his parents, dismissed the courtezans, and gave good advice to the citizens; and on leaving the city, he set off towards the north. The queen mother sent after them a thousand wagons, filled with all things useful and valuable, but they gave away the whole in alms.

Soon after their departure, two brahmans came to the city to enquire for Wessantara, and when they found that he had gone to the wilderness, they asked if he taken anything with him. Being told that he had taken nothing more than a chariot, they followed him, and requested him to stop, begging that he would give them the horses that drew the chariot. Without hesitation, the horses were given; but Sekra having observed what was taking place, sent four déwas under the disguise of horses, that yoked themselves to the chariot and drew it. On the way, another brahman cried out, " Sir, I am old, sick, and wearied; give me your chariot." The chariot was now given up as readily as he had previously given the horses. The prince then carried his son, and the princess her daughter; and though they suffered much from the roughness of the road, their minds were filled with pleasure from the remembrance of the alms they had presented. Giving the children fruits to eat, and water from the ponds, they thus went on until they came to a place in the kingdom of Chétiya, whence Madrídéwí sent to inform her father they were there; and when the king, with 60,000 princes, came to the place, surprised at what he saw, he enquired if Sanda was sick, or if some other misfortune had happened, and asked what they had done with their retinue and chariots. Wessantara told them the reason why they had left the city; on hearing which, Chétiya invited them to come and reign in his own city; and when they declined, he ordered the place in which they remained to be properly prepared and ornamented, and prevailed on them to tarry there seven days, during which period they had all delicacies provided for them; but at its expiration, they again set off on their journey towards Wankagiri. By command of Sekra, his wonder-worker, Wiswakarmma, had prepared them two pansals, in one of which Wessantara dwelt, and in the other Madrídéwí, with their two children. They all put on the dress of ascetics, and had no intercourse with each other, unless when the children went to the pansal of their father during the time their mother was in the forest collecting fruits. After they had lived in this manner for the space of seven months, there was an aged brahman, called Jújaka, who from the age of eighteen years had been a mendicant; he had accumulated a hundred masurans, which he delivered to another brahman, a poor man, to keep for him; but when he went to recover them, the brahman said that he had spent the whole to supply his wants, and that he had now nothing to give him but his daughter Amitta-tápa; so as he could get nothing more, he took away the brahman's daughter, and she became his wife. But the other females of the household became jealous of the stranger, and greatly persecuted her, particularly one day when she went to fetch water, at which she became angry and discontented; but Jújaka, in order to pacify her, said that he would himself in future fetch the wood, and attend to all the work that was necessary to be done, whilst she remained at ease. Amitta-tápa, however, informed him that the charitable Wessantara resided near the rock Wankagiri, and that if he applied to him he would be able to obtain a slave to wait upon her, and render her all the assistance she required. The brahman replied that the way was long, and he was old and weak; but she persisted in her demand, at the same time upbraiding the old man; so having prepared as much fuel and water as would be required during his absence, he set off on his journey to the rock. He first went to Jayaturá, and enquired for Wessantara; but the citizens, incensed that alms should still be asked from the prince, set upon him with sticks and staves, and drove him away. As he fled from the city, not knowing whither he went, he was guided by the déwas towards Wankagiri; but when he came near, he was seen by the guards who had been placed around the forest by the king of Chétiya, and would have been slain, had he not told a lie, and said that he was sent by the royal parents of Wessantara to enquire after his welfare. Proceeding on his way, he fell in with the ascetic Acchuta, who resided near the rock Wipula, to whom he said that he had been the preceptor of the prince in his youth. It was now noon, and thinking that at this time Wessantara would be away from the pansal collecting fruits, and that only Madrídéwí would be at home, who would probably hinder the granting of his request, he resolved to remain in an adjacent cave until the next morning. That night the princess had an uncomfortable dream, and early the next morning she went to the pansal of Wessantara, to have it explained. The prince enquired why she had come at an improper hour, when she said that she had been troubled by a dream, in which a black man came and cut off her two arms and plucked out her heart. Wessantara rejoiced to hear her dream, as he saw that the time for fulfilling the páramitás had come; but he told her that she had formerly eaten agreeable food and slept on pleasant beds, whereas she had now only fruits to eat and was obliged to lie on logs of wood; and with this intimation he sent her away. At the usual hour, she took the children and delivered them to his care, whilst she went into the forest. When the prince saw the brahman approaching, he told his son Jáliya to go and meet him, and carry his water-vessel. After the brahman had partaken of some fruits that were set before him, Wessantara enquired why he had come; and he replied that he had come to ask the gift of his two children. On hearing his request, the prince told him that he was the best friend he had yet met with, as others had asked only the elephant or the chariot; but that their mother was then absent, and as it would be right for her to see them before their departure, he would have to remain until the next day. The brahman said that he could not stay so long; and that if he did not receive the children now he must go away without them. Wessantara then informed him that if he took them to his royal parents, he would be rewarded with many gifts; but he replied that if he were to take them to the city it would cost him his life, when it became known in what way he had received them, and that the prince must decide whether he would give up the children or not. Jáliya and Krishnájiná, on hearing this conversation, fled away in extreme terror, and hid themselves under the leaves of a lotus growing in a pond near their dwelling.

By this time Wessantara had resolved upon giving his children to the brahman without any further delay; but when he called them they did not make their appearance. Upon this the old man began to reproach him, and said that he had not seen so great a liar in the whole country; as he must have sent them away purposely, though he had promised to give them in alms. To discover whither they had fled, the prince went to the forest, and when near the pond called out to Jáliya; and no sooner did the boy hear the voice of his father, than he said, "The brahman may take me; I am willing to become his servant; I cannot remain here and listen to my father's cries;" and tearing in two the leaf by which he was covered, he sprang up, and ran towards his father, weeping. Wessantara asked him where his sister was; and when Jáliya told him that they had fled away in fear and hid themselves, he called out to her; on which she came from under the lotus as her brother had done, and like him shedding tears, clung to the feet of her father. But as Wessantara reflected that if he did not give up his children he could not become a Budha, and would be unable to release sentient beings from the miseries of repeated existence, he called them to the pansal, and pouring water on the hands of the brahman, delivered them to him, saying, "May I by this become the all-knowing!"

The brahman took the children away, but he stumbled on going down a hill that he had to descend, and there remained, lying upon his face. The children embraced the opportunity of running away; and returning to their father, they put their hands upon his feet, and with many tears reminded him of the dream of their mother. Jáliya said how much they wished to see their mother before their departure, and requested that if it was necessary their father should give them to some brahman, he would give them to some one who was less ugly than this decrepid old man; and further, that as his sister was tender and delicate, and unfitted for work, it would be better to give him alone, and leave Krishnájiná with her mother. Wessantara made no reply, and as Jáliya was asking him why he was silent, Jújaka approached bleeding, and looking like an executioner who had just been taking the life of some criminal. The children trembled with fear when they saw him. Unable to retain them both, as Krishnájiná ran away when he seized Jáliya, and the sister when he seized her brother, he tied them together by a withe, and began to drive them along with a stick, beating them as they went. Looking at their father, they told him to see the blood streaming down their backs, and to consider the pain they endured. Wessantara reflected, "If my children have to suffer this before my eyes, what will they not have to endure when they are at a distance? How can they pass over hills, thorns, and stones? When they are hungry, who will feed them? When their feet are swollen who will give them relief? When the cold wind chills them, who will administer unto them comfort? How will the mother who has borne them in her bosom, grieve when she returns at night, and finds that they are gone? Thus thinking, he resolved to drive away the brahman, and receive them again. As they passed along the shady places where they had played together, and the cave in which they had been accustomed to make different figures in clay as a pastime, and the trees growing by the familiar pond, they said sorrowfully, "Fare ye well, ye trees that put forth the beautiful blossoms; and ye pools in whose waters we have dabbled; ye birds that have sung for us sweet songs; and ye kindurás that have danced before us and clapped your hands; tell our mother that we have given you a parting salutation! Ye well-known déwas, and ye animals with whom we have sported, let our mother know the manner in which we thus pass along the road!" When Madrídéwí was about to return home, Sekra sent four déwas to assume the form of wild beasts, and delay her return to the pansal; but as she went along, her mind dwelt upon the dream, and alarmed at the sight of the animals (not having previously met with any in the same place), she dreaded lest the children should come to meet her and so be devoured. And when she came near the pansal, and heard not their voices, she was still more afraid, and began to think that some eagle or sprite might have carried them off when they were sleeping; or else that perhaps her relatives had come and demanded them, in order to take them away. Going to the pansal she enquired of Wessantara where the children were, but he remained silent. This silence caused her to wonder, and the more so as he had not collected the wood and water as usual. Then he said to her that they had gone out when she delayed her return from collecting fruits; as he thought that her death might be caused if he informed her at once that he had given them in alms. On hearing this, the princess went into the forest, going from place to place, and examining every spot in which they had been accustomed to play; and as she did not find them, she became senseless. Wessantara followed her to learn the cause of her prolonged absence, and when he found her he sprinkled water upon her face, by which she recovered. Her first question was, "Where are the children?" The prince now informed her that he had given them away in alms to an aged brahman, that the pre-requisites of the Budhaship might be fulfilled. Then Madrídéwí replied, "The Budhaship is more excellent than a hundred thousand children!" and rejoicing in the reward that was to be obtained from this gift, wished that it might be extended to all the beings in the world.

When Sekra perceived that Wessantara had given away his children, thinking it would not be right that any one should take the princess in the same way, he assumed the appearance of an aged brahman, and went to the rock. Wessantara, on seeing him, asked him why he had come, and he replied, "I am now old and powerless; I have no one to assist me; I have therefore come to receive the princess as my slave." The prince looked in the face of Madrídéwí; and she, knowing his thoughts, expressed her willingness to comply with the wish that had been expressed; whereupon he delivered her to the supposed brahman, that the gift might assist in the reception of the Budhaship. When the brahman received her, he said, "The princess now belongs to me; that which belongs to another, you have not the right to give away; therefore keep her for me until I shall return." Then assuming his own form, Sekra informed Wessantara that all the déwas and brahmas had rejoiced in the gifts he had offered; and assuring him that he would most certainly attain the Budhaship, he informed him that in seven days his relatives would come to him, together with his children, and that he would again receive the kingdom. The earth had trembled at the presenting of each gift, and Maha Méru and the other rocks expressed their approbation.

Jújaka and the children were carried a distance of sixty yojanas before night, and placed under a tree that bent its branches over them as a canopy. Two déwas came to them in the shape of their parents, and ministered to all their wants. The brahman, overawed by this occurrence, took them the next day to the house of their grandparents. The previous night Sanda had had a dream, in which he saw a man bring to him two lotus flowers. Having assembled the brahmans learned in the four Vedas to know the meaning of this dream, they informed him that it betokened the coming of two children that would be to him the cause of much joy. Whilst they were speaking, the brahman approached with Jáliya and Krishnájiná; and the king asked them whence they came. The old man intended to say some other country, lest some harm should happen to him if the truth were known; but through the interference of the déwas he replied, "They were given to me as an alms-offering by Wessantara." When Sanda found that they were his grandchildren, he placed the boy upon one knee, and the girl upon the other, greatly rejoicing, and ordered many presents to be given to the brahman, who, however, from eating too much, died at midnight. The next day his body was burnt upon a costly pyre. The king, without further delay, went with the children, the citizens, and a grand array of nobles and princes, to the rock Wankagiri, that they might bring back Wessantara; who, when he heard the noise of their approach, sent the princess to the top of the rock to see whence it proceeded. On seeing the procession, she informed him that their relatives had come from the city. When the prince perceived that among the elephants was the animal he had given to the king of Kálinga he felt ashamed, as it had been presented in alms; when told, however, that it had been returned by the people, as there was now plenty in the land, he was satisfied. Thus the king Sanda, the queen Phusatí, the prince Wessantara, the princess, Madrídéwí, and their children Jáliya and Krishnájiná, accompanied by a great multitude of people from Jayaturá and Chétiya, went from the rock Wankagiri to the city. Wessantara and the princess again received the kingdom; and after reigning in conformity with the ten precepts of kings, he was reborn in the déwalóka called Tusita.

The brahman Jújaka afterwards became the prince Déwadatta; Amitta-tápa became the female heretic Chinchi; the brahman Acchuta became the priest Seriyut; the déwa Sekra became the priest Anurudha; the king Sanja became Sudhódana, the father of Gótama Budha; the queen Phusatí became Mahamáya-déwí, his mother; Madrídéwí became Yasódhara-déwí, his wife; Jáliya became Ráhula, his son; Krishnájiná became the priestess Upphala; and Wessantara became Gótama Budha.

VI. THE ANCESTORS OF GÓTAMA BUDHA.

THE FIRST MONARCH, MAHA SAMMATA.—HIS SUCCESSORS.—THE TREASURES OF THE CHAKRAWARTTI.—THE OKKÁKA RACE.—THE SAKYA RACE.—THE ORIGIN OF KAPILAWASTU AND OF KOLI.

In this chapter, the ancestry of Gótama Budha is traced, from his father, Sudhódana, through various individuals and races, all of royal dignity, to Maha Sammata, the first monarch of the world. Several of the names, and some of the events, are met with in the Puránas of the Brahmans, but it is not possible to reconcile one order of statement with the other; and it would appear that the Budhist historians have introduced races, and invented names, that they may invest their venerated sage with all the honors of heraldry, in addition to the attributes of divinity. Yet there may be gleams of truth in the narrative, if it were possible to separate the imaginary from the real. There are incidental occurrences that seem like fragments of tradition from the antediluvian age; and we might find parallel legends in the lore of nearly all nations that have records of remote antiquity. It will be observed that there are several discrepancies between the following narrative and the extract on the origin of caste, inserted in the third chapter.

In the beginning of the present antah-kalpa, the monarch Maha Sammata, of the race of the sun, received existence by the apparitional birth. As it was with the unanimous consent, or appointment, sammata, of all the beings concerned, that he was anointed king, he was called Maha Sammata. The glory proceeding from his body was like that of the sun. By the power of irdhi he was able to seat himself in the air, without any visible support. On the four sides of his person as many déwas kept watch, with drawn swords. There was a perfume like that of

VI. THE ANCESTORS OF GÓTAMA BUDHA.

sandal-wood, extending from his body on all sides to the distance of a yojana; and when he spoke, a perfume like that of the lotus extended from his mouth to the same distance. During the whole of an asankya* he reigned over Jambudwípa; and was a stranger to decay, disease, and sorrow. Indeed all the beings in the world of men were similarly situated; they lived an asankya; and as they committed no sin, the power of their merit freed them from all evil. They did not regard their age; they knew not at what period they were born, nor when they would die; and at this time a residence upon earth was more to be desired than in the déwa-lókas, as the happiness of the brahmas who resided here was greater than that of the déwas.

Sammata was succeeded by his son Rója, who reigned an asankya, and afterwards there reigned in lineal succession, Wararója, Kalyána, Wara-kalyána, Maha-mandhátu-upósatha,† and Maha-mandhátu, a chakrawartti. Each of these kings reigned an asankya.

The chakrawartti‡ is a universal emperor. There are never two persons invested with this office at one time. He is born only in an asunya kalpa; he never appears in any sakwala but this, nor in any continent but Jambudwípa, nor in any country but Magadha. He must have possessed great merit in a former state of existence. He is at first a yuwa-raja, or secondary king; then

* The ancient Egyptians had a king who reigned three myriads of years; but even this period is nothing to an asankya. Satyavarta, the first of the solar race of princes among the Hindus, reigned the whole of the satya-yug, or 1,728,000 years. Berosus informs us that the first ten kings of Chaldæa reigned 120 sari, the sarus being a period of 3600 years. Thus the ten kings give 432,000 years, the same extent as a kali-yug.

† Turnour in his Examination of the Pali Budhistical Annals (Journ. As. Soc. Nov. 1838), calls the sixth monarch simply Uposatho, and on the name of the succeeding monarch he has the following note: "In the Mahawanso I have been misled by the plural Mandáta, and reckoned two kings of that name. I see by the tika explanation that the name should be in the singular. The twenty-eight rajas who lived for an asankheyyan included therefore Maha Sammato."

‡ "A chakra-vartí is one in whom the chakra, the discus of Vishnu, abides (varttate); such a figure being delineated by the lines of the hand. The grammatical etymology is, He who abides in, or rules over, an extensive territory, called a chakra."—Wilson's Vishnu Purána. The ancient kings not unfrequently laid claim to universal empire. "Thus saith Cyrus, king of Persia, The Lord God of heaven hath given me all the kingdoms of the earth."—Ezra i. 2; Judith ii. 1. The Roman empire, as well as others that preceded it, was called οἰκουμένη, "the world."—Luke ii. 1. The same spirit still lives in the seven-hilled city, and the same pretensions are set forth; but it is in vain; as no chakrawartti will be permitted to appear, until the sceptre of Jesus Christ shall be extended over all nations.

the monarch of one continent only; and afterwards of all the four continents. There are seven most precious things that he possesses. 1. The chakraratna, or magical discus. 2. The hasti-ratna, or elephant. 3. The aswa-ratna, or horse. 4. The mánikya-ratna, or treasure of gems. 5. The istrí-ratna, or empress. 6. The grahapati-ratna, or retinue of attendants. 7. The parináya-ratna, or prince. On a certain day the chakrawartti ascends into an upper room of his palace, and reflects on the merit he has gained by his attention to the precepts in former births. At this moment a strange appearance is presented in the sky. Some think that another moon is about to appear; others that it is a sun with softened rays, or a mansion of the déwas; but the wise know that it is the chakra-ratna. It approaches the city with a sound as of music, and when near travels round it in the air seven times, after which it enters the palace. The elephant arrives in a similar manner, either of the Upósatha or Chaddanta race. The emperor ascends its back, and rides upon it through the air. The horse then comes, exceedingly swift, and able, like the elephant, to pass through the air. It is accompanied by a thousand other horses, each of which has similar powers. The gem is of the most dazzling brightness, so as to enlighten all around to a considerable distance; it has many most wonderful properties; and other gems are produced in numbers that cannot be told. The empress is in her person of the most perfect symmetry, and in every respect beautiful. When the emperor is too warm, she refreshes him by producing cold; and when he is too cold, she produces warmth. She fans him to sleep, and attends him with the constancy of a slave. The treasure of the grahapati consists of thousands of attendants. The prince is wise, excellent in disposition, and is attended by a numerous retinue.

There are times when the chakrawartti visits the four continents. On this occasion he is attended by the seven precious gems, as well as by an immense train of déwas and nobles, in all possible splendour of array. The discus proceeds first through the air, followed by the monarch and his host. Their first visit is to Púrwawidésa, when all the kings of that continent bring presents and pay their homage; and the emperor commands them not to take life, but to keep the precepts and reign righteously. The monarch then descends into the sea of that continent, a way having been opened into the waters by the discus; and he and

VI. THE ANCESTORS OF GÓTAMA BUDHA.

his nobles gather immense quantities of the most valuable jewels. After a similar manner, all the four continents are visited in order, and a repetition of the same circumstances occurs.

Though Maha-mandhátu possessed all these privileges, he was not contented with them, and said, "If I am indeed a powerful monarch, may the déwas as well be subject to my rule, and send a shower of gems that shall form a heap extending 36 yojanas." At the utterance of this command, the déwas were obedient, and produced the gems as he desired. After thus enjoying the blessings of earth, he went to a déwa-lóka, without dying, when he lived 129 kelas and 60 lacs of years, a greater age than that of 36 Sekras put together. At the end of this period he again came to the world of men, and reigned in all an asankya.

This monarch was succeeded by his son, Wara-mandhátu,[*] who, when he wished to present anything to his nobles, had only to stamp upon the ground, and he received whatsoever he desired. The succeeding princes, both of whom reigned an asankya, were Chara and Upa-chara. When Chétiya, the son of Upa-chara, began to reign, he appointed as his principal minister Kóraka-tamba, with whom he had been brought up, like two students attending the same schools, saying that he was senior to Kapila, his elder brother. This was the first untruth ever uttered among men; and when the citizens were informed that the king had told a lie, they enquired what colour it was, whether it was white, or black, or blue. Notwithstanding the entreaties of Kapila, the king persisted in the untruth; and in consequence his person lost its glorious appearance; the earth opened, and he went to hell, the city in which he resided being destroyed. Chétiya had five sons, and by the advice of Kapila he erected for one of them a city at the east of Benares, which he called Hastipura; for another son, at the south, he erected Aswapura; for another, at the west, Daddara; and for another, at the north, Uttarapanchála. The history of these transactions appears at greater length in the Chétiya Játaka. From the time the untruth was told, the déwas ceased to be guardians of the kings, and four princes were appointed in their place. The sons and grandsons of these princes multiplied, and until this day they retain the same office, and are called Ganawára.

Muchala, the son of Chétiya, from the fears that were induced

[*] This name is omitted in Turnour's list.

by seeing the destruction of his father, reigned in righteousness; and was succeeded by his son Muchalinda.* The sons of Muchalinda were 60,000 in number, who spread themselves through the whole of Jambudwípa, and founded as many separate kingdoms; but as they were all equally descended from Maha Sammata, they were all of the same race. In the course of time, however, their descendants neglected to keep up the purity of their blood, and other races were formed. The eldest son of Muchalinda was Ságara, who was succeeded in lineal order, by Ságara (or Ságara-déwa), Bharata, Bhagírata, Ruchi, Suruchi, Pratápa, and Maha Pratápa. The queen of Maha Pratápa, after she had been delivered eight months, refused to rise from her couch at his approach, as she was the mother of the heir-apparent, Dharmmapála. On this account the king was angry, and slew the prince; but the earth opened, and he went to hell. This was the first murder committed in the world. The evil that came upon these kings was a warning to their successors, so that they pursued a different course; and by this means they retained the same length of years, though the brightness of their bodies was gradually lost. The successor of Maha Pratápa was Panáda, whose son, Maha Panáda, had been a déwa; but at the command of Sekra he was born in the world of men, and reigned in great splendour. The successors of Maha Panáda were Sudarsana; Maha Sudarsana, a chakrawartti; Neru, Maha Neru, and Aswamanta.

The whole of the above named 28 kings reigned an asankya each; and resided in the cities of Kusáwati, Rajagaha, and Miyulu, which in the first ages were the three principal cities of the world.

From this period the age of the kings, as well as their splendour, began to decrease. The sons and grandsons of Aswamanta reigned, not an asankya, but a kela of years, at Miyulu, where the first grey hair appeared.† The last of these princes was Maha Ságara, who was succeeded by his son Makhá-

---

* Between Muchala and Muchalinda, Turnour inserts the name of Mahamuchalo.

† The Jews have a tradition that Abraham was the first man who ever turned grey. His beard became grey when Isaac attained the age of manhood, that he might be distinguished from his son, who exactly resembled his father. This was ordered by divine appointment, that the scoffs of those who doubted Sarah's innocence might be silenced.

déwa. When he had reigned 252,000 years, he saw the first grey hair, upon which he resigned the kingdom to his son, and became an ascetic in a forest that afterwards bore his name, where he resided 84,000 years, and was afterwards born in a brahmalóka. The Maha-sammata-wansa was now lost, and the Makhádéwa race commenced. There were 84,000 princes of this race, all of whom, when they saw the first grey hair, resigned the kingdom, and became ascetics; after which they were born in one of the brahma-lókas. The age of each was 336,000 years. The last of these kings, Káláranjanaka, did not become an ascetic, as his predecessors had done, and the Makhádéwa race ceased.

The son of Káláranjanaka was Asóka, whose successor was the first Okkáka king. Of this race were the kings Kusa, Dilípa, Raghu,* Anja, Dasaratha, and Ráma. Some of the monarchs of this race, of whom there were 100,000 in all, reigned 30,000 years, their age gradually diminishing, until it was 10,000 years. This history appears at length in the Dasaratha Játaka. The last of these kings was Okkáka the second; after whom, of the same lineage, were Udayabhadda, Dhananja, Kórawya, Wédéha, Sanja, Wessantara, and Jálaya, 100,000 in all, the length of whose ages gradually decreased from 10,000 years to the present age of man. The last of these princes had a son called Amba, or Okkáka the third.

The five principal queens of Amba (who is also called Ambatta) were Hastá, Chitrá, Jantu, Jálini, and Wisákhá. Each of these queens was the chief of 500 concubines. Hastá had four sons and five daughters. The names of the sons were Ulkámukha, Kalanduka, Hastanika, and Purasúnika or Sirinípura; and of the daughters, Priyá, Supriyá, Nandá, Wijitá, and Wijitaséna. After the death of Hastá, the king appointed a young maiden as his principal queen, who had a son, Janta. Five days after the birth of this prince, his mother arrayed him in a splendid robe, took him to the king, and placing him in his arms, told him to admire his beauty. The king, on seeing him was much delighted that she had borne him so beautiful a son

---

* The history of this king, written in Sanscrit by Kálidása, is still extant. It is said that there is a translation of it into Singhalese, but I have not met with the work. The history was printed at London, in 1832, with the title "Raghu Vansa Kalidassæ, Carmen, Sanskrite et Latine, edidit A. F. Stenzler."

in his old age, and gave her permission to ask from him anything she might desire. She replied that the king had already given her whatever she could possibly wish for, so that she had no want of her own; but she requested him to grant the succession of the kingdom to her son. The king, displeased at her request, said that he had four illustrious princes born prior to her son, and that he could not set aside their right to give it to the child of a low-caste woman; and he asked if it was her intention to put these sons to death? The queen said nothing at that time, but retired to her own apartments. But not long afterwards, when the king was talking to her in a pleasant manner, she told him that it was wrong for princes to speak untruths; and asked him if he had never heard of the monarch who was taken to hell for the utterance of a lie. By this allusion the king was put to shame.

Unable to resist the importunity of the queen, Amba called the four princes into his presence, and addressed them in these terms:—" My sons, I have thoughtlessly given to another the kingdom that of right belongs to you. These women are witches, and have overcome my better judgment by their wiles; Janta will be my successor; therefore take whatever treasures you wish, except the five that belong to the regalia,* and as many people as will follow you, and go to some other place that you may there take up your abode." The king then wept over his children, kissed them, and sent them away. The princes took with them abundant treasures and attendants, and departed from the city. When the five sisters heard of their departure, they thought that there would be no one now to care for them, as their brothers were gone; so they resolved to follow them, and joined them, with such treasures as they could collect. There was great lamentation in the city when the fate of the princes was revealed; but as the nobles felt assured that they would return and assume the sovereignty, in which case those who did not accompany them would be disgraced, 84,000 joined in the flight, and were followed by hundreds of brahmans and men of wealth, and by thousands of merchants and writers. On the first day, the retinue of the princes extended sixteen miles; on the second, thirty-two; and on the third, forty-eight miles. The

* These were, the golden sword, the ornamented slippers, the umbrella or canopy, the golden frontlet, and the chámara.

assemblage set off in a south-eastern direction from Benares, and when they had proceeded sixteen miles, a council was called. The princes said, "We have so large a retinue that there is no city in Jambudwípa which could withstand us; but if we were to seize on any kingdom by force, it would be unjust, and contrary to the principles of the Okkáka race; nor would it be consistent in us as princes to take that which belongs to another; we will therefore erect for ourselves a city in some unpeopled wild, and reign in righteousness." This advice met with general approbation, and they set out to seek a suitable locality.*

At this time, the Bódhisat who afterwards became Gótama Budha was the ascetic Kapila, and resided in a forest, near a lake, upon the borders of which were many umbrageous trees. The rite that he was practising was exceedingly difficult of observance. In the course of their wandering, the princes having come to the place of his retirement, did him reverence; and when he asked them, though he knew they were the Okkáka princes, why they were passing through the forest, they related to him their history. The ascetic was acquainted with the art called bhúmi-wijaya, by which he knew the whole history of any given spot, to the extent of eighty cubits, both above and below the ground. Near the place where he lived, all the blades of grass and the climbing plants inclined towards the south. When

* The following legend is translated (Journ. Bengal. As. Soc., Aug. 1833) by M. Alex. Csoma de Körösi from the 26th volume of the mDo class in the Ká-gyur, commencing on the 171st leaf :—" The five leaves, from page 171 to page 175, are occupied with an enumeration of the descendants of Maha Sammata down to Karna, at Potala (supposed to be the ancient Potala, or the modern Tatta, at the mouth of the Indus). He had two sons, Gótama and Bharadhwaja. The former took the religious character, but Gótama being afterwards accused of the murder of a harlot was unjustly impaled at Potala, and the latter succeeded to his father. He dying without issue, the two sons of Gótama inherit, who were born in a preternatural manner ; from the circumstances of their birth they and their descendants are called by different names ; as, Angirasa, Surya Vansa, Gautama, and Ikshwaku. One of the two brothers dies without issue, the other reigns under the name of Ikshwaku. To him succeeds his son, whose descendants (one hundred) afterwards successively reign at Potala, the last of whom was Ikshwaku Virudhaka (or Vidéhaka). He has four sons. After the death of his first wife he marries again. He obtains the daughter of a king, under the condition that he shall give his throne to the son that shall be born of that princess. By the contrivance of the chief officers to make room for the young prince to the succession, he orders the expulsion of his four sons." The princes set out to seek their fortune, and the narrative proceeds much in the same way as in the Singhalese legend. The descendants of Virudhaka, to the number of 55,000, reigned at Kapílawastu.

any animal was chased to that spot, fear fell upon the pursuer; hares and míminnás* overawed the jackal; frogs struck terror into the nayá; and deer were under no alarm from the tiger. This was perceived by Kapila, and he knew thereby that a chakrawartti and a Budha had resided there in a former age. It was on this account that he chose this place to be his own abode, and erected there his pansala, or hermitage; but on the arrival of the princes he offered it to them for the building of their city, telling them that if even an outcaste had been born there it would at some future period be honoured by the presence of a chakrawartti, and that from it a being would proceed who would be an assistance to all the intelligences of the world. No other favour did the sage request in return, but that the princes would call the city by his own name, Kapila. The city was built according to the advice they received, and was called after the name of the sage.† The princes then said to each other, "If we send to any of the inferior kings to ask their daughters in marriage, it will be a dishonour to the Okkáka race; and if we give our sisters to their princes it will be an equal dishonour; it will therefore be better to stain the purity of our relationship than that of our race." The eldest sister was therefore appointed as the queen-mother, and each of the brothers took one of the other sisters as his wife. In the course of time each of

---

* The míminna is found in Ceylon. It is of the deer species, but not higher than a lamb, and its limbs are shaped in the most delicate manner. The interpreter modliar of Negombo, M. L. E. Peréra, Esq., had one in his possession perfectly white, which he intended I should bring home and present to the queen in his name; but in an unhappy hour a pig got access to the cage in which it was confined, and destroyed its beautiful occupant.

† This was afterwards the birthplace of Gótama Budha. "The Chinese specify Kau-pi-le, the Burmese, Ka-pi-la-vot, the Siamese Ka-bi-la-pat, the Singhalese Kimboul-pat (Kimbulwat) and the Nepaulese Kapilapur, as the city in which their legislator was born . . . The precise situation of Kapila, it is not now easy to ascertain. The Tibetan writers place it near Kailas, on the river Bhagirathi, or as elsewhere stated, on the Rohini river. These indications, connected with its dependency on Kosala, render it likely that it was in Rohilkund, or in Kamaon, or perhaps even rather more to the eastward; for the river now known as the Rohini is one of the feeders of the Gunduk—at any rate it must have been on the borders of Nepaul; as it is stated that when the Sákyas were dispossessed of their city, those who escaped retired into that country."—Wilson, Journ. Bengal As. Soc., Jan. 1832. When visited by Fa Hian, Kapila had neither king nor people; it was absolutely one vast solitude. The Singhalese authors say that it is fifty-one yojanas from Wisála, and sixty from Rajagaha. In the Amáwatura, Budha is said to have passed from Sétawya to Kapila, and thence to Kusinára in going from Sewet to Rajagaha.

VI. THE ANCESTORS OF GÓTAMA BUDHA.

the queens had eight sons and eight daughters, or sixty-four children in all. When their father heard in what manner the princes had acted, he thrice exclaimed, "Sukká wata bho rájakumárá, parama sakká wata bho rájakumárayi." "The princes are skilful in preserving the purity of our race; the princes are exceedingly skilful in preserving the purity of our race." On account of this exclamation of the king, the Okkáka race was henceforth called Ambatta Sákya.

After 222,769 princes of the race of Sákya had reigned at Kapila, or Kapilawastu (Sing. Kimbulwat), the kingdom was received by Jayaséna, who was succeeded by his son Singha-hanu (so called because his cheek bones were like those of a lion). The principal queen of Singha-hanu was Kasayina, by whom he had five sons, Sudhódana, Amitódana, Dhotódana, Sukkódana, and Ghatitódana; and two daughters, Amitá and Párali. As Sudhódana was the eldest, he succeeded his father, and reigned at Kapilawastu. From Maha Sammata to Sudhódana, in lineal succession, there were 706,787 princes, of the race of the sun. Of these princes, Gótama Bódhisat was born as Maha Sammata, Maha Mandhátu, Maha Sudarsana, Makhádéwa, Nimi, Kusa, Ráma, Udayabhadda, Mahinsaka, Katthakári, Maha Sílawa, Chúlajanaka, Maha Janaka, Chullapaduma, Maha Paduma, Chullasutasóma, Maha Sutasóma, Pancháyudha, Dharmma, Satabhátuka, Sahasrabhátuka, Dharmmista, Bhágineyya, Rájówado, Alinachitta, Wédéha, Asadisa, Sakkaditti, Gandhára, Maha Gandhára, Adásamukha, Sudhábhójana, Anithigandha, Kurudharmma, Ghata, Dharmmapála, Dhígáyu, Maha Dhígáyu, Sussima, Kummásapinda, Parantapa, Udaya, Garata, Sádhína, Siwi, Sómanassa, Ayódhara, Alinasattu, Arindama, Temé, and Chandra. Nineteen times he was born as king of Benares. The last birth in which he was king was that of Wessantara.

The principal queen of Sudhódana was Maha Máya, daughter of Supra Budha, of the race of Anusákya, who reigned in the city of Kóli. The queen mother Priyá (of whom we have spoken in connection with the founding of the city of Kapilawastu), was seized with the disease called swéta-kushta, or white leprosy, on account of which she was obliged to reside in a separate habitation; and her whole body became white, like the flower of the mountain ebony, kobalíla. This disease was so infectious that even those who merely looked at her might catch it; and as the princes themselves were in danger of taking the infection, they took her to a forest near a river, at a distance from the city, in a chariot with drawn curtains. A hole was dug into which they put her, with fire and fuel, and all kinds of food; after which they went away weeping. The hole was of sufficient size to afford every necessary accommodation for the princess. It so happened that Ráma, the king of Benares, was seized by the same disorder, and the disease was so malignant in its type that neither the queen nor his concubines could approach him, lest they should be defiled. As the king was thus put to shame, he gave the kingdom to his son, and retired into the forest, thinking to die in some lonely cave.* After walking about some time, he was overcome by hunger, and ate of the root, leaves, fruit, and bark of a certain tree; but these acted medicinally, and his whole body became free from disease, pure as a statue of gold. He then sought for a proper tree in which to dwell, and seeing a kolom with a hollow trunk, he thought it would be a secure refuge from the tigers. Accordingly he made a ladder, sixteen cubits high, by which he ascended the tree; and cutting a hole in the side for a window, he constructed a frame on which to repose, and a small platform on which to cook his food. At night he heard the fearful roaring of wild beasts around; but his life was supported by the offal left by the lions and tigers after they had eaten their prey. One morning a tiger that was prowling about for food, came near the place where the princess was concealed; and having got the scent of human flesh, he scraped with his paw until the earth that covered the cave was removed, when he saw the princess, and uttered a loud roar. The princess trembled with fear at the sight of the tiger, and began to cry. As all creatures are afraid of the human cry, the tiger slunk away without doing her any injury. The cry was heard by Ráma as well; and when he went to see from whom it proceeded, he beheld the princess. The king asked who she was, and she said that she had been brought there that she might not defile her relatives. Ráma then said to her, " I am Ráma, king of Benares; our meeting together is like that of the waters of the rain and the

---

* The Ganésa Purána commences with the misfortune of Sómakánta. king of Surat, who, on account of the affliction of leprosy, left his house and kingdom to wander in the wilderness.—Dr. Stevenson, Journ. Royal As. Soc. viii.

VI. THE ANCESTORS OF GÓTAMA BUDHA.

river; ascend, therefore, from the cave to the light." But Priyá replied, "I cannot ascend from the cave; I am afflicted with the white leprosy." Then said the king, "I came to the forest on account of the same disease, but was cured by the eating of certain medicinal herbs; in the same way you may be cured; therefore at once come hither." To assist her in ascending, Ráma made her a ladder; and taking her to the tree in which he lived, he applied the medicine, and in a little time she was perfectly free from disease.

When the princess was thus restored to health, she became the wife of Ráma, and in the same year was delivered of two sons. Then, for the space of sixteen years, she had two sons every year, until the number amounted to thirty-two. It happened in the course of time that a man who knew the king saw him in the forest. When he said that he had come from Benares, Ráma enquired about his own family and the welfare of the city; and in the midst of their conversation the thirty-two princes gathered around them. The hunter asked in astonishment who they were; and when he was informed, he besought the king to leave the forest and come to the city; but Ráma was not willing to accede to this request. On his return to Benares, the hunter informed the reigning king that his father was alive. On receiving this intelligence, he went with a large retinue to the forest, and tried to prevail upon his father to return to the palace; but even his entreaties were in vain. The prince, therefore, commanded his servants to erect a city in that place, with walls, tanks, and every needful defence and ornament; and when this was done, he and his attendants returned to Benares. The newly-erected city was called Kóli, from the kolom tree (nauclea cordifolia) in which the king took refuge. It was also called Wyágrapura, (from wyágra, a tiger), because it was by means of a tiger that the princess was discovered in the cave. Another name that it received was that of Dewudæha. The descendants of the king received the name of Kóli.

The queen having informed her sons that there were four kings in Kapilawastu who were her brothers, and that they had thirty-two daughters, they sent to ask the hand of the princesses in marriage; but the four kings replied that though the race of the princes was good, as they were born in the hollow of a tree they could not consent to the proposed marriages, adding insult to their refusal. As it was known, however, that the princesses were accustomed to go to a certain place to bathe, the sons of Ráma sent letters to them privately, requesting an interview. A time being appointed, the princes, with their retinue, went thither, and taking the princesses by the hand, prevailed upon them to go to Kóli. When the four kings heard of this adventure, they were pleased with the courage of the young men; and as their race would still be kept pure, they became reconciled to the princes, and sent them presents.

From this time it became a custom for the Kóli and Sákya families to intermarry with each other. The thirty-two princes had separate establishments, and in due time thirty-two children were born to each family. After many generations Dewudæha was king, and was succeeded by his son Anusákya, whose principal queen was the younger sister of Singha-hanu. This queen had two sons, Suprabudha and Dandapáni, and two daughters, Maha Máya Déwí and Maha Prajápati. These princesses were beautiful as the queens of a déwa-lóka; no intoxicating liquor ever touched their lips; even in play they never told an untruth; they would not take life, even to destroy insects; and they observed all the precepts. It was declared by a brahman who saw them that they would have two sons, one of whom would be a chakrawartti, and the other a supreme Budha. No sooner was this noised abroad, than all the 63,000 kings of Jambudwípa sent to ask them in marriage; but the preference was given to Sudhódana, king of Kapilawastu; and they became his principal queens. Maha Máya was in every respect faithful to the king, and lived in all purity. In a former age she had presented an offering to the Budha called Maha Wipassi, saying, "I present this with the hope that at some future time I may become the mother of a Budha, who like thee shall be ruler of the world." Of Sudhódana and Maha Máya, Gótama Budha was born. (*Pújáwaliya, Amáwatura, &c.*)

VII. THE LEGENDARY LIFE OF GÓTAMA BUDHA.

I. THE CONCEPTION, BIRTH, AND INFANCY OF GÓTAMA.—II. THE MARRIAGE OF GÓTAMA, AND HIS SUBSEQUENT ABANDONMENT OF THE WORLD.—III. GÓTAMA AS AN ASCETIC, PREPARATORY TO THE RECEPTION OF THE BUDHASHIP.—IV. THE CONTEST WITH WASAWARTTI MÁRA.—V. THE RECEPTION OF THE BUDHASHIP.—VI. THE FIRST OFFERING RECEIVED BY GÓTAMA AS BUDHA.—VII. THE FIRST DISCOURSE DELIVERED BY BUDHA.—VIII. FIFTY-FOUR PRINCES AND A THOUSAND FIRE-WORSHIPPERS BECOME THE DISCIPLES OF BUDHA.—IX. BIMSARA, KING OF RAJAGAHA, BECOMES A DISCIPLE OF BUDHA.—X. THE TWO PRINCIPAL DISCIPLES OF BUDHA, SERIYUT AND MUGALAN.—XI. BUDHA VISITS KAPILAWASTU, HIS NATIVE CITY.—XII. NANDA AND RAHULA BECOME THE DISCIPLES OF BUDHA.—XIII. BUDHA VISITS THE ISLAND OF CEYLON.—XIV. BUDHA FORETELLS THE PROSPERITY OF A LABOURER'S WIFE.—XV. BUDHA ATTENDS A PLOUGHING FESTIVAL.—XVI. THE HISTORY OF ANÉPIDU.—XVII. THE HISTORY OF WISÁKHA.—XVIII. ANURUDHA, ANANDA, DÉWADATTA, AND OTHER PRINCES, BECOME PRIESTS; AND ANANDA IS APPOINTED TO THE OFFICE OF UPASTHÁYAKA.—XIX. BUDHA VISITS THE CITY OF WISÁLÁ.—XX. THE HISTORY OF JÍWAKA, WHO ADMINISTERED MEDICINE TO BUDHA.—XXI. THE HISTORY OF ANGULIMÁLA.—XXII. THE HISTORY OF SABHIYA.—XXIII. THE HISTORY OF SACHA.—XXIV. THE TWO MERCHANTS OF SUNAPARANTA.—XXV. THE YAKÁ ALAWAKA OVERCOME BY BUDHA.—XXVI. THE HISTORY OF UPÁLI.—XXVII. THE BRAHMAN KÚTADANTA EMBRACES BUDHISM.—XXVIII. THE BRAHMAN SÉLA BECOMES A PRIEST.—XXIX. BUDHA IS FALSELY ACCUSED OF INCONTINENCE BY THE FEMALE UNBELIEVER, CHINCHI.—XXX. THE FEMALE RESIDENT IN MATIKA BECOMES A RAHAT.—XXXI. THE PROWESS OF BANDHULA.—XXXII. THE KING OF KOSOL MARRIES THE NATURAL DAUGHTER OF MAHA-NAMA.—XXXIII. THE FLOWER-GIRL BECOMES A QUEEN.—XXXIV. THE PRIEST WHOSE BREATH IS LIKE THE PERFUME OF THE LOTUS.—XXXV. THE FIVE HUNDRED QUEENS OF KOSOL.—XXXVI. THE GIFTS PRESENTED TO BUDHA ON HIS RETURN TO SEWET.—XXXVII. BUDHA IS VISITED BY THE DÉWA SEKRA.—XXXVIII. THE TIRTTAKAS ARE PUT TO SHAME; A LARGE TREE IS MIRACULOUSLY PRODUCED; AND SEKRA MAKES A PAVILION FOR BUDHA.—XXXIX. BUDHA VISITS THE DÉWA-LÓKA TAWUTISÁ.—XL. THE NÁGA, NANDO-PANANDA, OVERCOME BY MUGALAN.—XLI. THE SIXTEEN DREAMS OF THE KING OF KOSOL.—XLII. THE QUEEN PRAJÁPATI BECOMES A PRIESTESS, AND OBTAINS NIRWÁNA.—XLIII. THE WICKED DEVICES OF DÉWADATTA AND AJÁSAT.—XLIV. THE CONVERSION OF AJÁSAT.—XLV. THE DESTRUCTION OF DÉWADATTA.—XLVI. THE HISTORY OF PRINCE

SUNAKHÁTA.—XLVII. THE HISTORY OF BAWÁRI.—XLVIII. BUDHA VISITS THE BRAHMA-LÓKA.—XLIX. MUGALAN ATTAINS NIRWÁNA.—L. THE PUNISHMENT OF SUPRA BUDHA.—LI. THE PRINCESS YASÓDHARÁ-DÉWI ATTAINS NIRWÁNA.—LII. THE DEATH OF GÓTAMA BUDHA.

THERE are ample materials for an extended life of Gótama; and the incidents that are recorded of his more immediate disciples are almost of equal extent. Of this matter the greater part may be a mass of mere absurdity, with as little of interest as would be presented by the detail of a consecutive series of the dreams of a disturbed sleep: but it is probable that nearly every incident is founded upon fact; and if we were in possession of some talismanic power that would enable us to select the true and reject the false, a history might be written that would scarcely have an equal in the importance of the lesson it would teach. It is said by Niebuhr that "unless a boldness of divination, liable as it is to abuse, be permitted, all researches into the earlier history of nations must be abandoned;" and a gifted critic may one day arise, who, by his discriminating skill, will be enabled to arrange every subject under one or other of these four classes—the pure fiction, the uncertain, the probable, and the established fact. In the mean time, we must be content with the legend in its received version, with all the accumulations it has gathered in successive ages. As no comment would be understood, until the legends have been read, I shall reserve all exegetical observations to the end of the chapter.

---

1. *The Conception, Birth, and Infancy of Gótama.*

After the Wessantara birth, Bódhisat was born in the déwa-lóka called Tusita, where he received the name of Santusita, and lived in the possession of every enjoyment for the space of 57 kótis and 60 lacs of years. At the end of this period, as it had been announced that a supreme Budha was about to appear, the déwas and brahmas of the various worlds enquired who it was to be; and when they discovered that it was Santusita, they went in a vast multitude to that déwa, and requested him to assume the high office, that the different orders of being might be released from the sorrows connected with the repetition of existence. To this request Santusita made no reply, but exercised the five great perceptions,* pancha-maha-wilókana, that he might discover, first, the character of the period in which the Budhas are born; second, the continent; third, the country; fourth, the family; and fifth, the day. As to the first perception, he saw that the age of man was about a hundred years,† and that therefore it was an auspicious period in which for the Budha to be born. As to the second, he saw that the Budhas are born in Jambudwípa. As to the third, he saw that they are born in the Madhya-mandala, or Magadha.‡ As to the fourth, he looked first to see whether the royal caste or the brahman was then the superior, and when he saw that it was the royal, he looked to see which of the 63,000 kings of Jambudwípa possessed the requisite merit to become the father of a Budha; by which he perceived that Sudhódana, king of Kapilawastu, of the Sákya race, was alone worthy of this honour. As to the fifth perception, when he looked to see on what day the Budhas are born, as he knew that the queen of Sudhódana would be his mother, and that the mother of a Budha dies on the seventh day after her confinement, he saw that he must be conceived in the womb of Mahamáya, 307 days previous to the time at which it was foreknown that her death would take place.§

When a déwa is about to leave the celestial regions, there are

* There are eight different kinds of beings who must look to the future before they attempt to carry into effect their intentions. The merchant, before he buys his goods; the elephant, before he makes use of his trunk; the traveller, before he commences a journey; the sailor, before he embarks on a voyage; the physician, before he administers medicine; the man who has to cross a bridge, before he ventures upon it; the priest, before he eats, that he may see whether there is sufficient time for him to finish his repast before the sun passes the meridian; and Bódhisat, before he receives his final birth.

† The theology of the Romans taught that twelve times ten solar years was the term fixed by nature for the life of man, and beyond that the gods themselves had no power to prolong it; that fate had narrowed its span to thrice thirty; that fortune abridges even this period by a variety of chances: it was against these that the protection of the gods was implored.—Niebuhr's Rome.

‡ This country was supposed to be situated in the centre of Jambudwípa. It would be difficult to define its limits, but it is generally regarded as answering to Central Bahar. In the reign of Bimsara, Rajagaha was its capital. It is called Makata by the Burmans and Siamese, Mo-ki-to by the Chinese, and Makala Kokf by the Japanese.

§ The matter contained in this chapter is principally translated from the Pújáwaliya; except in the few instances in which the name of a different work is inserted at the end of the section.

evidences of the fact. 1. His garments lose their appearance of purity. 2. The garlands and ornaments on his person begin to fade. 3. The body emits a kind of perspiration, like a tree covered with dew. 4. The mansion in which he has resided loses its attractiveness and beauty. The déwas having perceived these signs relative to Santusita, gathered around him, and offered him their congratulations. On the arrival of the proper person, he vanished from Tusita, and was conceived in the womb of Mahamáya. This event took place in the month Æsala (July, August), on the day of the full moon, early in the morning, the nekata being Utrasala.

The womb that bears a Budha is like a casket in which a relic is placed; no other being can be conceived in the same receptacle; the usual secretions are not formed; and from the time of conception, Mahamáya was free from passion, and lived in the strictest continence.* The inhabitants of Kapilawastu were accustomed to hold a festival, from the 7th day of the moon, to the 14th, in the month Æsala, during which period they spent their time in dancing and all other kinds of pleasure, so that at the conception of Budha the whole city was adorned like the heaven of Sekra. On the last day of the festival, Mahamáya bathed in fragrant water,† arrayed herself with flowers and ornaments; and after giving four lacs of treasure in alms, and taking upon herself the five obligations, she retired to her royal couch, and whilst reposing upon it had a dream.‡ In her dream she saw the guardian déwas of the four quarters take up the couch upon which she lay, and convey it to the great forest of Himála, where

* Plato passed among a large portion of his hearers for the actual son of Apollo, and his reputed father Aristo was admonished in a dream to respect the person of his wife Periktione, until after the birth of the child of which she was then pregnant by Apollo.

† Suetonius mentions that Caligula invented a new luxury in the use of the bath, by perfuming the water with an infusion of precious odours; but in the east this custom appears to have prevailed at a much earlier period.

‡ The last of the Jinas Vardhamána, was at first conceived by Dévanandá, a Brahmáná. The conception was announced to her by dream. Sekra being apprised of his incarnation, prostrated himself and worshipped the future saint; but reflecting that no great saint was ever born in an indigent or mendicant family, as that of a Brahmáná, Sekra commanded his chief attendant to remove the child from the womb of Dévanandá to that of Trisalá, wife of Siddhartha, a prince of the race of Jeswáca, and of the Kásyapa family. This was accordingly executed; and the new conception was announced to Trisalá by dreams, which were expounded by soothsayers as foreboding the birth of a future Jina.—Colebrooke's Miscellaneous Essays, ii. 214.

they placed it upon a rock, under the shade of a sal tree 100 miles high, and afterwards remained respectfully at a distance. The queens of the four déwas then brought water from the lake of Anotatta (after they had themselves bathed in it to take away from it all human contaminations), with which they washed her body; and they afterwards arrayed her in most beautiful garments, and anointed her with divine unguents. The four déwas then took her to a rock of silver, upon which was a palace of gold; and having made a divine couch, they placed her upon it, with her head towards the east. Whilst there reposing, Bódhisat appeared to her, like a cloud in the moonlight, coming from the north, and in his hand holding a lotus. After ascending the rock, he thrice circumambulated the queen's couch. At this moment Santusita, who saw the progress of the dream, passed away from the déwalóka, and was conceived in the world of men; and Mahamáya discovered, after the circumambulations were concluded, that Bódhisat was lying in her body, as the infant lies in the womb of its mother.*

In the morning, when the queen awoke, she told her dream to the king, who called together 64 brahmans, learned in the four Vedas, and gave them food in golden dishes, which he presented to them as gifts at the close of the repast. From these brahmans, Sudhódana enquired the meaning of the queen's dream; and they replied, that she had become pregnant of a son; if the child she would in due time bring forth continued a laic, they declared that he would be invested with the dignity of a Chakrawartti, but if he renounced the world, they foretold that he would become a supreme Budha. They then recommended the king to appoint a festival in honour of the event, and retired.

At the time of the conception, 32 great wonders were presented.

* The resemblance between this legend and the doctrine of the perpetual virginity of the mother of our Lord, cannot but be remarked. The opinion that she had ever borne other children was called heresy by Epiphanius and Jerome, long before she had been exalted to the station of supremacy she now occupies among the saints, in the estimation of the Romish and Greek churches. They suppose that it is to this circumstance reference is made in the prophetical account of the eastern gate of the temple: "The gate shall be shut, it shall not be opened, and no man shall enter in by it; because the Lord, the God of Israel, hath entered in by it, therefore it shall be shut."—Ezek. xliv. 2. The tradition inserted by Mahomet in the chapter of the Koran entitled "Mary," bears a considerable resemblance to this part of the history of Budha. Csoma Körösi says, that he does not find any mention in the Tibetan books "of Maha Devi's virginity, upon which the Mongol accounts lay so much stress."

The 10,000 sakwalas trembled at once; there was in each a preternatural light, so that they were all equally illuminated at the same moment; the blind from their birth received the power to see; the deaf heard the joyful noise; the dumb burst forth into songs; the lame danced; the crooked became straight; those in confinement were released from their bonds; the fires of all the hells were extinguished, so that they became as cool as water, and the bodies of all therein were as pillars of ice; the thirst of prétas and the hunger of all other beings were appeased; the fears of the terrified fled away; the diseases of the sick were cured; all beings forgot their enmity to each other; bulls and buffaloes roared in triumph; horses, asses, and elephants joined in the acclaim; lions sent forth the thunder of their voices; instruments of music spontaneously uttered sounds; the déwas put on their most splendid ornaments; in all countries lamps were lighted of themselves; the winds were loaded with perfumes; clouds arose though it was not the season of rain, and the whole of the 10,000 sakwalas were watered at one time; the earth opened, and fountains of water sprung up in various places; the flight of the birds was arrested as they passed though the air; the stream of the rivers was stopped, as if to look at Bódhisat; the waves of the sea became placid, and its water sweet; the whole surface of the ocean was covered with flowers; the buds upon the land and the water became fully expanded; every creeper and tree was covered with flowers, from the root to the top; the rocks abounded with the seven species of water lilies; even beams of dry wood put forth lotus flowers, so that the earth resembled one extensive garden; the sky was covered as with a floral canopy, and flowers were showered from the heavens; the 10,000 sakwalas were all thus covered alike: and great favours were everywhere received.

During the whole period of gestation, the déwas of the four quarters remained near the person of Mahamáya; and the 40,000 déwas from the 10,000 other sakwalas also remained on guard, with swords in their hands; some round the palace, whilst others guarded the city, or Jambudwípa, or the sakwala. The mother and the child were equally free from disease. The body of the queen was transparent, and the child could be distinctly seen, like a priest seated upon a throne in the act of saying bana, or like a golden image enclosed in a vase of crystal; so that it could be known how much he grew every succeeding day. The

VII. LEGENDS OF GÓTAMA BUDHA.

wonder of the queen was excited by these circumstances; and for the better preservation of her infant she moved about with care, like one who carries a vessel full of oil that he is afraid to spill; she did not eat any hot, bitter, or highly-seasoned food, nor did she eat to repletion; she did not lie upon her face, nor upon her left side; she used no exercise, nor did she use violent exertion; but kept herself calm and still.

At the conclusion of the ten months, Mahamáya informed the king that she wished to pay a visit to her parents; upon hearing which he commanded that the whole of the road between Kapilawastu and Kóli should be made level, strewed with clean sand, and have trees planted on each side, with water vessels at regular intervals. A litter of gold was brought, in which soft cushions were put, and it was carried by a thousand nobles in the richest dresses. The queen bathed in pure water, and put on robes of inestimable value, with all kinds of ornaments adorning her person, so that she appeared like a being from the déwa-lóka. When she entered the litter, and her journey commenced, she was accompanied by thousands of elephants, chariots like a cloud, banners, and music. Between the two cities there was a garden of sal trees, called Lumbini,* to which the inhabitants of both cities were accustomed to resort for recreation. At this time the trees were entirely covered with flowers; many swarms of bees sported among the blossoms, and culled their sweets; and there were birds of pleasant voice and beautiful plumage. Like an embassage coming to greet a king, grateful perfumes came from the garden at the approach of the queen. As she felt disposed to remain a little time in the garden, and enjoy the sight of its beauties, it was prepared in a proper manner for her reception. Attended by thousands of her maids, she entered, and passing on, admired the different objects that she saw, until she came to a sal tree, when she put forth her hand to lay hold of one of its branches; but it bent towards her of its own accord, and as she held it, the birth of Bódhisat commenced. The nobles then placed a curtain around her, and retired to a little distance. This being done, the déwas of the 10,000 sakwalas came to the same place as a guard. Without any pain whatever,† and entirely free

---

* This garden is said by Fa Hian to be situated about 50 li from Kapila, on the eastern side. It is called by the Chinese Lun ming, Loung mi ni, and Lan pi ni.

† My authority says, "without so much pain as would be produced by

from all that is unclean, Bódhisat was born. The face of the queen was turned towards the east, and the child was received by Maha Brahma in a golden net,* who, on presenting him to his mother, said, "Rejoice, for the son you have brought forth will be the support of the world!" Though the infant was perfectly free from every impurity, yet to render him and his mother still further clean, two streams of water were sent by the déwas, like pillars of silver, which, after performing that which was required immediately disappeared. The guardian déwas of the four quarters received the child from the hands of Maha Brahma, on the skin of a spotted tiger, extremely precious;† and from the déwas he was received by the nobles, who wrapped him in folds of the finest and softest cloth; but at once Bódhisat descended from their hands to the ground, and on the spot first touched by his feet there arose a lotus.‡ He then looked towards the east, and in an instant beheld the whole of the limitless sakwalas in that direction; and all the déwas and men in the same direction, presenting flowers and other offerings, exclaimed, " Thou art the greatest of beings; there is here no one like thee; no one greater than thee; thou art supreme!" Thus he looked towards the four points, and the four half-points, as well as above and below; and as he beheld the sakwalas in all these ten directions, the déwas and men acknowledged his supremacy; and he saw that there was no one greater than himself. Then the Maha Brahmas of the 10,000 sakwalas brought umbrellas 12 miles high, to be held over

the bite of a bug;" but in this part of the history there are many expressions that cannot be inserted in the text.

* The Mahomedans have a tradition that Abraham was received at his birth by the angel Gabriel, who immediately wrapped him in a white robe.

† The skins of animals were greatly prized by the ancients, and were considered as the attributes of many of the imaginary beings in their mythology. On certain occasions the high-priest of the Egyptians wore a leopard's skin.

‡ It was fabled of Apollo, who was also born whilst his mother was leaning against a tree, that immediately after his birth, he sprung up and asked for a lyre and a bow, and proclaimed that henceforth " he would declare unto men the will of Zeus." On the day that Hermes was born, he invented the lyre, stringing the seven chords upon the shell of a tortoise; escaping from his cradle, he went also to Pieiria, and carried off some of the oxen of Apollo. It is stated in the ancient Jewish traditions, that the mother of Moses was delivered without pain, and that when she looked at her beautiful child in sorrow, from the fear of the dangers that awaited him, he arose and said, "Fear nothing, my mother; the God of Abraham is with us;" and it is further stated, that at his birth a light appeared that shone over the whole world. But in more modern times, even these wonders have been exceeded, as it is said of St. Benedict that he sung psalms before he was born.

his head as a canopy; the Sekras brought conches 120 cubits long, the blast of which rolls on without ceasing during four months and a half; the Panchasikas brought harps 12 miles long; and the rest of the déwas presented golden caskets, chámaras, tiaras, frontlets, perfumes, red sandalwood and other gifts. When Bódhisat looked towards the north, he proceeded seven steps in that direction, a lotus rising up at every step; after which he exclaimed, " I am the most exalted in the world; I am chief in the world; I am the most excellent in the world; hereafter there is to me no other birth!" It was at the utterance of these words, which were spoken as with the voice of a fearless lion, and rolled to the highest of the brahma-lókas, that the brahmas and déwas assembled to do homage to the new-born prince. The thirty-two wonders seen at the moment of his conception were again presented. The queen did not proceed to Kóli, but returned to Kapilawastu, attended by 160,000 princes of both cities.

It was on Tuesday, the day of the full moon, in the month Wesak, the nekata being Wisá,* that Bódhisat was born; and on the same day the following were also born or produced: Yasódhará-déwi, who afterwards became his wife; the horse Kantata, upon which he fled from the city when he went to assume the Budhaship; the nobleman Channa, who accompanied him in the commencement of his flight; Ananda, his personal attendant after he became Budha; the nobleman Káludáyi, who was sent as a messenger by his father to prevail on him to visit his native city; the four mines of treasure;† and the bó-tree, near which he became Budha.

The chief counsellor of Singhahau, the father of Sudhódana, was Káladéwala; and it was he who instructed Sudhódana in

* Whenever an important event is recorded, the day of the week, the age of the moon, the month, and the nekata, are mentioned. But it is easy to be thus minute, when the annalist consults only his imagination. Thus, the giant Partholanus, the eighth lineal descendant from Noah, is said to have landed on the coast of Munster, the 14th day of May, in the year of the world 1978. The Mahomedans have a tradition that Adam was created on Friday afternoon, at the hour of Am, or between noon and evening.

† The four maha-nidhánas, or great mines of treasure, were formed at Kapilawastu, and became the property of the king. The first, Sankha, was four miles in circumference; the second, Phala, was eight miles; the third, Utphala, twelve miles; and the fourth, Pundaríka, sixteen miles. The depth of all the mines was equal to the thickness of the earth; and the treasures they contained were so vast, that if all the people in the world had taken from them as much as they desired, they would not have been decreased more than one inch.

the sciences. On the death of Singhahanu, the counsellor requested permission to retire from office, that he might become a recluse; but as the new king said that since the death of his father there was no one but he to whom he could apply for advice and direction, he consented to remain in a garden near the palace; where he received food from the king's table, but put on the garment of an ascetic. By the exercise of the necessary observances, and by meditation, he received power to see backward 40 kalpas, and forward the same number. By the acquirement of abhignyá, he overcame all passion, and arrived at the state of a rishi, so that he was enabled at will to visit the nága, garunda, and asura worlds, and the déwalóka of Sekra. One day, when in his lóka, he saw the déwas dancing hand in hand, most joyfully, in a manner that he had never previously witnessed; and when he enquired the reason, asking if they were about to receive another Sekra, they informed him that in eleven of their hours from that time, or thirty-five of the years of men, the son of the monarch Sudhódana would become Budha. On his return to the garden he was visited by the king, who informed him of the joyful event that had taken place; and as he expressed a wish to see the child, the infant was brought; but when his father would have had him worship the sage, in order to acquire merit, the venerable recluse prevented it by descending from his elevated seat; for were a Budha to bow to any other being whatever, the head of that being would instantly cleave into seven pieces. He then put the feet of the child to his forehead, as when the vivid lightning strikes against a cloud, and worshipped him. The king, unable to restrain his parental affection, presented the same mark of homage. Then the recluse said, "I pay no respect to Maha Brahma or Sekra; were I to forbid it, neither the sun nor the moon could proceed in its course; but I have worshipped this child." After thus speaking, he proceeded to examine whether the signs of a supreme Budha were to be found upon his person, viz. the 216 mangalya-lakshana, the 32 maha-purusha-lakshana, and the 80 anuwyanjana-lakshana; and when he saw that they were all present, smiling with joy like a full water-vessel, he declared that the prince would most certainly become Budha. Some of these signs, such as the teeth, were not then visible in the ordinary manner; but he saw them by anticipation, through the aid of his divine eyes. A little after he looked to ascertain whether he himself would be permitted to see the Budha that was thus to be revealed; when he perceived that before his manifestation he should be born in an arúpa world; and that a hundred, or a thousand, or a hundred thousand Budhas might be born, without his being able to derive therefrom any benefit. On learning his fate, he wept, like a water-vessel broken. The nobles who accompanied the king, seeing him at first smile and then weep, asked him why he did so, as they were afraid that he foresaw some danger that threatened the prince. The rishi informed them; and then again looked to see whether any of the members of his family would enjoy the privilege of which he was deprived; and as he saw that his nephew, Nálaka, would be thus favoured, he recommended him to become an ascetic. The nephew took this advice, and worshipped Bódhisat, after which he shaved his head, put on a yellow robe, and retired to the Himála forest, where he continued in the practice of the usual obligations. When the prince became Budha, he went to Benares, heard bana, retired to the forest a second time, and by meditation became a rahat.

Five days after the birth of Bódhisat,* a great festival was appointed, in order that his name might be given;† and 108 learned brahmans‡ were invited to attend, unto whom the king gave an offering of food. After they had eaten it, Sudhóna requested them to inform him what would be the destiny of his child. The brahmans were divided into eight companies, and one was chosen from each company to carry on the investigation. The names of these brahmans were Ráma, Dhaja, Laksana, Játi, Manta, Bhoja, Suyáma, and Sudanta. When they had examined the marks upon the prince's person, the seven senior

---

* "Seven days after the birth of Shakya his mother died."—Csoma Kőrösi.

† Among the Brahmans the ceremony of giving a name was performed on the tenth or twelfth day after the birth, "or on some fortunate day of the moon, at a lucky hour, and under the influence of a star with good qualities." —Inst, Manu, i. 30. The festival called Amphidromia, when the newly born child received its name, was held among the Athenians on the fifth day, according to Suidas.

‡ The number 108 is frequently in use among the brahmans, as the giving of 108 rupees in alms, the erection of 108 temples, &c. "If a member act meanly, and do not respect a brother's word, let him have 108 strokes of the red wood," is one of the 36 oaths of the Triad Society of China.

brahmans said that if he continued a laic he would become a Chakrawartti, but that if he became a recluse he would be a supreme Budha; and in token of this they lifted up two fingers.* The younger of them, Sudanta, said that if the lock on his forehead were red, he would be a Chakrawartti, but that if it were blue he would be a Budha; and when he had examined the signs, as he saw that he would most certainly become a supreme Budha, he lifted up one finger only in token. The brahmans collected at the festival said, "This prince will hereafter be a blessing to the world (sidhatta); to himself also will be great prosperity;" in consequence of which he was called Sidhártta.† The eight brahmans, on returning home, informed their sons that in thirty-five years the son of Sudhódana would become Budha, and recommended them, as they themselves were too old, to become ascetics, in order that they might secure the cessation of existence. The oldest of them soon afterwards died; when his son, Kondanya, became an ascetic, and went to Isipatana, in the forest of Uruwela, where he determined to remain until the prince became Budha; but when he went to call the sons of the other brahmans, and reminded them of the advice given them by their fathers, only four of them, Bhaddaji, Wappa, Mahanamá, and Assaji, were willing to accompany him to the forest.

The 80,000 relatives of the prince who were present on the day that he was named, reflected that if he became a Chakrawartti he would require a retinue; and that if he were a Budha, he would be attended by royal priests; so that in either case their children might through him obtain great advantages. They therefore sent their sons to be educated with him as his companions.

In order to procure a proper nurse for his son, Sudhódana assembled the princesses of the two cities of Kapilawastu and Kóli. She was not to be too tall, or the neck of the infant would be stretched: nor too short, or his body would be bent; nor too large, or his legs would be contracted; nor too weak, or his body would not acquire firmness; nor of too full a habit, or

---

* It was not unusual to recognise persons of superior power, or divine beings, by particular marks or signs. Twenty-nine signs were required in the bull that was chosen as the god Apis, the knowledge of which was regarded as a secret to be imparted only to the priests.

† The establisher.—Turnour.

her milk would be hot, and cause his skin to become red; nor of too dark a complexion, or her milk would be cold, and cause his flesh to be in lumps, in some parts hard and in others soft. A hundred princesses* were chosen, free from these faults.

Five months after the birth of Sidhártta there was a festival, at which the king was accustomed to hold the plough. With the rest of the royal household, the prince was taken to the field, where a couch was prepared for him with a canopy of many colours, under the thick foliage of a damba tree; and around this place curtains were hung, and a guard appointed to keep watch. The king was richly attired, and attended by a thousand nobles. At this festival all the people were accustomed to attend, in the gayest dresses, and with every token of pleasure. About a thousand ploughs start at once; of these, 108 are made of silver, and the horns of the bullocks that draw them are tipped with silver, and adorned with white flowers; but the plough held by the king is of gold, and the horns of the bullocks attached are also tipped with gold. The king takes the handle of the plough in his left hand, and a golden goad in his right; and the nobles do the same with their ploughs and goads of silver. The king makes one furrow, passing from east to west; the nobles make three: and the rest of the ploughmen then contend with each other who shall perform their work in the best manner. On the day that Sudhódana went to the field, the sight that was presented was extremely beautiful, as the ploughmen and drivers were dressed in garments of the gayest colours; gold and silver flags were seen, and banners, fans, vessels, and caskets; so that it seemed like a sky studded with shining stars. The one hundred nurses of the prince went outside the curtain, that was placed around him, attracted by the splendour of the sight. When Bódhisat saw that he was left alone, he arose from his couch by the power of ánápána-smerti-bháwaná, and ascended into the air, where he sat at a little distance from the ground, without any support. The nurses, on returning, saw him in this position; and running to the king they said, "Sire, this is the manner of *your* festival; but come and see the festival that is kept by the prince." No sooner did the monarch receive this intimation, than he went to the place; and as he approached the tree

* Some authorities say that the prince had sixty-four nurses, each of whom gave milk for a single day; and Csoma Körösi says thirty-two.

he perceived that the shadows caused by the sun's rays were not slanting, as they ought to have been from the early hour of the morning, but directly perpendicular, as if the sun were then in the zenith; by which means the spot was shaded in which the prince was placed. When the king saw his son sitting in the air, he wept with joy, and placing his feet upon his head, for the second time worshipped him,* saying, "Had your royal mother been here, and seen you, she would have made an offering to you of her life; but now that I am left alone, why do you exhibit to me these wonders?" Like the moon gradually increasing the prince continued to grow until he was seven years of age, when Wiswakarmma, the architect of the déwas, at the command of Sekra, made for him a magnificent bath, filled with water exceedingly cold.

When Sidhártta was twelve years old, the king assembled the brahmans, and enquired from what cause it would be, that he would become an ascetic; and they informed the king that he would see four things, viz., decrepitude, sickness, a dead body, and a recluse, which would induce him to leave the palace and retire to the forest. The king said, "I do not wish my son to become a Budha; as by so doing he will be exposed to great dangers from Wasawartti Mára and the yakás; I had rather that he were a Chakrawartti, as he will then be able to pass through the air, and visit the four continents." To prevent the prince from seeing the four signs that the brahmans had enumerated, Sudhódana commanded that they should be kept at a distance from him, and caused three palaces to be built, called Ramma, Suramma, and Subha, suited to the three seasons of the year.† They were all of the same height; but the first had nine stories, the second seven, and the third five. On all sides, extending to the distance of four miles, guards were placed;

---

* "One day the father of Thomas à Becket came to see his son, and when the boy was introduced into the presence of his father and the prior, the father prostrated himself at his feet. At seeing this the prior said in anger, 'What are you about, you foolish old man; your son ought to fall down at your feet, not you at his!' But the father afterwards said to the prior in private, 'I was quite aware, my lord, of the nature of what I was doing; for that boy of mine will one day or other be great in the sight of the Lord.'"—Giles's Thomas à Becket.

† The three capitals of Persia, Susa, Babylon, and Ecbatana, each enjoyed every year the privilege of being for a certain period the residence of the monarch. The spring was spent at Ecbatana, the three summer months at Susa, the autumn and winter in Babylon.

2. *The Marriage of Gótama, and his subsequent abandonment of the World.*

When the prince attained his sixteenth year,* his father, Subhódana, sent to Supra-budha, king of Kóli, to demand in marriage his daughter, Yasódhará-déwi; but that monarch thought that as Sidhártta was to become a recluse, his daughter would soon be left a widow; and he therefore refused to send her to Kapilawastu. The princess, however, firmly declared that even if Sidhártta were to become a recluse on the day after his marriage, there was no one else in the world to whom she would be united. When the prince was made acquainted with the opposition of Supra-budha, and with the reason upon which it was founded, he said that he had no wish to receive the kingdom though its rejection would include the loss of Yasódhará as his wife. But as Sudhódana was the lord paramount of the Sákya race, he went to Kóli, and notwithstanding the displeasure of her father, brought away the princess, with much state. On his return to Kapilawastu, after this successful expedition, he appointed Yasódhará to be the principal queen of Sidhártta; and placing them upon a mound of silver, he poured the oil of consecration upon them from three conches, one of gold, another of silver, and the third a shell opening to the right hand; after which he bound upon their heads the royal diadem, and delivered over to them the whole of his kingdom. He then sent to all their relatives on both sides, commanding them to bring their princesses, that they might be the inferior wives of Sidhártta, or remain as attendants in the private apartments of Yasódhará, but the relatives replied, "The prince is very delicate; he is also young; even to this day he has not learnt a single science; if hereafter there should be any war, he would be unable to contend with the enemy; he has not the means of maintaining our daughters; we cannot, therefore, consent to send them to one who is so utterly destitute of every endowment that he ought to possess." When the prince heard this, he resolved to

* According to Varro, boyhood ceased among the Romans with the fifteenth year, after the close of which the praetexta was exchanged for the manly toga at the next Liberalia.—Niebuhr.

exhibit his real strength; and caused it to be proclaimed throughout the city by beat of drum, that whosoever might be wishful to see his prowess, was invited to come to the palace in seven days from that time. On the day appointed, an immense pavilion was erected, and a vast multitude assembled in the court of the palace. Surrounded by a countless retinue, and in the presence of 160,000 of his relatives, he took a bow that required the strength of a thousand men to bend it; and placing the lower end on the nail of the great toe of his right foot, without standing up, he thrummed the string of the bow with his finger nail, as easily as if it were merely the bow by which cotton is cleaned. The sound produced by the vibration of the string was so loud, that it rolled to the distance of a thousand yojanas; and terror seized hold upon the inhabitants of Jambudwípa, as they supposed that it thundered, though it was not the season of rain. After this he placed four plantain trees at the corners of a square, and by one flight of the arrow pierced them all. Even in the dark he could send the arrow with so steady an aim as to split a hair from which anything was suspended. The prince also proved that he knew perfectly the eighteen silpas, though he had never had a teacher,* and that he was equally well acquainted with many other sciences. The relatives were thus convinced by what they saw and heard that he was no ordinary being; and soon afterwards 40,000 princesses† were sent to remain in the apartments of the palace.

* It is said in the Milinda Prasna that Sudanta became the preceptor of the prince, and that he was succeeded in his office by the learned brahman Sabbamitta, upon whose hands the king poured water, when he delivered him into his charge, as a token that he was entirely resigned to his care until he had acquired the knowledge it was necessary for him to know; whilst in other works it is said that he had had no teacher at the time of his marriage. Nágaséna says that he had five preceptors; some of whom are, however, not to be regarded as teachers in the ordinary sense of the term:— Sudanta; Sabbamitta; the charioteer by whom he was driven when he saw the four signs; and the ascetics Alára and Uddaka; as will afterwards be more fully explained.

† They are called nátaka-istri, literally, dancing women; but it is evident that they were considered as inferior wives, the same word being used here, both in Singhalese and Pali, that is used in reference to the hareems of other kings and princes. In many instances they are called queens, of whom Yasódhará is said to be the chief. The exaggeration in the text may throw light upon the conduct of Solomon (1 Kings xi. 3), as we may infer therefrom that it was common for the monarchs of that age to have an immense number of wives. Abu Fazel tells us that the hareem of Akbar was of such extent as to contain a separate room for every one of the women, whose number exceeded 5,000; and Ferishtah says that the emperor Shere was

Whilst living in the midst of the full enjoyment of every kind of pleasure, Sidhártta one day commanded his principal charioteer to prepare his festive chariot; and in obedience to his commands, four lily-white horses were yoked. The prince leaped into the chariot, and proceeded towards a garden at a little distance from the palace, attended by a great retinue. On his way he saw a decrepid old man, with broken teeth, grey locks, and a form bending towards the ground, his trembling steps supported by a staff, as he slowly proceeded along the road. The déwas had seen that the time was now approaching when he was to become Budha, and it was one of their number who had assumed the appearance that was presented to the prince; but it was seen only by himself and the charioteer.* The prince enquired what strange figure it was that he saw; and he was informed that it was an old man. He then asked if he was born so, and the charioteer answered that he was not, as he was once young like themselves. "Are there," said the prince, "many such beings in the world?" "Your highness," said the charioteer, "there are many." The prince again enquired, "Shall I become thus old and decrepit?" and he was told that it was a state at which all beings must arrive.† It was by the aid of the déwas that the charioteer was enabled thus pertinently to answer. The prince now saw that life is not to be desired, if all must thus decay; and he therefore proceeded no further towards the garden, but returned to the palace. When Sudhódana saw him, he enquired why he had returned so soon; and the prince informed him that he had seen an old man, which had made him resolve to become an ascetic; but the king conjured him to put away thoughts like these, and enjoy himself with the princesses of the palace; and to prevent him from carrying his resolution into effect, he placed an ad-

---

enraged because one of the viceroys who had reduced a neighbouring district kept no less than 2000 concubines and dancing girls in his hareem.—Calcutta Review, Jan. 1845.

* When Xerxes left Sardis in grand procession for the invasion of Greece, his charioteer, whose name is recorded, sat by his side, whence we may infer that this office must have been one of considerable dignity.—Herod. vii. 40.

† The charioteer was more honest than the French ecclesiastic. "Quoi donc," (exclaimed the young Dauphin to his preceptor, when some book mentioned a king as having died)—" Quoi donc, les rois meurent-ils?" "Quelquefois, monseigneur," was the cautious but courtly reply.—Brougham's Historical Sketches.

ditional number of guards, extending to the distance of eight miles round the city.

Four months after this event, as Sidhártta was one day passing along the same path, he saw a déwa under the appearance of a leper, full of sores, with a body like a water-vessel, and legs like the pestle for pounding rice;* and when he learnt from the charioteer what it was that he saw, he became agitated, and returned at once to the palace. The king noticed with sorrow what had occurred, and extended the guards to the distance of twelve miles round the city.

After the elapse of another period of four months, the prince, on his way to the garden, saw a dead body, green with putridity, with worms creeping out of the nine apertures, when a similar conversation took place with the charioteer, followed by the same consequence. The king now placed guards to the distance of sixteen miles.

There are some Budhas that appear when the age of man is immensely long, and in such instances the space of one hundred years elapses between these appearances. At the end of the next four months, on the day of the full moon, in the month Æsala, Sidhártta saw in the same road a recluse, clad in a becoming manner, not looking further before him than the distance of a yoke, and presenting an appearance that indicated much inward tranquillity. When informed by the charioteer whom it was that he saw, he learnt with much satisfaction that by this means successive existence might be overcome, and ordered him to drive on towards the garden. That day he sported in the water, put on his gayest apparel, and remained until the going down of the sun. The nobles brought the 64 different kinds of ornaments that are required in the complete investiture of a king, and a vast retinue of courtiers ministered to his pleasure. The throne of Sekra now became warm, and when he looked to discover what was the reason, he saw that it was the hour of the array of Bódhisat. He therefore called Wiswakarmma, and at

* The eastern pestle is about five feet long, and is made of wood, tipped with iron. It is found in every house, and is connected with as many superstitions and ceremonies as the besom or broom among the old wives of Europe. It is an instrument almost exclusively used by women, and it has often excited my pity when I have seen them at work; but not unfrequently two women are employed at the same mortar, and give alternate strokes, by which the process becomes less tedious, as they emulate each other in the giving of the stroke.

his command that déwá came to the garden in a moment of time, and arrayed Sidhártta in a celestial robe, more beautiful than all his previous magnificence. The prince knew that he was a déwa, and not a man, and allowed himself to be enveloped in the robe. It was of so fine a texture, that when folded it did not fill the hand, and was indeed no larger than a sesamum flower; yet when opened out, it was 192 miles in length. It was thrown round his body in a thousand folds, and a crown of sparkling gems was placed upon his head; the musicians were animated to play upon their instruments in the most perfect time; and the attendant brahmans chaunted the song of victory; after which the prince ascended his chariot, that he might return to the palace.

At this moment Yasódhará was delivered of a prince; and as his royal grandfather thought that this would be likely to prevent Sidhártta from becoming an ascetic, with all joy he sent a messenger to inform him of the auspicious event. The noble went in haste to the prince, and said, "Your highness, a son is born to you; and he is your second self." On receiving this intelligence he reflected that an object of affection was now received, and that it might lead him to dislike his intended renunciation of the world. On the return of the messenger, the king enquired what his son had said; and as he informed him that he exclaimed "Ráhula-játo," by which he intimated that something proper for him to love was born, the child received the name of Ráhula.* The prince resolved that as he had not only received a child, but what was a rarer occurrence, a son, he would not become an ascetic just then; but would go to the palace, and see his infant, after which he could abandon the pleasures of the world, and pass into retirement. In the full splendour of the festivity that had been held in the garden, he returned towards the palace. On the way he was seen by the princess Kiságótami, a relative who approached the window to look at him, as he appeared in sight, like a full moon emerging from an azure cloud. She then changed her position, so as to be able to speak to him, and repeated the following stanza:—

"Nibbutá núna támátá.
Nibbutá núna sopitá,

* The Karmikas of Nepaul assert that Ráhula remained six years in the womb of his mother. The pain and anxiety of mother and son were caused by the karma of their former births.—Hodgson's Illustrations.

Nibbutá núna sánárí,
Yassa-yan í-diso pati."

The purport of which is, that if his mother or his father, or any of his wives, were to see him (as he then appeared), they would be overcome. The prince thought within himself, as she repeated these words, "This female repeats the words nibbutá, nibbutá, reminding me of nibbuti (nirwána); as she has spoken to me so seasonably, I must make her a proper acknowledgment. Thus thinking, he took the collar from his neck, made of pearls, and worth a lac of treasure, and sent it to the princess. On receiving it, Kiságótami thought that he had sent her the present because he admired her, and that he would make her, as well as Yasódhara, one of his principal queens.

On reaching the palace, Sidhártta reclined upon a splendid couch, the lamps were filled with perfumed oil, and lighted, and around him were assembled his 40,000 queens. Some danced before him, whilst others played upon flutes, harps, and cymbals, and instruments made of the legs of fowls or of animals; whilst others again beat the drum, performed various evolutions, and tried in many ways to attract his attention; but the prince paid no regard to them, and fell asleep. The choristers and musicians, seeing that their attempts to amuse him were of no avail, placed their instruments under their heads as pillows; and they too fell asleep. When Sidhártta awoke, he saw the altered appearance of the revellers; some were yawning, the dress of others was in great confusion, whilst others again were gnashing their teeth, or crying out in their sleep, or foaming at the mouth, or restlessly rolling their bodies and placing themselves in unseemly postures; so that the place which a little time previous appeared like one of the déwa-lókas, now seemed like a charnel-house. Disgusted with what he saw, and roused to activity, like a man who is told that his house is on fire, he rose up from his couch, and resolved to enter at once upon the discipline it was necessary for him to pass through before he could become Budha. This was perceived by Wasawartti Mára, who came from the déwa-lóka of which he is the ruler; and appearing in the air at a little distance from the palace, he said to the prince, in order to induce him to put away the thoughts that were forming in his mind, "Sorrowless one, in seven days from this time you will receive the magical chariot; the divine horses, the precious jewel, and the other possessions of the Chakrawartti will come to you through the air; your commands will be obeyed throughout the whole extent of the four continents and the 2000 islands; you will also receive a prince, and have the four-fold army, attended by whom you will be able, like one of the déwas, to visit any part of your vast dominions; therefore put away these gloomy thoughts, and let them disturb you no more." But these words were to the prince like the piercing of his ear by an iron that had been heated during a whole day; so far from suffering his mind to be calmed by them, they only added to his previous agitation, like the heaping of fuel upon a fire. That which Mára said was false; but if it had even been true, Sidhártta would have refused to become a Chakrawartti; sooner would the water of the Anotatta lake, after passing along the Ganges, and entering the sea, and approaching the mouth of hell, return back from that dreadful place to the Ganges, and from the Ganges to the lake where it originally sprang; sooner would all the water of the ocean be dried up, so as to be no deeper than a bullock's hoof;* sooner would the sky become rolled together like a web of cloth; than the prince would resign the privileges of the Budhaship, after fulfilling the páramitás with the express design of obtaining them.

Then Siddhárta went to the golden gate, and called out to know who was on guard at the stairs; and when he discovered that it was Channa, he commanded this noble to bring forth his steed, properly caparisoned. As he chose the horse Kantaka, that animal thought he could not be required at such a time for any festival, and that therefore the period must have arrived to which he had so long looked forward. By this reflection he was filled with joy, and neighed so loudly that all the déwas heard it; but they prevented its being heard by men. Whilst Channa was absent in the stable, the prince, in order that he might see his son, went to the apartment of Yasódhará; and on opening the door he saw the princess upon a couch, surrounded by flowers, but she was asleep, her hand embracing the infant, which was also asleep, and laid upon her bosom. Sidhártta perceived that in order to take up his son Ráhula he must remove the mother's arm, which would probably cause her to awake; and as

---

* Hesiod speaks of the rain, "deep as the ox's hoof."—Works, 146.

he knew that if she awoke she would speak to him, which might shake his resolution, he remained upon the threshold, holding the doorpost with his hand, but not proceeding any further. He thought, "I can see my child after I become Budha; were I, from parental affection, to endanger the reception of the Budhaship, how could the various orders of being be released from the sorrows of existence?" Then resolutely, like a man attempting to root up Maha Méru, he withdrew his foot from the doorway, and descended to the court-yard of the palace. Putting his hand upon the back of the steed, as it stood proudly before him, he said, "Well, Kantaka, you must assist me to-night, that by your aid I may be enabled to release all sentient beings from the perils of existence;" and he then mounted upon his back. From his neck to his tail, Kantaka was 18 cubits in length, of proportionate height, and as white as the purest conch.* Strong was he and fleet, and when he pawed the ground, the whole city trembled; but upon the present occasion his footsteps were not heard, through the interposition of the déwas. The attendant noble, Channa, accompanied the prince, holding the horse by the tail.†

At the fifteenth hour after sunset, or at midnight, Sidhártta proceeded to the outer gate of the city. The king, who had foreseen that his son would attempt to escape by stealth, had placed a thousand men as wardens; and the gate itself was so ponderous that it required a thousand men to open or shut it. The noble resolved that if the gate were not open, he would take the prince on his right shoulder, and the horse on his left, and

* The easterns have a great predilection for horses of a white colour. When travelling in remote parts of Ceylon, where the animal upon which I rode was as much an object of attention as myself, I was frequently asked if I did not possess a white horse, and when I answered in the negative, I appeared to be much lessened in the estimation of the people.

† Horses that are nine yards high are not often found in our degenerate days; but at Madeira I have seen the grooms take hold of the tails of the ponies that traverse the narrow paths of its steep mountains; they retain their hold even when the animal is going at full gallop, and are thus carried along with fearful rapidity. We learn from Caesar that the Germans were so alert by continual exercise, that laying hold of the manes of their horses they could run with equal swiftness.—De Bel. Gal. vi. 13. The Arabs relate that when Moses fled from the palace of Pharaoh, he was carried over the Nile on the steed Hizan, provided for his escape by Gabriel. But both Kantaka and Hizan must bow before Borak, the miraculous horse of Mahomet, that enabled him to visit Medina, Bethlehem, Jerusalem, and Paradise, in so short a space of time that a water-vase which he overturned in rising from his couch was not emptied on his return.

leap over the ramparts of the city; and the horse resolved, in view of the same obstacle, to leap over the barrier with the prince on his back, whilst the noble held his tail. Thus, all exhibited the most determined courage, and were equally free from fear. But when they approached the gate, it was thrown open by the déwas, as they knew that in due time Budha would throw open to them the gates of the city of peace. Wasawartti Mára knew that if the prince proceeded on his journey, his own déwa-lóka would be emptied, and all beings become happy, by which he would lose the influence he then possessed; and he therefore came to him, and said, "Be entreated to stay, that you may possess the honours that are within your reach; go not; go not!" The prince asked who he was, and he said that he was lord of the sixth déwa-lóka, Paranirmmita Wasawartti; but on hearing this, in a way that made the sakwalas tremble, the prince declared, "A thousand or a hundred thousand honours such as those to which you refer would have no power to charm me to-day; I seek the Budhaship; I want not the seven treasures of the Chakrawartti; therefore, begone, hinder me not." Then Mára ascended into the air, and said to Sidhártta, gnashing his teeth with rage, "We shall see whether thou wilt become Budha; from his time forth I shall tempt thee with all the devices I can imagine; until the reception of the Budhaship, I will follow thee incessantly, like thy very shadow, and on the day of its attainment I will bring a mighty army to oppose thee." Throughout the whole of the seven years that followed this period, the assaults of Mára were continued.

Rejecting the offer of universal empire, as he would cast forth saliva from his mouth, in the month Æsala, on the day of the full moon, the nekata being Uttrasala, Sidhártta departed from the city. After proceeding some distance, he resolved to look once more at the place he had left; when the city, without his turning round, appeared as if it were before him. At the same time he foresaw that a dágoba would be erected to Kantaka, on the spot whence this view was presented. In this journey, 60,000 déwas preceded him with torches of jewels, and the same number were on each side. The light was so great, that in any part of the sakwala the smallest thing could be perceived. The déwas in attendance extended as far the sakwala rocks. The nágas, garundas, and other beings presented perfumes, and strewed flowers of various kinds, but all divine; floral showers also fell from the trees of Parasatu and Madara, filling the sky; the déwas played the five-fold music, the gandharwas from the summit of the sakwala rocks, and the rest from the further side, as there was no room for them within. The noise was like the raging of the sea. Attended in this magnificent manner, Sidhártta proceeded in the course of the night through three kingdoms; and having gone 480 miles, arrived in the morning at the river Anómá. This was not the full speed of Kantaka; such was his strength that he could have gone in a moment to the sakwala rocks, or have run round the outer circle of the sakwala between the time of the morning meal and noon; but on account of the number of flowers thrown in the path of the future Budha, and the great retinue by which he was attended, he went in that night only thirty yojanas. On arriving at the river, he enquired its name from the noble, and when he was told that it was Anómá, illustrious, or honourable, he received it as another omen in his favour. It was 800 cubits in breadth, but the horse carried both the prince and the noble across, at a single leap, and alighted on the other side upon a bank of sand as white as silver. At this place he presented the horse Kantaka, together with his personal ornaments, to Channa, and gave him permission to return to the city. The noble also wished to abandon the world; but the prince asked what, in that case, was to become of the horse and the ornaments of which he had divested himself, and how Sudhódana and Yasódhará were to learn whither he had gone. At a future time he promised his faithful attendant the accomplishment of his wish, but charged him now to go and inform his father, mother,* wife, and the people of the city, that as he had become a recluse they were not to sorrow for him; and he requested that care might be taken of his son Ráhula, as he would not see him again until he had become Budha. The noble wept on hearing these words. This was not the only occasion on which Bódhisat had received the assistance of Channa. In former ages he had derived from him the most efficient aid, in times of difficulty.† The horse under-

---

* The principal queen of Sudhódana, Prajápati, must be intended, as his own mother died soon after his birth.

† Numerous instances in which this aid was granted are inserted in the original text.

stood what was said by his master, and as he knew that he should never see him again, he became exceedingly distressed, his breast clove in sunder, and he fell dead upon the ground; but he was immediately born in Tawutisá as the déwa Kantaka. The noble, thus overtaken by a double affliction, then returned to the city, where he made known all that had occurred.

The prince knew that in order to become an ascetic his hair must be cut off; and as there was no one there to perform this operation for him, he took his sword in the right hand, and holding his hair by the left, he cut it off.* Then reflecting, "If I am to become Budha, my hair will remain in the sky, on being thrown upwards; but if I am not it will fall to the ground;" he threw it into the air, where it remained suspended, at the height of about sixteen miles from the earth, like the beautiful bird called a kála hansa. To preserve it, Sekra brought a golden casket sixteen miles in size, and having placed the hair in it, he deposited it in the déwa-lóka Tawutisá, in a dágoba called Salumini-sáeya, where it is worshipped by the déwas until this day. The brahma Ghatíkara, who had been the friend of Bódhisat, from the time of Kásyapa Budha, during a whole Budhántara, brought the eight articles requisite for a recluse, being the fourth set found in the petals of the lotus, at the beginning of the kalpa, and delivered them to Sidhártta, who, after putting on the robe threw his former garment into the sky, whence it was taken by Maha Brahma to the brahma-lóka, and deposited in a golden dágoba, 192 miles in size. After this, as he thought that some one might come from the city, in order to persuade him to return, he went to the mango garden called Anupiya, where he remained seven days without food, from an excess of joy; and at the end of this period, early in the morning, he went on foot 480 miles, to the city of Rajagaha,† which he

* The hair was then only two inches long; and it arranged itself (on his head), curling to the right hand; and during the rest of his life his hair remained of the same length. His beard also was proportionate, nor had he occasion to shave any more.—Turnour.

† This place is still known by the name of Rajagriha, and is situated about sixteen miles south of the city of Bahar. It was abandoned by Asóka, and when visited by Fa Hian was entirely desolate and uninhabited, though a few Budhistical remains could be traced. The surrounding country is covered with a great variety of ruins. It is a celebrated place of Hindu pilgrimage, and is also honoured by the Jains, who every year resort thither in great numbers, and have built temples on the five hills by which the valley is surrounded. In 1811 there was a Hindu hermit here who had seated himself in the open gallery of a thatched hut, where he sat all day in the

entered by the eastern gate, and went from house to house in regular order with the alms-bowl.

At this season there was celebrated in the city a nekata festival, called Æsala-keli, which commenced on the seventh day of the moon; and as all the citizens had left their usual employment to see the sports, not fewer than sixteen kelas of people gathered around him to gaze upon his beauty. Some said that the regent of the moon, from fear of the asur Ráhu had come down to the earth; others said that it could not be the regent of the moon, but that the déwa Ananga had come to see their festival; but others said that it could not be Ananga, as his body was half burnt by Maha Iswara, and upon this recluse they could see no marks of fire. It was then argued that he was Sekra; but others replied, "How you talk? How could it be Sekra? Where are his thousand eyes? Where are his elephant, his discus, and his throne? It must certainly be Maha Brahma, who has come to see if the brahman ascetics are diligent in the study of the four vedas." Others again maintained that it was neither the one nor the other of these beings, but a holy personage who had come to bless the world. The citizens informed the king, Bimsara,* that a mysterious being was seen; but whether he were a yaká, a déwa, a brahma, or Vishnu, they were unable to tell. The king went to look at him from one of the towers of the palace, but he said to his courtiers, "I cannot decide whether it be a déwa or not; but let some one follow him when he leaves the city, and watch him; if he be a demon (one not a man) he will vanish; if he be a déwa, he will ascend into the sky; if a nága, he will descend into the earth; if a garunda, he will fly away like a bird; but if a man, he will eat

---

posture in which Budha is represented, without motion or speech, but well besmeared with cow-dung.—Hamilton's Gazetteer. The Pújáwaliya says of this city, "It is called Rajagaha because it was founded by a king, and every house in it resembled a palace. It is surrounded by mountains. In the time of the Budhas it is like one vast round in which the priests can go from house to house to receive alms. At the birth of a Budha or a chakrawartti it is a city; but at other times it is a forest, inhabited by rákshas and yakás."

* It is said in the first volume of the Dulvá, in Tibetan, that the king of Anga, whose capital was Champá, conquered the king of Magadha, whose capital was Rajagaha, previous to the birth of Sákya (Gótama). When Vimbasara (Bimsara) grew up, he invaded Anga, and caused the king to be slain; after which he resided at Champá, until the death of his father, and then returned to Rajagaha.—Csoma Körösi.

the food he has received, in some convenient place." When the prince had received as much food as was sufficient, he retired from the city to the rock Pándhawa, and under the shade of a tree began to eat the contents of his alms-bowl. Previous to this time he had always been accustomed to the most delicate fare; but even the sight of what he had now to eat was enough to turn his stomach, as he had never seen or touched such food before; but he reflected that it was necessary he should endure many hardships if he wished to become Budha, and that he must conform in all things to the precepts. Thus he spake unto himself, "Sidhártta! thy body is not of polished gold; it is composed of many elements and members; this food, entering into the house of my body, will be received into the mortar of my mouth, where it will be pounded by the pestle of my teeth, sifted by the winnow of my tongue, and mixed with the liquid of my saliva, after which it will descend into the vessel of my abdomen, and pass into the oven of my stomach, there to be again mixed with the water of my gastric juice, and reduced by the fire of my digestive faculty; the fan of my wind will blow this fire; in sixty hours (a day) this food will turn to excrement, and be expelled. This food is therefore clean and pure in comparison with that into which it will be converted. Sidhártta! thy body is composed of the four elements, and this food is the same; therefore, let element be joined to element." By these meditations he overcame his antipathy to the food, and swallowed it. The messengers informed the king that the recluse had eaten the food; whereupon Bimsara went to the rock, and enquired what was his name and family, when he discovered that in former years he was his own friend. On learning the dignity of the prince's character he expostulated with him and said, "What is this that you are doing? No prince of your exalted race was ever before a mendicant. There are connected with Rajagaha 80,000 inferior towns, and 18 kelas of people; the countries of Angu and Magadha are 4,800 miles in extent, and bring me in a countless revenue. The city was once the residence of a Chakrawartti; and even now there are the five grades of nobles; therefore, come, and divide the kingdom with me." But the prince replied, "In seven days I shall reject the Chakrawarttiship; so that if I were to take the half of your kingdom, it will be like throwing away the magical jewel, chintá-mánikya, for a common stone. I want not an earthly kingdom; I seek to become Budha." The king tried in many ways to overcome his objections; but as he could not prevail, he received from him a promise that when he began to promulgate his doctrines, his first discourse should be delivered in Rajagaha. The king then returned to the city.

3. *Gótama as an Ascetic, preparatory to the reception of the Budhaship.*

When going away from the rock, Sidhártta fell in with two ascetics, Alára and Uddaka; but as from the dhyána he exercised in their company he was not able to attain the Budhaship, and as he reflected that he must endure many things to prove the firmness of his resolution to déwas and men, he went to the Uruwela forest,* where he remained in a place adapted to the exercises of meditation. In a former age there were 10,000 ascetics resident in that forest, and it was their custom that when any of them were troubled with evil thoughts, they arose early in the morning, and going to the river, entered it, and waded on until the water reached to their mouths, when they took up a handful of sand from the bottom and put it in a bag. They afterwards confessed the fault of which they had been guilty, in the midst of the assembled ascetics, and threw down the sand in their presence, as a token that the appointed penance had been performed. By this means, in the course of years, a sandy plain was produced, sixteen miles in size; and in after ages the kings of that country placed a fence around the spot, in order to do it honour, as it was considered to be sacred ground. At this place the prince began the exercise of the austerities he had to perform.

The five brahmans, Kondanya, Bhaddaji, Wappa, Mahanamá, and Assaji, in going from place to place, found out the retreat of Sidhártta; and they remained with him six years, practising austerities, as they thought thus continually:—" To-day he will become Budha, or to-day;" and during this period they assisted him by providing what he required to eat and drink. But the prince reflected that by living in this easy manner he was not

---

* The tíkáwa explains that the name Uruwélaya is derived from uru, sands, and wélaya, mounds or waves, from the great mounds or columns of sand which are stated to be found in its vicinity, and which have attracted the attention of modern travellers also.—Turnour.

taking the proper course to become Budha, and that he must endure hardships of a kind much more severe. "If I receive," he thought within himself, "as much food as a sesamum seed in size it would be sufficient; I require nothing more than a pepper pod, or a small fruit; with only this I can still live." The déwas, as he would not receive sustenance by the mouth, afforded him nourishment through the pores of the skin, by which they imparted moisture to his body. In this way his life was preserved; but from rejecting all solid food, his body became of a dark colour, and the thirty-two signs disappeared. From the same cause, though he had previously the strength of ten kótis and ten thousand elephants, he was now so reduced as to be unable to stand; and one night, after walking and meditating until the third watch, he fell senseless to the ground. The déwas assembled around him in sorrow. Some said, "The prince has endeavoured to become Budha, but has failed in the attempt; he is now dead." Others declared, "He is not dead: he will soon revive; he will yet become Budha, and until that time no harm can possibly happen unto him." A déwí who had seen him laid upon the ground, went to Kapilawastu, and entering the king's apartment, caused a light to appear. The king asked who she was, and she said that she had come to inform him that his son had just departed to the other world. Sudhódana then asked if the prince had become Budha before he died; and when she replied that the austerities he was practising in order to become Budha had caused his death, he said that he could not believe his son was dead, though a thousand déwas were to declare it, because he had himself tokens by which he knew that the wish of the prince would most certainly be accomplished. There were many other déwas who went to inform the king of his son's death, but he did not believe any of them. The déwí, on returning to the forest, saw that the prince had recovered, upon which she again went to the palace, and informed the king.

The efforts of Sidhártta to obtain the Budhaship were like those of a man trying to overturn Maha Méru. As his strength was so much reduced, in order to regain it he went from place to place with the alms-bowl, and again partook of food. By this means the beauty of his body was restored, as well as the thirty-two signs. The brahmans also, when they saw that he had begun to take the alms-bowl, after practising austerities during six years without becoming Budha, took their bowls and robes, and leaving the prince, went to Isipatana, near Benares.

At that time there was residing near the forest of Uruwela a noble whose name was Sénáni, in a village of the same name. His daughter, Sujátá, one day took an offering to the déwa of a nuga tree, called Ajápála, and made a vow that if he would procure her a noble husband, and her firstborn should be a son, she would present an offering of rice-milk yearly, with a lac of treasure. The wish of the maiden was accomplished; she married a nobleman of Benares, and had a son; and she now prepared to fulfil her vow. For this purpose she caused a thousand cows to be fed in a meadow of the richest grass; with the milk that these cows gave she nourished 500 other cows; with the milk that these gave she nourished 250; with the milk of the 250, she nourished 175; thus gradually decreasing to 64, 32, 16, and 8 cows. This was done that milk of the very best kind might be procured. On the morning of the day of the full moon, in the month Wesak, the cows gave milk of themselves, without its being drawn from them, sufficient to fill the vessels, before the calves were loosed to suck the teats.

In the night previous, Sidhártta saw a number of dreams. All the Budhas are accustomed to see dreams of a similar kind, on the night of the 14th day of the month Wesak. 1. After falling asleep, the whole earth seemed to be his couch, and the rocks of Himála were his pillow; the four seas overflowed until they reached his arms and feet; the sakwala-gala touched his fingers; and when he looked up he saw all the déwa and brahma lókas. On awaking, he considered what this could mean, and received it as a token that his wish was about to be accomplished. "The couch," said he, "represents my Budhaship; the pillow, my all-pervading wisdom; my doctrines will fill the whole sakwala; and as I saw all the three worlds, all the beings in the three worlds will receive my assistance; to-morrow I shall become Budha." 2. The second dream was this: From his navel there shot forth an arrow, which gradually increased in length, until it reached the brahma lóka. When he awoke, he reflected that as the arrow pierced the three worlds, so would his doctrines penetrate everywhere; and that as the arrow proceeded from his navel, so would he, himself, be the source of all truth. 3. He saw numberless worms with white bodies and black heads, which crept upon his foot and reached his knee; and he reflected that in this manner all beings would cling to him for protection. 4. Numbers of the bird called lihini flew to him from the four quarters; when at a distance they were of different colours, but as they approached him, they all became of a golden hue. By this he perceived that although men were at that time of different sentiments and religions, they would all embrace one doctrine, and put on the yellow robe. 5. In his dream he climbed a mountain, sixteen miles high; it was one mass of disgusting filth; but as he trod its surface, the sole of his foot was not in the least defiled. And he reflected, that though his followers would bring to him and his disciples the four necessaries of the priesthood, neither he nor they would fix their affections upon them, they would be free from all cleaving to them or defilement therefrom. These five dreams were received by the prince as encouraging signs; and having washed his mouth, he took the alms-bowl and robe, and after receiving alms in the village of Sénáni, sat down at the foot of the nuga tree, Ajápála, with his face towards the east. At this time the leaves of the tree shone like gold, in consequence of the splendour that proceeded from his body.

When Sujátá saw that the cows gave milk of their own accord, she took it in her own hand, and boiled it with sandal and other fragrant woods; but when placed upon the fire, along with rice, it did not boil over like other liquids. The bubbles that were formed all went towards the right side, and there was no smoke. The déwas of the four quarters now came, and kept watch on each side; Sekra kept the fire burning; Maha Brahma sat above the fireplace, holding an umbrella; and the déwas of the 10,000 sakwalas brought the most agreeable substances they could find, and put them in the vessel. The wonderful sight presented by the boiling liquid was observed by Sujátá, who said that such a thing had never been seen before. She then called her slave Púrnna, and told her to go and sweep carefully the ground near the tree. The slave ran quickly to the place, and saw the prince sitting, resplendent with the six rays, so that he seemed to be all of gold; and as she thought it was the déwa of the tree, who had come to receive the intended offering in his own person, she went and informed her mistress. Sujátá was greatly pleased with this intelligence, and said, that as Púrnna had been the bearer of information so important, she would adopt her as her eldest daughter, and give her ornaments suited to her rank. Then putting on her most costly garments, she poured the rice-milk into a golden vessel, worth a lac of treasure, with a golden cover; and placing it upon a tray of the same precious material, she carried it upon her head to the tree, accompanied by a procession of 16,000 maidens. When she saw the prince, her joy was further increased; and she approached him dancing, to present the food she had prepared. On its being offered, he looked behind for the alms-bowl given to him by Maha Brahma, but it had vanished; and as he had nothing in which to receive it, Sujátá took off the cover of the vessel, and presented it to him as an alms-bowl. She afterwards brought perfumed water that he might wash his hand; and saying, "The wish of my heart is accomplished; may your wish be accomplished as well;" she went away. It was in the time of Piyumatura Budha that she became wishful to have the opportunity of making the rice-offering to a Bódhisat; and from that period, through the whole of a kaplaksha, she was preserved, through the merit obtained by this wish, from being born in hell.

After receiving the food, the prince arose, and taking his alms-bowl he went to the river Níranjara; and after the manner of former Budhas, as he perceived what they had done, he bathed at a place called Supratishtita, and then sat down, with his face towards the east; and having divided the food in his bowl into forty-nine portions, being one for each day he had afterwards to fast, he ate it on the bank of the river. At the conclusion of the repast, he reflected that he must now, in the order of events, cast the alms-bowl into the river,* and that if it swam against the stream, it would be an evidence that he was upon that day to become Budha. When the bowl was thrown, it floated like a ship into the middle of the stream; and then, like a swift horse, it proceeded against the stream to the distance of 80 (or, as some authorities say, 87) cubits, and then sank. After this it descended to the lóka of the nága king, Maha Kálaná, with a tinkling noise, where it remained, surmounting the bowls of the three former Budhas. When Kálaná heard the noise, he said, "Yesterday a supreme Budha appeared; the day before that a supreme Budha appeared; to-day a supreme Budha will appear." This was said because a day in a nága-lóka is a Budhántara.

* On the day that Xerxes passed the Hellespont, he poured a libation into the sea from a golden vessel, and then threw the vessel into the water, together with a golden goblet.—Herod. vii. 54.

VII. LEGENDS OF GÓTAMA BUDHA. 173

From the river, Sidhártta went to a forest on its bank,* and sat down at the foot of a sal-tree, where he remained the rest of the day, during which period he gained the five supernatural endowments, pancha-abhignyá, and practised the eight modes of abstract meditation, ashta-samápatti. From the sal-tree to the bó-tree, soon to become so illustrious, the déwas made an ornamented path, 3000 cubits broad, and at night the prince proceeded along its course, attended by a vast concourse of déwas, nagas, and other beings. On his way, he was met by the brahman Santi, who gave him eight bundles of kusa grass, as he knew that they would be required, and prove a great benefit. On approaching the bó-tree, the prince first went to the south side, and looked towards the north; but the southern sakwalas appeared to him as if depressed, and the northern as if raised. He then went to the western side, and looked towards

---

* This country was afterwards called Budha Gaya. It was completely deserted when visited by Fa Hian, who calls it Kia ye. Hiuan Thsang says that the town is situated in a very strong position, but he found very few inhabitants. A few hundred yards west of the Nilajan river, in a plain of great extent, about five miles from Gaya Proper, there are remarkable remains, that now consist of confused heaps of brick and stone, exhibiting traces of having been once regularly arranged. There is a building called the temple of Budha, built of brick, and lofty, resembling at a distance a huge glass-house (probably a dágoba), and now so honey-combed with age as to excite surprise that it continues erect. The religion of Budha may be considered as completely extinct in this neighbourhood, but a few pilgrims come occasionally from distant countries to visit its monuments. On the terrace behind the temple a peepul tree is growing, which the Hindus suppose to have been planted by Brahma. It is supposed by the Budhists that it is exactly in the centre of the earth. In 1812 this tree was in full vigour, and appeared to be about 100 years of age; but a similar one may have existed in the same place when the temple was entire; a circular elevation of brick has been raised round its root, in various concentric circles, and on one end of these has been placed a confused heap of images and carved fragments of stone, taken from the ruins. Indeed the number of images scattered about this place, for 15 or 20 miles in all directions, is almost incredible; yet they all appear to have originally belonged to the great temple or its vicinity, which seems to have been the grand quarry for the whole, and carried from thence to different places. Many of these images are now worshipped by the Brahmanical Hindus. Besides inscriptions establishing the Budhist origin of many of these images, they may be distinguished by the enormous size and distension of their ears, and also by a mark on the palm of the hand and soles of the feet (the chakra).—Hamilton's Gazetteer. The statement is true that the Budhists believe the bó-tree to be in the centre of Jambudwípa. The Greeks had a similar superstition relative to Delphi, which they called umbilicus terræ. They said that two birds were sent by Jupiter, one from the east and the other from the west, in order to ascertain the true centre of the earth, which met at Delphi. In 1833, I saw the Greek Christians, in the Church of the Sepulchre at Jerusalem, offer lights to a short marble pillar, under the supposition that it stands in the centre of the world.

the east; but the eastern sakwalas appeared as if lowered, and the western as if elevated. He next went to the northern side, and looked towards the south, but in these directions also similar appearances were presented. By these tokens he knew that none of these sides were adapted to his purpose, as they wanted stability; he therefore went to the eastern side of the trees and looked towards the west; and as the side on which he stood was fixed and firm, he there remained. This was the place where the former Budhas overcame Mára, and all evil desire was destroyed.* Therefore, in the same place he threw down the bundles of kusa grass he had received from the brahman, and at

* In 1833, Budha Gaya was visited by two Burmese envoys from the king of Ava, accompanied by Captain G. Burney. In the 20th volume of the Asiatic Researches, there is a "Translation of an Inscription in the Burmese language," discovered at that time, in the court of the monastery called Guru Math. The translation is by Colonel Burney, who transmitted to the Bengal Asiatic Society a translation of the report made by the vakeels to the king, "together with a copy of a picture representing the peepul (bó) tree and the surrounding scenery, made by a Burmese painter in the suite of the vakeels." A fac-simile of the inscription appears in the Researches, but the picture is not given. The vakeels write to the king thus:—"Proposing to invite a piece from the western branch of Boodh's excellent tree, to proceed to the Burmese kingdom, to the spot where religion shines and the protector of religion dwells, your majesty's slave Mengyee Maha-tsee-thoo, walked round the tree from right to left, and poured out some rose water, when owing to the great virtues of your majesty, worthy to be styled protector of religion, your slave beheld within the brick platform of five gradations, which surround the body of the tree as high up as the branches strike off, what was wonderful, having never happened before, most curious and most excellent, and what contradicts the common saying, that a small peepul tree does not grow under a large one; it was a Boodh's adorable tree, of the size of a Chinese needle, with only four leaves, and evidently produced by and of the same constituent part as the (large) Boodh's excellent tree. Delighted with joy, your majesty's slave repeated his solemn appeal, and carefully gathered this plant. It is growing in your slave's possession, but in consequence of the stem and leaves being very tender, it cannot now be forwarded to your majesty." The junior envoy says in his journal. "The principal guardian of the tree, Muhunt Jogee, told us that the English chief has given him 27 villages contiguous to Boodh's tree, and that he lives on the revenue derivable from the same. He occupies a three-storied brick house, with all his disciples and subordinate jogees, living in the lower and uppermost portions of it. On asking him how many disciples and followers he had, he said upwards of 500, some near him and some at a distance. . . . The circumference of Boodh's tree, on a line with the top of the encircling brick platform of five gradations, which forms its throne, and is 35 cubits high, measured 19 cubits and 10 fingers' breadth. The tree rises 44 cubits above the brick platform. From the top of the tree to the terrace on the ground, on the eastern side, may be 80 cubits, or a little more only; apparently the boughs and small branches, which once grew upwards, have in consequence of the great age of the tree spread out laterally, and this is the reason why the present height of the tree does not correspond with that mentioned in the scriptures."— Col. H. Burney, Asiatic Researches, vol. xx.

the spot where they touched the ground, the earth opened, and by the power of his páramitás a throne arose, 14 cubits high, the roots of the grass being hid, whilst the blades appeared as a beautiful canopy, wrought by the skill of a clever workman. At the sight of this throne, the prince rejoiced; and when he sat down upon it, he was animated by the utmost courage. The déwas and brahmas, knowing that this was the day of the great triumph of the Budha, came from the 10,000 sakwalas that they might witness his battle and victory.

4. *The Contest with Wasawartti Mára.*

The déwa Wasawartti-mára* reflected thus:—This is the day on which Sidhártta will become Budha; but I must go and endeavour to prevent it; I have been trying for the space of six years to overcome him, but have not been able; if this opportunity be lost, no other will be presented." He then struck the great drum called Wasawartti-ghósá, and all the déwas and brahmas, on hearing its sound, trembled with fear and shut their eyes; but to the prince it was as the rolling of the timbili drum, struck in seasons of festivity. It was a sign to him that Mára would come to do battle; and as he knew who would be the conqueror, and that by this means his prowess would be proclaimed to the world, he sat in peace, undisturbed. When the retinue of Mára heard the sound of the drum, they concluded that their lord was about to fight some battle, and therefore gathered around him, all carrying weapons. The déwa mounted his elephant, Girimékhala, 150 yojanas high, and as he knew that he would not be able to conquer with one weapon alone, he made unto himself 500 heads, with 1000 red eyes, and 500 flaming tongues; he had also 1000 arms, in each of which was a weapon,

---

* Wasawartti Mára is the ruler of the sixth déwa-lóka. No reason is assigned for his opposition to Budha, but the fear that by his discourses many beings would attain the blessedness of the brahma-lókas and the privilege of nirwána, which would prevent the re-peopling of the inferior world in which he reigned, when the déwas then inhabiting it had fulfilled their period of residence. There can be no doubt that the whole history of this battle was at first an allegorical description of an enlightened mind struggling with the power of evil. It may refer to some reality experienced by Gótama, when in the solitude of the wilderness he was led to feel the "accusing thoughts" of which the apostle speaks, and to seek the attainment of a higher and better state of mind. Mára is called by Csoma' Körösi, "Káma-deva, or the god of pleasures."

and yet no two of these weapons were alike. As he knew that the task he had undertaken would be difficult to accomplish, from the power and wisdom of his opponent, he concluded that it would be better not to approach him in front, lest he should be seen from afar, and the mind of the prince be prepared for the attack; it might be that if he approached from behind and made a noise, Sidhártta would look to see what was the matter, which would be the proper moment in which to seize him. He therefore proceeded stealthily to the western side of the sakwala-gala. The army that accompanied him extended on every side 164 miles, and its weight was sufficient to overpoise the earth. No two of the warriors had the same appearance; they assumed the most frightful forms, appearing like lions, tigers, panthers, boars, bears, buffaloes, bulls, nágas, garundas, polongas, and pimburas, all with hideous faces; the snakes stretched out their necks; other animals tore up trees by the roots; they rolled round their heads, struck each other as if in mortal combat, made mouths in the middle of their bodies, from which they put out their tongues and caused dirty saliva to exude, chased each other hither and thither, manifested various kinds of evil dispositions, brought terror upon all who saw them, and extended themselves from the sakwala-gala to the bó-tree, without any intermediate vacancy.

When the déwas heard the noise of the army as it approached the tree, they all fled from the 10,000 sakwalas. Kálaná, who had come to dance in the presence of the prince, and sing hymns in his praise, accompanied by 60,000 nágas, descended 8000 miles into the interior of the earth, to the nága-lóka, Manjarika, on arriving at which he covered his face with both hands, and cried out, "Alas! the glory of Sidhártta will this day be extinguished!" and having said this, he fell flat upon his couch, with his face downwards. Then the Sekras of the 10,000 sakwalas threw down the shells that they held in their hands, and fled away; but Sujampati, the Sekra of our own favoured sakwala, because he was born here, and had the power resulting from great merit, and was moreover very courageous, did not leave his place; nor did he throw down his shell; mounting to the summit of the sakwala-gala, he stood looking towards the bó-tree. Thus also the Sujáma and Santusita déwas of the 10,000 sakwalas, throwing down whatever they had in their hands, fled away. The Sahampati Maha Brahmas of the 10,000 sakwalas fled away in like manner, after they had stuck their umbrellas, like so many moons, upon the summit of the sakwala-gala.

When the prince perceived that all the déwas had fled, without any exception, he still remained unmoved as the rock Maha Merú, and fearless as the king of the lions when he sees a herd of elephants. Then seeing the army of Mára coming towards him, he thought thus: "This great army comes to fight against me alone; my parents are not here: no brother is with me; nor is any one else present to assist me; therefore the páramitá of truth that I have kept perfectly during four asankyas and a kap-laksha must be to me as a mother; the páramitá of wisdom must be to me as a father; my knowledge of the dharmma must be to me as an assisting brother; my páramitá of kindness must be to me as most excellent friends; my firm faith must be to me as a beloved parent; my páramitá of patient endurance must be to me as a helping son; these six relatives have continually preserved me until now, not leaving me for a single day or hour; therefore my relatives that are as my life are here: the thirty páramitás that I have kept continually until now, without any intermission, shall this day be as thirty warriors to protect me; and thus I have powerful defenders; the thirty-seven great virtues of the Budhas are my nobles; the countless assemblage of my observances is as a powerful army. This powerful army of my observances will not leave me to-day. My profound endowments will be to me as a deep fosse; my renowned benevolence will be to me as water filling it; and with this fosse around me the approach of my enemies shall be prevented. My páramitás shall be to me as bricks for the building of a strong wall, so high that it shall touch the brahma-lóka; and this wall shall keep off my enemy Mára when he approaches. The four great duties, chatuparisudhi-sila, that I have constantly attended to, shall be as gates; the four observances of the senses, indrasangwarasíla, shall be as four trusty servants, who shall stand as wardens; and my wardens will not to-day open the gate to my enemies, but will protect me. This my throne shall be to me as the place of honour; this my illustrious bó-tree shall be to me as a triumphal canopy; and these two assistances, that have been produced by my own power, will not leave me to-day." Thus the prince was encompassed by his páramitás as by a fortification; and by his obedience to the precepts, as by a city surrounded with a wall and well defended; and he was therefore without fear.

At this moment Mára came behind the tree, but he was not able to approach it, on account of the splendour proceeding from the body of Sidhártta; so he caused a mighty wind to arise, that he might hurl him into the next sakwala; and a violent wind it was, as it tore up rocks twenty or thirty miles in size, threw down great trees, and blew as at the end of a kalpa; yet as it went and came, not even a leaf of the tree was shaken, not even the corner of his robe was disturbed, nor was a single hair of his head at all moved; like a gentle and agreeable breeze it refreshed him, did homage to him, and passed away. Then Mára, that he might see into what sakwala the prince was blown by the storm, mounted to the top of the Udayagiri rock; but when he saw his body still resplendent as the orb of the sun, he became angry as a stricken serpent, and thought within himself, "I will cause a thick rain to fall and destroy him by the force of the water;" intending to cause a rain like that which falls at the end of a kalpa.

By his great power, Mára caused a hundred and a thousand clouds to arise, and spread in the ten directions the noise of a thunder-storm; a hundred lightnings played, rain-drops fell, in size like a palm-tree, ploughing the earth, and bearing along many trees; but when it approached Sidhártta, it did not wet even the hem of his robe; it was refreshing to him, as it fell like a shower of water lilies, did him honour, and went away. Mára again looked to see whether he had given up the desire to become Budha, or to see into what ocean he had been driven by the force of the stream; but when he saw the renowned mouth of the prince, shining like a full moon, he became angry as a goaded elephant, and he thought, "I will now destroy him by crushing him to pieces," intending to bring upon him a shower of rocks. He therefore hurled through the sky a hundred thousand burning mountains, twenty or thirty miles in size; but when they approached the prince, by the power of his obedience to the precepts, they were converted into garlands of sweet flowers, and arranged themselves in order around him, like a floral offering.

"What," said Mára, "is Sidhártta not yet ground to powder?

Does he still wish to become Budha?" and when he saw his mouth shining like a golden mirror, he became angry as an elephant that has struck his foot against a stone. Then he thought, "I will cut his golden body, his ears, and his nose, by a shower of weapons," causing a shower of weapons to fall. Sharp on both sides were the weapons that fell, swords and spears, arrows and javelins, like a shower; but by the merit of his wisdom, the weapons were changed into flowers on their passage, and fell as if they were presented as an offering.

When Mára looked to see if the prince's body was not cut to pieces, he beheld his mouth beautiful as the water-lily; and at the sight he raged like straw cast into the fire. Now he thought, "I will at this time burn him," causing a shower of burning charcoal to fall; but it fell at his feet, by the power of his various páramitás, like an offering of rubies; and when the déwa looked again to see the effect produced by the fire upon his victim, or whether he yet desired the Budhaship, and beheld him like the summit of a golden mountain whence the darkness is receding, he became tremulous as grains of salt when cast into the fire. After this he resolved to try what a shower of fiery ashes would accomplish; but they vanished away, and in their stead there was an offering of fragrant sandal-powder.

The next attempt of Mára was to bring against the prince a shower of fine burning sand; but it fell at his feet like pearls; and he was still seen seated upon the throne in beauty, like a sal tree covered with flowers. The déwa now became agitated as a flame exposed to the wind, and rained a shower of burning filth; but it fell like an offering, as of perfumes presented at a festival, and Sidhártta was seen as a brilliant gem. Next there was caused by the same power a thick four-fold gloom; but when it approached the throne it vanished away, like darkness at the approach of the sun, and became an offering of light. When Mára looked to see what was the effect of the darkness, and beheld the prince yet unmoved, his mouth full of friendship, like a golden tal-fruit falling ripe from the stalk, he became angry as an elephant that has seen a préta.

Thus these nine dangers, wind, rain, rocks, weapons, charcoal, ashes, sand, mud, and darkness, did no harm whatever to Sidhártta, but were converted into offerings. When Mára perceived this, as he was unable to approach the prince, he said angrily to his army from a distance, "All of you, seize Sidhártta, pierce him, cut him, break him to pieces, grind him to powder, destroy his desire to become Budha, do not let him escape." Saying this, he mounted his elephant Girimékhala; and brandishing his formidable discus on every side, he approached the prince, and threw it towards him. Were this weapon to be thrown against Maha Méru, it would cleave the mountain in twain as if it were a bamboo; were it cast into the ocean, its waters would be dried up; were it hurled into the sky, it would prevent the falling of rain for twelve years; but though it has such mighty energy, it could not be brought to approach the prince who was seeking the Budhaship; through his great merit, it rose and fell in the air like a dry leaf, and afterwards remained in splendour above his head, like a canopy of flowers. The warriors of Mára meanwhile said to each other, "It is to no purpose now to look for Sidhártta, as he is undoubtedly destroyed; never before this time did our divine master throw the discus; to look for him now would be useless;" yet after poising for a time a hundred thousand rocks, they hurled them in the same direction, which however, became only like an offering of sweet-scented flowers. The déwas who had remained hid among the sakwala rocks now lifted up their heads to see what was going on; and exclaimed in fear, "This day the glory of Sidhártta disappears; Mára has thrown the discus!" But when Mára saw that he could not shake the prince by the power of this formidable weapon, he went in front of him, burning with anger like the fire at the end of a kalpa, and rolling round his red eyes he took his thousand weapons into his thousand hands, and brandishing them before the prince, he said, "I will take thee by thy two legs, and hurl thee into the next sakwala; begone from my throne!"

When former Bódhisats received the Budhaship, the Máras who came to oppose them saw at once the glory of their sacred mouth (which extended to the sakwala gala), trembled, and were overcome. But upon the present occasion, Mára had an advantage not possessed by his predecessors in the same struggle. For this there was a cause. In the Wessantara birth, Bódhisat gave away his children, Jáli and Krishnájina, to the brahman Jújaka, who beat them until they bled, and in other ways used them cruelly. On account of those hardships, Krishnájiná looked up submissively in her father's face, weeping; at which he felt exceedingly sorrowful, from the strength of his parental affection, and began to consider whether he should not by force take his children again. It was on account of this hesitancy that Mára now received power to approach the bó-tree, and say with a tremendous voice, "Begone from my throne!" Notwithstanding this stern command, the prince had no fear; he answered with a smile, speaking in a sweet voice from his lotus-like mouth, "Sinful Mara! to gain this throne I have practised the páramitás during four asankyas and a kap-laksha. I am therefore the rightful owner of this throne. How canst thou possess it, who hast never accomplished a single páramitá?" When he said this, Mára became still more enraged, like a fire into which oil is poured, and replied, "I have given more in alms than thou hast given: I have accomplished more páramitás. The prince asked, "Where are your witnesses?" on which Mára stretched out his thousand arms towards his attendant army, and said, "Here are my witnesses?" Then the warriors replied, "We are witnesses; we are witnesses!" lifting up their hands at the same time; and the sound was enough to cleave the earth; it was like the roar of the sea, and struck the brahma-loka. Mára proceeded, "Oh, prince Sidhártta! so great an army has become witness that I have accomplished the páramitás; that you have fulfilled them, produce a single witness." "Your witnesses," replied the prince, "are alive and partial; mine are not alive, and they are without any partiality;" and like lightning launched from a red cloud, he stretched forth his hand from his robe. He said further, "When it was announced by Dípankara Budha that in due time I should become a Budha, and I was reflecting on the accomplishment of the thirty páramitás, the ten thousand sakwalas cried aloud; and thou thyself didst say, Sádhu! Leaving out the other births, in the Wessantra birth, when I was eight years of age and determined to offer an alms; when I gave the elephants, and 700 of all the articles that I possessed, and went from the city to the rock of Wankagiri, and gave my children, and my queen Mandri déwí, and the shower of water lilies fell; at these seven periods thou thyself didst cry out (in approbation.) Why did not the earth cry out at the utterance of thy lying witnesses?" At the same time he stretched out his hand toward the earth; and the earth gave out a hundred and a thousand sounds at the same instant, like the striking of a drum the size of a sakwala with a stick the size of Maha Méru. Then the earth opened, and mountains of fire rose up from the 136 hells, and the army of Mára fled away with a great noise, like leaves driven by the wind, each in a different direction. They threw down their ornaments and weapons, and their outer garments; and covering their faces with both hands, without looking at their leader, they went off in great trepidation. The elephant, Girimékhala, fell upon his knees, trembled with fear, threw down Mára from his back, curled up his trunk and thrust the end into his mouth, put his tail between his legs, growled fiercely, and without looking at his master, fled away. When the déwa fell to the ground, bereft of his thousand weapons, he exclaimed, "Oh, prince Sidhártta, I perceive that thou art powerful, and that thou art glorious; thou hast fulfilled the thirty páramitás; I will proclaim thy courage to the world; I will proclaim thy power; forgive, forgive!" Three times did he make this exclamation, after which he fled to his own world; but being ashamed to look at his attendants, he lay down and concealed his face.*

The déwas of this sakwala now called out to the déwas of the next, "Mára is overcome, and has fled; our prince Sidhártta is conqueror!" The nágas of this sakwala called out to those in the next; as well as the garundas and brahmas. The Sekras of the 10,000 sakwalas, the Maha Brahmas, nágas, garundas, suparnnas, and other beings, brought celestial flowers and perfumes; and assembling around the prince, they put their hands to their foreheads, and made obeisance.

As Mára was unable to bear the ridicule that the déwas heaped upon him on account of his discomfiture, he arose from his couch, and came to a certain place in Jambudwípa, where he assumed the appearance of a traveller; but his mind was still filled with sorrow, as he reflected that notwithstanding all his opposition, the prince had become Budha, and would in a little time preach the bana, by which many beings would obtain nirwána. Whilst indulging these reflections he made ten marks

* In the Puránas there is an account of a battle between Durga and a giant called Durgu, which bears a considerable resemblance to this legend of the contest between the prince Sidhártta and Mára.

upon the ground, as there were ten things that were presented to his mind; and as he tried to reckon up the many hundreds of thousands of ways in which he was inferior to Budha, the marks were extended to twelve. When Tanhá, Rati, and Ranga, the daughters of Mára, perceived that their father had vanished from the déwa-lóka, they looked with their divine eyes to see whither he had gone; and when they had discovered the place of his retreat, they went to him in the snapping of a finger, and enquired why he was so disconsolate. Having learnt the cause, they told him to become cheerful, as they themselves would overcome the prince; and when Mára replied that their attempts would be in vain, they said that there was no being whatever who could withstand their wiles even for a single moment. They then transformed themselves into 600 beautiful maidens, of different ages, their dress being arranged in the most wanton manner. Approaching the prince, they praised the beauty of his person, and asked why he remained under the tree; had he no queen, or had he quarrelled with her, or was it to meet some one whom he loved that he had come to this spot? But Sidhártta remained unmoved. Tanhá continued to praise his beauty, and to flatter him; and when this was to no purpose, she reminded him that at other times he had sought the enjoyment of what he now refused. But Budha did not even look at the tempters, and after they had long tried to overcome him without effect, they fled away.

5. *The Reception of the Budhaship.*

The sun had not gone down, when the prince overcame Mára. At the tenth hour, he received the wisdom by which he knew the exact circumstances of all the beings who have ever existed in the endless and infinite worlds; at the twentieth hour, he received the divine eyes by which he saw all things within the space of the infinite sakwalas, as clearly as if they were close at hand; at the tenth hour again, he received the knowledge that unfolds the causes of the repetition of existence, paticha-samuppáda; and at the time that he received this knowledge, by which he was enabled to investigate these causes from their end to their source, and from their source to their end, the Great Earths of the 10,000 sakwalas called out in approbation, by sections of twelve and twelve, a hundred and twenty thousand times, and said, Sádhu. After this, Bódhisat obtained, in order, the privileges of the four paths and their fruition. Then at the dawn of the next day, every remain of evil desire being destroyed, the beings in the endless and infinite worlds, who had not before possessed this privilege, saw a supreme Budha; and as they manifested great satisfaction, the six-coloured rays from his body were extended to them. These rays, without staying for so short a period as the snapping of the finger and thumb, passed onward from sakwala to sakwala, resembling as they proceed (for they yet continue to spread, rejoicing the beings that see them in their beauty), a blue cloud, the rock rose, a white robe, a red garland, and a pillar of light. Those who see the rays exclaim, "See, what splendid colours!" and from their satisfaction merit is produced, from which they obtain birth in this favoured world, and having the opportunity of seeing a Budha, they are released from the repetition of existence. The thirty-two wonders presented at his conception and birth were this day repeated. Not even a hundred thousand mouths could enumerate the offerings now made to Budha, or repeat the wonders that were performed.

At the moment the prince became Budha, like a vessel overflowing with honey, his mind overflowed with the ambrosia of the dharmma, and he uttered the following stanzas;—

> Anékajátisangsárang
> Sandháwissang anibhisang
> Gahakárakangawesanto
> Dukkhájátipunappunang.
>
> Gahakárakadithósi;
> Punagehangnakáhasi;
> Sabhátephásukhábhaggá,
> Gahakútangwisangkhitang;
> Wisangkháragatangchittang;
> Tanhánangkhayamajhagá.
>
> Through many different births,
> I have run (to me not having found),
> Seeking the architect of the desire-resembling house.
> Painful are repeated births!
>
> Oh, house-builder! I have seen (thee).
> Again a house thou canst not build for me.

> I have broken thy rafters,
> Thy central support is destroyed;
> To nirwána my mind is gone,
> I have arrived at the extinction of evil-desire.[*]

After the repetition of these stanzas, Budha thought thus: "I have attained the Budhaship; I have overcome Mára; all evil desire is destroyed; I am lord of the three worlds; I will therefore remain longer at this place, which has been to me so propitious." Thus reflecting, he remained in a sitting posture upon the throne for the space of seven days. On this account, the déwas began to think that he had not yet become Budha, and that there were other acts he must perform. To remove these doubts, which were perceived by Gótama, he arose from the throne, and ascended into the air, where he remained for a moment, after which he descended to the earth on the north-east side of the tree; and then, as an act of pujá, he continued to look at the tree during seven days, keeping his eyes immoveably fixed upon it, animisa lóchana, and performing dhyána. The place where he did this is called the chaitya, or dágoba, of animisa lóchana. The déwas made a golden path from that place to the throne; and Budha continued during seven days to walk in it from end to end. This pathway is now called the chaitya of chankramana, or ambulation. The déwas then made a golden palace at the north-western side of the tree, where he resided other seven days, reflecting on the wisdom of the dharmma that he had acquired. Thus he thought: "I shall remain Budha forty-five years; Seriyut and Mugalan will be my principal disciples; I shall have a kela of followers; the religion that I shall establish will continue during 5000 years; and I shall pro-

---

[*] These stanzas are thus translated by Turnour:—"Performing my pilgrimage through the (sansáro) eternity of countless existences, in sorrow, have I unremittingly sought in vain the artificer of the abode (of the passions, i.e. the human frame). Now, O artificer! art thou found. Henceforth no receptacle of sin shalt thou form—thy frames (literally, ribs) broken; thy ridge-pole shattered; thy soul (or mind) emancipated from liability to regeneration (by transmigration) has annihilated the dominion of the passions." And by Gogerly, thus—

> "Through various transmigrations
> I must travel, if I do not discover
> The builder whom I seek:—
> Painful are repeated transmigrations!
> I have seen the architect (and said)
> Thou shalt not build me another house;
> Thy rafters are broken
> Thy roof timbers scattered;
> My mind is detached (from all existing objects)
> I have attained to the extinction of desire."

pound the discourses of the three pitakas." In this way the whole of the dharmma was presented before him, from the words "anéka játi sangsárang (the first line of the stanzas just recorded) to the words appámádéna sampádétha" (the last words spoken by Gótama previous to his death). The place where the dharmma was thus perceived is called the ratana-ghara chaitya. In the fifth week, he went to the tree Ajápála, where he enjoyed the fruition of nirwána. In the sixth week, he went to the lake Muchalinda, where he remained at the foot of a midella tree. At that time a rain began to fall, which continued during seven days without intermission, in all the four great continents. The nága Muchalinda having ascended to the surface of the lake, saw the darkness produced by the storm; and in order to shelter Budha from the rain and wind, and protect him from flies, mosquitoes and other insects, he spread over him his extended hood, which served the purpose of a canopy, and during the time the sage was in this position,* he enjoyed the satisfaction of dhyána. In the seventh week, he went to a forest of kiripalu trees, where he remained until the 49th day upon a couch of stone. Until this period he had remained without any other food than the fruition of nirwána; but on the 50th day, Sekra gave him a piece of amrata aralu, by which his body received strength; and after its reception he went to the lake Anotatta, where he washed his mouth with the water, and used the tooth-cleaner given by Sekra, after which he returned to the kiripalu forest.

6. *The first Offering received by Gótama as Budha.*

There were two merchants, Tapassu and Bhalluka, who had wished during a whole kap-laksha to have the opportunity of making an offering to a Budha; and they now came from the north towards the kiripalu forest, with 500 well-laden wagons. In the same forest was a déwí, who had formerly been their relative; and when she saw them coming, she thought it would confer on them a great blessing were she to cause them to present an offering to Gótama. To effect this, she made the wagons sink in the ground as far as the axle, and the oxen remained with their knees bent. The merchants concluded that this stoppage

* In painting and sculpture Budha is frequently represented as sitting under the extended hood of the nága.

was caused by some déwa,' and with perfumes and lights they offered up a prayer for assistance. The déwí then appeared to them in the sky, and said, "From the time that my Budha became supreme, that is to say, for the space of 49 days, he has not taken any food; those who have merit are now come to the forest; that both I and they may receive further merit, let them present an offering of acceptable food to our lord." After uttering these words, she released the wagons. The merchants, greatly pleased, presented some delicious honey to Budha. The almsbowl given by Maha Brahma vanished when Sujatá brought her offering of milk-rice, and the golden dish she gave him in its stead had been taken to the nága-lóka. As it was not the custom for the Budhas to receive anything in the hand, he considered in what way he should take the honey. The four guardian deities brought each an alms-bowl of emerald, but he did not accept them. They then brought four bowls made of stone, of the colour of the mung fruit; and when each entreated that his own bowl might be accepted, Budha caused them to appear as if formed into a single bowl, at the upper rim appearing as if placed one within the other. In this bowl he received the honey, and as it was the first food he had eaten since he became Budha, he taught them in return the three-fold protective formulary, and they became upásakas. The merchants then requested that he would give them something they might honour as a relic; upon which he lifted up his right hand, and gave them a lock of his hair. When the merchants had entered a ship to return to their own country, they passed in their way near Ceylon, and landed at a place called Girihandu, to take in wood and water. They placed the casket containing the relic upon a rock whilst they prepared some food; but when they attempted to take it again they were not able, as it had become attached to the rock. They therefore surrounded it with lamps and flowers, and went away. At this place the Girihandu wihára was afterwards erected.*

* This account is taken from the Pujáwaliya, but it differs from the legends I have seen in other works, which state that the relics were taken to their own country, Swarnna-bhúmi (Burma). In the inscription upon the great bell at Rangoon, as translated by the Rev. G. H. Hough, it is stated, "In the city Rangoon, in order that the religious dispensation (of Gótama) might be established during the period of 5000 years, to the merchant brothers Tapoktha and Pallika, he with his golden hand stroking his head, gave eight hairs, that to those coming to pay their respects and homage to the monuments in which they are enshrined . . . the immense advantages of merit

7. *The first Discourse delivered by Budha.*

In the eighth week, Budha went from the kiripalu forest to the tree Ajápála, where he reflected that the bana is deep, and that the beings of the world are unwise and filled with evil desire; he thought again, that though his own merit was great, the demerit of men was also great, and that in consequence, it would be to no purpose for him to declare the dharmma, as it would not be understood. When this hesitancy was perceived by Sahampati Maha Brahma, he exclaimed, "Nassati wata bhó lókó; nassati wata bhó lókó; the universe will most certainly be destroyed." This cry was immediately repeated by the other brahmas and déwas, and by the déwas of the clouds, cold, wind, and rain. All these beings then proceeded to the tree Ajápála; and Maha Brahma, bending his knee that was 48 miles high, said to Budha, "My lord, the Budhaship is difficult to acquire; but you have accomplished it, that you might release the beings of the world from existence; therefore proclaim the dharmma, that this may be effected; those who refuse to listen shall be chastised with my discus; désétha munindó dhámman; désétha bhagawá dhamman. Oh, wise one, let the dharmma be said! Oh, purified one, let the dharmma be said!" Budha promised that this prayer should be attended to; when all the déwas and brahmas thrice returned thanks, in such a manner that the noise might be everywhere heard; after which they retired to their several lókas.

When Budha looked to see unto whom he should first say bana, he saw that the ascetics Alára and Uddaka were worthy; but when he looked again to discover in what place they were, he perceived that the former had been dead seven days, and that the latter had died the day before; and that as they were now in an arúpa world, they could not receive its benefit. With affection for the two ascetics who were dead, he looked to discover in what place Kondanya was, and the four other recluses with whom he had practised austerities; and when he saw that

might be obtained." It is said in the additional remarks made by Mr. Hough, that the merchants on their way home were deprived of four hairs at two different places, but when they arrived at Ukkalaba, near the present Rangoon, they found that they had all the eight. The monument in which they are deposited is the far-famed Swa-da-gon.—As. Res. xvi.

they were in the Isipatana wihára, near Benares, he resolved that unto them first bana should be said.*

At the end of 60 days, in the eighth week after he became Budha, Gótama went alone from the Ajápála tree to Isipatana, a distance of 288 miles. All the Budhas begin to say bana in Æsala masa, on the day of the full moon. In the course of this journey he was seen by the ajíwaka mendicant, Upaka, who, as he noticed with what gravity the sage moved along, his body shining most beautifully, was pleased, and asked him if he were Sekra or Maha Brahma. Gótama replied, "I am neither Sekra nor Maha Brahma, but the supreme Budha; I know the manner in which the repetition of existence is to be overcome; all that is proper to renounce, I have put from me, as far as the sky is from the earth; all that is proper for me to acquire, I have in my possession, as if it were a portion of ambrosia; all the beings in the world are my servitors; Maha Brahma offers flowers to the cloth that cleans my feet; I am above all; I am the conqueror of Mára; my name is Ananta-Jinayo." On hearing this, Upaka said, "From this time you shall be my friend; but if I attach myself to you, is it in your power to protect me?" Budha informed him that it was in his power, and proceeded forward to Isipatana. Some time afterwards the mendicant went to the country called Wangahára,† where he entered a hunter's village in his usual scanty attire. The people flocked round him to look at him; and when they enquired who he was, he said that he was the rahat Ardhapála, and that he was so called because he did not put on clothing like other people, his shame being only half hid, and not entirely covered. The people of this country are at times tormented by a kind of fly about the size of a grain of sesamum, and when the insects are very numerous, they construct places like caves, to which they retire. As they believed the words of Ardhapála, they made him one of these places, and supported him. There was a maiden in the village, called Cháwi; and when the mendicant saw her, he wished to possess her, and from passion remained without food many days. The father wondered why he did not

---

* In a temple at Amoy, Bishop Smith saw eighteen images, which were said to represent the eighteen original disciples of Budha.

† The Vangas may be the people here referred to, who resided in Eastern Bengal.

come to receive alms as usual, and thinking that he must be sick, he went to his retreat to enquire what was the matter, when Ardhapála told him the whole truth. The father consented that he should come and live at his house, and gave him his daughter in marriage; but after this he had sometimes to work for the father, then to fetch fuel and water for the mother, and after that to pound rice for his wife, until his strength was nearly gone. A son, Bhaddaka, was born to him, but this increased his difficulties, as his wife now did nothing but nurse the child; and though he did all that was required, she continually abused him. Wearied out, he told his wife that he must leave her, at which she became more insulting, as she thought that she might get a younger husband; and when he could endure her abuse no longer, he left her as he had said, and going to Benares, he enquired if any one knew Ananta-Jinayo. From his description the people knew that he meant Budha, and directed him to the place where he was. Budha foresaw his approach, and told his attendants that if they met with any one enquiring for Ananta-Jinayo, they were to direct him to himself. On his arrival he requested permission to enter the priesthood, saying that though he was old, he could fulfil the duties required. Budha then admitted him, and taught him the discipline, when he entered the path anágámi, and after his death was born in one of the brahma-lókas, where he still remains.*

On the evening of the day on which Budha first spoke to Upaka, he arrived at Isipatana. When the five hermits saw him at a distance, they said, "Sidhártta has regained his strength and beauty; he must therefore have left off the practice of austerities; he now comes to us, as he is unable to gain the Budhaship; as he is of a royal family it is right that we should give him a seat, but we will not rise at his approach, nor go to meet him." Budha perceived their thoughts, and as the 11,500 inferior streams fall into the five great rivers, so the kindness that extended to infinite sakwalas was made to flow towards the five ascetics. As the withered leaf in the rapid stream cannot remain still a moment, but is continually driven hither and thither; so the ascetics, overcome by the force of Budha's kindness, were unable to remain upon their seats, and were com-

* When similar narratives occur, a mere outline of the matter in the original text, as in the present instance, will be given.

pelled to come towards him and worship. They afterwards washed his feet, and enquired familiarly about his health; but Gótama informed them, that they must not address him as an equal; he was now a supreme Budha. On receiving this intelligence, they rejoiced. In the place where the former Budhas said bana, the earth clove, and a throne arose, to which Gótama ascended, as the sun rises over Udayagiri. The evening was like a lovely female; the stars were pearls upon her neck, the blue clouds were her braided hair, and the expanse was her flowing robe. As a crown, she had the brahma-lókas; the three worlds were as her body: her eyes were like the white lotus, kowmada; and her voice was like the humming of the bee. To worship Budha, and listen to the first proclaiming of the bana, this lovely female came. Maha Méru leaped with joy; the seven circles of rocks did obeisance to Budha; and the sakwala-gala turned many times round. The various beings in the world all assembled, that they might receive the ambrosia and nectar of nirwána. They stood in circles, the room that they occupied being more and more compressed as each additional company arrived, until at last they were so close that a hundred thousand déwas had no more space than the point of a needle. All the déwa-lókas and brahma-lókas, except the arúpa worlds, were left empty, and the company extended from this sakwala to the brahma lókas. Though all space was thus filled, there was no impediment whatever to the spreading of the rays from the person of Budha. The sound was like that of a storm; but when the Sekras blew their conches, all became still as a waveless sea. Then Budha opened his mouth, and preached the Dhamsak-pæwatum-sútra (Dhamma-chakka). "There are two things," said he, "that must be avoided by him who seeks to become a priest; evil desire, and the bodily austerities that are practised by the (brahman) ascetics." The déwas on each side thought that he looked in their direction when he spoke; all the déwas and brahmas thought that he addressed himself to their own particular lóka; by this means the eyes of all were fixed upon him, and all hearts were offered to him. Although the stature of Maha Brahma is so great, he did not see the top of Budha's head, nor did any being from that time forth. The all-wise saw the exact disposition of every one in that assembly, and knew which of the sixty-three charitas each one cherished;

and he could say, the brahmas think thus, and the déwas thus, and the nágas thus, and so on of every separate order. Though he spoke in the language of Magadha, each one thought that he spoke in his own language; and all the different species of animals, both great and small, listened to him under the same supposition. The oldest of the five ascetics, Kondanya, entered the first path, as did also an asankya of déwas; an asankya of déwas also entered the second path, and another the third; and eighteen kelas of brahmas entered the fourth path.

8. *Fifty-four Princes and a thousand Fire-worshippers become the Disciples of Budha.*

Whilst Budha remained at Isipatana, Yasa, the son of Sujatá, who had been brought up in all delicacy, one night went secretly to him, was received with affection, became a priest, and entered the first path. The father, on discovering that he had fled, was disconsolate; but Budha delivered to him a discourse, by which he became a rahat. The fifty-four companions* of Yasa went to the monastery to induce him to return, and play with them as usual; but when they saw him, they were so struck with his manner and appearance, that they also resolved upon becoming priests. When they went to Budha they were admitted, by the power of irdhi received the pirikara requisites of the priesthood, and became rahats. Budha had now sixty disciples who were rahats, and he commanded them to go by different ways, and proclaim to all that a supreme Budha had appeared in the world.

When the disciples had departed on their mission, Budha set out to return to Uruwela, and by the way remained under the shade of a tree where four ways met. At that time there were thirty-two princes in Kosol,† who from being alike in beauty

* These are the same fifty-four persons who are represented under the head of asubha-bháwaná as having burnt the dead body of a woman that they found in the forest; and it was by the merit then obtained that they were now enabled to become rahats.

† Kosol, or Kósala, is the country along the bank of the Sarayu, forming part of the modern province of Oude. It was the pristine kingdom of the solar race. In the time of Gótama Budha, the principal city was Sewet. In the ninth century the authority of the king of Kósala extended into Gondwana, as appears from inscriptions yet extant. There are several Kósalas mentioned by Sanscrit authors, in different directions. Ptolemy has a Kontakussala in the south of India, probably one of the Kósalas of the Hindus.—Wilson's Vishnu Puráṇa.

and disposition were called Bhaddawaggi. They received from the king a province, which they ruled conjointly. Having heard that there was a very pleasant region called Kappasika, they went to see it. One of them, who had no wife like the rest, was accompanied by a courtezan, but she stole his ornaments and absconded; and when the princes went in search of her, they came to the place where Budha was seated under the tree, from whom they enquired if he had seen a courtezan, telling him what had happened. Budha asked them whether it was better to seek others or to seek themselves. As the princes knew his meaning, they said it was better for each one to seek for himself. Then Budha, seeing that they were willing thus to act, delivered to them an appropriate discourse, and the thirty-two princes became rahats; after which he sent them different ways to proclaim that the three gems had appeared. There were now ninety-two persons who had become rahats.

In the Uruwela forest, to which Budha repaired, near the river Niltará, three brothers resided of the same name, Uruwel Kásyapa, Gayá Kásyapa, and Nadi Kásyapa, who gave out that they were rahats, and thus deceived many people, whilst they lived in great plenty and splendour. The oldest brother had 500 disciples, the second 300, and the next 200; a thousand in all. As Budha wished to bring them all into the paths, he went to the residence of Uruwel, and requested permission to remain that night in the fire-hall, or temple. Uruwel replied that he himself had no objection, but that in the hall there was an immense nayá, the poison of which was most subtle; it did not hurt him or his brothers because they were rahats; but as Gótama was not a rahat, though his person was so beautiful, it would be dangerous for him to enter the hall. Budha, as if he had not heard what was said, again requested permission to remain in the fire-hall. Uruwel replied, "It is no matter to me whether you remain in the fire-hall or not; but remember the fatal serpent." As Budha could not ask him again, lest his head should be cloven, he fearlessly entered the hall, that he might repose there for the night. The nayá came forth, and asked in anger, "Who is this that has entered my mansion, as if it were his own?" at the same time sending forth a poisonous blast. Budha reflected, "Were I to send forth a blast, it would burn up the universe, as though it were only a cobweb; nevertheless, I must try to bring down this serpent's pride." Accordingly, he sent forth a fiery vapour, as from a burning wisp of straw, but it would not hurt an ant or a fly; and when it approached the nayá, he felt the pain of sorrow, but the flesh of his body received no injury. The nayá sent forth a flame to destroy Budha; but he made a flame seven times more powerful, and subdued the nayá. The light was perceived by Uruwel, and he said that Gótama must have perished from not attending to his advice. When Budha had overcome the nayá, he put it in his alms-bowl, after extracting its poison. The next morning he called Uruwel, and told him to look at the nayá about which they had boasted so much the day previous; and when he saw it in the alms-bowl, its attention was directed towards Budha, as if ashamed. The brothers said that he might subdue the nayá, but that still he was not a rahat.

At another time, Budha was not far from the residence of Uruwel, when the four guardian déwas came and kept watch around him; and he, like a golden dágoba surrounded by lamps, said bana to them. The next morning Uruwel asked him the meaning of the bright shining at the four quarters when he said bana, and was informed it was the four guardian déwas, who had come to listen. But the brothers were not yet convinced that he was a rahat equal to themselves, though Sekra and Maha Brahma came to do him homage, and hear bana. One day great multitudes came from Anga and Magadha, with offerings for Uruwel, who thought if the people were to see Budha, they would liken him and his brothers to monkeys, and therefore wished that he would not come in their direction that day. Budha knew his thoughts, and as he was desirous to bring him into the right way, he went to receive a repast in Uturukukuru, and drank water from the Anotatta lake, returning on the third day. Uruwel then invited him to pay him a visit, as he said that he had just received a great number of offerings, and enquired where he had been the two previous days. Budha replied, "I know the thoughts of all, from the lowest being to Maha Brahma; what has passed through your mind is open to me; you may deceive others, but me you cannot deceive." About the same period, Budha received the offering of a robe, and when he reflected where it should be washed, Sekra instantly caused a pool of water to appear, with two stones, one for the robe to be beaten against, and the other for it to be dried upon; and when the sage descended into the water, a déwa brought the branch of a tree upon which he laid hold. Thus assisted, he washed the robe; and the assistance he had received was known to Uruwel. On another occasion, he was invited by Uruwel to eat rice with him. Budha told him to go, and he would follow. In the interval he went to the forest of Himála, plucked a leaf from the jambu tree that is 100 yojanas high, and arrived at the residence before Uruwel. The fire-worshipper enquired how it was that he had arrived first, when Budha told him where he had been in the mean time; but said that this was nothing, as in the same period he could have gone round the sakwala gala a hundred thousand times. Another day Budha fetched two flowers, one from the forest of Himála, and the other from the garden of Sekra, and showed to Uruwel; but he said that though he could not, like Gótama, go useless journeys, he knew a road that Gótama did not know, the road to nirwána; and after all that he had seen, he would not confess the superiority of Budha.

One day Uruwel went with his 500 disciples to make preparation for a fire offering, and all at the same instant attempted to cleave the wood that was required; but Budha caused the wood not to cleave. The axes of some seemed like lead, and others like pitch: and some lifted up their axes and were unable to bring them down again. They concluded that it was the work of Budha. Then the sage looked in the face of Uruwel, and ordained that the wood should cleave; and before the axes could be brought down, the wood clove of its own accord. The jótis at another time intended to make an offering, but Budha would not allow the fire to burn though the smoke continued; and when they perspired with fear, he asked them if they wished the fire to burn, upon which the fire at once burnt brightly without their interference. When they wanted to put out the fire they could not; they brought water, but it acted like oil, and made it blaze more fiercely. Budha afterwards extinguished it in a moment. At another time, after the jótis had bathed, they were seized with a cold shivering; but Budha caused a fire to approach each of them, by which they were warmed. Again, out of the usual season there was a great rain; the waters overflowed; but when they approached Budha, they gathered round him like a silver wall. Uruwel went in a boat, thinking to rescue him; but found him in the manner described. Budha reflected, that from the time of the subduing of the nayá he had performed 3516 wonders; but that still the scepticism of the fire worshippers continued. He then said bana, and at once Uruwel was overcome; he confessed that Gótama was Budha, and entered the path sowán. The disciples of Uruwel, and his two brothers, with their disciples, followed his example. Then Budha went to the rock Gáya, at the head of the Gáya river, and delivered the discourse called Adittapariyá-sútra, by which the thousand priests became rahats.

9. *Bimasara, king of Rajagaha, becomes a Disciple of Budha.*

To fulfil the promise that he had given to Bimsara, Budha went to the forest of Yashti, twelve miles from Rajagaha, where he remained at the foot of a tree. The king was informed of his arrival by a forester, and with a retinue of 120,000 nobles, went to visit him. When the nobles saw Uruwel, who was as famous among them as the banner of the city, they knew not whether he or Budha was the superior, but Gótama looked in his face, and asked why he had forsaken the fire-worshippers; in answer to which, he rose into the air, by the power of dhyána, did reverence to Budha, and after performing many wonders, declared to the nobles that Budha was like the sun whilst he was like the fire-fly, by many other comparisons setting forth his own inferiority. Then the ruler of the world repeated the first játaka, called Mahánárada-kásyapa. It was to this effect:—There was a king in Miyulu,* called Angáti, who had a daughter, Ruchá. At first he lived correctly, but one day he heard some false teachers; who declared that there is no future world, and that the whole man at death is resolved into the four elements, the aqueous particles returning to water, the fiery particles to fire, and so forth; after which he thought it was better to enjoy the present moment; and he therefore became cruel, and ceased to give alms. The daughter, who was able to see the events of the fourteen preceding births, went to the king; and when he asked

* Miyulu, or Mithila, is the modern Tirhut. The Rámáyana places a prince named Mithi between Nimi and Janaka, whence comes the name Mithila.—Wilson's Vishnu Purána.

if all things were provided for her that she required, she said "Yes;" and then requested the king to give her a thousand masurans, as the next day was a festival, and she wished to make an offering. But the king replied that as there is no future world, no reward of merit, it was better to enjoy herself in the present life. Ruchá then related what had occurred to her in former births, and the reason why she was now only a woman. Fourteen births, previously she was a nobleman, but an adulterer. In the next birth she was again a noble, through the power of previous merit, and gave much alms. But when she died, she had to leave the merit thus acquired, like a mine of wealth hidden in the ground, and for her previous demerit she was born in the Rowra hell, where she remained 2880 kótis of years. She was next born as a vigorous ram in the country called Bhennuka; so powerful, that the shepherds taking it by the four feet, threw it on the ground, and deprived it of its virility; which was the punishment of her former deeds. Again, she was a monkey, and a draught bullock, in both of which births she had to suffer the same punishment; and was then born among savages, and was neither a male nor female. After this she was the déwí of Sekra; then the wife of a libertine; and last of all the daughter of the king. When she had related these things, the king smiled, but thought it was not right that the old should be taught by the young: and so he continued to be sceptic. Then Ruchá appealed to the déwas to render her assistance, and by the power of the satcha-kiriya charm, relating the merit she had acquired in previous states of existence, summoned them to come to her aid from the other world. At this time Bódhisat was Maha Brahma, and in answer to the charm he assumed the form of an ascetic and came to the city, illumining the whole place with his brightness. The king asked him whence he came, and when the ascetic said that he had come from the other world, he smiled, and said, "Well, if you have come from the other world, lend me a hundred masurans, and when I go to that world I will give you a thousand." Bódhisat replied, "When any one lends money, it must be to the rich, and he will receive his own again with interest; but if he lends to the poor, he will, from pity, allow him to keep the whole, and thus lose it; I cannot, therefore, lend you a hundred masurans, because you are poor and destitute." The king said, "You utter an untruth; does not this city, 100 miles in size, belong to me?" Bódhisat replied, "When you die you cannot take it with you to hell, as you will there be in unspeakable misery; you will be without raiment, and without food; you will not have a single masuran; how then could you pay me the debt?" As he thus set forth the misery of hell, the king trembled as if he already felt it, became alarmed, and renounced his scepticism. "That king," proceeded Budha, "is now Uruwel." At the end of this discourse, Bimsara and eleven nahutas of nobles entered the path sowán; a nahuta of the common people took refuge in the three gems; and as there are 10,000 in a nahuta, 120,000 persons were on this day released from the repetition of existence. At sixteen years of age Bimsara was crowned; he had now, on becoming an upásaka, attained his twenty-ninth year; he rendered assistance to Budha during thirty-six years; and in his sixty-fifth year attained nirwána.

When Bimsara returned to Rajagaha, it was reported among the people that the king had heard bana, and entered the path of nirwána. They enquired among each other, "What is this bana? what kind of a person is Budha? what can this nirwána mean?" As they could receive no satisfactory answer, they went to see for themselves; and the whole of the road from the city to the wihára was crowded with people, a distance of twelve miles. The garden also soon became filled, so that there was not room for a single priest to move about, nor could Budha or the priests eat their food. This was perceived by Sekra, who assumed a most beautiful form, and by his divine power cleared a space around Budha, after which he repeated his praises in hymns. When the people saw Sekra, they said, "Was ever so beautiful a person before seen? what princess can it be?" But the déwa said that he was only Budha's servant. Then Gótama went in the space cleared by Sekra to the city, along with a thousand disciples. The king gave alms to the priests, but said, "I cannot live unless I am near the three gems; whether it be at a proper hour or not, I must remain near Budha; this wihára is distant; but my own garden of Wéluwana is near; it is convenient for me to go and come; I will therefore present it to Budha." It was called Kalandaka-niwápa, or an offering made to the squirrels: on this account. There was in a former age a king, who was accustomed to go to this place for amusement. One day he became intoxicated, and fell asleep; when a nayá, angry at the smell of liquor, approached to bite him. The déwa of a tree, who saw his danger, reflected that if the king died, the garden would be suffered to go to ruin, and he would lose his pleasant residence. He therefore assumed the form of a squirrel, and going to the king, gently made a noise near his ear, by which he awoke, and saw the danger in which he had been placed, and the way in which he had been saved. Out of gratitude, he proclaimed, by beat of drum, that no one in his dominions should kill a squirrel upon pain of death and the destruction of his race; and he commanded that the squirrels in this garden should be regularly supplied with food. This was the reason why it was called Kalandaka-niwápa. When Bimsara presented the garden, the earth trembled. It also trembled when the garden called Ambátaka was given by Chittra, a rich citizen of Macchikásanda, to the priest Sadharmma; and when the Maha Mewuná garden, in Ceylon, was presented. But the earth trembled at the presenting of no other residence. As a token of the giving over of the garden, the king poured water upon the hands of Budha; and from this time it became one of the principal residences of the sage.*

When Budha entered upon the possession of the wihára 84,000 prétas, that had not eaten anything during three whole budhántaras, came and saw the sage, and obtained rice and water. This was their history:—In the time of Pussa Budha, they lived near his residence as cooks. When their master told them to prepare offerings of food for Budha, they began first to taste a little of it themselves, and then to give it to their children, (thus desecrating the sacred food). For this they were born in hell during ninety-one kalpas, and afterwards became prétas. In the time of Kakusanda Budha, they came to him and said that they had not tasted a morsel of food or a drop of water from the beginning of the kalpa, at the same time praying that he would release them. Budha felt pity for them, though he was not able to assist them; but he reflected that if he revealed their real condition, it would only be adding fire to fire; and he therefore said that at a future time Kónágamana Budha would be born, to whom they must apply. But Kónágamana, on his appearance in the world, said that they must apply to Kásyapa Budha; and

* It was called Wéluwana from the number of bamboos, wélu, by which it was surrounded. Its situation is described as being peculiarly delightful.

when he appeared, they were directed to Gótama, who would enable them to receive food. On hearing this they became joyful; it seemed to them as if they would be released on the morrow; and from this time they looked out for his appearance, as the husbandman looks out for the rain-cloud. At midnight they now appeared to Bimsara, and informed him what they had endured. The next day the king made known to Budha what he had seen, who told him that they would on that day receive food. They again appeared to the king, all naked, and when he informed Budha, the sage told him that they could only receive such things as were offered in alms to the priests. Bimsara therefore made an offering of robes, and the next night they appeared to him in garments splendid as those of the déwas. Budha delivered to them the Tirókudha-sútra, after which they were released from the préta birth, and entered the path to nirwána.

10. *The two principal Disciples of Budha, Seriyut and Mugalan.*

There were two brahman villages, Kólita and Upatissa, not far from Rajagaha, in which two families resided who had been upon terms of intimacy during seven generations; and now each of these families had a prince, called by the same names as their village, Kólita and Upatissa. The former had a retinue of 500 chariots, and the latter of 500 golden palanquins. They were equally clever; they sought the same amusement; what the one did the other did; and thus they were intimately united. But they thought that there could be no release from birth whilst they pursued their pleasures, and that therefore it behoved them to discontinue their pursuits, and seek nirwána. The question then arose, as to what place they should go. There was at this time in Rajagaha a famous paribrájika called Sanga. To him they went, and they remained with him some time; but he was unable to show them the paths. After this they went through all Jambudwípa, asking questions in every place, but no one was able to answer them. In this way they went through the 63,000 kingdoms, and then returned to Rajagaha. It was agreed that if one found a competent teacher, he was to tell the other. The residence of Gótama Budha was now at Wéluwana. When the priest Assaji had proclaimed through all Jambudwípa that a Budha had appeared, he returned to Rajagaha, and the next day went with his bowl to receive alms. In passing from place to place, he was seen by Upatissa, who greatly admired his appearance, and invited him to go and partake of food. Whilst they were together, Upatissa said, "From what I have seen of your deportment, I infer that you are acquainted with the path to nirwána; tell me, who was your teacher?" When the priest said that it was Budha, he enquired what were his doctrines; but the priest, under the supposition that the paribrájika was opposed to Budha, replied, "I am only a young disciple; the dharmma is deep; how, then, can I tell you?" Then Upatissa informed him that he need not give himself much trouble; if he only gave him a little information upon the subject, he could draw from it a hundred or a thousand inferences. The priest, in reply, repeated the following gátá:—

> Yé dhamma hétuppabhawá,
> Yésan hétun Tathágató,
> Aha yésan cha yo niródhó,
> Ewan wadi Maha Samano.*

"All things proceed from some cause; this cause has been declared by the Tathágata; all things will cease to exist: this is that which is declared by the Maha Sramana (Budha)." When the first two lines of this stanza were repeated by Assaji,

---

* This stanza, and another that will afterwards be introduced, beginning "Sabba pápassa," has been found on a slab taken from the dágoba at Sarnath, near Benares, as well as upon the image of Budha found at Tirhut, and upon monuments yet existing in other parts of India. It also appears at the beginning and end of many of the sections of the sacred books written upon the continent. It is thus translated by Dr. Mill:—"This is the generative source of the cause of meritorious duties. For the cause of these hath Tathágata declared. But as to what is the opposing principle of these, that likewise doth the Maha Sramana declare." By Csoma Körösi it is thus rendered from the Tibetan:—

> "Whatever moral (or human) actions arise from some cause,
> The cause of them hath been declared by Tathágata:
> What is the check to these actions,
> Is thus set forth by the great Sramanas."

After which is inserted the stanza translated, "No vice is to be committed," &c.—Journal As. Soc. No. 39, March, 1835. Mr. Hodgson says, that this confessio fidei can be repeated by almost every man, woman, and child, of the Buddha faith, at Kathmandu. His translation of the formula, with the help of the commentators, is as follows:—"The cause, or causes, of all sentient existence in the versatile world, the Tathágata hath explained. The great Sramana hath likewise explained the cause, or causes, of the cessation of all such existence."—Ib. No. 40, April, 1835.

the paribrájika embraced the doctrine, and entered the path sowán; and when the fourth line was concluded, he said, "I believe in thee; I believe in Budha; where is he?" On being informed, he went to Kólita, and informed him that he had found the path to nirwána; and as he repeated the same stanza, his companion also entered sowán, when he arrived near the end. The two friends then went to inform Sanga of what had occurred, and asked him to accompany them to the residence of Budha; but he said that it was not possible, as all Jambudwípa was filled with his fame, and he could not become the attendant of another. The 500 disciples of Sanga, however, resolved to accompany them; but when they saw that he became so sorrowful on this account as to vomit blood, 250 of them returned to him in consequence, and the rest went with the two companions. At the time they approached Budha, he was saying bana, and as he perceived their intention, he declared to those near him that the two individuals who were approaching would become his principal disciples.* After they had reverently worshipped him, they asked if they might be permitted to receive the benefit of his teaching. Budha replied by saying, "Come priests; in order to be released entirely from sorrow, embrace the brahma chariya ordinance; and I will declare to you the excellent dharmma." At its conclusion they all received the requisites of the priesthood by the power of irdhi, and had the appearance of persons who had been in the priesthood a hundred years. Budha then said bana, and the 250 disciples of Sanga became rahats. From this time, Kólita was called Mugalan; † and Upatissa, Seriyut.

Seven days after this event, Mugalan went to Kallawála, in Magadha, where he heard Budha explain the four dhátus, or elements; and he at once entered the second, third, and fourth paths, and received the wisdom necessary to an agra-sráwaka. Fifteen days after, Seriyut heard Budha deliver the Wédaná-

---

* Agasaw, or agra-sráwaka, from agra, chief, and sráwaka, a disciple, literally, one who hears. The disciples who receive this office must have practised the páramitás during one asankya-kap-laksha. They are never born of any other caste than the royal or the brahman. The two agra-srá-wikáwas, or principal female disciples of Gótama, were Khéma and Uppala-warnna.

† Csoma Körösi says, that Kolita, or "the lap-born," was also called Mongalyana, because he was one of the Mongol family or race.

parigrahana discourse, to his nephew, Díghanaka, a paribrájika, in the cave called Húrúkala, near Rajagaha, at which time he acquired the same privileges as Mugalan. In the following night, all the priests assembled together, and about this assembly* there are four things that are to be remarked. 1. It was held in the night of the full moon. 2. All the priests assembled without invitation. 3. All who were present had received ordination by the power of irdhi. 4. They were all rahats. Budha repeated to them the following gátá:—

> Sabba pápassa akaranan;
> Kusalassa upasampadá;
> Sa chitta pariyódapanan;
> Etan Budhánusásanan.†

"This is the advice of the Budhas; avoid all demerit; obtain all merit; cleanse the mind from all evil desire." This constitutes the discourse called Prátimóksha. In the time of Anomadassi Budha, one hundred thousand asankya-kalpas previous to the present age, one of the agra-sráwakas was an ascetic, and the other was his friend. They both gave great gifts to Anomadassi, and wished that they might become the principal disciples of a Budha. From that time they were always born together, either in the déwalókas or the world of men, like the two wheels of a chariot, and in their various births were associated with Bódhisat, to whom they rendered assistance.‡ At this time Gótama Budha had received, in different ways, 250,344 offerings.

11. *Budha visits Kapilawastu, his native City.*

During the residence of Budha at Wéluwana, his father Sudhódana, who had heard of his attainment of the Budhaship, sent to him a noble, with a thousand attendants, who delivered this message in the king's name:—"It is my wish to see you;

---

* This was the only convocation ever held by Budha; 1250 rahats were present.

† This stanza is thus translated by Csoma Körösi:—

> "No vice is to be committed:
> Every virtue must be perfectly practised:
> The mind must be brought under entire subjection;
> This is the commandment of Budha."

‡ About twenty examples are given; but it is stated that they were thus born many thousands of kótis of times.

therefore come to me; others have the benefit of the dharmma; but not your father or your other relatives; it is now seven years since we saw you." The noble arrived at the wihára at the time that Budha was saying bana, and with his attendants he went to the outer circle to listen; but they all became rahats, and remained at the wihára, without delivering their message. As they did not return, the king again sent a similar embassage, and after that seven more, but the consequence was the same; they all became rahats. The king thought that as none of them returned they had no affection for him, so he looked round for another messenger, one who would be more obedient to his commands; and when he saw the noble Kaludá, who is also called Udáyi, a man trustworthy, born on the same day as Budha, and who had been his playfellow from his infancy, he called him, and said:—"Nine times I have sent nine nobles, accompanied by 9000 attendants; but none of all these have returned; I wish to see my son before my death, as I cannot see him after; go to him, and request him to come and see me." The noble said that he would send him an account of his son, if he would allow him to embrace the priesthood; and the king gave him permission to do anything he liked, if he only succeeded in prevailing upon his son to visit him. This noble also, on his arrival at Rajagaha, heard bana, and became a rahat. Seven or eight days afterwards, the season of spring, wasanta, commenced; the ground was covered with grass, and the trees of the forest with flowers, Kaludá thought that this would be a favourable time in which for him to intercede with Budha to visit his royal parent. He therefore went to him, and began to extol the beauties of the road between Rajagaha and Kapilawastu. Budha asked him why he did this, and he replied, "Your father looks out for your coming as the lily looks out for the rising of the sun; and the queen as the night-blowing lily looks out for the rays of the moon." Gótama saw that the time had now arrived at which the former Budhas went to the place of their birth; and after giving, in sixty stanzas, an account of his lineage and of his native city, he informed Kaludá that he would set out the next morning. When Budha commenced his journey, he was attended by 10,000 priests of Anga and Magadha, and by 10,000 priests of Kapilawastu. Each day he proceeded sixteen miles, and as it was sixty yojanas' distance between Rajagaha and Kapilawastu, he accomplished the whole in two months, which were the months of Durutu and Medin-dina (February—March—April). Kaludá, now become a rahat, went through the air to Kapilawastu to inform the king of the approach of his son. Sudhódana was greatly pleased when he saw the priest, and ordered that food of the choicest kind should be given to him. When the priest received it, he put it in his bowl, and rose up as if to go; and when the king wished to detain him, he said that he must return to Budha. The king enquired where Budha was, and he replied, "He is on his way to see you, with 20,000 priests." On receiving this intelligence the joy of Sudhódana became still greater, and he requested that the priest would eat the food he had received, as food of a still better kind would be given for Budha; and when Kaludá had finished his repast, the king washed his bowl with fragrant water, and again filled it. He also told the priest that during the rest of the journey he must come daily to the palace for a supply of food; which he promised to do. Kaludá then, in the presence of all, rose up into the air and passing through it to Budha, presented the food: and the sage received it. This he did every day; and it was in this way that Budha received the food he ate during the rest of his journey.

The king prepared the garden called Nigródha for the reception of Budha. It was formed by one of the Sákya princes of the same name. In the procession appointed by the king to receive Budha, on his approach to the city, there were first 500 boys and girls, about sixteen years of age, the children of nobles; then 500 princes and princesses about twelve years of age; and afterwards the king, with 160,000 attendants, carrying perfumes and flowers. On arriving at the garden, Budha sat upon a throne, surrounded by the 20,000 priests. The seniors among the Sákya princes said, "Sidhártta is younger than we are; he is our nephew; we are his uncles and grandfathers." They therefore told the younger princes to worship him, whilst they sat down at a little distance. Budha knew their thoughts, and said, "My relatives are unwilling to worship me; but I will overcome their reluctance." Accordingly, he rose up from the throne, ascended into the air, and in their presence sent forth the six-coloured rays, and caused a stream of fire to proceed from his shoulders, ears, nostrils, eyes, hands, and feet, from the 99 joints and the 99,000 pores of his body; and this was followed by the issuing forth of a stream of water from the same places. At the time that the fire appeared, he exercised the téjo-kasina-samápatti; when the water appeared, he exercised the ápo-kasina-samápatti; when the blue rays appeared, he exercised the nílakasina-samápatti; and in the same way with the rest of the colours. The water was carried to the whole of the 10,000 sakwalas, so that there was not in any place so much as a hand-breadth that was not sprinkled; but it came only to those who wished to receive it, whilst it avoided the rest. The stream of fire, which was equally extended, did not in any place burn so much as a cobweb. Then Budha caused an image like himself to appear in the air; the two Budhas sometimes walked and sometimes sat; they paid each other the politest attention, and asked each other questions; their voice, size, and appearance were exactly the same. These things having been observed by Seriyut from Rajagaha, he came through the air with 500 disciples, to the same place. When the princes saw him at a distance, they said, "See! another Budha is coming; we shall now have three;" and when they saw the disciples, they said that there was not merely another coming, but five hundred. After Seriyut had worshipped Budha, he related the Budha-wansa, in a thousand stanzas; after which he requested Budha to relate the history of Maitrí Budha, which he did, by delivering the discourse called Anágata-wansa. At its conclusion, Budha descended from the sky to the throne he had previously occupied. Sudhódana then said to him, "My lord, my Budha, my prince Sidhártta, though I am thy father, as thou wert born of my house, yet will I not hereafter call thee my child; I am not worthy to be thy slave; I have already worshipped thee twice, and will now worship thee again; were I to offer thee my kingdom, thou wouldest account it but as ashes." The princes followed the example of the king, when he made obeisance to his son; like the bending of a forest of bamboos when agitated by the wind; the doubts of all were removed, as the clouds are scattered by the breeze. Budha informed them that this was not the only time in which their opposition had been overcome, and related to them the Wessantara-játaka. At this time Budha had received 420,001 offerings from the déwas and brahmas, the Sákya princes, Sekra, and the rahats.

The next day all the members of the royal family being beside themselves from joy, no one remembered that food was to be provided for Budha. In the morning he cleaned his teeth and washed his face, after which he went to a retired place, and performed the exercise of dhyána. At the time at which it was proper to set out to receive alms, he took his bowl and set out from the Nigródha garden, surrounded by the 20,000 priests. On looking to see how former Budhas had acted, he saw that they went from house to house, without omitting any. On this journey, wherever he put his foot down, a lotus previously arose from the ground, so that every step he made was upon flowers; but as he passed on, the lotus instantly vanished. The high places in the road became depressed, and the low places were elevated, so that the whole path became as level as the top of a drum. A wind came and removed all obstructions, freeing the road from all impurities; and a gentle rain fell to lay the dust. Rays proceeded from his body; they first came from his right side, went round him three times, and then extended on his right side 80 cubits; from his left side there was a similar appearance, as well as from behind. Rays also proceeded from his mouth to the same distance, as if to purify the path; and from his head, extending upward, as if to invite the presence of the déwas and brahmas. On approaching the city, the rays preceded him, went round it three times, and lighted up its gates, walls, monuments, and towers,* as if there had been poured upon them a stream of liquid gold. The whole city was full of light. In consequence of these wonders, all the citizens went forth to meet him. As the rays of the moon fall upon all places alike, whether they be clean and impure, so Gótama, like the former Budhas, manifested his affection equally to all, by going to all the houses in regular order, without omitting any. As the people were not accustomed to this mode of procuring alms, there was no one to carry his bowl or present him with food; all looked on in surprise. When he approached the palace, ladies who had never previously descended from the upper story, now came down and opened the windows, that they might look

* The word here used is attáli; there is a similar word in Spanish and Portuguese, atalaia or attalia, meaning a watch-tower.

at him. No sooner was Yasódhará-déwí apprised of what was done, than she exclaimed, "The prince Sidhártta is now going from house to house to receive alms, in the city where he was accustomed to ride in the chariot, with the sixty-four ornaments upon his person, and attended by a thousand nobles; his head is shorn; his robe is like a red clout; he holds in his hand an earthen bowl. This is what I have heard. I must go and see whether this guise befits him or not." As she stood near one of the entrances to the palace, she saw the rays proceeding from the person of Budha, and worshipped him; after which she said, "Sidhártta, on the night in which Ráhula was born, you went away secretly; at that time you rejected the kingdom of which you were heir, but you have received in its stead a more glorious kingdom." She then went and informed his father, Sudhódana, that the prince was begging from house to house; and in eight stanzas described the beauty of his appearance. The king went to him in haste, without staying even to adjust his garments, and said, "Why do you disgrace me thus? If you had even been accompanied by all the kings of Jambudwípa and their attendants, could I not have supplied the whole with food? How much easier, then, is it for me to supply you and your 20,000 priests?" Budha replied, "It is the custom of my race." But the king said, "How can this be? You are lineally descended from Maha Sammata; none of your race ever acted in this manner. Some of your ancestors could stamp with the foot, and they received whatever they wished." Budha then informed his father that he spoke not of the race of Sammata, but of the race of the Budhas; and said that when any one found a hidden treasure, it was his duty to make an offering of the most precious of the jewels to his father in the first instance; he therefore opened the mine of the dharmma, and delivered to him a discourse. "Do not procrastinate; listen to the excellent dharmma; he who thus listens, will attain prosperity." The king, whilst listening to this discourse, entered the first path. Budha then repeated another stanza: "Practise that which is enjoined in the dharmma; avoid that which is forbidden in the dharmma; he who listens to the dharmma will attain prosperity." On hearing this, the king entered into the second path. After thus hearing bana in the open street, Sudhódana carried the alms-bowl of Budha, and gave food to him and his attendant priests. When the repast was finished, the 40,000 ladies of the palace came and worshipped him.

The king then sent to inform Yásódhará-déwí that she also might come and worship Sidhártta; but she replied, "Surely, if I am deserving of any regard, he will come and see me; I can then worship him." Budha, however, went to her apartments. As they were going, he informed Seriyut and Mugalan that the princess had been an assistance to him in former births, and would now be released from the evils of existence. "I am free from evil desire," said he, "though the princess is not so; from not having seen me for so long a time, she is exceedingly sorrowful; unless this sorrow be allowed its course, her breast will cleave; she will take hold of my feet, but as the result will be that she and the other queens will embrace the priesthood, you must not prevent her." When Yasódhará-déwí heard that Budha was about to visit her, with 500 of her attendant ladies she cut off her hair, and put on mean garments, and then went to meet her lord. From the abundance of her affection, she was like an overflowing vessel, unable to contain herself; and forgetting that she was a mere woman, and that Budha was the lord of the world, she held him by the feet, and wept. But remembering that Sudhódana was present, she felt ashamed, and rose up; after which, she reverently remained at a little distance. It is not permitted even to Maha Brahma to touch the body of Budha. The king apologised for the princess, and said, "This arises from her affection; nor is it merely a momentary display; in the seven years that you were absent from her, when she heard that you had shaved your head, she did the same; when she heard that you had put on mean garments, she put on the same; when she heard that you had left off the use of perfumes and ornaments, she left off the same; like you, she has only eaten at appointed times, and from an earthen bowl; and like you she has renounced high seats, with splendid coverings; when other princes asked her in marriage, she refused their offers, and said that she was still yours; therefore grant unto her forgiveness." Then Budha related in what manner, when in a former age she saw the glory of the princess who was the wife of Paduma previous to his reception of the Budhaship, she had formed the wish to become the wife of a future Budha; and in what manner she had so assisted him during four asankya-kap-lakshas, as now to be the wife of Gótama Budha.* By this relation the sorrow of the princess, and the fears of the king, were overcome.

12. *Nanda and Ráhula become the Disciples of Budha.*

The next day Budha went from the Nigródha garden to a festival that was held in honour of Nanda, the son of Maha Prajápati, who was the sister of Maha Máya-déwi, and wife of Sudhódana. It was a three-fold festival, as on this day he was to be elevated to a new office, to enter upon a new residence, and to be married. Budha went with his rahats to the festival hall, that he might release Nanda from the sorrows of existence. When seated upon the throne that had been prepared for him, he repeated the following stanza :—"The destruction of evil desire; the keeping of the brahma-chariya, (or the continuing in continence); the knowing of the four great truths; and the comprehending of nirwána; these constitute the greatest festival." Having in this manner made him willing to follow the advice he received, he put the alms-bowl in his hand, which he took, though at that time he was arrayed in the richest ornaments. Budha then arose from the throne, and went to the wihára, followed by Nanda. The betrothed princess, Janapadakalyáni, called out to him from the window, to enquire why he went, but he gave her no reply. On arriving at the wihára, Budha said to Nanda, "Regard not the honors of the chakrawartti; become a priest like me." The thoughts of the prince still wandered after his betrothed wife, but as he said nothing against this advice, Budha directed Seriyut and Mugalan to admit him to the priesthood. Still, his mind was fixed upon the same object, and he became sorrowful. The other priests saw that he pined away, and asked him the cause of his sorrow; they wondered why he appeared so disconsolate, as he was the younger brother of Budha, a member of the royal family, and in every respect most fortunate. He then told them, that when he took the bowl from the hand of Budha, Janapadakalyáni looked after him, and told him, to return without delay, and that it was the princess who was the cause of his sorrow. This being known to Gótama, he enquired whether she were beautiful; and

* This account appears in the Sankindurá Játaka; the various births of the princes, after the formation of the wish, were related by Budha at length.

Nanda described her person in the most glowing terms. The sage thought to destroy the fire of this passion by the water of nirwána, and asked him if there was no one more beautiful than Janapadakalyáni. "No;" was the reply, " not in all Jambudwípa." Budha then enquired if he wished to see one that was more beautiful, but he thought that this was not possible; so the sage took him by the hand, and by the power of irdhi conveyed him to the world of Sekra. As they were going, he caused the withered body of an old female ape, burnt in the preparing of some forest-land for cultivation, to appear, and asked the priest if he saw it; who said that he did. On arriving at the déwa-lóka, he commanded 500 of the principal déwís of Sekra to come into his presence; and then enquired whether they or the princess were the most beautiful. Nanda replied, that in comparison to them his betrothed was like the burnt ape. When Budha again asked whether he would like to possess one of those beautiful déwís, he demanded in what way this could be brought about; and being informed that he might secure one by being obedient to the precepts, he set himself to their strict observance. By this means he was induced to keep the precepts, and in a little time became a rahat.

On the seventh day after the arrival of Budha at Kapilawastu, Yasódhará-dewí arrayed Ráhula, now seven years old, in all the splendor of a prince, and said to him, "This priest, whose appearance is so glorious, so that he looks like Maha Brahma, is your father; he possesses four great mines of wealth; since he went away, I have not seen them; go to him, and entreat him to put you in possession of these mines, and of the seven treasures of the chakrawartti; the son ought to inherit the property of his father." Ráhula replied, " I know of no father but the king, Sudhódana; who is my father?" The princess took him in her arms, and from the window pointed to Budha, who was at that time at the palace, partaking of food, and said that the priest he saw there was his father. Ráhula then went to Budha, and looking up in his face, said without fear, and with much affection, " My father;" and he further said, " Priest, your shadow is a place of privilege." When Budha had finished his repast, and given his blessing, he went away from the palace, followed by Ráhula, who asked to be placed in possession of the property named by his mother. None of the people did anything to prevent him, nor did Budha himself. The princess saw from the window that the child followed his father, and began to be fearful lest he should admit him to the priesthood, as he had done Nanda; at the thought of this, she wept. Ráhula had great merit, from having been the obedient son of Budha, when Bódhisat, in many births; and when he learnt that he was to be admitted to the priesthood, he was greatly pleased, thinking that now he could receive the inheritance. Budha then said to Seriyut, "My son asks his inheritance; I am not willing to give him that, which is connected with the sorrows of existence; I had rather give him the inheritance of the priesthood; the benefit arising from this does not perish." At the command of Budha, he was then admitted by Seriyut. When the king heard of what had been done, he was excessively grieved, and went to Budha to complain that he had in the same way lost his own two sons, Sidhártta and Nanda, and now his grandson was taken from him, who had ever been regarded by him as a son since the father became an ascetic; and he obtained a promise from Budha that henceforth he would ordain no one without the consent of his parents. The king also reminded him that he had not believed the report brought to him by the déwí that he was dead, immediately previous to his reception of the Budhaship. In return, Budha repeated the Dharmmapála Játaka, and informed him that in a former birth he was not willing to acknowledge his death, even when shewn one of his bones. By this discourse the king's sorrow was allayed, and he was enabled to enter the third path. Some time afterwards he became a rahat; and when on his royal couch, he attained nirwána.

13. *Budha visits the Island of Ceylon.*

In the ninth month after Gótama had received the Budhaship, he visited Ceylon. On the bank of the Mahawáluká river,* near which place he arrived, there was a garden called Mahanága (in Bintenne),† three yojanas in length and two in breadth. At

* This river, now commonly called Mahaweli, is the largest in Ceylon. Its source is near Nuwaréliya, and its main branch falls in the bay of Trincomalee. Near Kandy it is spanned by a bridge of one arch, the timbers of which are of sandal wood, 205 feet in span. In 1832 it was explored by R. Brooke, Esq., under the direction of the colonial government, who published an interesting account of the survey.

† This place is now called Myungana. According to Forbes, it is still a place of pilgrimage.

this time the garden was the seat of a great commotion, as two armies of yakás were fighting in it, with each other. Gótama approached them over the air, and made a louder noise than they did, which put them in fear. He then caused a great darkness, by means of a rain-cloud; and when he afterwards dispersed the darkness, he appeared to them in the sky, and put them to still greater terror by sending forth a volume of smoke from his body. After this he assumed the appearance of a moon. When the yakás had seen these wonders, they gave him, at his own request, permission to alight, and to occupy as much space as could be covered by a carpet of skin; but when he had descended to the ground, he caused pillars of fire to arise at each of the four corners of the carpet; and the fire extended itself on all sides, driving the yakás before it, until they had no place in which to remain but the sea-shore. The rock, or island, Giri, then approached, and the yakás took refuge upon it, after which it returned to its original position. In a moment, all the déwas of the air, the rocks, and the trees, and of Samastakúta, assembled in his presence, and made to him an offering of flowers.

To this assembly Gótama delivered a discourse, by means of which numberless déwas entered the path sowán; and before his departure he gave to Súmana, the principal déwa of Samastakúta, a lock of his hair as a relic, that it might become an object of worship. After going three times round the whole island in a moment, he returned to Uruwela.

The déwa Sumana made a dágoba of emeralds for the lock of hair he had received, seven cubits high, at the place where Budha first alighted. After the dissolution of Gótama, Sarabhu, a disciple of Seriyut, brought hither the thorax bone of the sage, and deposited it in the same place, which he covered with another dágoba, twelve cubits high. This was again covered by Chúlabhaya, brother of Déwánanpiyatissa, with a dágoba of brick, thirty cubits high; and lastly, Duttagamini encased the whole with another dágoba, which, with the golden tower at its summit, was eighty cubits high.

The second journey of Gótama to Ceylon was on this wise. In the fifth year after he became Budha, there was a dispute, in Nágadwípa,* between the two nága kings, Chulódana and

* This must have been an island connected with Ceylon, probably at its

Mahódana, relative to a throne of gems; and as war had been declared, two vast armies of nágas were assembled, in which there were thirty kelas of nágas from the rock Wedunna,* twenty kelas from Kælani,† or Kalyána, and thirty kelas from the nága island Mani; being in all eighty kelas, some from the waters and others from the rocks. They were armed with swords, spears, darts, shields, bows, crowbars, maces, clubs, and other weapons. The clash of these arms was like the stroke of the lightning; and the tumultuous commotion that was produced was like the waves of the sea. This account appears at length in the work called Samantakúta-warnnanáwa.

All this having been perceived by Budha, he left the Jétáwana wihára early in the morning, out of compassion to the nágas; and the déwa Samidhi-sumana, taking up a kiripalu tree that grew near the door, held it over his head as a screen or canopy, whilst he passed through the air. On arriving at the place of combat, Budha remained in the air, within sight of the warriors; and when he had attracted their attention, he first caused a thick darkness to appear, and then a dazzling light, like that of the sun. The sage also delivered unto them a discourse, by which he induced them to be reconciled to each other. The combatants then threw down the weapons that they held in their hands, and brought various kinds of offerings, which each yaká,‡ attended by a female demon, presented to Budha. They then requested him to alight, which he did, and sat upon the throne of gems. After he had partaken of some divine food that they brought him, he gave to them the three-fold formulary of protection, and delivered another discourse for their benefit. For the increase of their merit, he appointed as objects of worship the throne upon which he sat, and the tree that had been brought through the air by the déwa. In the name of the whole assembly of the yakás, these relics were received, and the three kings, Chulódana, Mahódana, and Mani, united together to secure their

northern extremity. The seaport Jambukóla was in it, supposed to be Colombogam, in the district of Jaffna. At this place a dágoba was erected, and Mallaka Nága built a wihára, A.D. 674.

* This rock is said to be in the Seven Korles.

† This is the second river in Ceylon, in point of magnitude, but its whole course is said not to exceed sixty miles. It rises in Adam's Peak, and falls into the sea a little to the north of Colombo, near which place it is crossed by a bridge of boats.

‡ They are first called nágas, and afterwards yakás.

preservation, that they might long continue to be a benefit and protection to Lanká.

The third journey of Gótama to Ceylon was made in the eighth year after he had received the Budhaship. At the request of the priest Sunáparantaka, he entered the golden palanquins presented by the guardian déwas, along with 500 rahats, and went to the hall built by some merchants, called Chandanamandala, in the forest of Mulu, in the region called Sunáparantaka, where he preached to those who were present, remaining there several days. After this, at the request of Punna, he went to the town of Suppáraka, where many merchants were congregated; and to them also he delivered a discourse. From this place, on his way to Sewet, he went to the Nirmmadá river,* at the request of the nága king of the same name; and at this place he partook of food presented by the nágas, to whom he preached, and gave the benefit of the three-fold protective formulary. In compliance with the earnest entreaty of the nága king, he left an imprint of his foot on the bank of the river, in the midst of a sandy desert, on a spot that is occasionally covered by the waves. This impression may still be seen in the Yon country, at a place where the waves strike upon a sand-hill, and they again retire. It is only on the retiring of the waves that the mark of the foot can be seen. From the river, Gótama went to the rock Sachabadha, upon the summit of which, at the request of a priest of the same name, he made an impression of his foot in clay.

From the rock Sachabadha, Budha came to Ceylon. The first place he visited was the residence of the nágas in the river Kalyána,† the water of which previously falls upon the mountain

---

* The geological features of the Nirmmadá, the present Nerbudda, and the Namadus of Ptolemy, appear to be more than usually interesting, from the various notices that are given of them in the Journal of the Bengal Asiatic Society. There are several remarkable waterfalls in the course of the stream, each of which has its peculiar tradition, but I have not been able to identify the spot that is said to have been visited by Budha. Ptolemy mentions a town called Siripala, on the Nerbudda, where it is joined by the Mophis or Mybes. This ought probably to be Srípáda, or "the illustrious foot," the name by which these impressions are still known. The present name of the river may have risen from some legend connected with Budha. The hill Téri Kothi, near Bhawun, of which a sketch is given in the third volume of the Journal, plate 23, is 150 feet high; both its name and appearance would indicate that it is of Budhistical origin.

† "The village of Kellania, or Kalyána, situated five miles from Colombo, possesses considerable attractions to those interested in the ancient history of

Sanantakúta, as if to clear it from all impurities. It is therefore called Kalyána, pleasing, or that which brings prosperity. The dágoba of Kalyána was subsequently erected upon the spot where Gótama sat at the residence of the nágas. After partaking of food, and delivering a discourse, he left an impression of his foot in the bed of the river, that it might be worshipped, and be an assistance to the nágas. The déwa of Samantakúta,*

Ceylon. It was probably the capital, as it has been the chief place for the worship, of Weebeesana, son of Pulastyia, friend of Ráma, the traitorous brother and deified successor of Ráwana. The following romantic events are to be found in Singhalese history. The beautiful queen of Kellania Tissa having been seduced by his brother, and their intercourse detected, he fled to Gampala, and from thence sent an emissary disguised as a priest; this person was instructed to mix in the crowd of those who went daily with the high priest to receive their alms, at which time he might find an opportunity of delivering a letter to the queen, who always assisted at this ceremony. The letter was full of the misery of the writer, and stated that his affection was undiminished; but neither the place from whence the letter came, nor the name of the writer, was mentioned. The disguised messenger dropped the letter, and the king hearing it fall, seized and read it. The writing convinced him that it was from the high priest, who was ordered to be thrown into a cauldron of boiling oil; the queen was bound and cast into the river; and the messenger cut in pieces. It afterwards appeared that the king's brother, having been a pupil of the high priest, had acquired the art of exactly imitating his writing. Not long after these events, the sea began to encroach rapidly upon the west and south coasts of Ceylon. The king believing that it was a judgment against him for the cruel and unjust death of the priest, determined to sacrifice his virgin daughter, as an offering to the god who controlled the waters. Having secured her in a covered canoe, on which was inscribed her fate and its cause, the canoe was launched into the ocean. The flood still increasing, the king mounted his elephant and proceeded to view the destructive effects of the raging waters. Whilst thus employed, the earth opened, and the king disappeared amidst flames which burst from the sinking wreck of his richest provinces. Before the waves ceased to encroach on the land, 640 villages (470 of which were principally inhabited by divers for pearls) had been overwhelmed, and the distance between Kellania and the sea coast had been reduced from twenty-five to four miles. The canoe in which the young princess was confined, having been driven towards the south-west of the island, was discovered and brought to land by some fishermen. This was in the Mágam-pattoo, at that time a separate kingdom, under Káwantissa, who hearing of the canoe and its mysterious appearance, went to examine it. On perceiving the inscription, he released the princess, whom he named Wiháré Déwi and afterwards married. Wiháré Déwi became the mother of Dutugemunu, a prince who restored the Singhalese power, and expelled the Malabars, to whom Kellania Tissa and Káwantissa had been tributaries. Many Budhists believe that in some future transmigration Wiháré Déwi will be the mother of Maitrí, the expected Budha."—Forbes, Ceylon Almanac, 1834.

* This mountain is called Sélésumano, Samastakúta, and Samanela. It is 7120 feet above the level of the sea, and was long considered as the highest mountain in the island; but it has been discovered, since the English came into possession of the interior, that there are at least three others that are higher, Pidurutalagala having an elevation of 8280 feet. It will, however, always be the most remarkable, from the many legends connected with it,

Samana, having heard of the arrival of Budha, went to the place where he was; and after he had worshipped him, he presented a request that he would leave an impression of his foot upon the mountain of which he was the guardian, that it might be worshipped during the five thousand years his religion would continue among men. To induce the sage to comply with his request, the déwa repeated before him at length the praises of the mountain he was invited to visit. The flowers that grew upon its sides and summit, he compared to a magnificent garment and head-dress; the hum of the bees, as they sped through the air laden with honey, was like the music of lutes: the birds upon the trees were like so many bells sending forth sweet sounds; doves and other birds uttered their peculiar notes; the branches of the trees, when agitated by the wind, appeared to dance, as at the command of the master of the revels; all seemed to acknowledge the supremacy of Budha; the trees presented offerings of flowers; in the pools of water were many reptiles; fishes sported in the streams; in the branches of the trees were birds of many kinds; in the shade, with their young, were elephants, tigers, bears, deer, monkeys, hares, and other animals; there were trees that struck their branches together, so as to produce fire; and there were others that appeared, from the mass of flowers by which they were covered, like a cloud from which the lightning flashed or around which it played. When the déwa had in this manner declared the greatness and the excellencies of the mountain, Budha went to it through the air, attended by the 500 rahats. At the right hand of the sage was Samana, in beautiful garments and rich ornaments, attended by all his inferior déwas, with their queens, who made music and carried flags and banners, and scattered around gold and gems. Sekra, Maha-Brahma, and Iswara, were all there with their attendant retinues; and like the rolling of the great ocean upon Maha Méru or the Yugandhara rocks, was their arrival at the mountain. The sun remained in the midst of the sky, but his rays were cold as those of the moon; there was a slight falling of rain, like the water that is sprinkled around a throne to allay

and the conspicuousness of its appearance, especially from the sea; it is an insulated cone, rising boldly into the sky, and generally cloud-capped. It is supposed by the Chinese (Davis's Chinese) that at its base is a temple, in which the real body of Budha reposes on its side, and that near it are his teeth and other relics.

218   A MANUAL OF BUDHISM.

the dust; and the breeze, charged with sweet perfume, came from all sides to refresh the illustrious visitant. At his approach, all the trees of the mountain were as though they danced in gladness at the anointing of a king. In the midst of the assembled déwas, Budha, looking towards the east, made the impression of his foot,* in length three inches less than the cubit of the carpenter; and the impression remained as a seal to show that Lanká is the inheritance of Budha, and that his religion will here flourish.

Gótama remained during the day in a cave of the same mountain, called Bhagawá. From thence he went to Díghanáka, in Ruhuna; and afterwards to the following places in order:—the spot where the bó-tree was afterwards planted by Mahindo, at Anurádhapura; Thupáráma, Lówámahapáya, and Lahabat-geya, which are also in Anurádhapura; the tank Danthádara; Ruwanpaya; and the summit of Mihintalá. From this mountain he returned to Jambudwípa, having visited in all fourteen different places in Lanká. (*Sadharmmaratnakáré.*)†

14. *Budha foretells the Prosperity of a Labourer's Wife.*

In the reign of Bimsara, there was in Rajagaha a couple extremely poor. The man's name was Kálawali, and he was a

* There is an indentation upon the summit of Adam's peak, commonly called the srí-páda, or illustrious footstep, which is annually visited by many pilgrims of different religious persuasions. The Hindus regard it as the footstep of Siva, and the Moors as that of Adam, whilst the Budhists affirm that it is the identical impression made by Budha when he visited the déwa Samana. It is said by Dr. Davy to be "a superficial hollow five feet three inches and three-quarters long, and between two feet seven inches and two feet five inches wide." The fakirs of the Mahomedan religion take impressions of the footstep on a piece of white cloth that has been previously covered with pulverized sander. The Mahomedan author, Masudi, A.D. 943, makes mention of mount Rahwan, on which Adam descended when expelled from Paradise, adding that a race of Hindus, in the island of Ceylon, descended from Adam, derived their origin from the children of Cain, and that the analogy between the traditions of the Arabs and Budhists may probably be traced to that period of early history when both people were Samaneans; maintaining, according to the authority of the Mefatih-el-olum, that the world had no beginning, that souls transmigrated from one body to another, and that the earth is constantly declining.—Bird's Anniversary Discourse, Journ. Bombay As. Soc. No. 5. It is probable that Rája Singha, A.D. 1581, would destroy the srí-páda then in existence, along with the other objects of Budhistical veneration that fell beneath his hand. Both Fa Hian and Hiuan Thsang met with srí-pádas in different parts of India.

† The whole of the three visits of Gótama to Ceylon are inserted together, as it is in this form they appear in the native authorities, though the two last are not in the proper order of time, as some of the legends subsequently inserted must have taken place at a previous period.

labourer. One day he went to seek work, but did not succeed, and all the food they had was a little pottage made of herbs. In the morning, Maha Kásyapa looked abroad to see whom he should benefit, and resolved on conferring a favour upon the labourer. When he came with his alms-bowl to the door, the wife reflected that they had nothing better to give the priest, so she presented to him the pottage, which he took to the wihára and gave some to Budha. The priest asked Gótama what would be the reward of the woman; and he said that in seven days she would be ennobled.

On the seventh day after, the king on passing a burial ground near the city, saw a man impaled, who cried out to him, requesting a supply of food from the royal table. The king, out of compassion, promised that he should have it. At night, when the king was at supper, he remembered the promise he had made, and told his nobles to call some one to take the food; but they could find no one who was willing to go. A second time they attempted, but did not succeed. On the third trial, the labourer's wife said she would go. The king asked her, if she, a woman, was not afraid to undertake the task; but she said she was not, if the five weapons were given her, and she was attired as a man. The king commanded that this should be done, and she took the food. In passing a tree on the way, a yaká who resided in it called out to her to stop if she had brought him food; but she said she was the king's messenger, and the food was for another. The demon then asked her if she could take a message for him also; and as she agreed, he told her to call out aloud at a certain tal-tree she would have to pass, that Káli, the wife of Díghatapla, daughter of the déwa Sumana, had been delivered of a son. On passing the tree that had been pointed out, she cried out aloud as she had been told; and the déwa Sumana having heard what she said, out of joy at the intelligence, commanded that as a reward she should be told of a treasure there was at the foot of the tree. When she had received this intelligence, she went forward to the place of execution, and informed the malefactor that she had brought him food from the king's table. On hearing this, as hunger was more powerful than the pain of impalement, the man ate the food with eagerness; and when he had finished, asked her to wipe his mouth. Whilst she was in the act of doing so, he seized her hair with his teeth; and as she could not otherwise release herself, she cut off the lock with the sword she had brought, and left it in his teeth. On returning to the king she informed him that she had executed his command; but he said that he must have some proof; on which she told him that a lock of her hair would be found between the malefactor's teeth, and further informed him respecting the treasure. Next day the king found out by her token that what she said was true, and also sent men, who dug up the treasure, and brought it to the palace. On seeing it he said that the woman must be possessed of great merit to have met with such good fortune; and he therefore, in the presence of the citizens, ennobled her, by which she was rewarded for her gift to the priest, and the words of Gótama were accomplished. (*Sadharmmaratnakáré.*)

15. *Budha attends a Ploughing Festival.*

When Budha resided at the wihára called Dakshinágiri, belonging to the village of Eknálaka, near Rajagaha, a ploughing festival was held by the brahman Kasíbháradwája.[*] There were a thousand oxen, the hoofs of which were cased with silver, and their necks were adorned with sweet-scented flowers; five hundred ploughs and goads tipped with gold;

[*] It is well known that in China and some other countries of Western Asia, ploughing festivals are still held. The following narrative is taken from Crawford's Embassy to Siam. "April 27, 1822.—This was a day of some celebrity in the Siamese Calendar, being that on which the kings of Siam, in former times, were wont to hold the plough, like the emperors of China, either as a religious ceremony, or as an example of agricultural industry to their subjects. This rite has long fallen into disuse, and given place to one which, to say the least of it, is of less dignity. The ceremony took place about two miles from Bangkok, and I am sorry to say we were not apprised of it in time to be present. A Siamese, however, who had often witnessed it, gave me the following description: A person is chosen for this occasion, to represent the king. This monarch of a day is known by the name of the King of the Husbandmen. He stands in the midst of a rice-field, on one foot only, it being incumbent on him to continue in this uneasy attitude during the time that a common peasant takes in ploughing once round him in a circle. Dropping the other foot, until the circle is completed, is looked upon as a most unlucky omen; and the penalty to the King of the Husbandmen is not only the loss of his ephemeral dignity, but also of his permanent rank, whatever that may be, with what is more serious, the confiscation of his property. The nominal authority of this person lasts from morning to evening. During the whole of this day the shops are shut; nothing is allowed to be bought or sold, and whatever is disposed of in contravention of this interdict is forfeited, and becomes the perquisite of the King of the Husbandmen."

five hundred ploughmen in gay attire; and many thousands of spectators. The wife of the brahman prepared a hundred thousand vessels of food, which were placed upon a wagon; and accompanied by a retinue of maidens, beautiful as déwís, she went to the field. The brahman took a vermilion wand in his hand, and directed that to this person rice should be given, and to that ghee, and to another some sweetmeat, whilst his wife dealt out the rice with a golden spoon. On the same day, early in the morning, Budha looked round the world with his divine eyes to see whom he should assist, when he perceived that the brahman who would hold a ploughing festival had the merit necessary to enable him to become a rahat. He therefore went to the field, and remained in an elevated place, whence he could be seen by the brahman. The rays from his person spread to every part of the field, causing all that was within it to appear of the colour of gold. This attracted the attention of the people, who having finished their repast, collected around Budha, and did him reverence. But the brahman was displeased when he saw what was going on, and said, "See now, this great mendicant has come to spoil our sport." When he had seen his person, he said again, "Were he to work like us who are husbandmen, he might become the king of all Jambudwípa; but now he does nothing, spending his time in idleness, and coming to ploughing festivals and such like places, that he may beg something to eat;" and then addressing himself to Budha, he said "Sramana, I plough and sow, and from my ploughing and sowing I receive grain, and enjoy the produce; priest, it would be better if you were in like manner to plough and to sow, and then you would have food to eat." Budha knew when the time had come in which it would be proper for him to speak, and replied, "Brahman, I do plough and sow; and from my ploughing and sowing I reap immortal fruit." On hearing this, the brahman thought thus, "The sramana says that he ploughs and sows; but he has neither plough nor any other implement; he must have spoken falsely." Yet on looking at the beauties of his person, he thought it impossible that he could tell an untruth; and he therefore said, "Bhagawat Gótama, I see no plough; no goad; no oxen; if you perform the work of the husbandman, where are your implements?" In reply to this question, Budha informed him that his field was the dharmma;

the weeds that he plucked up, the cleaving to existence; the plough that he used, wisdom; the seed that he sowed, purity; the work that he performed, attention to the precepts; the harvest that he reaped, nirwána; and when he had explained these matters at greater length, he exhorted the brahman to sow in the same field, unfolding before him the benefits of nirwána. The brahman, after hearing this discourse, brought forth the most excellent food, and with a joyful mind reverently presented it to Budha; but the sage informed him that he could not receive it, as it was not the custom of the Budhas to receive offerings after they had been setting forth the excellencies of the dharmma, and proclaiming its advantages, or they would be like musicians and dancers, who make a collection after they have amused the people. The brahman was therefore in doubt, as he thought that it would not be proper to present to any one else the food that had been offered to Budha. The sage perceived his thoughts, and told him that as the déwas had imparted to it the flavor they were accustomed to give to all food received by the Budhas, he might take it and place it upon the top of a rock where there was no grass, or throw it into water that was free from worms. Kasibháradwaja, accordingly, threw it into pure water, where it continued warm a whole day; first making a noise, as if it said "chiti, chita," like liquid boiling, and then sending forth smoke. The brahman took notice of this wonderful occurrence; then went to Budha, embraced the priesthood, and afterwards became a rahat. (*Milinda Prasna.*)

16. *The History of Anépidu.*

There resided in Rajagaha a rich merchant, who was intimate with Anépidu, a merchant of Sewet.* The two friends were accustomed to visit each other, with 500 wagons of merchandize, for the purpose of traffic. When they drew near to each other's city, it was the practice for one to go and meet the other at a distance of sixteen miles. One day Anépidu approached Rajagaha, but there was no friend to meet him; he came to the city,

* This city, which is also called Sáwathi and Sráwasti, was the metropolis of Kósala. It is termed by Fa Hian, She-wei; by Hiuan-tsang, She-lo-va-si-ti; and is placed by both nearly on the site of Fyzabad, in Oude. When visited by Fa Hian, there were in it not more than 200 families or houses.

the street, the house, but saw no one to welcome him, as had been usual. When he entered the house, his friend was there; but his greeting was hurried and brief. At night, however, he came to him to inform him of the reason of his conduct; he expected Budha and his priests the next day to receive an alms-offering at his dwelling, and he had been too much engaged in making the necessary preparation to show him the accustomed courtesy. At the mention of the name of Budha, Anépidu instantly formed the resolution to see the sage, which arose from the merit he had received in former births. Nor was he willing to delay his visit to the sage for a single moment, until his friend told him that Budha would be at that hour in retirement, and could not be disturbed. The merchant of Sewet retired to rest, but in the first watch of the night there was a preternatural light in his chamber; as he supposed that it was day, he arose, and it was only by seeing the moon shining in the sky that he was convinced of his error. In the second watch he was deceived by a similar appearance. In the third watch there was the same light, and as he was now certain that it was day, he proceeded towards the residence of Budha. The doors of the house and the gates of the city opened to him of their own accord. When he had walked some distance, he came to a cemetery, and saw a human body which he knew was a corpse, as it was cold, putrid, and emitted a most offensive smell. At the sight of it he became afraid, when the light vanished, and it was intensely dark all around. But a déwa who resided in the cemetery spoke to him on the great merit of those who set their feet to the hearing of bana, by which he was encouraged, and the light returned. As he proceeded further, he reflected, "There are many now who say that they are Budha, and I may be deceived; there was a name given me, Sudatta, by my parents, which is known only to them and me; if Gótama tells me what it is, when I ask him to repeat it, I will believe in him; but if he cannot repeat it, I will seek Budha elsewhere." Early in the morning, Budha, who knew what was passing in his mind, went to meet him, and on seeing him, said, "Sudatta, come hither!" On hearing this word, the faith of Anépidu was established, and he promised to cleave unto the sage until the end of his life. Then Budha repeated to him two stanzas; "He who is free from evil desire attains the highest estate, and is always in prosperity. He who cuts off demerit, who subdues the mind, and attains a state of perfect equanimity, secures nirwána; this is his prosperity." Anépidu now entered the first path, and requested Budha to receive from him on the following day an alms-offering, attended by his priests.

Anépidu, on returning to the house of his friend, informed him of what he had done; who said that when he went to Sewet, his host was at all charges, and that he must allow the same to be done at Rajagaha; but Anépidu refused his assistance, as well as that of the king and of the chief of the villages, which were offered, and purchased vessels, ovens, and all the requisite utensils, at his own expence. When the repast was concluded, he invited Budha to Sewet, telling him that the king of that city reigned over the countries of Kási and Kosol, 300 yojanas in extent, and that his own wealth was immense. The road between Rajagaha and Sewet, a distance of 45 yojanas, was richly ornamented, and resting-places were erected at the end of every yojana, as Budha accepted the invitation. When Anépidu returned to Sewet, he examined carefully the suburbs of the city, that he might find a suitable place for the erection of the wihára, not too near nor too distant. At last he found a place of this description, belonging to the prince Jeta. But when he asked the prince to dispose of it, he replied that he would not let him have it, unless he were to cover it over with golden masurans.* "It is a bargain," replied Anépidu, "upon these conditions the garden is mine." When the prince saw that he was serious, he was unwilling to abide by what he had said; and as Anépidu would not give up his right, the matter was referred to a court of justice, and decided against the prince. Jeta then reflected, "My garden is a thousand cubits in length and breadth; no one has wealth enough to be able to cover it with gold; it is therefore yet mine, though the case is decided against me." The prince and Anépidu went together to the garden, and saw that all the useful trees were cut down, only such trees as sandal and mango being permitted to remain; and the whole place was made perfectly level. Then Anépidu called his treasurer, and commanded that his stores of wealth should

* This is sufficiently extravagant. It was thought a great price when Kandaules, king of Lydia, paid Bularchus, for a picture of the battle of Magnetes, as much gold coin as would cover it.

be entered, and as many masurans brought out as would be necessary. The treasurer accordingly emptied seven stores, and measured the golden masurans as if they had been grain. The masurans were measured to the extent of ninety yalas, and were then brought and thrown down in the garden; and a thousand men, each taking up a bundle of money, began to cover the garden. Anépidu commanded his servants to measure the space occupied by the standing trees, and give as many masurans as would have been required if they had not been there, that he might lose no part of the merit he hoped to gain. When he saw that the entrance was not covered, he commanded his treasurer to break open another of the stores, and bring a further supply, though he knew by the plates of copper on which his wealth was numbered, that the store preserved by his forefather in the seventh generation backward had been opened, and that the whole sum disposed of amounted to 18 kótis of masurans; but when Jeta saw that although Anépidu had already given so much, he was equally ready to give more, he reflected that it would be well for him also to partake in the merit, and declared that the sum he had received was sufficient. After this was concluded, Anépidu began the erection of the wihára; around it were houses for the priests; offices that were suitable for the day, and others for the night; an ambulatory; tanks; and gardens of fruit and flower trees; and around the whole, extending 4000 cubits, was a wall 18 cubits high. The whole of these erections cost 18 kótis of masurans. In addition, Anépidu had many friends who assisted him, some by their personal labour, and others by their wealth. Jeta also said, "What has a prince to do with money procured from a merchant?" so he expended the whole of the 18 kótis he had received in building a palace seven stories high, at each of the four sides of the garden.

When all was finished, Budha was invited to visit the place; and he set off by easy stages, sixteen miles each day, so that he was forty-five days in travelling from Rajagaha to Sewet. On his approach to the city, he was met by a splendid procession, composed of different companies with 500 persons in each, carrying appropriate vessels and emblems, of the most costly description. One company was headed by Anépidu's two daughters, Maha Subadra and Chula Subadra. Anépidu escorted Budha to the wihára, and then enquired from the sage unto whom it should be offered, who said "Let it be offered to the whole priesthood, whether present or absent." Then Anépidu poured water from a golden vessel upon the hands of Budha, in token that he dedicated the wihára to all priests whatsoever, from whichever of the four quarters they might come; after which Budha repeated a stanza:—"He who resides in this wihára will be protected from heat and cold; from wild beasts, mosquitoes, and nágas; he who dedicated this wihára, if there be to him another birth, will in that birth be protected from all these dangers." By listening to the bana, many became rahats. Budha resided in the wihára nine months, and in the daily alms which Anépidu presented, he expended 18 kótis; so that the whole of the gifts that he presented would amount to 54 kótis of masurans. In former ages, the same place was given to the Budhas by other rich merchants.

17. *The History of Wisákhá.*

There resided in Anga and Magadha, five merchants, called Meda, Jóti, Jatila, Kákawali, and Punnaka; the wealth that they possessed was immense. In the family of Meda were five persons possessed of great merit from actions done in former births; viz., the merchant, his daughter Chandrapadumá, his son Dhananja, his daughter-in-law Sumana, and his secretary Punnaka. When Wisákhá, daughter of Dhananja and Sumana, was about seven years of age, Budha visited the village of Bhaddi, in Anga. On his approach to the village, Meda directed Dhananja to send his daughter to meet him, with a retinue of 500 maidens of the same age in chariots. Though so young, Wisákhá received this command with great joy; but when near the sage, she thought it more respectful to descend from her chariot and walk. When Budha saw her he knew that from the merit she possessed she would become the mother of his lay disciples, or his principal female disciple; and he therefore preached the dharmma, by which she and her 500 maidens entered the first of the paths. The next day Meda attained the same privilege from hearing bana, and gave alms to Budha and his priests during two weeks. After this Budha returned to the wihára of Jétáwana.

At this time the younger sister of Pasé-nadi, king of Kosol, was the principal queen of Bimsara; and the younger sister of Bimsara was the principal queen of Pasé-nadi. The king of Kosol thought that as there were many rich merchants in Rajagaha, he would request him to send one of them to reside in Kosol. After consulting with his nobles, Bimsara said that as it would be difficult to prevail upon one of the merchants of the first class to go, he would speak to Dhananja, who did not belong to the superior grade. When Dhananja was called into the royal presence for this purpose, he said that he was ready to go, if commanded by the king. This merchant therefore accompanied the king of Kosol on his return; and on their journey they arrived in the evening at an open space where four ways met. Dhananja having asked the king how large his city was, learnt that it was seven yojanas in size; but on hearing this, he said it would be difficult for his large retinue to find accommodation in such a city, and he therefore requested permission to remain in the spot where they then were, without proceeding further. The king acceded to this request, and remained there three or four days with his attendants to assist in forming places of shelter, after which he went forward to Sewet. This place was called Sákétu, from having been their evening resting-place, and Dhananja was appointed its chief.

There was in Sewet a merchant called Migára, who had a son, Púrnna-wardhana, a young man of excellent appearance. One day his parents said to him that he had arrived at a proper age to marry; but he said that he would never marry unless he could meet with a female possessed of the five beauties (pancha-kalyána). His parents asked him what they were; and he said, "1. Késa kalyána; hair that when spread out will be splendid as the feathers of the peacock's tail. 2. Mánsa-kalyána; lips, that whether betel has been eaten or not will always be red as the kem fruit. 3. Ashti-kalyána; teeth white, uniform, near each other, and of the same height. 4. Chawi-kalyána; the body of an uniform colour, without a single spot. 5. Waya-kalyána; though she should have twenty children, never to appear old, and though she should live to be a hundred years old, not to have a single grey hair." The parents, when they received this reply, collected 108 brahmans, from whom they enquired if there was such a female in the world; and they were told that there was. Then eight of the brahmans were selected and were sent to all parts of Jambudwípa to find a maiden of this description, a great reward being promised to the discoverer. They were long unsuccessful in their search, but arrived at Sakétu on a festival day, when the ladies of the city, at other times kept in the strictest privacy, were accustomed to make their appearance in public, and join in the amusements of the season. The nobles had now an opportunity of seeing their equals of the other sex; and they were accustomed to go to the corners of the streets to throw flowers and garlands at them as they passed. The brahmans thought that this would be a good opportunity to accomplish their design; and for this purpose they took their station in a certain hall. By and bye, Wisákhá, now fifteen years of age, came within sight, attended by her maidens; and as a shower of rain came on, the other ladies began to run towards the hall in great confusion; but Wisákhá continued to walk at her usual pace, just as if there had been no rain at all. As she came nearer, the brahmans saw that she had four of the beauties, but they could not see her teeth. They therefore entered into conversation with her, and said, as if in jest, "Unfortunate will be the man who has you for a wife; if you go for water in the morning you will not return before night, and so he will get nothing to eat." Sweetly she replied, "How so?" and they informed her that they judged thus, because she was the last to arrive at the hall and the last in putting off her ornaments that had been wet by the rain. But she said that it was not from indolence; it was not graceful in a female to run.* "There are four persons," said she, "who ought not to run. 1. The king, when the crown is upon his head, and he is arrayed in the royal ornaments; the people would be ashamed and compare him to a labourer. 2. The royal elephant, when his elegant trappings are on. 3. The recluse. 4. The female; lest the people should say she is a man. It was on this account I did not run. Again, a young maiden may be compared to merchandize on sale; were she to run, she might fall or dash her foot against some obstruction, and thus her palms and the soles of her feet would be damaged, and nobody would buy her." The brahman, who saw by this time that she was well fitted to become the wife of

* "The brahman must not run even when it rains."—Manu. Inst. iv. 38.

their lord, make known to her their intention, and put a chain of great value upon her neck. When Wisákhá had learnt the name and rank of Púrnna-wardhana, she sent to inform her father, and requested that chariots might be provided to convey her and her maidens home. The father asked the brahmans the wealth of their lord, and they said 40 kótis of treasure. Dhananjara said that this was only as much as his daughter would require for bathing money;* but as his rank was equal, he consented to her betrothal.

The brahmans now went to tell Migára of their success, who was well pleased, and resolved to set out for Sákétu without delay, but went first to inform the king of what had taken place. The king said that it was at his request the rich merchant had come to reside in those territories, and that therefore he would himself be present at the marriage. On hearing this, Migára, sent to inform the merchant of the king's intention; and said that as it was impossible he could provide for so large a retinue, the marriage had better be celebrated privately; but Dhananjara replied, that if even ten kings, with as many armies, were to come, he could provide for them all. Still Migára thought he said this as a mere boast, and sent again to tell him that only a few guards would be left in the city, and the king would be attended by 8 kótis of men; but he replied as before, that he could provide for them all. Dhananjara gave 70 measures of diamonds, pearls, and precious stones to the jewellers, to be made into different kinds of ornaments. When the king had arrived in the city and remained several days, he sent to tell the merchant that he had better not delay the marriage of his daughter, as the providing for so many people must be a burden to him; but Dhananjara said that the proper nekata for the marriage would not occur in less than four months, and that in the interval his majesty was to enjoy himself, and all his expenses would be defrayed. During the whole of the four months, the city was like a festive hall; through the liberality of the merchant no one wanted for anything. The firewood consumed in a single day amounted to 500 loads, which caused it to be deficient when all other things were in profusion; but Dhananjara, when informed of the circumstance, gave an order that the old

---

* It is said that Moeris gave the entire revenue of the lake known by his name to his queen for her personal expenses in dress and perfumes.

stables of the elephants and horses should be pulled down, and the wood taken for fuel. This only lasted a fortnight, after which he gave from the stores coarse cloth, then gradually cloth of a finer kind, and last of all sandal wood, as no fuel could otherwise be procured at that time, it being the rainy season.* At the conclusion of the four months the ornaments were brought by the jewellers. On the day of the marriage the whole body of the bride was covered with ornaments. On her head was an ornament in the form of a beautiful peacock, with feathers made of precious stones, the neck being composed of one single emerald; and the image was so constructed that when the wind blew it uttered sounds, so that those at a distance thought it was alive. She also possessed the ornament for the waist called mékhalá; and the value of the whole was nine kótis of masurans.† Dhananjara presented his daughter with 500 wagons laden with gold; and as many laden with silver and with all kinds of requisites and treasures; of each 500; and 500 in which were comely maidens. When the train left the city it extended twelve miles. The gates of the places where the other cattle, 120,000 in number, were confined, were also thrown open, when the whole herd of animals, of their own accord, through the merit of the bride, ran ahead of those attached to the vehicles, and remained in this position, extending twelve miles further. Previous to her departure, Dhananjara gave his daughter a number of advices, in figurative language, such as that she should never give fire from her house to another, nor receive fire into her house. This was overheard by Migára, who wondered what it could all mean. Next morning, in the presence of the royal guests, he appointed eight persons in whom he could confide, to accompany her as guardians, and presented her with the set of ornaments worth nine kelas and a lac. He also proclaimed to all his retainers, that whoever

* Vijaya Raghava Nayadu, king of Tanjore, daily fed 12,000 brahmans. In a rainy time he was advised to cease doing so; but when an entire want of fuel was stated to exist, he ordered every wooden material about his house to be taken down, or pulled to pieces in order to supply fuel. In three days this supply was exhausted: he then directed all the vestments in the palace to be dipped in oil, and made use of for fuel.—Rev. W. Taylor, Journ. As. Soc. June, 1838.

† Ornaments of the description now worn by Wisákhá have only been possessed by two other females, one the wife of Bandhula, and the other Sujátá, who presented the offering of food to the prince Sidhártta, immediately previous to his becoming Budha.

wished to accompany her might go, and those who preferred to stay might remain; but they all said that they would accompany the bride. The merchant then went with the king part of the way, after which he returned home.

Migára who was a sceptic, was the last person in the procession, and when he saw all the people before him, he was angry at their coming, as the whole would have to be provided for; and he would have driven them back, but was prevented. When they approached the city, Migára thought that if the bride entered it in a covered litter, all the people would say it was because her ornaments were of inferior value, or because she was not beautiful; he therefore requested her to enter an open chariot, that she might be seen of all. On their arrival at the house of Migára, the king and his nobles sent many costly presents to Wisákhá, in return for the attention that had been shewn to them by her father during four months; but she said she had no need of these things, and what she received from one she sent to another, according to their age and circumstances, and thus secured the friendship of all. Migára was at this time a follower of the tirttaka Nighanta. One day he invited Wisákhá to go with him to worship; and she, well pleased, put on her most splendid ornaments for the purpose; but when she saw that the persons she was to worship were naked tirttakas, she was ashamed, and asked her father-in-law why he had brought her to such a place.* The tirttakas overheard what she said, and addressed Migára thus: "This is an unhappy follower of Gótama; why did you choose such a person to be the wife of your son; it will be better to send her away at once, as if she remains she will undoubtedly be the destruction of your house;" but her father-in-law apologised for her, and said that she was young.

On a certain occasion, when Migára was in the mansion, a rahat came to the door with his alms-bowl; but Wisákhá told him to pass on, as the master of that house ate puráma (one meaning of which is, filth). This was overheard by Migára, who resolved at once to send her away. But she said that she

* A similar story is referred to by Csoma Körösi; but the heroine of the Tibetan tale is called Sumagadha; and several of the incidents here related are, on another occasion, spoken of in connection with a girl from Champa, called Sa-ga-ma.

was not a slave to go here and there at the bidding of another; her father had sent with her eight respectable persons to protect her, and they must be called. When they came, Migára said that she had spoken disrespectfully of him; but she declared that she had only said that he was eating puráma, meaning that he was suffering the consequences of deeds done in former births. At another time she went out of the house at night with a light, which was observed by her father-in-law, and he asked her why she had done it; when she informed him that a valuable mare had foaled, and she went to see what was going on in the stable. " But," said he, "did not your father tell you that you were not to give a light from the house to another?" She replied, "Yes; but my father was not talking about the light of a lamp, but about tittle-tattle and scandal, which I am neither to tell nor hear." In the same way she explained to him the nature of the other advices she had received, by which he was satisfied. In the presence of her eight guardians she then asked him if he had any other fault to find with her; and when he confessed that he had none, she said that she was now ready to take her departure, if he would summon her attendants for the purpose; but he now urged her to remain. She therefore said to him, "You are a sceptic; I am a believer in Budha and the gems; if I remain I must have permission to go and hear bana, and give alms." This was granted. Soon afterwards she invited Budha and his priests to partake of an offering of food at her house. When the tirttakas heard of it, they became alarmed, and thought that if Migára saw Budha, they themselves would only appear to him like apes; they therefore tried to persuade him not to be present, but he refused to listen to them, as he said that Wisákhá would only give him advice that was good. They then said that it would be a great sin for him to look at Budha, and that therefore if he was determined to go and hear bana, he must put a bandage over his eyes. The lord of the world knew all that was taking place, and as he saw that he had the necessary merit, he resolved to catch him that day as in a net. Migára accompanied his daughter-in-law, his eyes being covered; but when he heard the discourse of Budha, he was so charmed that he tore away the bandage, and beheld the beauties of the sage. Upon this he said to Wisákhá, that henceforth she should be to him as a mother; and approaching Budha, he declared that he would trust in him alone, and that this was the field in which he would sow his forty kótis of treasures. He also repeated a stanza to this effect: "He who gives to Budha will reap a benefit for that which he has given; this my journey has been to me a fortunate one." From this time the door of Migára was shut to all others, but open to the priests of Budha. As Wisákhá was thus the means of converting Migára, she was called in consequence Migára-Mátáwí, and became the mother, or chief, of the upásikáwas or female lay disciples of Budha.

Thrice each day Wisákhá went to the wíhára; in the day-time taking an offering of food, and in the evening flowers and lamps. On one occasion she asked permission to prefer eight requests to Budha. The sage replied that the Budhas were not accustomed to grant the requests of women; but when she said that they were relative to religion, permission was granted. "I request," she said, "1. That whatever priests come to you, you will send them to my house first, to receive alms. 2. That until my death, I may give alms daily to 500 priests. 3. That whenever a priest is sick, application may be made to me for what is necessary. 4. That I may give alms to those who assist the sick. 5. That the lord of the universe will partake of the rice-gruel and other things I provide for the 500 priests. 6. That yearly, at the end of wass, I may give 500 sets of pirikaras to as many priests. 7. That I may be applied to whenever any article of medicine is required. 8. That yearly I may give to all the priests of Budha the robes called kaspilisandan." The whole of these requests were granted by Budha.

Wisákhá had 20 children in 20 years, 10 sons and 10 daughters; each of these had 20 children; so that she had 400 grandchildren; and as each of these had again 20 children, she had 8000 great grandchildren; and all these were free from every kind of disease. Though she had the strength of five elephants, the king of Kosol was sceptical respecting it; and to ascertain its truth, he one day, on meeting her, urged his elephant towards her, but she held its trunk with two fingers, as if it had been merely a plantain tree, so that it roared out from pain. She afterwards thought it would be better to sell the ornaments she received at her marriage, and erect a wihára with the proceeds; but there was no one in Sewet who had wealth enough to purchase them. She therefore bought a garden at the east side of the city, and expended immense treasures in the erection of a wihára, which was called Púwáráma, from the place in which it stood. On the day when this wihára was presented to Budha, he declared that all her riches, strength, and prosperity, were the result of the merit she had received in former births.

18. *Anurudha, Ananda, Déwadatta, and other Princes, become Priests; and Ananda is appointed to the Office of Upastháyaka.*

The queen of Amitódana, younger brother of Sudhódana, was Sanda; and she had two sons, Mahanama and Anurudha, and a daughter, Róhini. When Anurudha was seven years of age, he one day played at a game called gula, with two other princes, it being agreed that the person who lost was to pay a rice-cake. As Anurudha lost the game, the brothers said they would play no more until the cake was produced; he therefore sent to his mother, and she gave him what he required. This occurred three times. A fourth time he sent for a cake, but the queen sent him word that there were "no more." When he received the message, he thought that the words "no more" were the name of some other kind of cake; and he accordingly dispatched a messenger to request that a "no more cake" might be sent him. But the queen, thinking that if he did not know the meaning of "no more," he would never be able to rule the kingdom, resolved that she would teach him; and for this purpose sent him a vessel with nothing in it. One of the guardian déwas of the city saw that it would be better for him not to learn the meaning of this term; and he therefore secretly placed a cake created for the purpose in the vessel that was carried by the slave. No sooner did the prince remove the cover and touch the cake with his finger, than he felt the rushing of its taste through all his veins; and its sweet savour filled the whole city. After dividing it to his companions, he went to his mother, and said, "How is it that if you have loved me before to-day, you have never given me any of those excellent 'no more' cakes?" The queen, surprised, asked the slave what had taken place; and when she was informed, she said that it must have been done by some déwa. The prince informed her that this was the only kind of cake he intended to eat in future, and then ran to rejoin his companions at their sport. From this time, when he wanted a cake, he sent to his mother for it, and she returned the vessel empty; but the déwa always provided a cake similar to the one first received by the prince.

When Anurudha was fifteen years of age, he was talking with the princes Bhaddi and Kimbila, and one asked the other whence rice was produced. Kimbila said it was produced from a vessel, naming the vessel in which rice is cleaned. Bhaddi said it was produced from another kind of vessel, naming that in which it is cooked. But Anurudha said that it is produced from a golden dish, with feet, about a carpenter's cubit in height, naming the vessel from which he had seen the rice poured out when brought to be eaten. Whilst the prince was thus ignorant of all that relates to the world, it was determined by Budha to ordain one from each of the families of the Sákya race; and as Mahanama was not desirous of enduring the privations of the priesthood, and feared that if his brother received the kingdom his ignorance would be the cause of many calamities, he thought he would try by a stratagem to prevail on him to abandon the world. He therefore said to him, "What do you say? How is it to be? Rice will have to be provided." "What," said Anurudha, "is not rice produced from the golden dish?" "No," he replied, "but from the labour of the husbandman (describing at length the manner in which agriculture was then carried on). There must be a plough, a yoke (in all eighteen different articles are enumerated). The labourer must clear a space from all obstructions, make ditches and banks, break the hard clods, and bring manure; the seed must be sown; for a week the field must be watched, that the seed may not be carried away by birds; fences will have to be tied; a lodge must be built for the watchers to sleep in at night; it must be guarded from rats, pigs, deer, and other animals; when the ear is formed, care must be taken to preserve it from the blast and other diseases; every day persons must go round, making a noise; and dry leaves must be hung, to frighten away the birds; if it be an inferior grain, it must be watched in this way three or four months, and if a superior, six or seven months; as it ripens, noises must be made without ceasing, and persons must run about in all directions to keep off parrots,* peafowl,

---

* In Ceylon there is a district called the Girwa-pattu, or Parrot-county. In the evening the parrots resort to the cocoanut trees that line the sea-

and other birds that steal the grain, shouting till they are hoarse; after it is reaped, the owner must receive his share, whether it be half, or two thirds, so that he has to give two shares and keep only one; if the whole has to be given (the husbandman being only a servant), none is to be reserved for himself; a portion must be given to the watchers and winnowers, and the washerman, tomtom-beater, and the beggar, must each have his share; when payment has been made for what has been borrowed, the remainder must be stored in the granary; of this, some must be kept for seed-corn; that which is not fit for seed, must be separated from the rest, and used for food; so much as is required for each day must be portioned out, that it may last until the next harvest. When all this is concluded, the same round must begin again; it is always work, work, without any leisure; the husbandman may be sick, or be called to go to the war, or old, but still the labour must be continued; at last he may have to go from place to place, leaning on two sticks, to beg; and after all this toil, the end may be that he falls into hell. Brother, I tell you all this, that you may see what awaits you; you can take possession of my wealth and honours, and I will go to Budha and become a priest." But Anurudha said that he was not previously aware the householder had so many troubles; and if this was the case, he would become the priest, and Mahanama might keep his possessions. At once he went to request the permission of his mother, that he might carry this design into effect; but she said, "Your father is dead; you are as my heart, as my two eyes; all my joy is to see you and your brother; I cannot bear the thought of your becoming a priest; therefore until my death, I must refuse my permission." Anurudha then said, "What do you tell me, mother? As the water of the river stays not till it has arrived at the sea, so will my mind continually be directed towards Budha; therefore, do give me permission to become a priest." But she still refused. Anurudha then said, "As the rain, when ascended into the sky, knows no place of rest until it has fallen to fertilise the ground, so will my mind

shore, and their screams are so loud as to overpower all other sounds. In the time of harvest, they bring with them ears of rice, and many people make a considerable profit by collecting the grain that falls to the ground.

know no repose until I have gone to the residence of Budha." But the mother was still relentless, and requested that words like these might not again fall upon her ear. The prince declared the third time, "As the river that ascends from a rock into the sky does not abide there, but again descends to the earth, so my mind will know no stay until it has proceeded to the place of consecration; therefore I again entreat your permission." The queen was unable to say more, from the excess of her grief; but by way of evasion she told him that his friend Bhaddi had now become a king, and if he could persuade Bhaddi to become a priest, her permission would no longer be withheld. She thought that no one who was a king had ever become a priest, and therefore gave her consent upon this condition.

When Anurudha set out to speak to Bhaddi upon the subject, he reflected upon what his mother had said, and saw that he must try to accomplish his purpose by a stratagem. "The Sákya princes," he thought, "do not lie even to save life; so I must try to catch him by inducing him to make a declaration, and then turn his words upon himself." Accordingly he went to the king, and after kissing him, said, "I cannot declare my affection for you; if you have the same regard for me, leave all these treasures, and let us both become priests; if I enter the priesthood first, we shall continue near to each other." As they had been friends from the time that they played together as children, Bhaddi, prompted by affection, but scarcely knowing what he said, gave his word that if Anurudha became a priest first, he would follow his example. The prince was greatly rejoiced at receiving this declaration, and said, "I intend to become a priest to-day, therefore come with me now." But Bhaddi began to repent of the promise he had made, and said, "We are both young yet; let us enjoy ourselves for the present, and when we are old we can embrace the priesthood." To this Anurudha replied, "There is no regularity in the order of old age and death; sometimes old age precedes death, but at other times death precedes old age; your declaration is not a wise one; the prince Sidhártta renounced the world at twenty-nine years of age, and many nobles of this city have done the same, whilst they were yet young; the receiving of the priesthood is a great privilege; therefore speak not another word, but come with me now."

Bhaddi respected the promise he had given, and said that in seven years from that time he would be prepared to become a priest; but Anurudha said he would not listen to this proposal. The king then mentioned six years, and gradually came down to two; but his friend was inflexible. Again he proposed a year, six months, and so on, until he came down to a fortnight; but the prince was equally unwilling to yield. At last Bhaddi declared, "I must have at least seven days to deliver up the kingdom, and give the necessary advices to my successor; if you love me, say no more."

At the end of seven days Bhaddi, Anurudha, Ananda, the son of Sudhódana's younger brother, the prince Kimbila, Déwadatta, the son of Suprabudha (the princess Yasódhará being his younger sister) and the prince Bhagu, went with a great retinue to a place about sixteen miles from the city, as if for the purpose of taking pleasure; but they contrived to steal away from their attendants, taking with them only Upáli, the king's barber. When they arrived at a private place, they took off their ornaments, gave them to the barber, and told him that he might keep them; but as they were going away, Upáli reflected thus: "If I take these ornaments to the city, the Sákya princes, who are wrathful, will deprive me of life; they are of no benefit to me; if these princes could leave all their possessions to become recluses, the same course will be much easier for me. He therefore hung the ornaments up in a tree, to be taken by the first comer, and pursued the direction taken by the princes, who enquired why he followed them; and when they were informed, they went on together.

Budha was at that time in a village called Anupiya, belonging to the princes of Malla. When the princes requested that he would admit them to the priesthood, they said that they were of an honourable family, so much so as not to pay respect even to him; but in order that their dignity might be lowered, they wished that the barber should be ordained first; they would then have to worship him, and if they even thought of returning to their possessions, they would know that the princes would say to them, "What, is it you who worshipped the barber?" and thus their return would be prevented. Budha approved of their resolution, and ordained the barber first, and then the princes. Bhaddi afterwards became a rahat, when observing the ordinance called widarsana, in the time of wass. Ananda entered sowán, and became the principal attendant on the person of Budha. Kimbilá and Bhagu became rahats, and each had 500 disciples. Déwadatta performed the ordinance called dhyána. Upáli became a rahat, and the chief of those who understood the Winaya-pitaka. Anurudha observed widarsana, and became a rahat; and from having formerly given a lamp-offering to Piyumatura Budha, he became the chief of those who have supernatural vision; and received divine eyes, by which he could see all things in a hundred thousand sakwalas, as plainly as a mustard seed held in the hand.

One day Anurudha went to the village of Munda, in which there resided a noble, Maha-munda, who requested him to perform wass; but he said that it was not in his power, as he had no sámanéra to assist him. The noble had two sons, Maha-sumana and Kudá-sumana, and he said that Anurudha might take the elder of the two and consecrate him; but he refused, as he saw that he was deficient in merit. He therefore received Kudá-sumana, at that time about seven years of age; who, as his hair was cut off, saw part of it, on which he reflected that a little time previous it had been the ornament of his head, and was now only a worthless thing to be thrown away. In the act of carrying on this meditation on the meanness of the body and its secretions, he became a rahat. After receiving the offerings of his parents on two póya days, as Anurudha said he must return to Budha, in their presence he ascended into the air, and accompanied the priest to a stone cave in the forest of Himála. At night, when walking for the purpose of religious meditation, Anurudha was attacked with flatulence; and when the sámanéra saw the pain that he endured, he asked him if he had ever suffered from the same complaint before, and in what way it was then cured. The priest informed him that it had previously been cured by some of the water of the Anótatta lake, on hearing which he said he would go and fetch some; and Anurudha said, though it was guarded by a nága called Pannaka, he would allow him to take some, when informed for whom it was intended. At the time he arrived at the lake, Pannaka was sporting in it, with 500 other nágas, who, when he saw him, said, "What is this young priest coming hither for with his vessel? I will not allow him to take away any of the water;" but as Sumana saw his anger, he remained in the air, and repeated a stanza, stating why he had come. Still the nága said, "Priestling, you may go and take water from the Ganges, but you shall have none from this lake." Upon this Sumana let him know that though he was only seven years of age, his power was immensely greater than that of the nága; he could take the earth and put it upon the top of Maha Méru; to him, water was not water; nor fire, fire; nor iron, iron; he was the sámanéra of Anurudha, and a priest of Budha. Pannaka said that if he were so clever, he had better try to get some of the water; but he would see that he could not succeed. The déwas from the different lókas now assembled, as it were in a moment, to see whether the nága or the priest of seven years would prove the stronger in the contest. Then Sumana assumed the form of a brahma, twelve yojanas in size, and entered the body of the nága, fifty yojanas in size, in which he walked about; but the pain he thereby caused made the nága cry out with a noise as if sea and sky were united. By his struggles, the water of the lake rose into high waves, which enabled him to dip his vessel into it as he walked; and when it was full, he said that he had got what he came for, and would now return. The déwas saw that he was the conqueror. Pannaka, angry at being thus defeated, set off to pursue him, upon which he assumed his own form; and when he presented the water to the priest, the nága declared that he had not given it; but as Sumana said that he had, and Anurudha knew that a rahat could not tell a lie he drank it. Pannaka thought still that he would be revenged; but the priest told him that Sumana had more power than a kóti of nágas; and when he heard this he went to the sámanéra, asked his pardon, told him he might take the water at any time he required it, and then went away.

The priest Anurudha, accompanied by Sumana, afterwards went to Budha, who was at that time residing in the wihára of Púrwáráma. The inferior priests of that place took the sámanéra by the ear, and asked him if one so young could fast after the turning of the sun, or perform the journeys required to be undertaken by the priests; and they enquired if he did not wish to return to his mother. They thus despised him, because they were ignorant that he was a rahat. When Budha perceived what was going on, he said that their conduct was as if one were to play with the trunk of an elephant; they did not know the power of the sámanéra, though it had been witnessed by all the déwas. At this time Budha wished for some water from Anotatta for the washing of his feet; but when Ananda informed the sámanéras, not one of them was willing to go, until he asked Sumana, who said that he was ready to go if directed by Budha. Taking a vessel, he went through the air, obtained the water without any difficulty, and returned in the manner in which he went. On his approach, Budha called to the priests to see in how beautiful a manner he was coming, and on his arrival received from him the water he had brought. He then enquired his age; and when he was told that it was seven years, he said that though others did not receive ordination until they were twenty years of age, he should receive it now; and accordingly he became of the upasampadá order from that time. Sópaka was the only person besides to whom was ever granted the honour of so early an ordination.

Previous to the ordination of Ananda, which took place in the twentieth year after the teacher of the three worlds became Budha, there was no one regularly appointed as his personal attendant; but the following persons waited on him at different times:—Nágasamála, Nágita, Upawána, Sunakkhatta, Chunda, Ságala, and Mesi. Budha now called together the priests, and said to them, "I am fifty-five years of age; I have not in any way begun to decline; yet sometimes the priest who carries my bowl lags behind, and talks to the sceptics, or he goes a different road to that which I have taken, and I have to submit to other inconveniences. It will therefore be better that some one be appointed as my regular attendant." Then Seriyut, Mugalan, and the rest of the priests, each said, "I will become your servitor; grant it me as a favour; let me be the recipient of this honour." But the sage said he would not give the office to a rahat, and therefore appointed Ananda, who agreed to undertake it if Budha would grant a favourable answer to eight requests he had to make. "The requests that I have to make," said he, "are as follows;—1. That I may never be required to put on a robe that has been worn by Budha. 2. That I never eat of the food that has been received in the alms-bowl of Budha. 3. That I do not accompany him when he is invited to any place to receive an offering of food. 4. That he will eat of the food I myself receive in the alms-bowl. 5. That when any one comes to a distance to speak to Budha, I may be allowed to go at that moment and inform him. 6. That when any doubt is formed in my mind, relative to the meaning of the dharmma, I may go at once to Budha and have it solved. 7. That I reside in a separate place. 8. That when Budha says bana in any place, I not being present, he will repeat the whole to me on his return." These requests were granted by the sage, as he saw that what was required had been the custom of the former Budhas. There were five things in which Ananda excelled all other beings:—1. In ministering to Budha. 2. In thankfulness for the favours he received. 3. In the receiving of the four requisites of a priest. 4. In the sweetness of his voice when saying bana. 5. In the power to listen attentively to the discourses of Budha." From the time of his appointment, Budha never had to call Ananda twice. During the three watches of the night, when necessary, he carried a light around his residence.*

19. *Budha visits the City of Wisálá.*

On a certain occasion, when Budha was delivering a discourse on the impermanency of all things, he declared that even the city of Wisálá,† usually so prosperous, would be visited at one

---

* On one occasion Ananda is represented as standing behind Budha, and fanning him.

† In a former age, according to a legend that appears in the Pújáwaliya, the queen of Benares was delivered of a piece of flesh, which was put into a vessel, sealed, and thrown into the river; but the déwas caused it to float, and it was seen by an ascetic, who caught it and took it to his cell. When he saw its contents, he put it carefully on one side; but on looking at it again some time afterwards, he saw that it had become divided into two. Then the rudiments of the human form appeared, and a beautiful prince and princess were presented, who sucked their fingers and thence drew milk. As it was difficult for the ascetic to bring them up, he delivered them to a villager; and from being so similar in their appearance, they were called Lichawi, which name was also given to the royal race that from them received its origin. The other children of the village were accustomed to revile them, and say that they had no father or mother, only the ascetic. The villagers said in consequence, Wajjatabba, meaning that they must be removed to some other place; and this name, Wajji, was afterwards given to the whole of that country, 300 yojanas in extent. After their removal from the village, they caused a city to be built in the place to which they retired. The prince and princess married, and had a son and daughter at one birth, and in due time sixteen sons and sixteen daughters, in the same manner. As their family increased, the city was enlarged, on which account it was called Wisálá. In the time of Gótama it was an extensive and splendid city. The princes lived together in great amity, and never intermarried with other races. There were 7707 princes, residing in as many separate places, each with a sub-king, treasurer, and other officers. They reigned in turn, each

and the same time by pestilence, famine, and sprites. And so it occurred. First there was the pestilence, and then came the famine, so that there was none to bury the dead, and the whole city resembled a charnel-house. The citizens informed the king of their calamities, who directed them to enquire whether in any way he were the cause; but they could not find that he was in any fault. Then some advised that application for assistance should be made to the rishis; but others who had heard of the miracles performed by Budha, recommended that his aid should be implored; and accordingly an embassage of princes was sent to invite him to the city. They knew that he was at that time resident in the Wéluwana wihára, but they first made application to Bimsara, the king; who informed them that the kindness of Budha was equally extended to all, and that therefore they

---

for an appointed time; and the city was like the lóka of Sekra in the magnificence of its appearance and the happiness of its inmates.

From the analysis of the Mahápariníbbána-suttan, by Turnour (Journal As. Soc. Dec. 1838), it appears that Ajásat, a short time previous to the death of Budha, meditated the subjugation of the Lichawi princes of Wisála, who were united in a confederacy, though still acknowledging the supremacy of one of their number, and calling him king. The princes were at that time plotting together, apparently with the intention of inflicting some injury upon the monarch of Rajagaha. In order that he might know in what manner his design could be best effected, Ajásat sent his prime minister, Wassakára, to ask the advice of Budha, from whom he learnt that the princes must either be propitiated by the payment of tribute, or that he must dissolve the compact that united them, without engaging in war. On receiving this advice, Wassakára, at his own request, was sent as a deserter to Wisálá, where he gained the confidence of the Lichawi princes, and then by insinuations sowed dissension among them; after which he communicated the result of his mission to Ajásat, who went with an army, and having subjugated all the princes to great calamities, returned.

According to the Vishnu Purána, Wisálá (Vaisáli) was founded by Visála, son of Trinávindu and the celestial nymph Alambushá. "Vaisáli is a city of considerable renown in Indian tradition, but its site is a subject of some uncertainty. Part of the difficulty arises from confounding it with Visálá, another name of Ujayın . . . According to the Budhists it is the same as Prayága, or Allahabad; but the Rámáyana places it much lower down, on the north bank of the Ganges, nearly opposite to the mouth of the Sone; and it was therefore in the modern district of Sáran, as Hamilton (Genealogies of the Hindus) conjectured."—Wilson's Vishnu Purána. Fa Hian visited Wisálá, but does not give any extended description of what he saw. Hiuan Thsang is more particular, and says that it had fallen into ruin, but the circumference of the ancient foundations was upwards of twenty miles. He saw the ruins of more than a hundred monasteries. The country was rich, the soil fertile, the climate equable, and the inhabitants were bland in their manners, and contented with their lot. There were a few monasteries, but the inmates were little better than heretics. It is said by Csoma Körösi, that the Tibetan writers derive their first king (about 250 years B.C.) "from the Litsabyis or Lichavyis."

might themselves go to him and make known their request. On receiving their petition, Budha consented to visit Wisálá; and when his determination was made known to the king, Bimsara prepared a road from Rajagaha to the Ganges, a distance of eighty miles. The moment he commenced his journey, rain began to fall, though there had been none for so long a period previous; but it was no inconvenience to those who did not wish to be wet. The Lichawi (properly Lich'hawi) princes also prepared a road on their side of the river, a distance of forty-eight miles. When Budha entered Wisálá, he commanded Ananda to go round the city, sprinkling water from his alms-bowl, and repeating the pirit. At once the sprites fled away; and the sick, restored to health, followed Ananda round the city, repeating the praises of Budha. The sage proceeded to the palace of the king, where he delivered the discourse called Ratana Sutra, and countless beings entered the paths. Two póyas he remained in the city, and as he was returning to Wéluwana, the nágas requested him to visit their residence, which he did, and he spent there a night; after which he proceeded to the other bank of the river, and accompanied Bimsara, who had been waiting to receive him, to Rajagaha.

20. *The History of Jíwaka, who administered Medicine to Budha.*

When Bimsara, king of Rajagaha, heard of the fame of Ambapáli, the chief courtezan of Wisálá, he became envious of the glory that by her means flowed to the Lichawi princes, as in this his own city was inferior to Wisálá. He therefore commanded that all the beautiful women in the neighbourhood should be collected, that the most beautiful of them all might be chosen; and the choice fell upon the princess Sáláwati. The king then levied for her a tax upon the city of 200,000 masurans, to which he himself added another 100,000 and made over to her many gardens, and buildings, and immense wealth. The price of her embrace was appointed to be 2000 masurans, being twice the amount received by Ambápáli. She thus became the principal courtezan of Rajagaha, and like the banner of the city, was known to all.

After some time she became pregnant, by Abhaya, the son of Bimsara; but the prince was not made acquainted with the circumstance. It was the custom of the courtezans not to make known that they were pregnant; and when the child was born, if it was a girl, she was brought up in private, but if it was a boy, he was taken to the forest and exposed. When any one came to the dwelling of Sáláwati, her attendants made known that she was sick, and thus she concealed her condition for the space of nine months. The child of which she was delivered was a boy, who was taken privately to a certain place in the forest, according to the usual custom. In due time the princess again anointed herself, and made her appearance in public, as if nothing had happened. On the day on which the child was taken to the forest, Abhaya went to the same place to walk, when his attention was attracted by a number of crows near a piece of flesh; they did not peck at it with their bills, but looked at it as if in kindness, without doing it any harm. The prince enquired what was the reason of this appearance, and was told that the crows were hovering round an infant, that had been thrown into a hole. He then asked whether it was alive or dead, and was informed that it was alive. It was because the infant was in that birth to enter the path sowán, that his life was thus preserved. When the prince saw it, he pitied it, from the force of parental affection, though he knew not that it was his own child; and commanding it to be taken to the palace, he appointed it a nurse and proper attendants. From having been told that it was alive, he called it Jíwaka, he who lives.[*]

When Jíwaka, who was also called Kómárabhacha, was seven or eight years of age, he was playing with the other princes in the hall, and they reproached him with having no mother. Ashamed, he went to Abhaya, and asked who was his mother; but he smiled and said, I am your father, who was your mother I know not; I found you exposed in the forest, and rescued you." Then Jiwaka reflected, when he heard this circumstance related, that he would receive no inheritance from relationship; so he resolved that he would learn some science, and then by his attainments he might be able to acquire both relatives and wealth. Again he considered the character of the eighteen sciences and the sixty-four arts, and determined that he would

[*] The history of Jíwaka is inserted at greater length than that of the other disciples of Gótama, as it is of greater interest, and illustrates the state of medical science in that early age.

study the art of medicine, that he might be called doctor, and be respected, and attain to eminence. With this intention he went to Taksalá,* and applied to a learned professor to receive him into his school. The professor asked him who he was; and as he thought that if he told the whole truth it would put him to shame, he replied that he was the son of Abhaya, and the grandson of Bimsara, king of Rajagaha. When he said that he wished to learn medicine, the professor asked what was the amount of the wages he had brought; and he replied, "I have come away by stealth from my parents; and therefore have not brought anything with me; but I will remain with you as a servant, if you will teach me." The professor saw that there was some appearance of merit about him, and agreed to teach him though from other pupils he received a thousand masurans. At this moment the throne of Sekra trembled, as Jíwaka had been acquiring merit through a kap-laksha, and was soon to administer medicine to Gótama Budha. The déwa resolved that as he was to become the physician of Budha, he would himself be his teacher; and for this purpose he came to the earth, entered the mouth of the professor, and inspired him with the wisdom he needed to teach his pupil in the most excellent manner. At once Jíwaka perceived that what the professor asked, and thought, and said, proceeded from a déwa, and not from a man; and he soon discovered that he could give relief in many cases where his teacher was not able. There are diseases that are mortal, and others that are not mortal, and about all these he was taught by Sekra for the space of seven years. With any other teacher he could not have learnt the same things in sixteen years. Then Jíwaka asked his preceptor when his education would be completed; and the old man, in order to try his skill, told him that he must go out of one of the gates of the city, and examine the ground around for the space of sixteen miles, during four days, after which he was to bring him all the roots, flowers, barks, and fruits he could discover that were useless in medicine. Jíwaka did so; but on his

---

* In almost numberless instances, Taksalá, or Takshalá, is represented as a collegiate city. It is most probably the Taxila of the Greeks, which was situated, according to Strabo, between the Indus and the Hydaspes, and is represented as being extensive and well-governed. The Hindu legends state that Taksha, the son of Bharata, reigned in Gandhára, his capital city being Takshasíla.

return informed the professor that he had met with no substance that was not in some way or other of benefit; there was no such thing upon earth. The teacher, on receiving this reply, told him that there was no one in the world that could instruct him further; and Sekra departed from his mouth. As he knew that his pupil had been taught by a wisdom that was divine, he gave him sufficient for his maintenance during three or four days, and sent people to accompany him to his own city.

In the course of his journey Jíwaka arrived at Sákétu, where he remained a little time to refresh himself. At that time the wife of one of the principal citizens had a violent pain in her head, from which she had suffered seven years. Many learned physicians had promised to cure her, but they only took her substance, and did not afford her a moment's relief. Jíwaka having heard of her situation, sent to inform her that a learned doctor was at her gate; but when she learnt his age, she said, "What can a little child do, when the cleverest physicians in Jambudwípa have failed? Tell him that if he is hungry, we will supply him with rice; or if it is something else that he wants, let him receive it, and be gone." On hearing this, Jíwaka replied, "Science is neither old nor young; wisdom does not come from age alone; what has the lady to do with my age, or how does this affect my ability? I will not go away until the head-ache is entirely cured; if I fail, no harm will be done; I will ask for nothing until my skill is clearly proved." The lady was pleased with the manner in which he spoke, and commanded him to be called; after which she offered him a seat, and said, "My son, can you give me relief for a single day, for it is seven years since I was able to sleep." Jíwaka promised to give her instant relief, and requested that a little butter might be boiled, on receiving which he poured from his hand a quantity of medicine into her nose, half of which went to her brain and the other half to her mouth. The part that went to her mouth, she spat out; but the husband told the servants to take it up with some cotton. When Jíwaka saw this, he thought to himself, "If these people are so niggardly that they take up even that which has fallen to the ground in spittle, I fear there is no chance of my receiving any great reward." The lady guessed his thoughts, and told him that it was done, not on account of their covetousness, but from the preciousness of the medicine; as if it remained on the ground it would benefit no one; but if taken up it might cure some other disease. She then informed her husband that her head-ache had all gone, and that Jíwaka was the cause of her recovery. For this the attendants praised him, and the noble, the lady, their child, and their relatives, each gave him 4000 níla-karshas, with chariots, and other gifts in abundance. With this wealth he went to Rajagaha, and told the prince he had brought him a first offering for the trouble he had had in bringing him up. But Abhaya replied that he had recently found out that he was his own son, by the courtezan Sáláwati, and that he had brought him up, not for a recompense, but from paternal affection. He also gave him permission to build a residence near his own palace, and to partake of his wealth.

At this time Bimsara was troubled with a fistula in ano, which sometimes caused his robe to be spotted, and exposed him to the ridicule of the queens. As the king was greatly ashamed on this account, he consulted the most renowned physicians in every part of Jambudwípa, but they could afford him no relief; so he one day called Abhaya, and asked if he knew of any other person that it would be well to consult. The prince recommended that his own son should be sent for; and when he came, Bimsara took him into a private apartment, and made known to him the nature of his complaint. Jíwaka had taken a little medicine in his finger nail, with which he anointed the fistula; in an instant the pain was gone, and the disease vanished, but in what way the king could not discover. Bimsara now thought that if Jíwaka was a good man, it was right that he should be honoured, but that if he was a bad man, it would be necessary to put him away; he was so exceedingly clever, that his presence would either be a great benefit or a great evil. To try him, he called his 500 queens, and after telling them of the wonderful cure that had been effected, he informed them that they might reward the physician in any way they thought proper. They therefore brought immense numbers of the richest robes, and presented them to Jíwaka.* Abhaya and the nobles who were

* By some of the ancient nations the medical profession was held in high esteem. The Egyptian surgeons were thought to excel all others in the exercise of their art. The surgeon Demokedes received from the citizens of

present, when they saw what was done, secretly wished that he would not receive them; and as he himself was wiser than any of them, he replied, "It is not proper that I, who am only a subject, should receive garments that belong to the king; I want them not; only grant me your protection and favour, and I require no more." The king returned to the queens their present, greatly praising Jíwaka; and appointing him the annual produce of many gardens and villages, he became his friend.

There was in Rajagaha a rich nobleman who had a pain in his head, like the cutting of a knife. Two medical men came to visit him, but they could do nothing for him; one said that he would die in five days, and the other in seven. The king was much concerned on receiving this intelligence, as the death of the noble would be a great misfortune to the city; and he requested Jíwaka to see him; who, when he had made the necessary examination, said that there were two worms in his head, one large and the other small; the large worm would cause his death in seven days, and the smaller in five. "Of the two physicians," he proceeded, "one saw the large worm only, and the other only the smaller one; but I will free you from danger in three days, though there is no other person in the world who could do the same." The noble, trembling from the fear of death, told him that he would give him all his property, and would become his servant, if he saved his life. Jíwaka promised to cure him, if he would grant him one request, and told him not to be afraid. The request was, that without removing from the same place, he would lie seven months on his back, seven months on his right side, and seven months on his left side, in all twenty-one months;* and Jíwaka said further, "If I give you pain, you must not attribute it to me as a crime, but must give me permission thus to afflict you; parents and teachers chastise their children, that they may be made obedient: and physicians

---

Aegina one talent, about £383 sterling, for remaining with them one year. Two years afterwards Polykrates, of Samos, offered him two talents. When he had cured Darius, that king sent him into the hareem to visit his wives. Being introduced as the man who had saved the king's life, the grateful sultanas each gave him a saucer full of golden coins.—Herod. iii. 130. Grote's Greece, iv. 341.

* If the medical men among the Jews treated their patients in a similar manner, the command given by God to Ezekiel, iv. 5, to lie on his left side 390 days, and on his right side 40 days, would appear less strange.

afflict their patients for their benefit, that by this means they may free them from disease." He then took the noble into an upper room, sat behind him, and taking a very sharp instrument,[*] opened his skull; and setting aside the three sutures, he seized the two worms that were gnawing his brain, with a forceps, and extracted them entire. One was the worm that would have killed him in five days, and the other in seven. He then closed up the wound in such a manner that not a single hair was displaced. He had made his patient promise to remain in one place twenty-one months; and under the hands of any other physician this would have been necessary, but he now declared that in twenty-one days he would be perfectly well, and no longer a detention would be required. The noble offered him in return an immensity of treasure, but he was not willing to receive it; he only took a lac of treasure from the king and another from the noble, with a few other things. The fame of Jíwaka now became everywhere known, like the banner of Jambudwípa.

There was a nobleman in Benares, who in his youth, whilst in the act of leaping, twisted one of his intestines into a knot, on which account he was not able to pass any solid food, and could only eat a little at a time, just enough to save life; his body gradually became like a piece of dry wood, and oil might be poured into the holes that presented themselves between his bones, and kept there as in a vessel. From all parts of Jambudwípa physicians came, so that the door of his mansion was beset by them continually; but they all declared, on seeing him, that they were unable to assist him. Then the father of the noble, who had heard of the fame of Jíwaka, took a rich present to Rajagaha, which he presented to Bimsara, and requested that he might receive the assistance of the renowned physician. At the request of the king, he went to Benares; and on being introduced to the noble, he asked him at once if he felt any symptoms as if his intestines were in a knot, and if it first came on when he was leaping or taking violent exercise. On being answered in the affirmative, he said that he could cure him, and putting everybody

---

[*] The ancients had arrived at very great perfection in the making of surgical instruments, as may be seen in many Egyptian paintings. The instruments found in a house at Pompeii, supposed to have belonged to a surgeon, have a great resemblance to those in use at the present day.

out of the room but the noble's wife, he bolted the door, then bound his patient to a pillar that he might not move, covered his face, bound him with a cloth, and taking a sharp instrument, without the noble's being aware of what was going on, ripped open the skin of his abdomen, took out his intestines, just showed the lady in what way the knot was twisted, and then replaced them in a proper manner. After this he rubbed some ointment on the place, freed the noble from the pillar, put him in bed, gave him a drink of rice-gruel, and in three days he was able to rise, and was as well as ever. The noble presented him as his fee 16,000 masurans, with horses, chariots, cattle, and slaves in abundance, and with these he returned to Rajagaha, as in grand procession. From all countries the people came to him, and requested his assistance as if they were asking for a divine elixir, or the water of immortality.

At that time Chandapprajóta, king of Udéni,* who had the jaundice, sent messengers to Bimsara,† with royal gifts, requesting the aid of Jíwaka, but he several times refused to go. This king had an unconquerable aversion to oil. He could not bear to have it in his food, nor to be anointed with it, nor to have it in the lamps by which his palace was lighted. They were therefore trimmed with malakada (tallow?). It was because his father was a scorpion, that this aversion arose. His mother accidentally imbibed the scorpion's emission, by means of which she conceived; but the child she brought forth was of a most cruel disposition, and was therefore called Chandapprajóta. It was on account of his aversion to oil, that Jíwaka was unwilling to go to Udéni, as it was not possible to cure him without using it in the preparation of the medicine. Other messengers, with greater gifts, succeeded the first, and at last Jíwaka was prevailed upon by Bimsara to go, as Chandaprajóta was his friend. When the great physician had seen the king, it occurred to him that he might endeavour to give the medicine by stealth; were he to administer it openly, it might cause both his own destruction and

---

* Ujjayani or Oujein, a city so called in Málava, formerly the capital of Vikramáditya. It is one of the seven sacred cities of the Hindus, and the first meridian of their geographers: the modern Oujein is about a mile south of the ancient city.—Wilson's Sanscrit Dictionary.

† The messengers made their first application to the king; and Naaman acted in a similar manner when he received a letter, not for Elisha, who was to heal him, but for the king of Israel.—2 Kings v 5.

that of the king. He therefore informed him that he could effect the cure of his disease; but there was one thing that he must mention to the monarch, which was, that doctors are unwilling to make known to others the ingredients of which their medicines are composed; it would be necessary for him to collect all that he required with his own hand, and therefore the king must give directions that he be permitted to pass through any of the gates of the palace whenever he might choose.

Chandapprajóta had four celebrated modes of conveyance. 1. A chariot called oppanika, drawn by slaves, that would go in one day 60 yojanas, and return. 2. An elephant called Nálágiri, that in one day would go 100 yojanas, and return. 3. A mule called Mudakési, that in one day would go 120 yojanas, and return. 4. A horse called Telekarnnika, that would go the same distance. In a former birth the king was a poor man, who was accustomed to carry the alms-bowl of a certain Pasé-Budha, more expeditiously than any other person; and on this account he was afterwards born of high or royal families and had the swiftest vehicles to convey him from place to place. When the king heard the request of Jíwaka, he gave him permission to use any of the royal modes of conveyance, and to pass out of the palace gates any hour of the day. Of this permission he availed himself, and went hither and thither at his will; now in this conveyance and then in that; so that the wonder of the citizens was greatly excited. One day he brought home an abundance of medicine, which he boiled in oil and poured into a dish. He then told the king that it was exceedingly powerful, so that it would be requisite for him to take it at once, without tasting it, or the virtue would be gone. The king stopped his nose with one hand, and with the other put the medicine into his mouth. At this moment Jíwaka, after informing the attendants what to give the king, went to the elephant hall, and mounting the elephant Baddrawati, set off towards Rajagaha like the wind. After going fifty yojanas, he arrived at Kosambæ,* where he remained a little to refresh himself, as he knew that the king had no army that could come so quickly; and that if any one came it would be either the slave, the elephant Nálágiri, the mule, or the horse, but that the elephant he had brought was five times swifter than any other animal.

* This city is mentioned in the Rámáyana and the Puránas.

When the king took the medicine, he knew instantly that he had swallowed oil; and in a rage he commanded that Jíwaka should be impaled; but the nobles informed him that he had fled away upon the elephant Baddrawati. He then sent for the slave Oppanika, and told him that if he would pursue the physician and bring him back he should receive a great reward. In an instant the slave was at Kosambæ, and told Jíwaka that he must return with him to the palace; but he said that he was hungry, and must have something to eat, and requested Oppanika to join him at his meal. As the slave refused, he gave him part of a fruit, in which he had previously put something from the tip of his finger; but when he had eaten about half of it, he fainted away, and Jíwaka was left to finish his repast at his leisure. After a little time he gave the elephant some water to drink, and going to the slave, enquired why he did not take him to the king; but Oppanika said that he would go with Jíwaka to any part of the world, and become his servant, if he would restore him. The physician laughed, and told him to eat the other half of the fruit; but he said that from eating the former half he was now unable to lift up his head, and if he ate any more he should certainly die outright. Jíwaka told him that he had never at any time taken life, and that this was the first time he had gone so far as to render any one unable to hold up his head. The slave then ate the other half of the fruit, and was in an instant well, like a man awaking out of a dream. Jíwaka delivered to him the elephant, and told him to return to Udéni, as by that time the king would be perfectly recovered from his disease; and he himself went on his way to Rajagaha, on arriving at which he informed Bimsara of all that had taken place.

It was after these events, that Jíwaka administered medicine to Budha, in the perfume of a flower; and it was because, in many previous births, he had wished for this opportunity, that he received his unexampled skill; it was the reward of his merit.

In this way was the medicine given. On a certain occasion, when Budha was sick, it was thought that if he were to take a little opening medicine he would be better; and accordingly Ananda went to Jíwaka to inform him that the teacher of the world was indisposed. On receiving this information, Jíwaka, who thought that the time to which he had so long looked forward had arrived, went to the wihára, as Budha was at that time residing near Rajagaha. After making the proper enquiries, he discovered that there were three causes of the disease; and in order to remove them he prepared three lotus flowers, into each of which he put a quantity of medicine. The flowers were then given to Budha at three separate times, and by smelling* at them his bowels were moved ten times by each flower. By means of the first flower the first cause of disease passed away; and by the other two the second and third causes were removed.

When this event was known to the faithful, persons from sixteen kelas of different tribes brought food of a kind proper for an invalid, each one according to his ability. But as Mugalan knew that it was requisite that food of the most delicate kind it was possible to provide should be procured, he looked with his divine eyes to see where it could be found, when he discovered that Sóna, of the city of Champá,† in Jambudwípa, had in his possession a kind of rice that would be better adapted for the sage than any other in the world.

The parents of Sóna were exceedingly rich, as they had thousands of houses surmounted by towers in the city, and possessed in addition 90,000 villages. From his childhood, Sóna never put his foot to the ground. Why? Upon the sole of his foot was a row of red hairs turning towards the right, like the flowers painted upon a drum, and appearing as if made by a vermilion pencil. It was because his parents saw this sign of greatness that they did not allow him to step on the ground; and they gave him many attendants. Greatly were the people of Jambudwípa astonished, when they heard of this remarkable

---

* By the ancients great efficacy was ascribed to perfumes. It is said of Democritus that being aware of his approaching end, but desirous to prolong his life beyond the festival of Ceres, he held hot bread to his nose, by means of which his wish was accomplished.

† Founded by Champapuri, a city of which traces still remain in the vicinity of Bhagalpur. It is the capital of Anga. Fa Hian says, that in following the course of the Ganges, there was upon the southern bank, the extensive kingdom of Tchen pho. The monasteries he saw appeared to be inhabited by priests. Hiuan Thsang describes the city as being about thirteen miles in circumference; the country was fertile, and the climate warm. There were about ten monasteries, for the most part in ruin, with not more than 200 priests, whilst there were twenty temples belonging to the heterodox fraternities.

appearance; they went in numbers to see it, like the pilgrims who visit the srí-páda, or impression of Budha's foot, upon Samanælla, in the island of Ceylon. Sóna resided in the upper story of a tower, surrounded by magnificent curtains, so that he could not even see the ground. His servants were never beaten, as in the families of other nobles, and yet were they all obedient. How was this? When any of them did wrong, Sóna said that he would put his foot to the ground if they were punished; and as all were afraid lest in this way they should cause the loss of so much merit, they were as attentive as if they had been coerced by being maimed, or their heads had been pounded by a hammer, or other severe modes of punishment had been used. In a former birth Sóna erected a wihára for a Pasé-Budha, who one day hurt his foot when he was walking, after which he provided him with a costly carpet upon which to walk. It was through the merit of this act, that he received in the present birth so great a distinction. And now as to the rice. There was a large field surrounded by a high fence, and covered by a network of hair. It was irrigated by water in which sandal-wood, camphor, and all kinds of fragrant substances had been steeped, so that their smell was imparted to the ground, the grain, and even to the husbandmen. At the harvest, the grain was cut, not with a sickle, but by the nails of the reapers. The rice was stored in a granary made of sandal-wood; first there was a layer of fragrant substances a cubit high, and then a layer of rice, and so on in succession. This granary was built in the most compact manner, and was not open until three years after it had been closed; and at that time, when the doors were thrown open, the perfume spread through the whole city, and every one knew whence it proceeded. Afterwards, as much was taken out every day as sufficed for the wants of the noble's family. When undergoing the usual preparation, it was pounded in a mortar of sandal-wood, and the grains resembled pearls. The husks were carefully preserved, and after being ground, were used by the people for the perfuming of their bodies. The rice was put in new vessels that had been purified seven or eight times, and when boiled the fuel was of some fragrant wood. This rice was received by Sóna because in the former birth he had faithfully fed a Pasé-Budha.

When Mugalan perceived in what part of the world the rice

was to be procured, he took his alms-bowl in his hand, and went through the air from Rajagaha to Champá, where he remained standing, near the house of Sóna, like a blue mountain covered by a cloud. The noble saw him, and filled his bowl with the most excellent rice; but when Mugalan received it, he said he had come to procure it for Budha, who had that day taken medicine. Then Sóna told him to eat what was in the bowl, and he would have it washed, and re-filled. The priest returned to Rajagaha in the same way as he left it, and presented the bowl to the illustrious sage. The king, Bimsara, also had food prepared, which he took to the wihára; but when he saw the rice that Mugalan had brought he enquired whether it had been procured in the dwelling of Sekra, or in Uturukuru, as it was impossible that it could have been grown in the world of men. Budha allowed him to taste of it, and told him it was from his own city of Champá, where a noble ate it every day. The king afterwards visited the noble, who in turn came to Rajagaha, when he saw Budha, and entered the path sowán. Sóna became a priest.

On the same day, Jíwaka presented a beautiful garment to Budha, which he himself had received as a present from one of his royal patients. It was a divine garment procured from the kalpa-tree in Uturukuru. One of the birds that take the dead bodies to the Yugandhara rocks to feed upon the flesh, in passing over a portion of the forest of Himála that belonged to Chandapprajóta, let two of the robes fall, when they were found by an archer, and brought to the king; and the king, in gratitude for the benefit he had received in being restored to health, sent them to Jíwaka. Budha reflected, that if the priests received robes of this costly description, they would be in danger from thieves; and he intimated the danger to Ananda. In consequence, Ananda cut them into thirty pieces, which he sewed together in five divisions, so that when the robe was completed, it resembled the patches in a rice-field divided by embankments. The great sage was pleased when he saw this contrivance, and ordained a law that his priests should only have three robes, and that they should always be composed of thirty pieces of cloth.

Jíwaka entered the path sowán, after hearing a discourse delivered by Budha; and as he wished to see the teacher thrice every day, but was unable to go so far as Wéluwanáráma he built a wihára in his own garden, and invited Budha to make it his residence. These things occurred in the twentieth year after the reception of the Budhaship.

21. *The History of Anguli-mála.*

The wife of the próhita of the king of Kosol, Bhárggawa, whose name was Mantáni, had a son. At the moment of his birth, all the weapons* in the city shone with a bright light; in consequence of which, the father consulted an astrologer,† who informed him that his son would become a robber. The father, on going to the palace the next day, asked the king if he had slept well the previous night; but he said that he had not, as his state sword had shone, which indicated that there was some danger coming, either upon himself or his kingdom. The brahman then informed the king that a son had been born to him, on whose account not only the state sword but all the weapons in the city had shone, which was a sign that his son would become a robber; and enquired whether the king wished him to put his son away; but the king said that as one single person could not do much harm, it would be better to bring him up. The child received the name of Ahingsaka.

When Ahingsaka grew up, he was sent to a college in Takshalá, where he excelled all the other pupils; which set them at enmity against him, and caused them to seek some mode of accusation, that they might have him punished. They could say nothing against his ability, or the respectability of his family; they, therefore, accused him of taking improper liberties with the professor's wife. For this purpose they divided themselves into three parties. The first party informed him of the pupil's crime; and the second and third party confirmed what the first had said; and as the professor could not believe that they spoke the truth, they told him that he must look to his own interests; they had done their duty, and could do no more. After this he noticed that his wife spoke kindly to Ahingsaka, which excited his suspicion, and he resolved upon his destruction; but he saw that it could not be accomplished openly, or no more pupils

* In an enumeration of the prodigies that occurred in Rome, A.U. 652, Julius Obsequens says that the spears of Mars, preserved in the palace, moved of their own accord.

† Nekata, one skilled in the prognostications of the nekatás or lunar mansions.

S

would place themselves under his care. He therefore said to the youth, "It will not be in my power to teach you further, unless you destroy a thousand men, and bring me one of their fingers as an evidence of their death." Ahingsaka replied that it was not the custom of his family to do evil to others; but still, from his love of learning, and as he thought that there was no other way by which he could prosecute his studies, he went to the forest, to a place where eight ways met, and began to murder those who passed in that direction. As it was observed that he cut off the fingers of his victims, he received the name of Anguli-mála. In a little time the people went to Sewet to inform the king that his country was becoming depopulated by the cruelty of a robber, and to entreat that he would come with an army and seize him, that they might be delivered from his power. The king resolved to accede to their request; but when the intelligence spread through the city, the próhita said to his wife that he feared the chief was none other than their own son, and asked her what was to be done. She said that he had better hasten to the forest before the departure of the king, and bring their son away; but the father replied that there were four things that could not be trusted,—a robber, a branch, the king, and woman. The mother, therefore, prepared to take upon herself this task.

At this time Budha was residing in the Jétáwana wihára, and he saw that Anguli-mála, from the merit he had received in former births, had virtue sufficient to enable him to enter the priesthood, and become a rahat, on the hearing of a single stanza of bana. He also saw that if the mother went she would be killed; and in order that this might be prevented, he took the form of a common priest, and went towards the forest. The herdsmen informed him that no one could pass that way alone; that men were obliged to go in companies of forty and fifty; and that even then they were sometimes cut off. That very day the number of victims was completed, except one, and Anguli-mála resolved that whosoever it might be that he saw, that person should be killed; yet it was now difficult for him to seize even a single individual, as the travellers always passed in large companies, well defended. At last he saw a priest, and as he was alone, and had no weapon, he thought it would be no difficult matter to slay him. For this purpose he pursued him, but after he had run twelve miles he could not overtake him. He thought within himself, "I have run after elephants, horses, chariots, and the swift deer, and have overtaken them, but this priest outstrips me." He then called out to the priest to stop; and Budha did so, but told him to remain where he was, and not come nearer. As Anguli-mála thought he must have some design in this, he was obedient; when Budha gave him good advice, telling him to be kind to all sentient beings, by which means he would save himself from the four hells. On hearing this, Anguli-mála knew that it was Budha, and that he had put himself to this trouble in order to assist him; he therefore, worshipped the sage, received the precepts, and requested ordination. Budha replied, "Ehi Bhikkhu; hither, priest!" at the same time lifting up his right hand. By this means Anguli-mála was enabled to receive the eight requisites of the priesthood at the same moment; and at once became of the upasampadá order, without being previously a sámanéra novice.

After this transformation, Anguli-mala went to reside as a priest in the Jétáwana wihára. His father and mother went to the forest, but were not able to find him. The king saw that it was necessary for him to exert himself, in order to save his people from this great danger. He was ashamed to remain in the city when his people were so urgent, and yet he was afraid to go; so he went to the wihára to ask the advice of Budha. The sage said to him, "What is the matter, oh king? Is Bimsara become your enemy; or are you afraid of the princes of Wisálá, or of some other monarch?" The king: "No; I am going to the forest to secure a noted robber called Anguli-mála." Budha: "If he should have become a priest, how would you act?" The king: "I should pay him due reverence;" but he thought it was impossible that Budha could receive into the priesthood so great a sinner. The king asked where he was at that time; and when informed that he was in the same wihára, he became greatly afraid; but Budha told him not to be alarmed. Then the king requested to be taken to his presence, and loosing his rich girdle from his loins, he laid it at the priest's feet; but like one keeping the ordinances called telesdhutánga, he would not receive it. At this the king was greatly surprised, and said, "This is a wonderful circumstance; the cruel has become kind; the covetous, liberal; the wicked, pure; this is through your influence; for we may crush the people with clubs, and scourge them, but there is no amendment in their conduct." Soon afterwards, Anguli-mála went to his own village with the alms-bowl; but when the people heard his name, they were afraid, and gave him nothing, so that he became very faint. On his return to the city, he saw a woman in severe labour, unable to bring forth; and he greatly pitied her. He who had slain 999 people, now felt compassion for an afflicted woman, from having entered the priesthood. On his arrival at the wihára, he informed Budha of what he had seen, who said to him, "Go to the place, and say, 'I have never knowingly put any creature to death since I was born; by the virtue of this observance may you be free from pain!'" The priest replied that he could not tell a lie, as he had knowingly put to death many persons; but Budha said, "Yes, but this was when you were a laic; you are now a priest; you have been born again; when you now say that such a thing is from the time of your birth, you mean that it is from the time you entered the priesthood." In consequence of this intimation, he went to the place; a screen was placed around the mother, and sitting upon a chair he repeated the words of Budha; when in an instant the child was born, with as much ease as water falls from a vessel. Upon the same spot a hall was afterwards erected, for the assistance of afflicted females, as the virtue communicated by Anguli-mála still continued; and other diseases were healed in the same way.

At times Anguli-mála was in great distress, because the people, from fear, were unwilling to give him alms. When he thought of the murders he had committed, how parents had entreated to be spared for the sake of their children, and how he had been deaf to the cries of the people when they pleaded for mercy, he felt the keenest sorrow. But Budha consoled him by saying, that these things were the same as if they had been done in a former birth, inasmuch as they were done before he became a priest. In a little time he became a rahat. When going to procure alms, if the people were throwing any missile to send away the dogs or the crows, it was sure to hit his body. One day when his head was thus laid open, streaming with blood he went to Budha; who told him he must endure all this patiently, as it was the consequence of the murders he had committed, and was instead of having to suffer a hundred thousand years in hell. "That which has been done in a former state of existence," said Budha, "will receive its reward in the present life, whether it was good or evil; but if it be deprived of its power (as by becoming a rahat), no further consequences are produced. So long as existence continues, the effects of karma must continue; and it is only by the cessation of existence that they can be entirely overcome." When any priest attains the rahatship, he cuts off the consequences of demerit as regards all subsequent existence; but if he has done any great misdeed in a former birth, the consequence will be felt in the present birth; yet in this alone, as it ceases on the attainment of nirwána. Reflecting on these things, Anguli-mála was comforted, and said, "The hook of the driver subdues the elephant and other animals; but Budha subdues by kindness." At different times many other robbers and murderers were overcome by Budha, as Sankicha, Atimuktaka, and Khánu-kondanya, each of whom had 500 companions, as well as Kelaruwan, who had 900 companions; and many hundreds and thousands of robbers were brought to nirwána by his assistance. (*Amáwatura.*)

22. *The History of Sabhiya.*

In a former age, after Kásyapa Budha had attained nirwána, the priests became negligent, and did not observe the precepts; but seven individuals, who were desirous of entering the paths before the power to do so was entirely lost, became priests, and ascended a high rock by a ladder; after which they threw down the ladder, and had no means of escape. The same night the oldest of the seven became a rahat, and went to Anotatta and Uturukuru, whence he brought water and rice to his companions; but they refused to receive them, until they also had become rahats. Soon afterwards the second priest entered the path anágámi, and he also urged the others to partake of the food, but they still refused. The first priest entered nirwána; the second was born in the Sudassa brahmalóka; and the rest, who died in seven days from the want of food, were born in different kámáwachara worlds. In the time of Gótama Budha, one of them was the maha-rája Poksí; another was Mahakásyapa; a third, the priest Dáruchí; a fourth, the priest Tissa, son of Dharmmapála; and a fifth, Sabhiya, a paribrájika. The last mentioned individual was the son of Sabhiyá, a paribrájikáwa, who at the time she was receiving the instructions of a certain teacher, became connected with another pupil, the consequences of which were soon apparent, and she was sent away. When the child of which she was delivered grew up, he was so exceedingly well skilled in argument, that no one was able to dispute with him. His residence was near the gate of the city, and he taught the princes. At the same time the abode of Budha was in the Wéluwana wihára, near Rajagaha; but Sabhiya did not know of his existence. The priest who had been born in the brahma-lóka one day examined into the cause of his prosperity; and when he discovered it he wondered what had become of the other priests who were with him upon the rock; and as he saw the situation of Sabhiya, he resolved that he would make known to him the merits of Budha. He, therefore, went to him by night, and called him by name; and when he arose and saw him, the brahman propounded to him twenty questions, and told him to go from place to place until he found some one to answer them; and when he had found such a one, to acknowledge him as his teacher, and embrace his doctrines. In accordance with this advice he went to Purána Kásyapa, and the other tirttakas, but they were not able to answer his questions; and as he was thus disappointed, he thought it would be better to become a laic, and enjoy himself, without any further thought about these matters. Though some one afterwards praised Gótama, he was at first unwilling to go to him, as he thought so young a teacher would be unable to assist him, when those of so much more experience had failed. But after a little further reflection, he was persuaded; and going to the wihára, he requested permission to propose the twenty questions. Budha replied, "You have travelled 700 yojanas in order that you might receive an answer to these questions; it is therefore right that your request should be granted." On hearing this, Sabhiya was greatly pleased, as no other teacher had received him with so much kindness. The answers given by Budha appear in the Sabhiya-sútra. Without any delay Sabhiya embraced the doctrines of Budha, and after a trial of four months, which was the usual custom when the tirttakas requested ordination, he was admitted to the priesthood, and became a rahat in due time. (*Amáwatura.*)

23. *The History of Sacha.*

There were two tirttakas, the one a female and the other a male, whose custom it was to go from place to place propounding 500 questions,* both of whom arrived at the same time at Wisálá, where they held a disputation in the presence of the Lichawi princes; and as they were both equally clever, the victory could be claimed by neither party. At the request of the princes, they took up their abode in the city, and after some time had a son, Sacha, and afterwards four daughters, Sachá, Lalá, Patáchárá, and Awáwataka. The parents had no dowry to give their girls; but they taught them the 500 questions. It was the custom of the tirttakas that if any laic overcame their daughters in argument, they were given to them as wives; but if overcome by priests, they embraced the priesthood. When arrived at the proper age, the four daughters took jambu branches in their hands, and went from place to place to hold disputations. In the course of their travels† they came to the city of Sewet, and as their manner was, they fixed their branches near the gate of the city, and made known that if any one was wishful to contend with them he might pluck the fruit.

At this time Budha resided in the Jétáwana wihára, and on the day when the four females arrived, it happened that Seriyut remained behind for a short time, when the others had gone with the alms-bowl, as he had to look after some priests that were sick. On arriving at the gate of the city, he saw the branches; and when he asked the reason why they were put there, and was told, he requested the persons near to pluck the fruit; and though at first they were afraid to obey his command, as they knew that they were not able to contend with the tirttakas, they took the fruit when he told them they might go to the wihára and present them there, by which they would find some one with the power that they themselves lacked. The females, on returning to

---

* In former times it was common for very learned pundits to go from kingdom to kingdom, challenging each king to bring forth his pundits to hold disputations on the subjects contained in the shastras. Uduyuna, in this manner, obtained the victory over all the pundits in the world. He was also the great instrument in overcoming the Budhists, and in re-establishing the practice of the Vedas.—Ward's Hindoos.

† "The Sibyllae were prophetic women, probably of Asiatic origin, whose peculiar custom seems to have been to wander with their sacred books from place to place."—Schmitz.

the gate, were told that the fruit had been taken by command of Seriyut; upon which they went as near to the wihára as was permitted to persons of their class, and told Seriyut that they had come to begin the disputation. The priest replied, that as they were females it was right that they should first propound their questions to him, and when they were answered he would become the examiner. Each of them was acquainted with a thousand questions, half of which had been taught them by their father, and the other half by their mother; but Seriyut answered the whole of the questions with as much ease as the nelum-beli creeper is cut with a sharp instrument. When their turn came to answer they were afraid, and declined any further contest; but as they were now to become priestesses, and it was necessary that their minds should previously be subdued, Seriyut said to them, "What does *one*, or unity mean?" None of the four could see beginning, middle, or end of this question, though they considered it well; and when the priest pressed them for an answer, they said, "Sir, we do not understand it." Seriyut: "Then I have answered a thousand questions that you put to me; but you have not answered one. With whom is the victory?" The females: "Venerable sir, you are the conqueror." Seriyut: "What will you now do?" The females: "According to the direction of our parents, we must now become recluses." Seriyut: "I am not allowed to receive you to profession; but I will give you a memorandum to take to the place where females are admitted." In a little time they learnt what was necessary, and were admitted to profession.

The tirttaka Sacha, who was more learned than his sisters, remained at Wisálá, instructing the princes. Such was the extent of his learning, that he feared his body would burst from its expansion; and to prevent this misfortune, he bound himself with an iron girdle.* To all he proclaimed, "There is no one so learned as myself;" and great numbers followed him on this account. At that time there was also in Wisálá a priest called Assaji, who, when going early in the morning with his alms-bowl, was seen by the tirttaka. On seeing him, Sacha

* This arises from the idea that the heart is the seat of the thoughts as well as of the affections. Elihu, the son of Barachel held sentiments in unison with those of Sacha. "I am full of words; the spirit of my belly constraineth me; behold, my belly is as wine which hath no vent; it is ready to burst like new bottles."—Job xxxii. 18, 19.

thought it would be well to hold a disputation with Budha, about whom he had heard so much; but that first he must learn from his disciples the nature of the doctrines he taught. He therefore asked Assaji by what means it was that Budha won over to his side those who embraced his doctrines, or by what means he subdued the minds of his followers. The priest considered that he must not inform him at first of the pains they had to endure before they could enter the paths, or he would be discouraged, and perhaps say that if such were the case, he had rather be born in hell. He, therefore, informed him of the impermanency of the panchaskhandas, the corporeal elements; and told him that this was the great truth that the teacher of the three worlds continually impressed upon his disciples. When the tirttaka heard this declaration, he said, "Never before did I hear of such a doctrine; I will go at once to Budha and convince him of the greatness of such an error." Before this he was afraid of disputing with Budha, as he was not aware of the character of his doctrines, but now he felt that his fears were removed; and he requested, with much boasting of what he was about to accomplish, the Lichawi princes to accompany him. The princes replied, that neither yaká, nor déwa, nor brahma, nor man, was able to contend with the great teacher; but 500 of them resolved to be present at the contest, and see the result.

It was about noon when Sacha arrived at the wihára. The priests had eaten their food, and were walking about. Budha had perceived that the tirttaka would come at that time; and on returning from the city with the alms-bowl, he did not retire as usual, but commanded the priests to prepare a seat in the adjacent forest, to which place he repaired; and Sacha, on his arrival, was directed to the same spot. When the citizens heard that he had gone to hold a disputation with Budha accompanied by 500 of the princes, they flocked in great numbers to the forest, that they might be present at the contest. The princes did reverence to the sage, when Sacha requested permission to ask a question; and Budha informed him that he might propose any question whatever, according to his own will. The same extensive permission was given on other occasions to the yaká Alawaka, to Ajásat, to Sekra, and to others; nor is this to be wondered at, as even in former births, previous to his reception of the Budhaship, his wisdom had enabled him to give the same liberty to his opponents. The question proposed by Sacha was the same that he had previously asked from Assaji; and Budha gave him the same reply, lest the doctrines of the teacher and the disciple should appear to be different. There are some persons whom none but a supreme Budha can convince of their error; and Sacha was of this description. After they had contended some time,* Sacha confessed that the declaration of Budha was right; when the sage declared to him, "As the man who goes to the forest with his axe, and cutting down a plantain-tree, examines it from top to root, but finds in it no hard wood; so I have found no profit in this conversation of yours, no worth in your argument. The woodpecker thinks that with his bill he can penetrate the ebony as easily as he has entered trees that are soft or decayed, but he only breaks his bill for his pains; so you, who have contended with others and been victor, thought that in the same way you could overcome the Tatágata, but you are foiled in the attempt, and your effort has been vain." The perspiration now fell from the tirttaka's body so copiously that his robe was saturated with it; and the princes thought, "This is the man who was so often angry with us on account of our dulness, when we were under his instruction; but now he receives the punishment that he was once accustomed to inflict upon others." The tirttaka perceived their thoughts, and resolving to put the best face he could upon the matter, said to Budha, "How many reasons are there why the priesthood is embraced by your disciples?" The sage replied, "There are eleven reasons why my disciples reject the thought that this is mine, or that I am, and despise the corporeal elements. Whether that which is spoken of be in past, present, or future time, whether great or small, whether illustrious or mean, whether it be that which is called their own or that which

* The argument is given in a subsequent part of this work under the head Panchaskhanda. Had it been inserted here, it would not have been understood without several notes.

† The stem of the plantain tree is composed of cellular tissue, and is entirely destitute of all woody substance. It has often occurred to me that from its peculiar structure and the rapidity of its growth, it must be admirably adapted to answer the purpose of the student of vegetable physiology. It has been supposed by Gesenius (Heb. Lex. art. תאנה), that it was with the leaves of the plantain-tree our first parents endeavoured to hide their nakedness; but no leaf could be less adapted to the purpose, as it tears with a slight touch, and when on the tree is frequently riven into shreds by the wind.

is said to belong to another, no one can say respecting it, this is mine." Again Sacha confessed that though he had despised Budha, he was now overcome; he was like a man exposed to an elephant or to a nayá, or to an extensive fire; but it was not from a sense of danger that he thus felt.

At the conclusion of this interview, Sacha invited Budha to partake of a repast at his dwelling on the following day, and the sage gave his consent in the usual manner. Of this he informed the princes, and told them that the 500 measures of rice they provided for him daily must on the following morning be offered to Budha. The next day, when all was prepared, Budha went to his dwelling, and Sacha presented to him the food with his own hand, saying, "May those who have provided this offering receive its reward;" but the great teacher told him that the reward would be his own, as the princes presented the food to him, and he presented it to the Tatágata. Still Sacha could not forbear the reflection that he had once been accounted as a learned man, and was honoured by all, but now he was despised. He, therefore, went once more to the wihára privately, and thought that if he was again overcome, he would sincerely embrace the doctrines of Budha. At this moment Budha was in the outer part of the wihára, and as the approach of the tirttaka was seen by Ananda, he requested him to await his arrival. Again Budha propounded to him the dharmma, but he neither entered the paths nor became a priest. Then why did Budha teach him? Because he foresaw that 246 years after he attained nirwána, Sacha would be born in Ceylon, of a noble family, not far from the Kinihiri wihára, where he would embrace the priesthood and become the rahat Kalubudharakhita. It was to this priest that the monarch of Ceylon presented the whole of the island, 100 yojanas in extent, when he heard him saying bana at the foot of a timbiri tree, near the wihára of Sægiri. (*Amáwatura.*)

24. *The two Mecrhants of Sunáparanta.*

There were two brothers resident in the country called Sunáparanta, merchants, who went to trade with 500 wagons; sometimes the elder brother accompanying the goods, and at other times the younger. On a certain occasion the elder brother, Punna, went to Sewet, and formed his encampment near the

Jétáwana wihára. When he saw the citizens taking offerings to Budha, he enquired where they were going, and they said that they were going to hear the bana of Budha. The mention of the name of Budha caused his bones to start within his flesh from joy; and he went with his attendants to the wihára, where, after hearing bana, he resolved upon entering the priesthood. Previous to his return he went to Budha, and informed him that he was about to become a priest in his own country, requesting some religious advices previous to his departure; and Budha said, "The people of Sunáparanta are exceedingly violent; if they oppose you and revile you, what will you do?" Merchant: "I will make no reply." Budha: "If they strike you?" Merchant: "I will not strike in return." Budha: "If they try to take your life?" Merchant: "There are some priests who from various causes are tired of life, and they seek opportunities whereby their lives may be taken; but this course I shall avoid." For these answers he received the approbation of Budha.

For some time Punna resided near his younger brother, at his own request; after which he went to reside at Mudugiri, but as it was near the sea, he was disturbed by the waves; and leaving this place he went to Mailigiri, but as there were many of the birds called minors that made a noise both at night and by day, he went to Muluaráma, which was also near his brother. Here he became a rahat. One day 300 of his former assistants were in great danger during a voyage; but he saw their situation, and saved them, enabling them to return home with a cargo of red sandal-wood. When they made an offering to Punna of part of the wood, he told them to build therewith a residence for Budha; and when it was completed he went through the air and invited Budha to visit the residence that they had prepared. On receiving the invitation, Budha said to Ananda,[*] "To-morrow it is my intention to visit Sunáparanta; inform 500 priests, save one, that they will have to accompany me." This information was imparted to the priests by laha.[†] The

---

[*] In a legend previously inserted (p. 57), it is said that this circumstance occurred in the eighth year after he had attained the Budhaship, on his third visit to Ceylon; but at this time Ananda had not become his attendant.

[†] The laha was a tablet hung up in some part of the wihára, upon which any matter might be written about which it was intended that the priests should be informed.

intention of Budha was perceived by Sekra, who provided the proper number of litters, and caused them to appear near the wihára. The first and best was entered by Budha, and the next in order were occupied by the two agra-sráwakas, after whom the other priests took possession of the rest. On their way to Sunáparanta they called at Sachabadda, where there was a mendicant with clotted hair. To him Budha delivered a discourse, as he saw that he had the merit necessary to enable him to become a rahat; and after he had attained this state, he entered the vacant litter, and accompanied Budha to the merchant's village. (*Amáwatura*).

25. *The Yaká Alawaka overcome by Budha.*

The king of Alow was accustomed, in order that he might prepare himself for the fatigues of war, to betake himself to the forest, and chase the game, without ceasing, for the space of seven days. On one occasion a part of the forest was surrounded, and the king gave orders that no animal should be permitted to escape; but a deer burst through the barrier near the king, and he pursued it alone to the distance of three yojanas before he killed it. Though he had no occasion for the flesh, yet to give proof of his prowess to his attendants, he divided it into two parts, and making a yoke of a piece of wood, attached one to each end, with which he proceeded towards the place where he had left the nobles. On the way he arrived at a banian tree, near a place where four roads met; and as he was very much fatigued, he remained a little time under the tree to rest. This banian was the residence of the yaká Alawaka, a subject of Wéramuna, who was accustomed to slay all persons who approached the tree. After his usual manner he came to slay the king, who was so terrified, that he promised, if his life was spared, every day to provide for the demon a victim and a dish of rice. But Alawaka replied, "When you return to the kingdom you will forget the promise you have made; I can only seize those who approach the tree, and therefore I cannot permit you to escape." But the king said, that on the day he omitted to make the offering, the yaká might come to the palace and seize his person. On receiving this promise Alawaka permitted him to return to the palace; and on his arrival he called the chief of the city, and told him what had occurred. The noble enquired if he had named a day on which the sacrifice was to cease; and when he said that he had not, he lamented that the king had committed so great an error, but promised to do his utmost to remedy the evil, without any care on the part of the king. For this purpose he went to the door of the prison, and said that those who were appointed to death for murder, and wished to live, might be reprieved, if they would only take a dish of rice and present it at the banian tree. The murderers embraced his offer; but when they approached the tree, they were caught by the yaká and slain. A similar offer was afterwards made to the thieves, and they too were killed in the same manner, until the prison was empty. Then innocent persons were accused falsely, and condemned to the punishment that had been inflicted upon the others. When this stratagem failed, the aged were taken by house-row; but the king told his noble that the people came to complain that their parents and grandparents were taken from them, and commanded him to resort to some other method to secure the daily victim. The noble said, that if he was not permitted to take the aged, he must seize the infants, for whom there would perhaps be less affection; but when this became known, the mothers who had children, or those who were pregnant, removed to other countries. In this way twelve years passed over. At last no child was left in the city but the king's own son, and as a man will rather part with anything than his life, permission was given to sacrifice the prince; and amidst the tears of the queens and courtezans, the nurse was directed to present him to the yaká.

On the morning of the same day, it was seen by Budha that the prince had sufficient merit to enable him to enter the path anágámi, and that the yaká might enter the path sowán. He, therefore, took his alms-bowl, and proceeded a distance of thirty yojanas from the Jétáwana wihára, in which he at that time resided, to the door of the yaká's dwelling. The porter, Gadrabha, asked him why he had come there at that hour; and he said that he had come to remain for a time in the dwelling of Alawaka. The porter informed him that this would be attended with danger, as his master was very cruel, not respecting even his own parents; but Budha said that no harm would happen to him, if he were allowed to remain there a single night. The porter again declared that his master tore out the hearts of all who came near, and taking them by the legs clove them in two; and when the sage still persisted in his request, the porter said he would go to the Himála forest, and ask the permission of his master. On his departure, Budha entered the dwelling, and sat down on the throne occupied by the yaká on days of festivity, upon which the courtezans of the place came and did him reverence; and the sage preached to them the bana, telling them to be kind to all and injure no one; on the hearing of which they said, Sádhu, in approbation. But when Gadrabha informed his master that Budha was at his dwelling, he became greatly enraged, and said that Gótama should suffer for this intrusion.

It happened that at this time the yakás Sátágera and Bémáwata were on their way, with their attendants, to worship Budha at the Jétáwana wihára. The yakás, in passing though the sky, must leave the paths that are frequented by the déwas. Around the dwelling of Alawaka there was an iron fence, and above it was protected by a net of gold. It was like a casket three yojanas in height. The two yakás had to pass near this place; but as no yaká is permitted to approach Budha (unless it be for the purpose of doing him reverence) they were arrested in their flight; and on looking to see what was the cause, they perceived that the great teacher was seated upon the throne in the yaká's dwelling; on which they went and offered worship, and afterwards departed to the Himála forest. Here they met with Alawaka, and informed him that a most fortunate circumstance had occurred to him, as Budha was in his dwelling, and he must go and entertain him. On hearing this, the heart of the yaká became agitated, and he asked, " Who is this Budha that has dared to enter my dwelling?" The two yakás replied, " Know you not Budha, the lord of the three worlds?" The yaká declared that whoever he was, he would drive him from his dwelling; but his companions said to him, "Why, yaká, you are like a calf, just born, near a mighty bull; like a tiny elephant, near the king of the tribe; like an old jackal, near a strong lion; like a crow, near a garunda 150 yojanas high; what can you do?" Then Alawaka arose from his seat full of rage, and placing his foot upon the mountain Ratgal, he appeared like a blaze of fire, and said, " Now we shall see whose power is the greater;" then he struck with his foot the mountain Kailása, which sent forth sparks like a red hot iron bar struck by the sledge hammer of the smith. Again he called out, "I am the yaká Alawaka!" and the sound reverberated through the whole of Jambudwipa.* Without delay the yaká went to his dwelling, and endeavoured to drive Budha away by a storm which he caused to arise from the four quarters, which had a force sufficient to bear down trees and rocks many yojanas in size; but by the power of Budha it was deprived of all ability to harm. After this showers were poured down of rain, weapons, sand, charcoal, ashes, and darkness; but they did no injury whatever to the sage. He then assumed a fearful form, as Budha did not stop him as he did Wasawartta, but let him weary himself by his exertions during the whole night. Yet he was no more able to approach the object of his hatred than a fly is to alight upon red-hot iron. He then threw the chéla weapon,† but it was equally impotent. By this time the déwas had assembled that they might see the contest. The yaká was surprised when he saw that his formidable weapon had no power, and looked to see what was the cause: by which he discovered that it was the affection or kindness of Budha, and that kindness must be overcome by kindness, and not by anger. So he quietly asked the sage to retire from his dwelling; and as Budha knew that rage was to be overcome by mildness, he arose and departed from the place. Seeing this, the yaká thought, "I have been contending with this priest a whole night without producing any effect, and now at a single word he retires." By this his heart was softened. But he

---

* There are four exclamations that were heard to the same distance. 1. When the yaká Púrnaku played with Dhananjayakórawya at dice, and overcame him, he cried out, "I am conqueror." 2. When the people of the world, in the time of Kasyapa Budha, had perverted the dharmma, Sekra assumed the appearance of a hunter, with Wiswakarmma as his dog, and going from place to place he told the unbelievers that they would be destroyed. 3. When the seven kings went to Ságal, to carry off Prabháwati, the queen of Kusa, he entered the street upon an elephant, accompanied by the queen, and called out, "I am king Kusa." 4. When the yaká exclaimed, "I am Alawaka."

† There are four weapons in the world that no one can withstand. 1. The chéla of Alawaka; 2. The wajra of Sekra; 3. The gadhá or gajá of Wésamuna; and 4. The mace of Yama, the regent of death. Were Alawaka to throw his weapon into the air there would be no rain for twelve years; if to the earth, no herbage could grow for twelve months; if to the sea, it would be dried up. Were Sekra to strike Maha Méru in anger with the wajra it would be cloven in two. Wésamuna could at once cut off the heads of many thousands of yakás. And the mere sight of the weapon of Yama scorches up the khumbandas.

again thought it would be better to see whether he went away from anger or from a spirit of disobedience, and called him back. Budha came. Thrice this was repeated, the sage returning when called, after he had been allowed so many times to depart, as he knew the intention of Alawaka. When a child cries its mother gives what it cries for in order to pacify it; and as Budha knew that if the yaká were angry he would not have a heart to hear bana, he yielded to his command, that he might become tranquillised. And as any one who intends to pour precious liquor into a vessel first cleanses the vessel, so Budha cleansed the heart of Alawaka that it might be prepared to receive the dharmma.

The yaká resolved on keeping Budha walking to and fro till night, when he would be tired, and so he could easily take him by the feet and cast him into the river; but when he a fourth time charged him to go away, he refused, as he knew his intention. Budha, however, said to him that he might ask any question, and it would be answered. It was the custom of the yaká to entangle the recluses and priests who came to his dwelling, by asking them questions; and thinking that he could now do the same again, he said that if Budha was not able to answer him, he should receive the same punishment as the priests, which was, to have his heart cloven, or to be cast into the river. The questions that he asked were thus learnt. In the time of Kásyapa Budha his parents asked the Budha eight questions, and the answers they received they taught their son. Gradually he forgot the answers; and lest he should forget the questions too, he wrote them upon a golden leaf. Then Alawaka asked Budha all the questions he had learnt; and when they were answered to his satisfaction, he entered the path sowán, and declared that from that time he would go from city to city and from house to house, proclaiming everywhere the wisdom of Budha and the excellence of the dharmma.

Whilst the yaká was in the act of making this declaration, the prince of Alow was brought to his dwelling; but as the attendants heard the repetition of Sádhu, Sádhu, and knew that this word was never uttered except in the presence of Budha, they approached without fear. On entering they saw that Alawaka was doing reverence to Budha; but they said that they had brought the prince as his victim for the day, and he might eat his flesh or drink his blood, or do to him whatever he pleased. The yaká was ashamed when he heard this declaration; and presented the prince to Budha, who blessed him and gave him back to the attendants; and as he was thus passed from hand to hand, he was called from that time Hastawaka-álawaka. The citizens were alarmed when they saw the prince brought back again to the palace; but when they heard the reason, they cried with one consent, Sádhu. Budha afterwards went to the city with his alms-bowl, and when he had eaten what he received, he sat down under a tree, where the king and many citizens came to visit him, and he preached to them the Alawaka-sútra, by which many thousands were enabled to enter the paths. When the prince had grown up, his father told him that as he had been saved from death by the sage he must go and minister to him; which he did, and with 500 attendants entered the path anágámi. (*Amáwatura.*)*

26. *The History of Upáli.*

At one time Budha, attended by his priests, departed from the Jétáwana wihára, and went to the mango garden of the noble Páwárika, near the city of Nálanda, in Magadha. In the same city resided the tirttaka Niganthanátha, who had many followers; and it so happened that one of them, Dírggha-tápasa, had one day a conversation with Budha. The sage said to him, "What does your teacher say is the principal cause (karma) of sin?" The tirttaka replied, "We speak not of karma, but of danda." Budha: "Then according to your teacher, how many of these causes (danda) of sin are there?" Tirttaka: "There are three: the body (káya); the speech (wák); and the thoughts (manó). Káya-danda is separate from manó-danda, or is achittaka; as when the wind blows, the branches of the tree are shaken, and the surface of the water is ruffled, without the intervention of any mind; so that which is performed by the body is equally without the intervention of the mind, or is achittaka. Again, when the wind blows, the branches of the palm and other trees

---

* Among the verses recited in the Pirit commemorative of Budha's triumphs, there is the following stanza:—" By the glorious power of the eminent sage who in addition to conquering Mára during the contest of the night overcame the fierce demon Aláwaka and others, by the force of his unmoved gentleness, may you obtain the feast of victory."—Gogerly, Friend, ii. 190.

give forth sound, without any intervention of a mind; so also speech is carried on without any intervention of the mind. It is thought (manó) alone that is influenced by the mind." Budha: "Then the acts of the body, of the speech, and of the thoughts, are three separate and independent processes?" Tirttaka: "They are." Budha: "Of these causes of sin, which is of the greatest consequence?" Tirttaka: "Káya-danda; that which relates to the body." Three times the last question was asked by Budha, as he knew that when the tirttaka went away he would repeat the conversation in the presence of Niganthanátha; which would lead to the conversion of Upáli, a grahapati, as he would be led to come and argue, after which he would embrace the dharmma, and enter the path sowán. Then the tirttaka asked Budha how many causes (danda) of sin he taught that there were. Budha: "The Tatágatas speak not of danda, but of karma." Tirttaka: "Then how many causes (karma) of sin do you teach that there are?" Budha: "There are three; the body, the speech, and the thoughts. If we divide each cause, there are three crimes (káya-charita) that are caused by the body (káya-karma); or káya-karma produces three káya-charita; the speech (wák-karma) produces four crimes (wák-charita); the thoughts (manó-karma) produce three crimes (manó-charita). There are these three causes; but the mind (chétaná) is the principal root of all three. It is not wrong to say that káya-karma and wák-karma, are the principal causes of demerit, or that manó-karma is the principal cause of merit. Of the five great sins for which the transgressor must suffer a whole kalpa in hell, four belong to the body; and one (the causing of divisions among the priesthood) belongs to the speech; and it is on this account that we hesitate not to say that the body and the speech are the principal causes of demerit. Again, one exercise of thought, in the performance of dhyána, secures prosperity for the space of 84,000 kalpas; and one exercise of thought directed to the acquirement of rahatship secures nirwána; and we therefore do not hesitate to say that the thoughts are the principal cause of merit." At the same time Budha declared the power of manó-karma in the production of demerit, inasmuch as it is the cause of scepticism; and repeated a stanza in which it set forth that scepticism is the worst of all modes of demerit, and that it is therefore to be avoided. The same questions were again asked by the tirttaka, before he retired from his interview with the sage, and the same answers were repeated.

Just at the time that Dírggha-tápasa came to Niganthanátha, he was surrounded by his disciples, among whom was Upáli, who had arrived from his village of Bálakalónaka with the offerings he was accustomed to present to his teacher. Niganthanátha enquired of Dírggha-tápasa whence he came; and when he told him that he had been speaking to Gótama, and repeated the conversation that had taken place, he told his disciple that he had answered discreetly, that neither manó nor wák, but káya-danda was the greatest cause of sin. Upáli, on hearing what had passed, said that he also would go and hold a controversy with Gótama, "I will hold him," said he, "as a man who seizes a sheep by its long hair, and it kicks and struggles, but cannot get away; or as a toddy-drawer who takes the reticulated substance he uses to strain his liquor, knocking it on the ground that it may be free from dirt; or as a flax-dresser who takes his flax, soaks it in water three days, and then tosses it about right and left that it may be suited to his purpose; or as an elephant sporting in a tank, that sends the water out of his trunk in all directions." Niganthanátha said it was a matter of little consequence who went to argue with Gótama, as any of them would be able to subdue him. Dírggha-tápasa, however, warned Upáli of the danger he would incur by conversing with Gótama, as he knew his artful method of gaining over persons to his opinion; and though their teacher ridiculed his fears, he thrice entreated Upáli not to go. The warning was given in vain, as Upáli went to the wihára, and made obeisance to Budha. All who approached the teacher of the three worlds did him reverence; some from respect to his office as teacher, and others because he was the son of a king. After Upáli, whose reverence arose from the joy he experienced, asked Budha upon what subject he had conversed with Dírggha-tápasa, and he had informed him, Budha said, "If a sick disciple of your master, who, on account of his disease, wished to drink cold water, from a fear of breaking the precepts you inculcate were, nevertheless, to refuse to drink it, and on that account die, where would he be re-born?" Upáli answered, "In the Manassatya-lóka; on account of having broken the manó-danda." The followers of Niganthanátha did not drink cold water at any time; all the water that they drank was made warm; because they thought that in small drops there are small worms, and in large drops large worms; even if a person's bile overflowed, he was not allowed to drink any water but warm, nor to wash his hands and feet in any other, though by so doing his disease became greater, and it was necessary for its removal that cold water should be used. When they could not procure warm water they drank rice gruel. Still, if they had a desire to drink cold water, though they neither asked for it nor made any movement to obtain it, they thereby became subject to be born again; though they kept the wák-danda and káya-danda, these alone would not enable them to attain nirwána; the manó-danda was broken, and they were therefore subject to future birth. It was thus evident that even according to their own rule, manó-danda was more powerful than the two other causes of sin.

Budha: "At first you said that káya-danda was the greatest, it now appears that manó-danda is the greatest (as it was from this that the supposed tirttaka was born in the déwa-loka); these two declarations do not agree with each other." Upáli then thought thus: "When a man is in a fit, there are no signs of breath, nor can he move his hands or feet: still it cannot be said he is dead so long as the hita, mind, is not destroyed; it cannot be learnt from the body alone that he is dead: his death and the birth he receives afterwards are from the mind, thus manó must be the greatest, and káya inferior." But in order that he might receive further instruction from Budha, he repeated his former declaration, that káya-danda must be superior. Then Budha said: "The tirttakas do not take life, nor cause others to take life, nor do they approve of those who take life; they do not steal, nor cause others to steal, nor approve of those who steal; they do not lie, nor cause others to lie, nor approve of those who lie; they do not indulge in evil desire, nor cause others to indulge in evil desire, nor approve of those who indulge in evil desire. In these things we are agreed. But they say that in cold water, decayed wood, leaves and sugar there are worms; now if any one crush an insect, when walking or from any similar cause, what will be the consequence, according to the teaching of Nighantanátha?" Upali: "If he kills the insect unwittingly, the fault is small." Budha: "But if he is aware of what he is doing, what will be the consequence?"

Upáli: "Then the fault will be great." Budha: "Think a little; this does not agree with what you said at the first." Upáli was now convinced that the tirttakas were wrong; but he did not declare his conviction, that he might learn more from the great teacher. Budha: "This Nálanda is a great city; in it are many horses, elephants, and men; if a man were to take a sword, and say he would destroy all these at one blow, could he accomplish what he said?" Upáli: "Even a thousand men could not do it; how much less one!" Budha: "But could a sramana, or a brahman, who had the power of irdhi, do it?" Upáli: "A rishi could destroy forty or fifty such cities; how much more, one!" Again Upáli was convinced that the tenets of the tirttakas were wrong (as the power of manó was thus distinctly proved), but he continued to argue as if he were still on their side. After instances of the power of the rishis had been repeated, Upáli declared that he had been convinced some time of the truth of Budha's doctrines, but that he appeared not to believe, that he might hear him deliver his arguments at greater length. Budha told him to ponder over the matter well; that now, whilst he saw the Tatágata he was on the side of the true dharmma, but that when he saw the tirttakas he might be drawn to their side; and that therefore he must be careful. Upáli said that it gave him pleasure to hear the sage speak thus, as when the tirttakas gained a convert they instantly proclaimed it through the city, that such a king, or noble, had embraced their doctrines. Budha said further, that the house of Upáli had been like a pool of water, free for all; and that he must still continue to assist all who came, even the tirttakas. Again Upáli expressed his satisfaction with what he heard, as the tirttakas forbade their followers to give to any but themselves, and for the third time, in honour of the three gems, took refuge in Budha; after which the teacher declared to him the four great truths, and he entered the path sowán. When Upáli returned to his own house, he told the porter that he was to give food to the tirttakas as before, but not to allow them to enter the dwelling; to the priests of Budha, however, he might grant this permission.

The disciple Dírggha thought much about the visit of Upáli to the wihára, as he knew well the power of Budha's words; and when he heard that he had taken refuge in the three gems, he went at once and informed Niganthanátha; the tirttaka, however, said that Upáli might have gained over Gótama, but it was impossible that Gótama could have gained over Upáli. To know the truth of the matter, Dírggha went himself to the house; but the porter would not let him enter, though willing to give him food in the place where he then stood, as he said that his master had embraced the doctrines of Budha. The disciple returned to the dwelling of Niganthanátha, and informed him of what had taken place; but still he would not believe what he heard, and went himself to the house. On his arrival the porter would not allow him to enter, so the tirttaka requested him to inform his master that he wished to see him; and when Upáli was made aware of his request, he gave permission that he should be admitted. There were seven walls and seven gates to the dwelling, at each of which there was a separate porter. Upáli seated himself on a high throne, near the seventh door. As the tirttaka proceeded, he became more and more sorrowful; it had been customary for Upáli to meet him at the fourth door, where taking him respectfully by the hand, he led him to the principal seat, upon which he placed him with all care, as a man would put down a vessel full of very precious oil; now there was no one to meet him, and Upáli himself occupied the most honorable seat. Niganthanátha asked him the meaning of this; and he replied, "I have embraced the doctrines of Budha, and I would that all my relatives, all déwas, brahmas, and men, would do the same." He then related a parable, by which he set forth the folly of those who trust in the tirttakas. "There was an old brahman," said he, "who had a young wife. One day she told him to go into the bazaar, to such a shop, where all kinds of things were sold for the amusement of children, and purchase a monkey that it might be a plaything for her son. The old man replied that they had better wait until the child was born; if it were a son he would buy a male monkey, if a daughter, a female; but as she urged him continually, he complied with her request. When the monkey was brought, she told him to take it to the dyer, and order him to make its skin perfectly sleek, and dye it of a golden colour; but the dyer, on receiving this strange order said that it was not possible to execute it, as the monkey would have to undergo all kinds of operations to receive the dye, by which its flesh, and brain, and other internal parts would be bruised, and the hair would be spoiled, without saying anything of its death. Now this is just like the teaching of the tirttakas, a thing without benefit, as useless as the tales called Bharáta, and Ráma, like the seeking for hard wood in the plantain, or rice in mere chaff. Afterwards the brahman took sundry pieces of cloth, and told the dyer to dye them of a golden colour, with a beautiful gloss; and the dyer said, that these were proper things to bring, as he could beat them, and pound them, and squeeze them without doing them any injury. Now this is like the teaching of Budha; you may examine them, and sift them even for a hundred years; but their full meaning it is difficult to acquire; they are deep, like the sea." When Upáli had concluded this discourse, Niganthanátha asked him whose disciple he was; upon which he descended from his seat, and reverently looking towards the place where Budha resided, said that he was the disciple of him whose praises he would now repeat, at the same time beginning to set forth the virtues of the teacher of the three worlds. Niganthanátha said that he had soon learnt his lesson; and he replied, "When there are beautiful flowers of many colours, it is an easy matter for the florist to form a nosegay; so also, the virtues of Budha are so many that it requires no skill to be able to recount them." In consequence of these things the tirttaka declared that his rice-bowl was broken, his subsistence gone; and he went to the city of Páwá, and there died. (*Amáwatura*).

27. *The Brahman Kútadanta embraces Budhism.*

It was one day perceived by Budha that the brahman Kútadanta would be caught in his net; and that he and his 500 disciples would embrace the faith of the dharmma. The sage, therefore, went to the village of Khánumat, in which Kútadanta at that time resided. A great offering had been prepared, in order that it might be presented to the brahman, consisting of seven hundred of each of the following animals:—bulls, cows, calves, goats, kids, deer, and minors. They were all tied ready in the hall of sacrifice. The brahmans who had assembled to partake of the offering, when they heard of the arrival of Budha, went to the mango grove in which he then was, that they might see him. This was observed by Kútadanta, who enquired where they were going; and when he was told that it was to see Budha, he also thought that he would go, and enquire from the sage what were the sixteen requisites of a proper sacrifice. His disciples, on learning his intention, tried to dissuade him from going, as he was older than Gótama; and it would be a disgrace to his own profession, as he had been made the chief of the brahmans by Bimsara. But Kútadanta said, that in many ways Budha was his superior; and that as he had arrived in the village a stranger, it was right that he should go and welcome him. When the disciples heard their master in this manner praise Budha, they resolved that they would accompany him to the mango grove. Kútadanta did homage to Budha on approaching him; but the rest of the brahmans did not properly salute him; they did it in such a way that they might either say that they had saluted him or that they had not. Then Kútadanta said to him, " I have heard that you have perfect understanding of the three yágas (modes of sacrifice) and the sixteen piriwaras; will you explain to me what they are ?" In reply, Budha related the history of Maja Wijita, who reigned over all Jambudwípa in a former age. This monarch was exceedingly rich in all treasures; and one day, on seeing a great number of vessels filled with gold, and enquiring of his treasurer who had collected them; he was told that they had been collected by his forefathers in seven previous generations. The king asked, "Where are they now ?" The treasurer said, "They are dead; they are gone to the other world." " Did not they take their treasures with them ?" enquired the king; and the treasurer replied, " What is it that you ask; how can a man at his death take his treasures to the other world ?" On hearing this the king lay down on his couch and reflected, "I have received in this world great possessions; in order that I may have possessions in the future world as well, I will celebrate a great yága." In this place the word yúga means an alms-offering. In order that the yága might be given in the most effectual manner, he consulted his próhíta respecting it, who gave him such advices as were necessary. When this recital was concluded, the brahmans praised Budha, but Kútadanta was silent. This excited the curiosity of the other brahmans, and they enquired the reason, when he said that it was not because he was in any way displeased; but that he was thinking that either the king or his próhita must have been Bódhisat. Budha told him that his conjecture was right, and that it was the próhita; and when he further enquired what was the most meritorious mode in which alms could be given, the sage instructed him upon this subject; and in such a manner, that Kútadanta, after ordering all the animals that had been prepared for the sacrifice to be released, took refuge in the three gems, and entered the path sowán. (*Amáwatura.*)

28. *The Brahman Séla becomes a Priest.*

On a certain occasion, Gótama went from the country of Anguttarápa, and entered the village of Apana, accompanied by 1250 rahats. The people of the village were made acquainted with his arrival, and having already heard much about his discourses and miracles, they deputed one of their number, Kéni, an ascetic, to visit him, and enquire into his character. The ascetic accordingly approached the sage in a reverent manner, and presented him with an offering of 500 vessels of different kinds of drinks, brought on as many yokes. After he had heard one of the discourses of Budha, he requested the teacher to partake of food at his dwelling on the following day; but Budha replied, "The priests with me are many; you have been accustomed to recount the praises of the brahmans." Kéni confessed that it was true; but on the next day he repeated the invitation, and received the same reply. A third time he requested the presence of Gótama and the priests at his dwelling; and as on this occasion he received no reply, he construed the silence of Budha as an acquiescence in his request. The reason why Budha delayed the reception of the ascetic's offering was this; he foresaw that in the meantime the brahman Séla, and 300 of his disciples, would become priests, by which his retinue would become greater, and the merit of the offering would be increased in proportion. On reaching home, Kéni called together his friends and the chiefs of the village, and addressed them thus:— "Good friends and faithful servants; sons, daughters, and other relatives, hear my words; the sage Gótama and the priests by whom he is accompanied, are invited to partake of food with me to-morrow; therefore let all things necessary be provided."

The friends and attendants of Kéni began with all readiness to obey this command; some set up the ovens; others clove the firewood, or cleaned the vessels, or poured pure water into the vessels, then covered them with plantain leaves, and arranged them, as well as the vessels of rice, in proper order; others again placed the seats; and Kéni erected the place of refection, with suitable canopies.

At that time there was in Apana a very learned brahman, Séla, who taught the Vedas, &c., to 300 disciples. Having taken out these disciples to walk, for the benefit of the exercise, they came to the house of Kéni, with whom he was intimate; but found that all the people were busily engaged in various ways. Surprised at what he saw, he enquired if some maiden was about to be given or received in marriage, or if some great sacrifice was about to be made, or if king Bimsara was expected, with his attendants? Kéni replied, "We are not about either to give or receive in marriage, nor do we expect the lord of Magadha and his attendants; but I am about to present an offering of alms; the illustrious Gótama has come from Anguttarápa, and on the morrow he and his priests will partake of the food we are now preparing." At the same time he recounted the praises of Budha. Then Séla enquired, "Did you say Budha?" Kéni replied, "I said, Budha." Again Séla made the same enquiry, and received the same answer. Having heard this, Séla reflected, "The saying of this word is a matter of no small difficulty; in a hundred thousand ages it is not heard." Further he reflected, that according to the Vedas, if any one be possessed of the thirty-two signs, he must be either a chakrawartti or a Budha; he can be no one else; and at the same time he called these signs to his remembrance. He then enquired in what direction he would be likely to find Gótama, as he wished to see him; when he was informed by Kéni that he must go towards the south, where he would find the sage in a grove of hopal trees. On receiving this information, he went thither with his 300 disciples, having previously given them the following charge:—"Take care that you do not make a noise, or speak in too loud a tone; do not make a disturbance with your feet; Budha is not to be approached too nearly; he is like the lion that needs no aid from any one, and does not wish to be disturbed. When I converse with Budha, you are not to interfere, but to listen in silence." After saluting Gótama, Séla remained at a little distance, noting the thirty-two signs of the Budha, with the exception of two, that were hidden from his observation. As Budha knew that he wished to see the whole, he exhibited one of the two in an image of his person that appeared by miracle; and the other, which related to the length of his tongue, he exhibited in his own person. By this means the brahman and his disciples were convinced that he was the supreme Budha; they accordingly embraced the priesthood, and received the pirikara requisites from the sky.

Next day the whole of the rahats attendant upon Budha, as well as the new converts, went to the residence of Kéni, and partook of the food he had prepared. At the conclusion of the repast Budha said, "As the offering of the brahman cannot be presented without fire, unto him fire is the principal requisite; as a knowledge of the science of recitation is requisite to him who repeats the Vedas; as the king is the chief of men; as all rivers are received by the sea; as the sun and moon are requisite to the exercise of the science of the astronomer; so to him who would acquire merit by the giving of alms, Budha and his priests are the principal requisite."—*Sélasútra-sanné.*

29. *Budha is falsely accused of Incontinence by the female Unbeliever, Chinchi.*

There were certain tirttakas who were envious when they saw the numbers who received the instructions of Gótama. They, therefore, cried out to the people in the corners of the streets, "What is it that you are doing? Is Gótama the only Budha? Are not we also Budhas? If those who make offerings to Gótama receive a reward, is the reward less of those who make offerings to us? If he imparts nirwána, do not we enable you to receive the same?" They then consulted together to see if they could not destroy the influence of the sage by some stratagem. There was at that time in Sewet, a young female, called Chinchi, an ascetic. One day she went to the residence of the tirttakas and worshipped them, but they remained silent. At this she became fearful, thinking that she must have done something wrong; and after worshipping them thrice, she asked what fault she had committed. The tirttakas informed her that they wished to hinder the success of Gótama, in which she would be able to assist them. She enquired in what way. They said that as the stream of the river is turned by the rising of the tide, so might she withdraw from Gótama the abundance he now received, and make it flow in their direction. As Chinchi was well versed in all kinds of female devices, when she perceived that the people of Sewet were accustomed to resort to Budha in the evening, that they might hear bana, she proceeded from her residence just at this time, arrayed in a crimson robe, with flowers and perfumes. The people asked her where she was going at such an hour, but she said it was no business of theirs; they had no right to be so inquisitive. Having thus put evil thoughts into the minds of the faithful, she went to the dwelling of the tirttakas, which was near the Jétáwana wihára where Gótama resided, and there remained all night. In the morning, when the upásakas were coming at an early hour that they might worship Budha, she returned towards the city, as if she had been remaining during the night at the residence of Gótama. When they enquired where she had slept she would not inform them. This she continued to do for a month or six weeks; but after this time, when they made the same enquiry, she said that she had spent the night in the apartment of Gótama. Then covering her person with her robe, she declared that she had become pregnant by the sage; by which those who had not yet attained divine knowledge were led to doubt, and much demerit was produced. After eight months she remained in private, and had the appearance of being pregnant; but it was produced in an artificial manner, by means of pieces of wood.

One day, when Budha was saying bana, she entered the hall, and said in his presence, "You are a priest; you say bana, and are surrounded by a numerous retinue; you have a pleasant voice and your appearance is beautiful; I am with child by you; you have appointed no place for my confinement, and in the place where we associated I cannot bring forth; I have neither oil nor pepper prepared; though it would not be proper for me to be confined here, you are Budha, and have friends, such as Anépidu and Wisákhá, both of whom are your associates; why do you not speak to them to render me such assistance as I require?" In this way she talked to Gótama, as if he were her lawfully received husband, and derided him; but her efforts were like those of the vilest filth to pollute the purity of the moon. After a little time Budha said in the midst of the assembly, "Chinchi, though your words should be true, is the truth known to you alone; must it not be known both to you and me?" She answered, "The words that proceed from the lips of the just are correct; it is not possible that they can be false; it is not therefore necessary to repeat what you have said; you must now provide a proper place and proper things for my confinement; it is to no purpose now to say bana, agitating the minds of the people."

The déwa Sekra now perceived that something extraordinary was going on in the world, and when he had looked to see what it was, he learnt that a falsehood had been uttered, equal to the saying that the dimbul tree had put forth flowers; so he took with him four other déwas, and they approached the assembly unperceived. They then transformed themselves into mice, went secretly behind her, crept up her back, and gnawed the thongs by which the pieces of wood were bound to her person. A wind came at the same time and blew aside her garments; and at the very moment when her person was thus exposed, the wood fell to the ground. The people assembled, when they saw the falsity of the accusation she had brought against Budha, took her by the hands and feet, beat her, and carried her out of the hall. As soon as she was out of the sight of Budha, the earth opened, and flames coming from Awíchi wrapped themselves around her, after the manner of her crimson robe, and she was carried to the midst of this hell. The stratagem by which the tirttakas had endeavoured to defame Gótama was soon proclaimed through the city, on which account their followers gradually left them and came over to the side of Budha; so that his fame increased from this time, as when oil is poured into a lamp nearly extinguished from the want of it, the flame becomes brighter and more powerful. The mouths of the four orders of the faithful were on that day insufficient to enable them to utter the praises of Budha.* (*Sadharmmaratnakáré.*)

* This account is cited as an example of drishta-dharmma-wédya-akusala.

30. *A Female resident in Mátika becomes a Rahat.*

There was a village belonging to the king of Kosal, called Mátika, surrounded by high mountains. Sixty priests, after they had worshipped Gótama set out to seek a place in which it would be convenient for them to perform the exercise of bháwaná meditation, and in the course of their search arrived at Mátika. At this time the chief of the village, who was known by the same name, was a lay devotee. His mother, when she had seen the priests, prepared food that it might be ready for them at the proper time; and when they came to her house with the alms-bowl, she enquired where they were going. They said that they were seeking a convenient place; and as she was wise, as well as old, she knew from this that they were in search of a place in which to perform wass, so she said that if they would keep it there, she would provide all that was necessary, and would herself keep the five precepts, and on póya days the eight precepts. As they consented, she prepared a proper place for them to reside in, and offered it to them as a wihára. One day, when the priests were assembled together, they said to each other, "In the present birth this woman is no relation to any of us, nor have we ever seen her before; but through our merit she expects to receive a great reward. We must, therefore, be careful to keep the precepts aright; we must not be indolent or negligent; otherwise we cannot be saved from hell. Our benefactress, whether we be faithful or not, on account of this good deed will be rewarded." They said further, that as the words of Budha were most certainly true, in order to receive what they thus sought, they must separate from each other, and only meet when they had to recite the pirit at night, or when in the morning they went to seek alms. Yet if any one were sick, the bell in the centre of the wihára might be rung, and they would all assemble to see what assistance was to be rendered. From that time they remained in separate places, apart from each other, performing the exercise of meditation.

One day the woman took oil, honey, and sugar to the wihára, at a time when all the priests had gone to their retirement; but as some one informed her that if she struck the bell with a piece of wood the priests would come; she did so, and they were all quickly assembled in the hall, as they supposed that some one was sick. When she saw them approach from separate places, she enquired if they had had a dispute, and were at enmity with each other; but they said that they had retired that they might meditate on the thirty-two impurities of the body, and on the three truths, its impermanency, pain and unreality. When she learnt that this exercise was good for all, like an universal remedy, she requested to know how it was to be performed; and as the priests gave her full instructions upon the subject, she commenced the same course, and entered the first of the paths before any of the priests had attained the same state. When she had proceeded further, and became a rahat, she looked with her divine eyes to see if the priests had received the same power; but she found that they had not. She then perceived that though other things were right, they did not receive such food as they wished; so she ordered the right kind of food to be prepared at her own house, and gave it to them. Their bodies were then comfortable, and they could give their minds to meditation, free from care, by which means they were soon enabled to become rahats. In three months the ordinance was concluded, and they resolved upon returning to Budha, to inform him of what had taken place. The sage was at that time in Sewet, and on arriving in his presence he enquired after their health, and how each one had succeeded, when they told him all that had occurred.

There was another priest, who, when he had heard the relation of these events, thought it would be well if he also were to go to a person who was possessed of so much merit. Accordingly he went, and on his arrival he reflected that the woman knew the thoughts of others; so, he was weary, he wished that some one might be sent to sweep the wihára; and it was done. As he was thirsty, he wished for some water mixed with sugar; and it was sent him. The next day he wished for some rice gruel and cakes, which he received; and he afterwards wished for some barley bread and other things, which the woman herself took. On seeing her, he asked if she knew the thoughts of others, and she said, "Are there not many priests that know the thoughts of others?" and when he said "I did not ask about the priests, but about yourself," she replied, "Can any one know the thoughts of others, but those who have entered the paths?" This she said, because it was a rule that those who had entered the paths should not inform others of the attainment, unless there was some adequate cause. The priest now thought that as he was not yet free from impurity, he would sometimes have evil thoughts, as well as good ones, which would be known to the woman; and she might proclaim them, and thus bring him into disgrace. To prevent this, he told her that he could not remain there any longer, and was going away; and though she wished him to remain where he was, his resolution was fixed, and he went to Budha. When Budha saw him he enquired how it was that he had returned so soon; and on learning the cause, the sage said that though he might not be able to perform all that was required, there was at least one thing he could do, and that was, he might subdue his mind by returning to the same wihára. "The mind not being subdued," said he, "a thousand thoughts enter into it; it wanders here and there, and runs after this and that; but it must be subdued. The mind is light, and easily moved, or overturned; it is heedless, not enquiring into the reason of things. It does not consider; wherever it wishes to go, there it goes. Therefore, as the sea does not retain any dead body or any manner of filth, but rejects it and casts it forth, so must the mind free itself from ignorance and evil desire. Again, as the sea does not cast forth the pearls and gems that are in it, but retains them; so must the mind retain and cherish the virtue that is produced by the keeping of the precepts and meditation. As the sea does not overflow, though it receives the waters of thousands of rivers, and infinite showers of rain, so must the mind be kept within bounds, in an even state, not passing to excess. And as the sea receives the waters that flow into it in succession, continually; so must the mind never be satisfied with the benefit it has gained, but continually seek for more and more accessions of good." The priest took the advice that was given him, went again to the village of Mátika, attained the state of purity, and saw nirwána.

The priest then looked to see if he had ever received any other benefit from the same woman in former states of existence, when he discovered that she had been his wife in ninety-nine different births, in all of which she had been faithless to him, and had been the means of his destruction. The woman also looked at the same things, but as she looked still further back, she saw that in the hundredth birth from that time she had saved him from death, and that it was through the merit of this act she had been enabled to render him the assistance he now received. The priest, after this, again returned to Budha, who informed him that he had accomplished his purpose, by the giving up of his will in returning to the village; as this subduing of his mind had enabled him to perform the exercise of meditation. (*Sadharmmaratnakáré.*)

31. *The Prowess of Bandhula.*

There was a powerful warrior, called Bandhula, who was the son of the sister of a Malwa king, who reigned at Kusinárá. No one in all Jambudwípa excelled him in the use of the five weapons—the sword, shield, bow, club, and spear. In his youth his royal uncle was desirous to see a display of his strength; and that this might be accomplished, he prepared sixty iron rods, which he concealed in as many bamboos, each of which had sixty knots. The whole were then made up into a bundle, or fascine; and Bandhula's uncle said to him, "If you can cleave this bundle of bamboos, cutting through the whole by a single blow of the sword, I will give you my daughter to wife; but if you fail, I will give her to some other person." The young man smiled on hearing this, and thought it would be no great feat. At once he drew his sword, and flourished it a little, and then lifted it up towards the sky eighty cubits. The courtiers who were looking on trembled, as they were apprehensive it might come down upon their own persons. But Bandhula struck the fascine sixty times, at each time cutting off a knot from each of the sixty bamboos. When the pieces fell to the ground he heard a jingling sound, and saw that there was iron. At this he was displeased; as he thought the king ought not to have placed him in a position where he might have been disgraced in the presence of the people. So he said in anger to the king, "I will remain no longer here; I will seek some other country;" and taking the king's daughter, who received the name of Bandhumalliká, he departed from the city, neither king nor princes being able to stop him.

First he went to the king of Kosol, as he had been educated with him in his childhood. The king received him gladly, saying, "Now that one so powerful is become my friend, all Jambudwípa is mine;" and made him the chief of his forces and the second person in the kingdom. The other kings were alarmed, when they heard that Kosol had received the assistance of the formidable Bandhula.

The wife of Bandhula had the strength of five elephants; in this respect being equal to Wisákhá; and like her also she possessed the ornament called mékhala, or méla, and was a disciple of Budha. But she had no child, which was a great disappointment to Bandhula, as he wished to have a son as powerful as himself. When, however, he determined to send her away to her father's house, and take to himself another wife, she received his command to depart with sorrow, as Budha then resided in Kosol, and she regretted the loss of the privilege she there enjoyed in being able to listen to his discourses. In her distress she went to the sage, resolved that she would do whatever he appointed. The sage, when he had heard her story, directed her to return to the house of Bandhula, who again received her, as they knew that something must be intended by the giving of this advice. From this time they lived together in harmony, and it soon became apparent that the wish of the warrior was likely to be gratified. Not long afterwards Bandhumalliká desired to bathe in the bath belonging to the princesses of Lichawi, but she knew that it was impossible, as it was protected by a network of metal, and if she could even approach it from the sky, her intention would be frustrated. When the wish was communicated to Bandhula, he said that as it was not an impossibility upon which her mind was set, he would see that it was accomplished. Taking his wife with him, the warrior left Sewet early in the morning, and arrived at Wisálá, a distance of fifty-four yojanas, about the middle of the day. Loudly did he knock at the gate, and when the princes heard the noise, they said that it could be none other than Bandhula that knocked with such force, and that it boded to them no good. After gaining an entrance into the city, he went at once courageously to the bath; and as the guards fled in terror, he cut the network with his sword, and entered the water with his wife; and after her wish was thus gratified, they set their faces to return to Sewet. A number of the Lichawi princes then went to the king, Maha-lí, and said that they were for ever disgraced by the presumption of Bandhula. They, however, made a vow that they would eat no rice until they had brought back his head; and 500 princes mounted their chariots to pursue him. The king tried to persuade them from their purpose, as he said that the warrior had strength sufficient to destroy them all at a single blow; but they replied, "Is he more than a man, and are we women?" When Maha-li saw that they were determined, he gave them advice by which they might deceive their enemy, and overcome him; but they heeded it not, and as they approached him in a line, one covered by the other, he sent an arrow towards them, by which they were all wounded to the death, though they did not fall. Bandhula, when this was done, went on his way, the princes calling to him to stop, that they might measure their strength with him; but he replied that he did not war with the dead. On hearing this, they thought he had become insane through fear; but when he said that if they did not believe him they might learn the truth by unloosing their armour, the first and second princes did so, and immediately expired. When the other princes saw this they set off in terror to return to the city, but on reaching their homes the whole number died. Bandhula and his wife reached Sewet in safety; after which they had two sons; and during sixteen years Bandhumaliiká had two sons each year, so that the number amounted to thirty-two. The good fortune of this princess came to her because in former years she had presented the requisites of the priesthood in alms, and had been charitable to the poor and aged.

32. *The King of Kosol marries the Natural Daughter of Maha-nama.*

Not far from the palace of the king of Kosol there was an alms-hall, in which he gave food daily to 500 priests; but the priests were not willing to receive it, or if they received it took it to other places to eat, as it was not given in a proper manner. The food presented by the common people might not be sufficiently boiled, or it might be black or dirty; but they received it in preference to that which was given by the king. One day, when the king had partaken of some food that he particularly relished, he commanded that a portion of it should be sent to the alms-hall; but when his servants arrived at the place, they found no one there. The king, on being informed of this circumstance, went to Budha, and after telling him that his priests were acting improperly, enquired what was the principal requisite of the dána almsgiving. Budha said to him, "Wiswása, faith, or sincerity, is the principal requisite of almsgiving: the food that you give is excellent in itself, but it is not given with sincerity; the food that others give is less excellent, but it is given with sincerity. If any one give only a spoonful of rice-gruel with faith and sincerity, the alms will be pre-eminently excellent." The king then enquired how he was to secure faith on the part of the priests;[*] and the sage told him that the priests had faith in those who had attained the paths, and in their relatives. After the return of the king to his palace, he thought that if he became a relative of Budha, all the priests would exercise faith in him; and as he was the principal king of Jambudwípa, he resolved that he would secure a Sákya princess, whether the princes were willing to give one or not. Sudhódana was dead, and Maha-nama had received the crown. To him the king of Kosol sent an embassage, the nobles of which were to demand a princess of the Sákya race. The Sákyas never intermarried with other families, as their race was of superior purity; and this they wished to preserve inviolate. When the princes received the message, they thought thus: "If we refuse one of our daughters, we shall excite the anger of this powerful king; if we give one, the purity of our race is gone." Maha-nama had a daughter, Wásabhakhattika, by the slave Maha-nunda. She was at this time about sixteen years of age. The king arrayed her in the most splendid manner, and presenting her to the nobles said, "This is our daughter; take her to become the wife of the monarch of Kosol." The nobles were suspicious when the maiden was given thus readily, as they knew that the Sákyas were extremely proud of their birthright. In order that they might not deceive their king, by taking a maiden who was not of the Sákya race, they demanded that Maha-nama should eat with her in their presence; and if this was done, they thought that they might reasonably dismiss their doubts. The king at once commanded her to be brought, that he might eat with her before the eyes of the ambassadors. On her arrival, he said to her, in apparent sorrow, "When shall I see you again? You are going away from me to become the wife of the king of Kosol?" and he wept as he spoke. He then put some rice in her hand, as a repast had been prepared, that she might eat it; and

[*] For the full merit of almsgiving, faith is required in the receiver as well as the giver.

before she had time to convey it to her mouth, he hastily ate a few grains himself. At that moment a noble who had before been instructed for that purpose, delivered a letter to the king, and said it had been brought from one of the border countries, and required an immediate answer. The king read it, and appeared to be greatly agitated; but he told the maiden to continue her meal, and talked away to pass the time over until she had done. She then washed her hands, and the king did the same in token of having eaten, by which the nobles were deceived, and without any misgivings took her to Sewet.* The monarch made her his principal queen. In due time she had a son, and when he heard of the event he sent a noble to inform the queen-dowager, who on hearing the news said, "Wallabha! wallabha!" as expressive of her joy. On his return, he asked him what his mother had said, and he, mistaking her words, replied that she had said, "widúdabha." The king gave this name to his son; and from this time he became more firm in the faith, and gave much treasure in alms.

33. *The Flower-Girl becomes a Queen.*

There were in Kosol 500 different families who gained a livelihood by the sale of flowers. The daughter of the principal florist, who was as beautiful as a déwí, one day put three cakes into her basket when she went to gather flowers, intending to eat them when she became hungry. On the morning of the same day, Budha looked to see unto whom he should render assistance, and perceived that the maiden of Kosol was worthy to receive it. As he was afterwards going with 500 priests to the city of Sewet to receive alms, he met the flower-girl and her companions on their way to the gardens. At the sight of the sage, she felt a desire to make him an offering, but had nothing she could offer besides the three cakes; so not knowing whether they would be received or not, she approached him reverently, and when Budha held his alms-bowl towards her to receive her gift, she presented them, and admiring him, worshipped. The

---

* When Cambyses required the daughter of Amasis, king of Egypt, in marriage, as Amasis knew that she would be, not the wife but the concubine of the Persian king, he sent Nitetis, daughter of the former king, who was extremely beautiful, as his own child. But the deception was discovered, and it is said to have been the origin of the invasion of Egypt by Cambyses. Herod. iii. 1.

teacher of the three worlds smiled, and told her that at a future time his religion would receive from her great assistance. Ananda knew that he would not smile without a reason, and enquired what it was; when he was told that the girl would on that day, through the merit of her gift, become the queen of the king of Kosol. The maiden overheard what he said, but wondered how it could be, as the king was not at that time in the city. On arriving at the garden, she thought of what she had heard, and began to sing as she plucked the flowers.

The monarch now reigning at Kosol was Pasé-Nadi, the son of Maha Kósala, whose daughter had been given in marriage to Bimsara, king of Rajagaha. As her portion she received the city of Sewet, which was situated on the border of each kingdom; but when her son, Ajásat, killed his father, Pasé-Nadi took back the city by force. A war ensued, as Ajásat was resolved to retain it; at one time the victory inclined to the side of Kosol, and at another to Rajagaha. At last Ajásat, to decide the contest, took his sword and shield, and rushed into the midst of his opponent's army, where he slew great numbers, so that the king of Kosol was obliged to retreat. Upon a swift horse he fled, and approached the city at the time the maiden was singing over the flowers she gathered. At the sight of him she thought of the saying of Budha, and continued her song, without manifesting any appearance of fear. The king enquired who she was, and whether she were married. Not long after his arrival, he sent a retinue to conduct her to the palace, and publicly anointed her his principal queen. As it was by means of Budha she attained this exalted rank, she daily sent many offerings to the three gems. Because she was first seen in a flower-garden by the king, she was called Malliká; and on account of her marriage to the king of Kosol, Kosála-malliká-déwí.

34. *The Priest whose Breath was like the perfume of the Lotus.*

In the time of Piyumatura Budha, a man who heard bana was greatly pleased, and at its conclusion said Sádhu, with much joy. By this act he was from that time preserved from being born in hell; and in the time of Gótama he had forty kótis of treasure. When he spoke, a smell as of the lotus proceeded from his mouth, and filled the whole house; and from this circumstance he was called Utphalagandha. Having one day heard Budha deliver a discourse on the disadvantages connected with the state of the laic, he embraced the priesthood, leaving all his treasures. The king of Kosol, when he heard of what had occurred, said that the treasure that had no owner belonged to the supreme lord; and he therefore took possession of it, as well as of his wife. One day the 500 flower-girls brought each a nosegay, which the king presented to his 500 queens. When the wife of Utphalagandha received hers, she thought of the sweet breath of her former husband, and smiled; but she again reflected that he was gone from her, and wept. This was observed by the king, who enquired the reason; but when she informed him, he would not believe it. She said that he might be convinced of its truth, if he would hear him when he delivered the bana. Next day the king invited Budha and Utphalagandha to partake of food at the palace, and prepared a place for the saying of bana. All flowers and perfumes were carefully removed, and the citizens were invited to be present. Budha was aware of the king's intention, and therefore directed the priest to say bana, when the time appointed had come. In compliance with this command, Utphalagandha fearlessly ascended the throne that had been prepared, and after a three-fold salutation, began the delivery of the dharmma. When he began to speak, a perfume like that of the lotus proceeded from his mouth, which filled the palace with its fragrance, and went out by the principal door towards the east. Greatly surprised, the king asked Budha the cause of this wonder, when the sage related to him what had occurred in the time of Piyumatura Budha. After this the king took the wife of the priest into his especial favor, and made her many presents.

35. *The Five Hundred Queens of Kosol.*

The 500 queens one day approached the king of Kosol, and said to him, that although he thrice every day went to the wihára of Budha, and Wisákhá and the other ladies of the city did the same, they were deprived of this privilege, as they were not permitted to leave the palace, by which the loss that they sustained was exceedingly great, a supreme Budha only appearing after immense intervals of time. The king knew that it would create confusion if they went to the wihára, and therefore thought it would be better to appoint some one to say bana daily in the interior of the palace. After speaking to Budha upon the subject, the upásaka Chattapáni was requested to undertake the office; but he excused himself, as he said that he was only a fit person to address the poor, and that it would be better to appoint some regularly ordained priest to go to the palace, as the queens would receive him with more respect. The king then called together 500 priests, and requested them to choose a proper person; in consequence of which Ananda was appointed, as he had the most pleasant voice. Having received a command to this effect from Budha, at the request of the king, he went daily to the palace to say bana, by which the queens obtained great merit. Because his voice was like a lute, and his personal appearance prepossessing, the minds of the queens were greatly affected towards him; and not long afterwards each queen had a son, in appearance like him. This gave occasion to the tirttakas to insinuate to the king, that the princes were not like him, but like Ananda; and as they did it again and again he was put to shame, but when he mentioned the subject to Budha, the sage repeated to him a stanza which removed his doubts.

36. *The Gifts presented to Budha on his return to Sewet.*

After visiting various places, Budha returned to Sewet, and as he had been long absent, the king of Kosol went to meet him, and congratulate him on his arrival. The next day he invited the sage to partake of a repast he had prepared; but on the day after that the citizens gave an alms-offering of ten times the value. The king was resolved not to be outdone, and on the third day presented an offering of greater value by twenty-three times than that of the citizens. On the fourth day, the citizens presented an offering more valuable by sixty or seventy times than that received by Budha on the preceding day. On the fifth day the king gave an alms a hundred or a thousand times more costly than that of the citizens. The citizens then conferred with each other and resolved to give an alms of superior value to any that had hitherto been presented. For this purpose a general contribution was levied, and even the unbelievers came forward with their share, in honour of the city; so that the offerings of all kinds of things necessary for the repast were incalculable. No one slept that night, as all were busy in making the preparations. The next day, when the gifts were presented, the king was overcome with astonishment, as he saw that the citizens had won the victory in this game of gifts; and when he returned to the palace he threw himself upon a couch, grieved and ashamed. The queen Mallika-déwi enquired the reason of his sorrow, and when she learnt the cause, she advised him to make a pavilion of sal trees, with all suitable ornaments, and having in it 500 thrones; then to invite 500 rahats to partake of a repast, with the 500 queens to wait upon them whilst they were eating, and with 500 elephants to hold canopies over their heads. The king commanded that all this should be done; but though there were many thousands of royal elephants, only 499 could be procured that were sufficiently tame. On hearing this Mallika-déwi directed that a wild elephant should be put near the priest Anguli-mála, as he would be able to keep it in awe. At the appointed time Budha came to the pavilion, accompanied by the rahats; all was carried on as the queen had directed, and the wild elephant appeared as tame as the rest. When the repast was concluded, the king presented to Budha the materials of the pavilion, the golden vessels, and all the other articles that had been provided, worth in all thirty-four kótis of treasure. This is called the asadrisa-dána, or the peerless offering. The citizens were not able to equal it, as they had neither sal trees, elephants, nor queens.

37. *Budha is visited by the Déwa Sekra.*

At one time Budha resided in the cave called Indrasála, in the rock Wédi, at the north side of the brahman village Ambasanda, on the east of Rajagaha. Sekra was long desirous of paying a visit to the teacher of the three worlds, but on account of the multitude of affairs that required his attention, he did not meet with a proper opportunity. When he thought about his death, he was greatly afraid, as he knew that he must then leave all his power and treasures. This made him look about, to see if there was any being in the three worlds who could assist him and take away his fear, when he perceived it was in the power of Budha alone to render him the aid he required. Accordingly he issued his command that the déwas should accompany him to the residence of Budha. There was a reason for this command. On a former occasion, when Budha was residing in the Jétáwana wihára, Sekra went alone to see him and hear bana; but as the sage foresaw that if he obliged him to come again, he would then be accompanied by 80,000 déwas, who would thereby be enabled to enter the paths, he did not permit him to come into his presence, and he had to return to his lóka without accomplishing the object of his visit. It was because he thought if he again went alone he would meet with a similar reception, that he now called the déwas to accompany him. In a moment's time the whole company came from the déwa-lóka to the rock Wédi, and rested upon it like a thousand suns. It was now evening, and the people were sat at their doors, either playing with their children, or eating their food. When they perceived the light upon the rock they said that some great déwa or brahma must have come to pay honour to Budha.

To announce his arrival to the sage, Sekra sent forward the déwa Panchasikha, who took with him his harp, twelve miles in length; and having worshipped Budha, he began to sing certain stanzas, which admitted of two interpretations, and might either be regarded as setting forth the honour of Budha, or as speaking in praise of Suriyawachasá, daughter of the déwa Timbara. His voice was accompanied by the tones of the harp. In this manner the praises of the pure being and the praises of evil were mingled together, like ambrosia and poison in the same vessel. Budha said to the déwa, "Thy music and thy song are in harmony," and then commanded that Sekra should be admitted, lest he should be tired with waiting and go away, whereby great loss would be sustained by him and his followers. From the delay, Sekra had begun to think that the dancer was forgetting his errand and speaking about his own matters to the sage; and he therefore sent to tell him not to talk so much, but to procure him permission to enter the honourable presence. The years appointed to Sekra being nearly ended, Budha knew that it would not be right to say to him on entering, in the usual manner, "May your age be multiplied!" and he therefore addressed him and the others collectively; but by this salutation, three kótis and sixty thousand years were added to his life, as the ruler of the déwa-lóka of which he was then the chief. Budha and Sekra alone knew of this result. When Budha said to him that it was well he had come to visit the fountain of merit at that time, he replied that he had long wished for the opportunity; and had indeed once come to see him when he resided at the Jétáwana wihára; but he was disappointed, as the ruler of the three worlds was then performing dhyána. After this Sekra stated that there were certain questions which he wished to have solved; and as Budha gave him permission to propose them, he asked thirteen questions, which, with their answers, appear in the Dik-sanga, in the Sekra-prasna-sútra. By the explanations which the sage gave to these questions, the 80,000 déwas were enabled to become rahats, and Sekra entered sowán. As it was by means of Panchasikha that Sekra was enabled to enter the first of the paths, by which, in eight births more, he will attain nirwána, he appointed that déwa as his teacher, and gave him Suriyawachasá as his wife. It was from cleaving to existence, and wishing to live long, that Sekra was able to enter only the first of the paths, whilst the rest of the déwas entered the last.

38. *The Tirttakas are put to Shame: a large Tree is miraculously produced: and Sekra makes a Pavilion for Budha.*

During the residence of Budha in the Wéluwana wihára, there was a rich man in Rajagaha, who one day found an alms-bowl of red sandal-wood when bathing. This he placed in the court-yard of his mansion, upon a frame of bamboo, and caused it to be everywhere proclaimed, that if there was any rahat in the world, he might come through the air and take it, and he would then believe in him and worship him. There were at that time six noted persons who were deceivers and sceptics.

1. Puráṇa-kásyapa.—He was so called because he was born in the house of a noble, of a girl who was a mellaka, or foreigner; there were previously ninety-nine of that race, and as his birth completed the hundred, he was called Púrna or Puráṇa, complete, or full, which was prefixed to his proper name, Kásyapa. From this circumstance his master was unwilling to put him to any hard work, and therefore made him the porter of his mansion; but he did not like this employment, and ran away. In the forest to which he absconded he was set upon by thieves, who stripped off his clothes and left him naked. In this state he approached a village, and when the people asked him who he was, he said that his name was Púrna, because he was full of all science;

Kásyapa, because he was a brahman; and Púrna-kásyapa-budha because he had overcome all evil desire. The people brought him clothes in abundance, but he refused them, as he thought that if he put them on he should not be treated with the same respect. "Clothes," said he, "are for the covering of shame; shame is the effect of sin; I am a rahat, and as I am free from evil desire, I know no shame." The people believed what he said, brought him offerings, and worshipped him. Five hundred other persons became his disciples, and it was proclaimed throughout all Jambudwípa that he was Budha. He had in all 80,000 followers, who were perverted from the truth, and went with their false teacher to hell.

2. Makhali-gósala.—His name was Makhali, and because he was born of a slave who at the time was confined in a cattle-pen on account of the displeasure of her master, he was called Gósala. After he had grown up, his master one day gave him a vessel of ghee to carry on his head; and when they came to a muddy place he told him to take care lest he should fall; but he did fall, and from fear of the consequences ran away. His master pursued him and caught hold of his garment; but he left it in his hand, and fled to the forest naked; whence he came to a village, and deceived the people in the same way as Kásyapa. He had the same number of disciples, and led the same number of followers to destruction.

3. Ajitákásakambala.—He was a servant, and ran away from his master; and as he had no livelihood, he became an ascetic. He put on a mean garment, made of hair, shaved his head, and taught that it is an equal sin to kill a fish and to eat its flesh; that to destroy a creeping plant and to take life is an equal crime.

4. Kakudasatya.—He was the son of a poor widow, of good family, who bore him at the foot of a kakuda or kumbuk tree. A brahman saw him, and brought him up, giving him the name of the tree near which he was born. When the brahman died he had no means of support, and became an ascetic. He taught that when cold water is drunk many creatures are destroyed, and that therefore warm water alone is to be used, whether for the washing of the feet or any other purpose. His followers never drank cold water, nor washed their bodies with it; and if obliged to pass through water or ford a river, it gave them

much pain, as they thought it caused a great destruction of life.

5. Sanjayabellanti.—He was called Sanja because he had on his head a boil like a sanja, or wood apple; and Bellanti, because he was born of a slave. He taught that we shall appear in the next birth as we are now; whosoever is now great or mean, a man or a déwa, a biped, a quadruped, or a millepede, without feet, or with one foot, will be exactly the same in the next birth.

6. Nighantanátaputra.—He was the son of Náta, the husbandman, and because he declared that there was no science with which he was not acquainted, he was called Nirggantha. He said that he was without sin, and that if any one had any doubt, on any subject whatever, he might come to him, and he would explain it. Each of the six sceptics had 500 disciples.

When these sceptics heard of the proclamation made by the rich citizen of Rajagaha, they went to his residence; and each one asked for the alms-bowl, saying that he was a rahat; but the citizen said that if they wanted it, they must come through the air and take it. Thus they remained for the space of five days. Nighantanátaputra reflected thus:—"The followers of Gótama Budha will come through the air and take the bowl, by which their fame will be everywhere diffused and we shall be put to shame; this must be prevented, in some way or other, even if it should be by the practice of a deception." He therefore directed his followers to go and ask for the bowl in the name of Budha, saying that he would not work a miracle for a thing so insignificant; but the citizen would not listen to this proposal. He then went to the place, accompanied by his followers, and said he was ready to pass through the air; but his followers, as he had previously instructed them to do so, held him as if by force, and said it was not worth while to pass through the air for such a purpose. Still the citizen refused to give up the bowl. After this Nighanta desisted from further attempts to obtain it, greatly mortified by his defeat.

On the seventh day Mugalan and Pindólabháradwája went to Rajagaha to receive alms, and on their way a woman informed them of what had taken place. When Mugalan heard this, he said to the priest who was with him that it would be a reflection on the truth if it were to continue, and that it would be better for him to go through the air and take the bowl, without keeping their adherents in any further suspense; but the priest said to Mugalan, that Budha, in the midst of the associated priesthood, had appointed him to be the chief of the rishis, and that therefore it would be right for him to take upon himself this service. Mugalan then said, that since he overcame the nágas and Sekra all were acquainted with his power; but they did not know the power of the priest. Upon receiving this reply, Pindólabháradwája rose into the air, and in the sight of all the people, who were at first afraid, went to the mansion near which the bowl was deposited. As he remained in the air, the owner and his family came out to worship him, and requested him to alight. Then filling the alms-bowl with sugar, oil, butter, and similar gifts, he gave it to the priest saying:— "Though it were to save my life, I will never deny that Gótama is Budha; I will be faithful to this system alone." On the return of the priest to the wihára, he was seen by the people at work in the fields, who had heard of his obtaining the bowl, and they requested him to shew them in what way he went through the air; which he did, sometimes leaving the bowl, and then taking it with him, in many different ways. As the warrior relates to his king, on returning from the field of battle, the victories he had gained, so the priest rehearsed the wonders he had accomplished.

When the circumstance was related to Budha, he said that it was not allowed to his disciples to receive an alms-bowl of wood, nor to perform a miracle to obtain any article whatever; so that the priests, from that time, ceased to exhibit wonders. This gave an opportunity to the tirttakas to show themselves again, and to boast that they could perform greater wonders than Gótama; but when Bimsara heard of what was said, he went to Budha, and told him that by this means many persons were deceived. The sage only remarked, smiling at the same time, that the boasting of the tirttakas against Budha was the same as if a pánsupisáchaka hobgoblin were to compare himself to Sekra; and declared that if the priests were forbidden by the precepts to perform wonders, he himself was not. The king asked if both he and his priests were not bound by the same precepts, when Budha said:—"The rays of Súrya-putra, the regent of the sun, are diffused to every part of the sakwala, but do not warm the hair upon his own body; the voice of the lion causes all creatures to tremble, but he himself is unmoved thereby. In like manner, the commands of the Budhas extend to one hundred thousand kelas of sakwalas, but he himself is free from their restraint. You, o king, give an order by beat of drum that no one shall eat the mangos of the royal garden; now after that order, if any one were to eat one of those fruits, what would you do to him?" The king: "I would impose a fine upon him." Budha: "But if you were to eat one yourself?" The king: "Then no fine would be exacted; who could impose a fine upon me?" Budha: "In the same way, I give commands to others, but am myself free from their restraint. The wisdom of the Budhas is underived, they have no teacher; they are therefore without an equal, and are not under the control of another. They take food from a golden alms-bowl; but this is forbidden to the priests. They live in the midst of a village, or inhabited place, but the priests must reside in the forest, and at the root of a tree."

After these statements had been made by Budha, the king enquired at what time the wonders he had spoken of would be performed, and in what place; when he was told that they would be seen after a lapse of four months, at the foot of a tree called Rajagandamba, near the city of Sewet. Bimsara offered to render any assistance in his power towards their accomplishment; but the ruler of the world said that he himself would create the tree, and that Sekra would cause a pavilion to appear, twelve yojanas in size. This was proclaimed to the whole city. The tirttakas knew that it would be their ruin, but they said that as even criminals were allowed a respite between the sentence and its execution, they would enjoy themselves during the four months, and make the most of their circumstances. They boasted that Budha could not then perform any miracle; in four months his wonder was to be seen; and it was not to be done at Rajagaha, but in a distant place.

In his journey towards Sewet, Budha went from village to village, in every place teaching the people, and many presents were brought to him. When informed of the intention of Budha, the principal supporters of the tirttakas set out to follow him; the place that he was at in the daytime, they came to at night;

and they went the next day to the place where he had spent the night. On the eighth day of Æsala the sage arrived at Sewet. The tirttakas also came to the city, that they might see the wonders; and having received a lac of treasure from their adherents, they erected a splendid pavilion. The king of Kosol, with Anépidu and others, went to the wihára to pay his respects to Budha; and when he learnt that the ruler of the three worlds had come to perform certain wonders, he asked where they were to take place, and was told that it was to be near the gate of the city. The king requested permission to erect a pavilion for Budha, larger and more magnificent than that which had been made for the tirttakas; but Budha said that it was not in his power to make one of the kind required. The king: "Who is able, if I am not?" Budha: "If it were possible for man to make it, you would have the power; but it will be made by Sekra."

The king sent nobles on elephants to every part of the city to proclaim by beat of the golden drum that on such a day, Budha would publicly perform a miracle, and that all people might come and see it. The déwas caused the sound of the drum to resound to every part of Jambudwípa, so that it was heard by all the inhabitants as plainly as if it were at their own door. The first proclamation was on the seventh day previous to the event, and it was repeated on each intervening day. Thus the information was received by all; and whosoever wished to be present was enabled to come to the city, from any part of Jambudwípa, through the power of the wish, without any other effort. Even by the unbelievers, the same power was received.

The tirttakas having heard that the miracle was to take place at the foot of a mango tree, were determined to prevent it; and for this purpose they collected their adherents, and purchased all the mango trees in and near the city at a high price, in order that they might destroy them. But on the day appointed, Budha took his alms-bowl as usual, and came with his priests to the gate of the city. On the morning of the same day the king's gardener, Gandamba, in passing through the royal orchard, found a cluster of ripe mangos, and as they were not then in season, he thought it would be well to go and present them to the king. But on his way to the palace, he saw Budha near the gate of the city, and reflected thus: "If I present the mangos to the king, he will perhaps give me a reward in gold; but if I offer them to the divine teacher, he will give me a reward more permanent, and will save me from the perils of existence." Thus thinking, he reverently approached Budha, and presented the fruit. Ananda took off the outer skin, and having prepared a throne for Budha in the same place, requested him there to eat it. The déwas assembled around, unseen by all but the gardener. After eating the fruit, the sage gave the stone to Gandamba, and directed him to set it in the ground near the same spot; and in like manner, after washing his mouth, he told Ananda to throw the water upon the kernel that had just been set. In a moment the earth clove, a sprout appeared, and a tree arose, with five principal stems and many thousand smaller branches, overshadowing the city. It was three hundred cubits in circumference, was laden with blossoms and the richest fruit, and because set by Gandamba, was called by his name. Some of the unbelievers who ate of the fruit that fell from the tree ran about hither and thither, as if deprived of their senses. When the king of Kosol perceived the tree from his palace, he went to the gate of the city with a great retinue, and expressed his regret to Budha that he had not known what was to take place, as, if he had known, he would have assembled a great multitude to witness the performing of the wonder; but he was told that it was of no consequence, as this was only an inferior matter. A guard was placed round the tree, that no accident might happen to it from the unbelievers.

The déwas of the wind and rain caused a great storm to arise, by which the pavilion of the tirttakas was carried through the air, and cast into the common sewer of the city. The regent of the sun poured down upon them his beams, making them perspire most profusely; and then the déwas of the wind covered them with dust, so that they looked like copper ant-hills; after which the déwas of rain sent against them a violent shower, which made them look like spotted deer. The citizens seeing them in this plight ridiculed them, and sent them away in disgrace. From this time Puránakásyapa, wherever he went, was abused by the people. One morning he was seen by one of his adherents, a husbandman, who told him that he was waiting to see one of the wonders he had promised to perform. The tirttaka told him to provide an earthen vessel and a rope, and his curiosity should be satisfied. After these were given, he went to the river, followed by the husbandman; and when they arrived at the bank, he fastened the vessel to his neck by the rope, and entered the water, in which he sank. The husbandman wondered what would be the end of all this, but he was no more seen.

The rays from the head of Budha proceeded thrice round the city, after which they passed round the sakwala, and thence to the déwa and brahma-lókas. The rays from his feet, in the same manner, passed through the earth, and the worlds beneath it. When those who were present saw this additional wonder, they called out Sádhu, and the déwas also did reverence. There was a woman called Gharani, who had entered the path anágámi. She requested Budha not to trouble himself by the performance of these wonders, as she could show her power to the people; and when the sage asked what she could exhibit, she said that she could cover the earth with water, and then diving come up with her head over the sakwala-gala, and still proclaim that she was only the handmaid of Budha. Sulu-anépidu offered to rise into the air, and assume a form so large that the sole of the foot should be seven and a half gows long. Others came forward with similar offers, but the services of all were alike rejected. It was declared by Mugalan that he could squeeze Maha Méru as a grain of undu, and hide it with his teeth, and in the same way hide the Maha Mérus of all the other sakwalas; that he could roll up the earth like a mat, and cover it with his finger; that he could turn the earth upside down, as if it were a water-pot; that he could take up the Maha Méru and Himála forest of this sakwala in his right hand, and the Maha Méru and Himála forest of another sakwala in his left hand, and put one in the place of the other; and that he could take the earth, and putting it on the top of Maha Méru walk about with it in his hand, as a priest carries an umbrella.

Budha refused permission to all, as there were thirty acts, called Budha-káraka-dharmma, it was necessary for him to perform, only fourteen of which had been hitherto accomplished, and the time for the accomplishment of another had arrived. After these events had taken place, he repeated the Kanka and Naudi-wisálá Játakas, and then looked towards the sky. By this token, Sekra knew that the period had come in which it would be proper for him to perform certain wonders. First, he caused a magnificent pavilion to appear, with all suitable ornaments, 12 yojanas in length and breadth; and afterwards a hall of ambulation, 203 kelas and 45 lacs of yojanas in length. When the people saw what was done, they clapped their hands in admiration, and waved their loose garments round their heads. Budha, in an instant, ascended to the hall, and was presented with offerings by the various orders of déwas and brahmas; after which, by the power of téjo and ápo kasina-samápatti, he caused a glory to proceed from his navel, which appeared to the three worlds.

39. *Budha visits the Déwa-Lóka Tawutisá.*

At three steps Budha went to the lóka of Sekra, that he might preach to the déwas and brahmas. The déwa thought within himself, when he knew of his approach, "My throne is 60 yojanas long, 50 broad, and 15 high; how then will Budha appear when seated on it, as he is only 12 cubits high?" But as this was the principal throne, and no other could be offered to Budha, he prepared it for his reception, and went with a great retinue to meet him. When Budha seated himself upon the throne, it became exactly of the proper size, being no higher than his knee. As he knew the thoughts of Sekra, in order to show his great power he caused his robe to extend itself on all sides, as the déwas were looking on, until it became more than a thousand miles long and eight hundred broad, and covered the throne, so that it appeared like a seat prepared expressly for the saying of bana. Then Budha appeared as if of proper size for the throne; the seat and its occupant were equal to each other. And when the déwas saw this display of his power, the whole assemblage offered him adoration.

As the people did not see Budha they began to be uneasy, and enquired of Mugalan whither he had gone; but he sent them to Anurudha, that that priest might have an opportunity of exhibiting his great knowledge. By the priest they were informed that the sage had gone to Tawutisá, where he would keep the ordinance called wass, so that three months must elapse before he could return. On hearing this, the people expressed their willingness to remain during that period, and pitched their tents in the same spot. Then Anépidu, the upásika, proclaimed that he would supply the whole company with whatever they might require, whether garments, food, water, or fuel, until the arrival of Budha. During this period Mugalan said bana, and answered the questions that were proposed to him. All lived together in friendship and peace; the natural secretions were not formed; they were like the inhabitants of Uturukuru. The multitude extended to thirty-six yojanas. When Budha said bana in Tawutisá, they heard his voice, and knowing whence it proceeded, they clapped their hands. By this hearing of bana many were enabled to enter the paths.

The déwas, with Mátru* as their chief, requested Budha to open the door of Abhidharmma, which had been shut during a whole Budhántara, and to agitate the sea of the Abhidharmma as the fish-king Timingala agitates the ocean, as from the day he became Budha, like men athirst seeking for water, they were continually looking out for the period when the unfolding of the Abhidharmma should commence. Then Budha lifted up his voice, the sound filling the whole sakwala as with a delightful perfume, and said, "Kusala dhammá, akusala dhammá, awyakta dhammá," these being the first words of the Abhidharmma, which is divided into eight prakaranas. The full meaning of the Abhidharmma is known to the Budhas alone; even the déwas and brahmas cannot attain to it; when, therefore, it was declared by Gótama to the beings assembled in Tawutisá, it was in a simplified manner, as they were capable of understanding it. When he began, the various beings reflected thus: "Is this the Abhidharmma? we had heard that it was so profound that no one could understand it." Budha saw their thoughts, and as he proceeded the manner of his discourse made its meaning gradually deeper. Then the beings were able to understand some parts and not others; it was like an image seen in the shadow. They said Sádhu, in approbation, the words still becoming more and more profound. The Abhidharmma now became to them like a form seen in a dream; its meaning was hid from them, and was perceived by none but Gótama. Not understanding any part, they remained like

* The mother of Budha, who had now become a déwa by the changing of her sex.

imagery painted upon a wall, in utter silence. In a little time Budha again simplified his discourse, when they once more expressed their approbation, and began to think, "The Abhidharmma is not so difficult; it is easy to understand," which, when the preacher perceived, he gradually passed to a profounder style. Thus, during half a night, Budha rapidly declared the bana of the Abhidharmma. In the time occupied by others to say one letter, Ananda says eight; in the time that Ananda says one, Seriyut says eight; in the time that Seriyut says one, Budha says eight; so that Budha can repeat 512 letters as rapidly as the priests can repeat one. When in Tawutisá he repeated the bana thus quickly, because the apprehension of the déwas was of equal celerity.

In one hundred of our years the déwas eat but once; and had Budha taken his accustomed meals in their presence during the period he performed wass in Tawutisá, they would have thought that he was always eating. Therefore, at the usual hours of refection he caused another Budha to appear and occupy his place, whilst he himself went to the Anotatta lake; and as his almsbowl here came to him in a miraculous manner, he took it to Uturukuru, where he received food. At this time Seriyut and 500 priests called Waggula were in Sakaspura, keeping wass. When Budha had eaten the food he received in Uturukuru, he went to the same city, and had at the request of Seriyut repeated all that he and the representative of Budha had said to the déwas. It would have occupied too much time to repeat the whole, and it was therefore spoken in an abridged form: but such was the wisdom of Seriyut, that when Budha declared to him one thing, from that one he learnt a hundred. The things he thus learnt, he was commanded by Gótama to teach in full to the 500 Waggula priests, who would afterwards be able to teach others; and thus the words of the Ahbidharmma would be preserved to future ages for the benefit of the faithful. When the rehearsal was concluded, Budha returned to the déwa-lóka, and causing the form to disappear, took its place. This occurred daily.

The Abhidharmma was completed when the three months of wass had passed over, and at its conclusion the déwa Mátru, now become a rahat, said to Budha, "You who have been born from my womb so many times, have now rendered me a recompence. In one birth, from being a slave I became the wife of the king of Benares, but that exaltation was not equal to the privilege I now receive. From the time of Piyumatura Budha, during a kap-laksha, you sought no other mother, and I sought no other son. Now, my reward is received." Not Mátru alone, but eighty kelas and a thousand déwas and brahmas entered the paths.

After eighty-three days had expired, the multitude assembled at Sewet enquired of Mugalan when Budha might again be expected to appear. To ascertain this, the priest departed, in the presence of the people, to Tawutisá, where he appeared before Budha, and asked when he would return to the earth, as the multitude of the faithful at Sewet had been waiting three months in the anxious expectation of seeing him. Budha informed him that in seven days he should proceed to Sakaspura,* to which place Mugalan was directed to bring the people from Sewet. On the return of the priest, after hearing the information he conveyed to them, the upásakas enquired the distance from Sewet to Sakaspura, and were told that it was thirty yojanas. They then asked how the young and the lame were to go such a distance; but Mugalan informed them that by the power of Budha, and his own power, they would be enabled to go without any inconvenience; and in the same instant, more quickly than if they had gone upon swift horses, sooner than betel† can be taken from the bag and mixed with the lime, they were transported through the air to Sakaspura, as if it were in a dream.

The time had now arrived when Budha was to take his departure from the déwa-lóka. Sekra reflected that he had come from the earth at three steps, but that it would be right to celebrate his departure with special honours. He therefore caused a ladder of gold to extend from Maha Méru to Sakaspura.‡

---

* This place is called in Pali Sankassa. A letter from Lieut. Cunningham, R.E. to Colonel Sykes, was read before the Royal Asiatic Society, Dec. 3, 1842, giving an account of the discovery and identification of the city of Sankasya, mentioned as the kingdom of Kusadwaja, in the Rámáyana. It is twenty-four miles from Farrakhabad, and fifty from Kanouj, on the north or left bank of the Kali Nadi. The ruins are very extensive, and there can be no doubt that they are of Budhistical origin.

† This masticatory is almost universally in use among the natives of Ceylon.

‡ It is said by Fa Hian that the three ladders disappeared under the earth; but that Asoka built a monument over the ladder by which Budha descended.

At the right side of this ladder there was another, also of gold, upon which the déwas appeared, with instruments of music; and on the left there was another of silver, upon which the brahmas appeared, holding canopies, or umbrellas. These ladders were more than 80,000 yojanas in length. The steps in the ladder of Budha were alternately of gold, silver, coral, ruby, emerald, and other gems, and it was beautifully ornamented. The whole appeared to the people of the earth like three rainbows. When Budha commenced his descent, all the worlds from Awíchi to Bhawagra were illuminated by the same light. The characteristic marks upon his person appeared to the multitude assembled at Sakaspura, as plainly as the inscription upon a golden coin held in the hand; and as they looked at him they said to each other, " Now he is upon the golden step, or the silver, or some other." Sekra preceded him on the same ladder, blowing the conch, whilst on the other ladders were the déwas and brahmas. The people who saw him thus honoured, all formed within themselves the wish to become Budhas.

The first to pay his respects to Budha on arriving at Sakaspura was Seriyut; and after he had worshipped the déwa of déwas he enquired if all who had formed the wish to become Budhas would have their wishes gratified. Budha replied, "If they had not performed the páramitás in former births, how could they have exercised the wish? Those who have superior merit will become supreme Budhas; the next in order will be Pasé-Budhas; and the others will be priests. Thus all will receive one or other of the three Bódhi."* After this declaration had been made, Budha resolved upon giving evidence before the people of the superior wisdom of Seriyut. In the first place he asked a question that those who had not entered the paths could answer; then he asked another, but they were silent, and those who had entered the first path answered. Thus each class was successively silent, and the one above answered, as he passed to those in the second path and the third; and then proceeded to the inferior (kshína), the middle (triwidyaprápta), and the chief (shatabhignyáprápta) sráwakas: then to Mugalan and Seriyut; and to Seriyut alone. Last of all he propounded a question that the Budhas alone could answer. After this exer-

* This is illustrated by the figure of the three landing places, in the rapid stream.

cise, Budha said to Seriyut the words bhuta-midang, which the priest explained in a kóti of ways, though none of the other sráwakas who were present understood the meaning. As Seriyut proceeded, Gótama listened with the pleasure a father feels when witnessing the cleverness of his son, and then declared that in wisdom he was the chief of his disciples. All this honour was received by Seriyut because in a former age he had given in alms a stylus and a blank book for the writing of the bana.

40. *The Nága Nandópananda, overcome by Mugalan.*

At the time that Budha visited the déwa-lóka Tawutisá, the nága king, Nandópananda, said to his subjects, " The sage, Gótama Budha, has passed over the world on his way to Tawutisá; he will have to return by the same way again, but I must try to prevent his journey." For this purpose he took his station upon Maha Méru. When one of the priests who accompanied Budha, Rathapála, said that he had often passed in that direction before, and had always seen Maha Méru, but now it was invisible, Budha informed him that it was the nága Nandópananda who had concealed the mountain. Upon hearing this, Rathapála said that he would go and drive him away; but the sage did not give him permission. Then Mugalan offered to go and subdue the nága, and having obtained leave, he took the form of a snake, and approached Nandópananda. The nága endeavoured to drive him to a distance by a poisonous blast, but Mugalan sent forth a counterblast; and there was a battle of blasts, but the blast of the priest was more powerful than that of the nága. Then the nága sent forth a stream of fire, and Mugalan did the same, by which he greatly hurt the nága, whilst the other stream did no injury whatever to himself. Nandópananda said in anger, "Who art thou who attackest me with a force sufficient to cleave Maha Méru? and he answered, "I am Mugalan." After this he went in at one ear of the nága, and out at the other; then in at one nostril, and out at the other; he also entered his mouth, and walked up and down in his inside, from his head to his tail, and from his tail to his head. The nága was still further enraged by this disturbance of his intestines, and resolved to squeeze him to death when he emerged from his mouth, but Mugalan escaped without his perceiving it.

Another poisonous blast was sent forth, but it did not ruffle a single hair of the priest's body. After this Budha imparted to Mugalan the power to overcome the nága, and taking the form of a garunda, he began to pursue him; but Nandópananda offered him worship, and requested his protection. By Mugalan he was referred to Budha, who delivered to him a discourse, in which he told him that they who exercised hatred, however beautiful they may be, will be regarded with aversion; and that their fate will be like that of those who are destroyed by their own weapons. And he further informed him that they who are cruel will have to suffer much in hell; or if born in this world, they will be diseased, one disease following quickly upon another; and that therefore it is better to avoid anger and love all sentient beings, to have a soft heart, and exercise compassion. (*Amáwatura.*)

41. *The sixteen Dreams of the King of Kosol.*

The king of Kosol, Pasénádi, had sixteen dreams in one night. In the morning, when the brahmans came to enquire respecting his health, he told them what he had dreamed, and enquired from them what it portended.* They said that great dangers were threatened, either to his kingdom, his treasures, or his life; and when asked further how they were to be averted, they told him that he must make a great sacrifice of animals, four and four of each kind. The king approved of this, and gave orders that it should be prepared. As the brahmans had thus advised the king, in order that they themselves might reap the benefit, they set about the work in all readiness. The queen, Malliká, having observed their eagerness, enquired what it was all about; and when the king told her, she said it would be better to go and ask the advice of Budha, who was living near, at Sewet. The king saw the propriety of this, and went at once to the residence of Gótama, who inquired why he had come so early; and when he was informed that the king had come to learn how he might avert the dangers that threatened him, without the sacrifice of so many lives, he told him to repeat the dreams, and as he repeated them he gave him the interpretation of each.

The 1st dream: Four fierce bulls approached each other to

* This is a favourite legend with the Singhalese. In the text it is much more extended than in the translation; but even in this abridged form it will be thought to have received more attention than it merits.

fight, but when the people gathered together to see them, they ran away. The interpretation: In time, men will become evil; the déwas will not give rain; as the four bulls came from the four quarters, so will the clouds be collected, with a great noise; but as the bulls ran away, so when the people are gathered together expecting rain, the wind will come and disperse the clouds.

The 2nd dream: There was a forest of large trees, but a little tree appeared, grew up, and overshadowed them. The interpretation: Men will become evil, but their children will be good, and will thus be superior to their parents.

The 3rd dream: Some cows drank milk from calves that were born on the same day. The interpretation: The time will come when children will not honour their parents, nor support them; the parents will thus be destitute, and be constrained to come and ask support from their children.

The fourth dream: There was a wagon heavily laden, to which two calves were fastened, and farther off were two strong bulls fastened to it by slight cords; as the calves alone were unable to draw it they threw the yoke from their necks, and went away. The interpretation: The time will come when princes will leave the cares of government to mean persons and children; but they will be unequal to the performance of the duties, and great loss will follow.

The 5th dream: There were two horses feeding, with two heads each, but however much they ate, they were not satisfied. The interpretation: Judges will take bribes from both parties, but however much they receive they will still require more.

The 6th dream; A jackal made water into a golden dish. The interpretation: Princes will give high situations to mean people; the noble will thus have no means of support; they will therefore give their children in marriage to the mean, and thus confusion will be produced.

The 7th dream: A man sitting upon a chair made a rope of skin, but a female jackal under the chair ate the part that hung down to the floor, as fast as he made it. The interpretation: Women will be faithless; they will spend with other men what their husbands have collected with great care.

The 8th dream: There was a large vessel near the gate of the palace, around it thousands of smaller vessels; people came with water, and poured it into the large vessel, until it ran over; this they did again and again; but they poured more into the smaller vessels. The interpretation: Princes and nobles will oppress the poor; if they have only one single piece of money left, they will take it from them, and thus leave them empty, whilst they put the wealth they had gained into their own treasuries that are already full.

The 9th dream: There was a pool to which birds came to drink; on the sides the water was good, but in the centre it was muddy. The interpretation: The people of the cities will be oppressed, and they will therefore retire into the forests; they will thus be at peace whilst the people in the cities are enduring misery.

The 10th dream: In a vessel, boiling at the same time, were three kinds of rice, good, ordinary, and bad. The interpretation: In one country, under one king, some people will have no rain, others too much, and others a proper quantity, by which their crops will be good.

The 11th dream: Sandal-wood, worth a lac of treasure, was sold for a little sour milk. The interpretation: Priests will say this bana, which I have proclaimed to impart nirwána, not from love to the beings, but for applause or a piece of cloth; in the highways, the corners of the streets, and sheds, they will repeat it, for the sake of gain.

The 12th dream: Large stones floated on the surface of water, whilst dry pieces of wood, gourds, and other light articles, sank. The interpretation: Foolish princes will give good situations to inferior persons; so the low will become high, and the high low.

The 13th dream: A frog as small as a grain of mí, chased and swallowed a large nayá. The interpretation: Unwise men will marry girls who will squander away their substance; and when they ask them where all their wealth is gone to, the girls will say, it is nothing to them, and abusing them, usurp the authority.

The 14th dream: A crow of most wretched appearance was surrounded by beautiful hansas. The interpretation; Princes will be idle, they will learn no science, and therefore be afraid to promote respectable persons to office; thus the noble will become dependent upon the mean.

The 15th dream: Goats and deer chased tigers; caught, killed, and ate them. The interpretation: Princes will appoint mean persons to respectable situations, who will oppress the rich; these will make complaints in the courts of law, but from thence they will be driven without redress, and their property will thus be lost. [One of the dreams is omitted.]

As each dream was related, Budha informed the king that he need not fear, as the fulfilment would not take place till a distant period. The sage further informed him that he had dreamed the same dreams in the Maha Supina birth. (*Sadharmmaratnakáré.*)

42. *The Queen Prajápati becomes a Priestess, and obtains Nirwána.*

This queen was the daughter of Suprabudha, who reigned in the city of Kóli. Her mother, Maha-yasódhará-déwi, was the aunt of Singha-hanu, the father of Sudhódana. On the day that the princess received her name, the diviners said that from the marks they saw upon her body, they could tell that if in after years she should have a son, he would be a chakrawartti, or if she should have a daughter, she would be the queen of a chakrawartti. It was on account of the good fortune that was to befall her she was called Prajápati, and as she belonged to the lineage of Gótama she was called Maha-Prajápati-gótama. On arriving at a proper age, she became, along with Mahadéwi, the wife of Sudhódana; and the two queens lived together like two srikántáwas in one lotus flower. Six days after giving birth to the prince Sidhartta, who afterwards became Budha, Maha-déwi died, and went to the déwa-lóka Tawutisá, when she became the déwa Mátru, and was the guardian déwa of the palace of Sudhódana. On the next day Prajápati also had a son, Nanda, afterwards a priest, who was given over to the charge of nurses, whilst Prajápati attended to the prince Sidhártta as if he were her own son, and fed him from her breast. Thus she became the foster-mother of the illustrious prince, and afterwards entered the path sowán on the same day as Sudhódana, which occurred on the first visit of Sidhártta to his native city after he became Budha.

Between the cities of Kapila and Kóli there was a river called the Róhini.* By the erection of an embankment, the inhabitants of both cities were enabled to irrigate the lands upon which they cultivated their rice; but it happened that in consequence of a drought the water became insufficient for the fields of both the parties. The people of Kapila put in a claim of exclusive right to the little water that flowed in the river; but the people of Kóli asserted a similar claim, and a feud commenced, which led to serious dissensions. At one time about a hundred persons were assembled on each side, and abuse was plentifully poured out. The people of Kóli said that the people of Kimbulwat were like pigs and dogs, as they intermarried with their sisters; and they in return said that the people of Kóli were descended from parents who were leprous, and who lived like bats in a hollow tree. This affair was related, with much exaggeration, to their respective kings. The Sákyas said that whatever might be the manner of their origin, they would prove that their swords were sharp; and the princes of Kóli were equally ready to shew the might of those who had come from the hollow tree. Both sides prepared for battle, and assembled their forces on the bank of the river. The princesses of the opposite parties, when they heard of these proceedings, went to the spot to entreat their relatives to desist from their intentions, but no regard was paid to their request.

At this time Budha was in Sewet, and when looking around the world, as he was accustomed to do in the morning watch, he saw that a battle was about to take place, and then looked further to see if it were possible to prevent it by his personal interference; when he perceived, that if he were to go to the place, and deliver a discourse, 500 princes would be induced to become priests. He therefore went, and remaining suspended in the air, caused a darkness to appear, so thick that the combatants were unable to see each other. The Sákyas, on seeing him, said that it would be wrong to fight in the presence of the jewel of their race, and threw down their weapons; and the princes of Kóli followed their example. Then Budha descended from the air, and sat on a throne on the bank of the river, where he received the homage of all the princes. The

---

* The Róhini, or Rohein, is said by Klaproth to come from the mountains of Nepaul, and after uniting with the Mahanada to fall into the Rapty, near Goruckpur.

teacher of the three worlds enquired why they had come together; was it to celebrate a river festival? They replied that it was not for pastime, but for battle; and when he asked what was the reason of their quarrel, the kings said that they did not exactly know; they would enquire of the commander-in-chief; but he, in turn, said that he must make enquiry of the sub-king; and thus the enquiry went on, until it came to the husbandman, who related the whole affair. Budha, after hearing their relation, said, "What is the value of water?" "It is little," said the princes. "What of earth?" "It is inconsiderable." "What of kings?" "It is unspeakable." "Then would you," said Budha, "destroy that which is of incomparable value for that which is worthless?" After this he repeated three játakas and a sútra, by which he appeased the wrath of the combatants. The kings now reflected that by the interposition of Budha the shedding of much blood had been prevented; that if the battle had taken place, none might have been left to tell their wives and children of what had occurred; and that if Sidhártta had become a chakrawartti the princes would have become his personal attendants; and they concluded that it was, therefore, right that they should still pay the same respect to him, as he was the supreme Budha. They accordingly directed that 250 princes from each of the two families should embrace the priesthood, who after receiving ordination resided with Budha at the Maha-wana wihára, whence they occasionally visited both the cities. But though they had become priests, it was not from their own choice, but from the wish of their parents; and they became additionally dissatisfied when their wives sent to inform them how much pain had been caused by their separation.

The dissatisfaction of the 500 princes was not hid from Budha, who, on a certain evening, asked them if they had seen the beautiful forest of Himála; and when they replied that they had not, he enquired if they were wishful to see it, but they said that they were not able to go because they did not possess the power of irdhi; yet they were willing to visit it if any one who had the power would take them. Then Budha took them through the air, and showed them all the treasures of the forest. They saw two kokilas take a sprig in their mouths, each holding it by the end; and the king of the kokilas alighting upon it, they flew through the air. Eight birds of a similar kind went before, and the same number behind, above, and below; and eight more carried in their beaks the most delicious fruits. The 500 priests were surprised by this sight, when Budha informed them that he was once the king of the kokilas in the same place, but at that time he had a retinue of 3500 birds, and not so small a number as they then saw. He then related the Kunála-játaka, in 100 stanzas, during the recital of which the priests entered the paths, and received the power of irdhi. They came by the power of Budha, but returned through the air by their own. After their arrival at the wihára, they were enabled to receive the rahatship, by which all evil desire was removed from them, as far as earth from heaven. When their wives again sent to them messages to entice them to leave their profession, they said that all further intercourse must now cease, as they had become rahats. (*Amáwatura*.)

It was during the residence of Budha at Maha-wana wihára, that he delivered the discourse called the Maha Samaya Sútra, when a kela-laksha of déwas and brahmas became rahats, and an asankya entered the three paths. With this discourse they are greatly pleased, and call it "*our* sútra."

The wives of the 500 princes, when they heard that their husbands had become rahats, thought it would be better for them also to become recluses, than to remain at home in widowhood. They therefore requested Prajápati to go with them to Budha, that they might receive consecration. At this time Budha was residing in the Nigrodáráma wihára, near Kapila, whither he had come on account of the festival to be held at the burning of the body of Sudhódana, who was now dead; and after the ceremony was concluded, he remained in the same place a short period that he might assist his relatives, by instructing them in the dharmma. The queen-mother, Prajápati, said to Budha that as Sudhódana was dead, and Rahula and Nanda were priests, she had no wish to reside alone; and therefore requested, that with the other princesses by whom she was accompanied, she might be admitted to profession. It was clearly perceived by the sage that if these females were admitted to profession, they would derive therefrom immense advantages; and he saw also that it was the practice of former Budhas to admit them; but he reflected that if they were admitted, it would perplex the minds of those who had not yet entered into the paths, and cause others to speak against his institutions. He therefore, thought it would not be right to accede to their request at once, and said, "Women, seek not to enter my immaculate order." Three times they presented their request, but as it was still refused, they were afraid to make it a fourth time, and retired to their homes.

From Kapila, Budha went to the Kútágára-sála, near Wisálá. Then Prajápati said to the other princesses:—"Children, Budha has thrice refused to admit us to profession; let us take it upon ourselves, and then go to him, and he cannot but receive us." On hearing this advice, they were pleased, and the whole of them cut off their hair, put on the proper robe, and taking earthen alms-bowls in their hands, prepared to depart from their homes. The queen-mother thought that it would not be right for them to go in chariots, as it would be contrary to the institutions of the recluse; they must travel in some manner that would be attended with fatigue; and they, therefore, set out for Wisálá on foot. Previously they had thought it a great thing to have to descend from the upper to the lower story of the palace; they were only accustomed to walk in places so smooth that they were like mirrors that reflected the image of all things near them; for fuel in the palace, when fires were required on account of the cold, they had only burnt cotton and silk cloth smeared with oil, as common wood would have caused too much heat, and sandal wood too much smoke; even when they went to the bath they were protected by curtains and canopies; and in every respect were brought up in the most delicate manner. In consequence of their extreme tenderness, their feet were soon covered with blisters, when they began to walk. The people of those parts, who had previously heard of their beauty, no sooner knew that they were on their way, than they came from all directions to look at them. Some prepared food, and requested they would do them the fávour to partake of it, whilst others brought vehicles and litters, and entreated that they would make use of them; but they resolutely refused to take advantage of these kind offers of assistance. The distance from Kapila to Wisálá was fifty-one yojanas. It was evening when they arrived at the wihára in which Budha was residing; they did not enter within but remained at the outside. When Ananda saw them, with bleeding feet, covered with dust, and half dead, his breast was full of sorrow, and his eyes filled with tears, and he said, "Why have you come? For what reason have you endured these hardships? Have the Sákyas been driven from their city by the enemy? Why does the mother of Budha remain in such a place?" An answer to these questions was returned by Prajápati; on hearing which Ananda requested them to remain there whilst he went and informed Budha of their arrival. To the sage he related all that he had seen, and described the wretchedness of the appearance presented by the princesses, at the same time informing him of their wish; but he merely said, "Ananda, seek not to have females admitted to profession." The priest then asked if the queen-mother was not worthy of being admitted, but he received only the same rebuke; and though he thrice repeated the question, no other reply was given. Then he enquired whether a female, on the supposition that she was admitted to profession, could enter the paths; and Budha said, "Are the Budhas born in the world only for the benefit of men? Assuredly it is for the benefit of females as well. When I delivered the Tirókudha-sútra, many women entered the paths, as did also many déwis when I delivered the Abhidharmma in Tawutisá. Have not Wisákhá, and many other upásikáwas, entered the paths? The entrance is open for women as well as men." No déwa or brahma would have been able to say more upon the same subject to the teacher of the world, but as Ananda knew his thoughts, he was bold, and said, "My lord, it is right that women should be admitted to profession; when you delivered the Budha-wansa discourse, you made known that this was one of the institutions of the twenty-four Budhas who have preceded you." With this reply of Ananda, Budha was pleased; but he said nothing, nor did he give permission to Prajápati to enter, that more might be elicited upon the subject. Ananda, therefore, continued; "It is evident that women may be admitted to profession; then why may not Prajápati, who has rendered so much assistance to Budha? What hinderance can there be?" And he proclaimed at length the benefits that Budha had received from Prajápati in his childhood.

When he had concluded, the great teacher saw that the time had now come in which it would be proper to admit the princesses to profession; and he therefore said, "Ananda, if Prajápati be admitted to profession, there are eight requirements to which the female recluses must attend.

The eight ordinances were repeated by Ananda to Prajápati and the other princesses, and when they heard the conditions upon which they could be admitted to profession, they were greatly delighted, and at once promised that all the ordinances should be strictly observed. They were admitted to profession in the presence of the priests; and when they had received upasampadá, Prajápati was appointed by Budha to be the chief of the female recluses, and to instruct her relatives in the necessary discipline. Not many days afterwards, when exercising bháwaná, she became a rahat: and the 500 princesses entered the paths at the time that Budha delivered the Nandakowáda-sútra to the priest Nanda. The number of the females who were admitted to profession after this period cannot be computed, but the chapters, both of the priests and priestesses, increased so greatly, that in all Jambudwípa it was scarcely possible to find a suitable place for the exercise of wiwéka, or solitary meditation.

On a certain occasion, when Budha was surrounded by his disciples, Prajápati began to utter his praises, and said, "May your glory increase continually. By means of your mother, Mahamáya, who brought you into the world, blessings without number have been conferred." And she proceeded in her speech and said, "May you live long; may you never decay or die; may you exist a whole kalpa, that you may continue to bless the world." All the orders of the priesthood who were present joined in this ascription of praise; but when the noise of their voices had passed away, Budha said, "The ornaments of a Budha are his sráwaka priests, as dutiful nobles are the ornaments of a king, and the stars of a moon; the Budhas desire to see their sráwakas many in number." He therefore directed his disciples to say, "May the pure priesthood continue and increase," but to express no desire for the increase of the age of Budha.

When Budha afterwards visited the city of Wisálá, the princes and others went to meet him; as from the time he had driven away the pestilence, the citizens had held him in great respect. During his residence there he took up his abode in the Kútágárasálá, where he was visited by Prajápati; and the queen-mother, after returning to her own wihára, and pondering in her mind over what she had seen, thus reflected:—"Budha is the glory of his sráwakas, and the sráwakas are the glory of Budha. I must look to see if any of them have ceased to exist. I see that none have ceased to exist since the prince Sidhártta became Budha. I must now look to see whether any of the sráwakas are near the attainment of this state. I see that it will soon be attained by Anya-kondanya, Seriyut, and Mugalan. I am now 120 years of age, though in appearance I am as young as when I was a maiden of sixteen; my teeth are perfect, and my hair is not grey; but it is meet that the child should see the departure of the parent, and not the parent the departure of the child; I will therefore request that I be the first of the faithful admitted to the city of peace." The earth moved as these reflections passed through her mind, which was perceived by the 500 princesses; and when they enquired the reason, she informed them of the resolution to which she had come. They replied that they had all been admitted to profession at the same time as the queen-mother, since which they had all lived together, and she had been their guide; and they now wished to attain nirwána at the same period. Soon afterwards they went to inform Budha of their request, when Prajápati said to the teacher of the three worlds:—" I paid you attention in your infancy, but you have repaid me in a way that no other son can assist his parent; I have sheltered you from the sun and storm, and you have protected me from the perils of existence; the mothers of the chakrawarttis are yet enduring the pains of existence, and after being the empresses of the universe they will become cattle, ants, and other mean creatures; but I have been the foster-mother of a Budha, and am therefore saved from future birth; I am the chief of women; and I have now to request that before any other of your disciples I may be permitted to attain nirwána. But previous to its attainment I request to see the beauties of the sacred person, and to be forgiven in whatever I have done wrong." Then Budha replied, "The water of the Anótatta lake needs not to be purified; the chintámánikya jewel needs not to be polished; the gold from the great jambu tree in the Himalayan forest needs not to be refined; nor does the queen-mother need to be forgiven, as there is nothing to forgive. It is not requisite that those who have seen nirwána should forgive each other. Yet as you have requested it, and it is the custom of the Budhas thus to forgive, what you seek is granted, as what you have asked is good. Therefore, be the first to enter nirwána;

and thus obtain the pre-eminence over all my other sráwakas, as all the stars are eclipsed by the superior light of the full moon." Anya-kondanya, Nanda, Rahula, the 500 princes, and others were present; and Ananda, as he was not yet a rahat, wept. But the queen-mother told him it was not a proper time in which to indulge in grief, as she was about to obtain a great privilege.

Before her departure, she was directed by Budha to exhibit some miracle in the presence of the faithful, that the error of those who supposed that it was not possible for a woman to attain nirwána might be removed. Then Prajápati rose into the air many times, and declared in such a way that the whole earth might hear it, that what she did was not by her own power but by the power of Budha. She then made as many repetitions of her own form as filled the skies of all the sakwalas, and the mouth of every image thus made repeated the praises of Budha. Then all the forms vanished but one, and afterwards this also disappeared. Many more wonders did she perform, by the power of dhyaná and kasina; making an image of herself so large that it reached to the brahma-lóka; causing a darkness that everywhere prevailed; taking the waters of the four oceans, and hiding them in the hollow of her hand; and making figures in the sky of elephants, lions, &c. When the whole was concluded, she descended to the earth, and worshipped Budha; after which she remained for some time in admiration of his mouth, footstep, and other beauties, and then retired, with her attendants. Having performed the four dhyánas from the beginning to the end, and from the end to the beginning, the chétana was extinguished, like a lamp going out, and she entered the city of peace, her body remaining like an image of gold. The 500 princesses attained the same privilege.

Wonders then appeared in heaven and earth; and the déwas going to Budha said, "The death of Prajápati and the princesses is like the passing away of the moon and the stars from the sky; the number of the faithful is diminished." Budha commanded Ananda to proclaim to his disciples in what manner the queen-mother had attained nirwána, and to summon them to her cremation. All who wished to come were enabled to do so in a moment of time, without any personal effort, by the power of Budha; so that there was the largest assemblage ever collected during the ministry of Gótama Budha. Wiswakarmma brought 501 golden litters through the sky, and the bodies were carried in them by the guardian déwas to the place of burning; an honour this, which was not received by Budha, nor by any other of his disciples. The Lichawi princes prepared a funeral pyre for each of the bodies, made of sandal-wood, saturated with perfumed oil; and after the burning had taken place, it was found that the bodies of the princesses were entirely consumed, but that that of Prajápati remained like a heap of pearls, which Ananda carefully collected, and placed in the alms-bowl of Budha.

43. *The wicked Devices of Déwadatta and Ajásat.*

In a former age, Déwadatta became the enemy of Bódhisat; and from that time, until he became Budha, the enmity continued through every successive birth. He was born in the city of Kóli, as the son of Supra-budha, and his mother was one of the sisters of Sudhódana. By the power of dhyána he became a rishi, so that he could pass through the air and assume any form. Others who attained this state were released by it from birth, but to him it was only as a curse. When the overflowing bile of a dog approaches his nose, he feels a courage so great that he will attack even an elephant, though it be to his own certain destruction; so Déwadatta, by possessing the power of irdhi, was led on to do that which involved himself in ruin. Thus he thought:— I am equally honourable, as to family, with Budha; before I became a priest I was treated with all respect, but now I receive even less than my previous followers. I must take to myself 500 disciples; but before I can do this, I must persuade some king or other to take my part; the great monarchs of Rajagaha, and other places, are all on the side of Budha; I cannot therefore deceive them, as they are wise. But there is Ajásat, the son of Bimsara; he is ignorant of causes, and disobedient to his parents; but he is liberal to his followers; so I must bring him over, and then I can easily procure a large retinue."

When the queen of Bimsara, who was the daughter of Maha Kosol, king of Sewet, was pregnant, she had a desire to drink blood drawn from the shoulder of the king. She told it to no one; but as it was not gratified, she continually faded away like a leaf; when the king insisted upon knowing the cause, she informed him. The king was greatly pleased that it only concerned himself, and having procured a golden dish and a sharp instrument, he at once permitted blood to be drawn from his shoulder, by a skilful surgeon, when the queen drank it, mixed with water, and was restored to health. The prognosticators having heard of it, declared that she would bear a son, who would be an enemy to his father, and cause his death. This being reported to the queen, she went to one of the royal gardens, and tried by compression to destroy the fruit of her womb; but when the king noticed the frequency of her visits to that place, he enquired the reason; and having learnt it he was angry, and commanded that there should be no repetition of her attempts, as the child might prove to be a daughter; and if other kings heard of it, they would be greatly displeased. Guards were set over the queen. She still determined, however, to destroy her infant after its birth, if it were a son; but the king gave orders to the midwives to convey the child away, without her knowledge. A son was born, and his life was preserved. When he was two or three years old, the king had him dressed in the most engaging manner, and took him to the queen, who on seeing him, no longer sought his death, but loved him with a sincere affection. The name given to him was Ajásat, because previous to his birth he was declared to be the enemy of his father. At sixteen years of age he was made sub-king.

At the time that Budha resided in Kosambæ, Déwadatta went to Rajagaha alone, where he remained in the Jétáwana wihára a single day, after which he assumed the appearance of seven nayás, and went through the air to the place where Ajásat was sitting with his attendants. Here he transformed himself into the appearance of bangles, one of which was entwined round each foot of the prince, one round each arm, one on each shoulder, and one in his lap; seven in all, formed of the seven nayás. Ajásat was greatly terrified, but as he was a royal prince he did not move from his seat; he merely called to his followers to destroy the serpents that were entwined around his person. Then Déwadatta told him not to be afraid, and informed him who he was; and Ajásat said if he would not frighten him in that way, he would become his disciple, and worship him. On hearing this, Déwadatta took the form of a recluse, and from that time the two princes became great friends. Ajásat built a wihára; and Déwadatta had soon 500 disciples, all of whom were provided for by the prince. The wihára was built upon the bank of the river Gayá. At this time he lost the power of dhyána.

The déwa Kakudha informed Mugalan, then at Kosambæ, of what had taken place; and the priest made it known to Budha, who said, "The boar roots up the earth, and eats mud; the elephant tries to do the same; but his body swells, and he dies; so also Déwadatta, by trying to imitate me, will bring about his own destruction." Soon afterwards Budha himself went to Rajagaha, when he was visited by Déwadatta and his 500 disciples. The prince said, "Kings have sub-kings; as you are the king of the dharmma, it is right that you should appoint a sub-king, and I request that this office may be given to me;" but Budha replied, that Seriyut and Mugulan were his principal disciples, and asked him if the snipe had power to draw the weight of an elephant. Déwadatta was unable to reply, but he retired from the presence of Budha; and in great anger, at the rebuke he had received, proceeded to his own wihára.

One day, when the two princes were together, Déwadatta said to Ajásat, "In former times men lived long, but it is not so now; there is no telling how short may be the period that you will have to enjoy the kingdom; you had therefore better put the king to death, that you may reign in his stead, and I will put Budha to death, and so become his successor." To this the prince agreed, and taking a javelin in his hand, he went to murder the king; but when in his father's presence he trembled greatly. The nobles knew from this agitation, and the sight of the weapon, that his intention was evil, and informed the king, who enquired of him why he sought his death. The prince said that he wanted the kingdom; but Bimsara kissed him, and told him it was not necessary for him in that manner to become a rebel, as he would deliver to him the whole kingdom; and accordingly he commanded that Ajásat should be proclaimed king. When the prince informed Déwadatta of what was about to take place, he was greatly displeased, and said that if Bimsara was permitted to live, he would undoubtedly attempt to regain the kingdom, and that, therefore, it was better to put him at once to death. Then Ajásat enquired in what way it could be done without using an instrument or weapon, as by this method he had failed in his intention; and Déwadatta recommended him to confine the king, and deprive him of food. This was done, and only the queen was permitted to see him; but when she went to visit him, she took with her a little rice, wherewith she nourished the king. When Ajásat found out the stratagem, he commanded it to be discontinued; and after this the queen took a small portion of food tied up in the topknot formed by her hair. Then Ajásat forbade her to tie up her hair; and she took food in her golden slippers. But this was forbidden. After this she bathed in water mixed with honey and other nutritious substances, and caused her body to be anointed, which enabled the king to draw from her skin a little nourishment with his tongue; until this also was discovered, and she was entirely prohibited from having access to the place of his confinement. At their last interview, she reminded him that it was her wish to destroy the prince in his infancy, but she was prevented by the king, and now his death was the consequence of the child's preservation; she also requested forgiveness for whatever she might at any time have done to grieve the king, and wept on account of the danger that awaited him. Notwithstanding, the king still lived; and when the prince enquired how it could be, he was told that his father walked about, though he had no food, and his body shone, because he had entered the path sowán. Then he commanded that the king's feet should be cauterized, and rubbed with salt and oil, to prevent him from walking. When the barber entered the prison to perform the operation, the king at first thought that his son had relented, and that he was about to be released; and when he learnt the truth, he felt no resentment against the barber, but told him to do as he had been commanded; but the poor man wept as he performed the operation. How was it that one who had entered sowán was thus to suffer? In a former birth he had walked with his slippers on near a dágoba; and he had also trodden on a carpet belonging to some priests without washing his feet. On account of these things he had now to endure great pain; and after calling upon the three gems, he died, and was born as the déwa Janawasabha, in the lóka called Chaturmaharájika.

On the same day that the king died, Ajásat had a son, and the nobles sent him two letters to inform him of these events. The first letter that was delivered to him informed him of the birth of his son; and when he had read it, he felt the rising of paternal affection, and thought, "In this manner my father must have felt when my own birth was made known to him;" his heart became softened, and he gave orders that his father should be spared. No sooner were they issued, than the other letter was put into his hand, informing him that his father was no more. On hearing this he went to the queen-mother, and asked her if his father had expressed pleasure when he was born. The queen informed him that his father was not only greatly delighted when he received a son; but when Ajásat was an infant, and had a sore upon his finger, such was the affection of his father, that he sucked the sore in the hall of justice where he was sitting, and retained the saliva out of respect to the sanctity of the place. The prince wept bitterly at the burning of his father's body.

About this time Déwadatta sent to Ajásat, now king of Rajagaha, to request a band of skilful archers, that they might slay Budha. The king called into his presence 500 archers, from whom he chose thirty-one who were more expert than the rest, and sent them to the priest, saying that they were to do whatsoever he commanded them. On their arrival, Déwadatta took their chief on one side, and told him that the order he was about to give was to be kept a profound secret, which the chief promised faithfully to keep. He then told the archer that his commission was, to slay Budha, when he was walking in the hall of ambulation belonging to the Gijakúta wihára, for the accomplishment of which he would receive a proportionate reward. The priest had resolved to set two of the men to kill their chief as he returned from the place of murder; and four others to kill these two, and eight others to kill these four, and sixteen others to kill these eight; and he intended last of all to kill these sixteen with his own hand, that it might not be known in what way Budha had been killed. Early in the morning of the same day, when the ruler of the three worlds looked to see whom he should catch in his net, he perceived that the thirty-one archers would receive the benefit of his teaching. Afterwards, in the hall of the wihára, he awaited their arrival with all affection, as the mother looks out for the coming of her only child. The chief of the archers came, and sent off an arrow; but it passed in a contrary direction to what he intended, and the twanging of the bow gave him great pain. Then Budha looked towards him, with the same kindness that he would towards any other being; and the archer in this manner overcome, went towards him, and offered worship, confessing that what he had done was at the instigation of Déwadatta; and when he requested forgiveness, Budha said bana to him, and he entered the path sowán. The other archers, in a little time, came to enquire into the reason why their chief did not return; and as the two, the four, the eight, and the sixteen successively arrived, although one company was unable to see the other, their eyes being purposely closed by the sage, they heard bana, by which they also were enabled to enter sowán; after which they became priests, and rahats. (*Milinda Prasna.*)

At another time, Déwadatta, from the top of the Gijakúta rock, by the help a machine, hurled an immense stone towards Budha, at a time when he was passing underneath, with the intent to kill him; but in its flight it broke into two pieces, and a small portion rolling towards the sage, struck his foot, whence it caused a drop of blood to flow, about the size of the kowakka (ocymum gratissimum) fruit. Budha suffered much from the wound, but Jíwaka opened it with a sharp instrument, and let out the extravasated blood, by which means it was cured.

The great enemy was now convinced that Budha could not be destroyed by a human being, and he therefore resolved to let loose upon him the Málágiri elephant, an animal exceedingly fierce and cruel. At the request of Déwadatta, the king commanded the keeper of the elephant to obey his orders, and to let the animal loose on the next day in the street of the city, when Budha came to receive alms. The elephant drank daily eight measures of arrack, but Déwadatta commanded that in the morning he should have sixteen. The next day a royal proclamation was issued that no one should appear in the streets; all the citizens were to remain within their houses. The upásakas, on learning what was intended to take place, went to the wihára and requested Budha not to visit the city next day, as a great danger awaited him; promising that they themselves would bring all that was necessary for the sage and his priests. But Budha declared that he would proceed in his usual course; and when the upásakas saw that they could not change his resolution, they went away. The next morning he called Ananda, and told him to inform the priests of the eighteen wiháras that they were to accompany him to the city. The citizens, both those who believed in him and those by whom he was opposed, assembled in great numbers upon an eminence; the former that they might see the triumph of their teacher, and the latter that they might witness the defeat of him whom they considered as an enemy. Budha at the usual hour entered the street where he was accustomed to receive alms, attended by the priests. Soon afterwards the elephant was let loose against him; at once it began to throw down the houses on each side, crushing their ruins to powder; its trunk was tossed about in the most terrific manner; its ears moved to and fro; and like a moving rock it rushed towards the place where the sage was walking. The priests entreated Budha to escape, as the savage animal was unacquainted with his merit, and was evidently set on his destruction; but he quietly told them not to be afraid. Seriyut asked permission to be the first to encounter the elephant; but the sage informed him, that the power of the Budha was one, and that of the disciple another, and forbade him to proceed towards the animal. Many other priests presented similar requests, but they were not granted. At last Ananda went a little in front of Budha, who thrice commanded him to retire to one side; and when he still refused obedience, the teacher of the three worlds, by the power of irdhi, obliged him to go behind. At this instant a little child wandered into the street, and the mother, without any apprehension of the danger in which she was placed, ran into the space between Budha and the infuriated animal; but when the elephant was about to destroy her, he called out, "The sixteen measures of arrack you this morning received were not given you that you might injure any other being but me; here am I; waste not your strength on a less noble object." On hearing the voice of Budha, the elephant looked to him; the effects of the arrack in a moment passed away; and the pacified beast approached him in the gentlest manner, and did him reverence. The sage charged him not to take life in future, to hate no one, and to be kind to all; and the elephant, in the presence of all the people, repeated the five precepts. Thus the rage of Málágiri was subdued, and had he not been a quadruped, he might now have entered the path sowán. The multitude, on seeing this great wonder, made a noise in approbation like the voice of the sea, and the clapping of their hands was like the thunder. They took off their ornaments and put them upon Málágiri, who from that time was called Dhanapála; and 84,000 of the people entered the path anágámi. As Budha had there performed a miracle, he reflected that it would be improper to seek alms in the same place, and in consequence retired to the Jétáwana wihára, without proceeding in the usual course.

44. *The Conversion of Ajásat.*

There was celebrated in the city of Rajagaha a festival called Sena-keli. On the evening of the full moon Ajásat was seated upon a throne, in the midst of all possible magnificence. From the time that he caused his father's death, he had been unable to sleep; and though the nobles asked the cause of his restlessness, he was ashamed to tell them, though he felt as if his body had been pierced by a hundred weapons. It was a beautiful night; but he was not at ease, and he enquired of the nobles who were near him whether they knew of any one expert in conversation who could beguile the time with instructive talk. The nobles recommended different persons, but they were all tirttakas; each one naming his own teacher; so that the king was like a man who wished for mangos and could only procure the poisonous kaduru. At some distance was Jíwaka; but as he remained silent, the king asked if no one else had a teacher to recommend. He was silent because he knew of the king's enmity to Budha; as he thought when the other nobles were severally recommending their teachers, that if he were to mention the name of Gótama, it would only add to the confusion. It was also his idea that if the king went first to converse with the tirttakas, he would learn their nothingness, and would then be better disposed to listen to the truth. But the king became increasingly sorrowful, as those only spoke whom he wished to be silent, and those were silent whom he wished to speak; and at last he said openly to Jíwaka, "Why are you silent when others are recommending their teachers; have you some cause of dissatisfaction?" Then the noble thought that the time for him to speak had come, and in a manner very different to the others, he descended from his seat, and reverently lifting up his hands towards the wihára in which Budha was residing, he began to recount his virtues. After this he said to the king, "Budha resides in my mango grove, with 1250 disciples; he can soothe the spirit of a hundred, or a thousand, or a hundred thousand persons, were they even all afflicted in an equal degree. You are at liberty to visit him, and put to him any question whatever, with the certainty that it will be answered." The heart of the king became joyful as he listened to these words, and he resolved at once to go to the wihára, accompanied by Jíwaka alone, for which purpose he commanded his elephant chariot to be prepared. He had horse and other chariots in great numbers, but he preferred the elephant chariot upon this occasion, as being more respectful to Budha, and as making less noise. But the noble reflected that kings have many enemies, and that if any harm were to happen to Ajásat, he alone would be blamed. He, therefore, recommended the king to take a guard; and as it would not be right to trust even the usual guards, as it was night, he had 500 females dressed in male clothing, who accompanied the king upon elephants, with weapons in their hands. Jíwaka knew that Budha only said bana to those who had merit to enter the paths; and as he thought that if a great multitude accompanied the king, there might be some among them who possessed the merit of which the monarch was deficient, he caused it to be proclaimed through the city that the king was about to visit Budha, and that any one was at liberty to join the procession. At the appointed time the concourse was great, and the scene magnificent. In addition to the females on elephants, there were 16,000 others on foot, and as many young maidens; then 60,000 nobles, 90,000 other chiefs, 10,000 brahmans singing joyful songs, and musicians, archers, and other warriors without number. The procession passed the thirty-two gates and the sixty-four posterns of the city by the light of thousands of torches, adorned with jewels. Between the outer wall and the Gijakúta rock was the garden of Jíwaka, and as it approached the wíhara the music suddenly ceased to play. The king became alarmed; and not knowing the cause why the noise in a moment ceased, he thought that he had been brought there to be slain; but Jíwaka, suspecting his fears, told him not to be under apprehension, as he had guards on each side of him, and the lights of the wihára already appeared in the distance.

When a little nearer the sacred habitation, the king alighted from his elephant, and the moment his foot touched the ground, the rays of Budha, out of mercy, were extended to the place where he stood. At this the king again became alarmed, so that his body broke out into a profuse sweat, as he remembered the many acts he had done in opposition to Budha. But on recovering himself, he expressed to Jíwaka his admiration of the architecture of the wihara he had built, and of the manner in which its walks and tanks were laid out. The king had not seen Budha since his youth; and though he could not mistake him when he saw him in the midst of his disciples, it was the manner of kings to appear ignorant, and he asked Jíwaka by what token he should recognize the teacher. The noble thought this was like asking where the earth was; or like a man looking in the sky and asking where the sun or moon was; or like a man at the foot of Maha Méru asking where there was a mountain. Then said Jíwaka, making a profound obeisance to the sage, "O king, this is our all-wise Budha;" and the king saw him seated near the centre pillar at the eastern end of the wihára. Not a single priest looked towards the king; they remained unmoved, like the lotus flowers upon the surface of a lake on a calm day. With this he was greatly pleased, and as it is natural that when any one sees that with which he is delighted, he should wish to impart the same pleasure to his children, he thought that if his own son were to receive an equal honour it would be all that he could desire. Budha perceived his thoughts, and said to him, "As the stream descends from an elevated place to the lower plain, so do your thoughts wander from me towards your son." The monarch was by this means convinced that the knowledge of Budha was beyond limit, and reflected, "No one has sinned against the goodness of Budha so much as myself; I have murdered my father, the friend of Budha; I have tried to murder Budha himself; I have joined the wicked company of Déwadatta, his enemy; and yet he speaks to me thus kindly." He then worshipped the sage, but did not worship the priests, as in that case he would have had to turn his back upon their chief.

Budha now gave the king permission to ask any question he wished; upon which he said, "Kings and nobles mount the elephant and subdue the horse; they collect wealth, and have families; they are charitable, and acquire merit; thus they have the benefit of both this world and the next. But the priests have no families; they go with the alms-bowl from door to door, and endure many hardships; by this means they secure a reward in the next world, but what benefit have they in this?"

The sage perceived that it would be necessary for him to be cautious in the reply he gave, as there were many present who were followers of the tirttakas, and it would not be right to proclaim these things indiscriminately to all; he, therefore, himself put a question to the king, and said, "Have you ever put the same question to other teachers: if so, did you receive satisfaction from the answers they gave?" The monarch replied, "When I made the same enquiry from Púrnnakásyapa he said that there is no reward in the next world either for virtue or crime; but this is as if I should ask him where there is a mango, and he should reply, There is a dell in such a garden. I asked one thing, and his reply related to another. I received no satisfaction from him whatever, but was like a man trying to squeeze oil from sand, and therefore I have come to you." Budha: "I will ask you another question. You have a slave; he wishes to obtain merit; he thinks thus—The king is a man; so am I; the king's wealth is like that of the déwas; I have only a small pittance in comparison. I cannot give a thousandth part of what he can, were I to give continually to my life's end. I will therefore become a priest. Now when such a one embraces the priesthood, and keeps the precepts, can you call him as aforetime, and bid him do the work of a servant?" The king: "No; I must worship him, and make to him offerings." Budha: Then there is one individual who is benefited, even in this life, by becoming a priest. But I will give you another instance. You have a husbandman; but he wishes to gain the same respect as the king. He, therefore leaves his farm, and becomes a priest. Can you then, o king, command him to take the plough, and prepare the ground?" The king: "No; so far from this, I must worship him." Budha: "There is yet a greater reward even than this; the priest enters the paths and becomes a rahat; than this there can be no greater privilege." This may be learnt at greater length in the Sámányasútra, in the Dik-sangha. The king, on receiving this information, said that he had applied to others without advantage, but that the replies of Budha were like the lighting of a thousand lamps. "I was hitherto," he continued, "ignorant of the goodness of Budha; I was like one bound; I have now received a five-fold joy; I will sooner lose my life than relinquish the protection of the dharmma; I will submit to the cutting off of my head rather than deny Budha, or the Truth, or the Associated Priesthood. I will become an upásaka." Then, in order that he might receive forgiveness for the murder of his father, he thrice worshipped Budha, after which he retired in a respectful manner, with his face towards the sage; and on entering the city proclaimed to all the excellency of Budha.

When Ajásat had left the wihára, Budha said to the priests, "Had not the king murdered his father, he might this day have entered the path sówan; even now, as he has taken refuge in the three gems, he will be saved from the hell Awíchi, where otherwise he must have remained a whole kalpa; but he will have to go to the Lóhakumbha-lóka, where he will remain 60,000 years, the half of this time in going from top to bottom, and the other half in returning from bottom to top. After this he will enjoy the happiness of the déwa-lókas during a kap-laksha, and at last become the Pasé Budha Wijitawisésa." Though the king had not been able to sleep from the time he murdered his father, this affliction now passed away. After this event he greatly assisted the three gems, and among all who have failed in obtaining an entrance into the paths, there has been no one equal to Ajásat. (*Amáwatura*).

45. *The Destruction of Déwadatta.*

As it was through the persuasion of Déwadatta that Ajásat was induced to murder his father, the nobles, who now saw the superiority of Budha, recommend their monarch to discontinue his intercourse with so wicked a priest; and the king, agreeably to their wishes, gave orders that no more food should be sent to his wihára. The supplies being thus cut off, his 500 disciples left him, and he was in indigence. Then he went to the city to receive alms; but the people indignantly drove him away, and broke his bowl. So he resolved to make a division among the priesthood of Budha, as a last resource, and succeeded in persuading Kókálika, Katamóratissa, Khandadéwaputra, and Samuddadattaya to espouse his cause. Accompanied by these four priests, Déwadatta went to Budha and said to him, "I have hitherto been refused that which I asked at your hands, but this is not right, as I am the nephew of Sudhódana; I have now five more requests that I wish to make." Though Budha knew the thoughts of all beings, he asked, smiling, what they were. Déwadatta replied, "I request that in future the priests be forbidden to reside in wiháras that are near villages and towns, and be required to retire to the forest, according to the ordinance áranyakanga." But Budha said, "No such ordinance as this was made by the former Budhas (as binding upon all). It would be like putting at once an axe to the root of the kalpa-tree of the dharmma, which is to remain many years. For this reason. Among those ordained, there are many persons of the royal, brahman, and merchant castes, who were previously unaccustomed to descend even from the upper story of their mansions to the lower; there are also young children, and aged people; how can these dwell alone in the wilderness? Princes and others resort to the priests to hear bana and gain merit; but they would object to go to the forest. It would be like cutting off the stream that irrigates the rice-field, were the ordinances to be enjoined that you propose. Females, the young, and the weak, could not observe it; and therefore the liberty to observe it is given only to such as have the power. They who keep the precepts, whether they live in a village, or in a hole, or upon a rock, or in a cave, are equally my children. What is your next request?" Déwadatta: "I wish that a command be issued, requiring the priests to eat only such food as they receive when going with the alms-bowl, according to the ordinance pindapátikánga, and forbidding them to eat what is brought by the people to the pansals." Budha: "This cannot be; how can the aged, or the sick, or children, take the alms-bowl to seek food? Who shall receive the food appointed to the priests who are strangers?" Then Déwadatta requested Budha to forbid the priests to make a robe of anything besides what was taken from a cemetery according to the ordinance pánsikúlakanga. But the teacher replied that there were many priests from the higher castes who had not even seen a dead body, and they would consequently be afraid to go near a cemetery: it would make them sick; and if the faithful were not allowed to give robes, how were they to acquire merit?" Déwadatta: "Then require all the priests to observe the ordinance werkshamúlakanga, and make them live at the root of a tree; never suffering them to enter a house covered with straw or protected by a roof."

Budha: "Were this ordinance to be enforced upon all, what could children do, and those priests who are weak, in the rainy season? And how are those to acquire merit who make residencies for the priests?" All the requests thus made by Déwadatta were refused, and he proceeded to the last proposition it was his intention to recommend. "It will be well," said he, "to issue an order that no priest be permitted to eat flesh of any kind; there are others who observe this ordinance; and as there are many persons who think it is wrong to eat flesh, the non-observance of this ordinance by the priests causes the dharmma to be spoken against." But Budha again replied, "I cannot consent to the establishment of such an ordinance. The Budhas are not like the blind, who require to be led by another; they do not learn from others, or follow the example of others. The faithful give to the priests flesh, medicines, seats, and other things, and thereby acquire merit. Those who take life are in fault, but not the persons who eat the flesh; my priests have permission to eat whatever food it is customary to eat in any place or country, so that it be done without the indulgence of the appetite, or evil desire. There are some who become rahats at the foot of a tree, and others in pansals; some when they are clothed in what they have taken from a cemetery, and others when clothed with what they have received from the people; some when abstaining from flesh, and others when eating it. If one uniform law were enforced, it would be a hindrance in the way of those who are seeking nirwána; but it is to reveal this way that the office of the Budhas is assumed."

The requests made by Déwadatta being all refused, he retired to his own wihára at the head of the river Gaya, with his four companions, and was soon joined by other dissatisfied priests, so that the number of his disciples again amounted to 500. When Budha saw that the time to reclaim the 500 priests had arrived, he commanded Seriyut and Mugalan to visit their wihára, and exert their influence for this purpose. On the arrival of the agra-sráwakas, Déwadatta was in the midst of his priests saying bana in imitation of Budha, and, when he saw them, he gladly gave them permission to enter, as he supposed they had come to join his party; but Kókálika said that it would be better to require them to keep at a distance, as it was most probable they had come to do him some injury. The one was placed on the right hand of Déwadatta and the other on his left, and Kókálika occupied the place of Anyakondanya, according to the arrangement when bana was said by Budha. After he had proceeded a little time, Seriyut said that he must be fatigued, and began to say bana in his stead, but in such a manner, that all the priests became rahats, with the exception of Déwadatta, who had fallen asleep. When he awoke, and found that all the priests were gone, he regretted that he had not followed the advice of Kókálika; and was so affected by this event, that he continued ill for the space of nine months. After this period he resolved to go to Budha, and entreat his forgiveness; and though his disciples tried to persuade him not to go, as they said that Budha would not see him, they were unable to induce him to alter his intention, as he knew that the great teacher felt no enmity towards him; and when they saw that he was determined, they took him in a litter, and conveyed him to the Jétáwana wihára. The priests informed Budha of his approach, but he said, " Priests, Déwadatta will not see Budha." They then said, he is at such a distance, now nearer, he is entering the court-yard; but the sage still declared that he would not see Budha. " His crimes are so great," said he, " that ten, or a hundred, or even a thousand Budhas would be unable to assist him; you will quickly see what will befall him." When near the wihára, the disciples put the litter upon the ground, whilst they washed themselves in the tank. The eagerness of Déwadatta to see Budha was so great, that he rose from the litter, though he had been unable to move for some time previous; but when he put his foot to the ground, flames came from the Awíchi hell, and enwrapped his body in their folds; first his feet, then to his middle, and at last to his shoulder. In terror he cried out, " Take me, children; take me; I am the brother-in-law of Budha. Oh Budha! though I have done all these things against thee, for the sake of our relationship, save me;" He also repeated a stanza in praise of Budha, by which he received the assistance of the three gems, which will benefit him eventually;* though he now went to hell and received a burning body, 1,600 miles high.

* In a future birth, Déwadatta will become the Pasé Budha Sattissara.

46. *The History of Prince Sunakháta.*

The Lichawi prince Sunakháta became a priest of Budha and ministered to him. One day he went to the sage to enquire what he must do to receive divine eyes, and he was informed. By this means he was enabled to obtain the eyes for which he wished, and to see the glories of the déwa-lókas. Soon afterwards he enquired what he must do to obtain divine ears, that he might hear the voices of the déwas; but Budha did not inform him, as he saw that in a former birth he had made a priest deaf by striking him on the ear, which would prevent him from now receiving this gift. At this the priest became angry, and thought, "I am a prince, as well as Budha; if I acquire the gift I seek, I, like him, shall be omniscient; it is on this account he refuses to give me the information." He, therefore, went to Budha, and informed him that he was about to leave him. The great teacher enquired if it was on account of anything he had ever said; but he replied that it was not; it was because he would not give him the information he wished to receive. Budha told him that if all he wished to know were declared to him, it would not enable him to become a rahat. The priest then said that he must proclaim to the citizens that the power of Budha had passed away. But the sage told him, "The citizens on hearing it will say, The same mouth that formerly declared himself unable to proclaim the excellencies of the three gems, now speaks against them, because he has not the power to keep the precepts; he wishes to become a laic. Thus the people will find out your design, but will continue to trust in the dharmma."

At one time Budha went with the alms-bowl to the village called Uturu; and to the same place went Sunakháta and other Lichawi princes. In this village were Kórakhatti, a tirttaka, and Balu, an ascetic. The tirttaka crept on his hands and feet; touched nothing with his hand, but took all things up with his mouth; even drank without using his hand; and lay in ashes. The prince thought, when he saw him, "This man has no clothes; he takes his food from the ground without using an alms-bowl; were he to become a priest, the rest of us would be put to shame (by his superior self-denial)." Budha, perceiving that he followed just after whatever he saw, that he had no stability, asked him why he thought thus foolishly; but Sunakháta supposed that it was because the sage was covetous of the rahatship he spoke to him in this manner. "I am covetous," said Budha, "that men and déwas should possess the rahatship; it was for this that I fulfilled the páramitás; I have no wish whatever to confine the privileges of the rahatship to myself. You, indeed, appear to think that you are already a rahat; you must leave this error, or it will bring to you great sorrow. In six days the ascetic will die, and will become the asúr Kálakancha, with a body twelve miles in height, but without flesh and blood, and like a scarecrow; his eyes will be on the top of his head, like those of a crab, so that when he seeks his food he will have to bend himself to find it; and you are at liberty to make enquiries from himself relative to those things." After Budha had returned to the wihára, Sunakháta went to Kórakhatti, and informing him what the sage had said, told him to be careful relative to the food he ate, lest some disease should be caused, and he should die; by attending to these things they might prove that Budha had spoken an untruth. When the tirttaka heard this, he lifted up his head from the ashes among which he was lying; and said that Gótama had declared these things on account of the enmity he bore him; but that the words of an enemy were not to be regarded, and he should not on account of these things alter his usual course. However, as Sunakháta entreated him to take warning, he remained six days without food. On the seventh day his followers thought, "Our teacher has not been near us for six days; he must be sick. They, therefore, prepared some pork, and took it to the place where he was, and put it down on the ground near him. At the sight of it he said, "I must eat it, die or not die;" so he rose up, and resting on his elbows and knees, he ate it; but he was unable to digest it, and died the same night, becoming an asúr as Budha had said. Though he thus died, his friends thought that they would still prove the falsity of Gótama's declaration, and for this purpose took his body to another place to bury him; but they were not able. As they were carrying him through Kírana-thamba the bier broke, and they were obliged to leave him there. Thus two of the declarations of Budha were proved to be correct; and to ascertain the truth of the third, he went to the body, and the body said to him "I am the asúr Kálakancha." After this he went to the wihára, and when Budha asked him if all things had not happened according to his prediction, he confessed that they had. "Then," said Budha, "why do you tell others that I have not the power of working miracles?"

At the time that Budha resided in the Maha-wana wihára, near Wisálá, there was a celebrated tirttaka called Kalaranamatthaka, who had many followers. There were seven sil, or precepts, that he observed, to this effect:—never to put on clothes; never to approach a woman; never to eat flesh, or rice; never to go further from Wisálá than the Udéna déwála, on the east side; nor further than the Gótama déwála, on the south side; nor further than the Satamba déwála on the west side; nor further than the Bahuputraka déwála on the north side. The citizens brought him many offerings. Sunakháta went to him, and asked him about the three signs, the impermanency, misery, and unreality of all things; but the tirttaka said that he had no time to answer such questions, and was angry with him. Now as the prince thought he was a great rahat, he asked his pardon, and promised no more to offend; but when he returned to Budha, the sage asked him if he did not boast much of his honourable descent; and when he enquired why he asked this question, Budha said, "Did not you ask pardon of the tirttaka, because you dreaded his wrath?" "If you follow that sceptic," said he, "you will come to destruction; in a little time he will break all his precepts and die." The declaration of Budha was true, as all that he had said came to pass.

There was another noted tirttaka, called Pathika, who said, "Gótama is a famous reasoner; I am the same; I must argue with him; if he be sixteen miles off, he must come eight miles, and I will go eight, to the place of contest; were either of us to exceed this distance, even by a single footstep, the person so doing would lose; if Gótama exhibits two wonders, I will exhibit four; I will double the wonders he exhibits, however many they may be." When the citizens heard that he had so spoken, they showed him great favour. Sunakháta also went to him, and told him not to be afraid, as he was the minister of Budha, and knew that the tirttaka would be able to exceed him in the number of his miracles. When, however, he returned to the wihára, Budha informed him that if he again denied that he was the supreme Budha, he was not to approach him any more, or his head would fall, like a tal fruit from its stalk, or would cleave into seven pieces. The prince said that the words of Budha would be proved to be false; when the sage declared to him, "No one, in the forty-five years of my ministry, has previously told me that the words I utter are false; the sakwala may be blown away by a storm; the sun and moon may fall to the earth; the rivers may turn back towards their source; the sky may be rent; the earth may be destroyed; and Maha Méru may be broken to pieces; but the Budhas cannot utter an untruth." Sunakháta enquired how he had become acquainted with the nature of the conversation he held with Pathika; did some déwá inform him? Budha replied, "Ajita, the commander of the Lichawi forces, is dead, and has gone to the Tusita déwalóka. It was he who came to me and said, 'Those who assisted at my cremation went to Pathika and enquired whither I had gone, and he told them that I am born in hell because I refused to listen to his doctrines, and embraced the dharmma; therefore, let it be proclaimed to the citizens, oh Budha! that I am born in Tusita; and let it be made known to the tirttaka that unless he sees Budha his head will cleave into seven pieces.' Therefore, Sunakháta, go and tell Pathika that after I have been with the alms-bowl to the city, I shall come to his residence." The prince made known to all the people, as he went along, that Budha was about to visit Pathika at his own dwelling, in consequence of which, great numbers were assembled; but the tirttaka knew that he had been practising a deception upon his followers, and that he should be exposed, if confronted with Gótama; he, therefore, ran away to the forest, and secreted himself near a rock in the midst of a thicket. Budha was aware that if he went to the same place it would cause the destruction of the deceiver, so out of pity he prevented him from leaving the forest. The people, not finding him at his residence, went to the forest to seek him; and were directed by a man who had seen him, to a timbari pillar. Having found him they said, "All the princes and nobles have gone to your dwelling that they may see your miracles; Budha is also at the same place; therefore, come without delay." And he said, "I come, I come," but was unable to move from the rock; so the people derided him, and went and informed the assembly. Then one of the princes, with his retinue, went to the rock, and told him that if he would come, they would assist him against Budha; but he made no reply and the prince returning, told the people that the tirttaka appeared as if dead. Budha also informed them that if they were to take a thousand yoke of oxen they could not compel him to come; either the ropes would break, or his body would burst. Then one Jalaya thought that he had the power to persuade him; but when he went, and told him how all the assembly was waiting, he still said, "I come, I come," but was unable to move. On seeing this, Jalaya said to him. "A lion, who lived in a retired part of the forest, sallied forth at night in search of prey. Three times he roared, and then commenced his expedition, thinking that he would kill deer in plenty, and eat them at his leisure. One day, when he had been hunting in this manner, he saw a jackal, whose name he asked, and was told it was Jambuka. The lion enquired if he was willing from that time to be his servant, and he agreed. When the lion killed any animal, the jackal came in for a share of the flesh, so that he became very fat, and he began to be playful with the lion, and to fawn upon him, and to be very proud. As he was drinking, on a certain occasion, at a stream of clear water, he saw the reflection of his own form, which led him to think thus, ' I have four feet, as the lion has; two cutting teeth; two ears; and a tail; I will therefore begin to hunt on my own account; why should I be contented to live on mere remains as I do now?' So he sallied forth, and roared; but no deer did he catch, and none did he kill. Now, if I were to apply this story, you would be the jackal, and Budha would be the lion." But even the ridicule he thus exercised was in vain; the tirttaka could not be moved from the rock. When it became evident to all that he would not return, Budha preached to the assembly near the tirttaka's dwelling, and 84,000 of those who were present entered the path anágámi. (*Amáwatura.*)

47. *The History of Bawári.*

Bawári was the próhita of Maha Kosol, and afterwards of Pasénadi. When wishful to retire from the cares of his office, he requested permission to become a recluse, which the king would not grant at first; but when he saw that he had no means of preventing him from fulfilling his wish, he built for him a residence in a retired part of the garden, near the palace, and went to see him at every convenient opportunity. The confusion of the city, however, prevented him from enjoying so much privacy as he required, and after a little time he requested to be allowed to retire into the forest. Three times the king refused his request, but afterwards gave two lacs of treasure to his nobles, and told them to look out for a proper place in which to build a residence for the recluse. Taking the money, they went north and south, but did not find a suitable place, until they arrived on the bank of the Gódávery,* where they found a spot in which a recluse had lived in a former age, situated between the dominions of the kings Assaka and Múlaka. One lac was given to each of the kings, for the purchase of the ground, after which the nobles returned to Sewet; and collecting all the requisite materials, they again went to the place, where they erected a pansal, and at a little distance from it a village. When the villagers, after they had begun to cultivate, went to Assaka to give the tenth of their produce, according to the usual custom, he refused to receive it, and told them to give it to the recluse and his associates.

The wife of a certain brahman one day said to her husband, that she could not always be toiling in that way, and that it would be better for him to go and ask for a part of the treasure given to Bawári. The recluse told him, when he asked for 500 of his treasure, that he did not possess so much money, as all he had received was given in alms; but the brahman made a hut at the door of his pansal, as if resolving to remain there, and said that if the money was not given the head of the recluse would speedily cleave into seven pieces. Bawári was greatly terrified at this threat; but the déwa of a tree, who took pity upon him, told him not to be afraid, as no one possessed this power but Budha. On receiving this information, the recluse became encouraged; and when he learnt that Budha was then at Sewet, he sent a number of his associates to pay him a visit. For this purpose they proceeded in order through the cities of Múlaka, Assaka, Máhissatí, Ujjáni, Gódhi, Diwisá, Wal Sewet, Kosambæ, and Sákétu. Budha perceived their approach, and as Sewet was not a proper place at which to

---

* The Gódávery is the largest river of the Dekhan, and falls into the bay of Bengal. The Singhalese have many legends relative to the contests that formerly took place in the regions near this river between the Budhists and Brahmans.

receive them, he went from thence to Rajagaha; and for this purpose he passed in order, after leaving Sewet, through Sétawya, Kapilawastu, Kusinára, Wisálá, and thence to Rajagaha, where he remained at the Ramaní-pásána wihára, which was situated upon a rock, and was formerly a déwála. Thither the associates of Bawári proceeded, and when they found Budha, and heard his bana, it was like water to one that is thirsty, or a shady place to the mid-day traveller, or the discovery of a cheap market by the merchant when he goes to purchase goods. At this time the sage was seated upon the throne presented to him by Sekra, surrounded by the priests, who extended on each side to the distance of six yojanas. The principal associate of the recluse was Ajita, who, when he saw Budha, resolved to test his knowledge by asking him the age of his teacher, his family, his peculiarities, his knowledge, and the number of his disciples. Budha at once said to him, (before his thoughts were uttered) "Your teacher is 120 years old; he is of the family of Prawara, but is commonly called Bawári; his peculiarities are the three maha-purusha-lakshana;* he teaches the three Vedas; and has 500 disciples." Upon receiving this answer, before the question was put, Ajita and those who accompanied him, were led to believe in the three gems. Budha afterwards gave him permission to make enquiry† about any subject whatever, respecting which he wanted information; and he subsequently became a rahat. After this the brahman Mogharája asked a question of Budha, but as the sage saw that he had not at that time (though he subsequently received it) sufficient merit to enable him to enter the paths, he gave him no reply. In the presence of the same assembly questions were subsequently asked by Tissametteyya, Punna, Mettébhútaka, Dótaka, Upasiwa, Nanda, Hémaka, Tódeyya, Kappa, Jatukanní, Bhadráwudha, Udhaya, and Posála, all of which were answered, and many thousands of those present entered the paths. When the associates of Bawári returned to the pansal, he saw them at a distance, as he was looking out for their return, and knew by their appearance that they had become priests, and that a

---

* The three peculiarities were these:—1. He could cover his forehead with his tongue. 2. There was a lock of hair upon his forehead. 3. The organ of generation was concealed.

† The questions proposed by Ajita, and by the other individuals mentioned in this section, appear in the Páráyana-sútra.

supreme Budha existed in the world. Joyfully he received the intelligence they conveyed; and by the favour of Budha he was enabled to enter the path anágámi, and his 500 disciples entered sowán. (*Amáwatura.*)

48. *Budha visits the Brahma-lóka.*

When Budha resided at the city of Ukkathá, he perceived that the brahma Baka was a sceptic. It was his idea that the Brahma-lóka had been always existent; that there is no decay or death; there is no passing from one world to another; that as things are, they will always continue; and that there are no paths, no fruition of the paths, there is no nirwána. Budha visited the brahma-lóka that he might convince him of his error, and enquired of him if these were the opinions that he entertained. The déwa Wasawartti-mára had perceived his intention; and resolving to prevent its being fulfilled, he also went to the same lóka. When Budha began to converse with the brahma, Mára replied that Baka was superior in wisdom and power to the other brahmas; that it was he who had made the earth, Maha Méru, and the other worlds; it was he that appointed who should belong to the different castes; it was he who ordained the existence of the different animals; and the déwa said, "Were there not sramanas before you who taught the impermanency of the world? and yet after teaching that all things are impermanent, they went to hell. There were brahmans who denied this, who declared that all things are permanent, and yet they were born in this brahma-lóka. It is, therefore, better to teach as the brahmans did. I give you this advice, that you listen to the same doctrines, and you will receive the same reward; but if you reject them you will come to destruction." But Budha replied, "I know you, who you are; the sinful Mára; think not that you can thus deceive me." Baka said that there were other Budhas before Gótama, but they had become extinct; no one could tell whither they had gone; and that therefore it would be better if Gótama would embrace his doctrines, and receive the same glory; but Budha showed that his knowledge was superior to that of Baka, by relating the circumstances of six former births of the brahma, with which he himself was entirely unacquainted. In one birth he was a hermit, and resided near a river. At that time 500 merchants came with their wagons to the same place, but were benighted. The first bullock turned back, and was followed by all the rest. The next morning the merchants had neither fuel nor water; they therefore lay down, with the expectation that they must die; but the hermit saw their danger and brought them water, by which their lives were saved. At another time, some thieves stole all the goods in a certain village; but as they were making off with their booty, he caused the five-toned music to be heard, so that the thieves threw down the goods and ran away, as they supposed that the king was coming. At another time, the people of two villages, who resided near the river, agreed to go together in boats to trade. Their progress was observed by a nayá, who thought to destroy them; but the hermit assumed the appearance of an immense garunda, and so frightened the nayá, that it fled away without doing any harm to the traders. For these acts of kindness the hermit was born in a brahma-lóka. When Baka heard this, he confessed that it was true, acknowledged the superiority of Budha, and took refuge in the three gems. (*Amáwatura.*)

49. *Mugalan attains Nirwána.*

In a former age, Mugalan was called Sumana, at which time his parents were blind; but he was very attentive to them, and devoted to them all his time. When they recommended to him to procure a wife, as they thought it a pity he should longer remain single, he resisted their importunities a considerable period; but as they pressed him continually, he at last consented, and was married. After he brought his wife home, she assisted his parents properly for one single day; but this was all. She soon became discontented; to deceive Sumana she put filth upon the hair of his parents, and said they had done it themselves after they were combed. As she insisted upon being allowed to return to her village, her husband was overcome, and he resolved upon putting his parents out of the way. To effect this, he took them to a certain forest, under the pretence of letting them visit some of their friends; and when they had arrived at a lonely place, he gave the reins of the animals by which they were drawn into the hands of his parents, and said that he must go forward a little to see if there were any robbers near the road, as it was a dangerous spot. He then imitated the onset of a robber, and his parents, thinking that some one else was attacking them, called out to him not to think about them, but to make his own escape. Still personating the thief, he took his parents into the thick forest, threw them down, and left them there, after which he returned to his wife. For this crime he was born continually in hell, during hundreds of thousands of years; but on his release therefrom, on account of his previous merit, and because he was free from any other crime, in the time of Gótama he became one of the two principal disciples of Budha.

One day when the tirttakas were met together, in the course of their conversation one of them enquired of the others, "Do you know from whom it is that Gótama receives the most efficient help?" They replied that they did not. Then said he, "I do: it is from Mugalan; and for this reason. At a certain time he went to heaven, and asked the déwas what they had done to secure so much happiness; he then went to hell, and extinguishing its fire for a moment, asked the dwellers therein what they had done to bring upon themselves the endurance of so much misery. When he had ascertained the cause of these things, he returned to the world, and proclaimed it to mankind. Therefore, when men hear the declarations he puts forth, as they know that he has actually seen what he describes, they give the more heed; and thus a great interest is excited in favour of Gótama; but if we can accomplish his destruction, the followers of Budha will leave him and come to us; it will be like the cutting off of the upper current from the stream." To this they were all agreed, and taking a thousand pieces of gold, they went to some robbers and said, "Go to the Black Rock, and murder Mugalan, who resides there," at the same time putting the gold into their hands. The robbers at once went to the place, and surrounded the dwelling of the priest, but he knew their intention, and escaped through the key-hole. The next day the robbers again surrounded the cave, but Mugalan ascended into the sky, as if by a ladder, from the summit of the conical roof.* In this way, two months were spent, after which

---

* There are frequent references in the native books to buildings of this description. At Pandrenton, near Kashmir, there is an ancient temple,

he remained at home; he knew that he could get away from the robbers, but that there was no escape, not even by the help of Budha, from the consequences of his former crime. The robbers accordingly caught him, pounded his bones as rice is pounded in the mortar; then thinking that he was dead, they took him into the forest, threw him down, and went away. Though he had been used in so cruel a manner, by the power of dhyána he put together the broken bones of his body, as an earthen vessel is repaired that has been broken in pieces. As he was now about to obtain nirwána, he went through the air to Budha, worshipped him, and informed him of his departure. Budha enquired the reason, when he related all that had occurred; after hearing which, Gótama said, "Go then, to nirwána; but first say to me bana, as there will hereafter be no one who can say it to me in a manner equally excellent." The priest was obedient, and performed the same wonders as Seriyut on a similar occasion; he then returned to the cave and attained nirwána. (*Sáleyya-sútra-banné.*)

50. *The Punishment of Supra Budha.*

When Supra Budha, a Sakya prince, and the father-in-law of Gótama, heard that he had left his wife, Yasódhará, and become Budha, and also, that although he had received his son Déwadatta into the priesthood, he had not given him any office suitable to his rank, and had moreover spoken evil of him before the world, he was greatly enraged.* One day as he was informed that Gótama was about to proceed to a certain place, he resolved to prevent his journey, and for this purpose remained in the road, drunk. When Budha approached, attended by his priests, the king was informed that he was coming, and was requested to make way for him to pass; but he said, "Gótama is younger than I; he is my son-in-law; inform him, therefore, that it is his duty to make way for me." As the procession advanced nearer, some one again requested the king to leave the path clear, but he was not willing. Budha quietly stopped. The king had sent a messenger privately to

---

supposed to be of Budhist origin, the ground plan of which is a square of twenty feet, and the roof pyramidal.

* This story is cited as an instance of drishta-dharmma-wédyn-kusala-karmma.

hear what Gótama said when the obstruction should be reported to him. Though he had not smiled from the time he became Budha, he smiled now; but though he smiled he did not show his teeth, or make a noise like some, as if water were poured from the mouth of a vessel: rays came from his mouth like a golden portico to a dágoba of emeralds, went thrice round his head, and then entered again into his mouth. When Ananda saw that he smiled, as he knew that there must be some reason for it, he enquired the cause. Budha replied, "In seven days, this Supra Budha, who will not permit us to go and receive alms, will be taken to hell; the earth will open for this purpose at the foot of the stairs that are near the lower story of his palace." The messenger who had gone to listen, went and informed the king what Budha had said. On hearing it, he said, "Our son-in-law will not say that which is false; nevertheless, we will prevent this occurrence by a stratagem; until the tenth day be passed, we will not go near the lower story of the palace; we will remain in the upper story; there will then be the boards of the floor beneath us, and not the ground, so that his declaration cannot take place." The king, accordingly went to the upper story, and had the necessary provisions brought thither for the appointed time; he also commanded the doors to be fastened with strong iron bars, and the stairs to be removed, placing two guards near each, that if he attempted to descend they might prevent him. But Budha said that if he were even to ascend into the sky, or to pass in a ship into the middle of the sea, or to conceal himself in the centre of a rock; still, what he had declared would most certainly take place, because of the king's demerit.

On the seventh day the king's charger went mad, and ran about in all directions. He asked what noise it was, and was told that his horse had become mad; and that no one could subdue him unless he saw his royal master. He then went to the door, in order to descend, which opened of its own accord, and the stairs returned to their place, by means of the king's demerit. The guards caught hold of him to convey him to the upper story, but instead of this he was precipitated to the ground. As the guards looked below, they saw the earth open; flames came from Awichi, enveloped him, and carried him away.—(*Sadharmmaratnakáré.*)

51. *The Princess Yasódhará-déwi attains Nirwána.*

The princess Yasódhará-déwi, who had been the wife of Bódhisat in many generations, and assisted him in the fulfilling of the páramitás, was born on the same day as the prince Sidhártta. At the age of sixteen years they were both anointed at the same moment. When Sidhártta became an ascetic, the princess resolved upon following his example, but Sudhódana, in order to prevent it, placed guards around the city, declaring to her that the prince would return; he was also fearful that as she was so extremely beautiful, unless she was well protected, the princes of other countries might hear of her situation and come and take her away by force. But although she was thus prevented from going to the forest, she resolved to keep the ordinances of the recluse in the palace; and for this purpose she had her head shaved, put on a yellow robe, and ate her food out of an earthen bowl. When Budha visited Kapilawastu, after the attainment of his office, and on the second day after his arrival visited the palace of Yasódhará-déwi, and repeated the Chanda-kinnara-játaka, she requested permission to become a priestess; but it was not granted, as Budha saw that the right of entrance into the order of the female priesthood belonged, first, to the queen-mother, Prajápati.

The princess was exceedingly sorrowful when Ráhula was ordained, but Sudhódana went to console her, and said, "Did you not hear that in the Wessantara birth, when your child was bound with a thong and given to the mendicant, you made no objection? Then why should you be grieved now? Were you to hear bana, you would give all your sons to be ordained, even had you a hundred. By and bye you also will become an ascetic; but it will be better to delay now, as people would say you have renounced the world on account of your sorrow." Then the princess thought she would carry her intention into effect when Sudhódana was dead. She was also informed by Prajápati that she herself had thrice requested to be admitted to profession, but had been refused by Budha. In due time Yasódhará-dewi became the rightful inheritor of all that had belonged to Sudhódana, Maha-máya, Maha-prajápati, Sidhártta, Nanda, Rahula, Déwadatta, and Supra-budha; but she regarded the whole with aversion, even as if it had been a dead nayá tied

2 A

round her neck. Accompanied by a thousand other princesses, she departed from Kapilawastu, in order that she might visit Maha-prajápati. When the inhabitants of Kapilawastu and Kóli heard of her departure, they came in immense numbers that they might prevail upon her to remain in the palace; but when she was still determined, they brought a thousand chariots, that the princesses might use them in their journey. Yasódhará-déwi, however, replied that it was right they should walk on foot, as all the luxuries of the world had been renounced; it was true that Sidhártta had fled on horseback, but he went away by stealth, and wished to escape quickly from his pursuers. The distance between Kapila and Wisálá was 49 yojanas, and after the princesses had seen Prajápati, and been admitted to profession, they went to Sewet, where Budha was then residing. By Budha they were admitted to upasampadá, on which occasion he proclaimed the merits of Yasódhará-déwi; in two póyas after this she became a rahat; and afterwards continued to reside at Sewet, whence she went, sometimes, to hear bana from Budha, and at other times to enquire after the health of Ráhula. The people of Jambudwípa brought her many presents; in consequence of which she informed Budha that she could not remain at Sewet any longer, as more offerings were made to her now than when she was a queen. She, therefore, went to Wisálá; but there it was the same, and she was obliged to go to Rajagaha. These gifts were received through the merit she had acquired in former births, when Bódhisat, with her full consent, gave away his possessions.

On the evening of a certain day, as Yasódhará-déwi was sitting alone, she thus thought: "Nanda, Ráhula, Seriyut, Mugalan, Khéma, Uppalawarnna, Sudhódana, Prajápati, and Anya-kondanya, have entered nirwána. I was born on the same day as Budha, and in regular order ought to enter the city of peace upon the same day; but this would not be decorous to the great teacher. I am now seventy-eight years of age. In two years from this time Budha will attain nirwána. I will, therefore, request permission to obtain this privilege from Budha." At the moment this resolution was formed, the earth shook, which was perceived by the other princesses; and as they knew the cause, they proceeded to the residence of Yasódhará-déwi, and accompanied her to the wihára of Budha. From the sage she asked forgiveness for the faults she might at any time have committed, and then presented her request. Budha said, "You are the most virtuous of women; but from the time you became a rahat, you have not performed any miracle, so that some persons have doubted whether you are a rahat or not. It is right that these doubts should be removed." The priests also had heard of what was about to take place, whence they inferred that the departure of Budha was not far distant. They therefore assembled around the sage, with a great number of the citizens. The princess thought that on account of the extreme beauty of her person it would not be proper to perform a miracle in the same way as others, lest evil thoughts should arise in the minds of such of the faithful as were not yet free from evil desire. She, therefore, related the history of her former births, then rose into the air and worshipped Budha; in this manner she rose and descended many times; and performed many other wonders, in the presence of men, déwas, and brahmas. The discourse that she delivered was upon the seven kinds of wives there are in the world of men. When all this was concluded, she retired to her own residence, and in the same night, whilst passing from dhyána to dhyána, saw the city of peace.

52. *The Death of Budha.*

When Gótama was about to receive nirwána, in the city of Kusinára,* he paid a visit previously to the city of Páwá, attended by a vast concourse of priests.† At this place he reposed for a short time, in the mango garden of Chunda, the smith; who, delighted with the honour thus conferred upon him, came without delay to offer worship; after which he invited the

---

* There is in Assam a district called Koch Vihar, or Coss Beyhar, derived from Kusha Vihar, which is by some supposed to be the Kusinára, at which Budha expired. By others it is placed at Hurdwar, not far from Delhi. There is a Kusina laid down in Hamilton's Map of Nepaul, which may possibly be the same place. Csoma Körösi calls it Kamrup, in Assam; but Klaproth thinks that this situation is too much to the east, and that it ought to be placed nearer the Gunduck. When visited by Fa Hian the population was small. In a temple at this place Hiuan thsang saw a picture representing the death of Budha.

† In the Journal of the Asiatic Society, No. 84, Dec. 1838, there is an analysis of the Parinibbána-suttan, by Turnour. It is the third suttan of the Mahawaggo in the Dighanikáyo of the Suttapitako; and Turnour calls it "perhaps the most interesting section in the Pitakattayan."

whole company of the priests to partake of food at his dwelling and prepared an offering of pork* to present to Budha.

This was perceived by the various déwas of the universe, who exclaimed, "From the time that the rice-mixture presented by Sujáta was eaten by the lord of the world, for the space of forty-five years, he has preached to us: now he will eat of the pork to be presented by Chunda, and enter nirwána: even in many millions of years the acquisition of the Budhaship is accomplished with difficulty." Then collecting together whatsoever is of the most grateful flavor in the four great continents, they imparted its richness to the food about to be presented.

The next day, Budha and his attendants were entertained by the smith, and in his presence the sage delivered a discourse on the benefit to be derived from the presentation of offerings, after which he said, "Let us go to Kusinára."

Like the radiant moon travelling amidst the hosts of the sky, surrounded by priests whom no arithmetic can compute, in number infinite, he commenced his journey towards Kusinára; but the pork that had been presented by Chunda, from some hidden cause, produced a diarrhœa (lóhita pakkhandika) in his body, and he endured the most intense suffering.† By his divine power he subdued the pain, then retired a little way from the road, and rested near the foot of a tree, saying to his attendant, "Ananda, I am weary, I wish to rest; let the outer robe be four times folded and spread out." Soon afterwards he said, "Ananda, I am thirsty; I wish for water, that I may drink." This was given, after which he proceeded on his journey and preached to the prince Pukkusa, giving him the benefit of the protective formulary. The prince presented him with a couple of robes, interwoven with gold, that were wrapped about his person. When he arrived at the river Kukutthá he

---

* Chunda was charged by Budha, who knew his intention, not to allow any portion of the pork to be given to the priests who accompanied him, and to bury what was left in the ground, as he knew that if any of them partook of it, disease would be produced.

† Bishop Smith, in his account of a visit to the temple of Honan, in China, says:—"We were conducted to the stall, or pen, in which the sacred pigs are domiciled. According to the popular theory, these pigs are maintained in a state of plenty, and are invested with a degree of sanctity, as a compensation to the species for the wrongs inflicted on them by the disciples of Budhism, in eating swine's flesh, contrary to the primitive laws of Budh." This custom may have arisen from some perversion of the legend contained in the text.

bathed, causing rays to emanate from his body and robe, that extended to both banks of the river; and after this he went to a mango garden not far distant, and said, " I am faint, I wish to lie down; spread out the robe." The robe was accordingly spread out, and he lay down, like a lion in repose. Thus, he who had the power of myriads of the strongest elephants, was unable to move without the utmost difficulty, from the time that his body was seized by the disorder. All this was endured that he might shew to the young the vanity of their strength, and to those cleaving to existence the sorrow connected therewith; and that he might make known to all, that none are exempted from old age, decay, and death. Those who hear of what he suffered must lament, as those who saw it wept; nor can it even be reflected upon without the most profound grief. It was, therefore, to teach the misery of existence to the beings in the world that he said, " Ananda, I am faint, I am thirsty, I wish to drink, I wish to lie down."

Though the whole distance that Budha had to travel was only about 12 miles, he was obliged to rest five-and-twenty times before he could accomplish the journey. At last, after repeated efforts, he reached a mango grove, near Kusinára, on which he said to Ananda, " Speak in this manner to the smith—'Chunda, as Budha, from having eaten of the pork you presented to him will attain nirwána, you will receive on this account an immense reward;' and if he should still appear doubtful, say to him again, 'Chunda, you will most certainly receive this reward; I heard it from the lord of the universe; it was from the sacred mouth I received my information.' Ananda, there are two offerings that will receive a greater reward than any other. Do you ask what they are? Before the Tatágata received the incomparable wisdom, an offering was presented to him by the daughter of Sujata; and now before he attains to the final rest of nirwána, another offering has been made by Chunda. These are the two most estimable gifts. The merit acquired by the illustrious Chunda, will endure long, and be exceedingly great. Thus, Ananda, the doubts of him who presented the pork will be removed."

When the déwas perceived that this was the last great offering that would be presented to Budha, they brought all kinds of agreeable ingredients and imparted their flavor to the pork, so that it was in every respect desirable and excellent. On this account, it could not be the pork that was the real cause of the illness of Budha. The elements of his body had become indurated by extreme old age, in the usual course of nature; and it was this that gave to the disease its power. In like manner, when one ignited substance is added to another, the fire burns with more destructive fierceness; or when to a common stream is added the volume of water poured down by the raging storm, its course is swelled to an impetuous torrent; or when more food is taken into the stomach already filled to repletion, the effects of indigestion are more clearly developed. We must not therefore, blame the ordinance of alms-giving, as if this were the cause of the disease.

After leaving the mango grove, Budha crossed the Hiranyawati, and entered the garden of sal trees, called Upawarttana, near Kusinára, to which the princes of Malwa were accustomed to resort in their seasons of recreation. On seeing it, he said again, "Ananda, I am weary, I wish to lie down; quickly place a couch between two sal trees, with the head towards the north." After the couch had been placed as he requested, he lay down upon it with his head in the same direction, never to rise again; but he still retained the full possession of his senses. He then addressed his faithful attendant, and said, " Ananda, were I to attain nirwána without the knowledge of the Malwa princes, they would exclaim, 'Alas, Budha, our king, has attained nirwána; alas, in his last moments we were not permitted to feast our eyes on his sacred presence; we did not hear bana, though he approached so near us; we had no opportunity of rendering to him our homage!" They will thus be brought to endure much sorrow. Therefore go, and inform them of our arrival." In compliance with this command, Ananda went to the place at which the princes were most usually to be found, and said, "Most excellent sirs, our Budha is now in the sal grove; this day he will attain nirwána; and he has sent me to inform you of it, lest you should afterwards say that his departure was from your own gate, and yet you were not permitted in his last moments to hear bana." On the delivery of this message, the 60,000 princes of Malwa, with as many princesses, nobles, and eminent ladies, cried out, "Budha, our king, will soon obtain nirwána; alas, our excellent Tatágata will soon be no more; the eyes that have looked upon all our sorrows will now become dim!" Some tore their hair; others struck their heads with their hands; they bowed this way and that, as the tree that has been cut nods to its fall; they threw themselves down, and rolled upon the ground in every direction; they cried out aloud; and there was a grievous mourning. Incessantly did they weep as they went towards the grove, and when they arrived in the presence of Budha, they threw themselves prostrate before him. In order to appease their grief, he gave them a suitable exhortation, and at this time the ascetic Subhadra attained rahatship.

The déwas and brahmas from the ten thousand sakwalas being assembled, Budha said to Sekra,* "Oh, divine Sekra! my religion will abundantly flourish in Ceylon; Wijaya Báhu, son of the monarch Síha Báhu, will proceed thither from the land of Láda, with 500 nobles, and there remain; therefore, take that prince and his kingdom under thy special protection." In this manner he delivered the realm of Ceylon, and the interests of his religion when therein established, into the hands of Sekra.

Early in the morning, Budha gave a charge to the assembled priests, and furthermore said to them, "Priests, if ye have any doubts as to the doctrines I have taught you for the space of forty-five years, ye have permission to declare them now; otherwise, ye may afterwards regret that ye had not the opportunity of stating them whilst I was yet in existence; or if ye hesitate to make these enquiries of me, make known your doubts to each other." As the priests did not entertain any doubts, they remained silent, and Budha proceeded, "Are there no doubts that you wish to have removed? Then I depart to nirwána; I leave with you my ordinances; the elements of the omniscient will pass away; the three gems will still remain." Thus having spoken, he ceased to exist. (*Milinda Prasna.*)

When the Malwa princes heard of the death of Budha, they were for some time overcome by grief, in which the princesses and royal maidens partook; but after a little time, having recovered from the excess of their sorrow, they brought the finest cloth, and cotton a hundred times sifted, in which the body of the sage was enwrapped.† First there was a fold of

* This account does not appear in Turnour's analysis of the Parinibbána-suttan, and is probably a comparatively modern interpolation.

† A pine tree was annually wrapt up in wool by the priests of Cybele, and

cloth, and then a layer of cotton, alternately, until a thousand folds had been completed. For this purpose 500 bales of cloth, and 500 bales of cotton were presented by the princes. The first, second, third, fourth, fifth and sixth days were occupied in the presenting of offerings and the preparing of the place where the body was to be burned. Every receptacle of filth in Kusinára was covered knee-deep with celestial flowers. On the seventh day the déwas and brahmas of 10,000 sakwalas brought flowers and perfumes, and appointed the choristers and musicians from their several lókas to be in attendance, so that there was offered to the corpse of the sage all that is pleasing to the eye or ravishing to the ear. For the place of cremation* the princes offered their own coronation-hall, which was decorated with the utmost magnificence, and the body of Budha being deposited in a golden sarcophagus† filled with sweet-scented oil, it was placed upon a pyre of sandal-wood, 120 cubits high.‡ When all was properly prepared, the four principal kings of Malwa, who had previously purified themselves and put on new robes, took fire in their hands and applied it to the pyre, but it would not ignite. The other princes, in sections of two and two, took golden fans, by which they endeavoured to increase the power of the flame, but all their efforts were in vain, though continued during seven days.

The chief of the priests who were endowed with divine wisdom, Anurudha, was then consulted as to the cause why the wood

---

with great solemnity carried into the temple of the goddess, in memory of her wrapping up in the same manner the dead body of Atys, and carrying it to her cave.

* We learn from Homer that the custom of burning the dead was in use before the Trojan war. The Jews burnt many spices at the funerals of their great men, but the bodies were interred.—2 Chron. xvi. 14; xxi. 19; Jer. xxxiv. 5. It is said that when Gamaliel, the son of Simeon, was buried, Onkelos burnt seventy pounds of frankincense upon his sepulchre. The funeral pile of the emperor Severus, erected near the city of York, was one of the most magnificent of which we have any record. Pliny complains that the people bestowed frankincense in heaps for the funeral pile of the dead, whilst they gave only a few crumbs when they made an offering in the temple.—Nat. Hist. xii. 18.

† According to the Parinibbána-suttan, eight of the princes attempted to lift the sarcophagus, with the intention of carrying it to the southward of the city, but they were unable to remove it. This was caused by the déwas, who themselves conveyed it to a spot at the eastern side of the city.

‡ The funeral pile erected by Alexander for Hephaestion was 130 cubits high; and the cost of the whole funeral was more than 12,000 talents.—Diod. Sic. xvii. 12.

would not ignite; and he informed them that no one but Maha-kásyapa had the power to bring about the ignition, and that therefore it was in vain to apply the fire until his arrival. The princes enquired, "Is that venerable personage dark or fair, tall or short, is he a powerful priest? Should he be like our Budha, we shall have no loss from his attainment of nirwána." At this time Maha-kásyapa was already on his way from Páwá to Kusinára; and when the princes heard from what direction he was to be expected, they took flowers and lamps and went to meet him, whilst others prepared the road; and all remained in anxious expectation. In due time he came, attended by 500 priests; and after he had properly adjusted his robe by leaving one shoulder bare, he thrice perambulated the pyre,* in a reverent manner, stopping at last in the direction where the feet of the sage were placed. Though the feet were enveloped in so many folds of cloth and cotton, he thought within himself, "May I once more see the glorious feet, and bow my head before them;" and by the power of this wish, the feet appeared, emerging from the pyre like the moon coming from behind a cloud; when he stretched forth his hand, and laying hold of the feet bowed his head towards them, and did reverence.† All that were present, when they saw this miracle, called out in approbation; and the 500 priests who accompanied Maha-kásyapa, with all the other priests who were present, worshipped the feet of Budha; not only so, but numberless déwas, brahmas, men, nágas, suparnnas, garundas, and gandhárwas, joined in the adoration. After this the feet, without putting anything out of its place, or in any way disturbing the pyre, returned to their original position, like the moon passing behind a cloud. Neither the cloth nor the cotton, nor a drop of oil in the sarcophagus, nor any part of the sandal wood, was displaced; all remained just as it was at first. When the feet had retired, like the rising of the sun or moon upon Hastágiri, Ananda, and the rest of the

* It is said that at the funeral rites for Patroclus,

"Thrice, in procession, round the course they drove
Their coursers sleek."—Il. xxiii. 13.

† "Just before a Jew is taken out of the house to be buried, the relatives and acquaintances of the departed stand round the coffin, when the feet are uncovered, and each in rotation lays hold of the two great toes, and begs pardon for any offence given to the deceased, and requests a favourable mention of them in the next world."—The Jew.

priests who were not rahats, the 60,000 princes of Malwa, and many upásakas and upásikáwas, wept with a loud voice, and their grief was even greater than on the day when Budha attained nirwána; but the rahats appeased them by repeating the four truths and the three signs. By the power of the déwas, the pyre* ignited spontaneously. The skin, flesh, and veins of the body were entirely consumed, so that not even the ashes were left; but the other parts of the body sent forth a delightful perfume, and afterwards remained like a heap of pearls. The principal relics were the four teeth, the two cheek-bones, and the skull.

To extinguish the fire a rain came down from the sky,† gradually increasing in size, though at first it was merely like a mist; water also arose from the earth, and was showered from the sal trees in the garden. Though the heat was so great, not a branch, or leaf, or flower, in the trees around was in the least scorched; the ants, beetles, spiders, and other isnects in the wood, as the fire increased, were sent forth without harm, just as if a gentle breeze had borne them. The princes examined the ashes with rods made of ivory, searching everywhere, that the whole of the relics might be collected and preserved; after which they were taken with a grand procession to the city, and deposited in one of the principal halls. The sacred spot was then ornamented in a proper manner, and concentric circles of guards were placed around it. It was feared by the Malwa princes that when the other monarchs of Jambudwípa heard of the death of Budha they would send and take away the relics by force, which would be a great loss to their city; and it was to guard them from such spoliation that the armies were placed.

When the nobles of Rajagaha heard of what had taken place, they thought within themselves, "Among all those who are yet subject to birth, there is no one equal to Ajásat, our king. When he hears of the death of Budha, his breast will cleave in two from

* An old priest, who had travelled extensively upon the continent of India, informed me that a brand taken from this pyre was afterwards worshipped at Juggernaut. This remark is worthy of notice, as it is well known that the temple at this place is supposed, from the distinctions of caste being abolished by the pilgrims when within its precincts, to be of Budhistical origin, and that the idol itself is "the coarsest image in the country." There are remains in Orissa which prove that Budhism once prevailed extensively in that province.

† When the vast pile of wood collected for the burning of Crœsus was already kindled, and the victim beyond the reach of human aid, Apollo sent a miraculous rain to preserve him.—Herod. i. 84; Ktesias, Persica, c. 4.

the greatness of his grief. We must therefore try to save him from so great a calamity." They, therefore, prepared three coffers, in which they put many sweet substances. They then went to the king and said, after saluting him, "Sire, we have something to mention," and when he gave them permission to proceed, a noble, who had put aside his ornaments and cut off his hair, looked in the direction of Kusinára, and said, "There is no one in the whole world free from death; Budha has attained nirwána." The king, on receiving this announcement, fell down in a fit, but was instantly put into one of the coffers, when his breath was warmed by the ingredients, and he revived. After this he was put into the second coffer, when he so far recovered as to be able to ask, "What was it you said?" But when told, he again fell into a fit, and was only revived by being put into the third coffer. He loosed the hair that had been anointed by so many perfumes, and beat his breast with his royal hands, calling out, "Oh my lord!" Like one distracted, he went into the street, attended by his nobles and the 16,000 princesses of his palace, after which he visited every place near the city, in which Budha had been accustomed to say bana, in deep sorrow. Still striking his breast, he exclaimed, "Here my lord said bana; giving joy to the sorrowful, and to the joyful still greater joy; it was thus that I received your sarana. You rejected the deceptive advantages of existence for the real benefits of nirwána; like the opening of a casket in which the most precious jewels are contained, so you opened your illustrious mouth, and the words of the bana proceeded from your heart." Weeping bitterly he proceeded, "Until this time I have heard of your going from place to place, attended by your priests; now it is different." The king repeated the virtues of Budha in sixty stanzas, when he thus reflected:—"It is of no benefit to indulge my sorrow in this manner; the ruler of the world must have left relics; I will go, and endeavour to secure some of them as my own." He, therefore, sent ambassadors to the Malwa princes with letters, of which this was the style:— "Most fortunate princes, Budha was a king; I also am a king. He was five years older than my father Bimsara; they were friends from their childhood; immediately previous to the time when he attained the Budhaship he went to my father's city, and after he had attained it, he again went there, and said bana to 110,000 brahmans and householders; my father entered the path sowán. Budha was my relative: I have received his sarana. It is, therefore, right that I should possess some relic of his body, now that he has attained nirwána; and I request that a dhátu be sent to me, in order that I may place it in a dágoba, and worship it." But immediately after Ajásat had dispatched this letter, he collected an army, and went in person, that if necessary he might take the relic by force.

The Sákya princes of Kapila, the princes of Wisálá, the princes of Allakappa, the princes of Rámagáma, the brahmans of Wétthadipa, and the Malwa princes of Páwá, when they heard of the death of Budha, severally collected armies, and went to Kusinára that they might obtain a portion of the relics. The seven kings having encircled the city, sent to the princes of Kusinára, to say, "We demand a portion of the relics, or we warn you to prepare for battle." The Malwa princes replied, "Budha received nirwána in our city; we did not invite him to come; he came of his own accord; the dhátu are therefore ours by rightful inheritance. There is nothing in the whole world so precious as the relics of Budha; we will give our lives rather than yield them up to another." Upon hearing this, the seven kings prepared to fight, but the princes, still without fear, said "You are not the only persons who have received the breast of the mother; we also are men, and have become strong; it is not we who seek the battle, but those who have approached our gate." In the event of a battle, the princes of Kusinára must necessarily have conquered, as their city was defended by an infinite number of déwas, from its being the depository of the precious relics.

At this critical moment, the brahman Dróha offered to mediate between the parties, as it would have been a dishonour to Budha, had there been any contention near the sacred spot where he attained nirwána. To induce the kings to alter their purpose he ascended an elevated place, whence he repeated aloud 500 stanzas. At first they paid no attention, but at the end of the second stanza, they said to each other, "How like the voice of our teacher," and then listened in silence. Nearly all present had been, at one time or other, the pupils of Dróha. When he perceived that their attention was secured, he said, "All ye kings, hear what I say; our departed lord, in the Kshánti and Dharmmapála births, as well as in many others, exercised the utmost patience and forbearance; it is therefore not right that with weapons in your hands you should attempt to seize his relics. Be at peace among yourselves, and dividing the relics into eight portions, let each take one, and retire to your separate cities. By this means many persons will have the opportunity of doing reverence to Budha." The kings were pleased with this advice, and agreed that the brahman should make the division; upon which he opened the golden casket in which the relics were deposited. The kings reverently approached the treasures weeping, and saying, " Oh, most glorious Budha! once we could look upon you, but this is not permitted unto us now!" and they beat their breasts as they repeated these words. The brahman seeing that the kings were off their guard, from being overcome with sorrow, privately took one of the teeth, and hid it in his hair, after which he divided the rest of the relics into eight portions. There were sixteen measures, according to the measure of Magadha, of the pearl-like substance that was collected when the fire was extinguished, and to each of the kings he gave two measures. But Sekra interfered, and enquired who was to possess the tooth from the right side of the sacred mouth; and when he found that Dróha had taken it by stealth, he took it from his head, and conveyed it to his own déwa-lóka, where he deposited it with the relic of Budha's hair. At the conclusion the brahman felt in his hair for the tooth, but it had gone; and he was ashamed to ask any one about it, because he had obtained it treacherously; he therefore requested as his share of the spoil, the golden vessel in which the relics had been measured, which was presented to him.

The princes of Pittali, on hearing of the death of Budha, sent to demand a portion of the relics, but the seven kings replied that they were already distributed, at the same time giving them permission to take the ashes of the pyre. At first they were reluctant to accept this as their portion, but as they were unable to contend with so many powerful kings, they went to the place of burning, and reverently collected the ashes.

The relic received by Ajásat was taken by him to Rajagaha, with a magnificent procession, and a powerful guard; and as they proceeded leisurely from place to place, that the necessary preparations might be made for its honourable reception, seven years, seven months, and seven days, were occupied in the journey. The tirttakas said that the king had brought the relic merely that he might benefit by the numerous offerings that were made to it; but for this declaration 96,000 persons went to hell. When the rahats saw in what manner the people were endangered, they requested Sekra to cause the king to hasten the passage of the relics to Rajagaha; but the déwa replied, "Among all those who are yet unpurified, there is no one so powerful as Ajásat; he will not pay any attention to what I say; but I will overcome him by a stratagem. I will cause the yakás to send a sickness among his attendants; and you who are rahats can go to the monarch, and tell him that as the yakás are angry, it will be better to take the relic to the city at once, without further delay." All this was done. The king said that he had not intended to hurry the relic on so irreverently, but as it was the request of the rahats, there should be no further protraction of the journey. Accordingly, he arrived at Rajagaha in seven days from that time, where he built a dágoba for the relic.

The other kings also erected dágobas over the relics they had received. The Sákya princes at Kapila; the Lichawi princes at Wisálá; the princes of Allakappa, Ramágama, and Wéthadípa, at cities of the same name; the Malwa princes at Páwá; and the Mallian princes of Kusinára, at Kusinára; and for the vessel in which the relics were measured, and the ashes of the funeral pyre, dágobas were erected by the brahman and the princes of Pittali. (*Th'úpa-wansa.*)

There have been various opinions as to the age in which Gótama lived;[*] but the era given by the Singhalese authors is now the most generally received. According to their chronology, he expired in the year that according to our mode of reckoning would be B.C. 543, in the eightieth year of his age. This was a period pregnant with events of great importance in the western world.[†]

[*] Professor Wilson, in the Oriental Magazine for 1825, quotes no less than eleven authorities, every one of which establishes the era of Budha more than 1000 years B.C., and five other authorities makes it above 800 years B.C. —Col. Sykes; Journ. Royal As. Soc. No. xii.

[†] In proof of this assertion, we may enumerate the following events, nearly all of which are mentioned by Grote (History of Greece) as coming within the period that includes the lifetime of Gótama. The taking of Jerusalem by Nebuchadnezzar, and the captivity of its citizens; the taking of Nineveh by the Medes; the circumnavigation of Africa by the Phoenicians; the

VII. LEGENDS OF GÓTAMA BUDHA.

In adopting the names Gótama and Budha to designate the great sage, I have taken the most simple form of the words. From the failure of the attempts that have been recently made, in the translations from other languages, to write proper names as nearly as possible according to the pronunciation of the original word, I have been led to adopt an opposite course; but the native authors use so many different modes of writing the name of the same person or place, that in some instances I have found it exceedingly difficult to preserve uniformity. I have generally inclined to the Sanskrit form, in the principal words, as being at once the most simple and the best known. The name of the founder of Budhism has been spelled by European authors in the following modes, and probably in many others that have not come under my notice: Fo, Fod, Foe, Fohe, Fohi, Fho, Fuh, Futh, Pot, Pott, Poot, Poota, Pootah, Poth, Poti, Pout, Phuta, Wud, Bod, Bot, Bud, But, Buth, Budh, Buddh, Bood, Boodh, Boudh, Bhood, Baoth, Bauth, Budo, Buto, Budu, Booda, Bodda, Budda, Butta, Budha, Buddha, Budhu, Buddhu, Budho, Buddho, Buddow, Budhow, Budhoo, Budsdo, Buhda, Boudha, Boudhu, Boudhoo, Bouddha, Bouddhu, Boutta, and Bouddho. The form Buddha is etymologically the most correct.* The name Gótama is a patronymic; in Chinese, it is Kiu tan; in Tibetan, Geoutam; and in Manchou and Mogul, Goodam. The origin of the word Sákya has been already explained, page 137. There

---

breaking down of the old routine of the Egyptian kings, and the display of a new policy towards foreigners by Psammetichus; the reformation of Zoroaster; the subjugation of the Asiatic Greeks by Lydia and Persia: the combined action of the large mass of Greeks under Sparta; the first diffusion and potent influence of distinct religious brotherhoods, mystic rites, and expiatory ceremonies; the agency of the Orphic sect; the founding of the most distant colony of the Greeks in the western regions, Massalia; the breaking up of the power of Sybaris, and the march of the Oscan population from Middle Italy towards the south; the burning of the Delphian temple; the accession of Peisistratus; the first application of writing to the poems of the Greeks, and the rise of their first prose writer, Pherekydes, of Syros; and the beginning of the exquisite statuary and architecture of the Greeks.

* Much erroneous speculation has originated in confounding Budha, the son of Soma, and regent of the planet Mercury, "he who knows," the intelligent, with Buddha, any deified mortal, or "he by whom truth is known."—Wilson's Vishnu Purána.

are several legends to account for the giving of the name Sidhártta to the infant prince; but they are at variance with each other. The epithet O-mi-to, used by the Chinese, is probably a corruption of amirta, a word which signifies deathless, and is used to designate nirwána. The word Samona Codam, in use among the Siamese, is the same as Sramana Gótama.

There can be little doubt that the founder of the religious system known as Budhism was a prince, and that he was born in the region called Magadha; but the illustrious genealogy that he has received is less to be relied upon, and it is evident that the dominions of his father were circumscribed. Setting aside the miraculous events that are said to have been attendant upon his infancy and youth, and the enormous exaggerations that are manifest in almost every sentence, there runs through the narrative a semblance of reality; and the reasons why he renounced the world, the austerities he practised in the wilderness, and his warfare with the powers of evil, have a parallel in the history of almost every ascetic saint whose life has been recorded. In some accounts, each onset of Wasawartti Mára is said to have been repelled by one particular páramitá virtue, the whole of the ten being taken in order.

I have not met with any eastern work that is exclusively confined to the biography of Gótama, or that professes to present it in its completeness. The incidents of his early life are repeated again and again, in nearly the same order, and with little variety of expression; but after he has assumed the high office of the Budha, the consecutiveness of the narrative ceases; and in the arrangement of the preceding legends, I have had to exercise my own judgment as to the order in which they ought to appear. It is only occasionally that an allusion is given, serving as a guide to the chronology of the event. The following extract from the Sadharmmaratnakáré is the only statement of the kind with which I am acquainted in any native author. "In the first year of his Budhaship, Gótama was at Isipatana, near Benares; the second, third, and fourth, at Wéluwana, near Rajagaha; the fifth, in the Kútágára hall, near Wisálá; the sixth, in the garden Kosambiya, near Kosambæ; the seventh, in the garden Pundaríka, in the déwa-lóka of Sekra; the eighth, at the rock Sungsumára (said by Turnour to be synonymous with Kapilawastu); the ninth, in the garden Ghósika, near Kosambæ; the tenth, in a cave at the foot of a sal tree, in the forest of Párali; the eleventh, in a garden belonging to the brahman village of Nalaka; the twelfth, in the hall Naléru, near the brahman village of Wéranja; the thirteenth, at the rock Chéliya, on the invitation of the déwa who inhabited it; the fourteenth, at the Jétáwana wihára, near Sewet; the fifteenth, in a cave of jewels connected with the garden Nigródha, near Kapilawastu; the sixteenth, in the city of Alow; the seventeenth, eighteenth, and nineteenth, at the Wéluwana wihára; the six following years in the mansion called Migáramátu, presented to him by Wisákhá; after which he had no fixed residence, but went about from place to place, preaching the bana, and spreading his religion." This account appears to be taken from Budhagósha's Commentary on the Budhawansa. It is elsewhere stated that he sojourned at Sewet for the space of nine years, and at Sáketu sixteen.

In the twenty-ninth year of his age, Gótama became a recluse; six years elapsed between this period and his attainment of the Budhaship; and he continued in the exercise of its privileges forty-five years. His first visit to Ceylon is represented as having taken place in the ninth month after he became Budha. This legend does not appear in the regular order of the narrative, in any of the native works I have read. From its position, it has the appearance of being an after-thought; and I was long under the impression that it was a modern invention, and probably of only local reception. But in this I was mistaken; as it was known nearly a thousand years ago to the people of Tibet. "The second treatise or sutra," says Csoma Körösi, "in the fifth volume of the Mdo (from leaves 81 to 298) is entitled in Sanskrit

A'rya Langkávatára maha yana sutra. A venerable sutra of high principles (or speculation) on the visiting of Lanká. This was delivered at the request of the lord of Lanká, by Shákya, when he was in the city of Lanká, on the top of the Malayar* mountain, on the sea shore, together with many priests and bodhisatwas. It was in a miraculous manner that Shákya visited Lanká. It is evident from the text that both the visitors and the pretended master of Lanká are fancied beings; but there is in the Langkávatára sutra a copious account of the Budhistic metaphysical doctrine, with some discussion on each. From leaves 298 to 456 there is again an explanation of the Langkávatára sutra, containing (as it is stated) the essence of the doctrine of all the Tathágatas. The Langkávatára sutra was translated by order of the Tibetan king Ral-pa-chan, in the ninth century. No Indian pandit is mentioned. It is stated only that it was translated by Lotsava Gelong, who added also the commentary (which must be the last part of the above-mentioned sutra) of a Chinese professor or teacher, called Wen-hi." It is stated by Hodgson that the Langkàvatára is regarded by the Nepaulese as the fourth dharmma. "The fourth (dharmma) is the Lankavatar, of 300 slokas, in which it is written how Ravana, lord of Lanká, having gone to the Malayagiri mountain, and there heard the history of the Budhas from Sakya Sinha, obtained Boddhynána."

A considerable number of the legends I have translated are known to the Tibetans, as we learn from Csoma Körösi;† to the Nepaulese, as we learn from Brian Hodgson;‡ or to the Chinese, as we learn from Remusat, Klaproth, and Landresse.§ The sacred books of Burma, Siam, and Ceylon, are

---

* Malaya is said by Professor Wilson to be the southern portion of the Western Ghauts.
† Asiatic Researches, vol. xx.—Journal Bengal As. Soc. passim.
‡ Illustrations of the Literature and Religion of the Buddhists, by B. H. Hodgson, Esq., B.C.S. Serampore, 1841.
§ Foĕ Kouĕ Ki, ou Relation des Royaumes Bouddhiques: Voyage dans la Tartarie, dans l'Afghanistan et dans l'Inde, exécuté à la fin du IVe Siècle, par Chy fă hian. Traduit du Chinois et commenté par M. Abel Remusat. Ouvrage posthume, revu, complété, et augmenté d'éclaircissements nouveaux, par MM. Klaproth et Landresse: Parie, 1836.

identically the same. The ancient literature of the Budhists, in all the regions where this system is professed, appears to have had its origin in one common source; but in the observances of the present day there is less uniformity; and many of the customs now followed, and of the doctrines now taught, would be regarded by the earlier professors as perilous innovations.

I am tempted by an almost irresistible impulse, to enter upon an extended examination of the personal character of Gótama, and of the religious system he established. But I forbear. The task I have undertaken is rather to impart information, than to assume the office of an expositor or controversialist. There is, nevertheless, something almost overpowering in the thought, that he was the means of producing a moral revolution more important in its results, and more extensive in its ramifications, than any other uninspired teacher, whether of the eastern or western world. The character of the instrumentality by which these mighty effects were brought about, has hitherto been little regarded; but the time is coming when it will engage the attention of our highest orders of intellect. With the founders of other creeds, and of other monastic orders, and of other philosophical systems, Gótama will have to be compared; nor must such beings as Melampus, Empedokles, and Apollonius, who, like himself, are invested with a shadowy existence and partook of supernatural powers, be overlooked. Though the great sage of Maghada has more disciples, by tens of millions, than Mahomet, or Anthony, or Aristotle, his name is scarcely heard beyond the limits of Asia; and in many cases where his history is partially known, he is regarded as a mere abstraction or as the subject of a myth.

VIII. THE DIGNITY, VIRTUES, AND POWERS OF BUDHA.

I. THE SUPREMACY OF BUDHA.—II. HIS MANHOOD.—III. HIS APPEARANCE AND STATURE.—IV. HIS MANNER OF WALKING.—V. THE BEAUTIES OF HIS PERSON.—VI. HIS DEPORTMENT AND VIRTUES.—VII. HIS KINDNESS. —VIII. THE MANNER IN WHICH HE SAID BANA.—IX. HIS SUPERNATURAL ENDOWMENTS.

THE Budhas are regarded by their adherents as the greatest of beings. The praises they receive are of the most extravagant description; and all the excellencies that the most fertile imagination can invent have been applied to them, in setting forth the beauty of their persons, the propriety of their deportment, the kindness of their disposition, or the greatness of their powers. The first sentence in all the óla books written in Ceylon is as follows:—Namó tassa bhagawató arhaható sammá sambuddhassa. Bhagawató, the virtuous, the meritorious;* araható, the perfectly pure, from having overcome all sensuousness; samma, in a proper manner; sambuddhassa, he who has ascertained the four great truths, by intuition; tassá, to him; namó, be praise, or worship.

In some of the translations now to be inserted, there is presented a more painful proof, if possible, of prostration of intellect, than in any of the preceding statements. But they are consistent in their wildness; and if the honours bestowed upon Budha are legitimately given, the rest of the story may

---

* The Brahmans give to this word a more recondite signification. "The word Bhagavat is a convenient form to be used in the adoration of that supreme boing, to whom no term is applicable; and therefore Bhagavat expresses that supreme spirit, which is individual, almighty, and the cause of causes of all things. The letter *Bh* implies the cherisher and supporter of the universe. By *ga* is understood the leader, impeller, or creator. The dissyllable *Bhaga* indicates the six properties, dominion, might, glory, splendour, wisdom, and dispassion. The purport of the letter *ca* is that elemental spirit in which all beings exist, and which exists in all things.— Wilson's Vishnu Puráňa.

follow as a matter of course. We have here a phase of mind that outstrips the utmost extravagancies of our own legends. The old monks have transmitted to us many most wondrous stories; but their most elaborated menologies must yield the palm to the narrative we have received of the prowess of Gótama.

Yet the relation has a melancholy interest, as it may be regarded as the prime effort of the mind of heathendom to present a faultless and perfect character. It is the eastern beau ideal of that which is the most beautiful, and praiseworthy, and great. There are, confessedly, some features that we are called upon to admire; but the folly in some instances, and the absurdity in others, mark the whole to be "of the earth, earthy."

1. *The Supremacy of Budha.*

It is said of Budha, that he is endowed with many virtues; he is the joy of the whole world; the helper of the helpless; a mine of mercy; the déwa of déwas; the Sekra of Sekras; the Brahma of Brahmas; the only deliverer; the very compassionate; the teacher of the three worlds; he who receives the homage of kings; the royal preacher; a diamond coffer to those who seek his assistance; a moon to the three worlds; he who gives the ambrosia of righteousness; the father of the world; the helper of the world; the friend of the world; the relative of the world; the gem of the world; the collyrium of the world; the ambrosia of the world; the treasure of the world; the magical jewel of the world; stronger than the strongest; more merciful than the most merciful; more beautiful than the most beautiful; having more merit than the most meritorious; more powerful than the most powerful; he who enables the being who only softly pronounces his name, or who gives in his name only a small portion of rice, to attain nirwána. The eye cannot see anything; nor the ear hear anything; nor the mind think of anything, more excellent, or more worthy of regard than Budha.

The following declaration, which appears in the Aggappasádasútra, was made by Gótama:—" Priests, there is no one superior to the Tatágata, whether it be among apods, bipeds, quadrupeds, or millapeds; among those that have rúpa, organized bodies, or those that are arúpa, incorporeal. He who trusts in Budha relies upon him who is supreme; and he who trusts in the supreme will receive the highest of all rewards. No one has been my teacher; there is none like me; there is no one who resembles me, whether among déwas or men."

Were a being possessed of all wisdom to repeat during an entire kalpa the praises of Budha, he would not be able to declare the whole. There are beings that are sentient, and beings that are not sentient; of these two classes, the sentient is the chief. There are two classes of sentient beings, animals and men; of these two classes, man is the chief. There are two classes of mankind, the male and the female; of these, the male is the chief. There are two classes of males, those who have fixed habitations and those who have none; of these the men who have no fixed habitation are the chief. Of those who have no fixed habitation, the priests, the Pasé-Budhas, and the supreme Budhas, are the chief.*

On a certain occasion, Jinorasa and Sákyaputra were walking together. He who went in the rear said to the other, "My lord, the excellence of Budha is immensely great; I have been thinking that if there were books written that contained a perfect account of the whole they would form a heap that would reach to the brahma lókas." "Friend," replied the superior priest, "by so saying you lower the dignity of our great monarch; such a comparison appears only like a mockery." The other priest then said, "I spoke according to the extent of my knowledge;" and as he had not said it with the intention of being disrespectful, but had spoken it out of a heart filled with affection for Budha, the superior priest forgave him.

The lofty Maha Méru may be reflected in a mirror; by putting out one finger, it may be said that the six déwa-lókas are there; a sign may be made to indicate that the sixteen brahma-lókas are in such a direction; taking up as much earth as is carried in the mouth of a white ant, it may be said that the earth is like that; a mustard seed may be used to declare

---

* "Of created things, the most excellent are those that are animated; of the animated, those which subsist by intelligence; of the intelligent, mankind; and of men, the sacerdotal class."—Manu, Inst. i. 96.

the size of the great ocean; the eye of a needle may be used as a comparison for the whole sky; even so may the words of a stanza be used to declare the excellence of Budha, but their power is utterly inadequate to accomplish this purpose in a right manner.

The appearance of a supreme Budha in the world is the greatest of all possible events. In the time of Kásyapa Budha, the kings of Káshtawáhana and Benares formed a league together; and it was agreed that if anything particular happened in either kingdom, it should be made known to the monarch of the other. On a certain occasion, the king of Káshtawáhana sent to the king of Benares eight robes of the description called palas, with a suitable embassage. On their arrival, the king called together his nobles to receive them; but when he saw the casket in which they were contained he was displeased, as he thought it could contain nothing of value, and was not worthy of any better use than to be given to his children for a plaything. It was opened, however, and then another that was inside; but when the king came to the robes, they shone like the sun, and were of the colour of the murutu flower. The principal treasurer declared that their value was beyond all computation. The king then resolved to send something in return that would be of double the value; and after meditating upon the subject some time, he wrote upon a leaf of gold that a supreme Budha had appeared, at the same time setting forth his virtue and power. This leaf he enclosed in rich caskets, and sent it upon an elephant to Káshtawáhana; and when the king of that country received the information it contained, he rejoiced greatly, and sent an ambassador to Budha, who did not arrive before he had attained nirwána; but on his return he brought with him the dabaráwa relic of the great teacher. The king heard bana, kept the precepts, and when he died was born in a déwa-lóka. At a subsequent period he was the próhita brahman of the king of Kosol, and was called Bawári.

The same praises belong to the whole of the three gems. Their excellence cannot be set forth by a comparison taken from any object existing in any of the three times, present, past, or future, nor in any of the three worlds; it is incomparable, unspeakable, inconceivable, peerless. It cannot be compared to space, because space can be comprehended by the rishis. It cannot be compared, as to stability, with the great earth; because the earth rests upon the Jala-polowa, and this upon the Wá-polowa; so that the earth may be shaken by the wind, and its summit may be gradually attained; but the three gems are firm and immovable. It cannot be compared, as to ponderosity, with Maha Méru; because the solid inches in the mass of this mountain can be computed, and at the end of the kalpa it will be destroyed; but the excellence of the three gems is incalculable, and they are indestructible. It cannot be compared, as to depth, with the great ocean; because at the appearance of the seventh sun its waters will be dried up; but the excellence of the three gems is unfathomable. It cannot be compared as to number, with the stars; because the size of the heavens in which the stars appear can be told; but the excellence of the three gems cannot be computed.

The rishis may tell the number of inches in the sky, the number of drops in the ocean, and the number of atoms in Maha Méru; they may hide the earth by the tip of the finger; and they may shake the vast forest of Himála, with all its high mountains, as by a cotton thread; but there is no being in the wide universe who has the hand of energy by which he can swim to the opposite side of the ocean of excellence possessed by Budha. Were a rishi to create a thousand or a thousand thousand mouths, and with these to repeat the praises of the three gems during the years of a maha kalpa, even in this period the whole would not be declared. Were he to collect a mighty assemblage of leaves, and to write upon them all, the number of letters they would contain might be told; but there is no method by which the excellence of the three gems can be adequately revealed. (*Wisudhi-margga-sanné. Pújáwaliya. Sadharmmaratnakáré.*)

2. *The Manhood of Budha.*

Though possessed of all this supremacy, the Budhas are men. Were Budha to appear as a déwa or brahma, the exercise of his powers would not be regarded as marvellous. It would be said that his miracles were performed by the power which he possessed as a déwa, and not as the Budha. The various orders of being would not love him; they would not attend to his bana, nor seek to be delivered from error. It is for these reasons that he is born as a man. Still, though born as a man, he might appear by the opapátika, or apparitional birth. But to remove the doubts of all beings, to show that what he does is not by the power of irdhi, or from any other cause of a similar description, he receives the supreme Budhaship as a man, born from the womb.

The body of Budha was subject to pain and disease, and it was argued by the king of Ságal that on this account he could not be the all-wise. But Nágaséna replied that there are various causes of disease, of which the karma of previous births is only one. All the pain felt by Budha was from some present cause, or from the contrivance of others. Thus the harvest may be poor, from the badness of the seed, without any fault whatever on the part of the husbandman. When a stone is thrown into the air, it falls on the ground, not from any previous karma, but naturally, from a cause then present. The purest vessel may have poison put within it. And when the earth is cleared and ploughed, it is not from any previous karma that it is thus lacerated, nor from any appointment of its own; but from the will of another. In like manner, the pain felt by Budha was without any cause on his part; it came naturally from some cause then present, or from the contrivance of some other person. (*Milinda Prasna.*)

3. *The Appearance and Stature of Budha.*

Budha is sometimes said to be twelve cubits in height, and sometimes eighteen cubits; but in the latter case either a different measure is used, or the nimbus on the top of his head is included, which extended above him six cubits.

When Budha resided in the wihára called Purwáráma, built by the upasikáwa Wisákhá, he overcame the asúr Ráhu, in the following manner. The déwas and asúrs having heard bana, expressed their delight to Ráhu, recommending him to go and hear for himself the same good word. The asúr enquired what kind of a person Budha was, when they described a few of his characteristics, but declared that they were unable to tell all. Among other things they told him that Budha was twelve cubits high; but on hearing this he said, "Why should I, who am 4,800 yojanas high, go to see Budha, who is only twelve cubits high?" The déwas replied that if a hundred or a thousand asúrs were placed one upon another, they would be unable to reach the height of Budha. Ráhu then resolved that he would go and see him, that it might be known which was the taller. His intention was perceived by Gótama, who commanded Ananda to spread a carpet, that he might recline upon it. Upon this carpet he lay down, with his head towards the south, and his face towards the east, like a lion in repose. When the asúr had seen his beauty and remained looking at him in astonishment, the sage asked what it was that he was noticing with so much interest. Rahu said that he was trying to discover the end of his foot, but was not able to reach it. "No," exclaimed Budha, "nor would you be able to reach it, were you even to see the highest of the brahma-lókas." When this was said, the asúr had not seen his mouth; but he thought that if his feet were thus wonderful, his mouth must be above all praise. And now he confessed that he was a believer in Budha; and promising to become his devoted servant, he requested his protection. Then the sage permitted him to see his mouth, and preached to him the bana, by which many déwas were enabled to see the fruition of nirwána.*

At a time when Budha visited the city of Rajagaha, there resided in the same city a brahman, called Atula, who having heard that neither Sekra, Maha Brahma, Vishnu, Mahéswara, nor any of the rishis was able to measure the height of Budha, thought within himself it was a singular thing that they were unable to tell the height of one who was only of the ordinary stature: about twelve cubits. He, therefore, procured a bamboo sixty cubits long; and when Gótama entered the city, he stood near him with it; but it did not reach even to his knees. He went home in sorrow, at not succeeding in his attempt; but the next day he fastened another bamboo of the same length to the end of the former one, so that it was now 120 cubits long; and when Budha approached, he stood with it at the entrance of the city; but he soon found that it was still insufficient. Budha then enquired why he stood near him, with his two bamboos fastened together, and placed erect; and when he replied that it was to ascertain his height, the teacher of the three worlds said,

* Neither the asúrs nor the dwellers in the Wasawartti déwa-lóka can enter the paths.

"Brahman, if you were to fill the whole circuit of the earth with bamboos, and could find out a way of fastening all these together, end to end, even this would be an insufficient instrument to measure my stature. No one can compute the number of the garments, ornaments, couches, chariots, slaves, cattle, villages, fields, pearls, and gems, I have given in alms since the time when I resolved upon becoming Budha; nor can any one calculate the number of eyes, heads, and children I have given; and if a lac, a kela, or an asankya of brahmans like yourself were to try to discover the virtue of my páramitás, all that they could discover would be only like the eye of a needle in comparison to the sky, or a mustard seed to the great ocean, or the portion of mould taken into the mouth of a worm to the whole earth. In like manner, no creature whatever is able to comprehend my stature; therefore, cease, brahman, from thy attempt." (*Sadharmmálankáré.*)

It is difficult to describe the appearance of Budha; and for this reason. He could walk in a space not larger than a mustard seed; yet on one occasion, he placed his foot on the earth, then on the rock Yugandhara, and next on the summit of Maha Méru, by which means, at three steps, he reached the heaven of Sekra. This was done with as much ease as a man crosses the threshold of his house; yet the stature of Gótama remained the same; he did not increase in size, nor did the mountains become less.

4. *Budha's manner of Walking.*

The manner in which Budha walked excited universal admiration. At the time he resided in a cave, near some sal trees, at the rock Wédiya, he was seen by an owl of the race of Kosiya, who greatly admired his manner of walking, as he went to the village to receive alms. On his return, the owl again looked at him with the utmost affection, and on his arrival at the cave paid him adoration. Budha then smiled, and when Ananda asked the reason, he said that the owl, by reason of the merit it had thus received, would hereafter be free from disease, and would escape birth in any of the four hells during many ages, as it would always be born either as a man or as a déwa; and that it would afterwards become the Pasé-Budha, Sómanassa, and attain nirwána. (*Sadharmmálankáré.*)

At another time, when Gótama was walking in a manner that was marked by the utmost propriety, he was asked by the ascetic Ardha who was his preceptor. He replied that he was self-taught. When he went abroad with his attendant Ananda, that he might bless the world, he appeared like the full moon accompanied by the planet Guru (Jupiter). If there were any thorns, stones, roots, potsherds, rocks, or other substances that would hinder him or obstruct his progress, they removed from his path of their own accord, and left it clear; if there was mud, it became dry; or if there were holes, they became filled up; if there were any elevations, they passed away, like butter that sees the fire, until the whole path was as level as the head of a drum, and the air appeared as if sweetened by perfumes. If he passed any being that was in pain, though it were in an agony equal to hell, it ceased in an instant; and when his foot touched the earth, a lotus sprang up at every step. (*Sadharmmálankáré.*)

The foot of Gótama came to the ground as lightly if it had been cotton wool. When the winged horse passes swiftly over water lilies, its course may be seen by the bending of the flowers, but it leaves no impression of its footstep: and in like manner, the footstep of Budha was without a trace. It was in kindness that this was appointed. Budha was usually surrounded by a crowd of people; and if he had left the impression of his foot, as he walked along, they would have been wishful to honour it; they would not have trodden in the same place; and thus their progress would have been impeded. (*Sadharmmaratnakáré.*

On some occasions, when Budha was about to ascend the throne upon which he sat, he came through the ground, and rose up at the place, like the sun rising over Yugandhara: and at other times he went through the sky. During his progress from place to place, the light that shone from his body was like the glory proceeding from Maha Brahma, or the splendour of the gems in the royal diadem on the day of the king's anointing, or a canopy adorned with gold and silver, or a garland of the most beautiful flowers, or an alms-hall filled with sweet-scented flowers and perfumes. (*Pújáwaliya.*)

5. *The Beauties of Budha's Person.*

These are divided into three kinds:—1. The 216 Mangalya-lakshana, of which there were 108 on each foot. 2. The 32 Mahapurusha-lakshana, or superior Beauties. 3. The 80 Anuwyanjana-lakshana, or inferior Beauties.

(1.) The 216 Mangalya-lakshana.—1. The chakra circle. 2. Two thousand lines proceeding from the centre of the circle, like the spokes of a wheel. 3. The rim round the extremity of these lines, like the outer frame of a wheel. 4. Small circles between the lines, within which were the representations of flowers. These four were called the chakrawartti-lakshana. The remaining 212 were as follows: on each foot was a small drum, a swastika,* a cymbal, a frontlet, the hood of a nayá, an ornament in which flowers are placed, a garland, a gem, an ornament for the head, a royal couch, a palace, a festive arch, a white umbrella, an elephant's tusk, a sword of state, a talipot fan, a peacock's tail, two chámaras of different kinds, a jessamine flower, a blue water lily, a red water lily, a red lotus, a white lotus, a full vessel, an alms-bowl, a white sea, a blue sea, a coral sea, a golden sea, a sakwala-gala, the forest of Himála, a Maha Méru, a discus, the palace of the sun, the mansion of the moon, the isles of the east, the isles of the west, the isles of the north, the isles of Jambudwípa, a chakrawartti surrounded by his retinue, a right-handed conch, a golden fish, the seven rivers, the Yugandhara and six other concentric circles of rocks, the Anótatta and six other lakes, the king of the garundas, a makara,† two festive flags, a golden litter, the rock Kailása, a royal tiger, a lion, a horse of the breed Walahaka, an elephant of the breed Upósatha, a nayá, a hansa, a bull, an elephant of the breed Eráwana, a mariner, a surabhi-dénu or cow that gives

---

* A kind of mystical figure, the inscription of which on any person or thing is generally considered to be lucky; amongst the Jainas it is the emblem of the seventh deified teacher of the present age.—Wilson's Sanskrit Dictionary. This figure is found in many magical diagrams, and in Runic inscriptions and amulets; it is the hammer of Thor; and is seen on some ancient Etruscan vases that were dug up at Rome, in 1817. It is also very commonly seen on the ancient coins that were struck by the Budhist monarchs of India.

† A sea-monster; the upper extremity of its body being like an antelope, and the lower like a fish. It answers in the Indian zodiac to the Capricornus of the west.

whatever is desired, a kindurá, a chanda-kindurá, an Indian cuckoo, a peacock, the bird kos-libiniyá, a brahmany kite, a Greek partridge, the six déwa-lókas, and sixteen brahma-lókas.*

(2.) The thirty-two Maha-purusha-lakshana or superior Beauties.—1. The feet of Budha were like two golden sandals. 2. There was a chakra, or wheel, in the centre of the sole. 3. His heels were like balls of gold, but extremely soft. 4. His fingers tapered gradually to the end. 5. The palms of his hands, and the soles of his feet, were as soft as cotton dipped in oil. 6. The palms and soles appeared like richly ornamented windows. 7. His instep was high. 8. His legs were like those of an antelope, round and full. 9. His arms were straight, and so long that without bending he could touch his knee. 10. His secret parts were concealed, as the pedicle of the flower is hid by the pollen. 11. His skin was soft and smooth, as an image polished by the tooth of a tiger. 12. His body did not collect dust or dirt, as the lotus is not defiled by the mud in the midst of which it grows. 13. The hair on his body was smooth, not rough or straggling. 14. All the hairs of his body curled towards the right hand. 15. His body was perfectly straight. 16. The soles, palms, shoulders, and back, were rounded and full. 17. The upper part of his body was full, like that of a lion. 18. His antarásas were like a golden oven. 19. His body was high, like a banian-tree, and round, like the same tree, i.e. the breadth was proportioned to the height. 20. His neck was like a golden drum. 21. The seven thousand nerves of taste all bent towards the tongue, so that he was sensible of the slightest flavour. 22. He had a lion's strength. 23. His forty teeth were all of equal size. 24. His teeth were perfectly white, as if made from a conch shell. 25. His teeth were like a row of diamonds, without any orifices. 26. His teeth shone like the stars of a constellation. 27. His tongue was so long that by putting it out he could touch his forehead, or the orifices of his ears. 28. His voice was eight-toned, like that of Maha Brahma, and melodious as that of the Indian cuckoo. 29. His eyes were blue, and sparkled like sapphires. 30. His eyes were round, like those of a new-born calf. 31. Upon his forehead

---

* The order in which these signs are enumerated is not always the same. I have taken more pains than the matter is worth, to procure a perfect list, but some signs are yet wanting to complete the number required.

VIII. DIGNITY, VIRTUES, AND POWERS OF BUDHA.

was a lock of hair, curling towards the right.* 32. Upon his forehead, extending from ear to ear, was, as it were, a frontlet.

(3.) The eighty Anuwyanjana-lakshana, or inferior Signs.— 1. The form of Budha was beautifully moulded; the members of his body were proportioned to each other; his body was round or plump; his nails were of a copper colour, high in the centre and sloping to the sides, and smooth; the calf of the leg was strong and firm; the sole was flat, so as to touch the ground in all places alike; his gait was like that of the royal elephant, lion, hansa, and bull; the hair of his body inclined towards the right hand; his knees were well rounded; the navel had no perforation, it was deep, and bent towards the right hand; his shoulders were like those of the royal elephant; his members were properly divided; proportionate, full, extremely soft, and well put together, so as to be easily known or distinguished; his body was without a spot, symmetrical, pure, and clear; he had the strength of a kela of elephants; his nostrils were high; his gums were red; his teeth were clean, round, and well set; his senses were very acute; his lips were red; his mouth was long; the lines on his hands were long, deep, straight, and auspicious; his temples were full; his eyes were long and broad, and of five rays; his hair was gradually turned; his tongue was soft, thin, and red; his ears were long; his head was well made, round, without any irregularities, and not thick; his body was erect, like an umbrella; his forehead was long and broad; his eye-brows were soft, uniform, large and long; his body was soft, shining, and emitted a pleasant smell; the hair of his body was uniform, soft, and of a blue colour; the drawing of his breath was gentle, almost imperceptible; his mouth smelt sweetly; the hair of his head was blue, soft, uniform, not tangled, and in just proportion; and his body emitted rays to the distance of a carpenter's cubit.† (*Pújáwaliya*.)

---

* Among the ancient Egyptians, figures of the gods were distinguished by the beard turning up at the end.—Wilkinson's Ancient Egyptians.

† It is difficult to tell why many of the signs here enumerated are called beauties; and the whole series taken together presents a singular standard of taste. The superior signs are repeated among the inferior; and even in the same class there is a constant repetition of the same idea, which renders the translation of some of the terms difficult; different epithets being used, particularly with regard to the attribute of softness, but all having the same

6. *The Deportment and Virtues of Budha.*

There are sixty hours in the day, thirty of which belong to the night, which is divided into three watches, of ten hours each. Budha slept during one-third of the third watch, or three hours and one third. In the first watch he said bana; in the second watch he answered questions put to him by the déwas; and in the first division of the third watch he slept, in the second exercised meditation, and in the third looked abroad in the world to see what being or beings should be caught in the net of truth during the day. (*Amáwatura.*)

There was a learned brahman, called Brahmáyu, who resided in the city of Mithila. To the same place came Gótama Budha; and when the brahman heard of his arrival, knowing his fame, he commanded his disciple Uttara to go and test his knowledge. The disciple enquiring how he was to know Budha, Brahmáyu replied, "You might as well ask how you are to know the earth upon which you tread; have you not read, and have I not taught you from the four Vedas, that such and such are the signs of a Budha." Uttara then went to the wihára, where he remained seven months; after which he returned to Brahmáyu, and informed him in what way the sage conducted himself, setting forth at length the beauties of his person, and the propriety of his behaviour in all circumstances and upon all occasions.

Uttara proceeded: When Budha walks, he places his right foot first, whether he has been sitting, standing, or lying. He does not take wide strides, but walks at a solemn pace; nor does he take short steps; even when late, he does not walk too quickly, but like a priest passing along with the alms-bowl. He does not wait for the priests when they have lagged behind; he does not strike his knees or his ankles against each other when he is walking; he does not lift his shoulders up, like a man in

signification. In some instances there appear to be contradictions.—The king of Ságal objected that the prince Sidhártta could not have had the beauties that are attributed to him, because they were not possessed by either of his parents, and the child must be like its father or its mother; but Nágaséna referred him to the beautiful lotus, with its hundred different hues, which is formed in the water and springs from the mud, but neither in colour, odour, or taste, is like the elements from which it is produced.—One of the titles of the king of Siam is, "the pre-eminently merciful and munificent, the soles of whose feet resemble those of Budha."

the act of swimming; nor does he throw them back, like the branch of a tree bent in the form of a snare; nor does he hold them stiffly, like a stake stuck in the soft ground or a person who is afraid of falling when walking in a slippery place; nor does he throw them hither and thither like the movements of a doll with wires. Only the lower part of his body moves when he walks, so that he appears like a statue in a ship; the upper part being motionless, those at a distance cannot perceive that he moves. He does not throw his arms about, so as to cause perspiration or produce fatigue. When he wishes to see anything that is behind him, he does not turn his head merely, but at once turns round the whole body, like the royal elephant. He does not look upwards, like a man counting the stars, nor does he look downwards, like a man searching for some coin or other thing that he has lost. He does not look about him, like a man staring at horses or elephants, nor does he look before him further than the distance of a plough or nine spans; anything further than this distance he sees only by his divine power, not with the natural eye. When he enters any place, he does not bend his body, nor carry it stiffly. When about to sit down, moving gracefully, he does not place himself at a greater or less distance from the seat than a footstep; he does not take hold of the seat with his hand, like a person sick, nor does he go to seat himself like a person who has been fatigued by working, but like a person who suspends something very carefully or who puts down a portion of silk cotton. When seated in any place, he does not remain doing something foolish, like a priest playing with drops of water in the rim of his alms-bowl, or twirling his fan. He does not scrape his foot on the floor, nor does he put one knee above the other. He does not place his chin upon his hand. He never appears as if he was in any way afraid, or in any trouble. Some teachers, when they see any one coming to them to make enquiries upon religious subjects, are in doubt, not knowing whether they will be able to answer them or not; others are in perplexity, not knowing whether they will receive the necessary alms or not; but Budha is subject to none of these trials, as he is free from all the doubts and fears to which others are subject. When receiving gruel, or other liquid, he does not hold the alms-bowl too firmly, nor does he place it too high or too low, or shake it; holding it in both hands, he neither receives too much nor too little, but the proper quantity. He does not scrape the bowl when washing it, nor wash the outside before the inside. He washes his hands at the same time, and not after he has put down the bowl. He does not throw the water to too great a distance; nor near his feet, so as to wet his robe. When receiving solid food, he holds the bowl in the same manner as when receiving liquids. When eating, three parts are rice, and only a fourth part condiment (curry). Some persons, when eating, take more condiment than rice, and others more rice than condiment; but Budha never exceeds the proper proportion. The food taken into his mouth he turns over two or three times; not a single grain is allowed to pass into the stomach without being properly masticated, so that it is like flour ground in a mill. No part is retained in his mouth; nor does he take more until the previous mouthful has been swallowed. The déwas always give to his food a divine flavour, and it does not produce the same consequences as in other men. He does not eat to gratify his appetite, like the common people; nor to increase his size, like kings and other great ones; nor to render his body beautiful, like those who are licentious; nor to render his person agreeable, like dancers and others. He merely eats to sustain existence, as a prop is put to a falling house, or oil to the wheel of a wagon, or salve to a wound, or medicine is taken by the sick, or a raft is used to cross the river, or a ship the sea. When he has done eating, he does not put his alms-bowl by as if it were a thing he cared about; nor does he, like some persons, wash it or dry it or fold it in his robe, to preserve it from dust. His meal being finished, he remains a moment silent; unless he has to give the benediction in favour of the person who has presented the food. There are some priests who hurry over the bana spoken as a benediction, if there be a child crying, or urgent business, or if they be suffering from hunger. There are some again who talk with the people about sowing and ploughing and such matters, instead of saying bana. But Budha says it deliberately, and on no account omits it. Nor when eating the food given him, does he wish for any other, or ask what kind of rice it is, or disparage it. He does not say bana in such a way as to make it appear as if he wished to be invited again the next day, or the day after; nor when he sees any one cooking does he begin to say bana with the hope of receiving a portion when it is ready. Budha says bana that he may impart instruction. When passing from one place to another, he does not go too fast, so as to fatigue his attendants, nor too slowly; but at a becoming pace. He does not let his robe come too high or fall too low. There are some priests who put the robe close to the chin, or let it come so low as to cover the ankles, or put it on awry, or so as not to cover the breast. Budha avoided these extremes; he does not put on his robe so loosely as to allow it to be ruffled by the wind, nor so tightly as to cause perspiration. After walking, his feet are washed, unless he has walked upon the pavement alone. He then reflects on the inspirated and expirated breath, and practises meditation. When he enters a wihára, he delivers his discourse to the priests in kindness. He does not address the great ones of the earth by high titles, but speaks to them as to other men; nor does he address any one in jest; but speaks as if what he says is of importance. His voice is pleasant in its tone, and his manner of speaking is free from hesitation; his words come forth continuously, and being uttered from the navel they are loud, like the rolling thunder. (*Brahmáyu-sútra-sanné.*)

Budha took no thought relative to the retinue of priests by which he was attended; he did not reflect that it was by his means they had received these privileges; he did not think within himself, They are mine. True, upon one occasion he said, that like as he was the means of privilege to a great number of priests, so when Maitrí Budha appeared, he would be the same; but he said this without reflecting on what he said, or thinking for a moment relative to the priests, They are mine; even as the earth sustains the beings that are upon it, or the shower brings gladness to those who partake of its effects, without reflecting in any way that these consequences have taken place. (*Milinda Prasna.*)

In the practice of things difficult to be performed, Budha had no equal. Rejecting all kinds of garments that would be beautiful to look upon, or in their texture pleasant to the body, he wore only the simple robe, made of thirty pieces of cloth; but he was in this way a myriad times more beautiful than if he had been arrayed in the most costly ornaments. Rejecting all golden vessels, he took his food from a vessel of dark clay. Avoiding palaces, couches, and splendid coverlets, he reposed at the foot of a tree, in the forest, in lonely places. What others could not do he accomplished in a manner the most excellent. (*Sadharmmálankáré.*)

There were eight things required of those who approached Budha :—1. Not to look at him in a sideway direction. 2. Not to take a more honourable place than that which was occupied by the sage. 3. Not to go so near as that when speaking saliva would fall upon him from the mouth. 4. Not to remain so far off as to oblige him to shout when speaking. 5. Not to stand to windward, so that the breeze would strike first upon their bodies, and then upon Budha. 6. Not to stand to leeward, so that the breeze would strike first upon Budha, and then upon them. 7. Not to stand in a higher place, so as to require him to lift up his head. 8. Nor in a lower place, so as to require him to bend his head. These observances were required when approaching any great man, but more especially in the presence of Budha. (*Pújáwaliya.*)

7. *The Kindness of Budha.*

The words of Budha were never intended to cause pain. The strongest term of reproach that he ever addressed to any one was, mogha purisa, vain man. On one occasion he reproved the priest Kalandaka-putra; but it was as the physician who uses powerful medicine for the curing of his patient; or who prescribes the most loathsome medicaments for the same purpose; or it was the parent who from affection chastises his child. A profusion of fine cotton, though in size it were like a rock, might fall upon any one without his being hurt; and thus lightly fell the words of Budha upon those whom he addressed.

The methods that he took, in order that he might the more effectually teach those who came to him, were many; as when he made an image of himself, in which he revealed to Séla the sign that he could see in no other way, which sign was seen by the brahman alone, though at the time he was accompanied by 300 disciples; just as when a man feels pain, it is felt by himself alone, and not seen by another, and as a sprite may appear to one person alone, though he be in the midst of many. To Nanda he exhibited a beautiful déwi in the world of Sekra, that he might be induced thereby to despise the earthly princess upon whom he had placed his affections. In other ways also, or by other stratagems, he imparted instruction to his followers. In this he acted like the skilful physician, who tries the emetic or the purgative, and who at one time cures by anointing and at another by injection.

It was declared by Budha to Ananda, that there are no concealed doctrines belonging to the Tatágatas; nevertheless it is said in the Málunka-sútra that when Málunka asked Budha whether the existence of the world is eternal or not eternal, he made him no reply; but the reason of this was, that it was considered by Budha as an enquiry that tended to no profit; and it was not the practice of the Budhas to reply to any question, the purport of which was not designed in some way or other to assist in the overcoming of successive existence and the reception of nirwána.

It is said that at one time, when Budha was preaching the bana, about sixty priests, who were imperfect in the faith, vomited forth warm blood. The king of Ságal objected to Nágaséna that this was contrary to the declaration that Budha is a benefit to all, and a disadvantage to none. Nágaséna: "The throwing up of the blood by the priests was not caused by Budha; it was their own act." Milinda: "But if Budha had not said bana, would it have taken place?" Nágaséna: "It would not; whilst the priests were listening to the bana, a fire was kindled within their bodies, and this fire caused the coming forth of the warm blood." Milinda: "Nevertheless, it must have been Budha who was the principal cause of their destruction. Thus, there is a nayá, that lives in an ant-hill; but a man comes and breaks down this mound, that he may take away the earth, by which means the hole in which the snake lies is filled up, and because it cannot breathe it dies; now is not the death of the snake most clearly caused by the man?" Nágaséna: "It is." Milinda: "Just in the same way, the death of the priests was caused by Budha." Nágaséna: "When Budha says bana, it is not to produce anger in any one; it is to preserve those who hear it from anger and hatred. When any one receives it with a willing mind, it brings forth the fruition of the paths (to nirwána); but when any one hears it with an evil mind, he is brought to destruction. Thus, a man shakes a tree laden with fruit, whether it be of mango, jambu, or some other kind; the fruits that have a strong stalk remain upon the tree, but, if there are any of which the stalk is decayed, they fall to the ground; just so it is with the bana of Budha; they whose minds are prepared receive from it benefit, but they whose minds are averse receive from it no benefit; they fall again into the ocean of existence. Again, in ploughing a field, for whatever kind of grain, many thousands of blades of grass are destroyed; or in putting the sugar-canes to be crushed in the mill, any worms that there may be upon them must perish: in the same way, the mind that is rightly disposed receives benefit from the bana, whilst that which is evil is still exposed to the sorrows of existence." Milinda: "But was it not through the preaching of the bana that the priests died?" Nágaséna: "The carpenter, in preparing the tree that has been felled, cuts off the knots and branches, that all may be made smooth, whilst he leaves untouched the parts that are free from these excrescences; and in the same way, by the preaching of Budha those who are seeking the paths are assisted, whilst the others perish. Again, when the plantain tree has borne fruit, it dies; and when the mare of the breed call Ajána has foaled, she also dies: and when the robbers who have pillaged a country are doomed to punishment, it is by their own act; in like manner, when the sixty priests vomited forth warm blood, their destruction was not caused by Budha, nor by any other being; it was their own act."

At another time, when Budha resided in the garden called Amalakí, belonging to the Sákya princes, near the city of Chátumá, he was visited by Seriyut and Mugalan, who were accompanied by 500 other priests; but when they proceeded to meet the resident priests, so great a noise was made in placing their seats and putting down their alms-bowls and robes, that Budha called out, "Ananda, who are these persons that are making a noise, like so many fishermen drawing their nets?" Ananda informed him that it was occasioned by the arrival of some stranger priests; on hearing which, he said further, "Ananda, assemble the whole priesthood, and tell the priests who have acted like fishermen, no longer to remain near the place where I am." The priests, on receiving this command, retired to the council-chamber of the Sákya princes, who said to them when they had been informed of their arrival, "Sirs, where are so many of you going at this unseasonable hour?"

The priests told them what had occurred; upon which they went to Budha to intercede in their behalf, and said, "My lord, the seed newly sown, if it be not watered, perishes; the calf that is away from its mother dies; so also will these priests, newly appointed to their office, be discouraged if they see not the great teacher; therefore, let them be forgiven." Sahampati Maha Brahma also came from the brahma-lóka, and entreated forgiveness for the priests. This being perceived by Mugalan, by means of his divine eyes, he said, " Priests, Budha grants us permission to return; let us hasten to see him." After they had worshipped the sage, he said to Seriyut, "What were the thoughts that you entertained when you were sent away?" Seriyut replied that he began to think it would be better to leave the practice of the precepts, and return to the world. Upon hearing this, Budha said, "Seriyut, Seriyut, this is enough; let no such thought hereafter be formed." The same question was then put to Mugalan; who replied, "I began to think that Budha had abandoned the truth, and that I or Seriyut must see to the preservation of the priesthood." For this resolution he was commended by the great teacher, who said that it was eminently good. When a man stumbles over a root, or stone, or uneven ground, it is not the earth that throws him down in anger, because the earth is incapable of feeling either displeasure or satisfaction; nor is it from aversion that the sea casts the dead body upon the shore; in like manner, it was not the anger of Budha that caused the retirement of the priests, as he was entirely free from any such feeling; it was the act of the priests themselves, that forbade them to remain. It was foreseen by Budha that the retirement of the priests would have a beneficial influence upon them; and it was on this account, out of kindness to them, that he exercised this act of discipline. (*Milinda Prasna.*)

8. *The Manner in which Budha said Bana.*

When Budha said bana, if it were so designed, all the beings in the sakwala might hear it, but if it were only designed for some particular being or beings, others were unable to hear it, though they might be only an inch away from those to whom it was addressed. Thus when Budha, on a certain occasion, said bana to Sekra, Mugalan, who was at that time in his own dwelling, heard the Sádhu uttered by the déwa, but did not hear the voice of Budha. (Amáwatura.)

By listening to the discourses of Budha, even animals were assisted to enter the paths. On account of the want of merit, they might not be able to enter upon this privilege at once, but after one or two subsequent births they were prepared to receive it. When Gótama was preaching by the side of a pond near the city of Champá, his sermon was heard by a frog, which praised the sweetness of his voice, and exercised faith in him. Immediately afterwards, a man who was watching some calves, drove a stake into the ground, and inadvertently pierced the head of the frog, so that it died; but it was born in the Tawutisá déwa-lóka, and had a mansion of gold twelve yojanas in size. The déwa looked to see how it was he had attained this distinction; and when he discovered the cause, he went to the place where Budha was preaching, and worshipped him. Budha was aware of all that had occurred; but for the benefit of those who were standing near, he said, "Beautiful déwa, who are you? why do you worship my feet?" The déwa then related the circumstances under which he had gained his present happiness; after which Gótama delivered a discourse to him, and 16,000 people attained the paths. The déwa entered the path sowán, and addressing the assembly, he said, "If I, who have heard bana during so short a period only, have gained all this beauty and splendour, undoubtedly those who listen long to the great teacher will attain nirwána." (Wisudhi-margga-sanné.)

The saying of bana by any one else, to those who were accustomed to hear Budha, was like the giving of a gem to those who live in a palace of jewels, or a plantain to those who are in the midst of a forest of sugar-cane, or the lighting a lamp in the broad sunshine. Thus the upásaka Atula, with 500 others, went to their religious preceptor, Rówata, to hear bana; but he informed them that he was performing the exercise of dhyána, and could not be disturbed. Dissatisfied with this reception, they resolved to leave him, and went to Seriyut, who, without delay preached to them part of the Winaya-pitaka; but they said that this was like a torrent of rain that filled the ponds and overflowed the fields; and they were still not contented. They then went to Ananda, who said so little, that it was like the thunder-cloud, which promises much but lets fall only a few drops. Last of all they went to Budha, who said neither too much nor too little, but just sufficient for the mind to retain. By this means Atula and the other upásakas were enabled to enter the paths, and attain nirwána. (*Sadharmmaratnakáré.*)

In a ná-tree, at the door of a léna, or cave, near the wihára of Kelapaw, in Ceylon, resided a déwa. A young priest within the léna one day repeated the Maha-samya-sútra, when it was heard by the déwa, who called out loudly, Sádhu. The priest enquired, "Who are you?" and the voice replied, "I am a déwa." The priest then asked, "Why do you call out, Sádhu?" and the déwa said, "I heard the same sútra delivered by Budha when he preached it in the great forest; you have now said it exactly as it was spoken by him, without adding or retrenching a single word." The priest: "At that time the assembly was immensely large; in what position were you when you heard the words of the sútra?" The déwa: "I resided in the same forest; so many superior déwas arrived that there was no room for me in all Jambudwípa; I therefore came to Dimbultota, in Ceylon; but even there I was not able to remain; I was driven onward by the pressure of the crowd, until I arrived in Mágam, in the province of Ruhuna, whence I had to enter the sea called Golu, until the water was as high as the neck; from this place I heard the sútra." Priest: "Could you see Budha from thence?" Déwa: "Yes; as plainly as if he had been close to me." Priest: "On that occasion many déwas became rahats; did you?" Déwa: "No." Priest: "Perhaps you entered the path sowán?" The déwa was ashamed to reply, as he had not entered even the first of the paths, and said that this was not a proper question for the priest to ask. The priest then requested to see the déwa, but he replied that it was not possible for him to exhibit his whole body; he therefore put forth only a part of one of his fingers, when the whole léna became full of light, as if the full moon had risen. The déwa then worshipped the priest, and retired. (*Amáwatura.*)

The king of Ságal enquired of Nágaséna how it was that Budha, when at the foot of the bó-tree, refused to say bana until entreated to do so by Maha Brahma, saying his conduct was like that of a bowman who should take pains to acquire the art of archery, and then never touch a bow, or that of an athlete, who should study attentively the art of wrestling, and then never enter the arena. Nágaséna replied, "Budha perceived that the dharmma is exceedingly subtle and occult; like a hair that is split a hundred times, or a treasure covered by a great rock; and that to release men from existence, on account of the prevalence and power of evil desire, would be like snatching the prey from the mouth of an alligator. He therefore, paused before he began the preaching of the bana; just as a skilful physician, when he approaches his patient, considers what medicine it will be proper to administer for the overcoming of the disease; or a king, when anointed, thinks in what manner all the various orders of his attendants and ministers will have to be supported. When so exalted a being as Maha Brahma entreated Budha to say bana, all the déwas and brahmas learnt therefrom the greatness of its excellence, and were willing to receive it, as when a king or principal noble pays respects to any sramana priest, the worship of all the other orders in the state follows as a natural consequence.

On a certain occasion, when Nanda was expounding the bana, Budha reflected that as his religion would endure so long, and be beneficial to so many, it would be right that as a mark of respect he should go and hear it preached. So he went in disguise, and listened during the whole of the three watches, until the dawn began to appear; when he came forth from his concealment, crying out Sádhu, Sádhu, and declared that the meaning of what he taught had been correctly explained. On hearing this, Nanda arose from his seat, worshipped Budha, and asked how he could endure the fatigue of listening so long. The sage replied, "Is it at all wonderful that I have listened to you during the three watches? I could remain to hear bana, not merely during a single day, but through a whole kalpa." From that time the people listened with greater delight to the bana, as it had thus been praised by Budha. (*Sadharmmaratnakáré.*)

9. *The supernatural Endowments of Budha.*

The dasa-bala, ten powers, or modes of wisdom, were possessed by Budha. 1. The wisdom that understands what knowledge is necessary for the right fulfilment of any particular duty, in whatsoever situation. 2. That which knows the result or consequences of karma. 3. That which knows the way to the attainment of nirwána. 4. That which sees the various sakwalas. 5. That which knows the thoughts of other beings. 6. That which knows that the organs of sense are not the self. 7. That which knows the purity produced by the exercise of the dhyánas. 8. That which knows where any one was born in all his former births. 9. That which knows where any one will be born in all future births. 10. That which knows how the results proceeding from karma may be overcome.*

The eighteen budha-dharmma were as follows :—1. The seeing of all things past. 2. The seeing of all things future. 3. The seeing of all things present. 4. Propriety of action, or that which is done by the body. 5. Propriety of words, or that which is done by speech. 6. Propriety of thought, or that which is done by the mind. 7. The establishment of his intentions, so that they cannot be frustrated by another. 8. The similar establishment of his doctrines. 9. The same with that which proceeds from samádhi. 10. The same with that which proceeds from wírya. 11. The same with that which proceeds from wimukti. 12. The same with that which proceeds from pragnyáwa. 13. Avoiding pleasures, or anything that might excite ridicule. 14. Avoiding strife and contention. 15. The possession of a wisdom from which nothing is hid, in any place whatever. 16. Doing all things with due deliberation. 17. Having some meaning, or intention, in all that is done. 18. Not doing anything from an unwise partiality.

There is no limit to the knowledge of the Budhas; and they are the only beings ever existent of whom this can be predicated. To the knowledge of all other beings there is a limit, differing in extent according to the merit of the individual. From the Budhas nothing can be hid; all times as well as places are open to their mental vision; they see all things as distinctly as a man in a small apartment can see all things in it, at high noon, in clear weather. The mind of the Budhas, when it goes out after anything, is sure to discover it, as the well-directed arrow of the skilful archer flies at once to the hair it is intended to split; it does not go too far, it does not come too

---

* The three last powers are called triwidyáwa.

short; it passes exactly to the right place. (*Wisudhi-margga-sanné.*)

In the conversations that were held between Milinda and Nágaséna, the king brought many objections against the supremacy and wisdom of Budha. It is said that all that it was necessary for Budha to receive, such as robes, food, and medicine when sick, he received without any trouble or effort beyond that which was implied in the carrying of the alms-bowl, as was his usual custom; but one day when he visited the brahman village of Panchasála, no alms were given him, and he returned with an empty bowl. The king of Ságal asked Nágaséna how this occurred, and was told that it was through the influence of Mára. "Then," said the king, "the demerit of Mára was more influential than the merit of Budha." But Nágaséna replied, "A man brings a present of honey to the palace gate of a chakrawartti; but the porter, out of envy tells him that the emperor cannot be disturbed at that untimely hour, and sends him away without receiving the present. In this case, the porter prevents the emperor from receiving the honey; but he is not more powerful than the emperor, inasmuch as presents are pouring into the palace by a thousand other channels; and in the same way, though Mára prevented the people of Panchasála from presenting alms to Budha, the déwas nourished his body with divine aliment, and he suffered no loss from the withholding of the alms. There are four modes in which alms may be prepared. 1. Adrishta, as when food is prepared without the intention of presenting it to Budha. 2. Uddissakata, as when food is prepared with the express intention of giving it to Budha. 3. Upakkata, as when food is placed before Budha. 4. Paribhóga, as when any article has been presented to Budha, and become his personal possession, whether it be a robe, alms-bowl, or other requisite. When food comes under the head of adrishta, Budha may be prevented from receiving it; but in those things that relate to the other heads, no prevention can be exercised; their reception is certain. Whatever being were in any of these instances to attempt to hinder Budha from receiving that which was intended for him, or to take from him that which he has received, his head would cleave into a hundred or a thousand pieces. There are four privileges that exclusively belong to Budha, viz.,

VIII. DIGNITY, VIRTUES, AND POWERS OF BUDHA. 397

No one can take from him the food that has been set before him, or prepared for him, nor any of his personal possessions; no one can prevent the shining of the rays that proceed from his body; no one can prevent the exercise of the power he possesses of knowing any matter with which he wishes to be acquainted; and no one can take his life. Mára was in the brahman village in disguise; but as the thief when detected is cut into a thousand pieces, or the adulteress impaled, so will Mára suffer for his opposition to Budha; and therefore his demerit was not more powerful than the merit of Budha.

It is said that when Budha walked abroad, though the earth does not possess a mind (achétaná), the low places in his path became elevated, and the high places plain. Nevertheless, on one occasion the fragment of a stone struck the foot of the great teacher. These declarations appeared to Milinda not to coincide; but Nágaséna informed him that the fragment did not strike the foot of Budha from any inherent or natural cause. A large stone was aimed at his head by Déwadatta; but through the merit of the sage two large rocks arose from the earth, and at the distance of twenty cubits from Budha met the stone that had been hurled against him, when a small fragment was broken off by the concussion, which on falling struck his foot. Thus, when any liquid, whether it be milk, honey, ghee, or gruel, is taken up by the finger, part of it is lost; as it drops from the end; it does not come to the proper place; or when fine sand is taken in the hand, part of it escapes; or when rice is eaten, part of it falls from the hand as it is conveyed to the mouth; and the breaking off of the fragment of a stone was only like the remnant or part that is wasted and lost, of which no notice is taken. When dust is raised by the wind, it falls here or there as it may happen, and the withered leaf when it falls from the tree is in the same manner carried in this direction or in that as the case may be; in the same way, the fragment, when broken from the stone, must fall in some direction, and it fell upon the foot of Budha; the stone was arrested in its course, but the breaking off of the fragment was a casual circumstance, exterior to the main occurrence.

It might be said that if Budha was all-wise, he would not have been moved to forgive Seriyut and Mugalan, when the priests who accompanied them made a noise near the wihára in which the sage resided, at the intercession of the Sákya princes and Maha Brahma. But the wife gratifies her husband by displaying before him his own treasures, and even the barber pleases the king when he dresses and combs his hair; in like manner, the princes gained forgiveness for the priests by repeating to Budha what he already knew.

The king of Ságal one day said to Nágaséna, "Did you ever see Budha?" and the priest replied that he had not. Milinda: "Did your preceptor ever see him?" Nágaséna: "No." Milinda: "Then there is no Budha." Nágaséna: "Did you ever see the Uhá river, in the forest of Himála?" Milinda: "No." Nágaséna: "Did your father ever see it?" Milinda: "No." Nágaséna: "Then there is no Uhá river." Milinda: "Though neither I nor my father ever saw it, still there is such a river." Nágaséna: "So also, though neither I nor my teacher ever saw Budha, there is such a being." Again, the king enquired how Nágaséna knew that Budha, whom he had not seen, was supreme; and the priest replied that he knew it in the same way as persons who have never seen the sea know that it is broad and boundless, and receives the waters of the five great rivers. The priest said also, "There was formerly in this city of Ságal a learned preceptor called Tissa; though he has been dead many years, we know that such a person existed by the writings he has left; in like manner, any one who reads the discourses of Budha now extant, may learn therefrom that he is supreme."

The king, on another occasion, said to Nágaséna, "Did Budha know all things? Did he see all things?" Nágaséna: "Yes." Milinda: "Then why did he forbid things after they had been done by his disciples; would there have been any harm in forbidding them previously?" Nágaséna: "There is in this your city a wise physician; he is acquainted with the properties of all kinds of medicine; does he administer the medicine previous to the disease, or after?" Milinda: "After its appearance." Nágaséna: "Even so, though Budha knew all things; he did not forbid that which was done by his disciples previous to the performance of the act, but after it was accomplished."

Another objection was brought by Milinda against the perfection of wisdom claimed by Budha, in this form: "It was declared by Budha that he perfectly understood all that he taught or enjoined, and that he enjoined nothing whatever that he did not thus understand; and yet at another time he gave the priests permission, if so disposed, to omit attending to some of the ordinances he had enjoined; now they must at first have been propounded in ignorance, or without an adequate cause." Nágaséna replied, "This was done merely that he might try the priests. Thus, the chakrawartti addresses the prince who is to be his successor, and says, Son you will have to reign over the whole of the people of Jambudwípa; the cares of state are many; it will therefore be better for you to take no notice of the more barbarous nations. But the prince, from his love of power, pays no attention to this advice. In like manner, though Budha gave permission to his priests to omit attending to some of his ordinances, he knew that they would not do so, from their love to the dharmma, and their wish to be relieved from the evils of existence."

The ordination of Déwadatta by Budha was commented on by the king of Ságal, who said to Nágaséna, "If Budha knew, when he ordained Déwadatta, that he would cause a division of the priesthood and have to suffer during a whole kalpa the punishment of hell, it cannot be true that he loves all sentient beings, pities them, and turns away the misfortunes that threaten them; or if he did not know that he could commit the crime, he is not all-wise, and the declaration that he knows all things is false; if he is all-merciful he is not all-wise; if he is all-wise, he is not all-merciful." Nágaséna: "Budha is all-merciful, and yet he is all-wise, though he ordained Déwadatta, and thus gave him the power to commit the sin for which he must suffer during a whole kalpa in hell. The apparent contradiction is thus explained. Budha saw that on account of the sins committed in former births, Déwadatta was doomed to pass from hell to hell, during many lacs of kelas of years, so that his punishment would be almost endless; but he also saw that if he were ordained, though he would cause a division of the priesthood and thus have to suffer during a whole kalpa in hell, yet that the merit he would gain thereby would set aside the severer punishment, and cut it off, so that it would not have to be endured. Thus, if he had not been ordained, his punishment would have been immensely greater than that which he has now to suffer; and it was from seeing this that Budha ordained him. Therefore Budha may be all-merciful, and yet all-wise." Milinda: "Then Budha's mercy is on this wise; he punishes a man, and then anoints his body with sesamum oil; he casts him down, and then raises him up; he takes his life, and then causes him again to live; see, what mercy! When he would favour any one, he first causes him sorrow, and the consolation comes afterwards." Nágaséna: "When Budha punishes any one, or casts him down, or takes his life, it is that he may be benefited thereby; for the same reason that a father chastises his child. Budha ordained Déwadatta, because he saw that thereby a great degree of suffering would be prevented. As when a noble who is in favour at court sees that a relative or friend is about to suffer some severe punishment, he pleads for him with the king, and mitigates the sentence, or obtains forgiveness; so Budha interfered to arrest the punishment that awaited Déwadatta. It was like the act of a skilful physician, who cures a disease by the application of a powerful medicine. When he sees a putrid and offensive sore, he cleanses it, cuts it open with a sharp instrument, and cauterises it; but will any one say that he does all this wantonly, or that he does wrong? When a man, carelessly walking along the road, runs a thorn into his foot, and another who follows him sees his misfortune, and with another thorn, or some instrument, extracts the thorn that has caused pain, does he do this wantonly, or from a cruel disposition? Is it not rather in mercy, that a greater evil may be prevented? It was for the same reason, and with the same intention, that Budha ordained Déwadatta." When the king heard this explanation, he acknowledged that his doubts were removed.

The king of Ságal repeated the question that he had asked on a previous occasion respecting the wisdom of Budha, and again enquired, "Does Budha know all things?" Nágaséna replied, "Yes; he knows all things, but the power that he possesses is not at all times exercised; this power is attached to thought, or there must be the exercise of thought in order to discover that which he wishes to know; what he wishes to know he discovers in a moment by the exercise of thought." Milinda: "Then if Budha must seek before he can find; if that which he sees has to be discovered by searching, he is not all-wise."

Nágaséna: "The power of thought in Budha is exceedingly quick and subtle. I will explain to you how it is, but I can only do it in a very inadequate manner. Thus, in one gela, or load of rice, there are 63,660,000 grains; each of these grains can be separately considered by Budha in a moment of time. In that moment the seven-times gifted mind exercises this power." (*Milinda Prasna.*)

IX. THE ONTOLOGY OF BUDHISM.

I. THE ELEMENTS OF EXISTENCE.—II. THE ORGANIZED BODY.—III. SENSATION.—IV. PERCEPTION.—V. DISCRIMINATION.—VI. CONSCIOUSNESS.—VII. IDENTITY; INDIVIDUALITY; AND MORAL RETRIBUTION.—VIII. REPRODUCTION.—IX. KARMA.

WE have now done with the ancient legend, and its supernatural accompaniments. We have to enter into another region, and commence a course of observation that in its character will differ widely from that which we have hitherto pursued. We have, for a time, to shut out from our vision the various orders of existence that have flitted before us in bewildering profusion, and to chain down our attention to a silent contemplation of the elements of our own being. We are still in a world of mystery; but this arises as much from the difficulty of the subject, as from the manner of its illustration.

Before we commence our task, it will be well to ascertain the object, or motive, of our investigation. We should have supposed, from what we have already seen, that the teachings of Budha were of too practical a nature to allow of much attention being paid to so abstract, and apparently unprofitable, a subject, as the one now before us. But it is not from a vain curiosity, or to discover new objects of admiration, or to enlarge the domain of science, we are to continue our researches. It is to find out the highest illustration of the great principle, that all being, every possible mode of existence, partakes of "impermanency, misery, and unreality." The Spartan prayer was, "Give us what is good and what is beautiful;" and Coleridge says, "Poetry has given me the habit of wishing to discover the good and the beautiful in all that meets and surrounds me;" but the Budhist seeks to realise the truth of a more ancient axiom, "All is vanity and vexation." The essential properties of existence are enumerated, in order to convince us that there is no self, or soul. We are to contemplate the unreality of our being, that we may learn to despise it, and place ourselves in such a position that we may live above its agitations and secure its cessation.

The elements of sentient existence are called khandas, of which there are five constituents; literally, five sections, or heaps (1). 1. The organized body (2), or the whole of being, apart from the mental processes. 2. Sensation (3). 3. Perception (4). 4. Discrimination (5). 5. Consciousness (6).

In the Brahma Jála Sútra (Rev. D. J. Gogerly, Ceylon Friend, Sept. 1838), we have an account of sixty-two heterodox sects, which enumeration is said to include "all the different modes of belief that were then in existence or could exist." They are divided into two great sections.

1. Those who reason on the past, containing eighteen classes. 1—4. Those who hold the eternity of existence, which arises from their having a recollection of former births, or from induction. 5—8. Those who hold that some beings are eternal and some mutable. 9—12. Those who affirm that the world is finite, or that it is infinite, or infinite laterally but not perpendicularly, or that it cannot be predicated as either finite or infinite. 13. Those who doubt, or equivocate, from various causes. 14—18. Those who suppose that they and the world are uncaused, from their having previously existed in the brahma world in which there is no consciousness.

2. Those who reason as to the future, containing forty-four classes. 1—16. Those who hold a future state of conscious existence, and that it is either material, immaterial, a mixed state, or neither material or immaterial: that it is either finite, indefinitely extended, a mixture of both states, or neither the one nor the other; or that its perceptions are either simple, discursive, limited, unlimited, happy, miserable, mixed, or insensible. 17—24. Those who hold a future

state of unconscious existence. 25—32. Those who hold a state between consciousness and unconsciousness. 33—39. Those who hold that death, at once, or ultimately, is annihilation. 40—44. Those who reason on the mode in which perfect happiness is to be obtained.

According to Gótama, the pure unmixed truth is not to be found anywhere but in his own bana. To other teachers the truth may appear partially; but to him alone does it appear in unshrouded clearness and in its utmost amplitude. In him it is not an acquisition, gained by means of some mental process, nor is it a lesson taught by another. It is an intuitive underived power; a self-generated effulgence. By this unerring sage it is declared, that none of the sixty-two opinions above enumerated are consistent with the truth; so that, according to him, there is no state of future existence, either conscious or unconscious, material or immaterial, miserable or happy. And yet death is not annihilation. We exist, and we do not exist. We die, and we do not die. These appear to be contradictions; but we shall afterwards learn that the seeming discrepancy arises from the complexity of the system. There will be a future state of existence, but not of the individuality that now exists; and though death is the dissolution of that which now exists, it is not the annihilation of a potentiality inherent in that existence.

It is evident that the four last of the khandas are results, or properties, of the first; and if there be anything equivalent to that which we call the soul, it must be found under the first class. Now there are twenty-eight members of the organized body, but among them no single entity is presented that we can regard as the primary and essential principle to which all the other parts are accessories. It is the office of life, or vitality, to keep together, or preserve, the constituents of the organized body; and here its office appears to cease. We are told that it is a wind, or air, that imparts the power by which the hand or foot, or any other member is moved; but it is said again that the principal cause of muscular action is the hita, or mind. When we search further, to find out what the mind is, we are still left in uncertainty as to its real nature. There are mental operations presented, of various classes, but we can find no instrumentality by which these processes are conducted. The second khanda, sensation, is the result of contact, and cannot exist without it. The third, perception, and the fourth, discrimination, are equally derived or dependent; they commence and cease simultaneously with contact. And of the fifth, consciousness, it is expressly stated it can only exist contemporaneously with the organized body. On some occasions, mind is represented as being merely a result, produced by the impinging of thought upon the heart, as sight is produced by the contact of the eye with the outward form, or of the ear with sound. At death, or consequent upon it in the course of time, there is a dissolution, a " breaking up" as it is called, an entire evanishment of the whole of the khandas, and of every part of them. The elements, that whilst in juxta-position, formed what we, in our ignorance, call a sentient being, no longer produce the same effect, as their relation to each other has ceased. Nor is it from want of precision in the language, or defect in the enumeration, that we are led to form these conclusions; as it is expressly stated to be a heterodox idea that represents the soul as "flying happily away, like a bird from its cage." At another time we are informed by Gótama that none of the khandas taken separately are the self, and that taken conjointly they are not the self. There is no such thing as a soul, the home of a self, apart from the five khandas. There can therefore, according to Budhism, be no such process as a transmigration, in the usual sense of the term, and I have not used it in any of my illustrations.

The eastern mind has suffered much from its fondness for analogy and metaphor. With the native authors the inconclusiveness of an argument is overlooked if it be supported by a striking figure. By this means, they set aside the existence of the man (7). It is asked, What is a chariot? Are the wheels (each part of the chariot being separately named) the chariot? It is evident that they are not. Then, most conclusively, there is no chariot. The chariot is a mere name. In like manner, it is asked, What is a man? Are the eyes (each member of the body being separately named) the man? It is evident that neither the eyes, the feet, the heart, nor any separately-named member of the body is the man. Therefore, most conclusively, there is no man. The man is a mere name. But they forget that whilst between the wheel and the axletree there is no connection but that of position, subjectively, and of name, objectively, there is a mysterious communion between one member of the body and another, so that "if one member suffer, all the members suffer with it; or one member be honoured, all the members rejoice with it." Even upon their own system the comparison fails, as they acknowledge a nexus of vitality in what we call the man, to which there is nothing analogous in the chariot.

A formula has been propounded by Gótama, called the paticha samuppáda, or the causes of continued existence. Like the successive footsteps of the bullock when drawing the wagon or the plough; or like the repeated undulations of a wave, one flowing into the other; a process is continuously in operation, in which there is the recurrence of certain educts, in uniform regularity of sequence. "On account of ignorance," said Budha, in one of the Discourses that appear in the Sanyutta, as translated by the Rev. D. J. Gogerly (Ceylon Friend, April, 1839), "merit and demerit are produced; on account of merit and demerit, consciousness; on account of consciousness, body and mind; on account of body and mind, the six organs of sense; on account of the six organs of sense, touch (or contact); on account of contact, desire; on account of desire, sensation (of pleasure or pain); on account of sensation, cleaving (or clinging to existing objects); on account of clinging to existing objects, renewed existence (or reproduction after death); on account of reproduction of existence, birth; on account of birth, decay, death, sorrow, crying, pain, disgust, and passionate discontent. Thus is produced the complete body of sorrow. From the complete separation from, and cessation of ignorance, is the cessation of merit and demerit; from the cessation of merit and demerit is the cessation of consciousness; from the cessation of consciousness is the cessation of (the existence of) body and mind; from the cessation of (the existence of) body and mind is the cessation of (the production of) the six organs; from the cessation of (the production of) the six organs is the cessation of touch; from the cessation of touch is the cessation of desire; from the cessation of desire is the cessation of (pleasurable or painful) sensation; from the cessation of sensation is the cessation of the cleaving to existing objects; from the cessation of cleaving to existing objects is the cessation of a reproduction of existence; from a cessation of a reproduction of existence is the cessation of birth; from a cessation of birth is the cessation of decay. Thus, this whole body of sorrow ceases to exist." There are three terms in this series that will require further explanation: 1. Ignorance. 2. The cleaving to existing objects. 3. Merit and demerit.

1. The first term in this circle of generation is ignorance, awidya. It is an abstract quality producing another abstract quality, merit and demerit, karma; which karma produces a third abstraction, consciousness; and this consciousness is endowed with physical power, and produces body and mind, in which is included all the particulars that in their aggregation form what is called a sentient being. We have no information as to the origin of awidya. How did it first arise? To what was it then attached? These are questions to which we have no answer, as no one but a Budha can tell how karma operates, or how the chain of existence commenced. It is as vain to ask in what part of the tree the fruit exists before the blossom is put forth, as to ask for the locality of karma. We can learn how error is produced in a being already existent; but we are not taught, in any work I have seen, how the primary karma, the first link (not in the circle,

but in the series of circles) was produced. We are told that each circle comes from a previous circle; as any given flame comes from a previous flame; or any given tree comes from a previous tree; or any given egg comes from a previous egg; but, as in all similar arguments, the declaration is unsatisfactory. It only carries back the process to a more distant period. We want to know whence came the first egg, or tree, or flame, or circle. We cannot think of a second, or of any number in a series, however extended, that is not dependent on a first. The brahmanical account of the origin of awidya is more intelligible, though not more satisfactory. "Whilst Brahmá formerly, in the beginning of the kalpa, was meditating on creation, there appeared a creation beginning with ignorance, and consisting of darkness. From that great being appeared fivefold ignorance, consisting of obscurity, illusion, extreme illusion, gloom, and utter darkness. The creation of the creator thus plunged in abstraction, was the fivefold (immovable) world, without intellect or reflection, void of perception or sensation, incapable of feeling, and destitute of motion. Since immovable things were first created, this is called the first creation."—Wilson's Vishnu Puŕana. But as this was an imperfect creation, it was succeeded by eight others, each more perfect than the preceding act. According to this theory, awidya is the primary operation of the divine energy. Nearly all the ancient cosmogonies commenced in a similar manner, which is only a poetical mode of confessing ignorance of the Great First Cause, by changing the subjective into the objective. In the Orphic fragments, Night is called "the source of all things." With this agrees the well-known passage in Hesiod's Theogony:—
"First of all was Chaos. Afterwards arose the wide-bosomed Earth, the firm resting-place of all things; and gloomy Tartara in the depth of the earth; and Eros, the fairest of the immortal gods." The world was called by Democritus, "an egg of the night." From the worship of the mus araneus by the Egyptians, we may learn that amidst the gloom of their solemn temples a similar idea was entertained. There

is this difference between the east and west, that whilst the Greeks personified what are called the powers of nature, the Hindus give to them intelligence and efficiency, without personification.

2. The cleaving to existing objects is upádána. There are two properties inherent in all sentient beings, except the rahats:—first, upádána, and secondly, karma, literally action, the aggregate result of all previous acts, in unbroken succession, from the commencement of existence, in the births innumerable that have been received in past ages. At death, the five khandas are dissolved. As they no longer exist in combination, they can maintain no reciprocity of influence; their mutuality of operation has ceased for ever. But the upádána still exists, and the karma lives on. The cleaving to existing objects, or the breaking up of the khandas, by some unexplained instrumentality, produces another being. The upádána cannot but exert its power; another being must necessarily be produced. It is as impossible, under ordinary circumstances, to separate reproduction from upádána, as it would be to separate heat from fire or solidity from the rock; the one follows as naturally as the other, and all are equally mysterious in the manner of their operation. As it is the grand tenet of Budhism, that all existence is an evil, it thus becomes consistent with right reason to seek the destruction of upádána, which alone can secure the reception of nirwána, or the cessation of being.

3. By upádána a new existence is produced, but the manner of its operation is controlled by the karma with which it is connected. It would sometimes appear that upádána is the efficient cause of reproduction, and at other times that it is karma. But in all instances it is the karma that appoints whether the being to be produced shall be an insect in the sunbeam, a worm in the earth, a fish in the sea, a fowl in the air, a beast in the forest, a man, a restless demon, or a déwa or brahma of the celestial world. The renewed existence may be in any world of any sakwala; it may be in any species of being; and in that species it may be of any grade.

Thus, if the existence be as a man, it is the karma that appoints whether it shall be as a male or female, as a monarch or as an outcaste, as beautiful or ugly, or happy or miserable. The karma is itself controlled by its own essential character. If it be good, it must necessarily appoint the being that will be produced to a state of happiness and privilege; but if it be evil, it must as necessarily appoint the being to a state of misery and degradation. In the act of reproduction, karma can work without the aid of a material instrumentality, as some beings in this world, and all in the déwa-lókas, are produced by what is called the apparitional birth (8).

It is difficult to speak with technical precision on Budhistical subjects, in another language, unless great circumlocution be used. We have to alter the meaning of words, if we would rightly understand the system. We may notice, for instance, the personal pronoun . . . I. With the Budhist, this is a non-entity. And it is not because he is a nominalist rather than a realist. He knows all that constitutes what is regarded as a sentient being. He can enumerate all the parts that enter into its composition. But he denies that there exists anything equivalent to that which, in other systems, is called the soul. It is true that the five khandas exist. There is no delusion as to them. But when we assert the existence of any element or essence in addition, we deceive ourselves; it is not a reality. Uttering the sentiments of Budhism, rather than adopting its language, I may regard myself as a sentient being, now existent in the world of men. But I have existed, in a similar manner, in many myriads of previous births, and may have passed through all possible states of being, from the highest to the lowest, and have been in some of them repeatedly. I am now under the influence of all that I have ever done, in all these ages. This is my karma, the arbiter of my destiny. Until I attain nirwána, I must still continue to exist; but the states of being into which I shall pass, as duration rolls on, I cannot tell. The future is enshrouded in impenetrable darkness.

This wonder-working karma is a mere abstraction. It is

declared to be achinteyya, without a mind. In this respect, it is allied to the earth. The earth, naturally, enables the seed to germinate, and produces plants and lofty trees; and in the same manner, karma, naturally, produces a new existence, in conjunction with upádána. Neither the earth nor the seed, neither the karma nor the upádána, possesses a mind. Yet the way of karma is intricate and involved. No sentient being can tell in what state the karma that he possesses will appoint his next birth; though he may be now, and continue to be until death, one of the most meritorious of men. In that karma there may be the crime of murder, committed many ages ago, but not yet expiated; and in the next existence its punishment may have to be endured. There will ultimately be a reward for that which is good; but it may be long delayed. It acts like an hereditary disease; its evil may be latent through many generations, and then break out in uncontrollable violence. The Budhist must therefore, of necessity, die "without hope." It is by the aggregate karma of the various orders of living being that the present worlds were brought into existence, and that their general economy is controlled. But it is difficult to reconcile the unerring rectitude of karma with the recurrence of events in uniform cycles and with the similarity of all the systems of worlds; unless it control, absolutely, the will of sentient being, in which case it is no longer a moral government, but necessity or fate (9).

It will have been observed, that if there be a dissolution of all the elements of existence at death, and there is no hereafter, no future world, to that existence, there is then no moral responsibility. To set aside this conclusion, there are many arguments presented in the native works, particularly in the one from which I have so often quoted, Milinda Prasna. Thus, a man plants a mango, and that fruit produces a tree, which tree belongs to the man though that which he planted was not a tree but a fruit. A man betroths a girl, who, when she has grown into a woman, is claimed by the man, though that which he betrothed was not a woman but a girl. A man sets fire to the village, and is punished for it, though it was not he who burnt the village but the fire. The tree came by means of the fruit; the woman came by means of the girl; and the fire came by means of the man; and this " by means of," in all the cases, is the only nexus between the parties, whether it be the fruit and the man, the girl and the woman, or the fire and he who kindled it. In like manner, when the elements of existence are dissolved, as another being comes into existence by means of the karma of that existence, inheriting all its responsibilities, there is still no escape from the consequences of sin. To this we might reply, that by this process the crime is punished; but it is in another person; and the agent of that crime is less connected with that person than the father is with the child. The parent may see the child, and know him; but the criminal has no knowledge whatever of the being who is punished in his stead, nor has that being any knowledge whatever of the criminal. We shall be told that this process is not inconsistent with the other speculations of the Budhists on identity, who teach that the flame is as much the same flame when transferred to another wick, as the flame of one moment is the flame of a previous moment when proceeding from the same wick; in both cases, one is the consequence of the other. But the moral objections to the doctrine still remain in full force.

The difficulties attendant upon this peculiar dogma may be seen in the fact that it is almost universally repudiated. Even the sramana priests, at one time, denied it; but when the passages teaching it were pointed out to them in their own sacred books, they were obliged to acknowledge that it is a tenet of their religion. Yet in historical composition, in narrative, and in conversation, the common idea of transmigration is continually presented. We meet with innumerable passages like the following:—"These four, by the help of Budha, went (after death) to a celestial world." At the end of the Apannaka Játaka, Budha himself says, " The former unwise merchant and his company are the present Déwadatta and his disciples, and I was then the wise merchant." The whole of the Játakas conclude with a similar declaration.

These speculations are peculiar to Budhism; and although they produce contrivance without a contriver, and design without a designer, they are as rational, in this respect, as any other system that denies the agency of a self-existent and ever-living God. The origin of the world has been attributed to nature, order, symmetry, number, arrangement, association, harmony, irritability, love, attraction, fortuity, infinite intelligence, a plastic energy, a seminal principle, creative power, an emanation from the supreme spirit, eternal necessity, material necessity, mechanical necessity, the force of circumstances, an operative fire, a generative water, a vital air, an unfathomable depth, &c. With none of these systems has Budhism any agreement. Nor do I know of any modern theory that resembles it, unless it be that of Johan Gottlieb Fichte, who taught that "the arrangement of moral sentiments and relations, that is, the moral order of the universe is God." Among men who ought to have been wiser, we have many instances of a similar want of definiteness, in their ideas of creative power; as when Kepler thought that "comets arise as a herb springs from the earth without seed, and as fishes are formed in the sea by a generatio spontanea;" with whom we may class the philosophers who taught that petrified shells have been formed "by the tumultuous movements of terrestrial exhalations," and all who held the doctrine of equivocal generation. As to the supreme controlling power, apart from the creative, there has been equal uncertainty of opinion. The Greeks worshipped Zeus as the ruler who "according to his own choice assigned their good or evil lot to mortals;" but more potent than "the most high and powerful among the gods" were the inflexible Moirae, and the dreaded Erinnyes were equally unrestrained by his decrees.

Inasmuch as Budhism declares karma to be the supreme controlling power of the universe, it is an atheistic system. It ignores the existence of an intelligent and personal Deity.

It acknowledges that there is a moral government of the world; but it honours the statute-book instead of the lawgiver, and adores the sceptre instead of the king.

I have dwelt longer upon these topics than has been my usual custom, from the abstruseness of the subject and the novelty in the mode of its development.

---

1. *The Elements of Existence.*

All being exists from some cause; but the cause of being cannot be discovered.

It is declared by Budha that the essential properties of being are five, called the five khandas, viz. 1. Rúpan, the organized body. 2. Wédaná, sensation. 3. Sannyá, perception. 4. Sankháro, discrimination. 5. Winyána, consciousness.*

2. *The Organized Body.*

The Rúpakkhando are twenty-eight in number, viz.: 1. Pathawi-dhátu, earth. 2. Apó-dhátu, water. 3. Téjo-dhátu, fire. 4. Wáyo-dhátu, wind. 5. Chakkhun, the eye. 6. Sótan, the ear. 7. Ghánan, the nose. 8. Jiwhá, the tongue. 9. Káyan, the body. 10. Rúpan, the outward form. 11. Saddan, the sound. 12. Gandhan, the smell. 13. Rasan, the flavour. 14. Pottabban, the substance, or whatever is sensible to the touch. 15. Itthattan, the womanhood. 16. Purisattan, the manhood. 17. Hadayawatthun, the heart. 18. Jíwitindriyan, vitality. 19. Akása-dhátu, space. 20. Káya-winnyatti, the power of giving, or receiving information, by gestures or signs. 21. Wachí-winnyatti, the faculty of speech. 22. Lahutá, the property of lightness, or buoyancy. 23. Mudutá, softness, or elasticity. 24. Kammannyatá, adaptation. 25. Upachayan, aggregation. 26. Santati, duration. 27. Jaratá, decay. 28. Anichatá, impermanency.

1. Earth.—The parts of the body that are formed of this element are twenty in number; viz., the hair of the head, the hair

---

* The definitions in this chapter are taken from the Súryódgamana-sútra (a discourse delivered by Gótama, by means of which 500 priests entered the paths); Milinda Prasna: Bála-pandita-sutra (a discourse delivered by Gótama, when resident in the Jétáwana-wihára): Amáwatura; and Wisudhimargga-sanné.

of the body, the nails, the teeth, the skin, the flesh, the veins, the bones, the marrow, the kidneys, the heart, the liver, the abdomen, the spleen, the lungs, the intestines, the lower intestines, the stomach, the feces, and the brain.

2. Water.—The parts of the body that are formed of this element are twelve in number; viz., bile, phlegm, pus, blood, sweat, fat, tears, serum, saliva, mucus, the oil that lubricates the joints, and urine.

3. Fire.—There are four different kinds of fire in the body; viz., the fire that prevents it from putrifying, as salt prevents the corruption of flesh; the fire arising from sorrow, that causes the body to waste away, as if it were burnt; the fire that produces decay and infirmity; and the fire in the stomach that consumes the food.

The absence or diminution of heat is called cold. Some have said that ápo-dhátu is the cause of cold; but this is not correct. For this reason. When any one goes from the sunshine into the shade he feels cold; but if he was to come from the interior of the earth to the same place he would feel warm. Therefore cold does not proceed from ápo-dhátu; and to maintain this would be to say that ápo-dhátu and wáyo-dhátu are the same.

4. Wind.—There are six different kinds of wind in the body; viz., the udwángama wind, that ascends from the two feet to the head, and causes vomiting, hiccough, &c.; the adhógama wind, that descends from the head to the two feet, and expels the feces and urine; áswása and práswása, the inspired and expirated breath; the kukshira wind, that is in the stomach and abdomen, exterior to the intestines; the kotthása wind, that is within the intestines; and the angamangánusári wind, that pervades the whole of the body, being conveyed in vessels like the veins, and imparts the power by which the hand or foot, or any other member, is moved. By these six winds, or airs, the body is prevented from being like a mere log of wood, and is enabled to perform whatever action is required; but though it is said that they are the cause of motion, it must be understood that the principal cause is the hita, or mind. The first five airs are connected with karma, the season, thought, and food; but the last only with the mind.

The element of earth may be distinguished by its smell; water, by its taste; fire, by its light; and wind, by its sound.

Thus one element is perceived by the nose; another by the tongue; another by the eye; and a fourth, by the ear.

The essential property of earth is solidity; of water, fluidity; of fire, heat; and of wind, expansiveness or diffusion.

The body is indurated by the earth of which it is composed, as if it were bitten by a serpent with a dry mouth; by the water it is corrupted, as if it were bitten by a serpent with a putrid mouth; by the fire, it is burnt, as if it were bitten by a serpent with a fiery mouth; and by the wind, it is lacerated, as if it were bitten by a serpent with a weapon-like mouth.

5. The eye. 6. The ear. 7. The nose. 8. The tongue. 9. The body.—These five are called prasáda-rúpas, or organs of sense. 1. The eye, that which receives the impression of colour, whether it be green or yellow. 2. The ear, that which receives the impression of sound, whether it be from the drum, harp, or thunder. 3. The nose, that which receives the impression of smell, whether it be grateful or unpleasant. 4. The tongue, that which receives the impression of taste, whether it be from a solid or liquid. 5. The body, that which receives the impression produced by the touch, or contact, of substance, whether it be of a garment or a living being.

When the karma by means of which these impressions are produced is deficient, or when any of the four principal elements of which the organs are composed, are either absent or too abundant, the office of the eye, ear, &c., cannot be fulfilled; there is no sight; no hearing, &c.

As the nayá, alligator, bird, dog, or jackal, goes to the ant's nest, the water, the sky, the village, or the cemetery, in search of food; so the five senses go out after the various objects that are suited to their particular nature. The eye is like a serpent in an ant-hill; the ear is like an alligator lurking in a hole or cave filled with water; the nose is like a bird flying through the air to catch flies; the tongue, ready for all flavours that are presented to it, is like a dog watching for offal at the door of the kitchen or some part of the village; and the body, gratified by that with which it comes in contact, is like a jackal feeding with delight on a putrid carcase.

10. The outward form. 11. The sound. 12. The smell. 13. The flavour. 14. The substance, or whatever is sensible to the body when in contact with it.—These five are called wisaya-

IX. THE ONTOLOGY OF BUDHISM.

rúpas, or qualities of nourishment. 1. For the nourishing of the eye, or the production of sight, there must be a communication between the eye and the outward form. 2. For the nourishing of the ear, or the production of hearing, there must be a communication between the ear and the sonorous body. 3. For the nourishing of the nose, or the production of smell, there must be a communication between the nose and the object smelled. 4. For the nourishing of the tongue, or the production of taste, there must be a communication between the tongue and the object tasted. 5. For the nourishing of the body, or the production of the feeling that arises from touch, or contact, there must be a communication between the body and some substance, or sensible object; pottabban being the power of feeling, or sensibility; as, when a garment is put on, the body is conscious of a sensation, either comfortable or unpleasant, according to the material of which it is made.

The khandas that are thus connected with some sensible object, and by that object are nourished, are called ábáraja; those that are connected with the mental faculties, and cannot be divided, are called chittaja.

15. The womanhood.
16. The manhood.
17. The heart, the seat of thought. The heart may be said to feel the thought, to bear or support it, and to throw it out or cast it off. It is the cause of mano-winyána, or mind-consciousness.

18. Vitality, the principle of life, the essential of existence. It is produced at the same time as the organized body to which it is attached, by means of karma. It is that which forms the aggregation of the rúpa-khandas, and is the cause of their (temporary) preservation, as water nourishes the lotus, and it is the means by which they exist; it is the medium by which they are sustained, as the infant prince is supported by the milk of his nurse. When the principle of life is extinguished, there is an end of rúpa-khandas, as death ensues.

19. Space.—There are in the body nine apertures, vacuities, or spaces; the orifices of the ears, the nostrils, the mouth, the throat, the orifices whence proceed the feces and the urine, and the stomach and intestines. These are not rúpa-khandas in the strict sense of the term; but as their existence is continuous, and they are essential to the body, they are so called.

20. The power of giving, or receiving, information by signs or gestures.

21. The faculty of speech.

22. The property of lightness, or buoyancy, possessed by the body, which in its character is similar to that of iron which has been heated during a whole day. There is both kaya, corporeal, and chitta, mental, lightness.

23. Softness, or elasticity, a property like that of a skin that has been well anointed or beaten. This property is also both corporeal and mental.

24. Adaptation, a property like that of gold that has been exposed during a whole day to the influence of a strong fire, which enables the body to accommodate itself readily to any work it may have to perform.

25. Aggregation, the result of the continued production of the rúpáyatanas, or organs of sense and their respective objects, like the entrance of water into a well dug near a river.

26. Duration, also the result of the continued production of the rúpáyatanas, like the constant overflowing of the water in the well.

27. Decay, the breaking up, or destruction, of the rúpáyatanas.

28. Impermanency, the liability of the rúpáyatanas to change; their instability.

Of these twenty-eight rúpa-khandas, some are called wastu and some dwára; thus the heart has wastu, substance; but no dwára, aperture, or door, like the eye; and there are some that have neither substance nor aperture, they are invisible. Again, some are called ékaja, as proceeding from one cause, and others dwija, as proceeding from two causes, &c.

3. *Sensation.*

The Wédaná-khando, or sensations, are six in number. They are produced by communication with that which is agreeable, disagreeable, or indifferent. When an agreeable object is seen there is gratification; when a disagreeable object is seen there is aversion; and when an object is seen that is neither pleasant nor unpleasant, neither agreeable nor disagreeable, as the ground, rocks, and similar objects, there is indifference. So also with that which is presented to the ear, tongue, nose, body, or mental faculties; some of the sensations thus produced are pleasant, some unpleasant, and others indifferent.

4. *Perception.*

The Sannyá-khando, or perceptions, are six in number, and are on this wise. When an object is seen, whether it be green or red, there is the perception that it is of that particular colour. So also when any sound is heard, whether it be from the drum or any other instrument, there is the perception that it is such a sound; when there is any smell, whether it be agreeable or disagreeable, there is the perception that it is such a smell; when there is any flavour, whether it be sweet, sour, milky, saline, or oily, there is the perception that it is such a taste; when the body comes in contact with any substance, there is the perception that it is agreeable to the touch or disagreeable; and when the mind considers any matter or subject, and examines it, there is the perception that it is of such a character or kind.

5. *Discrimination.*

The Sankháro-khando, or powers of discrimination (including the moral faculties), are fifty-five in number; viz.:

1. Phassá, touch, the first thought produced in the mind from the touching of the eye by the figure, of the ear by the sound, &c., as when at the dawn of day the first rays of the sun impinge upon a wall.

In answer to the question of the king of Ságal, "What are the signs, or properties of contact? Will you explain them to me by a comparison?" Nágaséna replied, "We will suppose that two rams are fighting with each other; one ram is the eye, the other is the figure, or outward form, and the meeting of their heads is contact. Again, a man claps his hands; one palm is the eye, the other is the outward form, and their meeting together is contact. And again, a man plays upon the cymbals; one cymbal is the eye, the other is the outward form, and their meeting together is contact."

2. Wédaná, sensation, as that of flavour; like the king who eats delicious food.

The property of wédaná is sensation, or experience; it is that which arises from enjoyment, or possession. Thus, a man renders a service to the king; and the king, well-pleased, appoints him to some office, by means of which he is enabled to enjoy the pleasures of the world; he thus reflects, By rendering such and such a service to the king I have been put in possession of these advantages (sepa-wédaná-windimi); in this way he has the sensation of enjoyment. Again, a being obtains merit, and by means of it, after his death he is born in a déwa-lóka; in the midst of his happiness he thus reflects, In former ages I have obtained merit, and by means of it I am now enabled to enjoy the blessings of the déwa-lóka (sepa-wédaná-anubhawakeremi); in this way he has the sensation of enjoyment.

3. Sannyá, perception, as the distinguishing of the different colours, when thinking about them, whether they be blue, golden, red, or white, like the placing of a mark by a carpenter upon timber that he may know how to cut it, or work it in the form he wishes.

4. Chétaná, thought, that which exerts itself more quickly than any other of the fifty-five faculties in all mental exercises, as when a husbandman goes with fifty-four of his friends to plough, or perform any other agricultural operation, he himself works more actively and laboriously than any of the rest. It is one, though it is produced by many different series of karma.

It is by the action of the mind upon the power of reflection that thought is produced. The manner in which it thus acts is called touching, though there is no actual contact. When a man, standing on the ground, sees another man at the top of a high tree, or at the extremity of one of its branches, he feels fear, and his knees smite one against the other; in like manner, the eye does not touch the object of vision, nor the ear the instrument of sound, yet sight and hearing are produced. In none of these instances is there actual contact. The medium by which this communication takes place is, as it were, an act of striking, as when one hand is struck against the other.

This action is unceasing, as when a cow has a sore from the abrading of the skin, she feels continual pain when anything touches it, wherever she may be; so also when the eye, in the manner thus set forth, touches any object, or when any object is seen, there is the production of sensation, either pleasant, or disagreeable, or indifferent. If a mother has to go to some other place whilst her child is left near a deep well, she incessantly fears for its safety; and equally unceasing is the action of the mind; the exertion of the thought is incessant.

The principal faculty connected with chétaná is the mind, hita, producing volition, manákota karana, (which may have an influence upon others, as well as upon the individual in whose mind it is produced). Thus, a man prepares poison, and drinks some of it himself; if he gives to others also to drink, he brings sorrow upon himself, and upon the others who have drunk with him; so also, a man resolves on the taking of life, and for this crime he is born in hell, and if he persuades others also to commit the same crime, they will receive the same punishment. Again, the man mixes together ghee, butter, sugar, curd, and other kinds of savoury ingredients, and drinks the compound, by which he is nourished and made strong; and if he gives of it to others also, and they drink it, they too are nourished; so also, a man resolves upon acquiring merit, and from the good acts that he performs, he is born in one of the déwa-lókas; and if he persuades others to perform the same acts, they too receive the same reward.

The king of Ságal said to Nágaséna, "How can we now have thought of, or remember, that which happened at some former time?" Nágaséna: "Thought comes from the memory, sihiya." Milinda: "How can that be? thought, chétaná, comes from the mind, chitta, and not from the memory, sihiya." Nágaséna: "Do you ever forget that which you have once known?" Milinda: "Yes." Nágaséna: "Then at the time when the thought passes away, does the mind pass away too; or, when you are without thought are you also without mind?" Milinda: "It is not the mind that passes away, but the thought." Nágaséna: "Then how is it you say that when the remembrance of that which has happened in some former period has passed away, this remembrance comes again from the mind, and not from the thought?" The king, upon hearing this question, acknowledged that he was overcome.

Again, the king said to Nágaséna, "Does all thought come from the memory, or is it also imparted by others?" Nágaséna: "It is received in both ways; it comes from the memory, and is imparted by others; if there were no imparted thought, the office of the teacher would be assumed without any result; the scholar would be unable to learn. Thought is produced in sixteen different ways:—1. From reflection; Ananda, the upásaka Khujjutara, and many others, were enabled by this means to know what happened to them in former ages; not in this birth alone but in previous births. 2. From the instruction of others; a man forgets something that he has once known, and his neighbours say, What, do you not remember such or such a thing? and by this means the thought is again received. 3. From consciousness; a man is anointed king, or he enters the paths, after which he is conscious of what has taken place. 4. From satisfaction; a man has something that he enjoys, and he afterwards remembers that in such a place he received enjoyment or satisfaction. 5. From aversion; a man meets with something that causes sorrow, and he afterwards remembers that in such a place he received sorrow, by which aversion is produced. 6. From similarity, or resemblance; a man sees another human being, and it reminds him of his father, or his mother, or his brother, or some other relative; he sees a camel, or a bull, or an ass, and it reminds him of other camels, bulls, and asses. 7. From separation, or analysis; a man sees some one, and he thinks that his name is so and so; and that his voice, smell, taste, touch, &c., are so and so. 8. From conversation; a man entirely forgets some matter, but by conversing with others he is reminded of it again. 9. From signs; a man sees the signs or attributes of a bull, by which he knows that it is a bull, or he is reminded of a bull. 10. From assistance; a man forgets something, but another person tells him to try and think about it, and he then remembers. 10. From impressions; a man sees a certain letter in any writing, from which he knows what letters are to come next. 11. From numbers, or computation; an arithmetician sees a number, by which he is led to calculate other numbers, or is reminded of them. 12. From instruction; a man is instructed by others concerning that of which he is ignorant. 13. From meditation (bháwaná); a priest meditates on some former birth, whether it be one, ten, a hundred, or a thousand, previous to the present birth. 14. From books; a monarch wishes to know what has occurred in former times in his kingdom; he therefore sends for the chronicles that were then written, and by reading them he learns it. 15. From proximity; a king sees a vessel that is placed near him, by which he is reminded of some other vessel. 16. From experience, or habit; when a man sees anything, he thinks of its shape; when he hears anything, of its sound; when he smells anything, of its odour; when he tastes anything, of its flavour, when he touches anything, of how it feels; when he is conscious of anything, he reflects on it; and thus thought is produced."

5. Manaskára, reflection, that which exercises the thought, turns it over and over, as a charioteer exercises a high-bred horse.

6. Jíwiténdriya, that which is the principle of life, sustaining the co-existent incorporeal faculties, arúpa dharmma, as water sustains the lotus.

7. Chittakágratáwa, individuality, that which is the centre of the phassá, and other faculties of discrimination, uniting them together, and causing them to be one, as when a king, surrounded by a numerous army, goes to war, he alone is the ruler and guide of the whole host.

8. Witarka, attention, consideration, or impulse towards an object; that faculty of the mind which is first exercised when thought arises, as the blow that first strikes the bell. It is said in the tikáwa to be the power by which thoughts arise in the mind. There are ten winyánas, and there is wíraya, that may arise in the mind without the intervention of witarka, on coming in contact, or being associated with certain objects, some through meditation, bháwaná, and some through habit.*

"The property of witarka," said Nágaséna, "is that of fixing or establishing. Thus, a carpenter takes a piece of wood, prepares it, and puts it in its proper place."

9. Wichára, investigation, examination, continued impulse or tendency, that which prolongs the witarka that has arisen in the mind, as the sound that continues to proceed from the bell.†

"The property of wichára," said Nágaséna, "is that of investigation. Thus, when a gong is struck by a mallet, it gives forth sound; the stroke is witarka, and the sound is wichára."

Witarka is an enemy to thína and mijja, or sleep and drowsi-

---

* Witarka: reasoning, discussion; doubt, deliberation; consideration of probabilities, mental anticipation of alternatives, conjecture; from the root wi, implying discrimination, and tarka, to reason, or doubt.—Wilson's Sanskrit Dictionary.

† Wichára: the exercise of judgment, or reason, on a present object, investigation, consideration, deliberation; dispute, discussion.—Ibid.

ness; wichára is an enemy to wichikicháwa, or doubt. Witarka precedes wichára; it is that which causes the rising of the aramunu, thoughts that proceed from contact with sensible objects, in the mind: wichára is that which lays hold upon these thoughts and examines them. Witarka is the first movement or trembling of the thought; it is like the bird that is spreading out its wings in order that it may rise into the air, or the bee as it flutters near the flower when about to enter its bell: wichára is like the bird pursuing its course through the air, or the bee walking over the petals of the flower and collecting pollen. Witarka is like the moving of the golden eagle through the air, when the movement of its wings cannot be perceived; wichára is like the struggles of the smaller eagle to lay hold on the air that it may preserve its elevation. The first is like a man who holds a vessel made of any kind of metal in his hand; the second is like one who holds in his hand the cloth made of goat's hair, and anointed with oil, for the purpose of shampooing the body. The one is like the clay held in the hand by the potter, ready to be turned upon the wheel and made up into some kind of vessel; the other is like the kneading of the clay that it may be brought to the proper consistency or shape. Witarka is like the leg of a pair of compasses that is at rest in the centre of the circle; wichára is like the leg that traverses the circumference. In this way witarka and wichára are connected with each other, as the flower and the fruit of the tree.

10. Wíraya, or wírya, persevering exertion, effort, resolution, courage, or determination; that which prompts to all kinds of exertion, like the powerful man who shrinks at nothing. Its opposite is kusíta, indolence. All the other faculties are assisted by its exercise. The sceptical tirttakas possess it, but it only leads them to more certain destruction.

The property of wíraya is to afford support, as by a prop; it prevents the downfall or destruction of merit. When a house leans to one side a prop is placed against it that it may not fall; in like manner, this principle is, as it were, a prop to prevent the downfall of merit. When a king, with a large army, engages another king, with a small army, he overcomes by the superiority in the number of his men; and as the victorious king is thus assisted by his army, so is the man who seeks nirwána assisted by this principle. The same truths have been declared by Budha :—" By wíraya, the sráwaka disciple keeps at a distance all akusala, or demerit, and is enabled to practise all kusala, or merit; keeps at a distance that which is evil, and receives into the mind, and continually increases, that which is pure or good; thus he possesses a mind which is free from all evil desire."

There were three novices who came to the priest Tissa. The first said that he would do whatever was required of him, even though it should be to jump into a pit as deep as one hundred men placed one upon the other. The second said that he would do it, though his body in the effort should be worn away, as by the trituration of a stone. And the third said he would do it so long as he had breath. The priest, seeing the strength of their resolution, assisted them to obtain the object they had in view, which was to acquire a knowledge of the essentialities of abstract meditation.

11. Prítiya, joy, that which causes gladness, as when a man travelling through the desert, in the hot season, and overcome by thirst, sees a pond in which the five kinds of water lilies are growing. It is the opposite of wyápáda, the wish to injure another. It is accompanied by sepa, satisfaction or enjoyment; where there is the one, there is always the other. Prítiya is like the finding of the water, whilst the drinking of it is sepa.

There is pharana-prítiya, which like wind in an instrument, or water in a cave, pervades every part of the being by whom it is possessed; it is sometimes so powerful as to cause the hair of the body to become erect.

There is a second kind of prítiya that is again and again repeated, with intervals between, like the flashes of the lightning; and a third that is no sooner present than it is gone, like the waves of the sea that expend themselves, and lose their existence, by rolling upon the shore.

There is also udwéga-prítiya. The priest Maha Tissa resided at the wihára of Panágal. It was his custom to worship at the dágoba, and on a certain festival he looked towards the place where the principal relics were deposited, thinking thus within himself, " In former periods many priests and religious persons assembled here that they might worship;" and as he was in the act of making this reflection, he received the power of udwéga-prítiya, by which he was enabled to rise into the air, and go to the sacred place.

Near the Girikanda wihára was a village called Wattakála, in which resided a respectable woman who was a devotee, upásikáwa. One evening, when her parents were about to go to the wihára to hear bana, they said to her, "On account of your present situation it will not be proper for you to accompany us to the wihára; we will go alone, and hear bana, and whatever benefit we receive we will impart to you." She was exceedingly desirous to hear bana, but as she could not disobey her parents she remained at home. The wihára could be seen from the court-yard of her house; so from that place she looked towards it; and seeing the lights of the festival and the people in the act of worship, whilst at the same time she could hear the voices of the priests, she thought within herself, "They who can thus be present at the festival are blessed." Thus udwéga-prítiya was formed in her mind, and in an instant she began to ascend into the sky, so that she arrived at the wihára before her parents; who, when they entered and saw her, asked how she had come, and she replied that she had come through the sky. When they further asked how she had thus become a rahat, she said, "I only know that I did not remain in the same place any longer after I felt the joy; I know nothing more."

As when the water of many different rivers, or many different kinds of oil, are poured into the same vessel, it is difficult to separate the water of one river from that of another, or one kind of oil from another; so is it difficult to separate the three states, prítiya, sukha (pleasure or delight), and winyána.

12. Chanda, determination, that which carries the intention into effect, as when the hand is stretched out in the house-resembling thought.

13. Adhimokha, steadfastness, that which gives stability to the mind, as the firm pillar of emerald.

14. Sardháwa, purity, that which cleanses the mind from evil desire; as when a chakrawartti travels, and the feet of his soldiers foul the water through which they pass, the water is cleansed by the udakaprasanna jewel, in order that he may drink it.

When sardháwa is carried out to its most powerful exercise it is called ógha (stream, or torrent). In this way. There are many persons assembled on both the banks of a rapid river who are wishful to cross; but their timidity prevents them, until one, more daring than the rest, plunges into the flood, and crosses the stream. This man is to the other persons what ógha is to sardháwa.

"There are," said Nágaséna, "two principal properties of sardháwa, viz., purification, sangprasádhana, and progress, sangpakkhandana (literally, leaping). By the former, evil desire is subdued, and that clearness of the mind is produced which brings with it tranquillity, or freedom from all agitation. When the four-fold army of a chakrawartti passes a brook in which there is only a small quantity of water, it is fouled by the feet of those who pass, and becomes muddy; the water and the mud are mixed together, until it becomes like the pool in which buffaloes have wallowed. The emperor, when he also has passed over, tells his nobles to bring him some of the water to drink. But how can his majesty drink water that is thus defiled? In his possession there is a magical jewel; and when this is put into the water, the mud falls to the bottom, and it becomes perfectly clear, so that it is now fit for the chakrawartti to drink. The muddy water is the mind. The noble who cast the jewel into the water is he who is seeking nirwána. The mud and other impurities in the water are evil desire. The jewel is sardháwa. The water when cleared is the mind freed from impurity. Thus sardháwa subdues evil desire, and the mind, when free from evil desire, becomes pure; and it is in this way that sardháwa produces purity.

"Again, when he who is seeking nirwána sees that evil desire is overcome by some other being, he endeavours to enter, as it were by a leap, one or other of the four paths; he exerts himself to gain the advantages not yet gained, to attain that which is not yet attained, and to accomplish that which is not yet accomplished. When the waters of a heavy rain fall upon a rock, they do not remain upon the summit, but fall to the low places and fill the rivers. A traveller arrives at the bank of a swollen river, where others have preceded him, but they know not the depth of the stream, and are afraid to venture across. By and bye a more courageous man arrives, who arranges his garments, enters the stream, and gains the opposite bank. This is seen by the others, who soon follow his example in crowds. In like manner, when he who is seeking nirwána, sees in what way others have become free from impurity, he enters, as by a leap, one of the four paths; and it is in this way that sardháwa leads to progress. The same truths are declared by Budha in the Sanyut-sangha : ' By sardháwa the four rivers, viz., evil desire, the repetition of existence, scepticism, and ignorance, may be crossed; by assiduity, the ocean of birth may be crossed; by resolution, all sorrow may be driven away; and by wisdom, freedom from impurity may be obtained.

15. Smirti, the conscience, or faculty that reasons on moral subjects; that which prevents a man from doing wrong, and prompts him to do that which is right; it is like a faithful noble who restrains and guides the king, by giving him good advice, and informing him of all things that it is necessary for him to know.

"It is the property of smirti," said Nágaséna, "to divide that which is united or combined, one kind or species being separated from another, or distinguished from it, according to its own essential nature. It distinguishes the four satipatthánas, the four samyakpradhánas, the four irdhi-padas, &c.; kusala and akusala; that which is criminal and that which is not criminal; that which is low and that which is exalted; and that which is white and that which is black. Thereby he who seeks nirwána unites that which it is proper to unite, and refrains from uniting that which it is improper to unite; he separates that which it is proper to separate; and refrains from separating that which it is improper to separate. The treasurer, or high steward, of the chakrawartti informs him every morning and evening of the extent of his retinue, saying, Your elephants are so many, your cavalry so many, your chariots so many, and your infantry so many; your gold is so much; you have so many pieces of coin, and so many stores; your majesty will be pleased to take note of these things. In like manner, he who seeks nirwána, by smirti distinguishes the four satipatthánas, the four samyak-pradhánas (the whole series being repeated as before); he does that which it is proper for him to do, and leaves undone that which it is proper for him to avoid; he sees that this will be a hindrance to him, and avoids it, and that that will be a help to him, and seeks it. The prime minister of the chakrawartti knows who are on the side of the king, and encourages them, whilst all others are banished from the court; in like manner, by smirti the good is distinguished from the evil. The teaching of Budha is to the same effect, who says, 'I declare that by smirti all meanings, or tendencies, are discovered.'"

16. Hiri, shame, that which deters from the performance of what is improper to be done, through the influence of shame.

17. Ottappa, fear, that which deters from the performance of what is improper to be done, through alarm for its consequences.

18. Alóbha, indifference, that which causes him who sees or hears to be as though he heard not, or saw not, like the water that floats upon the surface of the water lily (without in any way affecting it, or entering its pores).

19. Adwésa, affection, that which bears no enmity, and is free from anger, like a faithful friend.

20. Pragnyáwa, wisdom, that which dispels ignorance, revealing what is good and what is not good, like the burning lamp that brings to view the figures that would otherwise be hid by the darkness. Its opposite is awidya, ignorance.

The locality of pragnyáwa cannot be pointed out. It is like the wind; it has an existence, but no one can tell where it is.

To have pragnyáwa is to possess a mind inclined towards the practice of merit, with an understanding of its properties. It is the result of understood meanings; when the meaning of a matter is understood, wisdom is produced. It is difficult to acquire, as well as to explain. It is extensive, multiform, and scattered in various places; brings fatigue to him who would find it; and requires perseverance in the search. It is the principal power by which the Budhaship is obtained; without it, all else is but like a sword put into its scabbard.

One of the causes or sources of pragnyáwa is the voice; but dharmma-pragnyáwa is the result of the exercise called widarsana, which is itself produced by the practice of sámádhi.

Pragnyáwa is the body of the five wisudhi, as séla-wisudhi, drishti-wisudhi, chitta-wisudhi, &c. It is so called, because it is that of which they are composed, their substance, as the body is the support of the different members. The power of the wisudhi is increased or decreased according to the strength of the pragnyáwa.

"Pragnyáwa," said Nágaséna, "is equivalent to light; it dispels the darkness of ignorance; produces the ashta-widyá, or eight kinds of knowledge possessed by the rahats; declares the four great truths; and perceives that the five khandas are impermanent, associated with sorrow, and unreal. The man who lights a lamp in a house where there is darkness, thereby dispels that darkness and produces light, by which the form of the different articles in it is revealed; and it is in the same way that wisdom produces the effects that have already been declared. Again, wherever wisdom is produced, in that place móha, ignorance or deception, is destroyed; as when a man takes a lamp into a dark place, the darkness is destroyed, and light is diffused.

"When any one has gnyána, knowledge, he had also pragnyáwa; the one is similar to the other. He who possesses them is ignorant concerning some things; and concerning others his ignorance has passed away. He is ignorant of the precepts that he has not yet learnt, of the paths in which he has not yet walked, and of the institutes that he has not yet heard; but he is not ignorant that all things are impermanent, subject to sorrow, and unreal."

This question was asked of Nágaséna by the king of Ságal, "Where is pragnyáwa? or, In what place does wisdom appear?" and this is the substance of the reply that he received. "When wisdom has effected that for which it has been called into existence, it passes away, or is destroyed; but that which it has revealed still remains; as when it imparts the knowledge of impermanency, &c., this knowledge abides, though the wisdom that produced it has passed away. This may be illustrated by a figure. A respectable man wishes to write a letter in the night season; he calls for his secretary, commands a lamp to be lighted, and causes the letter to be written; after this, the lamp is extinguished, but the writing remains. In like manner, pragnyáwa passes away, but the knowledge that it has imparted, still abides. Again, a village is on fire, to each house five vessels of water are brought and their contents poured upon the flames, by which the fire is extinguished; after this, there is no further necessity for any water; the vessels are useless. Now the water vessels are the five indrayas; the man who throws the water is he who is seeking nirwána; the fire is evil desire; the water is sardháwa and the other powers that destroy evil desire; the evil desire, when once destroyed does not again exist; even so wisdom passes away, but that which it has produced still abides. Again, a medical man takes five kinds of roots, earths, and other drugs, with which he compounds a medicine; it is given to the patient for whom it was prepared, and by this means he recovers; the medicine is then of no further use, though the recovery is permanent; and it is the same with wisdom."

There is a difference between manaskára and pragnyáwa. The former is possessed by sheep, cattle, and camels; but the latter is not. Again, the property of the former is úhana, combination; that of the latter is chédana, separation or excision. The man who reaps barley takes the stalks in his left hand, and a sickle in his right hand, and thus severs or cuts the stalks; so the man who seeks nirwána lays hold of his hita, mind, by manaskára, and cuts off evil desire by the sickle-resembling pragnyáwa.

The difference between sannyá, winyána, and pragnyáwa may thus be known. By the first is learnt the difference in the colours of things, but it is insufficient to discover their impermanency. By the second is learnt the difference in the colours of things and their impermanency, but it is insufficient to discover the paths. By the third may be learnt the whole of these things; colour, impermanency, and the paths. There is another method by which this difference may be understood. When a heap of gold coin is seen alike by a child, a peasant, and a citizen, the child will perceive the beauty of the colour; but he does not know what kind of articles it will purchase. The peasant perceives the beauty of the colour, and knows that he can purchase with it such and such articles; but he does not know the name or the value of each particular coin. The citizen, however, perceives all these things; he knows each coin by its colour, taste, and sound, and by its weight when held in the hand; he knows also in what city, province, or kingdom it was struck, or at what rock or forest, or on the bank of what river; and he knows the name of the artist by whom it was made. Sannyá is like the knowledge of the child, derived from what he saw; winyána is like that of the peasant, who knows the uses to which the coin may be put but pragnyáwa is like the knowledge of the citizen, who understands the whole, and understands it well.

There is a kind of wisdom called chintá-pragnyáwa, which is received by intuitive perception, and not from information communicated by another. It is possessed in an eminent degree by the Bódhisats; but the wisdom that discovers the four great truths is received only by the Pasé-Budhas and the supreme

Budhas in their last birth. With this exception, all other kinds of wisdom may be gained by any being who will practise the paramitas.

There are eight causes of the increase of pragnyáwa:—age, the company of the wise, investigation, association with the good, reflection, conversation, the friendship of the kind, and the aid of the three gems.

21. Madhyastatá, impartiality, that which is equally disposed to whatever may be the subject of thought, referring all things to their own proper cause.

22. Káya-prasrabdhi, the repose or tranquillity of the body, that which prevents udacha, disquietude, and other consequences arising from wédaná.

23. Chitta-prasrabdhi, the repose or tranquillity of the mind, that which prevents disquietude, and other consequences arising from winyána.

24. Káya-lahutá, body-lightness, that which allays the desire of sensual gratification.

25. Chitta-lahutá, mind-lightness, that which prevents sleep and drowsiness.

26. Káya-mirdutwa, body-softness, that which prevents scepticism and deception.

27. Chitta-mirdutwa (is explained in the same way as No. 26.)

28. Káya-karmmanyatá, body-adaptation, the power of causing the body to be in any state that is desired, so as to be free from all uneasiness, a power which aids in restraining the desire of sensuous gratification.

29. Chitta-karmmanyatá, mind-adaptation, (is explained in the same way as No. 28, but must be considered in its application to the mind).

30. Káya-prágunyatá, body-practice or experience, that which prevents impurity.

31. Chitta-prágunyatá, mind-practice or experience (is explained in the same way as No. 30).

32. Káya-irjutwa, body-uprightness or rectitude, that which prevents the deception arising from wédaná, &c.

33. Chittairjutwa, mind-uprightness or rectitude (is explained in the same way as No. 32).

34. Karuná, kindly regard, favour, pitifulness, that which desires the destruction of the sorrow of the afflicted.

35. Mudita, benevolence, that which rejoices in the success of the prosperous.

36. Samyak-wachana, truthfulness of speech, that which avoids the utterance of that which is untrue, and seeks to utter the truth, like the husbandman who, by the act of winnowing, drives away the chaff whilst he retains the grain.

37. Samyak-karmmánta, truthfulness or propriety of action, that which performs whatever is fit or proper, like the wise man, and not like the child that defiles itself in various ways.

38. Samyak-ajíwa, truthfulness of life or conduct, that which purifies the life, like the goldsmith who refines the precious metals.

39. Lóbha, covetousness, that which cleaves to sensible objects.

40. Dwésa, anger, that which is wrathful, like a serpent struck by a staff.

41. Moya, móha, ignorance, that which knows not the four great truths.

42. Mityá-drishti, scepticism, that which teaches there is no present world, no future world; it is the principal root of all akusala, or demerit.

43. Udacha, disquietude, that which keeps the mind in continual agitation, like the wind that moves the flag or pennant.

44. Ahiriká, shamelessness, that which is not ashamed to do that which it is improper to do, like the hog that openly wallows in the mire.

45. Annottappa, recklessness, that which does not fear to commit evil deeds, like the moth that fearlessly casts itself into the flame of the lamp.

46. Wichikichá, doubt, that which questions the existence of Budha, his discourses, and the priesthood; previous birth, future birth; the consequences resulting from moral action, and the entrance into the dhyánas by means of the exercise of kasina. He who is under the influence of this principle is like a man held by a serpent; he trembles from the doubts that agitate him; he does not continue in one mind, and is perpetually led hither and thither, without any abiding place of rest; and when he sees any object, he is unable to tell whether it be a pillar or a man.

47. Mánya, self-conceit, that which indulges the thought that I am above all other persons, superior to all.

48. Irsyá, envy, that which cannot bear the prosperity of others.

49. Mátsaryya, selfishness, that which leads me to wish that the prosperity which has come to me may not come to another. If any one under the influence of this principle sees even in a dream that the advantages he enjoys are imparted to others, he is unable to bear it; his mind thereby becomes debased, and the features of his countenance are changed, so that it becomes painful to look at him; he wishes not the prosperity of another, and loves only his own.

50. Kukhucha, moroseness, or the disposition to find fault, querulousness, that which is equally dissatisfied with what has been done and what has not been done, and can never be pleased. He who is under the influence of this principle is like the slave who is subject to the caprice of an imperious master.

51. Thína, sleep, that which refreshes, or calms the mind.

52. Mijja, drowsiness, that which prevents the body from performing any work. It is sometimes said that thína has the same effect upon the body that mijja has upon the mind. The body is supposed to be asleep when the mind is awake, and the mind to be active when the body is in unconscious repose.

The fifty-two modes of sankháro here enumerated, together with wédaná, sannyá, and winyána complete the category of discrimination.

6. *Consciousness.*

The Winyána-khando, or faculties of consciousness, are eighty-nine in number, viz.:

1. Chaksu-winyána, eye-consciousness, in the eye, about the size of a louse's head, is that which perceives, or is conscious of, the sensible object, whether it be blue, golden, or any other colour. It receives its birth from the eye and the outward form. It was possessed by Gótama before his birth, whilst he was yet in his mother's womb; all other beings, in the same situation, possess only káyawinyána.

The eye of the body is surmounted by the eye-brow, and has within it a circle of a black colour, and another that is white; thus it is beautified, as the water-lily by its petals. As a drop of oil poured upon the uppermost ball of cotton, when there are seven balls suspended from each other, or poured upon the outermost when there are seven balls one within the other, soon makes its way through the whole of the seven balls; so the light entering into the eye by one of its folds or concentric layers, passes from that fold to the next, and so on in succession through the whole of the seven folds of the natural (as distinguished from the divine) eye. The four elements enter into the composition of the eye, but the winyána is its principal faculty, as the prince is the chief of his followers or retainers.

It is not the eye that sees the image, because it has got no mind, chitta. If it were the eye that sees the image, it would see also by the other winyánas. Nor is it the mind that sees the image, because it has got no eye. If it were the winyána that sees the image, it would see the image within the wall; it would penetrate into the inside of the solid opaque substance, as there would be nothing to prevent it: but it does not thus happen. When the eye and the image communicate with each other, or come into contact, then there is sight. It is necessary that there be the coming of light from the object to the eye. As the light does not come from within the wall, that which is within the wall cannot be seen. From within such substances as crystals and gems the light proceeds, so that that which is within them can be seen. When any object is seen it is not seen by the eye alone, nor by the winyána alone. It is the chaksu-winyána that sees it, though we say, in common language, that it is the eye. When the winyána that is united to the eye, communicates, by the assistance of light, with any object that is presented before it, we say that the man who possesses that winywána sees that object. Thus we say that such an object is shot with the bow; but in reality it is not with the bow, but with the arrow, that it is shot; in like manner, it is not the eye that sees the image, but the winyána; or rather, not the eye alone, nor the winyána alone, but both united.

2. Sróta-winyána, ear-consciousness, in shape like a thin copper ring, or like a lock of copper-coloured curled hair, or a finger covered with rings, is that which perceives the various sounds.

3. Ghrána-winyána, nose-consciousness, in the nose, like the footstep of a goat in shape, is that which perceives smell, whether it be agreeable or disagreeable.

4. Jiwhá-winyána, tongue-consciousness, in the tongue, like the petal of a water-lily in appearance, is that which perceives the different flavours.

5. Káya-winyána, body-consciousness, is the perceiving of touch by the body. The exercise of this power is immediate, which none of the other winyánas are, as they require some medium of communication with the object before any effect is produced.

6. Manó-winyána, mind-consciousness, is the perceiving of the thoughts that are in the mind. Manó (in other places called hita, sita, and chitta) is the chief of the winyánas. It is like an overseer who continually urges on his labourers to work; like the first scholar in the school, who repeats his lesson, and is then followed by all the other scholars; or like the head workman, who sets all his men in motion when he himself begins to work.

As a large fish agitates the water in which it swims or sports, so the hita moves the rúpa, or body. Its powers are brought into exercise rapidly, like the quick movements of a mother, when she sees her child in danger of falling into a well.

The king of Ságal said to Nágaséna, "Is mano-winyána produced wherever there is the production of chaksu-winyána?" Nágaséna: "Yes." Milinda: "Is eye-consciousness first produced, and afterwards mind-consciousness; or is mind-consciousness first produced, and afterwards eye-consciousness?" Nágaséna: "First, eye-consciousness is produced, and afterwards mind consciousness." Milinda: "What, does the eye-consciousness say to the mind-consciousness, I am going to be born in such a place, and you must be born there too? Or does the mind-consciousness say to the eye-consciousness, Wherever you are born, there I will be born also?" Nágaséna: "They have no such conversation with each other. Milinda: Will you explain to me, then, by a figure, how it is that these two modes of consciousness always accompany each other?" Nágaséna: "What think you; when it rains, where does the water go to?" Milinda: "It goes to any low place or declivity that there may happen to be." Nágaséna: "When it rains again, where does this other water go to?" Milinda: "To whatsoever place the first water goes, to the same place goes the second." Nágaséna: "What, does the first water say to the second, Wherever I go, thither you must follow me? Or does the second water say to the first, Wherever you go I will follow?" Milinda: "They have no conversation of this kind; they go to the same place because of the declivity in the ground." Nágaséna: "Even so, when eye-consciousness is produced, in the same place is produced mind-consciousness. The one does not say to the other, Where you are born there I will be born: they are produced in this manner because it is natural to them thus to be produced." Milinda: "Will you now explain to me by another figure, how it is that when these two modes of consciousness are thus produced together they both proceed by the same door or aperture?" Nágaséna: "There is a fort in some distant part of the country, with walls and ramparts, but only one single gateway; now when any one wishes to retire from the fort, by what means does he go out?" Milinda: "By the gateway." Nágaséna: "There is afterwards another man who wishes to retire; by what means does he go out?" Milinda: "By the same gateway as the first man." Nágaséna: What, does the first man say to the second, You must come out of the fort by the same gateway that I do? Or does the second man say to the first, I will go out of the fort by the same gateway that you do?" Milinda: "They do not hold any conversation of this kind with each other; they both retire from the fort by the same gateway, because it is the right and proper road." Nágaséna: "Even so, there is no conversation held between the two modes of consciousness; it is because of the door or aperture that they are born together." The priest afterwards illustrated the same process by the figure of two wagons (the bullocks of which), from custom, follow each other in the same path; and by the figure of a pupil, who at first is unable to understand what he is taught, and his mind is confused; but by practice, or habit, he becomes calm and collected, and retains the remembrance of what he is told. "In like manner, from custom, and from practice, or habit long continued, the production of mano-winyána follows the production of chaksu-winyána." The king asked the same question relative to the other winyánas; if, where nose-consciousness or body-consciousness is produced, there mind-consciousness is produced also; and was answered in the affirmative.

After receiving this answer, the king asked Nágaséna another question, and said, "Wherever mind-consciousness is produced is sensation, wédaná, produced in the same place?" The priest replied, "Wherever mind-consciousness is produced, there is also produced touch, or contact, phassá; sensation, wédaná; perception, sannyá, thought, chétaná; attention, witarka; and examination, wichára.

Of these various modes of winyána, eye-consciousness and ear-consciousness are produced by communication; there must be a communication between the object seen and the eye, and between the object that produces the sound and the ear; images and sounds are, as it were, the food of the eye and ear. The other winyánas, as taste and smell, are produced by contact. Unless there be actual contact between the tongue and the object tasted there is no production of jiwhá-winyána; but when anything is in contact with the eye, whether it be the collyrium by which it is anointed, or the grain of sand by which it is annoyed, there is no consciousness of its colour or shape; notwithstanding, the eye can discern the hare in the moon,[*] though it is at so great a distance. With regard to ear-consciousness there is a difference; some sounds are heard when afar off, but others must be near, or they are not perceived. Between the birth of the sound and its being heard there is the lapse of a short period of time; and sound is not heard at the same moment by one who is near and one who is distant. There are instances in which the sound is produced in one place and heard in another, as in the echo. By the rushing of sound, even a large vessel, if it be empty, may be shaken.

The meaning of winyána may be learnt in this way. The watchman of a city remains in its centre, at the place where the four principal streets meet; by this means he can discover who comes from the east, and who from the south, or the west, or the north; in like manner, form is seen by the eye; sound is heard by the ear; odour is smelled by the nose; flavour is tasted

---

[*] The easterns speak of the hare in the moon as we do of the man in the moon. The following passage occurs in the Sanskrit poem called Naishadha Charita, in speaking of the rising sun, as translated by Dr. Yates:—

> "The moon beheld the hawk of day fly up,
> And with his bright and heavenly rays give chase
> Unto the raven night: alarmed with fear
> For the dear hare reclining on his breast,
> He fled precipitate; and all the stars,
> Like doves afraid, betook themselves to flight."—
> Asiatic Researches, vol. xx.

by the tongue; contact, or touch, is felt by the body; and thoughts are perceived by the mind. All these things are discovered or ascertained by means of winyána.

7. Akusala-wipáka-winyána-dhátu-chitta, that which is the cause of birth in the four hells; akusala, demerit, without any admixture of kusala, merit.

8. Kusala-wipáka-winyána-dhátu-chitta, that which is the cause of birth as man; imperfect kusala, which from its imperfection brings blindness, deafness, disease, &c.

9—16. The eight sahituka-kámáwachara-sit, that are the cause of birth in the déwa-lóka, or if in the world of men, as possessing great prosperity.

17—21. The five rúpáwachara-wipáka-sit, which are the cause of birth in one of the rúpa brahma-lókas.

22—26. The five arúpawachara-wipáka-sit, which are the cause of birth in the arúpa brahma-lóka.

27. The thoughts that cleave to sensible objects, not perceiving the impermanency of the body; and are sceptical relative to the consequences of merit and demerit.

28. The thoughts that rest in the supposition that the circumstances of the present birth are not controlled by that which has been done in a former birth.

29. The thoughts that conclude there is no evil consequences resulting from sin, when these thoughts arise spontaneously in the mind, and not from the suggestion of another.

30. The same thoughts when they arise from the suggestion of some other person.

31. The thought that there is neither happiness nor sorrow.

(The rest of the winyánas are of a similar description, all of them being states of the mind, or thoughts; some of which, like the above, are connected with demerit, and others with merit. Among the states of mind connected with merit are the following:—the performance of good actions from the spontaneous suggestion of a man's own mind, in the hope of receiving a pure reward; the performance of the same at the suggestion of some other person; the performance of the same from imitation, as when a child follows the example of its parents; the giving of good advice by parents to their children, such as to worship Budha, &c. All these modes of merit and demerit being referred to in other places, it is not necessary to enumerate them here.)

It has been declared by Budha that the five khandas are like a vessel in which all sentient beings are placed. The rúpakkhando are like a mass of foam, that gradually forms and then vanishes. The wédanákhando are like a bubble dancing upon the surface of the water. The sannyákhando are like the uncertain mirage that appears in the sunshine. The sankhárokhando are like the plantain-tree (without firmness or solidity). And the winyánakhando are like a spectre, or magical illusion. In this manner is declared the impermanency of the five khandas.

7. *Identity; Individuality; and Moral Retribution.*

1. (As all the elements of existence are said to be included in the five khandas, it is evident that Budhism does not recognize the existence of a spirit or soul; and that this assertion is not made without adequate authority will be seen from the additional extracts now to be made upon the same subject, taken principally from the Questions of Milinda.)

2. In the commencement of the conversations that were held between Milinda and Nágaséna, the king said, "How is your reverence known? What is your name?" Nágaséna replied, "I am called Nágaséna by my parents, and by the priests and others; but Nágaséna is not an existence, or being, pugala."* Milinda: "Then to whom are the various offerings made (that are presented to you as priest)? Who receives these offerings? Who keeps the precepts? Who enters the paths? There is no merit or demerit; neither the one nor the other can be acquired; there is no reward; no retribution. Were any one to kill Nágaséna he would not be guilty of murder. You have not been instructed; nor have you been received into the priesthood. Who is Nágaséna? What is he? Are the teeth Nágaséna? Or is the skin, the flesh, the heart, or the blood Nágaséna? Is the outward form Nágaséna? Are any of the five khandas (mentioning each of them separately) Nágaséna? Are all the five khandas (conjointly) Nágaséna? Leaving out the five khandas, is that which remains Nágaséna?" All these questions were answered in the negative. Milinda: "Then I do not see Nága-

---

* Nágaséna declares that rupa, wédana, sannyá, and winnyáno, do neither jointly nor severally constitute the man (puggalo) and yet that without them he does not exist.—Rev. D. J. Gogerly.

séna. Nágaséna is a mere sound without any meaning. You have spoken an untruth. There is no Nágaséna." Nágaséna: "Did your Majesty come here on foot or in a chariot?" Milinda: "In a chariot." Nágaséna: "What is a chariot? Is the ornamented cover the chariot? Are the wheels, the spokes of the wheels, or the reins, the chariot? Is the seat, the yoke, or the goad, the chariot? Are all these (conjointly) the chariot? Leaving out all these, is that which remains the chariot?" All these questions were answered in the negative. Nágaséna: "Then I see no chariot; it is only a sound, a name. In saying that you came in a chariot, you have uttered an untruth. There is no chariot. I appeal to the nobles, and ask them if it be proper that the great king of all Jambudwípa should utter an untruth?" The five hundred nobles who had accompanied the king declared that his majesty had not previously met with any one whose arguments were so powerful, and asked him what reply he would give. Milinda: "No untruth have I uttered, venerable priest. The ornamented cover, the wheels, the seat, and the other parts; all these things united, or combined, form the chariot. They are the usual signs by which that which is called a chariot is known." Nágaséna: "In like manner, it is not the skin, the hair, the heart, or the blood that is Nágaséna. All these united, or combined, form the acknowledged sign by which Nágaséna is known; but the existent being, the man, is not hereby seen. The same things were declared by Budha to the priestess Wajíra:—'As the various parts, the different adjuncts of a vehicle, form, when united, that which is called a chariot; so, when the five khandas are united in one aggregate, or body, they constitute that which is called a being, a living existence.'"

3. (Though an interruption to the narrative of Nágaséna, an extract from the work called Amáwatura will be explanatory of his argument relative to the Ego, the self). When Budha was visited by a tirttaka called Sachaka, the sage declared to him the impermanency of all the elements of existence. Sachaka replied, "If there be in any field plants or seeds, it is from the earth that they receive their increase; agriculture and commerce are also carried on by means of the earth. In like manner (it has been declared by some) the rúpa, or outward form is the átma, the self, the man, and that by means of the rúpa merit and

demerit are acquired; the wédaná are the self (others have said), and that by means of the wédaná merit and demerit are acquired; the sannyá are the self (others have said), and that by means of the sannyá merit and demerit are acquired; the same has been said of the sanskhára and the winyána (by others); the five khandas are to the sentient being like the earth to the plants and seeds, as by means of them merit and demerit are acquired. But you, sir, deny that there is an átma, that the being possesses a self; you say that the five khandas are anátma, unreal, without a self." Budha replied, "You say that the rúpa is yourself; that the wédaná are yourself; the sannyá are yourself; the sanskhára are yourself; the winyána are yourself; is it not so?" Sachaka: "This is not my opinion alone: it is that of all who are around me." Budha: "It is with you that I argue; let there be no reference to those who are around." Sachaka: "I repeat what I have said: the rúpa and other khandas are myself." Budha: "To prove that the five khandas are not the átma, the self, and that they exist without an átma, I will ask you a question. The authority of the anointed king, born of the royal caste, is supreme in the country that he governs; whom he will, he appoints to death; whom he will, he reduces to poverty; whom he will, he banishes from the country. Kosol, and Ajasát, and the Lichawi princes, and the princes of Malwa, all possess this power; in their several countries their authority is supreme; is it not so?" The tirttaka replied that this statement was correct, but by so doing he forged a weapon for his own destruction; because, if the people were killed, or fined, or banished, it must have been contrary to their own will; and therefore the átma can have no power over the rúpa and other khandas; it cannot preserve them. Budha: "You say that the rúpa is yourself; that it exists by means of the átma; now if you determine that the rúpa shall be in this way, or that it shall be in that way, will it be obedient to your will, or to the authority of the átma?" It is evident that if we will our body to be of such a colour, or not of such a colour, or to be beautiful as a gem, we have no power to determine these things; we cannot carry our will into effect, it will not be accomplished. The tirttaka saw, therefore, that he was conquered; and he reflected thus:—" If I say that the rúpa and other khandas are sustained by the átma, the Lichawi princes will say to me, 'Then how is it that your person is not as comely and beautiful as ours?' and if I say that it is not thus sustained, Gótama will say that it is contrary to my former declaration." He, therefore, remained silent. Budha again said to him, "You say that the rúpa is the self, that it is sustained by the átma. Now if you determine that your outward form, rúpa, shall be beautiful, will it thus happen, will your wish be accomplished? You say that the wédaná are the self, that they are sustained by the átma; now if you determine that the wédaná shall be pleasant, will it thus happen? The same question was asked relative to the other khandas, and to all the tirttaka replied in the negative. Budha: "Are the five khandas permanent or impermanent?" Sachaka: "Impermanent." Budha: "Is that which is impermanent connected with satisfaction or sorrow?" Sachaka: "With sorrow." Budha: "If death is followed by life, and thus a repetition of sorrow is endured, is it not from ignorance that any one says, I belong to that, or, that belongs to me; the átma belongs to the five khandas, or the five khandas belong to the átma?" Thus was Sachaka overcome, as he was brought to confess that the five khandas are impermanent, connected with sorrow, unreal, not the self.

4. (To return to the narrative of Nágaséna). The king enquired of the priest how old he was when he was ordained, and he replied that he was seven years of age? Milinda: "Is the 'seven' of which you speak attached to you or to the years; does the seven exist because of you, or do you exist because of the seven?" At this moment the fine form of the monarch, with all his royal ornaments, was reflected on the ground, and Nágaséna said to him, "When your shadow appears in a vessel of water, are you the king, or is the shadow the king?" Milinda: "I am the king; the shadow is not the king; because of me the shadow appears." Nágaséna: "In like manner, I was ordained when I was seven years of age; but I was not the seven; because of me the seven existed."

5. The king requested to hold further conversation with Nágaséna; and when the priests said that kings are impatient of contradiction and sometimes punish their opponents, he replied that he did not wish to be regarded as a king whilst they were carrying on their argument. Milinda said it was then late; and after requesting that the discussion might be renewed on

the following day, in the interior of the palace, he mounted his chariot and returned home. The next morning Nágaséna, attended by 80,000 priests, went to the palace, when one of the nobles respectfully said, "We call you Nágaséna; who is Nágaséna?" The priest replied, "Who do you think is Nágaséna" The noble: "The living breath, pránawáta, that is within Nágaséna; that which is inspirated and expirated; this is Nágaséna." The priest: "Does the breath of those who play upon reeds, or horns, or trumpets, or who sound the conch return to them again?" The noble: "No." The priest: "Then how is it that those who blow these instruments do not die?" The noble: "I am not able to argue with so acute a reasoner; pray tell me how it is." The priest: "The breath is not the life; it is only áswása and práswása, that which is inspirated and expirated, it is merely an element of the body, káya-sanskára."

6. The king said to Nágaséna, when the discussion was recommenced, "A being is born from his mother's womb. Does that being continue the same until his death, or does he become another?" Nágaséna: "He is not the same; neither is he another." When the king requested him to explain this by a figure he said, "What think you? At one time you were a child, young in years, small in person, and unable to rise; are you now that child, or have you become an adult?" Milinda: "I am not that child now; I am another; an adult." Nágaséna: "Then if this be the case, if you have become another, there is no mother, no father, no teacher, no disciple, no one who obeys the precepts, no wise person; the embryo in its different stages is not nourished by the same mother; he who learns the sciences is another; he who commits sin is another; he who is punished is another." Milinda: "Why do you state these things?" Nágaséna: "I was once a child, carried in the arms, but now I am an adult; by means of this body, the embryo in its different stages, the youth, and the adult, are united together, or connected. When a man lights a lamp, does the same lamp continue to burn during the whole night?" Milinda: "Yes." Nágaséna: "What, is there the same flame in the middle watch that there is when the lamp is first lighted?" Milinda: "No." Nágaséna: "Is there the same flame in the morning watch?" Milinda: "No." Nágaséna:

"What, is there one wick in the evening watch, and another in the middle watch, and another in the morning watch?" Milinda: "No; the lamp burns through the whole of the night, because it has the same wick." Nágaséna: "In the same way, great king, one being is conceived; another is born; another dies; when comprehended by the mind, it is like a thing that has no before, and no after; no preceding, no succeeding existence. Thus the being who is born, does not continue the same, nor does he become another; the last winyána, or consciousness, is thus united with the rest (or, he is thus connected with the last winyána).* Again milk that has been put by for a night becomes curd; from this curd comes butter; and this butter turns to oil; now if any one were to say that that milk is curd, or that it is butter; would he speak correctly?" Milinda: "No: because of the milk, oil has gradually been produced." Nágaséna: "In the same way, one being is conceived, another is born, another dies; when comprehended by the mind, it is like that which has no before and no after; no preceding, no succeeding existence. Thus the being who is born does not continue the same, neither does he become another; the last winyána is thus united with the rest (or, he is thus connected with the last winyána)."

7. Again, the king said to Nágaséna, "What is it that is conceived?" Nágaséna replied, "These two: náma and rúpa." Milinda: "Are the same náma and rúpa that are conceived here, or in the present birth, conceived elsewhere, or in another birth?" Nágaséna: "No: this náma and rúpa (or mind and body) acquires karma, whether it be good or bad: and by means of this karma, another náma and rúpa is produced." Milinda: "Then if the same náma and rúpa is not again produced, or conceived, that being is delivered from the consequences of sinful action." Nágaséna: "How so? If there be no future birth (that is, if nirwána be attained), there is deliverance; but if there be a future birth, deliverance from the

* I am not able to translate the last clause of this sentence in any way that does not leave it doubtful whether I have rightly apprehended the meaning. By one priest whom I consulted, it is said to mean, "The last winyána is the real being; emphatically, the man." But the whole sentence is thus translated by Mr. Gogerly from the original Pali, "Thus, great king, a living being flows on; one is conceived, another born, another dies; flows on as being neither the preceding nor the succeeding; it is not the same, or yet another; and so proceeds to the last accession of consciousness."

consequences of sinful action does not necessarily follow. Thus a man steals a number of mangos, and takes them away; but he is seized by the owner, who brings him before the king, and says, 'Sire, this man has stolen my mangos.' But the robber replies, 'I have not stolen his mangos; the mango he set in the ground was one; these mangos are other and different to that; I do not deserve to be punished.' Now, your majesty, would this plea be valid; would no punishment be deserved?" Milinda: "He would certainly deserve punishment." Nágaséna: "Why?" Milinda: "Because, whatever he may say, the mangos he stole were the product of the mango originally set by the man from whom they were stolen, and therefore punishment ought to be inflicted." Nágaséna: "In like manner, by means of the karma produced by this náma and rúpa another náma and rúpa is caused; there is therefore no deliverance (in this way) from the consequences of sinful action. (The same process is illustrated by the sowing of grain and the setting of the sugarcane). Again, a man lights a fire in the dry season, and by his neglecting to extinguish it another fire is produced, which sets fire to his neighbour's rice-field, or to his field of dry grain. The owner of the field seizes him, and bringing him before the king, says, 'Sire, by this man my field has been burnt; but the man replies, 'I did not burn his field; true, I neglected to put out a fire I had kindled, but the fire kindled by me was one, the fire that burnt his field was another; would it be right that upon such a plea he should be released?" Milinda: "No; because the fire that did the damage was produced by the fire that he kindled and neglected to put out." Nágaséna: "Again, a man takes a light, and ascending into an upper room there eats his food; but whilst doing so the flame of his lamp sets fire to the thatch of the roof; by this means the house is burnt, and not this house alone, but the other houses of the village. Then the villagers seize him, and say, 'Man, why did you burn our village?' But he replies, 'Good people, I did not burn your village; I was eating my food by the light of a lamp, when the flame rose and set fire to the thatch of the roof; but the flame that I kindled was one, and the flame that burnt the house was another, and the flame that burnt the village was another.' Now were he to persist in this plea when brought before the king, the decision would still be given against him; for this reason, because the flame that burnt the village was caused by the flame from the thatch, and this flame was caused by the flame from the lamp. Again, a man gives money to a girl for a maintenance, that afterwards he may marry her; the girl grows up, when another man gives her money and marries her. Hearing this, the first man demands the girl, as he has given her money; but the other man replies, 'No; the girl to whom you gave the money was a child, but this is a grown-up young woman; she cannot therefore belong to you.' Now if such a plea as this were set up in the court, it would be given against the man who made it; for this reason, that the child had gradually grown into the woman. Again, a man purchases a vessel of milk from the cowherd, and leaves it in his hand until the next day: but when he comes at the appointed time to receive it, he finds that it has become curd; so he says to the cowherd, 'I did not purchase curd; give me my vessel of milk." Now if a case like this were brought before your majesty, how would you decide it?" Milinda: "I should decide in favour of the cowherd, because it would be evident that the curd had been produced from the milk." Nágaséna: "In like manner, one mind and body dies; another mind and body is conceived; but as the second mind and body is produced by (the karma of) the first mind and body, there is no deliverance (by this means) from the consequences of moral action." *

8. The king then said to Nágaséna, "You have spoken of náma and rúpa; what is the meaning of these terms?"† The priest replied, "That which has magnitude is rúpa; náma is the exceedingly subtle faculty that exercises thought." Milinda: "How is it that the náma and rúpa are never produced separately?" Nágaséna: "They are connected with each other, like the flower and the perfume. And in this way: if no germ be formed in the fowl no egg is produced; in the ovarium of the fowl there is the germ and the shell, and these two are united to each other; their production is contemporaneous. In like manner, if there

---

* This argument appears in the Friend for Sept. 1838, translated from the Pali by the Rev. D. J. Gogerly.

† "The words translated body and soul are náma and rúpa; they are of frequent occurrence, and are clearly defined in several parts of the Pitakas: rúga signifies the material form: náma signifies the whole of the mental powers; the two combined signifies the complete being, body and mind."—Rev. D. J. Gogerly.

be no náma there is no rúpa; they are consociate; their existence is coeval; they accompany each other (as to the species, but not as to the individual), during infinitude."

9. The king enquired what was the meaning of this infinitude; or period of time, or duration, infinitely long; and Nágaséna replied, "It is divided into past, future, and present." Milinda: "Has time an existence (or is there such an existence as time)?" Nágaséna: "There is time existent, and time not existent." Milinda: "What is time existent, and what is time not existent?" Nágaséna: "When a sentient being, after repeated births, is no more, or becomes extinct, to him time is not existent. But when a being is still receiving the reward of moral action, or doing that for which he shall afterwards receive a recompense, and is subject to a repetition of existence, to him there is time. When a being dies, and receives another birth, there is time existent; but when a being dies, and is not subject to a repetition of existence, does not receive future birth, then time is not existent; nirwána is attained, time is no longer."

10. After this explanation, the king said, "What is the root, or beginning of past duration, what of future duration, what of present duration?" Nágaséna replied (repeating the pratitya-samuppáda-chakra, or circle of existence), "The beginning of past, future, and present duration is awidya-nam-móha, ignorance, or deception, which is like a bandage tied over the eyes, and is deceived relative to the four great truths, not knowing them. Móha is so called because it cleaves to that which is evil, and does not cleave to that which is good; it does not understand the union of the five khandas, nor the nature of the sight and other senses proceeding from the six áyatanas, or sentient organs; it does not perceive the nothingness of the eighteen dhátus, or elements; it does not regard the superiority of the shad-indrayas; and it is subject to repeated birth in different worlds and various modes of existence. By means of móha the twenty-nine descriptions of chitta, or modes of thought possessing merit or demerit, are produced; by means of the twenty-nine descriptions of chitta, or merit and demerit, the nineteen descriptions of pratisandhi-winyána (pilisanda-ganna-chitta) or actual consciousness, is produced; by means of actual consciousness náma and rúpa, body and mind, or the five khandas is produced; by means of náma and rúpa the six áyatanas, or

organs of sense are produced; by means of the six organs of sense the six modes of phassá, contact, or touch are produced; by means of the six modes of contact, the three modes of wédaná, or sensation, are produced; by means of the three modes of sensation the 108 modes of trisnáwa, or evil desire, are produced; by means of the 108 modes of evil desire, the four modes of upádána, or the cleaving to existence, are produced; by means of the four modes of cleaving to existence, the three modes of bhawa, or actual existence, are produced; by means of the three modes of actual existence játiapadíma, or birth, is produced; by means of birth the breaking up of the five khandas, called death; as well as the excess of maturity, called decay; and sorrow, weeping, pain, and mental anguish, are produced. In this way it is that the beginning of duration does not appear."*

* In the Kármika system of the Nepaulese there is a similar arrangement. "The being of all things is derived from belief, reliance, pratyaya, in this order; from false knowledge, delusive impression; from delusive impression, general notions; from them, particulars; from them, the six seats, (or outward objects of) the senses; from them contact; from it, thirst or desire; from it, embryotic (physical) existence; from it, birth, or actual physical assistance; from it, all the distinctions of genus and species among animate beings; from them, decay and death, after the manner and period peculiar to each. Such is the procession of all things into existence from awidya, or delusion; and in the inverse order to that of their procession, they retrograde into non-existence. And the egress and regress are both karmas, wherefore this system is called kármika. (Sákya to his disciples in the Racha Bhagavatí.)"—Hodgson's Illustrations. By Csóma Körösi it is called "a dependent connexion or casual concatenation (of twelve things):—1. Ignorance. 2. Composition, or notion. 3. Cognition. 4. Name and body. 5. Six senses. 6. Touch. 7. Perception. 8. Affection. 9. Ablution. 10. Existence. 11. Birth. 12. Old age and death. Everything, but especially the human soul, depends for its existence on the causal concatenation." We have the same scheme in the brahmanical accounts of the Budhist system. "Ignorance, or error, is the mistake of supposing that to be durable which is but momentary. Thence comes passion, comprising desire, aversion delusion, &c. From these, commencing in the embryo with paternal seed and uterine blood, comes the rudiment of body; its flesh and blood: it is name and shape. Thence the sites of six organs, or seats of the senses, consisting of sentiment, elements, name and shape (or body) in relation to him whose organs they are. From coincidence and conjunction of the organs with the name and shape (that is, with body), there is feeling or experience of heat or cold, &c., felt by the embryo or embodied being. Thence is sensation of pleasure, pain, &c. Follows thirst, or longing for renewal of pleasurable feeling and desire to shun that which is painful. Thence is effort or exertion of body or speech. From this is condition of merit or demerit. Thence comes birth or aggregation of the five branches. The maturity of those five branches is decay. Their dissolution is death . . Upon death ensues departure to another world. That is followed by return to this world. And the course of error, with its train of consequences, recommences."—Colebrooke, Miscellaneous Essays, i. 394. The Chinese scheme agrees, in a remarkable manner, with the preceding extracts. I give

Milinda: "Will you explain what you have said by a familiar figure?" Nágaséna: "A man sets a seed, or nut, in the ground; from this seed proceeds a germ, which gradually increases in size until it becomes a full-grown tree, and produces fruit; in that fruit is another seed or kernel which is put into the ground, and this also germinates, gradually comes a tree, and bears fruit; of this process no beginning can be perceived; and in like manner the beginning of duration does not appear. Again, a fowl produces an egg, and this egg produces another fowl, and this fowl produces another egg; in this way, no end can be perceived to this process; and it is the same with duration." The priest then drew a well-defined circle on the ground, and asked the king if he could show him the beginning of it or the end; but he replied that he was not able. Nágaséna: "It is in this way that Budha has propounded the pratitya-samuppáda-chakra, or circle of existence. On account of the eye and the outward form, eye-consciousness, or sight is produced; from the union of these three, contact is produced; from contact, the three modes of sensation are produced; from sensation, evil desire is produced; from evil desire, karma is produced; so again, from karma, by means of the eye, eye-consciousness is produced. There is no end to this order of sequences. Again,

---

it in the words of M. Klaproth. We may hereby learn that the grand principles of Budhism are the same in nearly all countries, and that there is also great uniformity in the renderings of its principal expositors. "L'origine des douze Nidâna est l'ignorance ; l'ignorance agissant, produit la connaissance ; la connaissance agissant, produit le nom et le titre ; le titre agissant, produit les six entrées ; les six entrées agissant, produisent le plaisir renouvelé ; le plaisir renouvelé agissant, produit le désir ; le désir agissant, produit l'amour ; l'amour agissant, produit la caption ; la caption agissant, produit la possession ; la possession agissant, produit la naissance ; la naissance agissant, produit la vieillesse et la mort, la douleur et la compassion, le chagrin et la suffrance, qui sont les peines du cœur et l'instrument de grandes calamités. Quand l'âme est une fois tombée dans cette alternative de la vie et de la mort, si elle veut !obtenir la doctrine, elle doit interrompre l'amour et éteindre et supprimer les passions et les désirs. Quand la quiétude est venue, alors l'ignorance s'éteint ; l'ignorance étant éteinte, alors l'action s'éteinte ; l'action s'eteignant, alors la connaissance s'éteint ; la connaissance s'eteignant, alors le nom et le titre s'eteignant ; le nom et le titre étant éteints, alors les six entrées s'éteignant ; les six entrées s'éteignant, alors le plaisir renouvelé s'éteint : le plaisir renouvelé étant éteint, alors le désir s'éteint ; la douleur éteinte, alors l'amour s'éteint ; l'amour étant éteint, alors la caption s'éteint ; la caption étant éteinte, alors la possession s'éteint ; la possession s'eteignant, alors la naissance s'éteint ; la naissance s'éteignant, alors la vieillesse et la mort, la tristesse, la compassion, la douleur et la souffrance, les peines du cœur et les grandes calamités ont pris fin : c'est ce qu'on appelle avoir trouvé la doctrine."

from the ear and sound, ear-consciousness, or hearing, is produced; from the nose and perfume, nose-consciousness, or smell, is produced; from the tongue and flavour, tongue-consciousness, or taste, is produced; from the body, and the tangible object body-consciousness, or touch, is produced; from the mind and the object of mental perception, mind consciousness, or thought, is produced. From the union of the three in each of these classes, contact is produced; from contact, sensation; from sensation, evil desire, from evil desire, karma; from karma, consciousness; and so on without any limit to the process. In like manner, the beginning of duration does not appear."

The king again said to Nágaséna, "You have declared that the beginning does not appear; of what is it that this beginning has been predicated?" Nágaséna: "It is spoken of past duration." Milinda: "Is it true of all things that the beginning does not appear?" Nágaséna: "Of some things it appears, and of some it does not appear." Milinda: "In what way?" Nágaséna: "Formerly all things, of whatever kind, were entirely awidyamána, lost in confusion, or covered from the sight; their beginning does not appear; but when that which was not existent comes into existence, is produced and destroyed, of this (which may be regarded as referring to each separate individuality in the sequence of existence) the beginning does appear." Milinda: "If that which was non-existent comes into existence, and after coming into existence is destroyed, is not its destruction entire and absolute, from being thus, as it were, cut off at both ends?" Nágaséna: "It receives the destruction of awidyáwa, or non-perception." Milinda: "But can that which is awidyáwa, and cut off at both ends, continue to exist?" Nágaséna: "It may." Milinda: "But can it exist from the beginning." Nágaséna: "It may exist from the beginning." The priest then repeated the comparison of the seed and the tree; the khandas are like the seed (the beginning and the end of each separate tree being apparent, though the beginning of the process by which this sequence of trees came into existence cannot be traced).

11. The king enquired of Nágaséna if any sanskhára-dharmmakenek, or sentient being, exists; and if so, what is the nature of that being? In reply, the priest repeated the circle of existence.

On receiving this answer, the king said, "Does the being that has no existence come into existence?" Nágaséna: "Is this palace, or any house in which you may happen to be, a non-existent object brought into existence?" Milinda: "The timbers were produced in the forest; the clay used in its construction was in the ground; by the exertions of men and women (from these materials), the palace was produced." Nágaséna: "In like manner, no being is produced from that which is non-existent; there is no such being. All sentient beings are produced from something that previously existed. Thus, if a seed or root be cast into the ground, it gradually increases in size, and becomes a tree, which bears flowers and fruit; the tree is not a non-existent thing brought into existence; there is no such tree. Again, a potter takes clay from the earth, and therewith manufactures different kinds of vessels; these vessels are not something non-existent brought into existence; they are produced from that which previously existed. Again, for the production of sound from the wéná (a stringed instrument frequently referred to in eastern story) there must be the frame, the skin, the body, the wood, the strings, and the handle, together with the skill of the player, or no sound is produced; all these things are previously requisite that the sound may be elicited. Again, if there be no piece of wood to be rubbed and no upper piece, and no string for the binding of the pieces together, and no exertion of the man, and no rag, fire cannot be produced; but if there be all these things, fire may be elicited. Again, unless there be the jóti-pásána, or burning-glass, and the rays of the sun, and the dried cow-dung, no fire can be produced; but if there be all these things, fire may be elicited. Again, if there be no mirror, and no light, and no face, no reflection of the features is produced; but if there be all these things, an image of the features may be produced. In all these instances it is not a non-existent object that is produced; the production is from something that previously existed; and the same is to be predicated of the sentient being."

12. Again, the king said to Nágaséna, "Is there such a thing as the wédagu, is such a thing received?" Nágaséna; "What is this wédagu of which you speak?" Milinda: "It is prána-jiwa, it is inward life, or the internal living principle, by means of which figure is seen by the eye, sound is heard by the ear, odour is smelled by the nose, flavour is tasted by the tongue, the tangible object is felt by the body, and thoughts are perceived by the mind. Thus, we sit in this palace, and when we are wishful to

see any object through any of the windows, we look out of that particular window, whether it be towards the east, the south, the west, or the north; even so, if the inward living principle be wishful to look out by the eye, or any other of the sentient organs, it looks out by that particular aperture or door." Nágaséna: "I also will say something relative to the six organs of sense; you must pay attention to what I say. If the inward living principle sees objects by the eye, we who are sitting here ought to see the same object by whatever window we might look out,* whether by the eastern window, the southern, the western, or the northern; so also the inward living principle would see the outward object by means of the eye, but not by that alone; it would see as well by the ear, the nose, the tongue, the body, and the mind; and it would hear sound equally by the eye, the nose, the tongue, the body, and the mind; it would smell, in the same way, by the eye, the ear, the tongue, the body, and the mind; it would taste by the eye, the ear, the nose, the body, and the mind; it would feel by the eye, the ear, the nose, the tongue, and the mind; it would think by the eye, the ear, the nose, the tongue, and the body. We who are in this palace, by putting our heads far out of the window, can clearly discern various objects; in like manner, by the same rule, when the inward living principle opens the window of the eye, it ought to see clearly all the objects in an extended prospect; and when it opens the window of the ear, and that of the nose, or the tongue, it ought distinctly to hear the sounds in the same space, and to smell the odours, and to taste the flavours, and to feel the objects. Were the noble, Dinna, who is near you there, to go out of the door, could you tell that he had left this place, and gone out?" Milinda; "Yes." Nágaséna: "And if he were to return into the interior of the palace, could you tell that he had returned, and was standing in your presence?" Milinda: "Yes." Nágaséna: "And can the inward living principle, when it has anything upon the tongue possessing flavour, tell whether it be sweet, sour, salt, bitter, acrid, or pungent?" Milinda? "Yes." Nágaséna: "And when that which possesses flavour enters into the stomach, can the inward living principle

* And they who say, as some do, that the eye sees not anything, but it is the soul only that seeth through them, as through open doors, observe not, that if the eyes were like doors, we might see things much better if our eyes were out, as if the doors were taken away.—Epicurus, according to Laertius and Lucretian.

tell whether it be sweet, sour, salt, bitter, acrid, or pungent?" Milinda: "No." Nágaséna: "Then your two declarations do not agree with each other. Suppose a man to have a hundred measures of honey, the whole of which is poured into one large vessel; now if he puts his head into the vessel, whilst his mouth is bound over with a cloth tightly drawn, can he then discern whether the honey be sweet or sour?" Milinda: "No." Nágaséna: "Why?" Milinda: "Because the sweetness did not enter into his mouth." Nágaséna: "Then your two declarations do not agree with each other." Milinda: "Will you be kind enough to explain these matters to me?" The priest then again repeated the circle of existence, and said, "There is no such thing as the inward living principle of which you speak; there is no wédagu; besides that which is set forth in the circle of existence, there is no such a thing as the wédagu connected with the body."

But the king (as if not satisfied by the answer he had received) again said to Nágaséna, "Is there such a thing as the wédagu?" Nágaséna: "There is not." Milinda: "Is there any separate being, any distinct principle of existence, connected with (or attached to) the náma-rúpa?" Nágaséna: "There is not." Milinda: "Then there is no one to endure the consequences of sin; there is no responsibility." Nágaséna: "If there were not conception in some other place, then there would be no responsibility; but there is this conception, and therefore the consequences of sin are endured. When a man steals a mango that belongs to some other person, is he not punished?" Milinda: "Yes." Nágaséna: "But the mango that he steals is not the mango that the other man set in the ground as seed; then why is he to be punished?" Milinda: "Because the mango that he steals was produced from the tree that grew from the mango that the other man set in good ground." Nágaséna: "Even so, from the karma, whether it be connected with merit or demerit, belonging to this náma-rúpa, another náma-rúpa is produced (to which the karma is transferred); thus there is no release, in this manner (apart from the reception of nirwána), from the consequences of sin."

13. The king again said, "Do the winyána, consciousness; pragnyáwa, wisdom; and the life that is in the body composed of various elements, produce one effect and embrace one idea, or are the effects and ideas multiform?" Nágaséna replied, "The winyána is like a man who, when he sees the gold coin called a

masuran, knows its denomination. Pragnyáwa is like the goldsmith who when he sees the masuran, knows whether it be a counterfeit or a genuine coin. The life within the body is not a living soul that enables the being who possesses it to eat, and drink, and go from place to place." Milinda: "Then if there be no living principle what is it that sees colours, shapes, &c., by the eye, hears sounds by the ear, smells by the nose, and so on?" Nágaséna: "If there were a living soul that saw by the eye, it would still see clearly though the eye were plucked out, and the socket were empty; though the ears were destroyed, it would still distinguish sounds; though the tongue were cut out, it would still be able to discern flavours, &c. But we know that these consequences do not take place; as when there is no eye, there is no sight, when there is no ear, there is no distinguishing of sounds, &c.; and therefore there can be no such thing as a living soul that enables the being who possesses it to eat, and drink, and go from place to place. It has been declared by Budha that it is exceedingly difficult to say, this is touch, this is sensation, this is perception, this is thought; or to tell in what place the incorporeal thought resides. Were a man to go in a ship far out to sea, and take up a portion of water therefrom, could he say, this is from the Ganga, this from the Yamuna, this from the Achirawati, this from the Sarabhu, or this from the Mahí? We know that he would not be able; and equally difficult, it has been declared by Budha, would it be to say, this is touch, this is consciousness, this is perception, &c. The king's cook prepares delicious food for the royal table, in which there is milk, pepper, onions, ginger, and many other savoury ingredients. His majesty on receiving the food says, 'Oh, cook, separate from each other the flavour of the milk, ginger, pepper, and other ingredients, and give each to me separately and alone.' But this cannot be; they are all mingled together, and the taste of each may be perceived, but one flavour cannot be separated from the other. In like manner touch, sensation, perception, &c., may be severally experienced, but they do not admit of individual separation."

"So is it with the sad-indrayas," said Nágaséna, "and the other faculties; they produce one effect, inasmuch as they destroy evil desire. There are various sections in an army, but the object of all is the same; in the field of battle they subdue the opposing host: in like manner, the indrayas and other faculties are many, but their object is the same: they overcome evil desire."

14. The king enquired the meaning of the word sangsára; and Nágaséna replied, "There is birth in this world and then death; after death there is birth in some other place; in that place also there is death; and then there is birth again in some other place. Thus a man, after eating a mango, sets the stone in the ground; from that stone another tree is produced, which gradually comes to maturity, and bears fruit; the stone of one of these fruits is again set in the ground, and another tree is produced; from this tree there are other fruits; and thus the process goes on continually without any appearance of its end. It is the same with sangsára, or the sequence of existence."

15. The king again said, "You have declared, venerable priest, that the átma-bháwa (that which constitutes, or is included in, individual existence) does not go to any other place after death; then is it born, or produced, or does it appear, in any other place?" Nágaséna: "It is." Milinda: "Will you explain this by a figure?" Nágaséna: "A man from one lamp lights another; by so doing does he extinguish the light of the first lamp?" Milinda: "No." Nágaséna: "In like manner the kaya (literally the body, but here put as a synonyme for átma-bháwa), though it does not pass away from the place where it is, is nevertheless produced in another place," Milinda: "Will you favour me with another explanation?" Nágaséna: "When you were a boy you were taught different slókas, or stanzas; but these slókas did not, when communicated to you, pass away from the mind of your teacher; and it is the same with the átma-bháwa."

16. Another enquiry made by the king was this, "A man dies here and is born in a brahma-lóka; another dies here at the same time, and is re-born in Kásmíra; which of these two will receive birth the first?" Nágaséna: "There will be no difference." Milinda: "Will you explain to me how this can happen?" Nágaséna: "In what place were you born?" Milinda: "In the village of Kalasí." Nágaséna: "How far is it from hence?" Milinda: "About 200 yojanas." Nágaséna: "How far is it to Kásmíra?" Milinda: "Twelve yojanas." Nágaséna: "Quickly think of your native village." Milinda: "I have done so." Nágaséna: "Now quickly think of Kásmíra.." Milinda: "I have done so." Nágaséna: "Which of

these places did you think about in the shortest space of time?" Milinda: "There is no difference: I can think of one as soon as the other." Nágaséna: "So also, when one being is re-born in a brahma-lóka and another in Kásmíra, they are both born at the same moment." The priest illustrated the same position by the figure of two crows alighting on a tree at the same moment, one on an upper branch and the other on a lower; but the shadows of both reach the earth at the same instant.

17. "The same náma and rúpa," it is said in the Wisudhi-margga-sanné, "is not reproduced. As there is a different karma, that which is produced is a different being. When the elements of the body are broken up, or destroyed, they are never again produced, or brought into existence. They pass, as it were, into deep darkness, where they cannot be discovered by the unwise. As the karma has the power to produce new elements, it is not necessary that the same elements should be produced again."

8. *Reproduction.*

1. All quadrupeds, men, déwas, brahmas, and those who live in the arúpa worlds, all beings that have náma and rúpa, a mind and a body, are born because of karma, and are therefore called karmaja; fire, and all things proceeding from seed, being produced without any hétu, or cause exterior to themselves, are called hétuja; and earth, rocks, water, and wind, being produced by irtu, season or time, are called irtuja; but space and nirwána are neither karmaja, hétuja, nor irtuja; we cannot say of nirwána that it is produced, nor can we say that it is not produced.

2. When birth is ruled by karma, and there is the possession of much merit, it causes the being to be born as a kshastriya-mahasála, brahmana-maha-sála, or grahapati-maha-sála, or as a déwa in one of the déwa-lókas; sometimes by the oviparous (andaja) birth, as Kuntraputra; at other times by the viviparous (jalábuja) birth, as men in general; or from the petal of a lotus, as Pokkharasatiya; or by the apparitional (opapátika) birth, (in which existence is received in an instant in its full maturity), as Ambapáli. There is also the sédaja birth, as when insects are produced from perspiration or putridity.*

---

* According to the Nyáya system, the distinct sorts of body are five: 1st, ungenerated, as the gods and demi-gods; 2nd, uterine, or viviparous; 3rd, oviparous; 4th, engendered in filth, as worms, nits, maggots, &c.; 5th, vegeta-

3. When conception takes place, it is by a portion of the karma possessed by some previous being, whilst the other portions of the karma form the different members, as the eye, ears, &c.

4. The wind causes fowls to conceive, and the sound of rain has the same effect upon cranes. Déwas, prétas, and the beings in hell, are born by the apparitional birth, not from the womb; men, cattle, and other animals, are born from the womb, but their destiny is different, as some are born to the crown, some to the yellow robe, and some to the covering of skin.

5. In the forest of Himála there is a rock called Néru, of a golden colour, and it has this property, that whatever animal approaches it is turned to the same colour; in like manner, whatever being receives birth, whether it be viviparous, apparitional, or any other, he loses his previous nature, and receives that of the species to which he is attached by his birth.

6. There are living things that eat grass; they nip the green or dry grass with their teeth, and eat it; they are horses, cattle, asses, goats, deer, and many others. Through the karma of previous births, sentient beings are thus born as graminivorous animals. There are living things that feed upon dung; they scent it from afar, and hasten towards it with the expectation of receiving the richest treat. As when the Brahmans have scented the sacrifice, they hasten towards it that they may partake of it, so when these have scented the filth, they fly towards the spot that they may enjoy the feast; they are fowls and swine, dogs and jackals. This also is the consequence of crimes committed in previous births. There are living things that are born in darkness, and in the same darkness they live and die; they are grubs and worms. This also is the consequence of previous karma. There are living things that exist in water, in which element they decay and die; they are fish, turtle, and alligators. This also is the consequence of previous karma. There are living things that are born in dunghills and filthy places; and others in putrid flesh, the corpses of animals, stale food, in cesspools, and places that receive the refuse of cities;

tive, or germinating.—Colebrooke's Miscellaneous Essays, i. 270. The sceptics taught that some living things are generated from fire, as the cricket of the hearth; some from stagnant water, as gnats; some from sour wine, as scnipes; some from slime, as frogs; some from mould, as worms; some from ashes, as beetles; some from plants, as caterpillars; some from fruits, as maggots; and some from putrified flesh, as bees from cattle and wasps from horses.

but to give a perfect description of all that is suffered by the beings that are born as animals, even an age, or a hundred thousand ages, would not suffice.

7. A man throws a perforated yoke into the sea. The east wind sends it in a westerly direction, and the west wind sends it in an easterly direction; the north wind sends it in a southern direction, and the south wind sends it in a northern direction. In the same sea there is a blind tortoise, which after the lapse of a hundred, a thousand, or a hundred thousand years, rises to the surface of the water. Will the time ever come, when that tortoise will so rise up that its neck shall enter the hole of the yoke? It may; but the time that would be required for the happening of this chance cannot be told; and it is equally difficult for the unwise being that has once entered any of the great hells to obtain birth as man.

8. When the power to receive birth as man has been obtained, conception takes place in various ways. Not long after Ananda began to say bana in the palace of the king of Kósala, his 500 queens each brought forth a son, and the whole of the 500 princes bore a striking resemblance to the priest. The tirttakas insinuated that Ananda had been acting improperly; but Budha, in order to remove the doubts of the king, repeated a gátá, to this effect:—"There are nine ways in which conception may be produced.* 1. In the usual manner. 2. By the simple attrition of two bodies of different sexes. 3. By umbilical attrition. 4. By looking steadfastly in the face of a man. 5. By the use of flowers or perfumes that have previously been in the possession of a man. 6. By eating the food left by a man. 7. By putting on, or using the garments that have been worn by a man. 8. By the season, or time, as in periods of great heat living beings are rapidly produced. 9. By listening wantonly to the sweet voice of a man."

9. The ascetic Dukula, and his sister Pariká, were born in Benares, of most respectable parents, who were of the brahmanical caste. Their previous birth had been in a déwa-lóka. Though they were so nearly related, yet as it was the custom of their family, and they were very like each other, both being exceed-

* Before the time of the patriarch Daksha, living creatures were variously propagated by the will, by sight, by touch, and by the influence of religious austerities.—Professor Wilson.

ingly beautiful, they were married to each other by their relatives, notwithstanding their repugnance, as they were free from all evil desire. After living together some time in the city, they retired to a forest, where they began to practise the necessary discipline, in order that they might attain nirwána. But the déwas were jealous on account of the great merit they acquired; in consequence of which Sekra went to them, and told them it would be of great advantage if they had a son, as they were living alone in the forest; but they resolutely rejected his advice. The déwa, however, told them that it might be done without transgressing the rules of asceticism, merely by umbilical attrition; and upon hearing this, they took his advice, by means of which a son was conceived and born, who was called Sáma. Thus there was conception without personal union, as fire imparts warmth to the substance with which it is not in actual contact.*

10. In that which is said of sentient beings, trees are not included, as they do not possess a mind. In a former age when Bódhisat was the déwa of a tree, he said to a brahman who every morning asked the protection of the tree, and made offerings to it continually, "The tree is not sentient; it hears nothing, it knows nothing; then why do you address it, or ask from it assistance?" At another time he said that a tree called out to the carpenter, a brahman, who was about to cut it down, "I have a word to say; hear my word." But when he said that the tree called out, it was a figurative expression, as it was not the tree that spoke, but a déwa who resided in the tree; just as we say of a cart laden with grain, that it is a grain-cart, though in reality it is not a grain-cart, but a cart laden with grain; or a man says that he will churn cream, when in reality it is not cream that he churns but butter; or a man says that he will make such a thing, though the thing of which he speaks is not in existence; he regards a non-entity as if it were an entity."

11. The king of Ságal said to Nágaséna, "When water is boiled, it makes a noise, as if it said chichitá, or chitichita; is this on account of the sufferings endured by living beings who are in the water, or from what cause does it proceed?" Nágaséna replied, "The water is not alive; nor in the water is there anything that has life." Milinda: "But the sceptics say that there is life

* Numerous instances are given of similar modes of conception, but they are too gross for publication.

in the water; they therefore forego the use of cold water, and use it only when it is warm; and they speak against the priests of this religion, saying that by the use of cold water they take life, and thereby transgress the precept. It would be well if this objection were removed." Nágaséna: "It is on account of the fierceness of the fire alone that these noises are heard. When the ponds and other places dry up on account of the drought are there any noises? If there were life in the water, they would be heard then, as well as in the other case. Again, when water and rice are put into a vessel and covered over, they remain still; when put upon the fire they make these noises; the water trembles, runs here and there, boils over, and makes a regular commotion. When water that has been received by the priest in his alms-bowl in going from house to house is put into a vessel, and covered over, it remains still; there is no noise, no commotion; but it is not so with the water of the sea; you know how that rolls and roars." Milinda: "Yes; I have heard the waves of the sea and seen them rising to the height of a hundred or two hundred cubits." Nágaséna: "It is the wind that causes this difference. Again, when the drum is struck it gives forth a sound; but there is no life in it; when it is not struck it is silent. It is thus evident that though the water makes a noise when it is boiled, this is no proof that there is life in it, or any living existence."

9. *Karma.*

1. Karma includes both kusala and akusala, or merit and demerit; it is that which controls the destiny of all sentient beings.

There are three principal meanings of the word kusala, viz., freedom from sickness, exemption from blame, and reward; but as used by Budha its primary idea is that of cutting, or excision. It has a cognate use in the word kusa, the sacrificial grass that cuts with both its edges the hand of him who lays hold of it carelessly. That which is cut by kusala is klésha, evil desire, or the cleaving to existence. Akusala is the opposite of kusala. That which is neither kusala nor akusala is awyákrata; it is not followed by any consequence, it receives no reward, either good or bad.

Akusala is divided into wastu-káma and klésha-káma. To wastu-káma belongs pancha-káma, the modes of evil desire that are connected with the five senses. Klésha-káma is the same as trisnáwa (which may here be considered as the cleaving to existence, whilst wastu-káma is the cleaving to existing objects). When the two kámas are conjoined, the state is called kámá-wachara.

There are eleven káma-bhawa, or states of existence in which there is káma. Even those who reside in the arúpa worlds are figuratively called kámáwachara, as well as those in the rúpa worlds. Thus we call a man a warrior though he may not at the time be actually fighting; it is his profession, that to which he is most accustomed, and which he may at any hour be called to exercise, though now living in peace; in like manner, the inhabitant of the arúpa world, though he may not just now exercise káma, is exposed to its influence in the other states of existence that await him when this is concluded. That which is neither rúpa nor arúpa is called lókottara, a state in which there is entire freedom from all káma.

2. At the time that Gótama resided in the wihára of Jétáwana, there went to him a young brahman, named Subha, son of the próhita of the king of Kosol, who said, "From some cause or other mankind receive existence; but there are some persons who are exalted, and others who are mean; some who die young, and others who live to a great age; some who suffer from various diseases, and others who have no sickness until they die; some who have disagreeable persons, and others who are beautiful; some who are strong, and others who are weak; some who have great authority and extensive possessions, as kings, and others who have none; some who are of mean birth, and others who belong to the kshatra, brahman, and other high castes; some who are destitute of wisdom, and others who are extremely wise; among individuals of the same species, man, these differences occur. What is their cause? what is it that appoints or controls these discrepancies?"

Budha made the same reply to all these queries, and it was as follows:—"All sentient beings have their own individual karma, or the most essential property of all beings is their karma; karma comes by inheritance, or that which is inherited (not from parentage, but from previous births) is karma; karma is the cause of all good and evil, or they come by means of karma, or on account of karma; karma is a kinsman, but all its power is from kusala and akusala; karma is an assistant, or that which promotes the prosperity of any one is his good karma; it is the difference in the karma, as to whether it be good or evil, that causes the difference in the lot of men, so that some are mean and others are exalted, some are miserable and others happy.

When Budha had made this reply, Subha still remained like a man with a bandage fastened over his eyes; he was unable to comprehend its meaning; and he therefore requested the sage to explain these things to him at great length, that he might understand them more fully.

Budha informed him that he would find it difficult to understand them, unless he paid the most profound attention; but as he promised thus to listen, the teacher of the three worlds proceeded:—" A woman or a man takes life; the blood of that which they have slain is continually upon their hands; they live by murder; they have no compassion upon any living thing; such persons, on the breaking up of the elements (the five khandas), will be born in one of the hells; or if, on account of the merit received in some former birth, they are born as men, it will be of some inferior caste, or if of a high caste, they will die young, and this shortness of life is on account of former cruelties. But if any one avoid the destruction of life, not taking a weapon into his hand that he may shed blood, and be kind to all, and merciful to all, he will, after death, be born in the world of the déwas, or if he appear in this world, it will be as a kshatra, or brahmau, or some other high caste, and he will live to see old age."

By many other examples of a similar kind did Budha illustrate the effects of karma; proving thereby, to the satisfaction of Subha, who became a convert to the faith of Gótama, that the differences in the lot of men, as at present seen, are produced by the karma of previous births. (*Chúlakamma wibhanga-sútra.*)

3. There are eleven descriptions of karma:—1. Drishta-dharmma-wédya. 2. Upapadya-wédya. 3. Aparapariya-wédya. 4. Yatgaru. 6. Yadásanna. 7. Kritatwá. 8. Jana. 9. Upasthamba. 10. Upapidaka. 11. Upagháta.

The first, drishta-dharmma-wédya karma, whether it be kusala or akusala karma, is accomplished in the present birth; or if not in the present birth, not at all, in which case it is called abháwa karma. It is then like grain that has been boiled, which will not germinate or grow, though it should be sown in the ground. Another comparison may illustrate this result. A hunter goes to shoot deer. He plants his trusty bow well, the arrow flies in a straight direction, and the animal is killed. But at another time the arrow misses its aim, the deer escapes; and as the hunter cannot find it again, its fear having now led it far away, its escape is permanent; it cannot again be caught. In like manner, when this description of karma does not produce its rightful consequences in the present birth, as to all future births it is ineffective, no result can be accomplished.*

The second description of karma is accomplished in the next birth, or not at all. Out of many results that are connected with this karma, only one is produced. Thus, when it is kusala karma, birth may be obtained in the brahma-lóka; and in this case, though other rewards may be due for other acts, they are not received. Again, when it is akusala karma, one of the five deadly sins may be committed, which will cause the being to be born in hell, in the next birth, where he will have to remain during a whole kalpa; but if the whole of the five sins were committed, the punishment would be the same.†

The karma called yadásanna is received when at the point of death.

4. When the king of Ságal enquired where karma resides, its locality; Nágaséna replied, "Karma is like the shadow, that always accompanies the body. But it cannot be said that it is here, or that it is there; in this place, or in that place; the locality in which it resides during the sequence of existence cannot be pointed out. Thus, there is a tree, a fruit tree, but at present not in bearing; at this time it cannot be said that its fruit is in this part of the tree, or in that part, nevertheless it exists in the tree; and it is the same with karma."

5. On a certain occasion, when the priests had repeated to each other many things in praise of the power and greatness of Budha, the sage informed them that they were not to suppose that these advantages were produced by the Budhas themselves, irrespective of other causes; but to remember that they were entirely the result of merit acquired in previous ages. Then one of the priests, rising from his seat, reverently said, "My lord, the power and greatness you possess are seen by us; but we wish also to know what was done by you in former ages by

---

* The stories of Púrnnaka, Chinchi, and Supra Budha, are cited as instances of this karma.

† I have not met with any description of the other modes of karma.

reply, like a person taking a golden mirror from a bag, related what he had done; shewing that neither by his own inherent power, nor by the assistance of the déwas, had he obtained the Budhaship, but by the kusala karma of previous births.

6. As men cannot fly through the air unless they have the power of the irdhis; so no being can be born in a state of happiness who has not acquired merit.

The wise man, who would obtain merit, bends his mind to the avoiding of all demerit, and to the destruction of the demerit he has already received; he regards with indifference, or he does not regard at all, the objects that are presented to the eye and other organs of sense. He also endeavours to gain all merit, and to retain the merit he has already gained. In this way, his mind is like a circle divided into four segments.

The kusala-chitta, or mind endowed with merit, is received and retained by the hearing of religious discourses; the performance of acts that in themselves are free from evil, and the studying of such lessons of wisdom as are beneficial in their tendency. To those who dwell in the déwa-lókas the kusala-chitta is natural, they receive it with their birth. It is also natural to those who have overcome evil desire, or have attained to the state of rahats.

In the kalpas in which there is no Budha, there are no years, seasons, months, titis, or nekatas. There is no teaching of the dharmma, or law. There is no saying, This is right, or, This is wrong. There is no acquiring of merit.

Even when there is a Budha, they cannot acquire merit who are born in any of the eight hells, or in the hell called Osupat; they cannot receive the news of his birth, and there is no cessation to their torments.

The beasts that are born upon the earth, because they are devoid of wisdom, cannot distinguish right from wrong. They are under the influence of fear, and they possess evil desire and anger, but nothing more. They are therefore unable to acquire merit.

There are beings called prétas, who continually think with sorrow on their fate, from not having acquired merit in former births; they are now tormented without ceasing by hunger and thirst, and have not the power of obtaining merit.

Neither can merit be acquired by the beings in the four arúpa

2 H

worlds, as they cannot seë Budha, nor hear his discourses. And those who live in the outer sakwalas, even though it be in the time of a supreme Budha, are unable to acquire merit, for a similar reason.

There are also other places in which merit cannot be obtained, such as Uturukuru, Púrwawidésa, and Aparagódána, and the 500 islands connected with each of these continents; and in the same class are to be included the 500 islands of Jambudwípa, except Ceylon; and the barbarous countries of Jambudwípa. And even persons who are born in Jambudwípa, if they are maimed, deaf, blind, outcastes, idiots, or sceptics, are unable to acquire merit.

It is only in this sakwala that nirwána can be secured; and it is therefore called the magul-sakwala, or most favoured world; literally, the festive sakwala.

Budha has declared that men are few in number, but that the other beings are many; and that there are more in the sea than upon the land. The water of the great ocean is to the four continents as the water of the pond to the lotus; yet in every part there is an abundance of fish. Were the branches of all the trees in Jambudwípa and its 500 islands to be stripped of their leaves, and every blade of grass to be rooted up, and a fish were to be pierced with each leaf and blade, there would still be a multitude of fishes in the ocean remaining unpierced. The living things upon the land are also numerous, as in the body of a man there are ninety different species of worms. The hells too are filled with beings who are continually passing from one state of torment to another; and in the préta-lóka it is the same. Thus it is difficult, even in a kap-asankya, to obtain deliverance from the sequence of existence.

7. There was a nobleman, in whom the king delighted, and he was entrusted with the government of a country; but as he began to oppress the people, the king commanded him to be cast into prison, and slain. It is thus with men who have the opportunity of acquiring merit, and neglect it. As the nobleman enjoyed the royal favour, but was afterwards cast into prison; so may a man be prosperous for a time, on account of the merit he has received in former births; but if he does not continue to keep the precepts, his next birth will be in one of the hells; he will then be born in this world as a beast;

afterwards as a préta; and again in one of the hells. The same succession of punishment will be many times repeated. Therefore, let him who has the opportunity of acquiring merit, by being born when the precepts of Budha are taught, be careful not to let his privileges pass away without improvement.

Budha one day took up a small portion of mould in his finger nail; and said that those who die in this world, and are afterwards born again in the same world or in one of the déwa-lókas; or those who die in one of the déwa-lókas, and are afterwards born again in a déwa-lóka or in this world; are in the same proportion to those who are born in some inferior form, as the mould in his nail to the whole earth.

He who is born as man in the time of a Budha, and refuses to acquire the merit necessary to attain nirwána, is like one who having swam across the seven seas, surmounted the eight concentric circles of rocks, and succeeded in climbing to the summit of Maha Méru, for some frivolous reason falls back into the sea, whereby he places himself in the position he occupied before his toils commenced, rendering them, after all their arduousness and difficulty, utterly without profit.

The man who thus allows himself to be led away by evil desire will receive the destruction of the crow, which was on this wise. An elephant feeding on the banks of the Ganges, at a place where it is four miles broad, fell into the stream, and was drowned. As the body floated down the river, it was seen by a crow, who in his ignorance thought thus within himself; "Here is food for more than a thousand crows; this body shall be my permanent abode." Thus thinking the crow flew to the carcase, and remained upon it night and day. It had all his thoughts; he fed upon its flesh, and from the water of the river quenched his thirst. Though he saw upon the banks many forests of mango, jack, and other fruit trees, and the sacred trees upon which were the fish that had been offered in sacrifice, he regarded them not. Thus he was hurried on by the stream, until carried far out to sea, whence even a bird would have attempted in vain to reach the shore. The flesh of the elephant was soon washed from the bones, or it was all eaten and there remained nothing but the skeleton. The crow then flew away in the direction in which he had come, but he could not discover the land; he flew north, in great alarm, and he flew south, but his efforts were all in vain. At last he fell into the sea, exhausted, and there perished. And so perish all who are under the influence of evil desire, and cleave to existing objects.

8. The king of Ságal said to Nágaséna, "Is kusala, merit, or akusala, demerit, the more powerful?" Nágaséna: "Merit is more powerful (in its effects) than demerit." Milinda: "This I cannot believe: when a man commits murder, theft, or any other great crime, he is beheaded, or eaten by dogs, or perishes in some other way. Not unfrequently the punishment is awarded the next day or at most a very little time after; but do we ever see that when an upásaka gives alms to a priest, or ten priests, or even a hundred thousand priests, the reward for so doing is received in the same birth?" Nágaséna: "Yes; there have been four persons who by this means have gone from the same body in which the alms were given to enjoy the happiness of the déwa-lókas; viz., the monarchs Maha Mandhátu, Nimi, and Sádhína, and the famous musician Guttíla." Milinda: "But these things happened ages ago; they are doubtful matters, such as no one has recently seen; can you not tell me of something that has happened since the appearance of our present Budha?" Nágaséna: "The slave Púrnna, from having presented alms to Seriyut, in the same birth became the wife of a nobleman. The daughter of a poor noble, Gópála-mátru-déwi, cut off her hair, and sold it for eight pieces of gold, which she gave to eight priests, and in the same birth became the principal queen of Udéni. The upásikáwa Suppiya, cut a piece of flesh from her thigh, which she presented to a priest who was sick, and the next day the wound in her thigh was healed. These and others, as Sumana, Mallika, and Ekasátika, received the reward of their merit in the same birth." Milinda: "True; but this is only like finding a few pearls in the great ocean; therefore, I still think that demerit is more powerful than merit. Sometimes in one single day I punish a hundred or a thousand men for their crimes. Again, in the battle that was fought between the brahman Bhadrasála, of the race of Nandagutta, and Chandragutta, of the race of Sákya, there were slain on both sides as follows:—About eighty persons had their heads cut off, 10,000 elephants, 100,000 horses, 50,000 charioteers, and a hundred

kelas of infantry, were slain; the eighty headless trunks rose up in the field of battle, and danced. Now all this bloodshed arose from the influence of demerit. But the monarch of Kósala presented an offering of unequalled value; for which he received no increase of wealth or prosperity. Therefore, that which I have declared must be true; merit must be far less powerful than demerit?" Nágaséna: "The power of demerit is small, and therefore its effects soon appear; the power of merit is great, and therefore its effects do not appear with the same rapidity. Thus, the esculent water lily, so much used in the region called Aparanta, is ready to be cut in one month after it has been sown, but the best rice requires five months in which to ripen. The value of the rice, however, is far greater than that of the water lily; the one is the food of kings, whilst the other is only eaten by labourers and slaves." Milinda: "This may be; but that warrior is the most famous who enters into the battle, seizes his powerful adversary, overcomes him, and at once drags him into the presence of his commander; that surgeon is accounted the most skilful, who quickly takes out the nail or the stake, and heals the wound that has thereby been caused; and that wrestler is the most applauded, who speedily throws down his opponent. In like manner, whether it be merit or demerit, that which produces its effects in the shortest period will be considered the most powerful." Nágaséna: "Demerit is connected with crime; but merit is not; when a man commits any crime he is speedily punished; but it is not so with a man who in a place of trust acts with integrity; his reward is delayed. The criminal is sought for that punishment may be administered; but when a reward is to be given, there is no seeking of the individual who has proved himself to be thus worthy. Therefore, notwithstanding these objections, merit may be more powerful than demerit; a fact that is not to be controverted."

When merit and demerit are both acquired, the former increases in a greater degree than the latter. In this way. The man who acquires demerit reflects that he has done wrong, and is brought to repentance, by which he is prevented from again committing the same crime. The man who acquires merit reflects that he has done right, by which satisfaction is produced in his mind; from satisfaction comes pleasure; from pleasure, joy; from joy, comfort of body; from comfort of body, tranquillity;

by which he perceives the good effects of merit. Thus demerit decreases, and merit increases. Again, a man who (for some crime) has his hands and feet cut off, presents a bunch of flowers to a Budha, by which he is prevented from entering hell during ninety-one kalpas; and in this manner he learns the manner in which the increase of merit is obtained.

9. The reward of merit is according to its character, as well as its degree. When it arises from something unconnected with the dharmma, worldly prosperity is received, or birth is secured as a garunda, suparnna, or nága. When it arises from something connected with the dharmma, it secures birth in a déwa-lóka or brahma-lóka, or an entrance into the paths.

10. The king of Ságal propounded this question to Nágaséna. " Is happiness connected with merit, or with demerit, or with a combination of the two ? " Nágaséna replied, " It is connected with merit, and with demerit, and with the combination of the two." Milinda: " But if there be merit, there is no sorrow; if there be sorrow, there is no merit; if happiness be connected with merit, it must be with that alone; if with demerit, it must be with that alone; merit and sorrow cannot appear together." Nágaséna: " There is a man who holds in his hand a bar of iron that has been heated during a whole day, and in the other hand a piece of ice from the forest of Himála; will both the iron and the ice burn the hand of him who holds them ? "* Milinda: "Yes, they will." Nágaséna: " What, are the iron and the ice both of them hot ? " Milinda: " No." Nágaséna: " Are they both cold ? " Milinda: " No." Nágaséna: " Therefore you see into the futility of your argument; if it be heat alone that burns, it is evident that they are not both hot; therefore it is not true that happiness and sorrow cannot exist together; or if it be cold alone that burns, it is evident that they are not both cold; therefore it is not true that merit and sorrow cannot exist together; they are not both hot, neither are they both cold; the one is hot, and the other is cold; yet they both burn, they both produce the same effect: in the same way, merit and sorrow may exist together."

11. In reply to questions that were put to him by Sekra, Budha said, " There are five kinds of pride. 1. Of possessions.

---

* I have seen the sensation of cold, on grasping iron, compared to that of heat; I think, by one of our north-polar navigators.

2. Of family or caste. 3. Of benefits that have been gained. 4. Of personal character. 5. Of religious knowledge. Whosoever is proud of his possessions will afterwards be born an asúr, a préta, or a yaká, living on a dunghill and delighting in filth. Whosoever is proud of his family may be born a man; but he will vomit warm blood, or flames will proceed out of his mouth, or his bowels will burst. Whosoever is proud of benefits that have been gained, will be born a préta, a yaká, or a worm. Whosoever is proud of his personal character, will be born ugly, with large lips. Whosoever is proud of his religious knowledge, will be born in the hell of ashes. They who are thus unwise place themselves at a distance from the paths; yet until they attain them these evils must continue to be endured, however much they may try to free themselves therefrom."

12. It was said by Budha in the Síwaka-sútra that disease may arise from an excess of the morbid humours, without any reference whatever to the karma of the individual by whom the pain is felt. "If any one," said he, "declares that all sensation, whether it be pleasure, pain, or indifference, is caused by the merit or demerit of former births, be he priest or be he brahman, his declaration is false."

13. The happiness and misery that may be alternately received by the same being, were thus described by the prince Mahanama to his brother Anurúdha, when he was endeavouring to prevail upon him to become a priest:—"The being who is still subject to birth may at one time sport in the beautiful garden of a déwalóka, and at another be cut to a thousand pieces in hell; at one time he may be Maha Brahma, and at another a degraded outcaste; at one time he may eat the food of the déwas, and at another he may have molten lead poured down his throat; at one time he may sip nectar, and at another be made to drink blood. Alternately, he may repose on a couch with the déwis, and writhe on a bed of red hot iron; enjoy the society of the déwas, and be dragged through a thicket of thorns; bathe in a celestial river, and be plunged in the briny ocean of hell; become wild with pleasure, and then with pain; reside in a mansion of gold, and be exposed on a mountain of lava; sit on the throne of the déwas, and be impaled with hungry dogs around; drawn in a chariot of the déwas, and dragged in a chariot of fire; drawn by an elephant, and yoked like a beast, to the chariot of others;

adorned with a crown, and carrying fuel; clothed in a robe of the déwas, and covered with a garb vile and filthy; ornamented with pearls, and clothed in rags; like Brahaspati in wisdom, and utterly ignorant; have a melodious voice, and be dumb, speaking only by the eyes and hands; a man with a retinue of females, a female in attendance upon a man; loved by others, and hated by others; and he may now be a king who can receive countless gems by the mere clapping of his hands, and now a mendicant, taking a skull from door to door to seek alms."

14. In many births Déwadatta was superior to Bódhisat, which may appear to contradict the assertion that prosperity is the reward of merit and calamity of demerit; but though he was continually the enemy of Bódhisat, he was not the enemy of others; and in the births in which he was king, he did many things that were good, for which he received the due reward. In the course of the sequence of existence the good and the evil are connected together in different relationships, as the stream of the river, in its onward career, meets with and bears on its surface that which is excellent as well as that which is mean; but though Déwadatta and Budha were thus frequently connected, in the last birth the former went to hell, and Budha attained nirwána.

15. The king of Ságal said to Nágaséna, "It was declared by Budha that Mugalan was the chief of those who possessed the power of irdhi; and yet it was said on another occasion, that the same Mugalan was assaulted by thieves, who pounded his body with staves, and broke his bones, after which he attained nirwána; now the one declaration is contrary to the other; if Mugalan had the power of irdhi, he could not have been exposed to the endurance of this calamity." Nágaséna: "It is perfectly true that the bones of Mugalan were broken, but it was by means of karma that this was effected." Milinda: "But are not irdhi and karma equally achinteyya, without mind, or beyond thought; and if so, does it not follow that the irdhi is able to overcome the karma, in the same way as we take one wood-apple to break another with, or one mango to break therewith another fruit of the same kind?" Nágaséna: "Among things that are achinteyya one may be more powerful than another. Thus, there are many princes who have authority, but one is more powerful than the rest; he is the king; all the others must attend to his com-

mands: in like manner, of all things that are achinteyya, karma is the most powerful, whether it be kusala or akusala, the karma of merit or of demerit. Again, when a man commits a crime, neither his father, his mother, his relatives, nor his friends can save him from punishment. Why? Because the will of the king is supreme; he is more powerful than all; and it is the same with karma. Again, when a fire breaks out in the forest, and the whole land is in a blaze, the water from many thousands of vessels would be insufficient to quench it; and in the same way, nothing can overcome the force of karma. In a former birth, far distant from the last, in which he attained nirwána, Mugalan was the murderer of his aged parents; and it was in consequence of this crime that in his last birth a similar calamity was inflicted on him by the thieves."

16. A female, of extremely beautiful appearance, was born, by the apparitional birth, at the foot of a mango (amba) tree, in a garden belonging to the Lichawi princes, near the city of Wisála. On account of the place of her birth she was called Ambapáli, and was a courtezan. The cause of her being a courtezan may be learnt from the following narrative. In the thirty-first kalpa previous to the present age, when Sikhi was Budha, Ambapáli was one of his female relatives; but she renounced the world, and though a member of the royal family became a priestess. One day when going to worship a certain dágoba, in company with other priestesses, in the course of their circumambulation of the relic, one of them happened to sneeze, and a part of the mucus, without her perceiving it, fell on the ground. The princess, however, who was next in the order of the procession, saw that the court was defiled, and exclaimed, " What rude person can have been here?" Though she did not discover the delinquent, she still abused her, whoever she might be.

In consequence of having thus offered an insult to a sacred person, she was next born in the Amédya hell, which caused her to wish that when again born of the race of man, she might receive the apparitional birth. She was afterwards an immense period in different hells, enduring great pain; was a hundred thousand times a female beggar; and ten thousand times a prostitute; but in the time of Kásyapa Budha she remained in perfect continence, and was then born a déwi, and after enjoying the pleasures of the déwa-lóka for the proper period, she was finally born in the garden of the Lichawi princes.

The gardener informed the princes that he had found a beautiful female at the foot of a mango tree; and on hearing this news they hastened to the place, and were in great amazement at her appearance. They all wished to possess her; but as this was not possible, in order to end the dispute that arose from their conflicting claims, that otherwise appeared to be interminable, it was decided that the eldest prince should take her; after which she was placed in the office of courtezan, and received as a gift the garden in which she had appeared.

At this time Gótama went with a large retinue of priests to the village of Kótigráma, near Wisála. When the Lichawi princes heard of his arrival, they put on their royal garments, and went to see him. But before their appearance, Ambapáli had gone to pay him her respects. On approaching the sage, she offered him the most profound reverence, and listened with great delight to a discourse that he delivered; after the conclusion of which she requested that he would next day do her the favour of receiving a repast at her dwelling. In returning home, as the people crowded forward on their way to the wihára, her chariot came into collision with that of one of the princes; but she heeded it not, and passed on. When she arrived at her dwelling, she set about the preparation of various kinds of the most delicious food. The princes, on arriving within a certain distance of the wihára in which Budha was residing, descended from their chariots, and as they approached nearer, reverently bowed themselves. The coming of the princes was perceived by Budha, who, as he noticed the different colours of their garments and ornaments, and the varied splendour of their array, said to his attendant retinue, "Priests, those of you who have not seen the glory of the Tusi déwa-lóka, look at the Lichawi princes; behold their grandeur, and learn therefrom the magnificence of Tusi." After remaining with the sage some time, listening to his instructions, they requested him to receive an offering at the palace the next day, but as he had already accepted the invitation of Ambapáli, he could not comply with their request. From this place he went to Gijjakáwásaya, in the village of Nádika. The next day Ambapáli informed Budha that all was prepared; when the great teacher, accompanied by a retinue of rahats, went to partake of the offering. At the conclusion of the repast, he repeated the usual benediction; and the courtezan, in return, presented the garden to the priesthood, and subsequently erected in it a wihára, which she gave to Budha.* She also renounced the world, became a priestess, and attained the state of a rahat.

17. The king of Ságal said to Nágaséna, "There are some persons in the world who present alms, and say at the same time, May this alms-offering be a benefit to my relatives who are dead, and have become prétas! Tell me, will their departed relatives receive any benefit from such an offering?" Nágaséna: "There are some prétas who receive a benefit therefrom, and others who will not: those who are born in any of the 136 hells will derive no benefit from the offering or the rice that is presented; nor will those who are born in the déwa-lókas, or those who are born as animals. There are four kinds of prétas:—1. Wantásikás, who live countless ages in great sorrow, eating the most disgusting substances. 2. Khuppipásikas, that live a whole budhántara without tasting either meat or drink. 3. Nijjhámatrisnikas, that live in the hollow of decayed trees which have been set on fire. These three kinds of prétas derive no benefits from offerings; but there are others that may receive assistance therefrom." Milinda: "Then it will frequently happen that no benefit is derived from the alms that are thus presented; and they will thus be fruitless and vain." Nágaséna: "Not so; there is a man who takes fish, flesh, toddy, rice, and cakes to present to his relatives; but he is not able to find them. On this account, is the food lost that he has prepared? Does he not enjoy it himself? And it is the same with alms (in such instances as have been referred to); the giver receives the benefit." Milinda: "Be it so; the deceased relatives will in some instances receive benefit from the alms that are presented; but if I become a cruel murderer, putting many persons to death without mercy, will my relatives in any way reap the reward of my evil actions?" Nágaséna: "No." Milinda: "What is the reason of this difference? The reward of good actions is received by the deceased relatives, but the reward of evil actions is not; tell me the cause of this distinction?" Nágaséna: "You are asking a profitless question; it is just like asking why the sky does not fall, or why

---

* When Fa Hian visited Wisála, the garden was yet in existence.

the stream of the river does not go upward rather than descend, or why men and birds have only two feet, whilst the beasts of the field have four; these are not proper questions at all for any one to ask.". Milinda: "I do not make this enquiry merely to trouble you; I ask it that my mind may be relieved, and that others also who have doubts upon the subject may be instructed." Nágaséna: "The reward of merit may be divided, and a portion of it imparted to another; but that of demerit cannot. Just in the same way, water may be carried by bamboo spouts to a great distance, but the rocks and hills cannot be removed at will; the lamp may be fed with oil or grease, but it cannot with water; water taken from the pond fertilises the soil, but that which is taken from the sea cannot be used for the same purpose." Milinda: "Will you explain to me how it is that the reward of demerit cannot be imparted to another? I am like a blind man; I want instruction." Nágaséna: "The reward of demerit is small and insignificant; that of merit is vast, and spreads to the déwalóka; and this is the reason why the one can be divided and not the other. A single drop of water cannot be made to spread over the space of ten or twelve yojanas; but a heavy shower fills the lakes, rivers, brooks, rills, and channels, and spreads over this space. And in like manner, demerit, on account of its littleness, cannot be received by another, whilst merit, because of its greatness, admits of participation." Milinda: "Whence is this greatness of merit derived?" Nágaséna: "A man gives alms, or keeps the precepts; by this means his mind is filled with satisfaction; again and again this satisfaction wells up within him, and he is induced to acquire a greater degree of merit; it is like a perpetual fountain, continually flowing over; but when a man does that which brings demerit, his mind becomes sorrowful, and he is deterred from pursuing the same course, like a river that is lost in the sand of the desert. It is in this way that merit increases and becomes great, whilst demerit is diminished."

X. THE ETHICS OF BUDHISM.

I. THE TAKING OF LIFE.—II. THEFT.—III. ADULTERY.—IV. LYING.—V. SLANDER.—VI. UNPROFITABLE CONVERSATION.—VII. COVETOUSNESS.—VIII. SCEPTICISM.—IX. INTOXICATING LIQUORS.—X. GAMBLING.—XI. IDLENESS.—XII. IMPROPER ASSOCIATIONS.—XIII. PLACES OF AMUSEMENT.—XIV. THE PARENT AND CHILD.—XV. THE TEACHER AND SCHOLAR.—XVI. THE PRIEST AND HOUSEHOLDER.—XVII. THE HUSBAND AND WIFE.—XVIII. THE MASTER AND SERVANT.—XIX. THE FRIEND.—XX. MISCELLANEOUS ADVICES.—XXI. THE SÍLA PRECEPTS.—XXII. TERMS AND CLASSIFICATIONS.

THERE are three sins of the body:—1. The taking of life, Murder (1). 2. The taking of that which is not given, Theft (2). 3. The holding of carnal intercourse with the female that belongs to another, Adultery (3).

There are four sins of the speech:—1. Lying (4). 2 Slander (5). 3. Abuse. 4. Unprofitable Conversation (6).

There are three sins of the mind:—1. Covetousness (7). 2. Malice. 3. Scepticism (8).

There are also five other evils that are to be avoided:—1. The drinking of intoxicating Liquors (9). 2. Gambling (10). 3. Idleness (11). 4. Improper Associations (12). 5. The Frequenting of Places of Amusement (13).

There are additional obligations that are binding upon particular classes of individuals, among whom may be reckoned:—1. The Parent and Child (14). 2. The Teacher and Scholar (15). 3. The Priest and Householder (16). 4. The Husband and Wife (17). 5. The Master and Servant (18). 6. The Friend (19).

There are Miscellaneous Advices and Admonitions (20) that form another section.

The Síla Precepts are almost limitless in their extent (21). The most celebrated are the ten Obligations of the Priest.

In the native works, certain terms are continually met

with, an understanding of which is necessary to a right acquaintance with Budhism. A few of the more important of these Terms are inserted, with their explanation (22).

---

1. *The Taking of Life.*

Pránagháta is the destruction of the life of any being, the taking of it away. The prána is here put for the being, but it is only by a figure of speech. In reality the prána is the same as the jíwitindra (the eighteenth rúpa-khanda, the principle of life. He who takes away this principle, whether it be done immediately or by instigation (by the body or by the speech) is guilty of this crime. He who takes away the life of a large animal will have greater demerit than he who takes away the life of a small one; because greater skill or artifice is required in taking the life of the former than of the latter. When the life of a man is taken, the demerit increases in proportion to the merit of the person slain; but he who slays a cruel man has greater demerit than he who slays a man of a kind disposition.

There are five things necessary to constitute the crime of taking life. 1. There must be the knowledge that there is life. 2. There must be the assurance that a living being is present. 3. There must be the intention to take life. 4. With this intention there must be something done, as the placing of a bow or spear, or the setting of a snare; and there must be some movement towards it, as walking, running, or jumping. 5. The life must be actually taken. (*Sadharmmaratnakáré.*)

Again, it is said, when any one injures a tree, or root, or rock, with the intent to take life, not knowing its nature; when any one takes life, knowing it is life that he takes; when any one intends to take life; when any one actually takes life, whether it be done by himself or through the instrumentality of another, he is guilty of this crime. (*Milinda Prasna.*)

Pránagháta may be committed by the body, as when weapons are used; by word, as when a superior commands an inferior to take life; or by the mind, as when the death of another is desired.

There are six ways in which life may be taken:—1. By the person himself, with a sword or lance. 2. By giving the command to another. 3. By the use of projectiles, such as a spear, an arrow, or a stone. 4. By treachery, as the digging of pits and covering them slightly over, setting springs, or poisoning ponds. 5. By magical rites. 6. By the instrumentality of demons. (*Pújáwaliya.*)

There are eight causes of the destruction of life:—1. Evil desire. 2. Anger. 3. Ignorance. 4. Pride. 5. Covetousness. 6. Poverty. 7. Wantonness, as in the sport of children. 8. Law, as by the decree of the ruler.

This crime is committed, not only when life is actually taken, but also when there is the indulgence of hatred or anger; hence also lying, stealing and slander, may be regarded in some sense as including this sin. (*Sadharmmaratnakáré.*)

Under certain circumstances one's own life may be given up, but the life of another is never to be taken.

If the person who is killed is the person who was intended to be slain, the crime of murder has been committed; but if it is intended to take the life of a particular person, by throwing a dart, or javelin, and the weapon kill another, it is not murder. If it is intended to take life, though not the life of any particular person, and life be taken, it is murder. When a blow is given with the intention of taking life, whether the person who is struck die at that time or afterwards, it is murder.

When a command is given to take the life of a particular person, and that person is killed, it is murder; but if another person be killed instead, it is not murder. When a command is given to take the life of a person at a particular time, whether in the morning or in the evening, in the night or in the day, and he be killed at the time appointed, it is murder; but if he be killed at some other time, and not at the time appointed, it is not murder. When a command is given to take the life of a person at a particular place, whether it be in the village, or city, or desert, on land, or on water, and he be killed at the place appointed, it is murder; but if he be killed at some other place, and not at the place appointed, it is not murder. When a command is given to take the life of a person in a particular position, whether it be walking, standing, sitting, or lying down, and he be killed whilst in the position appointed, it is murder: but if he be killed whilst in some other position, and not in the position appointed, it is not murder. When a command is given to take the life of a person by a particular weapon, whether it be sword or spear, and he be killed by the weapon appointed, it is murder; but if he be killed by some other weapon, and not by the weapon appointed, it is not murder.

Were a command to be given to take the life of any person fifty years afterwards, or even at a period still more distant, and the person giving the command were to die a moment after it was issued, he would be guilty of murder, and as such would be born in one of the hells.

The crime is not great when an ant is killed; its magnitude increases in this progression—a lizard, a guana, a hare, a deer, a bull, a horse, and an elephant. The life of each of these animals is the same, but the skill or effort required to destroy them is widely different. Again, when we come to men, the two extremes are the sceptic and the rahat (as no one can take the life of a supreme Budha).

In the village of Wadhamána, near Danta, there was an upásaka who was a husbandman. One of his oxen having strayed, he ascended a rock that he might look for it; but whilst there he was seized by a serpent. He had a goad in his hand, and his first impulse was to kill the snake; but he reflected that if he did so he should break the precept that forbids the taking of life. He therefore resigned himself to death, and threw the goad away; no sooner had he done this, than the snake released him from its grasp, and he escaped. Thus, by observing the precept, his life was preserved from the most imminent danger.

A certain king, who reigned at Anurádhapura, commanded an upásaka to procure him a fowl and kill it. As he refused, the king issued a decree that he should be taken to the place of execution, where a fowl was to be put into his hand, and if he still refused to kill it, he was to be slain. The upásaka, however, said that he had never broken the precept that forbids the taking of life, and that he was willing to give his own life for the life of the fowl. With this intention he threw the fowl away unhurt. After this he was brought back to the king, and released, as he had been put to this test merely to try the sincerity of his faith. (*Pújáwaliya.*)

In the city of Wisála there was a priest, who one day, on going with the alms-bowl, sat down upon a chair that was covered with a cloth, by which he killed a child that was underneath. About the same time there was a priest who received food mixed with poison into his alms-bowl, which he gave to another priest, not knowing that it was poisoned, and the priest died. Both of these priests went to Budha, and in much sorrow informed him of what had taken place. The sage declared, after hearing their story, that the priest who gave the poisoned food, though it caused the death of another priest, was innocent, because he had done it unwittingly; but that the priest who sat upon the chair, though it only caused the death of a child, was guilty, as he had not taken the proper precaution to look under the cloth, and had sat down without being invited by the householder.

It was said by Budha, on one occasion, that the priests were not to throw themselves down (from an eminence, in order to cause their death). But on another occasion he said that he preached the bana in order that those who heard it might be released from old age, disease, decay, and death; and declared that those were the most honourable of his disciples by whom this purpose was accomplished. The one declaration (as was observed by the king of Ságal), appears to be contrary to the other; but the apparent difference may be reconciled by attending to the occasions on which they were delivered. There was a priest who was under the influence of passion; and as he was unable to maintain his purity he thought it would be better to die than to continue an ascetic. He therefore threw himself from a precipice, near the rock Gijakúta; but it happened that as he came down he fell upon a man who had come to the forest to cut bamboos, whom he killed, though he did not succeed in taking his own life. From having taken the life of another he supposed that he had become párájiká, or excluded from the priesthood; but when he informed Budha of what had taken place, the sage declared that it was not so (as he had killed the man unintentionally, his intention being to take his own life). Nevertheless, though Budha declared that he delivered the bana in order that old age and decay might be overcome, he made known that the priests were not permitted, like the one abovementioned, to throw themselves from an eminence in order that their lives may be destroyed. The members of the priesthood are like a medicine for the destruction of the disease of evil desire in all sentient beings; like water, for the washing away of its dust; a talisman, for the giving of all treasures; a ship by which to sail to the opposite shore of the sea of carnal desire; the chief of a convoy of wagons, to guide across the desert of decay; a wind, to extinguish the fire of anger and ignorance; a shower of rain, to wash away earthly affection; an instructor, to teach the three forms of merit, and to point out the way to nirwána. It was, therefore, out of compassion to the world that Budha commanded the priests not to precipitate themselves (or to cause their own death). The benefit of the priesthood was also declared by the priest Kumára Kásyapa to a certain brahman. But as the repetition of existence is connected with many evils, Budha delivered his discourses in order that by their means it might be overcome or destroyed. (*Milinda Prasna.*)

The unwise man is cruel; to all beings he is unkind, and he takes life. For this he will in the present world be in danger from sharp instruments, the horns of animals, &c. He will then be born in hell, and after remaining there hundreds of thousands of years, he will again be born in this world; but if he belong to a rich or illustrious family, he will not be permitted to enjoy the privileges of his birth; he will die whilst he is young. (*Sáleyya-sútra-sanné.*)

He who keeps the precept which forbids the taking of life will be thus rewarded:—He will afterwards be born with all his members perfect; he will be tall and strong, and put his feet firmly to the ground when he walks; he will have a handsome person, a soft and clear skin, and be fluent in speech; he will have the respect of his servants and friends; he will be courageous, none having the power to withstand him; he will not die by the stratagem of another; he will have a large retinue, good health, a robust constitution, and enjoy long life. (*Pújáwaliya.*)

2. *Theft.*

When anything is taken that is not given by the owner, whether it be gold, silver, or any similar article, and it be hidden by the person who takes it, in the house, or in the forest, or in the rock, the precept is broken that forbids the taking of that which is not given; it is theft.

Again, it is said, when any one takes that which belongs to another, or that which he thinks belongs to another, or takes that which is not given, whether it be taken by himself or through the instrumentality of another, the precept is violated.

There are five things necessary to constitute the crime of theft:—1. The article that is taken must belong to another. 2. There must be some token that it belongs to another. 3. There must be the intention to steal. 4. There must be some act done, or effort exerted, to obtain possession. 5. There must be actual acquirement. (*Sadharmmaratnakáré.*)

When any one conceals near the road or in the forest that which belongs to another, breaks into houses, uses false scales, demands too large a share of profit, uses a false measure for oil or grain, or utters false money, it is theft. When any one takes more than is due, or extorts a fine larger than is allowed by the law, it is theft. When any one procures for himself that which belongs to another by the giving of false evidence, it is theft.

This crime may be committed by making signs to any one to take that which belongs to a third person.

When that which belongs to another is taken so much as a hairbreadth, with the intention to keep it, it is theft; but if it be taken even the distance of a cubit, and then returned, it is not theft. To take an ear of corn from the field, or a fruit from the tree, or a flower from the garden, is theft. When a piece of money is left upon the ground by mistake, or through forgetfulness, to put the foot upon it in order to conceal it, it is theft. When any one causes a person carrying any article to throw it down and run away from fear, whether he takes the article or not, it is theft. When an article is given on loan, or in pledge, and the person receiving it keeps it, it is theft. When a number of persons agree to commit a robbery, though only one takes the article, the whole are guilty of theft.

When a command is given by any one to take that which belongs to another, at the distance of thirty or forty years, though he dies immediately after giving the command, he is guilty of theft, and as such will be born in one of the four hells.

To take that which belongs to a sceptic is an inferior crime, and the guilt rises in magnitude in proportion to the merit of the individual upon whom the theft is perpetrated. To take that which belongs to the associated priesthood, or to a supreme Budha, is the highest crime.

He who keeps the precept that forbids the taking of that which is not given, will in future births receive abundance of wealth and of golden vessels, he will have no desire for that which is not in his possession, no anxiety for the property of another; he will be able to preserve all that he has acquired; he will not have to endure affliction from kings or robbers, from water or fire; he will acquire many things that are not in the possession of others; he will be exalted in the world; his requests will not be denied; and he will live in comfort. (*Pújáwaliya.*)

3. Adultery.

When any one approaches a woman that is under the protection of another, whether it be her father, if her mother be dead; or her mother, if her father be dead; or both parents; or her brother, sister, or other relative of either parent; or the person to whom she has been betrothed: the precept is broken that forbids illicit intercourse with the sex. Whosoever does this will be disgraced by the prince; he will have to pay a fine, or be placed in some mean situation, or have a garland of flowers put in derision about his neck.

There are twenty-one descriptions of women whom it is forbidden to approach. Among them are, a woman protected by her relatives; or bought with money; or who is cohabiting with another of her own free will; or works for another person for wages, though she is not a slave; or who is betrothed; or a slave living with her owner; or working in her own house; or taken as a spoil in war. All these are to be regarded as the property of another, and are therefore not to be approached.

When any one approaches a female who is the property of another, with the intent to commit evil, and practises some deception to gain his end, and accomplishes his purpose, he transgresses against the precept.

Four things are necessary to constitute this crime:—1. There must be some one that it is unlawful to approach. 2. There must be the evil intention. 3. There must be some act or effort to carry the intention into effect. 4. There must be the accomplishment of the intention. (*Sadharmmaratnakáré.*)

The magnitude of this offence increases in proportion to the merit of the woman's protector; and when she has no protector, in proportion to her own merit.

In the time of Piyumatura Budha there was a female who exercised the wish to become the principal priestess of a future Budha. Accordingly, in the time of Gótama, she was born in Sewet, of a noble family, and was called Utpalawarnna. She was so extremely beautiful that her father thought if he gave her to the king, or the sub-king, or to any prince or noble, the others would be envious, and become her enemies. He therefore resolved upon making her a priestess, to which she herself was perfectly agreeable. Soon after her initiation, as she was looking at the flame of a lamp hung up at a festival, it became to her a sign, by which she practised téjo-kasina, and became a rahat. In the Andha forest, near Sewet, there was a cell, to which she retired that she might perform the exercises of asceticism. At this time it was not forbidden by Gótama that priestesses should reside in the forest alone. One day she went with the alms-bowl to Sewet, which became known to Nanda, the son of her mother's brother, who had loved her before she assumed the robe. Whilst she was absent, he went secretly to her cell, and concealed himself under her couch. On returning, as she could not see clearly from coming immediately out of the strong sunshine, she lay down upon the couch, when Nanda came from his concealment and violated her person; but the earth opened, and he was taken to hell by the flames arising from Awichi.

He who keeps the precept that forbids the approach to a woman who is the property of another, will afterwards have no enemy, as all persons will love him; he will possess food, garments, and couches in abundance; he will sleep soundly, and have no unpleasant dreams; he will not be born a female, will be placid in his disposition, and free from anger, and have all his senses perfect; he will have an agreeable person, and possess the confidence of all persons; all things will happen to him according to his wishes, with little effort on his part to secure their gratification; he will have prosperity, be free from disease, and retain that which he possesses. (*Pújáwaliya.*)

4. *Lying.*

To deny the possession of any article, in order to retain it, is a lie, but not of a heinous description; to bear false witness in order that the proper owner may be deprived of that which he possesses, is a lie, to which a greater degree of culpability is attached.

When any one declares that he has not what he has; or that he has what he has not; whether it be by the lips, or by signs, or in writing, it is a lie.

When any one says that which is not true, knowing it to be false, and gives it actual utterance, the person addressed receiving it as true, it is a lie.

The first lie ever spoken in the world was uttered by Chétiya, king of Jambudwípa.

There are some persons who regard the telling of a lie as a trifle; they speak falsely, in the court of justice, or in the presence of the multitude, or when deciding a case of inheritance, or when in the court of the king. They say that they know, though they do not know; that they do not know, though they know. They say that they saw, though they did not see; that they did not see, though they saw. About the members of the body, or the wealth of relatives, or because they have received a bribe, they knowingly speak that which is not true.

Four things are necessary to constitute a lie:—1. There must be the utterance of the thing that is not. 2 There must be the knowledge that it is not. 3. There must be some endeavour to prevent the person addressed from learning the truth. 4. There must be the discovery by the person deceived that what has been told him is not true. (*Sadharmmaratnakáré.*)

The magnitude of the crime increases in proportion to the value of the article, or the importance of the matter, about which the lie is told.

From the time that Gótama became a Bódhisat, through all his births, until the attainment of the Budhaship, he never told a lie; and it were easier for the sakwala to be blown away than for a supreme Budha to utter an untruth.

It is said by the brahmans that it is not a crime to tell a lie on behalf of the guru, or on account of cattle, or to save the person's own life, or to gain the victory in any contest; but this is contrary to the precept.

On one occasion Budha said that when a lie is uttered knowingly it is párájiká, or excludes from the priesthood; yet on another occasion he said that it is a venial or minor offence. It was in this manner that it occurred. A number of priests kept was near the river Waggumudá, in the country called

Wœdæ; but as the people were remiss in providing them with food and other requisites, they falsely gave out that they had attained to the first dhyána, or had entered the first path, or had become rahats, by which means they obtained abundance of all that they wanted. At the conclusion of the ceremony they went to Budha, who, after enquiring about their welfare, began to reprove them, and said, "Foolish men, for the sake of the belly you have assumed to yourselves the glory of the dharmma, as if you yourselves had promulgated it. Better would it have been for you, than to have practised this deception for the sake of a little food, to have had your intestines torn out, or to have swallowed molten metal. There are five opponents of my religion who for their crimes are afterwards born in hell:—1. The priest who places himself at the head of a hundred, or a thousand others, merely that he may obtain a livelihood from the laity. 2. The priest who understands the bana, but proclaims it as his own. 3. The priest who falsely accuses another of having violated the law of chastity. 4. The priest who takes the lands, couches, chairs, pillows, vessels, axes, hoes, withes, and other things that have been presented as an offering to the associated priesthood, and gives them to the laity that he may secure their favour. But worse than any that have yet been named, is the priest who proclaims himself to be a rahat, that he may gain respect and assistance. Therefore, priests, as you have practised this deception, you are declared to be párajiká." The other occasion on which Budha spoke about lying was when he declared that if a priest knowingly utters a falsehood relative to anything that he has said or done, and in an humble manner shall confess it to another priest, it is páchiti, a minor fault, or one that requires only confession in order to secure absolution. Thus, if one man strikes another in the street, he is merely fined for the offence; but if he were to strike the king, his hands and feet and then his head would be cut off, and all his relatives, both on the side of his father and mother to the seventh degree of relationship, would be destroyed.* In

* In 1846, when the life of the king of the French was attempted, and the criminal was only sentenced to perpetual imprisonment, though found guilty, I had the opportunity, in a small periodical I then published in Singhalese, of showing the great change that has taken place in the severity of punishments, by publishing the above sentence in juxta-position with this extract from the Questions of Milinda.

like manner there is a difference in the amount of culpability between one lie and another. (*Milinda Prasna.*)

He who keeps the precept that forbids the uttering of that which is not true will in future births have all his senses perfect, a sweet voice, and teeth of a proper size, regular and clean; he will not be thin, nor too tall nor too short; his skin will smell like the lotus; he will have obedient servants and his word will be believed; he will have blue eyes, like the petal of the nelum, and a tongue red and soft like the petal of the piyum; and he will not be proud, though his situation will be exalted. (*Pújáwaliya.*)

5. *Slander.*

When any one, to put friends at enmity, or to sow dissension between societies, says here what he heard there, or there what he heard here, it is slander; or if he speaks evil of persons and places that are esteemed by others, or if by insinuation he leads friends to question the sincerity of each others' professions, it is also slander. He who does these things will be born in hell, there to remain during many ages; and when released from this misery he will become a préta, and endure great privations during a whole kalpa.

The brahmans say that it is no crime to utter slander, when it will tend to the benefit of the guru, but this also is contrary to the precept.*

6. *Unprofitable Conversation.*

When things are said out of the proper time, or things that cannot in any way tend to profit are spoken of, the precept that forbids unprofitable conversation is broken. (*Sáleyya-sútra-sanné.*)

7. *Covetousness.*

When any one sees that which belongs to another, and desires to possess it, or thinks, It would be good were this to belong to me, he transgresses the precept that forbids covetousness.

---

* I have not met with any advices or explanations relative to the third crime connected with speech, abuse, or railing; and have to say the same of the second crime connected with the mind, malice.

8. *Scepticism.*

A man thinks thus:—There is no reward for alms-giving, or for that which is offered to the associated priesthood, or for service done in the temples; there are no consequences proceeding from merit or demerit; those who are in another world cannot come to this, and those who are in this world cannot enter any other world, as there is no passing from one world to another; there is no apparitional birth; there is no one in the world who can teach the true way, no one who has attained it; there is no Budha, no bana, no priesthood, no present world, no future world, no future existence. This is scepticism.

The sceptic induces many to leave the right path, thus causing grief to both déwas and men; but the wise man prevails on others to leave the wrong path and enter the right one. The sceptic will be punished in one or other of these two ways; he will be born in hell, or as a beast. The wise man will be rewarded in one or other of these two ways; he will be born in a déwa-lóka, or as a man. There are five great crimes, but scepticism is a still greater crime. At the end of a kalpa, they who have committed any of the five great crimes will be released from hell, but to the misery of the sceptic there is no end appointed.

Scepticism is the root or cause of successive existence; there is no release for the sceptic; he cannot enter the paths, neither can he enter a déwa-lóka. The being that is born in hell, may, at the end of a kalpa, be born in a brahma-lóka, on account of previous merit, but the sceptic has no such privilege; he will be born in the hell of some outer sakwala, and when this is destroyed he will be born in the air, but still in misery. This is declared in the prakarana Sárasangraha. (*Sáleyya-sutra-sanné.*)

The folly of the sceptic is like that of the brahman who was deceived by the jackal. One night, a jackal entered a certain city, and finding some refuse of toddy that had been thrown away, he devoured it, and became drunk. When he came to his senses it was already light, and he was greatly afraid; but he resolved to put forth all his cunning in order that he might rescue himself from the imminent danger. Soon afterwards he offered a brahman whom he met two hundred pieces of gold if he would assist him in his escape. The man was willing, and took him by his legs to carry him out of the city; but the jackal said, "Is this a proper manner in which to carry me, when so much gold is to be your reward?" Then he wrapped the animal up in his outer garment, and threw it across his shoulder. When they had passed the gate, the man asked if he should put him down there; but the jackal said it was too public a place in which to expose so much money; he must take him a little further. Then the jackal told him to wait a little, and he would go and fetch the money, as he had an immense store, and it was not right that the brahman should know where he kept it. Until sunset did he wait, but the jackal did not return. The déwa of a tree, who had watched the proceedings, then reproached him for his folly; and asked him how he could suppose that the jackal could give him two hundred pieces of gold, when he had not as many coppers? Thus will it be with those who listen to the teachings of Siva or Vishnu; they will be deceived, and the object at which they aim will not be attained. (*Pújáwaliya.*)

There are four kinds of questions that belong to the class called wyákarana:—

1. Ekansa:—The questions belonging to this division do not admit of doubt; they are asked with a certainty of the result; as when any one enquires if the five khandas are impermanent, it is known that they are so.

2. Wibhajja.—The questions belonging to this division are the same as those belonging to the first, but they are asked with some doubt as to the result.

3. Pratipuchhá.—When it is asked, Is the knowledge of all things received by the eye? the question belongs to this class.

The questions in any of these three classes may be asked without any impropriety, but those belonging to the next division are to be passed by, they are not to be regarded.

4. Thápani.—The questions belonging to this division are numerous. When it is concluded that the world is permanent, this is séswata-drishti. To conclude that the world is impermanent, but that after death there is no other existence, is uchhédadrishti. To conclude that the life and the body are the same thing, is uchhéda-drishtirwáda. To conclude that the life

and the body are separate and distinct existences, is séswata-drishti-wáda. To conclude that the same individual being will exist after death, or that he will not exist after death, or that he will neither exist after death nor not exist after death, or that he will exist after death and will not exist after death, is amaráwikshépika-drishti. All these questions are to be put on one side, and avoided.* (*Wisudhimargga-sanné.*)

9. *Intoxicating Liquors.*

When any intoxicating liquor has been taken with the intention that it shall be drunk, and something is actually done to procure the liquor, and it has passed down the throat, the precept is broken that forbids the use of toddy, and other intoxicating drinks.

When intoxicating drink is taken that robbery may be committed, whether on the highway or in the village, the crime is presented in its worst form.

When only so much toddy is drunk as can be held in the palm of the hand, it is a minor offence; it is a greater when as much is drunk as can be held in both hands; and a greater still when so much is drunk that all things appear to be turning round.

Of the five crimes, the taking of life, theft, adultery, lying, and drinking, the last is the worst. Though a man be ever so wise, when he drinks he becomes foolish, and like an idiot; and it is the cause of all other sins. For this reason it is the greater crime. (*Pújáwaliya.*)

To constitute the crime of drinking, four things are necessary:—1. There must be intoxicating liquor, made from flour, bread, other kinds of food, or a collection of different ingredients. 2. There must be actual intoxication produced by these liquors. 3. They must be taken with the intention of producing this effect. 4. They must be taken of free will, and not by compulsion. (*Sadharmmaratnakáré.*)

There are six evil consequences from the continued use of intoxicating liquors:—1. The loss of wealth. 2. The arising of disputes, that lead to blows and battles. 3. The production of various diseases, as soreness of the eyes, &c. 4. The bringing

---

* Under this head are also enumerated the errors inserted at page 10.

of disgrace, from the rebuke of parents and superiors. 5. The exposure to shame, from going hither and thither unclothed. 6. The loss of the judgment required for the carrying on of the affairs of the world.

If a man has a friend in the tavern, he is only a liquor friend: before the face he says, My friend, my friend, but behind the back he seeks some hole by which he may do an injury; he is a friend without friendship, a mere image or picture; he is a friend where there is gold and wealth.

The man who frequents the tavern, and drinks, will be like water falling upon a rock; his desire of liquor will only become the more powerful, and he will lose his respectability. (*Singálówáda-sútra-sanné.*)

He who observes this precept will in future ages have an intelligent mind and a sound judgment; he will not lose his senses; he will not be an idle man, nor mean, nor addicted to liquor; he will not stray from the right path, nor will he be envious; he will be prompt in the giving of an answer, and know what is profitable and what is dangerous. (*Pújáwaliya.*)

10. *Gambling.*

There are six evil consequences that result from frequenting places of gambling:—1. The man who loses is angry with him who wins. 2. He is sorrowful, because another has seized his substance. 3. His poverty is wasted. 4. When the gambler gives evidence in a court of justice his testimony is not believed, even though he should speak the truth. 5. He is not trusted either by his friends or superiors. 6. He cannot procure a wife, from being unable to provide the proper ornaments and jewels.

The gambler first loses his child, then his wife, and afterwards all his substance; he is left in perfect solitude (literally nottwoness); but this is a minor affliction; he will be born in hell. (*Singálówáda-sútra-sanné.*)

11. *Idleness.*

He who says it is too hot, or too cold, or too early, and on this account refuses to work, is an idle man, and will be deprived of the means of existence; but he who is neither afraid of the heat nor of the cold, nor of the grass,* will possess continued prosperity.

There are six evil consequences that arise from idleness:—1. The idle man thinks in the morning that the cold is enough to break his bones, so he does not set about any work, but lights a fire; thus his business suffers, whether it be merchandise or husbandry. 2. If any one at a later hour calls him to work, he says it is too hot, and so does nothing. 3. At night he says it is too late; his flocks are not folded, his cattle are neglected. 4. In the morning he says it is too early; so his work remains undone. 5. At another time he says he is too hungry, he must eat; so he is again prevented from attending to his duty. 6. When he has eaten, he says that his stomach is too full; so his labour comes to nothing. In this way, that which he requires is not obtained, and the wealth he has previously gained is wasted away. (*Singálówáda-sútra-sanné.*)

12. *Improper Associates.*

The man who has sinful friends, unwise associates, and frequents the company of those who follow evil practices, will come to destruction, both in this world and the next.

There are six evil consequences that result from associating with improper companions:—1. The man who frequents the company of gamblers will become a gambler. 2. If he associates with those who are attached to women, he will become licentious. 3. If with those who are addicted to the use of intoxicating liquors, he will become a drunkard. 4. If with those who speak evil behind the back, he will become a slanderer. 5. If with those who flatter, he will learn to practise deception. 6. If with those who commit sin, he will become a transgressor.

It has been declared by Budha that he who avoids the company of the wise, and associates with the evil, will be born in one of the four hells, and have no opportunity of entering the déwa or brahma-lókas; and even birth in the world of men cannot be attained by him without great difficulty. (*Singálówáda-sútra-sanné.*)

---

* This appears to refer to the dew. I have sometimes, when passing through the high grass that grows on the mountains of Ceylon, early in the morning, been made as wet as if I had waded through a river.

13. *Places of Amusement.*

There are six evil consequences that arise from frequenting places of amusement. The mind is ensnared by the following practices:—1. Dancing. 2. Singing. 3. The beating of drums. 4. Gambling. 5. The clapping of hands. 6. The game of water-jars.

Dancing, beating the drum, and singing are to be avoided; also, the seeing others dance, and the listening willingly to those who play or sing, But when dancing is seen, or music is heard, without the consent of the mind, the precept is not broken; nor when meeting persons in the way by chance who are dancing or playing; and if the bana be chanted, or listened to when chanted by others, it is an act of merit.

14. *The Parent and Child.*

It is right that children should respect their parents, and perform all kinds of offices for them, even though they should have servants whom they could command to do all that they require. In the morning, if it be cold they are to collect fuel, and light a fire. In extreme age, if they become filthy in their habits, they are cheerfully to cleanse them, remembering how they themselves were assisted by their parents, when they came polluted into the world. They are to wash the feet and hands of their parents, thinking how they themselves were washed when they were young. If attacked by any disease, they are to see that they have medicine provided, and to prepare for them gruel and suitable food. They are to see also that they have such clothing as they require, a bed upon which to lie, and a house in which to live. When needful, they are required, with their own hands, to rub their limbs with scented oil; but they must not take life for them, nor steal for them, nor give them intoxicating liquors; if so, all will be born in hell. Were the child to place one parent upon one shoulder, and the other parent upon the other, and to carry them without ceasing for a hundred years, even this would be less than the assistance he has himself received. The man who gains a livelihood for his parents by honest means, is a greater being than a Chakrawartti.

In a former age Mugalan, one of the two principal disciples of Gótama, caused the death of his parents, for which crime he was born in hell, where he had to suffer for many hundreds of thousands of ages. If a person possessed of so much merit had thus to suffer, great indeed must be the misery of an ordinary being, when guilty of the same offence.

Were the murderer of his parents, in order to obtain release from the consequences of this crime, to fill the whole sakwala with golden dágobas, or to present to the rahats an offering that would fill the entire sakwala, or to take hold of the robe of a Budha and never leave him, he would still be born in hell. This is declared in the Sárasangraha.

Among all who have not attained the paths, there has been no one equal to the monarch Ajásat, who, when he heard of the death of Budha, fainted three times, and was deprived of his senses. He it was who made a splendid receptacle for the depositing of the sage's relics, and appointed Maha Kásyapa and 500 rahats to assemble at the rock Wébhára, near Rajagaha, in order that they might declare authoritatively what were the sayings of Budha, what it was that was to be received as belonging to the tun-pitaka. But even this king, when he died, was born in hell, on account of the murder of his father.

There are five ways in which children should assist their parents:—1. When their parents, who in their infancy gave them milk, and rendered them all needful assistance, are old, they should wash their feet, and do all similar offices. 2. They must cultivate their fields. 3. They must see that their property is not wasted, in order that the respectability of the family may be kept up. 4. They must act according to the advice they give. 5. They must give alms in their name when they are dead.

There are five ways in which parents should assist their children:—1. They must prevent them from transgressing the precepts. 2. They must encourage them to do that which is right. 3. They must have them taught arithmetic and the other sciences. 4. They must provide the son with a beautiful wife, who has attained sixteen years of age. 5. They must give him a share of the wealth belonging to the family. (*Singálówáda-sútra-sanné.*)

15. *The Teacher and Scholar.*

It was ordained by Gótama, that the disciple should be in all respects obedient to the teacher, and render him all honour. When he rises in the morning he must place the teacher's sandals, robe and tooth-cleaner in proper order, present him with water that he may wash, prepare a seat, and give him rice-gruel from a clean vessel. All that is written in the Khandaka he must perform. The teacher may ask him why he has come, and he must then inform him; but if he does not make the enquiry, he must remain ten or fifteen days; and when the teacher dismisses him, he may respectfully ask leave to tell his wishes and wants. When he is told to come early in the morning, he must do so; but if he is taken ill, he may go at any other hour and inform the teacher.

There are five ways in which the scholar ought to honour the teacher:—1. When the teacher approaches, he must rise to meet him; if he has anything in his hand, he must ask permission to carry it for him; and he must wash his feet. 2. Thrice every day he must go to him, and render such assistance as he may require. 3. He must try to gain instruction from him by making enquiries, or he never can become properly learned. 4. He must bring water for the washing of his teacher's face, prepare the tooth-cleaner, and perform other similar offices. 5. Whatever he learns from the teacher, he must try to remember and put in practice.

There are five ways in which the teacher ought to assist the scholar:—1. He must teach him how to behave and how to eat, to avoid evil companions, and associate only with the good. 2. If the scholar pays attention, he must explain all things to him in a plain and intelligible manner. 3. What he has learnt from his own teacher, he must impart at length to his scholar. 4. He must tell the scholar that he is becoming as learned as himself, speaking to him in a friendly manner, that he may be encouraged. 5. He must teach him to please his parents by attention to his studies.

There are twenty-five rules that the teacher must observe in reference to his scholar:—He must be continually solicitous about his welfare; appoint the relative portions of time in which he is to work, to rest, and to sleep; when he is sick, he must see whether or not he has such food as is proper for him; encourage him to be faithful, persevering, and erudite; divide with him what he has received in the alms-bowl; tell him not to be afraid; know who are his associates, what places he frequents in the village, and how he behaves in the wihára; avoid conversing with him on frivolous subjects; bear with him, and not be angry when he sees a trifling fault in his conduct; impart to him instruction by the most excellent method; teach him in the fullest manner, without abridgment, whether it be relative to science or religion; try each fond endearment to induce him to learn, as with the heart of a father; with an enlarged mind teach him to respect the precepts and other excellent things; subdue him to obedience, in order that he may excel; instruct him in such a manner as to gain his affection; when any calamity overtakes him, still retain him, without being displeased when he has some matter of his own to attend to; and when he is in affliction, soothe his mind by the saying of bana. By attending to these rules the duty of the master to his scholar will be fulfilled. (*Singálówáda-sútra-sanné.*)

16. *The Priest and Householder.*

When the upásaka, though he may have entered the path sowán, sees a priest, whether that priest be of the superior or inferior order, he must do him honour; he must rise from his seat, and offer him worship; just as the prince, though he may afterwards be king, pays his teacher all respect and reverence.

There are five ways in which the householder ought to assist the priest:—He must render him any service that he requires, in a kind spirit; he must address him in a pleasant manner; he must wish that the priest who is accustomed to come to his house to receive alms may be free from disease and sorrow; in the morning he must present the priest with food, and when he is sick with medicine.

There are five ways in which the priest ought to assist the householder:—He must avoid the taking of life, and keep the precepts; he must wish that all creatures may be without sorrow; when anything is declared on the subject of religion that he has not heard before, he must listen attentively; he must explain the truths of religion properly to the upásakas, that they may be able to understand and practise them. (*Singálówáda-sútra-sanné.*)

17. *The Husband and Wife.*

There are five ways in which the husband ought to assist the wife:—1. He must speak to her pleasantly, and say to her, Mother, I will present you with garments, perfumes, and ornaments. 2. He must speak to her respectfully, not using low words, such as he would use to a servant or slave. 3. He must not leave the woman whom he possesses by giving to her clothes, ornaments, &c., and go to the woman who is kept by another. 4. If she does not receive a proper allowance of food she will become angry; therefore she must be properly provided for, that this may be prevented. 5. He must give her ornaments, and other similar articles, according to his ability. (*Singálówáda-sútra-sanné.*)

In the discourse delivered by Yasódhara-déwi, in the presence of men, déwas, and brahmas, immediately previous to her death, she described the seven kinds of wives that there are in the world of men.

1. Wadhaka, the executioner.—This woman always thinks ill of her husband, though protesting continually that she loves him; she associates with other men, and flatters them; if her husband be a poor man, she asks him for something it is not in his power to give her, and then reproaches him because she does not receive it; and she sits on a higher seat in his presence. Though such a woman should have a person beautiful as that of a déwi, be of a respectable family, and possess many slaves; she is not the wife of her husband; she is like a manacle tightly fastened by the executioner, or an iron collar encircling his neck, or a weapon always prepared to wound him, or a sword so sharp that it will cut a hair.

2. Chóri, the thief.—This woman is seldom in the house of her husband, but goes to the market-place, or the field, or wherever there is a multitude of people; she is acquainted with many ways of sin; she hides whatever property is brought into the house by her husband, hides it from him, but reveals it to other men; she tells abroad his secrets; she appears to despise any ornaments and other things that he gives her, and asks

pettishly for what he does not give; she shows no kindness to her husband's relatives or friends; she shuns the company of the good, and associates with the bad. She is not like his wife, but like an ulcer on his body, or a cancer, or an incurable disease; she is like a fire in a dry forest, or an axe for cutting down the tree of merit.

3. Swámi, the ruler.—This woman does not in any way strive to benefit her husband, but to injure him; she leaves the house, and runs hither and thither; she lets the work of the house remain undone; her mind goes out after other men; she is continually eating; she hankers after things that do not belong to her station; she proclaims her own fame, and gives no credit to others; she despises her husband, and rules him as if he was her slave, and is like a messenger sent from Yama to frighten him.

These three descriptions of women, when they die, will be tormented in hell; therefore their ways are to be avoided.

4. Mátu, the mother.—This woman loves her husband as a mother, takes care of his property, provides his meals at the proper time, and is always anxious for his prosperity; when he does anything wrong she affectionately reproves him, and threatens to return to her own relatives if he will not do that which is right; she gives him good advice and recommends him to be industrious, loyal, and to go and hear bana. She is like a divine medicine, for the curing of all diseases, or a branch of the kalpa-tree, that gives whatever is requested from it.

5. Bhágini, the sister.—This woman pays the same reverence to her husband that a sister does to her brother; she gives him all that is in the house; she wishes that he may receive whatever she sees others possess; and she loves him alone, and no other man.

6. Sakhi, the faithful friend.—This woman is always thinking about her husband when he is absent, and looks out continually for his return; it gives her pleasure to hear of him, and when he returns she is delighted to see him; she associates with his friends, and not with his enemies; his friends are her friends, and his enemies are her enemies; she hides his faults and proclaims aloud his goodness; she stops those who are abusing him, and encourages those who praise; she tells others of his virtues and greatness; she keeps no secrets from him, and does not reveal those with which he intrusts her; she is sorry when any

misfortune happens to him, and rejoices in his prosperity; and she provides for him the best food.

7. Dási, the slave.—This woman does not resent the abuse of her husband, however brutal it may be; she does all that is required of her with alacrity; she keeps at the utmost distance from all improper conduct with other men; she first gives food that has been nicely prepared to her husband, or any guest there may be in the house, and then eats herself; she retires to rest after her husband, and is up before he rises; she is economical in her expenditure; she commends and exalts her husband, but is herself lowly as a slave; and she is like a helper in the procuring of merit, or a shield in warding off demerit."

18. *The Master and Servant.*

There are five ways in which the master ought to assist the slave:—He must not appoint the work of children to men, or of men to children, but to each according to his strength; he must give each one his food and wages, according as they are required; when sick, he must free him from work, and provide him with proper medicine; when the master has any agreeable and savoury food, he must not consume the whole himself, but must impart a portion to others, even to his slaves; and if they work properly for a long period, or for a given period, they must be set free.

There are five ways in which the slave must honour his master: —He must rise before his master awakes, and must not sleep until after he has retired to rest; he must not purloin his master's property, but must be content with what is given him; he must not think as he works, I shall receive no benefit from this toil, but must go about his business cheerfully; and when people are at any time collected together he must say, Who is like our master? we do not feel that we are servants, or that he is a master, thus proclaiming to others his praise. (*Singálówáda-sútra-sanné.*)

19. *The Friend.*

There are five ways in which one friend must assist another: —By imparting to him of his own substance; by speaking kind words to him; by assisting him in his work; by acting in the same way to him as he has done to you; and by giving him a portion of your garments, and ornaments, if you have any, not hiding them from him.

There are five ways in which the friendship of a superior must be returned:—He must be protected from harm when he is in liquor; if he be sick, his cattle and property must be taken care of; when under the displeasure of the king, he must not be forsaken; when under any misfortune he must be assisted, and when he is disabled, his children must be assisted.

There are four kinds of persons who appear to be your friends, but they are not so in reality:—Those who come empty, but go away with a portion of your wealth; those who give assistance only in words; those who speak to you in an improper manner, or give bad advice; and those who waste your substance.

The friend who takes away part of your wealth is he who gives you a little, with the hope of receiving much in return; if any necessity comes upon him, he is your lowly slave, that he may gain your assistance; he does not associate with you because of affection, but to gain his own ends.

He who is your friend only in word, reminds you of obligations under which you were indebted to him long ago; he promises, when you are in difficulty, to assist you at some future time, but he forgets his promise; if he sees you in the street, he asks you to mount his elephant, and plies you with unmeaning words; if you really require his assistance, and ask him for it, he says falsely that his wagon is broken, or his oxen are diseased.

He who speaks to you in an improper manner, or gives you bad advice, may be known thus:—When you are meditating to take life, or do something that is contrary to the precepts, he encourages you in your evil design; when you are resolving to give alms, or do something that is good, he discourages you; when he is near you, he speaks well of you, and praises you, but when away, he says something that is to your discredit.

He who wastes your substance is he who tells you that in such a place there is good liquor, and says, Let us go and drink; he loiters over the liquor, and entreats you to drink again and again; he entices you to lounge in the streets at improper hours; and tempts you to visit places of amusement.

From such friends as these the wise man turns away, as he would avoid the road in which he knew that there was a lion or a tiger.

The real friend will at any time render you assistance; he is equally faithful in prosperity and adversity; he is a friend in meaning, and not in the promise alone; and he sympathises with you.

He who renders you assistance is he who, when he finds you in a state of intoxication, at the road side, thinks that some evil may happen to you, or that your clothes or ornaments may be stolen, so he stays to protect you; if he finds that you have gone out of the village, and that there is no one in charge of your property, he takes care of it in your stead; if you are tormented by any fear, he says, I am your friend, why are you alarmed? thus encouraging you; when you are in want, and go to ask a single piece of coin, he is ready to divide with you half his substance.

He who is equally faithful in prosperity and adversity, reveals a secret to you alone; if you reveal a secret to him, he faithfully keeps it; he does not turn away from you in adversity; he sacrifices even his life to assist you.

He who is your friend in meaning, and not in word alone, is he who prevents you from taking life, or doing any other evil; he urges you to almsgiving and other good deeds; he informs you of that which you did not previously know; and he tells you what is to be done in order that you may enter the paths.

He who sympathises with you rejoices in your prosperity; he is pleased when you receive any increase of honour; when he hears any one disparaging you, he says, Do not say so; he is a good man: and if he hears any one speak well of you, he confirms it.

The wise man searches for the friend thus gifted, even as the child seeks its mother.

He who is thus wise, and keeps the precepts, shines resplendent, as a flame of fire upon the top of a rock at night dissipates the surrounding darkness. He who does no evil, but increases his substance in a righteous manner, will be blessed with abundance. As the bee, without destroying the colour or perfume of the flower, gathers the sweetness with his mouth and wings, so the riches of the true friend gradually accumulate; and the increase will be regularly continued, like the constant additions that are made to the hill formed by the white ant. (*Singálōwada-sútra-sanné.*)

20. *Miscellaneous Advices and Admonitions.*

The benefits that accrue from the possession of riches may be divided into four parts:—1. They enable the possessor to gain friends. 2. A fourth part is required for his own personal expenses. 3. One half is required for the outlay attendant on the carrying on of husbandry or merchandise. 4. A fourth part must be hid as a resource when any case of necessity occurs, arising from the oppression of the king or the chiefs of the land.

There are six causes of the destruction of substance:—1. The repeated use of intoxicating liquors. 2. The tarrying in the streets at improper hours. 3. The frequenting of places of amusement. 4. The continued practice of gambling. 5. The associating with persons that are ignorant, or addicted to vice. 6. Idleness.

The practice of the six following things will be followed by destruction:—To sleep until the going down of the sun; to have intercourse with women that are under the protection of another; to be filled with anger, like a nayá that has received a blow; to seek to injure others; to associate with evil persons, like Déwa-datta or Kokálika; and to be covetous, like Illísa. (*Singálówáda-sútra-sanné.*)

It is declared by Budha, in the Bála-pandita-sútra, which he delivered when residing at Jetáwana, that the conduct of the unwise man may be set forth under three heads:—1. He cherishes evil thoughts, and thoughts that are contrary to the truth. 2. He utters falsehoods, and uses contemptuous expressions. 3. He takes life, steals, approaches women who belong to another, and drinks. In like manner, there are three modes in which he receives punishment. 1. He is constantly fearful; whether he be in the crowd, or in the street, or in a square, when he hears any one speaking of the consequences of sin, he becomes uncomfortable, thinking that he also may one day receive the consequence of his crimes; and because these are his thoughts, he is unwilling to remain, he goes away. 2. When he sees the infliction of any punishment by command of the king, he thinks that if the king knows all he has done, he will punish him in the same way; when alone, when seated in his chair, when reclining on the bed, or in any other place, he thinks of these things, and is sorrowful; even the crimes committed long ago trouble him; as the shadow of a great rock is thrown to a distance, and extends far, at the setting of the sun. 3. He is sorrowful again when he thinks how much merit he might have gained; but that he has neglected this opportunity, and instead has continually added to his crimes.

The six directions are not to be honoured with any outward ceremony.

On a certain occasion, when Budha was returning to the wihára, from the city of Rajagaha, whither he had been with the alms-bowl, he saw a grahapati, Singálóha, with wet hair and streaming garments,* making obeisance in the six directions. The sage enquired why he was acting thus; and when he said that it was in obedience to the command of his deceased parents, Budha gave him the advice contained in the Singálówáda-sútra. After hearing it, he saw the folly of the act that he was performing, and became a disciple of Budha, declaring that the instructions he had received were like the right placing of a vessel that had been turned upside down; or like the laying open of treasures that had been covered over with refuse and grass; or like the taking of a man by the hand who has lost the road and guiding him aright; or like the holding forth of a torch amidst the midnight darkness (effects that under similar circumstances are in the native works very frequently represented as being produced).

In their stead, our parents, who have assisted us in our infancy, are to be regarded as the east; our teachers, as being worthy to receive assistance, are to be regarded as the south; our children, as those by whom we are afterwards to be assisted, are to be regarded as the west; our friends and rulers, as those who will assist us in times of sorrow and misfortune, are to be as the north; our servants, salves, and retainers, as being under our authority, are to be as the under side; and the priests and religious advisers, as assisting us to put away that which is evil, are to be regarded as the upper side. (*Singálówáda-sútra-sanné.*)

---

* The men and women are seen coming dripping from the banks of the Ganges.—Ward's Hindoos.

As the man whose head is on fire tries to put the flame out quickly, so the wise man, seeing the shortness of life, hastens to secure the destruction of evil desire.

As the jessamine is the chief among flowers, and as the rice called rat-hel is the chief among all descriptions of grain, so is he who is free from evil desire the chief among the wise.

This advice was given by Budha. He who would attain nirwána must not trust to others, but exercise heroically and perseveringly his own judgment. The wagoner who leaves the right path and enters into the untrodden wilderness, will bring about the destruction of his wagons and endure much sorrow; so also will he who leaves the appointed path and enters upon a course of evil, come to destruction and sorrow.

The unwise man cannot discover the difference between that which is evil and that which is good, as a child knows not the value of a coin that is placed before him; he cannot tell whether it is gold or copper, or whether it is a genuine coin or a counterfeit.

As the hirala defends its eggs at the risk of its own life, as the Indian yak tries by every means to keep its tail from injury, as the man with only one son is careful of that son, as he who has only one eye takes great pains to preserve that eye; so ought the wise man continually to exercise thought, lest he break any of the precepts. Even should the forfeiture of life be the consequence, the precepts are to be observed.

When acts are done under the influence of favour, envy, ignorance, or the fear of those in authority, he who performs them will be like the waning moon; but he who is free from these influences, or avoids them, will be like the moon approaching its fulness.

When the seed of any species of fruit that is bitter is sown in moist ground, it gathers to itself the virtue of the water and the earth, but because of the nature of the original seed, all this virtue is turned into bitterness, as will be seen in the fruit of the tree that it produces; in like manner, all that the unwise man does is an increase to his misery, because of his ignorance. On the other hand, when the sugar cane, or rice, or the vine, is set in proper ground, it gathers to itself the virtue of the water and the earth, and all is converted into sweetness, because of the sweetness of the original plant or grain; in like manner, all the acts of the wise man tend to his happiness and prosperity, because of his wisdom.

The door of the eye* must be kept shut. When the outer gates of the city are left open, though the door of every separate house and store be closed, the robber will enter the city and steal the goods; in like manner, though all the observances be kept, if the eye be permitted to wander, evil desire will be produced.

It is better to have a red-hot piece of iron run through the eye, than for the eye to be permitted to wander, as by this means evil desire will be produced. It must be carefully guarded against, or the breaking of all the precepts will follow. The mind will then be like a field of grain that has no fence, or a treasure house with the door left open, or a dwelling with a bad roof through which the rain continually falls. The same may be said of all the other senses. (*Wisudhi-margga-sanné.*)

When dissensions take place, the mother is divided against the son, and the son against the mother; the father against the son, and the son against the father; the nephew against the niece, and the niece against the nephew; and friend against friend; as the laden ship beats against the waves, and the fruit upon the tree is shaken by the wind, and the fine gold is worked by the hammer of iron. (*Wisudhi-margga-sanné.*)

It was declared by Mahanama to his brother Anurudha, that repeated existence is like a mockery; it appears to the wise man like a ball made of straw, without top or bottom; or the nest of the bird gula, made without order; or an entangled thread; or an oscillating swing; or an image reflected in a mirror; a thing utterly worthless. (*Pujáwaliya.*)

21. *The Síla Precepts.*

The dasa-sil, or ten Obligations binding upon the priest, forbid: 1. The taking of life. 2. The taking of that which is not given. 3. Sexual Intercourse. 4. The saying of that which is not true. 5. The use of intoxicating drinks. 6. The eating of solid food after mid-day. 7. Attendance upon dancing, singing, music, and masks. 8 The adorning of the body with flowers, and the use of perfumes and unguents. 9.

---

* The eye is sometimes called daiwadípa, the divine lamp; or if daiwa be derived from déwa, an organ of sense, it will be the lamp of the body.

The use of seats or couches above the prescribed height. 10. The receiving of gold or silver.

The first five of these obligations are called the pancha-sil. They are repeated by some persons every day at the pansal, especially by the women. The first eight are called the ata-sil, and they are repeated only on póya days, or festivals. When taken by a laic, they involve the necessity of his living apart from his family. These obligations are most usually taken in the presence of a priest, who may either be a sámanéra or an upasampadá; but they are sometimes received from an upásaka, without the intervention of a priest.

The obligations may be taken for a limited period, or for as long as the person has power to observe them, or to be observed until death. When they are not taken for a limited period they are called nitya-síla.

They may be taken either separately or together. When taken to be kept separately, though one should be broken, it does not impair the merit of the rest; but when they are taken to be kept collectively, if one be broken, the whole are impaired.

There are three degrees in the manner of keeping the precepts: —1. They may be kept inadvertently, without any intention of acquiring merit thereby. 2. They may be kept at the recommendation of another, or to please another. 3. They may be kept from free choice, from having seen their excellence or advantage. The third is the superior síla.

There was a man who during fifty years had gained his living by catching fish, but he had committed no other crime. When he was near death a priest, who perceived his danger, went to his house, but the man's wife ordered him away. The priest, however, gained access to him, and prevailed on him to repeat the five precepts, by which he received power to be born in one of the déwa-lókas; at the very last moment, he again repeated the precepts, and received power to be born in a déwa-lóka higher than the former. But this species of merit is received by few, as there is frequently the obstruction of the usual secretions; dangers from yákas; the distress of friends; thoughts about the property that is to be left, about his children, and about death; so that the man has not the opportunity of receiving yadásanna (the merit that is obtained when at the point of death). And even when he enters a déwa-lóka from this kind of merit alone, he does not remain there long, but soon falls into hell. Its benefit is therefore small.

In a former age, there was a king who, with his courtiers, kept the eight obligations. This was observed by a poor woman, who reflected that if persons so exalted kept the síla, it must be an excellent observance. She therefore kept the ata-sil one day, for which she was born in a déwa-lóka, and afterwards became a rahat.

In a former age there was a certain village in which all the people, headed by Magha-mánawaka, kept the obligations continually. But the chief of the district became enraged against them, as he got no bribes from them for the appeasing of quarrels. He therefore went to the royal court and accused them as thieves; on hearing which the king commanded them to be trampled to death by elephants. Though Magha-mánawaka heard the sentence, he felt no resentment, either against his accuser, or the king, or the elephants. In the court of the palace the elephants were turned upon the people; but they ran away, and refused to do the villagers any harm. The king, on perceiving it, enquired if they had any charm upon their persons; and they were searched, but none was found. He then asked if they were acquainted with any mantra; and they said that they were, but it was only this, that they had kept the obligations, built places of shelter for travellers, and given alms. The king, thus convinced of their innocence, commanded that their accuser should be given to the village as a slave, and that the elephants should also be presented as a gift. Magha-mánawaka was afterwards born as Sekra.

In the time of Anómadarsa Budha there was a poor labourer, who resided in the city of Hangsawatí. Having heard Budha say bana, he thought thus:—" All the beings in the world are enveloped in darkness; evil desire, anger, and ignorance, like three fires, burn within the mind; but if I wish to cross the ocean of successive existence, what can I do? I have no wealth by which I can give alms; I will therefore observe the five precepts." He then received the pancha-sil from Nisabha, one of the principal disciples of Budha. At that time men lived to the age of 100,000 years; and during the whole of this period he kept the five precepts, without once breaking them. When near death the déwas

came to call him with a retinue of a thousand chariots drawn by divine horses, in one of which he ascended to Tusita. After this he was born thirty times as a déwa, seventy-five times as a chakrawarti; he was from time to time king of Kósala, but never of any other country; and in the time of Gótama he was born as a rich man in the city of Wisálá. One day reflecting that he had kept the precepts for so long a period, he became a rahat, and was ordained by Budha, on which occasion he uttered these words:—
"I have kept the precepts during 100,000 kalpas; in no part of this period was I born in hell; I have ever been endowed with length of days, wealth, wisdom, and courage; all evil desire is now destroyed, and I have become a rahat; therefore let all who would attain nirwána keep the five precepts."

The observance of síla is an aid in the practice of all other rites and in all other modes of acquiring merit. All trees, whether they be produced from seed or spontaneously, receive their increase and maturity from the earth; the man who would build a city first clears the ground from all obstructions, and then lays out the streets and the principal squares; the mountebank who would turn a somerset first prepares the area in which he intends to perform, by clearing away the stones, thorns, and other things that might prevent the right exhibition of his skill. In like manner, he who seeks nirwána is assisted in the attempt, and clears the way before him, by the practice of síla. The same things have been declared by Budha:—"The wise man, by the observance of síla, continually enlarges his mental faculties and his wisdom, and is freed from the perturbation produced by evil desire. The observance of síla is an assistance to the man who has formed the hope of nirwána, as the earth renders benefits to all things that have life; it is the root of all merit, and the most productive mode of acquiring merit that is practised by the all-wise."

There is greater benefit from keeping the ata-sil during a short period than there would be from the possession of the whole sakwala filled with treasures; as the keeping of the ten obligations will ensure birth in one of the déwa-lókas, where the age of the déwas is immensely great, whilst any benefit arising from riches will quickly pass away.

Síla purifies whatever proceeds from the three doorways of the body, the speech, and the mind. There are two things that are greatly allied to it, shame and the fear of doing wrong. As the other elements, heat, air, and water, are necessary to the fertilising of the earth; as the skill of the weaver is necessary for the clearing away of the refuse of the cotton; so shame and fear are necessary to the perfecting of síla; without them it is nothing. When these are all united there is the driving away of the perplexity that as an enemy lurks in the mind, and the certain reception of an adequate reward. There are three kinds of joy that arise from its observance; he who possesses it reflects thus, " Truly, this is to me a benefit; truly, I have received that which is good; my síla is pure." Budha has declared that the reward of síla is the destruction of all perplexity, but that is only a small part; its principal reward is freedom from fear, and peace. When he who possesses síla approaches kings, brahmans, householders, or priests, he is devoid of fear; and when he comes to die, as he can reflect on the merit he has gained, he dies in the full possession of his senses; afterwards he is either born in a déwa-lóka, or in the world of men. No one is able to tell how great is the reward of síla; all the water of the five great rivers, added to that of the Chandrabhaga, Saraswatí, and other inferior rivers, is insufficient to extinguish the fire of evil desire; but it is destroyed by síla. It is thus destroyed, even as heat is overcome by the wind that accompanies the rain-cloud, or by various kinds of precious stones, or by the rays of the moon. The perfume of the flower spreads only in the direction of the wind, but the greatness of him who possesses síla spreads on all sides without exception. It is as a ladder by which to ascend to the déwa-lóka; like a gateway that enters upon nirwana. The priest who is arrayed in the robe of síla has a more real splendour than the monarch in his royal garments and ornaments of gold.

The word síla is the same as sísan, the head, because síla is the head, or principal method by which merit is to be obtained. When the head is severed from the body there is no life, so when síla is disregarded there is no merit.

There are numerous divisions of síla, though all possess something in common.

There are various sílas that are divided into two classes.

1. Cháritra-síla is the keeping of all the precepts of Budha; for its right performance, purity and persevering exertion are required. 2. Wáritra-síla is the avoiding of all things that are

forbidden by Budha; for its right performance, purity alone is required.

1. Abhisamáchára-síla is thus called on account of its being the chief síla, the practice of which leads to the four paths and their fruition: it is not used in reference to the eight kinds of action, three of which belong to the body, four to the speech, and one to the life or conduct. 2. Adibrahmachariya-síla is so called (from ádi, prior, first, ancient) because it must be produced previous to the margga-brahmachariya; it is used in reference to the eight kinds of action, and precedes that which leads to the paths; it must be observed without ceasing, even by the householder; by its observance the body, speech, and conduct become purified; it is used in reference to the obligations that appear in the Ubhatowibhanga and Khandakawatta.

1. Wirati-síla is the avoiding of such crimes as the taking of life. 2. Awirati-síla is the avoiding of such evils as proceed from the mind.

1. Nisrata-síla belongs to trishná and drishti; to the former belongs the wish to become Sekra; to the latter, the wish to gain nirwána. 2. Anisrata-síla is that which aims at an earthly reward.

1. Kálapariyanta-síla is when the obligations are taken for a single day, or a night, or any definite period. 2. Apánakótika-síla is the taking of the obligations for life.

1. Sapariyanta-síla is when no definite period was originally fixed for the observance of the precepts, but afterwards, for some cause or other, the period is limited. 2. Apariyanta-síla is when the precepts are kept until death, but not from a religious motive, or to receive nirwána.

1. Lowkika-síla is when the observance is for the purpose of obtaining some reward less than nirwána. 2. Lókóttara-síla is when the observance is not to attain anything in any of the three worlds, but to attain nirwána.

There are various sílas that are divided into three classes.

1. Hína-síla is when the desire, mind, exertion, and wisdom are in an inferior degree. 2. Madhyama-síla is when they are in a middle degree. 3. Praníta-síla is when they are in a superior degree. When the obligations are kept for praise, fame, or any similar attachment, it is hína; if for merit, it is madhyama; if for nirwána, it is praníta. Again, when the obligations are kept

to gain wealth, it is hína; when to overcome the repetition of existence, it is madhyama; and when to obtain a Budhaship, that all sentient beings may be released from birth, it is praníta.

1. Atmádhipateyya-síla is when the obligations are kept from the fear of blame, or in order to gain personal praise. 2. Lókádhipateyya-síla is when they are kept not from these motives. 3. Dharmmádhipateyya-síla is when they are kept from affection for the precepts themselves.

1. Parámarshta-síla is the avoiding of that which prevents an entrance into the paths. 2. Aparámarshta-síla is an approach to the paths. 3. Patippassadha-síla is a more immediate approximation to the paths.

1. Wisudhi-síla is the keeping of the obligations perfectly. 2. Awisudhi-síla is the keeping of them imperfectly. 3. Wématika-síla is the keeping of them without any fixed intention, like the man who does not know the difference between the flesh of a bear and that of a boar.

1. Sékha-síla is the observance of the precepts in order to enter the paths, or gain the three benefits of the priesthood. 2. Asékha-síla is their observance in order to gain rahatship. 3. Néwasékha-násekha is their observance from a different motive, in order to gain some worldly advantage.

There are various sílas that are divided into four classes.

1. Parihání-síla is when a priest falls into any crime, shuns the company of wiser priests, or gives his mind to wealth. 2. S'thiti-síla is when a priest observes the precepts with the expectation of receiving something connected with existence, and not nirwána. 3. Dhyána-síla is when the priest practises the dhyánas. 4. Balawa-wipassanáwa-síla is when the priest enters upon the course by which he expects to arrive at the attainment of widarsana in its most powerful form.

1. Bhiksu-síla is the observance of all the precepts binding upon a priest. 2. Bhiksuni-síla is the observance of all the precepts binding upon a priestess. 3. Anupasampanna-síla is the observance of the precepts, or the dasa-sil, by the male and female sámanéras. 4. Grahasta-síla is the continued observance of the panchasil, and the occasional observance of the dasa-sil, by the male and female upásakas.

There are also various other sections of the sílas.*

Swabhháwa-síla is the constant observance of the five precepts naturally, by all the inhabitants of Uturukuru. Achára-síla is the observance of different sílas in various countries. Kuladharmma-síla is the proscription of intoxicating liquors by the brahmans, an observance belonging to a particular race. Désa-dharmma-síla is the rule not to slay animals or take life. Pásandha-dharmma-síla is the observance of the precepts of the tirttakas. Bódhisatwamátu-síla is the continence of the mother of Budha after his conception. Púrwahétuka-síla is the continued observance of the precepts during many ages, as by Mugalan and Bódhisat.

The unwise call many other things by the name of síla, as when any being endures sorrow, or is peaceable in his conduct, they call it his síla of sorrow or of quietness. Síla is also sometimes divided into that which is merit, or demerit, or neither one nor the other; but though demerit may thus be connected with síla, it is merely a name, not a thing really belonging to síla. (*Wisudhimargga-sanné.*)

23. *Terms and Classifications.*

1. *Triwidhadwára; the three Doors.*—There are three entrances whence proceed that which is good and that which is evil:—1. The body. 2. The speech. 3. The mind.

2. *Triwidhasampatti; the threefold Advantage:*—There are three modes of happiness that will be received by the wise. 1. The benefits of the world of men. 2. The enjoyment of the déwa and brahma-lókas. 3. Nirwána.

3. *Triwidhágni; the threefold Fire:*—There are three principles to which all are subject who have not attained to the state of a rahat:—1. Rága, evil desire. 2. Dwésa, hatred. 3. Móha, ignorance.

4. *Tilakuna; the three Signs:*—There are three subjects upon which the mind of the ascetic ought constantly to dwell:—1. Anitya, impermanency. 2. Dukha, sorrow. 3. Anátma,

---

* The subdivisions of the sílas are almost limitless; but the enumeration is too uninteresting to be further pursued.

unreality. Of all that exists these three may be predicated. The right understanding of these three subjects is called triwidyáwa.

5. *Tunbhawa, or Tunlóka; the three Worlds :*—The regions in each sakwala are divided into three sections :—1. Káma, the regions in which there is form and sensuous gratification. 2. Rúpa, the regions in which there is form, without sensuous gratification. 3. Arúpa, the regions in which there is neither form nor sensuous gratification, but a state of unconsciousness.

6. *Trisnáwa; Evil Desire, or the Cleaving to Existence:*— Sentient beings are bound about by evil desire, as by a net. It is like a net that has 138 meshes; it is like the entanglement of the branches in a forest of bamboos : it continually passes from rúpa to dharmma; and from dharmma to rúpa. As the branches of the bamboo become interwoven, so that they cannot be separated; as the hair of the head becomes matted together, so that it cannot be got loose; in the same way evil desire seizes upon the objects that are presented to it, and becomes entangled by them to such a degree that it cannot be loosed therefrom. As the worm becomes entangled by the contortions of its own body, so evil desire becomes more hopelessly entangled by its own motions and passions. As it is exercised to an individual's own possessions or those of another, to his own existence or that of another, it is relatively called anto, inner, or bahira, outward.

7. *Sat-charita; the six Principles, or States of the Mind:*—1. Rága. 2. Dwésa. 3. Móha. 4. Sardháwa. 5. Budhi. 6. Witarka. By the uniting together of the first three, four more are produced; and there are four more produced by the uniting together of the last three; so that there are in all fourteen charitas. By another mode of union, sixty-three charitas are produced, the nature of which may be learnt from the tíkáwa on the Asammósasútra.

8. *Chaturwidha-ásrawa : or four Principles by which the Cleaving to Existence is produced.*—1. Káma, evil desire. 2. Bhawa, existence, the being subject to a repetition of birth. 3. Drishti, scepticism. 4. Awidya, ignorance. They are sometimes called chaturwidha-ógha, the four streams.

9. *Chaturwidha-árya-satya, or four great Truths.*—1. Dukha-satya.—By the cleaving to existence or to sensible objects, and the agitation of mind arising therefrom, are produced:—(1.) The sorrow arising from birth, decay, and death. (2.) The coming of that which is not desired. (3.) The absence of that which is desired. (4.) The non-reception of wealth and other things upon which the affections have been placed. (5.) The five khandas, or existence as an organised being. (6.) The misery of hell.

2. Dukha-samudya-satya.—The three modes of existence, in the káma, rúpa, and arúpa worlds, are produced by the continued cleaving to existence, or to sensible objects.

3. Dukha-niródha-satya.—There is no escape from the repetition of existence but by an entrance into the paths, and the reception of nirwána.

4. Dukha-niródha-gámini-patipada-satya.—There is no reception of nirwána, but by the destruction of the cleaving to existence.*

* *The four chief Truths:*—That every existent thing is a source of sorrow. 2. That continued sorrow results from a continued attachment to existing objects. 3. That a freedom from this attachment liberates from existence. 4. The path leading to this state, containing eight sections.—Gogerly.

The four sublime Truths which Budha apprehended by the light of Budha-gnyána, when the same had dispelled the darkness of awidya were:—

1. Dukha-satya: the reality of misery, has been explained as inherent in the system of the panchas-khanda.

2. Samudaya-satya: the reality of aggregation, or the progressive accumulations of evil, by the agency of káma-tanhá, bháwa-tanhá, and wibhawa-tanhá. Káma-tanhá signifies lust, avarice, and love. Bháwa-tanhá signifies the pertinacious love of existence induced by the supposition that transmigratory existence is not only eternal, but felicitous and desirable. Wibhawa-tanhá is the love of the present life, under the notion that existence will cease therewith, and that there is to be no future state.

3. Nirodha-satya, or the reality of destruction, signifies the destroying of the desires above-mentioned, and thereby the causes which perpetuate the misery of existence; and this is also the signification of the word nirwána.

4. Márga-satya, the reality of means, signifies the efficiency of the exertions and operations whereby those desires are destroyed, and their concomitant miseries extinguished.—Armour.

The four excellent Truths:—1. There is sorrow or misery in life. 2. It will be so with every birth. 3. But it may be stopped. 4. The way or mode of making an end to all miseries. With respect to these four truths little further explanation is afforded. Ignorance is the source of almost every real or fancied misery; and right knowledge of the nature of things is the true way to emancipation; therefore, they who desire to be freed from the miseries of future transmigrations, must acquire true knowledge of the nature of divine and human things.—Csoma Körösi.

1. Sorrow is like a disease. 2. The cleaving to existence is like the cause of that disease. 3. Nirwána is like the curing of the disease. 4. The four paths are like the medicine that causes the cure.

1. The repetition of existence, or the continuance of birth, may be called dukhá, sorrow. 2. This sorrow is produced by the cleaving to the three modes of existence. 3. There is no escape from sorrow but by the destruction of the cleaving to existence. 4. The cause of the destruction of sorrow is the gaining of the paths.

10. *Chaturwidha-dharmma-pada, or Four Divisions of the Dharmma.*—1. The sentient being is subject to decay; he cannot remain long (under one form of existence.) 2. He has within himself no protection; no adequate defence. 3. He has no real possession: all that he has he must leave. 4. He cannot arrive at perfect satisfaction, or content: he is the slave of evil desire.

11. *The Thirty-seven Bodhi-pákshika-dharmmas.*—They are:—
1. The four satipatthánas; the four samyak-pradhánas; the four irdhipádas; the five indrayas; the five balayas; the seven bódhyángas; and the eight árya-marggas.

12. *Satara-satipatthána.*—There are four subjects of thought upon which the attention must be fixed, and that must be rightly understood. 1. Káyárúpapassaná, the body is composed of thirty-two impurities. 2. Wédanánupassaná, the three modes of sensation are connected with sorrow. 3. Chittánupassaná, the mental faculties are impermanent. 4. Dharmmánupassaná, the five khandas are unreal, not the self.

13. *Chaturwidha-samyak-pradhána.*—There are four great objects for which exertion must be used:—1. To obtain freedom from demerit, or the consequences of sins already committed. 2. To prevent the birth of demerit, or of sin not in existence. 3. To cause the birth of merit not in existence. 4. To increase the merit already received.

14. *Chaturwidha-irdhi-páda.*—There are four modes by which the power of irdhi is to be attained:—1. Chandidhi-páda, firm

determination. 2. Chittidhi-páda, thoughtful meditation. 3. Wiriyidhi-páda, persevering exertion. 4. Wimansidhi-páda, close investigation. The priest thinks that by these exercises he may attain the supreme Budhaship, or see nirwána. The samádhi that is produced by the first exercise is called chanda-samádhi; the second, chitta-samádhi, &c. By means of samádhi the power of irdhi is received. It is called páda, a foot, on account of the assistance it renders to those who possess it.

It was declared by Budha to Ananda, that whosoever possesses the power of the four irdhi-pádas, should he desire it, may live a kalpa, or any part of a kalpa.

15. *Panchindra.*—The five indrayas, or moral powers are:—1. Sardháwa, purity. 2. Wiraya, persevering exertion. 3. Sati, or smirti, the ascertainment of truth. 4. Samádhi, tranquillity. 5. Pragnyáwa, wisdom. In some instances príti, joy, is inserted instead of the third power, persevering exertion. The five balayas are the same as the five indrayas.

16. *Satta-bódhyánga.*—The seven sections of wisdom are:—1. Sihi, or smirti, the ascertainment of truth by mental application. 2. Dharmmawicha, the investigation of causes. 3. Wiraya, persevering exertion. 4. Príti, joy. 5. Passadhi, or prasrabdhi, tranquillity. 6. Samádhí, tranquillity in a higher degree, including freedom from all that disturbs either body or mind. 7. Upékshá, equanimity.

17. *Arya-ashtángika-margga.*—The eight paths of purity are:—1. Samyak-drishti, as opposed to mityá-drishti, or correct ideas upon religious subjects, as opposed to those that are erroneous. 2. Samyak-kalpanáwa, correct thoughts. 3. Samyak-wachana, correct words. 4. Samyak-karmánta, correct works. 5. Samyak-ajíwa, a correct life. 6. Samyak-wyáyáma, correct energies or endeavours. 7. Samyak-sihi, a correct judgment. 8. Samyak-samádhi, correct tranquillity.

18. *Chaturwidha-pratisambhidá; or four Modes of Perfect Understanding.*—The wisdom that enables the priest to understand aright the four following sections of knowledge:—1. Arttha, the meaning of any matter, in its separate divisions. 2. Dharmma, the doctrines of Budha. 3. Nirutti, the power of

the Budhas to perceive all truth intuitively, without study, and without the teaching of another. 4. Pratibhána, the power of the rahats to know the roots and the properties of things.

The power of pratisambhidá is obtained by the exercise of meditation in former births and the acquirement of great merit in the present birth. This attainment is less than that of widarsana.

The priest who is arrayed in the glory of the pratisambhidá is utterly fearless when in the presence of others by whom he may be questioned or examined. He reflects thus:—"If I am asked the meaning, arttha of any matter or thing, I will answer according to the proper rules, explaining the whole, meaning by meaning, cause by cause, and point by point, thus removing doubt and producing satisfaction. If I am asked anything relative to the sacred institutions, dharmma, I will explain the whole, institution by institution, eternal by eternal, infinite by infinite, nirwána by nirwána, void by void, &c. If I am asked anything relative to the wisdom of the Budhas, nirutti, I will explain the whole, nirutti by nirutti, the four pádas by the four pádas, letter by letter, section by section, sign by sign, class by class, and accent by accent. If I am asked anything relative to the wisdom of the rahats, pratibhána, I will explain it, figure by figure, sign by sign, and character by character."

19. *Chaturwidha-áhára, or four Kinds of Food.*—The word áhára, food, is from a root that signifies to convey, and it is so called because it brings or conveys to the body strength, beauty, and length of days. There are four kinds:—1. Kabalinká. 2. Phassá. 3. Manósanchétaná. 4. Winyána.

(1.) The first, kabalinká, is the common nourishment of men. It is made into balls, and is mixed with liquid or moisture. It produces that which is connected with rúpa; and from it comes sorrow, when evil desire exists in him by whom it is taken; but when he who takes it is free from evil desire, no sorrow is produced.

(2.) Phassá, the second, includes those things that have no rúpa, but are apprehended by the mind; it produces the three sensations, pleasure, pain, and that which is indifferent, neither the one nor the other, and from it, as from the first, comes sorrow. As it is connected with the body, sorrow is produced by means of thought (aramunu, the thought that arises from contact with sensible objects) and thought and sorrow united produce fear.

(3.) Manosanchétaná, the third, includes the thoughts that have entered into the mind and there abide, continued thought, or reflection; it produces birth in one or other of the three modes of existence.

(4.) Winyána, the fourth, includes all that is the subject of consciousness, and produces náma and rúpa.

As when a parent, in order that he may be enabled to cross a wide desert, when all other food fails him eats the flesh of his own son, but with the utmost disgust; so must these four kinds of nourishment be regarded with absolute aversion, inasmuch as they produce birth and the sorrows connected therewith.

When a cow has a sore that breeds worms, pain is produced through phassá, touch; but he who is without phassá is like a cow that has got no skin. As when a weak man is taken by two strong men, and cast into a pit of burning charcoal, so by the power of karma, derived from its two constituent properties, merit and demerit, through the instrumentality of manosanchétaná, are the unwise beings cast into the pit of successive existence. As the man who is pierced by 300 darts endures severe pain, so is he who is under the influence of winyána. They who are released from the influence of the four modes of áhára are not subject to birth.

20. *Dasawidha-irdhi, or ten Supernatural Powers.*—There are ten irdhis, the first three of which are accounted as the chief.

(1.) Adishtána, the power to produce, by an effort of the mind, a hundred, or a thousand, or a hundred thousand figures, like the person's own.

(2.) Wikurwana, or wikumbana, the power to disappear from the sight of men, or to assume any form that is different to the person's own, whether it be that of a child, young man, nága, garunda, yaká, or ráksha.

(3.) Manóma, the power to make any figure whatever, according to the person's own will.

(4.) Gnyánaweppára, the power received from the former possession of gnyána, knowledge, which preserves its possessor from the consequences of any danger to which he may be exposed, either at the moment when the danger occurs, or at some other time.

During the childhood of Bakkula there was a festival at his father's house in the city of Kosambæ, when his mother took him to the river Yamuna to bathe. After she had washed him, she placed him upon the bank, and returned to bathe herself; but in the mean time he fell from the bank into the river and was swallowed by a fish, that swam towards Benares, a distance of thirty yojanas, where it was caught in a net. The fisherman who took it sold it to a nobleman, whose wife, on seeing it, said that she would prepare it herself, as it was too fine a fish to be entrusted to the hands of a servant; but when the lady ripped it open, she saw that it contained a child, at which she was greatly pleased, as she said she must have done some meritorious act in a former birth to have received in this way such a beautiful child; so she adopted it as her own. But as Bakkula's own mother heard of the manner in which he had been preserved, she went to Benares and claimed him. The wife of the nobleman was unwilling to give him up; so they referred the matter to the king; who said that as one had borne him and the other had bought him, their interest in him was equal, and he decided that he should belong to both. On this account he was called Bakkula, as belonging to two kulas, or races. After he grew up he resided, in great splendour, six months at Benares and six at Kosambæ, and went between the two cities in a boat by the river Mahí. When ninety years of age he heard bana from Budha, at the time he resided at Kosambæ, by which he was induced to leave all his possessions and become a priest. After this he lived ninety years more; and throughout the whole of this period he never felt any disease for a single moment. By Budha he was declared to be the chief of that class of his disciples who were free from disease; and he became a rahat.

The mother of Sankicha was near the time of her confinement when she died; but as her friends were preparing her body to be burnt upon the funeral pile, the child cried. Those who were near heard the voice; and as they knew thereby that the child was alive, they took the body down, and released it from its confinement after which they delivered it to its grandmother to be brought up; and in time he embraced the priesthood and became a rahat.

Bhupála was born in Rajagaha, of a poor family. One day he went with his father into the forest to procure firewood; but on their return, when near the gate, the bullock that drew their cart slipped the yoke over his neck, and ran away into the city. The father then left the cart under the care of Bhupála, whilst he attempted to catch the bullock; but in the mean time the gate was shut, and he was unable to return to his child. In the night Bhupála saw many yakás and prétas come out of the city that were going to the cemeteries in search of flesh, but none of them did him the least harm, and he remained in perfect security. In the course of time he became a rahat.

Thus it is not possible that any one can perish, or be exposed to a danger ending in death, who has the merit to obtain nirwána in the same birth.

(5.) Samádhi-wippara.—The power that is received from having possessed samádhi in a former birth, which preserves its possessor from danger, either immediately or at some other time.

At one time Seriyut and Mugalan resided together at Kapótakandara, which was so called from the number of doves in its neighbourhood. Early one morning Seriyut went into the open air, when he saw two yakás, one of whom struck him a blow upon the top of his head, the sound of which reverberated loudly in the ten directions; but in the moment when the hand of the yaká was uplifted, Seriyut thought of nirwána, by means of which the blow to him was but as the alighting of a fly upon his head, whilst to the yaká it was as painful as if he had struck a solid rock.

The priest Sajíwa resided near a village of herdsmen, who one day found him in abstract meditation at the foot of a tree. Supposing that he was dead, they prepared a funeral pile, wrapped the body in his robe, covered it over with dry grass, and then set it on fire in two places. But though the pile and the grass were consumed, no harm happened to the priest, not even a thread of his robe was singed.

Another priest, Khánu-kondanya was lost in meditation at the foot of a tree, when 500 robbers came up, who had been plundering a neighbouring village; and as they thought it was a quiet place, where no one could disturb them, they resolved upon remaining there a little time to rest. When they saw the priest, they took him for a pillar, so they heaped up around him their loads of plunder; but after they had rested awhile, and were about to resume their loads, as the time appointed by the priest for the exercise had passed away, he was restored to consciousness, and began to move. On seeing this the thieves cried out in alarm, and were about to prepare for their safety in flight, when Khánukondanya called out to them and said, " Be not afraid; I am a priest." Being thus encouraged, they approached him reverently, when he said bana to them; and they subsequently became priests, and finally rahats.

There was an upásikáwa called Uttará, daughter of Púrnaka, upon whose head the courtezan Sirima, out of hatred, poured a vessel of boiling oil. But Uttará looked at her in the same moment with affection, and the oil fell harmless to the ground, like water poured upon the lotus.

Sámawati was the faithful queen of the monarch of Udéni; but there was a brahman, Mágandhiya, who thought to have her disgraced, that his own daughter might be elevated in her place. For this purpose he secretly put a nayá in the lute of the queen, and then told the king that she had a serpent concealed, with the intent to kill him. No sooner did the king hear this, than he took up a bow, and placed it to his shoulder with a poisoned arrow; but at the same moment the queen looked at him with affection, and he remained motionless as a statue, unable to send the arrow. The queen, therefore, asked him what was the matter, as he appeared to be suffering pain; when he informed her that he was paralysed, and unable even to put the bow down again that he had taken up. The queen said, "Let your anger pass away, and your arm will be set at liberty;" and as he took her advice, he was in the same instant released from the spell. Sámawatí said further, "Sire, whenever you wish to overcome the anger of any one, exercise affection towards them, and their anger will pass away." The king received this declaration, afterwards reigned righteously, and at his death entered a déwa-lóka.*

---

* When Sihabahu, the father of Wijayo (the conqueror of the demon race in Ceylon), proceeded to the door of his father's den, and saw him approaching, impelled by his affection for his child, he let fly his arrow at his lion parent, that he might transfix him. On account of the merit of the lion's good intentions, the arrow, recoiling in the air, fell on the ground at the feet of the prince. Even until the third effort it was the same. Then the king of animals losing his self-possession (by which the effect of the charm that preserved his life was destroyed) the impelled arrow, transpiercing his body, passed through him.—Turnour's Mahawanso.

It was by the power received from samádhi-wippara that the above-mentioned individuals were prevented from receiving harm in the several dangers to which they were exposed.

(6.) Arya-irdhi.—When the priest who possesses this power sees anything decayed or disagreeable, he thinks that it was once beautiful; when he sees anything young or immature, he thinks that in time it will decay; whether the object be pleasant or unpleasant he regards all with an equal mind; and as this is the characteristic of the rahats, it is called árya-irdhi.

(7.) Karmma-wipákaja-irdhi.—This power is possessed by all birds and déwas, by some men, and by some yakás. All birds can fly through the air, though they do not enter the paths; so also all déwas have the same power, though they do not attain to the wisdom of the rahats; in a former age there were some men who were equally gifted, and there have been certain yakás with the same power.

(8.) Punyawato-irdhi.—By this power the Chakrawartti is enabled to convey his army through the air, with its elephants, chariots, &c., and its accompaniment of retainers, herdsmen, artisans, and others.

There was a nobleman, Jótiya, for whom there appeared a cleft in the earth, out of which there sprung a golden palace, and a magical tree, sixty-four cubits high. For the noble Jatika a golden rock was formed, eighty cubits high. The noble Ghosika was seven times saved from the most imminent dangers. When the noble Médaka had bathed, he looked towards the sky, and there came down a fine kind of rice, which filled 12,500 large granaries. His wife boiled a single measure, and gave a portion to every person in Jambudwípa; but still the measure was not exhausted. His son put a thousand pieces of gold in a bag, and gave one to every person in Jambudwípa; but still his store was not done. When his servant ploughed, fifteen furrows were made at the same time, seven on each side of the furrow along which the plough was carried. All these occurrences resulted from punyawato-irdhi.

(9.) Widyáma-irdhi.—They who possess this power can, by means of magic and mantras, cause armies, whether of elephants or horses, to appear in the air, and can themselves pass through the air.

(10.) Samyak-prayóga-pratya-pratilábharttha-irdhi.—This power is possessed by those who have overcome the cleaving to existence, and have entered the paths; and by those who know the three vedas, the three pitakas, and the sixty-four sciences.

Eight years after Budha-rakkhita had received the upasampadá ordination, he went to minister to the priest Maha Róhana-gutta, who was sick. In the same place there was a nayá that was accustomed to assist the priest, but one day a garunda was about to swallow it, when Budha-rakkhita, by the power of irdhi, caused a rock to be formed, which prevented it from being destroyed.

21. *Upékshá.*—This power is so called, because it includes freedom from all kinds of desire, as of uppatti, or birth; also, because it has no paksha, or preference, for one thing more than another. It is opposed to individuality, as it regards all things alike; and its principal attribute is indifference, or equanimity. There are ten kinds :—

(1.) Sadangopékshá, when there is neither pleasure nor displeasure.

(2.) Brahma-wiháropékshá, when the mind is equally affected towards all beings, not loving one more than another, and not disliking one more than another.

(3.) Bódhyangopékshá, when the mind is equally affected towards all the thoughts that arise within it, not having more complacency in one than another.

(4.) Wíryopékshá, when the mind is always affected by the same force of determination.

(5.) Sankháropékshá, when the mind is equally affected towards all the various kinds of wisdom that are necessary for the attainment of the paths.

(6.) Wédanópékshá, when the mind is sensible to neither pleasure nor pain.

(7.) Widarsanopékshá, when the mind is not affected by that which is seen.

(8.) Tatramadyastopékshá, when the whole of the ten modes of upékshá are exercised together.

(9.) Dhyánópékshá, when the impermanency of sensible objects is regarded with an even mind.

(10.) Parisudhi-upékshá, when the mind is equally affected towards all that is necessary to secure freedom from the cleaving to existence.

As the same person may be a prince, young man, the first-born, general, and king, so all the upékshás may be possessed at the same time; they have different characteristics, but all partake of one nature. There may be the first upékshá without the second, but the second is never possessed without the first.

Our development of this great system is now completed. The present chapter contains the most rational of its phases, and the one in which its greatest superiority is maintained. It discountenances all licentiousness. It inculcates an affection for all orders of being; and shrinks from the inflicting of pain, even as a punishment. Yet from no part of heathenism do we see more clearly the necessity of a divine revelation than from the teachings of Budha. The moral code becomes comparatively powerless for good, as it is destitute of all real authority. Gótama taught the propriety of certain observances, because all other Budhas had done the same; but something more is required before man can be restrained from vice and preserved in the path of purity. The words of John Foster might have been written with express reference to this system. "Man," says that profound thinker, "is not a being to be governed by principles, detached from an overawing power. Set them in the best array that you can in his mind, to fight the evil powers within and from without,—but refuse them weapons from the armoury of heaven; let no lightning of the divine eye, no thunder of the divine voice, come in testimony and in aid of their operation—and how soon they will be overwhelmed and trampled down!"—Broadmead Lectures.

There is properly no law. The Budhist can take upon himself certain obligations, or resolve to keep certain precepts; as many or as few as he pleases; and for any length of time he pleases. It is his own act that makes them binding; and not any objective authority. Even when he takes the obligations, there is this convenient clause, in the form that he repeats to the priest. "I embrace the five precepts (or the eight, as the case may be) to obey them severally, *as far as I am able,* from this time forward." The power of the precepts is further diminished, as they are repeated in Pali, a language seldom understood by the lay devotee.

From the absence of a superior motive to obedience, Budhism becomes a system of selfishness. The principle set forth in the vicarious endurances of the Bódhisat is forgotten. It is the vast scheme of profits and losses, reduced to regular order. The acquirement of merit by the Budhist is as mercenary an act as the toils of the merchant to secure the possession of wealth. Hence, the custom of the Chinese is in entire consistence with the teachings of the bana. They have a work called "Merits and Demerits Examined," in which a man is directed to keep a debtor and creditor account with himself of the acts of each day; and at the end of the year he winds it up. If the balance is in his favour, it is carried on to the account of next year; but if against him, something extra must be done to make up the deficiency.—Davis's Chinese. The disciple of Budha is not taught to abhor crime because of its exceeding sinfulness; but because its commission will be to him a personal injury. There is no moral pollution in sin; it is merely a calamity to be deprecated or a misfortune to be shunned.

With these radical defects, it is not needful to point out minor errors and contradictions; of which many will have been observed in perusing the elucidations and comments of the Sińghalese authors, in the extracts we have inserted from their works. They explain the system as it is now practically understood. The world is, happily, in the possession of "a more excellent way." The life of the angels in heaven, and of men redeemed upon earth, is to be one continued act of consecration to God; and in all the movements of their existence they are to seek, with a sacred intensity, the promotion of the divine glory. They are brought to the fulfilment of this duty by motives that are overpowering in their grandeur, and mighty in the potency of their influence. The Budhist can discover no permanent rest, no eternity of peace, in any world; and he therefore concludes that there can be no deliverance from change and sorrow but by the cessation of existence. The book of revelation, however, offers to us now, " a peace that passeth all understanding," and opens before us the prospect, of " a far more exceeding and eternal weight of glory," through the redemption that is in Christ Jesus. Whosoever will, may come to the cross, and be made happy. The stream that issues therefrom " cleanses from all sin." This doctrine may be, as in the days of its first manifestation, " unto the Jews a stumbling-block, and unto the Greeks foolishness," but unto all who are willing to test its truthfulness, it will prove to be " the power of God and the wisdom of God." The time is coming when these sublime principles will govern the world. All systems that have not arisen from the inspiration of God will then have passed away: the now myriad-worshipped Budha will not have a single votary; and Jesus of Nazareth, " who is over all, God blessed for ever," will be the life, and the blessedness, and the glory of universal man.

APPENDIX.

As it appears desirable that the sources whence I have drawn my information should be known, I have prepared the following notices of the works from which I have principally quoted. During my residence in Ceylon, I collected a list of the native works now to be obtained in the island, in the Sanskrit, Páli, and Singhalese languages. The number amounted to 465, of which about one half are in Páli, either in that language alone, or with a Singhalese sanné. About 80 of the works are in Sanskrit; and 150 in Elu, or Singhalese. This list must necessarily be imperfect; as it is only by the labours of many individuals, continued through a period of years, that it can be rendered complete. The books are written upon the leaves of the talipot, with a stylus, and are bound, literally, in boards. In the island there are a few books brought from Burma, composed of plates of silver, upon which the letters are beautifully painted; and I have seen some belonging to the Daladá wihára, at Kandy, that are of laminated gold, with the letters engraved. There is a great difference in the style of the Singhalese works, scarcely any two being alike; and even in the same work the difference is, in some instances, striking; one part being almost in pure Sanskrit, and another in colloquial Singhalese. The date at which many of them were written cannot now be ascertained.

The works I shall more particularly notice are the following: —1. Pansiya-panas-játaka-pota. 2. Wisudhi-margga-sanné. 3. Milinda Prasna. 4. Pújáwaliya. 5. Sadharmmálankáré. 6. Sadharmmaratnakáré. 7. Amáwatura. 8. Th'upáwansé. 9. Rájawaliya. 10. Kayawirati-gátá-sanné. 11. Kammawáchan. 12. The Sannés of various Sútras.

1. *Pansiya-panas-játaka-pota.*—This work has already been noticed in the introduction to the fifth chapter, page 101.

2. *Wisudhi-margga-sanné.*—This work was written by Budhaghósa, of whom the following account appears in the Mahawanso:—"A brahman youth, born in the neighbourhood of the terrace of the great bó-tree (in Magadha), accomplished in the wijja and sippa; who had achieved the knowledge of the three wedos (Védas), and possessing great aptitude in attaining acquirements; indefatigable as a schismatic disputant, and himself a schismatic wanderer over Jambudipo, established himself, in the

character of a disputant, in a certain wihára, and was in the habit of rehearsing, by night and by day, with clasped hands, a discourse which he had learned, perfect in all its component parts, and sustained throughout in the same lofty strain. A certain maha théro, Réwato, becoming acquainted with him there, and saying to himself, 'This individual is a person of profound knowledge; it will be worthy of me to convert him,' enquired, 'Who is this that is braying like an ass?' The brahman replied to him, 'Thou canst define, then, the meaning conveyed in the bray of asses?' On the théro rejoining, 'I can define it,' the brahman exhibited the extent of the knowledge he possessed. The théro criticised each of his propositions, and pointed out in what way they were fallacious. He who had been thus refuted said, 'Well then, descend to thy own creed;' and he propounded to him a passage from the Abhidammo. The brahman could not divine the signification of that passage; and enquired, 'Whose manto is this?' 'It is Buddho's manto.' On his exclaiming, 'Impart it to me,' the théro replied, 'Enter the sacerdotal order.' He who was desirous of acquiring the knowledge of the Pitakattaya, subsequently coming to this conviction, 'This is the sole road to salvation,' became a convert to that faith. As he was as profound in his ghósó (eloquence) as Buddho himself, they conferred on him the appellation of Buddho-ghósó (the voice of Buddho), and throughout the world he became as renowned as Buddho. Having there (in Jambudipo) composed an original work called Nanódayan, he, at the same time, wrote the chapter called Atthasalini, on the Dhammasangini (one of the commentaries on the Abhidammo). Réwato théro then observing that he was desirous of undertaking the compilation of a Parittatthakathan (a general commentary on the Pitakattaya), thus addressed him, 'The text alone (of the Pitakattaya) has been preserved in this land; the Atthakathá are not extant here; nor is there any version to be found of the wída (schisms) complete. The Singhalese language, by the inspired and profoundly wise Mahindo, who had previously consulted the discourses of Buddho, authenticated at the three convocations, and the dissertations and arguments of Sariputto and others, and they are extant among the Singhalese. Repairing thither, and studying the same, translate them according to the grammar of the Mághadas. It will be an act conducive to the welfare of the whole world.'"

The particulars of Budhaghósa's visit to Ceylon are next related. "Having been thus advised, this eminently wise person rejoicing therein, departed from thence and visited this island in the reign of the monarch Mahanámo. On reaching the Mahawiháro, at Anurádhapura, he entered the Mahapadháno hall, the most splendid of the apartments in the wiháro, and listened to the Singhalese Atthakathá, and the Thérawádá, from the beginning to the end, propounded by the théro Sanghapáli, and became thoroughly convinced that this conveyed the true meaning of the doctrines of the lord of dhammo. Thereupon, paying reverential respect to the priesthood, he thus petitioned: 'I am desirous of translating the Atthakathá; give me access to all your books.' The priesthood, for the purpose of testing his qualifications, gave only two gáthá, saying, 'Hence prove thy qualification; having satisfied ourselves on this point, we will let thee have all our books.' From these, (taking these gáthá for his text) and consulting the Pitakattaya, together with the Atthakathá, and condensing them into an abridged form, he composed the commentary called the Wisuddhimaggan (Sing. Wisudhimargga). Thereupon having assembled the priesthood, who had acquired a thorough knowledge of the doctrine of Buddho, at the bó-tree, he commenced to read out (the work he had composed). The déwatás, in order that they might make his (Buddhaghósó's) gifts of wisdom celebrated among men, rendered that book invisible. He, however, for the second and third time recomposed it. When he was in the act of reproducing his book for the third time, for the purpose of propounding it, the déwatás returned the other two copies also. The assembled priests then read out the three books simultaneously. In those three versions, neither in a signification, nor in a single misplacement by transposition; nay, even in the théro controversies, and in the text (of the Pitakattaya) was there in the measure of a verse, or in the letter of a word, the slightest variation. Thereupon the priesthood rejoicing, again and again fervently shouted forth, saying, 'Most assuredly this is Mettéyyo (Buddho) himself'; and made over to him the books in which the Pitakattaya were recorded, together with the Atthakathá. Taking up his residence in the secluded Ganthákaro wiháro at Anurádhapura, he translated, according to the grammatical rule of the Mágadhas, which is the root of all languages, the whole of the Singhalese Atthakathá (into Páli). This proved an achievement of the utmost importance to all languages spoken by the human race. All the théros and ácharayos held this compilation in the same estimation as the text of the Pitakattaya. Thereafter the objects of his mission having been fulfilled, he returned to Jambudipo, to worship at the bó-tree (at Uruwélaya, in Magadha)."*

The character and contents of the Wisudhi-margga have been thus described by the lamented individual to whom we are indebted for the translation from the Mahawanso:—"The Wisuddhimaggo, a compendium formed by Buddhaghósó, presents an abstract of the doctrinal and metaphysical parts of the Budhistical creed, which, as being the work of the last commentator on the Budhistical scriptures, acquires an authority and authenticity which no compendium exclusively formed by any orientalist of a different faith, and more modern times, can

* Mahawanso, cap. xxxvii.

have any claim to . . . . . In the Atthakathá, by Buddhaghósó, called Sumangala Wilásini, is the following sentence, giving an account of the contents of the Wisuddhimaggo:—The nature of the sílakathá, dhútadammá, kammathánáni, together with all the chariyáwidháni, jhanáni, the whole scope of the samápatti, the whole of abhinnáno, the exposition of the panna, the khandá, the dhátu, the áyatanáni, indriyáni, the four aryáni-saccháni, the pachchayákárá, the pure and comprehensive nayá, and the indispensable maggá, and wiphassanabháwaná—all these having, on a former occasion, been set forth by me in the Wisuddhimaggo, I shall not here examine into them in detail."*

The Burmans ascribe a new era in their religion to the time that Budhaghósa arrived in that country from Ceylon; and even among them the Wisudhi-margga is celebrated, though their idea of its contents, as expressed by Ward, is not correct. "They believe that 650 years after Budha's death, in the reign of Muha-munee, Bouddhu-goshu, a brahman, was deputed to Ceylon to copy the work Vishoddhimargu, which includes all the Jutus, or histories of the incarnation of Budha; and it is fabled that the iron stile with which he copied this work was given him by a heavenly messenger."†

The word wisudhi means "pure," and margga, "path;" hence the title would be, the Path of the Pure, or, the Path by which Purity may be obtained. The sanné was written by Prákrama Báhu. There are several kings of this name, and I cannot discover from the work itself which of them is to be understood, but it was most probably Pandita Prákrama Báhu, who reigned A.D. 1471. It is a work of great importance; but the repetitions are so numerous, the explanations of words are carried out to so great a length, and the details, both of doctrine and discipline, are divided and subdivided into so many sections, that the reading of it is extremely tedious. I may mention as a mark of the respect in which it is held, that one of the most learned priests with whom I am acquainted, who happened to come into my study one day when I was reading it, said that any one who read through this work would be able to fulfil the office of sanga rája, or supreme ruler of the priesthood. But notwithstanding the high estimation in which it is held, I must confess that I have been somewhat disappointed in it, as it is rather an assistance to the understanding of other works, than in itself a body of information. It contains, upon the same scale as the Játakas (page 101), rather more than 1200 pages.

3. *Milinda-prasna.*—This work, though the incidents that gave rise to it occurred in a period much more recent than the time of Budha, is one of the most popular in Ceylon; and it is almost the only one that in the manner of its origin, independent of its con-

---

* Turnour, Journ. Bengal As. Soc. July, 1837.
† Ward's Hindoos: see also, Crawford's Embassy to Ava.

APPENDIX.

tents, is of general interest. The word Milinda designates a king of that name, and prásna means "questions," so that the title of the work is, The questions of Milinda. These questions were asked by Milinda, king of Ságal, and were answered by Nágaséna, a Budhistical sage, whose history is narrated in the introduction to the work.

In the time of Kásyapa Budha there was a noted wihára, near a certain river, in which resided many associations of priests. These priests, when they arose in the morning, took their brooms to sweep the sacred enclosure. One day a priest told one of the sámanéra novices to throw away the dirt that he had collected; but the novice went away as if nothing had been said; and though the command was repeated a second and a third time, he still paid no attention. The priest then struck him with the handle of the broom; upon which he went and did as he was directed, at the same time expressing the following wish:— "May I arrive at nirwána for having thrown away this dirt; and in the mean time, in my various births, may my glory be resplendent as that of the meridian sun." After this he went to the river to bathe, and as he saw the roaring waves following each other in rapid succession, he expressed the wish that he might ever receive wisdom suitable to the situation in which he was born. This wish was overheard by the priest, who concluded that his own reward would be proportionately greater, and said within himself, "From this time to the reception of nirwána, may I ever receive the wisdom necessary to enable me to unravel and clear up the questions this novice may ask me!"

A few years previous to the commencement of our era, as had been foretold by Gótama Budha, the novice was born in the world of men, and became Milinda, king of Ságal, in the country called Yon. This king was wise, a ready speaker, and learned in all the sciences. One day, when he had reviewed his troops, he said to his nobles that there was yet much time before the setting of the sun; and enquired if there was any sramana priest or brahman who could explain to him the manner of the rahats or of the Budhas. The names of six persons were mentioned, who all professed to be Budhas; and to each of them the king went, but they all proved to be deceivers; and as they were unable to answer satisfactorily the questions put to them by the monarch, he exclaimed, "All Jambudwípa is empty!" For the space of twelve years, whenever he heard of any learned person, of whatever caste, he went to him that his doubts might be satisfied; but in vain, as there was no one who was able to answer his arguments; and though many, in other places, were regarded as wise, they were silent when they came to Ságal. This was perceived by the priest Assagutta, who resided with his fraternity at the rock Rakkhita; and as he lamented the evil consequences that it produced, he assembled, upon the Yugandhara rocks, many thousands of rahats and a hundred times asked if any of them were able to overcome the doubts of Milinda; but even in this vast assembly no one equal to the task could be found. Then the whole of the rahats, vanishing from the rock, went to the celestial world called Tawutisá, as they perceived that the déwa Mahaséna possessed the requisite qualifications. On their arrival, they requested that he would receive birth in the world of men; he alone being able to solve the doubts of Milinda, a king who perplexed all with whom he conversed by the subtlety of his questions. This Mahaséna was the priest who in a former age struck the novice with a broom. To the request of the rahats, though with some hesitation, he consented, and became the son of a brahman, Sónuttara, who resided in the village Kajangalá, near the forest of Himála. The name that he received was Nágaséna; and as it is fabled that Gótama foretold his appearance 500 years after his own death, he must have been born in the year 43 B.C. From the time of his conception, a Budhist priest, Róhana, by the appointment of Assagutta, went daily to the house of his father, with the almsbowl; though he went six years and nine months without receiving anything further than scorn. When Nágaséna arrived at seven years of age, his father told him that he must now be taught according to the customs of their caste; and when the son asked what it was that he was to learn, he was informed that he must learn the three Védas, and many other branches of knowledge. Nágaséna was willing to be taught, and a learned brahman was appointed as his preceptor; but he learnt by heart the whole of the three Védas after once hearing them, and with equal facility gained a knowledge of grammar, history, and the other sciences. He then enquired from his father if there was anything more that he would be required to learn, and was told that there was not. After this, as he was one day near the entrance of the house, he saw the priest Róhana approaching; and as he felt drawn towards him by a secret affection, he went to him and said, "Who are you, with your shaven head and yellow garments?" The priest replied, "I am one who has abandoned the world." The youth enquired why he had done so; and when he was informed, he further asked why his head was shaven, and why he wore garments of that peculiar appearance. His curiosity being satisfied upon these points, he enquired if the priest was acquainted with any of the sciences, and was told that he had an ample knowledge of these matters; but that before he could teach them to the youth, he must receive the permission of his parents to embrace the priesthood. Accordingly he went to his parents, and entreated that they would allow him to become a priest, in order that he might learn the sacred sciences which he would become acquainted with in no other way. His parents told him that he might become a priest in order to learn the truths that he wished to know; but that when he had learnt them, they should expect him to resume his former state as a laic. He was, therefore, ordained by Róhana, who at once taught him the Abhidharmma, the most difficult of the three Pitakas. Not long afterwards he thought disrespectfully of the knowledge of the priest; but having learnt his error, he asked forgiveness; and Róhana told him, that in order to receive it, he must go to the court of Milinda, king of Ságal, and answer the questions that he would put. Soon after this appointment he went to the place where Assagutta resided, who sent him to the Asókáráma wihára, near Pelalup (Pátalíputra),* where dwelt the priest Dharmmarakshita. This was a distance of one hundred yojanas; but he went, and there became a rahat. After this he returned, in a moment of time, to Rakkhita, where the rahats had already assembled to congratulate him on the attainment of this great privilege; and after their respects were paid, they requested that without further delay he would encounter the king of Ságal, and free him from the darkness in which he was involved.

About this time Milinda heard of the fame of the priest Ayupála, and having received permission to visit him, he enquired why he had become a priest. Ayupála said it was in order that he might attain nirwána. The king then asked if no laic had ever attained that state; when the priest related to him many instances in which the brahmans of Benares, and others, who were yet laics, had seen nirwána from hearing the discourses of Budha. "Then," said the king, "it is evident that the reason you assign is not a sufficient one. You have garments of one colour, no settled habitation, and you deprive yourself of sleep; you must, therefore, in a former birth, have been a robber, and are now reaping the reward of your crimes." Thus the priest was put to silence.

It was to the wihára called Sankeyya that Nágaséna repaired, in order that he might meet the king; and Milinda was informed of his arrival by one of his nobles, Déwamantri. No sooner did he hear the name of the sage, than he began to tremble; but he went to the wihára, accompanied by a hundred of the Yon nobles; and though Nágaséna was in the midst of 80,000 priests, the king knew him at once. The conversations that ensued are detailed at length in the Milinda-prasna; and the result was, that the doubts of the king were removed, and he became a convert to the Budhist faith.

Nágaséna has been identified with Nágárjuna, through whose influence the people of Kashmir embraced Budhism, in the time of certain Turushka princes, or Tartars, as mentioned in the Rája Tarangini, translated by Professor Wilson.

It has been supposed, with much probability, that Ságal is the

* In Sanskrit, Kusama-pura. It is the Palibothra, near the modern Patna, to which Megasthenes was sent by Seleucus Nicator, to renew a treaty with Sandracottus, supposed to be the Chandragupta of the Hindus.

Sangala of the Greeks, the inhabitants of which resisted Alexander in his Indian expedition. After passing the Hydraotis, the Macedonian warriors pursued their way to Sangala, near which the Kathayans were encamped, upon an eminence fortified by a triple row of chariots. The first attack was unsuccessful; but at the second assault the barrier was forced, and the Kathayans, after a desperate resistance, retired to Sangala. The city was of great extent, protected on one side by a lake, and strongly fortified; but a breach was soon made, and the place was taken by storm. It is said that 17,000 of the citizens were massacred, and 70,000 made captives, whilst the Macedonians lost only 100 men and 1200 wounded. Soon afterwards Alexander commanded that Sangala should be entirely destroyed; but if this place be the Ságal of Milinda, it must have arisen from its ashes at a subsequent period, and again become the metropolis of the country. In one of the conversations held with Nágaséna, the king stated that he was born at Alasanda,* which he said was 200 yojanas from Ságal.† But this statement is indefinite; and though the reference is undoubtedly to Alexandria, there were so many cities of this name that we cannot exactly tell what place is intended by the king. We may, however, conclude therefrom that Milinda was not a Hindu, but probably an Asiatic Greek. In the same conversation he stated that Kásmíra, or Cashmire, was only twelve yojanas from Ságal, which agrees well with the position of Sangala. The nobles who accompanied the king are called Yons, or Yonikas,‡ a word which has been considered as synonymous with Yawan, or Ionia. It is said by Turnour that Yóna, or Yawana, is mentioned in the ancient Páli books, "long anterior to Alexander's invasion;" but to what books he refers is not apparent, as only 187 years elapsed between the death of Budha and the birth of Alexander; and it is evident that the Pitakas, in their present form, must have been composed many years subsequently to the events that they relate. The Singhalese authors place the Yon country on the banks of the Nirmmadá, or Nerbudda; but this is too much to the south of Sangala; and as the legend in which this statement

* It is stated in the Mahawanso that Alasaddá is the capital of the Yoná country.

† It is supposed by Masson that the Sangala of Arrian was at Harapa, a village of the Punjab, close to the left bank of the Ravi, and seated amid very extensive ruins (Journ. Bengal As. Soc., Jan. 1837); but Professor Wilson observes, "whether they (the Macedonians) followed the Iravati (Ravi) to Harapa, may be reasonably doubted." By Isidorus, Ságal and Alexandria are mentioned in the same sentence, "―― et Sigal urbs;" ubi regia Sacarum, propeque Alexandria urbs et non procul Alexandriopolis urbs."

‡ It is perhaps worthy of investigation whether the Yons may not be the same as the Huns, Ουννοι. By Moses of Choroene, in his Armenian History, they are called Hounk, which bears a considerable resemblance to Yonika.

is made appears to be of comparatively modern origin it may be incorrect.

By the Tibetans Nágaséna is regarded as the author of the Madhyámika school of Budhism. "In the Bstan-hgyur," says Csoma Körösi,* "the sixteen first volumes of the Mdo class are all commentaries on the Prajná Páramitá. Afterwards follow several volumes explanatory of the Madhyámika philosophy, which is founded on the Prajná Páramitá. The Prajná Páramitá is said to have been taught by Shákya, and the Madhyámika system by Nagarjuna (Nágaséna) who is said to have lived 400 years after the death of Shakya, who had foretold of him that he would be born after so many years, to explain his higher principles laid down in the Prajná Páramitá. With Nagarjuna originated the Madhyámika system in philosophy. The philosophers in India, before his time, were in two extremes, teaching either a perpetual duration, or a total annihilation, with respect to the soul. He chose a middle way; hence the name of this philosophical sect. There are in the Bstan-hgyur, several works of him, as also of his successors, explanatory of the Madhyámika school. Beside other matters of speculation, the following twenty-seven subjects are to be discussed and analyzed in the Madhyámika system :—1. Efficient (accessory or secondary) cause. 2. The coming (into the world) and going away. 3. Organs (of sense). 4. Aggregate, or body. 5. Province, or region, (viz. of senses). 6. Passion and affection. 7. The state of coming forth, duration, and cessation. 8. The maker, or doer, and the work, or deed. 9. Former existence. 10. Fire, and the burning wood. 11. Anterior and posterior limits (or worldly existence). 12. Done by one's self, and done by another. 13. Composition, or the forming of notions. 14. The act of meeting. 15. Self-existence, or nature. 16. Tied and liberated. 17. Work and fruit. 18. I, or ego. 19. Time. 20. Union (or cause and efficient causes). 21. Origin, or beginning, and destruction. 22. Tathágatha, or Buddha. 23. Wrong, error, or falsehood. 24. Excellent truth. 25. Deliverance, or delivered from pain. 26. Dependent connexion, or casual concatenation. 27. Critique of theories. These are the principal topics of the Madhyámika philosophy. I have thought proper to enumerate them here, because they are similar to the subjects of the Prajná Páramitá."†

* Asiatic Researches, vol. xx. p. 400.

† From the prominent place that Nágaséna occupies in the history of Budhism, and the frequent reference made to his opinions in these volumes, it may be interesting to add another extract, from an Essay that recently came under my notice, in which some of the statements in the preceding paragraphs are confirmed. "Nagarjuna, the same as Nágaséna of the Páli work Milindipanno, was, as would appear, a Bauddha hierarch, who lived B.C. 43. He is celebrated for a controversy on the subject of his religion, with Milinda, the rajah of Sagaia, a city well known to Greek history, and otherwise named Euthymedia, or Euthydemia, having been so called in honour of the Bactrian king Euthydemus; who, after successfully directing an insurrection in Bac-

538   A MANUAL OF BUDHISM.

In the Singhalese version of the Milinda-prasna there are 262 questions, but it is stated by the translator that in the original Páli there are 42 more.* Why they were omitted, or upon what subjects they treat, I am unable to say. The translation was made at Kandy, A.D. 1777, in the reign of Kírtisrí Rájasingha, by Hímati Kumburé Sumangala, who is said to have been the disciple of Aharagama Trirájaguru Bandára. He was at first a priest, but subsequently commenced a seminary in Kandy, in which he was patronised by the king; and his name is still held in high honour, from the knowledge he possessed of Singhalese, Elu, and Páli, and for his great attainments, not only in matters of religion, but also in the sciences, particularly astrology. The translation forms a work of about 720 pages.

4. *Pujáwaliya.*—This work was composed by Mayurapáda, who flourished in the reign of Prákrama Báhu III. A.D. 1267—1301. It contains thirty-four sections, or chapters, nearly all of which refer to some incident in the life of Gótama Budha. It has afforded me more ample materials for translation than any

---

tria, against the Seleucidæ, pushed his conquests into India, and established this city under his own name. . . Difference of opinion exists as to the site of this city, which, in the time of Alexander the Great was called Sangala, and is said in Arrian's History of India, to be situated between the two last rivers of the Punjab, the ancient Hydrastes and Hyphasis, or the modern Ravi and Pipasa. The town of Hurrepah, south-west of Lahore, and distant from it somewhat more than 60 miles, has been, with apparent truth, identified by Mr. C. Masson, as the site of Sagala, which, in Alexander's time, was the capital of the Kathai (Kshatriyas); and is mentioned in the Kerna Parva of the Mahabarat, under the name of Sakala. In the latter, it is called a city of the Bahikas, otherwise named Arattas; who are said to be without ritual or religious observances; and who, as distinguished from the pure Hindus, or followers of the Vedas and orthodox system, must have been Bahalikas, Bactrians, or of Indo-Scythian extraction. The inference that the people of Sangala belonged to the latter, is rendered more certain by facts, that this city is mentioned by Isiodorus Characenus, as belonging to the Sacæ or Scythians; and by Ferishta's history and the Persian romances, again mentioning that one of its rajahs was assisted by Afrasiab, in a war against the celebrated Kaikhusrau, or Cyrus. A point of connection between the Greco Bactrian kingdom and one of the earliest schools of Bauddha philosophy seems thus established with tolerable certainty; and the name of the city of Sagala, met with in the western cave inscriptions, must afford additional proof that the religious opinions and ritual of Budhism were not uninfluenced, in the north of India, by the mythology, if not the philosophy of the Greeks. Nagarjuna's principal disciples, according to the Tibetan books, were Arya Deva and Budha Palita.—Bird on the Bauddho and Jaina Religions; Journ. Bombay Branch, Royal As. Soc., Oct. 1844.

* As it is said by Turnour, that "the Milinda-panno, extant in Ceylon, contains 262 dissertations, as well as the designations of the dissertations that are missing, being forty-two," it would appear that the omission is not in the Singhalese translation alone, but also in the Páli version whence it is taken. It is probable that when this work was written, there was some extended life of Nágasóna extant. Being incomplete, neither the date nor the author of the Milinda-panno can now be ascertained.—Turnour, Journ. As. Soc., Sept. 1836.

other work in all that relates to the personal acts of the sage. The original occupies 800 pages, of which I have translated the greater portion.

5. *Sadharmmálankáré.*—This work is a collection of legends and tales, many of which refer to times long subsequent to Budha, and illustrate the history of Budhism during the periods of its ascendancy and decline on the continent of India. It contains 800 pages, and was written by Siddhartta, or Dharmmaditta-charya-wimalakirtti, the disciple of the sanga rája, Dharmmakirtti, whilst residing at the Maha Wihára of Anurádhapura, in the reign of Prákrama Báhu VI. A.D. 1410.

6. *Sadharmmaratnakáré.*—This work is of a similar description to the one last mentioned, but contains a greater portion of matter relative to the rites of Budhism, and the meaning of Budhistical terms. Its style is very unequal. It has 360 pages; but I do not know by whom it was written.

7. *Amáwatura.*—I have not been able to ascertain in what age this work was written. Its style is very different to any other work I have read; but this appears to arise rather from the caprice of its author than from its antiquity. There is another work by the same author, called Pradípikáwa, written in the same style. The Amáwatura contains an account of the birth of the prince Sidhártta, and of his reception of the Budhaship; after which, in eighteen sections, is given an example of the manner in which different classes of individuals were converted by Budha, including a brahma, déwa, yaká, king, brahman, householder, tirttaka, digambara, jatila, tápasa, thief, &c. It was written by Gurulugowina, and contains 256 pages.

8. *Th'úpawansé.*—The word thúpa means a conical erection, containing a relic, the more common term in Singhalese being dágoba. This work contains an account of the manner in which the relics of Budha were apportioned after his cremation, of the places to which they were taken, and of their subsequent fate. It has 250 pages.

9. *Rájawaliya.*—This work contains a connected history of Ceylon, with the names of all the kings, from the death of Budha to the arrival of the English. The former portion bears a considerable similarity to the Mahawanso, for the compilation of which it has furnished materials. It was composed by different authors, at various periods. Some copies close at the time of the arrival of the Portuguese; others, of the Dutch; and a few are brought down to the beginning of the present century. The copies most commonly met with contain about 260 pages.

10. *Kayawiratigáthá-sanné.*—This work contains an account of the anatomy of the human body, setting forth its offensiveness, and the folly of bestowing attention upon a thing so worthless. It was written by a priest, but I know neither his name nor the age in which he lived. It is read to condemned

criminals, that they may not grieve at being obliged to leave a state that is connected with so many evils.

11. *Kammawáchan.*—This is one of the formularies used by the priests, containing the ritual to be observed at the ordination of an upasampadá, the dedication of a temple, &c. A translation of some of its principal parts, as well as of some other works of a similar description, appears in the chapters of Eastern Monachism that treat of the discipline of the priesthood.

12. *The Sannés of various Sútras.*—The Sútra Pitaka is the second division of the sacred code, and contains the discourses of Budha that were addressed to the laity, in contradistinction to those that were addressed to the déwas and priests. The word sanné means a translation or paraphrase. It usually includes both a translation and a commentary or explanation. In some instances the translation is almost literal, whilst in others the comment is so extensive as to form almost an original work. The sannés are of various value, according to the ability of the priest by whom they were made. In the Singhalese copies the text of the original Páli always accompanies the paraphrase.

INDEX.

A.

A, a negative, 1.
ABHASSARA, a rúpa-brahma-lóka, 26, 29, 65, 66.
ABHAYA, son of Bimsara, 244.
ABHIBHU, a priest, 9.
ABHIDHARMMA, 309.
ABHISAMÁCHÁRA-SÍLA, chief síla, 511.
ABRA, the déwas of rain, 22.
ACHÁRA-SÍLA, 513.
ACHÉTANÁ, not possessing a mind, (said of the earth), 397.
ACHINTEYYA, without a mind, 411, 472.
ACHIRAWATI, a stream, 17.
ACCHUTA, an ascetic, 122.
ADA, lunar mansion, 24.
ADHIMOKHA, steadfastness, 426.
ADHIMUKTI, kind of death of the Bódhisats, 108.
ADHÓMUKHA YUGA, 7.
ADIBRAHMACHARIYA-SÍLA, 511.
ADISHTÁNA, the power to produce by an effort of the mind, 519.
Adittapariyá-sutra, 196.
Adultery, 484.
Advantages, the thirteen, of the Bódhisat, 107.
ADWÉSA, affection, 429.
ÆSALA-KELI, a nekata festival, 166.
ÆSALA MASA, a month (July, August), 23, 144, 158, 189, 305.
Agappasádasútra, quoted, 373.
AGASAW or AGRA-SRÁWAKA, chief disciple, 202.
Aganna-suttán, 82.
AGGIDATTA, father of Kakusanda Budha, próhita to the monarchs of Kohéma, 87.
AGGISÉNA, the cake-giver of Kónágamana, 99.
AGNIMALI, 13.
AGNYÁSÉTRA, 2.

AHÁRÁJA, khandas connected with some sensible object, 417.
AHINGSAKA (afterwards Angulimála, the finger cutter), 257.
AHIRIKÁ, shamelessness, 433.
AJA, goat path, 20.
AJÁPÁLA, a tree, 180.
AJÁPÁLA, the déwa of a naga tree, 170.
AJÁSAT, son of Bimsara, king of Rajagaha, 265, 295, 326, 362, 495.
—— his conversion, 333.
AJÁSAT, Pasé Budha, Wijitawisésa, 337.
AJATÁKÁSA, 12, note; 33, 65.
AJHÁRÓHA, 13.
AJITÁKÁSAKAMBALA, a deceiver and sceptic, 301.
AKÁSA, aerial abode, 33.
AKÁSA DHÁTU, space, 417.
AKÁSÁNANCHÁYATANA, a rúpa brahma lóka, 26.
AKANISHTAKA, a rúpa brahma lóka, 26.
AKÁSAGANGA, the passage through the sky of, 17.
AKINCHANNYÁYATANA, a rúpa brahma lokas, 26.
AKUSALA, demerit, 425, 461, et pass.
AKUSALA, Wastu-káma, klésha-káma, 461.
AKUSALA-WIPÁKA-WINYÁNA-DHATU-CHITTA, cause of birth in the four hells, 439.
ALÁRA, an ascetic, 168, 188.
ALAWAKA, a yaká, 265.
ALÓBHA, indifference, 429.
AMALAKÍ, a garden near the city Chátumá, 390.
AMANUSA (not men), 47.
AMARAPURAS, sect of priests in Ceylon, 38.
AMBATOARALU, 186.
Amáwatura, description of, 539.

INDEX.

Amawatura, quoted, 56, 57, 59, 140, 261, 262, 267, 269, 274, 314, 320, 345, 348, 349, 384, 392, 393.
AMBA, a king, his five principal queens, 133.
AMBAPÁLI, chief courtezan of Wisálá, 473; the history of, 244.
AMBASANDA, a brahman village, 298.
AMBÁTAKA, a garden, 199.
AMBATTA SÁKYA, a name of the Okkáka race of kings, 137.
AMÉDYA, hell, 473.
AMITTA-TÁPA, daughter of a brahman, 122.
ANÁGÁMI, a path, 91, 190, 433.
Anágata wansa, 206.
ANANDA, a fish, 13.
ANANDA, the personal attendant of Gótama, 9, 149, 238, 241, 242, 295, 297, 306.
ANANGA, the dewá, 166.
ANANTA-JINAYO, 189.
ANÁPÁNA-SMERTI-BHÁWANÁ, the power of, 151.
ANATHAPINDIKA (Anépidu), 47.
ANÁTMA, unreality, 514.
ANDAJA, oviparous birth 457.
ANDHA, forest near Sewet, 485.
ANÉPIDU, a nobleman, an upásika, 114, 222, 223, 224, 305, 309.
ANGA, a country, 194.
ANGÁTI, a king in Miyulu, 196.
ANGULI MÁLA, history of 257, 298.
ANGUTTARÁPA, a country, 282.
ANICHATÁ, impermanency, 418.
Animals, 17.
ANIMISA LÓCHANA, the keeping eyes immoveably on the tree, 185.
ANISRATA-SÍLA, 511.
ANITYA, impermanency, 513.
ANIYATA-WIWARANO, the indefinite assurance to become a Budha.
ANJA, a monarch, 133.
ANKOTTAPPA, recklessness, 433.
ANÓMÁ, a river, 164.
ANOMADASSI, a Budha, 79, 203, 508.
ANÓTTATTA, one of the great lakes, 71, 31, 145, 194, 261.
ANÓTATTA-WILA, a lake, 16.
ANUPASAMPANNA-SÍLA, 512.
ANUPIYA, a mango garden, 165.
ANURA, lunar mansion, 24.
ANURÁDHAPURA, a city in Ceylon, 53, 60, 218.

ANURUDHA, attendant to Kondannya Budha, 97.
ANURUDHA, a priest, the déwa Sekra, 127, 238, 308, 360.
ANUSÁKYA, a king, 149.
ANUWYANJANA LAKSHANA, inferior beauties, the, 80; of a supreme Budha, 150, 381.
ANYA-KONDANYA, 324, 340.
APÁKAKÓSIKA-SÍLA, 511.
APANA, a village, 282.
Apannaka Játaka, quoted, 110, 412.
APARAGÓDÁNA, a continent, 7, 466.
APARÁMARSHTA-SÍLA, 512.
Aparanita Dharmi, quoted, 91.
APARANTA, a region, 469.
APARARIYA WÉDYA, karma, 463.
APARIYANTA-SÍLA, 511.
APÓDHÁTU, 415.
APO SANGWARTTA, destruction by rain, 33.
APPRAMÁNASUBHA, a rúpa brahma lóka, 26.
ARAMUNU, thoughts that proceed from contact with sensible objects, 424.
ÁRANYAKANGA, an ordinance to retire to a forest, 338.
ARDHA, an ascetic, 380.
ARDHAPÁLA, the mendicant Upaka, 189.
ARINDAMA-RÁJA, name of Gótama Bódhisat, 97.
ARPPANI, 7.
ARTHADARSHI, a Budha, 97.
ARTTHA, the meaning of any matter, 517.
Arunawatí-sutra, 9.
ARÚPA WORLDS, 44.
ARÚPA-BRAHMA-LÓKAS, the four, 26.
ARÚPAWACHARA, 3.
ARÚPAWACHARA-WIPÁKA-SIT, cause of birth in the arúpa-brahma-lóka, 439.
ARYA, or ARYAHAT, the fourth of the paths leading to nirwána, 39.
ARYA ASHTÁNGIKA-MARGGA, the eight paths of purity, 517.
ARYA-IRDHI (the power of the rahat,) 523.
Arya langkávatára maha yana sutra, 370.
ASADRISA-DÁNA, the peerless offering, 298.
Asadrisa Jataka, 116.
ASALA, fury, 21.

INDEX.

Asammósasutra, the tikáwa of, 514.
ASANKYA, a numeral, 1.
ASANKYA-KAP-LAHSHA, numeral 91.
ASANYASATYA, rúpa-brahma-lóka, 26, 105.
ASEKHA-SÍLA, 512.
ASLISA, lunar mansion, 24.
ASHTÁ-SAMÁPATTI, the eight modes of abstract meditation.
ASHTA-WIDYA, eight kinds of knowledge, 430.
ASÓKA, son of Kálaranjanaka, a monarch, 133.
ASSAGUTTA, a priest, 533.
ASSAJI, a priest, 152, 200, 264.
ASSAKA, a king, 346.
ASUBHA-BHÁWANA, 192, note.
ASUNYA-KALPA, 129.
ASURS, the, 5, 47, 59.
ASWAKARNNA, 12, 13, 31.
ASWAMANTA, 132.
ASWAPURA, a city, 131.
ASWARATNA, horse.
ATWÁRA, inspirated, 444.
ÁTÁNÁTIYA, defence, 47.
ATAPPA, a rúpa-brama-lóka, 26.
ATA-SIL, the eight precepts, 507.
ATAWAKA, the first quarter of the moon, 22.
ATIDÉWA-BRÁHMANA, name of Gótama Bódhisat, 97.
ATIMUKTAKA, a robber, 261.
ÁTMABHÁWA, constituting individual existence, 456.
ATMÁDHIPATEYYA-SÍLA, 512.
ATTHASALINI, 530.
ATÚLA, an upásaka, 378, 292.
ATULA-NÁGA-RÁJA, name of Gótama Bódhisat, 97.
AWAKÁSA-LÓKA, 3.
AWANTI, the king of, 83.
AWICHI, a naraka, 27, 31, 286, 312, 337, 485.
AWIDYA, ignorance, 407, 514.
AWIDYAMÁNA, lost in confusion, 457.
AWIDYÁWA, non-perception, 457.
AWIHA, ruler of the brahma-lóka, 28, 29.
AWIRATI-SÍLA, 511.
AWISUDHI-SÍLA, 512.
AWYÁKSATA, not followed by any consequence, 461.
ÁYATANAS, sentient organs, 448.
AYUPÁLA, a priest, 535.
AYODHA, a great town in Oude, 88.

B.

BADALÁTÁ, a climbing plant, 67.
BADDRAWATI, an elephant, 252.
BAHIRA, outward, 514.
BAHUPUTRAKA-DÉWÁLA, 343.
BAKA, a brahman, 348.
BAKHAS, a month, 23.
BAKKULA, history of, 520.
BÁLAKALÓNAKA, a village, 276.
Bála-pandita - sútra-sanné, quoted, 61.
Bála-pandita-sútra, 503.
BALU, an ascetic, 341.
BALAWA-WIPASSANÁWA, a sila, 512.
BANA, 9, 38.
BANDHULA, a warrior, the prowess of, 290.
BANDHUMATTIKÁ, wife of Bandhula, 290.
Bath of the supreme Budhas, 16.
Battle fought between Bhadrasála of the Nandagutta race, and Chandragutta of the Sákya race, 468.
BAWÁRI, the próhita of Maha Kosol and Pasénadi, history of, 345.
BHADDAJA, a brahman, 168.
BHADDAJI, son of, a brahman, 152.
BHADDAKA, son of Upaka, 190
BHADDAWAGGI, a condition, 193.
BHADDI, a prince, 235, 237, 238.
BHADRA, disciple of Kondannya Budha, 97.
BHADRÁWUDHA, a brahman, 347.
Bhagavata, (quoted) 12.
BHAGAWÁ, a cave, 218.
BHAGINEYYA, a nobleman, 63.
BHÁGINI, the sister, 499.
BHAGÍRATA, a monarch, 132.
BHAGU, 238.
BHALLUKA, a merchant becomes an upásaka, 186.
BHANNUKA, a country, 197.
BHÁRADDWAJA, disciple of Kásyapa Budha, 99.
BHARATA, a monarch, 132.
BHARUKACHA, 13.
BHAWA, existence, 514.
BHAWAGRA, a world, 312.
BHÁWANÁ, the meditative rite, 33, 287.
BHIKSUNI-SÍLA, 512.
BHIKSU-SÍLA, 512.
BHOJA, a brahman, 117.
BHÚMATU-DÉWATÁ, a terrestrial deity, 19.

BHÚMI, the period required for the exercise of a páramitá, its length, 105.
BHÚMI-WIJAYA, the art to know the history of any given spot, 136.
BHUPÁLA, history of, 521.
BHUSIDATTA BIRTH, 104.
Bears, 17.
BÉMÁWATA, 271.
BIMSARA (BIMASARA), king of Rajagaha, 166, 196, 218.
BIMSARA, king of Wéluwana, 283.
BINARA, a month, 23.
BODHI-PÁKSHIKA-DHARMMA, the thirty-seven, 516.
BÓTREE, 27, 177, et pass.
—— its birth, 149.
BÓDHA, bótree, 4.
BÓDHI-MANDALA, 4.
BÓDHISATS, the beings who will become Budha, their number, 90, 91.
—— *Three* kinds of, 106.
—— their birth-place in the world, 105.
BÓDHISAT-GNEYYA, who attains least quickly.
BÓDHISAT-UGGHATITAGNYA, who attains quickly, 106.
BÓDHISAT-WIPACHITAGNYÁ, who attains less quickly, 106.
BÓDHISAT-MAHA-BRAHMA, 197.
BÓDHISAT-SUPPÁRAKA, 13.
BÓDHISAT-WAMÁTU-SÍLA, 513.
BÓDHYANGÓPÉKSHÁ, 524.
BRAHMA-CHARIYA, ordinance, 202, 210.
BRAHMADATTA, father of Kásyapa Budha, king of Benares, 99, 110.
Brahma Jála Sútra, 403.
BRAHMA-LÓKAS (system of worlds), 2.
BRAHMANS, the eight chosen to investigate a name for Gótama, 157.
BRAHMANS, ten kinds of, 75, 83.
BRAHMA PARISADYA, (rúpa brahma lóka), 26.
BRAHMA PUROHITA (rúpa brahma lóka), 26.
BRAHMANÁ, suppressors, 68.
BRAHMA-WIHÁROPÉKSHÁ, 524.
BRAHMÁYU, a brahman, 384.
Brahmáyu-sútra-sanné, 387.
BRÁHMO (Brahman), 82, note.
BUDHA-DHARMMA, the eighteen, 395.

BUDHA, Mercury (planet), 24, 67.
BUDHA, warning, 30, note.
BUDHAGHÓSA, 530.
BUDHAJÁNA, attendant of Kakusanda, 98.
BUDHA-KÁRAKA-DHARMMA, thirty wonders, 307.
BUDHÁNTARA, a period, space, 60, 168, 309.
BUDHA-RAKKHITA, 524.
BUDHAS, the sixteen, their appearance, 88; their dharmma, birth, age, nirwána, size, 89.
—— who preceded Gótama, 88.
BUDHAS, names of 143, quoted in Hodgson: illustrations of the literature and religion of the Budhists, 90.
Budha-wansa, 206, 322.
BUDHA-WISAYA, 9, note.
Buffaloes, 17.
Bulls, 17.
Burning of the dead, 325, et pass.

C.

Castes, origin of, 68.
—— institution of, and transmigration of souls, connection between, 79.
—— no distinction at first, according to Budhists, 80.
—— among the Budhists of Ceylon, 80.
—— in Budhistic countries, 84.
—— uncertainty in Ceylon respecting them, 84.
—— its influence, 85.
Causes the, of Sidhártta becoming a Budha, 154.
CHADDANTA, one of the seven great lakes, 17.
CHAITYA, of Chankramana, 185.
CHAITYA (dágoba), of animisa lochana, 185.
CHAKRARATNA, magical discus, 30.
CHAKRAWARTTI, warning, 30, note.
CHAKRAWARTTI, his state and condition, 129; his seven precious things, 130.
CHAKRAWARTTA-LAKSHANA, 381.
CHAKSU-WINYÁNA, eye conciousness, 434.
CHÁMARAS, 120.
CHAMPA, a city in Jambudwípa, 254.
CHANDA, formation of the, 67.
CHANDA, determination, 426.

CHANDALA (Sadol), 82.
CHANDANA-MANDALA, a hall in the forest of Mulu, 215.
CHANDRABHAGA, a river, 510.
CHANDRA, moon (Planets), 42 et pass.
CHANDRAWATI-DÉWI, the daughter of the king of Benares, 51.
CHANNO, a nobleman, 141.
—— his birth, 149.
—— his assistance to Gótama in former ages, 164.
Chanda Pirit, moon's protection, a part of the pitakas, 47.
CHANDA, the god (moon), 47.
Chandakinnara játaka, 353.
CHANDAPPRAGÓTA, king of Udéni, 251.
CHANDIHI-PÁDA, firm determination, 517.
CHANDRAPADUMÁ, daughter of Meda, 226.
CHARA, a monarch, 131.
CHÁRITRA-SÍLA, keeping of all precepts, 510.
CHATTAPÁNI, an upásaka, 297.
CHÁTURMAHARÁJIKA (adéwa-loka), 20, 25, 329; its extension, 24.
—— residence of the gandhárwas, 44.
CHATUPARISUDHISÍLA, the four great duties, 177.
CHATURWIDHA-ÁHÁRA, four kinds of food, 518.
CHATURWIDHA-ÁRYA-SATYA, four great truths, 515.
CHATURWIDHA-ÁSRAWA, four principles by which the cleaving to existence is produced, 514.
CHATURWIDHA-DHARMMA-PADA— four divisions of the dharmma, 516.
CHATURWIDHA-ÓGHA, the four streams, 514. *See* the Chaturwidha-ásrawa.
CHATURWIDHA-IRDHI-PÁDA, four modes by which power of irdhi is to be attained, 516.
CHATURWIDHA - PRATIRAMBHIDA four modes of perfect understanding, 517.
CHATURWIDHA - SAMYAK - PRADHÁNA, four objects for which exertion must be used, 516.
CHÁWI, a girl, 189.
CHÉDANA, separation, 431.
CHÉLA, a weapon, 272.
CHÉTANÁ, thought, 325, 420.

CHÉTIYA, a monarch, son of Upachara, 131.
CHÉTIYA, king of Jambudwípa, lie the first spoken by, 486.
Child, duties of, towards parents, 476.
CHINCHI, a female heretic, formerly Amitta-tápa, 63, 127, 284.
CHINDUKA, the grass-giver of Kónágamana, 99.
CHINTÁMÁNIKYA, the magical jewel, 167, 324.
CHITRÁ, queen of Amba, 133.
CHITRAKÚTA, 15, 16.
CHITTA, modes of thought, 448.
CHITTAJA, khandas connected with the mental faculties, 417.
CHITTAIRJUTWA, mind uprightness, 432.
CHITTAKÁGRATAWA, individuality, 423.
CHITTA - KARMMANGATA, mind adaptation, 432.
CHITTA-LAHUTÁ, mind-lightness, 432.
CHITTA-MIRDUTWA, mind-softness, 432.
CHITTA-PRÁGUNYATÁ, mind-practice, 432.
CHITTA-PRASRABDHI, repose or tranquillity of the mind, 432.
CHITTÁNUPASSANÁ, 516.
CHITTIDHIPÁDA, thoughtful meditation, 517.
CHITTA, a rich citizen of Macchikásanda.
CHÓRI, the thief, 498.
CHÚLABHAYA, brother of Dewanan piyatissa, 203.
Chúlakamma-wibhanga-sútra, 463.
CHULA SUBADRA, daughter of Anépidu, 225.
CHULLA SUTTASOMA, birth, 104.
CHULODANA, a naga king, 214.
CHUNDA, Budha's attendant, 241.
CHUNDA, a smith, 355.
Coins, masuran, nilakarsha, karsha.
Consciousness, 408, et pass.
Covetousness, 488.
Crimes, the three of the body, káya charita; the four of the speech, wák; the three of the mind, manó, 275.

D.

DABARÁWA, relic, 375.
DADDARA, a city, 131.

DADHIMALI, 13.
DAGOBAS 52, 88, et pass.
DAIWADIPA, the divine-lamp; name of the eye, 506, note.
DAKSHINAGIRI a wihára, belonging to the village of Eknálaka, 220.
DÁLIDDI, a village.
DAMBA TREE (jambu,) 19.
DÁNA, almsgiving, the three kinds of—páramitá, ' rupa páramitá, paramartha-páramitá, 104.
Dancing women, 161.
DANDA, (cause,) 274.
DANDAKI, the king of Khumbáwáti, 55.
DANTHÁDARA, 218.
DARUCHI, a priest, 261.
DASABALA, ten powers, 394.
DASARATHA, a monarch, 133.
Dasaratha Jataka, quoted, 153.
DASA SÍL, 506.
DASAWIDHA IRDHI, ten supernatural powers, 519.
DASI, the slave, 500.
Dasa-brahma-játaka, 75.
Deer, 17.
DEGASAW, male disciple of Dípankara, 96.
DENATA, lunar mansion, 24.
DÉSADHARMMA-SÍLA, 513.
Destruction, the, of the universe, 33.
DEODAR, (Himalayan cedar, cedrus deodara) 19.
DETA, lunar mansion, 24.
DEWADATTA, the brahma Jújaka, 127.
DEWADATTA, the son of Supra Budha, 63.
DEWADATTA, destruction of, 337.
—— in a future birth, the Pasé Budha Sattissara, 340.
—— and AJÁSAT, the wicked devices of, 326.
DÉWA-LÓKAS and BRAHMA-LÓKAS, 24.
DEWAS, the, 16, 50.
—— their functions, 41.
—— their birth, 33.
—— their residence, 40.
DEWAS, the four guardians, 24, 52.
DEWALAS, places of worship dedicated to the dewas, 43.
DEWUDABHA, a king, 178.
Dhamsak-pawatum-sutra, 191.
DHANAPÁLA, an elephant, formerly Malágiri, 332.
DHANANJA, son of Méda, 13, 226.
DHANNYA, 95.

DHANA, a rási, 23.
DHARATI ASANKYA, 95.
DHARMMA, knowledge of, 37, 93, 177.
—— the doctrines of Budha, 517.
DHARMMA, the throne of Sekra, 52.
DHARMMÁNUPASSANÁ, 516.
DHARMMAPALA, heir-apparent of Maha Pratápa, 132.
DHARMMADHIPATEYYA-SILÁ, 512.
DHARMMARAKSHITA, a priest, 535.
DHARMMADARSHI, a Budha, 97.
DHAMMAWATÍ, mother of Kasyapa Budha, 99.
Dharmmapálá Játaka, 212.
DHÁTU, elements, 367, et pass.
DHAYA, a brahman, 151.
DHRATARÁSHTRA, a guardian déwa, 24.
DHUMA, the dewas of mist, 22.
DHYANA, an ordinance, exercise of, 31, 44, 91, 239, et pass.
DHYANA-SILÁ, 512.
DHYÁNÓPEKSHA, 524.
DÍGHANAKA, nephew of Gótama Budha, a paribrájika, 203.
Diksangha, (Diksanga) 300, 336.
DILÍPA, a monarch, 133.
DIMBUL-TREE, 286.
DIMBULTÓTA, in Ceylon, 393.
DIPANKARA, a Budha, 96, 107, 181.
DÍRGGHA-TÁPASA, one of the followers of Niganthanátha, 274.
Disciples of Budha, fifty-four princes and a thousand fire-worshippers become, 182.
Diseases, the four to which the regent of the sun is subject, 21.
DÓTAKA, a brahman, 347.
DRISHTA - DHARMMA - WEDYA, KARMA, 351.
DRISHTA -DHARMMA- WÉDYA- AKUSALA, (the history of Chinchi) quoted as an example of, 286.
DRISHTA - DHARMMA - WÉDYA - KUSALA-KARMMA, 351, note.
DRISHTI, scepticism, 514.
DRÓHA, a brahman, 383.
DUKHA, sorrow, 513.
——— NIRODHA GÁMINI PATIPADA SATYA, 515.
——— SAMUDYA-SATYA, 515.
——— NIRODHA-SATYA, 515.
——— SATYA, 515.
DUKULA, an ascetic, 453.
DURUTU, a month, (January, February, March) 21, 23, 205.

INDEX.

DUTTHAGÁMINI, a monarch, 23, 25, note.
DWÁRA, aperture, 418.
DWESA, anger, hatred, 433, 513.
DWÍPA, 4.

E.

Earth, its revolutions, 5.
Eclipses, 5, et pass.
Elements of existence, 414.
Elephants, 17.
EMASUNANDA, cake giver of Kasyapa B, 99.
Era, the, of resolution, 91.
—— the, of nomination, 96.
—— the three which succeed the appearance of Budha, 90.
ERAKA, a rock, 94.
Erecting, the, of dagobas over Budha's relics, 366.
Ethics, the, of Budhism, 477.
Evidence of the fact that a déwa leaves the celestial regions, 144.
Existence, the circle of successive, 407.

F.

FA-HIAN, 88, et pass.
Festival, the, of the king's plough-holding, 153.
Formula, the threefold protective, 187.
Forest, the Great, 15.
Friend, the, 500.

G.

GADRABHA, porter of the yaká Alawaka, 270.
GAL-POLOWA, a stratum of earth, 3.
Gambling, 492.
GANAWARA, the guardian princes of the monarchs, 133.
GANDHAMÁDANA, 15, 16.
GANDAMBA, a gardener, 305.
GANDHÁRWAS, the attendants of Dhratarásḥtra, 24.
—— their number, 24.
—— their garments, 44, 164.
GANGA, wave, 13; river, 17.
GARUNDAS, 31, 45, 182, et pass.
GANDHAN, smell, 416.
GANTHÁKARO WIHÁRO, 531.
GAYA, a river, 339.
GELA, load of rice, 401.
GHARANA, a woman, 307.
GHATÍKARA, a brahman, 165.
GHEE, or sesamum oil, 32.

GHOSIKA, a noble, 523.
GHÓSÓ, eloquence, 530.
GHRANA-WINYANA, nose consciousness, 435.
GIJAKÚTA, a rock, 481.
—— WIHARA, 330.
GIMHANA, summer season, 21.
GIRIHANDA, a place near Ceylon, where afterwards the Girihanda Wihára was erected, 187.
GIRIMÉKHALA, elephant of Mára, 175, 180.
GIWALU, forest, 55.
GNYÁNAWEPPPÁRA, the power received from the possession of gnyána, 519.
Go, Bull path, 20.
GÓDAWARI, a river, 55, 346.
GOGERLY, "Ceylon Friend," ii, 228.
Golden eagles, 17.
GOLWA, a sea, 393.
GÓPÁLA-MATRU-DÉWI, daughter of a poor noble, 468.
GÓTAMA-DEWALA, 343.
GÓTAMA BÓDHISAT, a yáka, 46, an ascetic, 93, 97; takes the name Sestratápa, 92; pursuing elephants, 92; born in a dewa-lóka, 94: a chakrawartti, 95; born as the son of the monarch of Dhannya, 95; born as the son of Sunanda, king of the city Paraspawatí, 96; born as the king of Benares, 92; sailing to Swarnna Bhúma, 92; a késara lion, 97; number of times in which he appeared in particular states of existence as recorded in the Játakas, 102; a merchant, 110; a bull, a tradesman, a lion, 115; as Wessantara, 118; as Sujáta, 100; the ascetic Kapila, 135; name of the princes as which he was born, 137.
—— the sakwala in which he appeared, 4.
GOTAMA BUDHA, his notions of the world system, 35, note.
—— the teacher of the three worlds, 37.
—— delivers the *Arunawati Sútra*, 9.
—— delivering the discourse *Maha Samaya*, 41.
—— interview with the déwas, 42.
—— the rishi Lomasa Kásyapa, 51
—— acknowledging the superiority of the Brahman, 74.

GOTAMA BUDHA, protects the moon, 23.
—— relating the *Dasa brahma játaka*, 75.
—— inquiring after castes, 79.
—— a philosophical opponent of popular superstition and brahmanical caste, 79.
—— rejects caste, 80.
—— his eight hairs, 88.
—— enumerating the qualities he would require in his wife, 80.
—— recites the *Aganna suttan*, 82, note.
—— a Bódhisat, 92.
—— residing in Jétawana, a wihára, 109.
—— his ancestors, 112.
—— conception, birth, and infancy of, 142.
—— his growth, 154.
—— marriage, the, of and his subsequent abandonment of the world, 155.
—— exhibits his strength, 156.
—— disgust with the life in the palace, 160.
—— preparations for his travel, 161.
—— his meeting with Mára, 163.
—— the food of, in Rajagaha, 167.
—— vanishing of his strength, his food as an ascetic, 167.
—— as an ascetic, preparatory to the reception of Budhaship, 168.
—— his dreams, 170.
—— his contest with Wasawartti Mára, 175.
—— at the Ramaní pásána wihára.
—— reception of the Budhaship, 183.
—— performs the act of animisa lochana, 185.
—— his promise to propound the three pitakas, 186.
—— goes to the tree Appálá, 186.
—— goes to the lake Muchalinda, 186.
—— enjoys the satisfaction of Dhyána, 186.
—— receives a piece of amrata aralu, goes to the lake Anotatta, 186.
—— teaches the two merchants the three-fold protective formulary, 187.
—— delivers his first discourse, 188.
—— preaches the *Dhamsak-paewatum-sutra* (*Dhamma-chakka*), 191.

GOTAMA BUDHA, returns to Uruwela, 192.
—— speaks in the language of Magadha, 192.
—— with the naya, 193.
—— receives the offering of a robe, 195.
—— with the jótis, 195.
—— delivers the *Adittapariyá-sútra*, 196.
—— delivers the first játaka *Mahánárada-kásyapa*, 196.
—— in Wéluwana, 200.
—— delivers the *Tirokudha-sútra*, 200.
—— delivers the *Wédana-parigrahana discourse*, 203.
—— visits Kapilawastu his native city, 203.
—— exercises the Téjo-kasina-sanápatti; Apo-kasina-sanápatti; Níla-kasina-sanápatti, 206.
—— delivers the *Anágata-wansa*, 206.
—— relates the *Wessantara-játaka*, 206.
—— exercises dhyána, 206.
—— visits Yasódhará-déwí, 209.
—— visits the island of Ceylon, 212.
—— recites the *Dharmmapála Játaka*, 212.
—— at the nágas, delivers discourses, 214.
—— second journey to Ceylon, 214.
—— third journey to Ceylon, 215.
—— fortells the prosperity of a labourer's wife, 218.
—— attends a ploughing festival, 220.
—— visit to the garden of Anépidu, 225.
—— visits the village of Bhaddhi, in Anga, 226.
—— in the village Anupiya, 238.
—— attendants, his, Nágasamala, Nágita, Upawána, Sunakkhatta, Chunda, Ságala, Mesi, 241.
—— visits the city of Wisálá, 242.
—— delivers the *Ratana-sútra*, 244.
—— being sick receives medicine of Jíwaka, 253.
—— ordains a law concerning the robes of priests, 256.
—— delivers the *Sabhiya-sútra*, 262.
—— dispute with Sacha, 265.
—— dispute with Niganthanátha a tirttaka, 274.

GOTAMA BUDHA, at the ascetic Kéni, 283.
—— is falsely accused of incontinence by the female unbeliever, Chinchi, 284.
—— the gifts presented to, on his return to Sewet, 297.
—— is visited by the Déwa Sekra, 298.
—— repeats the *Kanka* and *Nandiwisálá Játaka*, 307.
—— visits the déwa-lóka Tawutisá, 308.
—— interprets sixteen dreams to Pasénádi, king of Kosol, 314.
—— takes 500 princes through the air to the Himála forest, 319.
—— delivers a discourse to the people of Koli and Kapila, about to fight, 319.
—— relates the *Kunála-játaka*, 320.
—— delivers the *Maha Samaya Sútra*, 320.
—— delivers the *Tirokudha sutra* and *Budha wansa*, 322.
—— delivers the *Nandakowáda sútra*, 323.
—— resides in Kosambae, 327.
—— converts Ajásat, 335.
—— at the Maha-wana-wihára, 342.
—— visits the brahma-lóka, 348.
—— with Supra Budha, 351.
—— repeats the *Chandakinnara-játaka*, 353.
—— in the city of Páwá, 355.
—— death of, in Kusinára, 355.
—— preaches to the prince Pukkusa, 356.
—— preparations for his burial, 360.
—— in the Kshánti and Dharmmapála birth, 364.
—— Chinese: Kiu tan, Tibetan: Geoutam Manchou: Goodam, 367.
—— the dignity, virtues, and powers of, 372.
—— his supremacy, 373.
—— his manhood, 376.
—— overcomes the asúr Ráhu, 377.
—— his appearance and stature, 377.
—— with the brahma Atula, 378.
—— manner of walking, 379.
—— the beauties of his person, 381.
—— his deportment and virtues, 384.

GOTAMA BUDHA, his kindness, 388.
—— the manner in which he said bana, 391.
—— his supernatural endowments, 394.
—— repeats a *gáthá on conception*, 459.
—— resides in the garden Amalakí, 394.
—— with the brahma Subha, 462.
—— visited by the tirttaka Sachaka, 441.
—— in the village Kótigráma, near Wisála, 474.
—— recites the *Bála pandita sútra*, 503.
—— with the householder Singálóha, 504.
GOY-WANSA (or Wellála), the first caste with the Singhalese.
GRAHASTA-SÍLA, 512.
GRAHAPATI-RATNA, retinue of attendants, 130.
GRAHANAS, seizures or eclipses of the moon, 5.
GRAHAS, planets, 24.
GULA, a game (play), 234.
Guna Játaka, 115.
GUNASUBHADRA, the grass-giver of Kakusanda, 98.
GURU, 67.
GURU, Jupiter, planet, 24.
GURULUGOWINA, author of the *Amáwatura*, 539.
GUTTÍLA, a famous musician, 468.

H.

HANGSAWATÍ, a city, 508.
Hansas, 17.
HASTÁ, queen of Amba, 133.
HASTAGIRI, a mountain, 31.
HASTANÍKA, son of HASTÁ, 133.
HASTAWAKA-ALAWAKA, name of the yaká Alawaka after his conversion, 274.
HASTIPURA, a city, 131, et pass.
HASTIRATNA, an elephant, 130.
HATA, lunar mansion, 24.
HÉMAKA, a brahman, 347.
HÉMANTA, the winter season, 21.
Heterodox sects, account of, 403.
HÉTUJA, things proceeding from seed, 457.
HÍMATI KUMBURÉ SUMANGALA, translator of the Milinda Prasna, 538.
HINA-SÍLA, 511.

HIRANGAWATI, 358.
HIRI, shame, 429.
HITA, mind, 277, 405.
Horses, 17.
HÚRÚKALA, a cave near Rajagaha, assembly of the priests at, 203.
Husband, the, and wife, 498.

I.

Identity, 440.
Idleness, 492.
IL, a month, 493.
Improper associates, 493.
Impurities, the thirty-two of the body, 288.
INDRASÁLA, a cave in the rock Wédi, 298.
INDRASANGWARASÍLA, the four observances of the senses, 177.
INDUPAT, a city in Kuru, 75.
Intoxicating liquors, 491.
IRDHI, the power of working miracles, 36, 202.
IRDHI-WISAYA, 9, note.
IRSYÁ, envy, 434.
IRTU, time, 457.
IRTUJA (earth, rocks, water, wind, produced by irtu), 457.
IRADHARA, 12.
ISTRÍ-RATNA, empress, 130.
ISWARA, 217.
ITTHATTAN, the womanhood, 417.

J.

JALÁBUJA, viviparous birth, 457.
JALA-POLOWA, 3, 33.
JALAYA, a citizen, 345.
JALÁYA, a monarch, 133.
JÁLI, BÓDHISAT child in the Wesantara birth, 180.
JÁLIYA, son of Wesantara Bódhisat, 119, 123.
JAMBUDWÍPA, 4, 13, 15, 17, 21, 118, et pass.
JAMBUKA, a jackal, 345.
JAMMAK-SÉTRA, 2.
JANA-KARMA, 463.
JANAPADAKALYÁNI, betrothed princess to Nanda, 210.
Janawansa, quoted, 74.
JANAWASABHA, a déwa, formerly Bimsara, 329.
JANTA, son of Amba, 133.
JANTU, queen of Amba, 133.

JARATÁ, decay, 418.
Játakas, 81.
—— Asadrisa, Apannaka, Chandapennara, Dharmapala, Guna, Kanka, Kunála, Mahánárada Kasyapa, Makasa, Munika, Nandiwisálá Sakindurd, Sankuta, Sujáta, Tinduka, Wessantara.
Játaka Gáthá, birth stanzas, 101.
JATAWANY, a city, 47, et pass.
JÁTI, a brahman, 151.
JATIKA, a noble, 523.
JATILA, a merchant, 226.
JATILARÁSHTRIKA, name of Gótama Bódhisat, 97.
JÁLIMÁLÁ, garland of classes, creation of men, 70.
JÁTIPADÁMA, birth, 449.
JATUKANNÍ, a brahma, 347.
JAYASÉNA, a king, 137.
JAYATURÁ, a city, 118.
JETA, a prince, 224.
JINORASA, 374.
JÍWAKA, history of, called Kómárabhacha, 244, 245, 331, 333.
JÍWITINDRIYAN, vitality, 417, 423.
JIWHÁ-WINYÁNA, tongue curiousness, 436.
JÓTI, a merchant, 226.
JÓTIPÁLA, a brahma, Gótama Bódhisat, 99.
JÓTI-PÁSÁNA, burning-glass, 452.
JÓTIS, 195.
JÓTIYA, a nobleman, 523.
JÚJAKA, a brahman, 180.

K.

KABALINKÁ, common nourishment of men, 518.
KADURU, poisonous plant, 333.
KAELANI (Kalyána), 214.
KAILÁSA, a mountain, 15, 271.
KÁKAWALI, a merchant, 226.
KAKUDA-TREE, 301.
KAKUDASATYA, a deceiver and sceptic, 301.
KAKUDHA, a déwa, 328.
KAKUSANDA, a Budha, 89, 98, 199.
KÁLA, the caste of lions, 18.
KÁLADÉWALA, father of Sudhódana, chief counsellor of Singhahanu, his acquirements, 149.
KÁLA-HANSA, a bird, 165.
KÁLAKANCHA, an asúr, 342.

INDEX.

KÁLAKANJAKA, a préta birth, 60, 108.
KÁLANÁ, 176.
KALANDAKA-PUTRA, a priest, 388.
KALANDAKA-NIWÁPA, an offering made to squirrels, 198.
KÁLANDUKA, son of Hastá, 133.
KÁLAPARIYANTA-SÍLA, 511.
KALABANAMATTHAKA, a tirttaka, 343.
KÁLABANJANAKA, the last king of Makhádéwa race, 133.
KÁLASÚTRA, naraka, 27.
KÁLAWALI, a labourer, 218.
KÁLI, wife of Dighatapla, daughter of the déwa Sumana, 219.
KALINGA, the destruction of, 57.
KALLAWÁLA in Megadha, 202.
KALUDÁ, a noble (ÚDÁYI), 204.
KÁLUDÁYA, a nobleman, his birth, 149.
KALPA, 5, 7, 8, 9.
—— Yugs (the periods of the brahmans); satya yug; tréta; dwapar; kali, 8, note.
KALPA-WURKSHA, 15.
KALYÁNA, monarch, successor of Maha Sammata, 129.
KÁMA, evil desire.
KÁMA-BHAWA, the eleven states of existence, 462.
Kammawáchan, description of, 540.
KÁMÁWACHARA, a déwa-lóka, 3, 30, 261.
KAMMANNYATA, adaptation, 418.
KANAKAWASSAN, a golden shower, 98.
Kanka játaka, 307.
KANTATA, the horse of Gótama, 161; its birth, 149, 165.
KANYÁ-RASÍ, a virgin, 23.
KAP-ASANKYA, numeral, 91.
KAPILA, the elder brother of Chétiya, 131.
KAPÍLAWASTU, 80, 147; its site, 136, note, et pass.
KAPÓTAKANDARA, a town, 521.
KAPPA, a brahman, 347.
KAPPA-KÓLÁHALA, a warning before the destruction of the world, 30, note.
KAPPASIKA, a country, 198.
KAPPAWATÍ, 94.
KARAWIKA, 12.
KARKKATA, a rási (red crab), 23.
KARMA, moral action, 261, 274, 461, et pass.

KARMA, principal cause of sin, 274.
—— the cause of reproduction, 40
KARMA WISAYA, 8, note,
KÁRMIKA, system, the, of the Nepaulese, 449, note.
KARMMA,-WIPÁKAJA-IRDHI, 523.
KARSHA, coin, 1.
KARUNÁ, kindly regard, 432.
KASAYINA, queen of Singha-hanu, her five sons and two daughters, 137.
KÁSI, a country, 224.
KASÍBHÁRADWÁJA, a brahman, 220.
KARMAJA, all beings having náma and rúpa, 457.
KASI, a country, 110.
KASINA, a rite, 206, et pass.
KASPILISANDAN, robes of the priests, 233.
KÁSYA BUDHA, 261.
KASYAPA BUDHA, 89, 98, 99, 199, 375.
—— the relics of his body, 88.
KATAMÓRATISSA, a priest of Budha, 337.
KATTÁ, a nobleman, 119.
KÁYA (danda), body, 274.
KÁYA-IRJUTWA, body-uprightness, 432.
KÁYA-KARMMANAYATÁ, body-adaptation, 432.
KÁYA-LAHUTÁ, body lightness, 432.
KAYA-PRAGUNYATA, body practice, 432.
KÁYA-PRASRABDHI, repose or tranquillity of the body, 432.
KÁYÁRÚPAPASSANÁ, 516.
KÁYA-WINNYATI, power of giving, 418.
KÁYA-WINYÁNA, body consciousness, 436.
Kayawiratigáthá-sanné, description of, 539.
KELA, 2.
KELALAKSHA, numeral, 24.
KELAPAW, in Ceylon, 393.
KELABUWAN, a robber, 261.
KÉNI, an ascetic, 282.
KÉSARÁ, caste of lion, 18.
KETI-NEKÁTÁ, 21.
KÉTU (Planet), the asúr, 24.
KHADIRANGARA, birth, 103.
KHANU-KONDANYA, a priest, 521.
KHÁNU-KONDANYA, a robber, 261.
KHANDADÉWA-PÚTRA, a priest of Budha, 337.
KHANDAKA, the, 496.
KHANDAKAWALLA, 511.

KHANDA, elements of sentient existence, 403.
KHANDATWA-ASANKYA, 96.
KHÁRODAKA, rain, 32.
KHATTIYO (KSHATRIYÁ), 68.
KHETTÁNI, the cultivated lands, 68.
KHUMBANDAS, 47.
KHUMBÁWATÍ, a city in Kalinga, 55.
KHUPPIPÁSIKAS, prétas.
KHUPPIPÁSA, the préta birth, 60, 108.
KHURAMALI, 13.
KIMBILA, a prince, 235.
KINDURAS, 17.
KINICHIRI, a flower, 29.
KÍRANABHAMBA, 342.
KIRIPALA, tree, 186, 214.
KISAWACHA and NALIKÉRA, the legends of, 55.
KISAWACHA, a follower of Sarabhanga Bódhisat, 55.
KISÁGÓTAMI, a princess, a relative to GÓTAMA, 159.
KITULPAW, 53.
KLÉSHA, evil desire, 461.
KOBALÍLA, a flower, 137.
KOETI, lunar mansion, 24.
KÓKÁLIKA, a priest of Budha, 337.
KOKILA, a bird, 319.
KÓLI, a city, 139, 147.
KÓLITA, a prince, afterwards Mugalan, principle disciple of Budha, 200.
KÓLITA, a brahma village, 200.
KÓMÁRABHACHA, 245.
KÓNÁGAMANA BUDHA, 89, 98, 199.
KOSAMBAE, 252.
KOSOL, a country, 224.
KOSOL, the king of, marries the natural daughter of Mahanama, 292.
KOTI KELA, (numeral,) 6.
KOWAKHA, a fruit, (ocymum gratissimum,) 331.
KOWMADA, the white lotus, 191.
KRISHNAJINA, daughter of Wesantara, 119, 180.
KRITATTRÁ, 463.
KSHANTIWÁDA, birth, 104.
KONDANNYA BUDHA, 96, 188.
KONDANYA, son of the brahman Rama, becomes an ascetic, 152, 168.
KONÍSWARA-PARWATIYA, a peak of Maha Méru, 59, note.
KÓRAKATAMBA, principal minister of Chétiya, 131.

KÓRAKHATTI, a tirttaka, 341.
KORAWYA, king of the city of Indupat, 75, 133.
KOSÁLA MALLIKÁ DEWÍ, the flower-girl, wife of Ajásat mallliká, 294.
KSHÁNTI-PÁRAMITÁ, virtue proceeding from forbearance, 104.
KSHATRIYA, 83.
KSHEMA, a king, afterwards Gótama Bódhisat.
KSHÍRANÁGA, a temple, 54.
KUDÁSUMANA, son of Munda, 239.
KUJA, planet, 24, 67.
KUKHUCHA, moroseness, 434.
KUKKUTTHA, a river, 356.
KULADHARMMA-SÍLA, 513.
KUMÁRA KÁSYAPA, a priest, 482.
KUMBHA, (rási) a white man, 23.
KUMBHANDAS, the attendants of, 21.
KUNÁLA, one of the seven great lakes, 17.
KUSA, a monarch, 133.
KUSAMALI, 13.
KUSALA CHITTA, mind endowed with merit, 465.
KUSALA-WIPAKÁ-WINYÁNA-DHÁTU CHITTA, cause of birth as man, 439.
KUSA, sacrificial grass, 461.
KUSALA, merit, 461, et pass.
KUSALÁ DHAMMÁ, AKUSALÁ DHAMMÁ, AWYAKTÁ DHAMMÁ, the first words of the Abhidharmma, 309.
KUSINÁRÁ, a city, 290.
KUSITA, indolence, 424.
KÚTADANTA, a brahman embraces Budhism, 280.
KÚTÁGARA, 41.
KÚTÁGA-SALA, near Wisálá, 321.

L.

LAHA, a tablet hung up in the Wihára for communication to the priests, 268.
LAHABAT-GEYA, 218.
LAHUTA, the property of lightnes, 418.
Lakes, the seven great, 17.
LAKSHA, 6.
LAKSANA, a brahman, 157.
LÉNA, a cave, 393.
LICHAWI PRINCES, the, 244.
LIHINI, a bird, 171.
Lie the first, 486.
Life of man, 1.

INDEX.

Lions, 17.
LÓBHA, covetousness, 433.
LÓHAKUMBHA-LOKA, 337.
LÓHITA PAKKHANDIKA, a diarrhœa, 356.
LÓKÁDHIPATEYYA-SÍLA, 512.
LÓKANTARIKA NARAKA, the residence of the Pretas, 2, 48, 28.
LÓKOTTARA, a state with entire freedom from all káma, 462.
LÓKÓTTARA-SÍLA, 511.
LOMASA KÁSYAPA, a rishi, the legend of, 51.
LÓWAMAHAPAYA, 218.
LOWKIKA-SÍLA, 511.
LUDDA, 68.
LUMBINI, a garden between Kapilawastu, and Koli, 147.
Lying, 485.

M.

MADARA, a tree, 164.
MADAYAWATTHUN, the heart, 417.
Madhura-sútra, quoted, 82.
MADHYAMA-SÍLA, 511.
MADHYÁMIKA SCHOOL, 537.
MADHYASTATÁ impartiality, 432.
MADRIDÉWI, wife of Wessantara, 119.
MA-DROS, (Tibetan for Anóttatta wila,) 16.
MAGADHA, the language of, 192, et pass.
MAGAN, in the province of Ruhuna, 393.
MÁGANDHI, a brahman, 63.
MÁGANDHIYA, a brahman, 522.
MAGHA-MÁNAWAKA, chief of a village, the history, 508.
MAGUL, festive, joyous, 4.
MAGUL-SAKWALA, the most favoured world, 466.
MAHA BHADRA KALPA, the present kalpa, 65, 91, 98.
MAHA BRAHMA, a rupa brahma lokas, 26, 30, 31, 42, 148, 166, 217.
MAHA ISWARA, 166.
MAHA-JANAKA BIRTH, 104.
MAHA KACHÁNO, 82.
MAHAKALA, the fruit of the damba tree, 19.
MAHA KÁLANÁ, the nága king, 172.
MAHA KALPA, 1, 6.
MAHAKÁSYPA, 219, 261, 361.
MAHA-LI, a Lichawi king, 291.

MAHA-MANDHATU, a chakrawartti, monarch, successor to Maha Sammata, 129, 131.
MAHA-MANDHATU UPOSATHA, a monarch, successor of Maha Sammata, 129.
MAHA MÁYA, mother of Gótama, principal queen of Sudhódana, 137, 144, 323.
—— during the period of gestation, 147 ; of confinement, 148.
MAHAMÁYA-DEWI, formerly queen Phusatí, 127.
MAHA MAYA DÉWÍ, MAHA PRAJÁPATI, daughters of Singhahanu, 140.
MAHA MÉRU, 2, 3, 10, 14, 177, 217, et pass.
MAHA MEWUNÁ, a garden in Ceylon, 199.
MAHAMUNDA, a slave, 293.
MAHAMUNDA, a noble, 239.
MAHANÁMA, son of SANDA, 234.
MAHANÁMA, a brahman, 152, 168.
MAHANÁMA, a monarch in Ceylon, 530.
MAHANÁMA, a Sakya prince, 293.
Mahánárada-kásyapa, the first játaka, 196.
MAHA NERU, a monarch, 132.
MAHA-NIDHÁNAS, mines, the four, of treasure, 149, note.
MAHA PANÁDA, a monarch, his successors, 132.
MAHA POLOWA, 3.
MAHA PRATÁPA, monarch, 132.
MAHA-PURUSHA-LAKSHANA, the three signs of a great man, 347.
—— superior beauties, 381.
—— the, 32, of a supreme Budha, 150.
MAHA ROHANAGUTTA, a priest, 524.
MAHA ROWRAWA, a naraka, 27.
MAHA SÁGARA, a prince, 132.
MAHA-SAMMATA, a monarch at the beginning of the present antahkalpa, 112, 208.
Mahasamya-sútra, 41, 320, 393.
MAHASÉNA, afterwards Nágaséna, 534.
MAHA-SUBADRA, the daughter of Anépidu, 225.
MAHA-SUDARSANA, a monarch, chakrawartti, 132.
MAHASUMANA, the son of Manda, 239.
MAHA-SUPINA, the birth of Pasénádi, 317.

INDEX.

Maha Suttasóma, birth, 104.
Maha-timi, 13.
Maha-wana Wihára, 319.
Maha-yasódhará-déwi, mother of Prajápati, 317.
Mahésákya - yaksha - séná - pati, name of Gótama Bódhisat, 97.
Mahí, 17.
Mahika, the déwas of dew, 22.
Mahinda, a wave, 13.
Maitrí, the coming Budha, (a Bódhisat) 19, 94, 98, 206.
Maitrí-bháwaná, a form of meditation, 53.
Maitreya, 91.
Maitrí-páramita, virtue from kindness and affection, 54.
Maja Wijita, monarch of Jambudwipa, 281.
Majjhima-nikáyo, 82.
Mahawáluká, river in Ceylon, 212.
Mahanága, a garden on the bank of the Mahawáluká river, 212.
Mahindo, 218.
Mahódana, a nága king, 214.
Makara, a rási, a marine monster, 381.
Makasa Játaka, 115.
Makhádéwa, a prince, 133.
Makhali-gósala, a deceiver and sceptic, 301.
Málágiri, elephant, 331.
Maligiri, 268.
Malakada, (tallow), 251.
Malunka-sutra, 389.
Malliká, the flower girl, becomes a queen, 294.
Malwa-princes, the, 359.
Manákota-karana, volition, 421.
Manaskára, reflection, 423.
Manassatya-lóka, 276.
Manda-asankya, 95.
Manda-kalpa, 97.
Mandakini, one of the seven great lakes, 17.
Mandridéwá, 181.
Mánekata, lunar mansion, 24.
Mangala, disciple of Dipankara, 97.
Mangala brahman, a name of Gótama Bódhisat, 97.
Mangalya - lakshana, the, 216; signs of a superior Budha, 150, 381.
Mani, a nága king, 214.
Manibhadda-asankya, 95.

Mánikya-ratna, treasure of gems, 130.
Manjarika, a nága lóka, 176.
Manjusaka, a tree, 16, 50.
Manner of spelling the name of Budha by the Europeans, 367.
Manó (Danda), thought, 274.
Manóma, the power to make any figure, 519.
Mano-winyána, mind consciousness, 417, 436.
Mantra, charm, 38.
Mangala, a warning, 30.
Mangala-sutra, 30, note.
Manipur, the, 45.
Manópranidhána, the resolution or wish to become a Budha, 93, 103.
Manosanchátana, continued thought, 519.
Manu, 78, 81.
Manya, an evil spirit, self-conceit, 433.
Mára, causes a rain, sends weapons, 178.
—— causes a storm, the effect of on Gótama, 178.
—— causes a fire, 173.
—— his daughters, 183.
Master, the, and servant, 553.
Masuran, a gold coin, 117, 455.
Mátali, the charioteer of Sekra.
Mátika, a village, 287.
Matru, chief of the déwas, 309.
—— becomes a rahat, 310.
Mátsaryya, selfishness, 434.
Mátu, the mother, 499.
Mayurapáda, composer of the Pujawaliya, 538.
Méda, a merchant, 226.
Médaka, a noble, 523.
Médhankara, a Budha, 96.
Medin-dina, (a month) March, April, 21, 23, 205.
Mégha, the path in which the moon moves, 22.
Mékhalá, birth place of Kahusanda Budha, 28.
Mékhala, or Mela, an ornament, 230, 291.
Mellaka, foreigner, 300.
Merchants, rank of the, in India, 78.
Merchants, the two, of Sunáparanta, 267.
Méru, 21.
Mesha, a rási (a red ram), 23.
Mettébhútaka, a brahman, 347.
Midháta, a tree, 54.

INDEX. 555

MIGÁRA, a merchant in Sewet, 227, 229.
MIHINTALÁ, 218.
MIJJA, drowsiness, 424, 434.
Mí, a grain of, 316.
MILINDA, king of Ságal, 12, 62, 396, 398, et pass.
Milinda Prasna (Milinda Panha), 22, 62, 89, 156, 222, 359, 377, 387, 452, 488, 391, 478.
—— *description of*, 533.
MÍMINNAS, an animal, 136.
MÍNA, a rási, two fishes, 23.
Miscellaneous advices and admonitions, 503.
MITHILA, a city, 384.
MITHUNA, a rási,
MITYÁ-DRISHTI, erroneous thoughts upon religious subjects, scepticism, 433, 517.
MIYALU, (Mithila) the modern Tirhut, 196.
Modes, the four, in which alms may be prepared, ADRISHTA, UPAKHATA, UDDISAKATA, PARIBHOGA, 396.
MOGHA-PURISA, vain man, 388.
MÓHA, ignorance, 430, 448, 513.
Moneyya-piliwet, the ordinances of rahats as explained by Budha, 30, note.
Months, the, of the year, 23.
Moon, 20.
—— speed of her travel, 22.
MOYA (MÓHA), ignorance, 433.
MUCHALA, son of Chétiya, 131.
MUCHALINDA, son of Muchala, a monarch, 152.
MUDAKÉSI, a mule, 252.
MUDITA, benevolence, 433.
MUDUGIRI, residence of Punna, 268.
MUDUTÁ, softness, 418.
MUGALAN, principal disciple of Gótama, 15, 185, 202, 209, 256, 302, 307, 308, 313, 324, 339, 349, 421, et pass.
MULA, lunar mansion, 24.
MULUARÁMA, 268.
MÚLAKA, a king, 346.
MUNDA, a rock afterwards called Ereka, 94.
Munika Játaka, 115.
Murder, the first committed on earth, 133.
MURUTU, a flower, 375.
MUWASIRISA, lunar mansion, 24.

N.

NÁGA, serpent path, 20.
NÁGAS, the attendants of Wirupaksha, 25, 31, 45, 182, et pass.
NÁGADWÍPA, probably an island, 213.
NÁGASÉNA, 38, 62, et pass.
NAHUTA, 6.
NÁLÁGIRI, Chandapprajota's elephant, 252.
NÁLAKA, nephew of Sudhódana, 151.
NALAMALI, 13.
NÁLIKÉRA, a king of Kalinga, 56.
NÁMA, 445, et pass.
NAMÓ TASSA BHAGAWATÓ ARAHATÓ SAMMÁ SAMBUDDHASSA explanation of this formala, 372.
Name giving, the festival of Bódhisat, 157.
NANDA, a brahman, 347.
NANDA, cousin of Utpalawarnna, 485.
NANDA, son of Prajápati, becomes a rahat, 210, 211, 317.
NANDA AND RAHULA become the disciples of Budha, 210.
NANDÁ, daughter of Hastá, 133.
NANDA-ASANKYA, 95.
Nandakowáda-sútra, 323.
Nandiwísá Játaka, 307.
NANDÓPANANDA, the nága overcome by Mugalan, 313.
Nanódayan, a Budhistic work, 530.
NÁRADA, a Budha, 97.
NARAKAS, inhabitants of, 5, 49, 61.
NÁTREE, 51, 393.
NAWAN, a month, 23.
NAYA, 193.
NEKATAS, lucky hours, 75.
NEKATAS, the twenty-seven mansions of the moon, 24.
NÉMENDHARA, 12.
NÉRU, a rock in the forest Himála, 458.
NÉRU, monarch, 132.
NÉWASÉKHA-SÍLA, 512.
NÉWÁSANNYANÁSANNYÁYATANA, arúpa-brahma-lóka, 26.
NIBBÁNA (nirwána), 50, note.
NIGHANTA, a tirttaka, 231.
NIGHANTANÁPUTRA, a deceiver and sceptic, 302.
NIGANTHANÁTHA, a tirttaka, 274.
NIGRODÁRÁMA-WIHÁRA, 320.
NIGRÓDHA, a garden, 205.
NIGRODHA, an ascetic, 40.

556 INDEX.

NIGRODHANIGA BIRTH, 104.
NIJJHÁMATATANHÁ-PRÉTA WORLD, 107.
NIJJHÁMÁTANHÁ, a préta, 59.
NIJJHÁMATRISNIKAS, 475.
NIKINI, a month, 23.
NÍLAKARSHA, a coin, 1, 248.
NILTÁRA, a river, 193.
NIMI, a monarch, 468.
NIMMÁNARATI, a déwa-lókas, 25.
NINNAHUTA, (numeral) 6.
NÍRANJARA, a river, 172.
NIRMMADÁ, a river, 215.
NIRUTTI, the power of the Budhas to perceive all truth, 518.
NIRWÁNA, 36, 91, 82, 186, 192, 198, 210, 222, 224, 261, 516, 200, 275, 289, et pass.
NISABHA, one of the principal disciples of Anómadarsa Budha, 508.
NISRATA-SÍLA, 511.
NITYA SÍLA, precepts taken for an unlimited period, 507.
NUGA, sacred tree of Kásyapa, 99.
Nurse, choosing the, of a, for Gótama, 152.
Numerals, 7; asankya, antah-kalpa, maha-kalpa, laksha, koti, kela, prakóti, kótiprakóti, nahuta, ninnahuta, hutanahuta, khamba, wiskambha, ababa, attata, ahaha, kumuda, gandhika, utpala, pundarika, paduma, katha, mahakatha.

O.

Oceans, the, 12.
Offering, the first received by Gótama Budha, 186.
OGHA, stream, 426.
O-mi-to (Chinese), probably deathless, 368.
Ontology of Budhism, 402.
OPAPÁTIKA BIRTH (apparitional), 377, 457.
Opinions as to the age of Budha, 366.
OPPANIKA, a slave of Chandapprajáta, 253.
Opponents, the five, of Gótama, who for their crime are born in hell, 487.
Orders, the various, of intelligence, 38.
OSUPAT, a naraka, 27, 465.
OTTAPPA, fear, 429.

P.

PACHITI, a minor fault, 487.
PÁDAS, the fourth part of a nekáta, 22.
PADUMA, a Budha, 97, 209.
PADUMA, the wife of Dípankara, 96.
PADUMA, a numeral, 7.
PAHOLAWAKA, day of the full moon, 22.
Palaces, the three, built by Sudhódana, 154.
PALAS, a kind of robes, 375.
PANÁDA, a monarch, successor of Maha Pratápa, 132.
PÁNCHA-KALYÁNA, five beauties, Késa, Mánsa, Ashti, Chawi, Waya } kalyána, 227.
PANCHA-MAHA-WÍLÓKANA, the five great perceptions, 143.
PANCHA-ABHIGNYÁ, the five supernatural endowments, 173.
PANCHASÍLA, the five precepts, 507.
PANCHASKHANDAS, the corporeal elements, 265.
PANCHASIKHA, a déwa, 299.
—— the prime minister of Sekra, 52.
PANCHINDRA, the five moral powers, 517.
PÁNDHAWA, a rock, 167.
PÁNDU, caste of lion, 18.
PANNAKA, a nága, 239.
PANSAL, 338.
PANSALA, (hermitage), 136.
PÁNSIKÚLAKANGA, an ordinance regarding robes, 338.
Pansiya-panas-játaka-pota, the book of the 550 births, 101, 529.
Panthers, 17.
PÁNSU-PARWATA, five mountains, 17.
PÁNSUPISÁCHAKA, hobgoblin, 303.
PÁRÁJIKÁ, excluded from the priesthood, 481.
PARAMARSHTA-SÍLA, 572.
PÁRAMITÁS, practice of the, (prescribed virtues), 50, 342.
—— the, of truth, 177.
—— the ten, 100.
PARANIRMITA WASAWARTTI, a déwa-lóka, 26.

INDEX.

PARANIRMITA WASWARTTI, the lord of the 6th déwa-lóka, 163.
PARASATU, a tree, 164.
Páráyana-sútra, 347.
Parent, the, and child, 494.
PARIBRÁJIKA, a class of religionists, 197, et pass.
PARIHÁNI-SÍLA, 512.
PARIKÁ, sister of the ascetic Dukuta, 459.
Parinibbána-suttan, 360, note.
PARINÁYA-RATNA, a prince, 130.
PARISUDHI-UPÉKSHÁ, 524.
Parittatthakathan, a commentary on the pitakas, 530.
PARITTASUBHA, a brahma-lóka, 26, 31, 33.
PARITTÁBHA, a rúpa-brahma-lóka, 26.
PARWÁTA, a monarch, Gótama Bódhisat.
PÁSANDHA-DHARMA-SÍLA, 513.
PAS-POLOWA, 3.
PASÉ BUDHAS, the sages of wondrous power, 16, 38, 50, 255, 312, et pass.
PASÉNÁDI, king of Kosol, his sixteen dreams, 227, 314.
PATHAWI-DHÁTU, 414
Passion and sexual intercourse, origin of, 67.
PATHIKA, a tirttaka, 343.
Paths, the three, of the Chaturmaharajika world, 20.
PATICHA-SAMUPPÁDA, causes of continued existence, 183, 406.
PATIPPASSADHA-SÍLA, 512.
Patisamdhidan, commentary on the, 28, note.
PÁWÁ, a city, 280.
PÁWÁRIKA, a noble, 274.
Pea-fowl, 17.
PELALUP, a city (Pátalíputra), 53, 535.
PHASSÁ, touch, things that have no rúpa, but are apprehended by the mind, 419, 518, et pass.
PHUSATÍ, wife of Sanda, 118.
PHUSSA, a Budha, 97.
PINDAPÁTIKANGA, an ordinance regarding food, 338.
PINDÓLABHÁRADAWÁJA, a follower of Budha, 302.
PIRIKARAS, the requisites of the priesthood, 29, 233.
PIRIT, an exorcism, 47, 244.
PIRIWARA, 281.
Pitakas, the three, 186.

PIYUMATURA BUDHA, 94, 172, 239, 255, 485.
PIYADARSHI, a Budha, 97.
Places in which Budha lived after attaining Budhaship, 369.
Places of amusement, 494.
Planets, 20.
POKSÍ-MAHA-RÁJA 261.
POLONNARUWA, city in Ceylon, 18.
PORISA, measure.
POSÁLA, a brahman, 347.
POSON, a month, 23.
POTTABBAN, power of feeling substance, 416, 417.
Powers, the, possessed by an arhat, 39.
PÓYA, dark day of the new moon, a sacred day, 22, 50, 52, 239.
PRACHANDA, wind by which the earth is destroyed, 33.
Pradípikáwa, a Budhistic work, 539.
PRAGNYÁ-PÁRAMITÁ, virtue proceeding from wisdom, 104.
PRAGNYÁWA, wisdom, 429, 454, 517.
PRAJÁPATI, queen, daughter of Suprabudha, monarch of Kóli, becomes a priestess, and obtains nirwána, 317.
—— performs wonders by the force of dhyaná and kasina, 325.
PRAKÓTI, 6.
PRÁKRAMA BÁHU, monarch of Ceylon, 18.
PRÁKRAMA-BÁHU, author of the *sanné* to the *wisudhimargga*, 532.
PRÁNA (put for being), 478.
PRÁNA-JIWA (inward life), 452.
PRÁNÁGHÁTA, destruction of life, 478.
PRÁNAWÁTA, living breath, 444.
PRANÍTA-SÍLA, 511.
PRÁSWÁSA, expirated, 444.
PRASÁDA-RÚPAS, organs of sense, chakkhun, eye; ghannan, nose, jiwha, tongue; káyan, body; sótan, ear, 416.
PRATÁPA, a naraka, 27.
PRATÁPA, monarch, 132.
PRATHUWÍ-ASANKYA, 95.
PRATIBHÁNA, the power of the rahats to know the roots and properties of things, 518.
Prátimoksha, a discourse, 203.
PRATISANDHI-WINYÁNA (pilisanda ganna chitta), actual consciousness, 448.

PRATITYA - SAMUPPADA - CHAKRA, circle of existence, 448, 450.
PRAWÁLA-NALAMALI, 151.
PRÉTAS, the, 48, 59, et pass.
—— the 84,000, history of, 199.
PRÉTI, 60.
Pride, five kinds of, 470.
Priest, the faithful, legend of, 53.
Priest, the, and householder, 497.
PRÍTIYA, joy, 425.
PRIYÁ, daughter of Hastá, 133.
Probability of Gótama's history, 368.
PUDUMA-ASANKYA, 95.
PUGALA, being, 440.
PUJÁ, act of, 185.
Pújáwaliya, quoted, 15, 109, 140, 376, 380, 383, 388, 478, 480, 482, 484, 485, 488, 490, 491, 492, 506.
Pújáwaliya, description of, 538.
PULÍLA, sacred tree of Dípankara, 96.
PUNÁWASA, lunar mansion, 24.
PUNDÁRIKA-ASANKYA, 95.
PUNNA, a merchant, becomes a rahat, 58, 267.
PUNNA, a brahman, 347.
PUNNAKA, a merchant, secretary of Meda, 226.
PUNYAWATO-IRDHI, 523.
PURANA DIPANKARA BUDHA, 94.
PURÁMA (filth), 231.
PUNYA-KSHÉTRAYO, more honourable castes, almsgiving to, 82.
PURÁNA-KÁSYAPA, a tirttaka, a deceiver and sceptic, 262, 300; his death, 307.
PURASÚNIKA, son of Hastá, 133.
PURISATTAN, the manhood, 417.
PÚRNA (purána), complete, 300.
PURNNA, slave of Sujátá, 171, 468.
PÚRNNA-WARDHANA, son of Migára, 227.
PÚRNNAKÁSYAPA, 336.
PURÓHITA, vizier, 55.
PÚRWÁRÁMA, the wihará of, 240.
PÚRWAWIDÉSA, a continent, 4, 138, 466.
PÚRWAHÉTUKA-SÍLA, 513.
PUSA, lunar mansion, 24.
PUSPAWATI, a city, 96.
PUSSA BUDHA, 199.
PUSU-NEKATA, 21.
PUWAPAL, lunar mansion, 24.
PUWAPUTUPÁ, lunar mansion, 24.
PUWASALA, lunar mansion, 24.

Q.

Qualifications, the eight, possessed by beings who receive the assurance of becoming a Budha, 106.
Queens, the 500, of Kosol, 297.
Questions of Milinda, see Milinda Prasna (Milinda Panha).

R.

RÁGA, evil desire, 518.
RAGHU, a monarch, 133.
RAHAT, an ascetic, who has entered the fourth path leading to nirwána, 16, 39, et pass.
RAHENA, lunar mansion, 24.
RÁHU, an asúr, 5, 21, 23, 24, 48, 166, 378.
—— his size, 59.
RÁHULA, formerly Jáliya, 127.
RÁHULA, the son of Gótama, 159, 211, et pass.
RAJA, the déwas of dust or motes, 22.
RAJAGAHA, a city (Rajagriha), 46, 165, et pass.
RAJAGANDAMBA, a tree, 304.
Rájawaliya, description of, 539.
RÁKSHAS, their residence, 48.
RAL-PA-CHAN, a Tibetan king, 370.
RÁMA, king of Benares, 133, 138.
—— a brahman, 151.
RAMMA, a palace, 154.
RAMMAWATÍ, birthplace of Kondannya Budha.
RANGA, daughter of Mára.
RANGOON, inscription upon the great bell at, 88.
RASAN, flavour, 416.
RÁSIS, the twelve collections, signs of the zodiac.
Ratana-sútra, 244.
RAT-HEL, a sort of rice, 505.
RATANA-GHARA-CHAITYA, the place where the Dharmma was perceived, 186.
RATGAL, a mountain, 271.
RATHAPÁLA, a priest, 313.
RATI, daughter of Mára, 183.
RAWA, planet (sun), 24.
Relics, the, of Budha, 362; dividing of, 365.
Reproduction, 457.
Requests, the five, of Déwadatta, 338.
Requirements, the eight, to which the female recluse must attend, 323.
Revolutions, mundane, 6.

RÉWATA, a Budha, 97.
RÉWATI, lunar mansion, 24.
RÉWATO, a mahathéro, 530.
Reward, the, of merit, 470.
RISHI, men performing wonders by certain rites, 2, 9, 10, 16, 38, et pass.
ROCHANÍ, principal queen of Kakusanda, 98.
ROCKY CIRCLES, the, 12.
RÓHANA, a wave.
RÓHINI, daughter of Sanda, 234.
RÓHINI, a river between Kapila and Kóli, 318.
RÓJA, successor of Maha Sammata, 129.
ROWRAWA (Rowra), a naraka, 27, 197.
RUCHÁ, daughter of Angáti, 197.
RUCHI, a monarch, 132.
RUCHIGÁTRÁ, principal queen of Kónágamana, 98.
RUHUNA, a province of Ceylon, 54.
RÚPA (RÚPAN) the aggregate of the elements that constitute the body, outward form, 44, 514, 416, 445, et pass.
RÚPÁ-BRAHMA-LÓKAS, the, 16, 26.
RÚPAKKHANDA, the twenty-eight, 414.
RUPANWAYA, 218.
RÚPAWACHARA, 3.

S.

SÁ, lunar mansion, 24.
SABHIYA, a praribrájika, history of, 261.
Sabhiya-sútra, 262.
SACHA, son of a tirttaka; in a later birth, the rahat Kalubudharakhita, history of, 263, 267.
SACHABADHA, a rock, 215.
SADANGOI ÉKSHÁ, 524.
SADDAN, sound, 416.
SADHARMMA, a priest, 199.
Sadharmmálankáré, quoted, 379, 88, 380, 385.
—— described, 559.
Sadharmmarat-nakáré, 10, 54, 99, 109, 218, 220, 286, 290, 352, 376, 393, 394, 478, 479, 433, 484, 486, 491.
—— described, 539.
SÁDHINA, a monarch, 468.
SÁDHU, a saying, 181.
SADOL CHANDÁLA, 82.
SAENI, Saturn, planet, 24, 67.

SÁGAL, a city (probably the Sangala of the Greeks), 536, et pass.
SAGARA, attendant of Dípankara, 96.
SÁGARA, son of Machalinda, a monarch, 132.
SÁGARA ASANKYA, 95.
SAHAMPATI MAHA BRAHMA, 177, 188.
SAHITUKA-KÁMÁWACHARA, cause of birth in the déwa lóka, 439.
SAÍHA, a nobleman, 51.
SAJÍWA, a priest, 521.
SAKASPURA, a city (páli Sankasso), 310, 311.
SÁHÉTU, a resting-place, 227, 247.
SAKHI, the faithful friend.
Sankindurá Játaka, quoted, 209.
SAKRADÁGÁMI, a path, 91.
SAKWALA (system of worlds), 2. et pass.
SAKWALA-GALA, 10, 12, 13.
SÁKYA, a Budha, 95.
SÁKYAPUTRA, 374.
SAL, the sacred tree of Kondannya, 97.
SALA POLOWA, a stratum of earth, 3.
SÁLAWATI, a princess, chief courtezan of Rajagaha, 244.
Sáleyya-sútra-sanné, 482, 488, 489.
SALUMINI-SÁRYA, a dágoba, 165.
SÁMA, son of Dukula and Pariká, 460.
SAMA, female disciple of Kakusanda.
SAMÁDHI, tranquillity, 517.
Samadhi-Raja, quoted, 90.
SAMÁDHI-WIPPARA, the power that is received from having possessed Samádhi, 521.
SAMANO, the déwa of Samantakúta, 216.
SAMANAELLA, in the island of Ceylon, 255.
SAMANYA, a king, 117.
Sámányasútra (Diksangha), 336.
SAMARTTHAKARA-MÉGHA, a rain, 65.
SAMASTAKÚTA, 213.
SÁMAWATA, queen of the monarch of Udéni; history of, 241.
SAMBAHULA, disciple of Kónágamana, 99.
SAMIDHI SUMANA, a déwa, 214.
SAMMATA, the appointed, the supreme ruler, 68.
SAMONA CODAM, Siamese title of Gotama Budha, 369.

SAMPATI MAHA BRAHMA, the chief of the brahma-lókas, 44, 57, et pass.
SAMPATTIKARA-MAHA-MÉGHA, the rain falling at the commencement of a kalpa, 28.
SAMPATTIKARA MÉGHA, a rain, 65.
SÁMUDDÁ, female disciple of Kónágamana, 99.
SAMUDDADATTAYA, a priest of Budha, 337.
SAMYAK-JÍWA, correct life, truthfulness of life, 433, 517.
SAMYAK-DRISHTI, correct ideas upon religious thoughts.
SAMYAK-KALPANÁWA, correct thoughts, 517.
SAMYAK-KARMMANTA, faithfulness of action, correct works, 433, 517.
SAMYAK-PRAYÓGA-PRATYA-PRATI-LÁBHARTTHA-IRDHI, 523.
SAMYAK-SAMÁDHI, correct tranquillity, 517.
SAMYAK-SIHI, correct judgment, 517.
SAMYAK-WACHANA, truthfulness of speech, correct words, 433, 517.
SAMYAK-WYÁYÁMA, correct energies, 517.
SANCHI, the Budhist temple at, 89.
SANDA, queen of Amitódana, younger brother of Sadhódana, 234.
SANDA (Sanja) king of Jayaturá, 118, 133.
SANGA, a parabrájika, 200.
SANGHAPÁLI, a théro, 530.
SANGHATA, a naraka, 27.
SANGPAKKHANDHA, progress (literally leaping), 427.
SANGPRASÁLHANA, purification, 427.
SANGSÁRA, 456.
SANGWARTTA-ASANKYA-KALPA, 5.
SANGWARTTASTÁYI - ASANKYA - KALPA, 5.
SANJA, wood apple, 302.
—— (Sanda), monarch, 118, 133.
SANJAWÍ, disciple of Kakusanda, 88.
SANJAYABELLANTI, a deceiver and sceptic, 302.
SANJÚVA, naraka, 27.
SANKHÁRO-KHANDO, powers of discrimination, 419.
SANKICHA, a robber, 201, 520.
SANNÉ, translation, paraphrase, 540.
SANNYÁ-KHANDHO, perception, 419.

SANSKÁRA-LÓKA (system of worlds), 3.
SANSKHÁRA-DHARMMA-KENEK, sentient being, 451.
SANKHÁROPÉKSHÁ, 524.
SANTATI, duration, 418.
SANTI, a brahman, 173.
SANTUSITA, name of Bódhisat in the déwa-loka Tusita, 142, 145, 176.
SANYADATTA, father of Kónágamana, 38.
SAPARIYANTA-SÍLA, 511.
SÁRA-KALPA, 97.
SARA, a birth, 104.
SARABHANGA BÓDHISAT, 55.
SARABAHU, a disciple of Seriyut, 213.
SÁRANANDA-KALPA, 97.
SARANANKARA, a Budha, 96.
Sarasangraha, 489, 495.
SARASWATÍ, a river, 510.
SARDHÁWA, purity, 426, 517.
SARWACHITRA, attendant of Kásyapa, 99.
SARWA-RATNA ASANKYA, 95.
SARWA-SÉLA ASANKYA, 96.
SARWA BHADRA ASANKYA, 95.
SARWA PHULLA ASANKYA, 95.
SÁRWARTHASIDDHA (Sákya before he became a Budha), 90.
SASÉ NADI, monarch of Kosol, 295.
SATÁGERA, a yaká, 271.
SATAMBA DÉWALA, 343.
SATARA-SATIPATTHÁNA, subjects of thought, 516.
SATCHARITA, the six principles or states of mind, 514.
SATCHA-KIRIYA, 197.
SATI (smirti) ascertainment of truth, 517.
SATTA-BÓDHDYÁNGA, the seven sections of wisdom, 517.
SATTÁ-PÁRAMITÁ, virtue proceeding from truth, 104.
SATTUABHÁTTA, birth, 104.
SATWA-LÓKA (system of worlds), 3.
Scepticism, 489.
Scholar, duties of the, 496.
SÉDAJA, a birth (perspiration or putridity), 457.
Seasons, the, 21.
SÉKHA-SÍLA, 512.
SEKRA, 3, 11, 41, 42, 109, 166, 21 247, 265, 280, 298, et pass.
—— causes a pavilion to appear for Budha, 304.
—— the throne of, 51.
—— his voice, 53.
—— the mansion of, 29.

INDEX.

SEKRA, a planet, 67.
SEKRAS, the, 149.
SEKRADEWENDRA, name of Gótama Bódhisat, 27.
Sekraprasna-sútra, 300.
SÉLA, a brahman becomes a priest, 282.
Sélasútra-sanné, 284.
SENA-KELI, a festival, 333.
SEPA, satisfaction.
SÉRIYUT, principal disciple of Budha, 185, 209, 212, 312, 324, 332, 339, 521.
—— disputes with the tirttaka's daughter, 263.
—— relates the *Budha wansa*, 106.
—— his superior wisdom in answering questions, 313.
—— a priest formerly Acchuta, a brahma, 127.
SEWET, a city, 109, 222, et pass.
"SIDHÁRTTHA, the name of Gótama as a Budha blessing to the world," 94, 97, 152.
SIDHÁRTTHA, oil of white mustard seed, 94.
SIDDHARTTA, or DHAMMADITTA-CHARYA-NIMALAKIRTTI, composer of the *Sadharmmálankáré*, 539.
SIDHAS (men performing wonders by the aid of herbs), 38.
Signs, the, of a supreme Budha, 150.
SIHAPRATÁPA, one of the seven great lakes, 17.
SIHIYA, memory, 421.
SIKHI, a Budha, 9, 97.
SÍL (SÍLA), precept, 343, 506, et pass.
SÍLA-PÁRAMITA, observance of the precepts, 107.
SILPAS, the eighteen, 156.
SINGÁLÓHA, a householder, 504.
Singálówáda sutra sanné, 492, 493, 488, 497, 498, 500, 502, 503, 504.
SINGHA, lion (rasí) 23.
SINGHA-HANU, a king, 137.
Singhalese era, 366.
SIRIMA, a courtezan, 522.
SIRIMATI, a city afterwards called Benares, 92.
SIRISA (márá) a tree, 98.
SÍSAN, head, 510.
SITA, lunar mansion, 24.
Siwáka-sútra, 471.
SIYÁWARA, lunar mansion, 24.
Slander, 488.

SLÓKAS, stanzas, 456.
SMIRTI, conscience, 428.
SNÁPARANATA, a city, 58.
SÓBHITA, a Budha, 97.
SÓDHAWATI, birthplace of Kónágamana, 98.
SOMANASSA, the grass giver of Kásyapa, 99.
SÓMANASSA, a Pasé Budha, 379.
SÓNA, of the city Champá, 254.
SÓPAKA, 241.
SORTTHIJANA, attendant of Kónágamana, 99.
SRÁWAKAS, 312, 323, 324.
—— kshína (inferior).
—— triwidyaprápta (middle).
—— shatabhignyáprápta (chief).
SRIKÁNTÁWA, 317.
SROTA-WINYÁNA, ear consciousness 435.
STHITI-SÍLA, 512.
SUBHA, a palace, 154.
SUBHA, a brahman, 462.
SUBHADRA, an ascetic, 359.
SUBHADRA, disciple of Kondannya Budha, 97.
SUBHAKÍRNNAKA, the ninth brahmalóka, 26, 33.
SUDANANA, a monarch, 132.
SUDARSANA, a mountain, 12, 16.
SUDARSHANA-RÁJA, name of Gótama Bódhisat, 97.
SUDASSA RÚPA BRAHMA LÓKA, 26.
SUDASSIK RÚPA BRAHMA LÓKA, 26.
SUDDA, 68.
SUDDARMMA, the hall of Sekra, 52.
SUDDO, 82, note.
SUDÉWA, the father of Dípankara, 96.
SUDHÓDANA, father of Gótama Budha, 203, et pass.
SUDHÓDANA, formerly king Sanju, 127.
SUDRA, his origin, 68, 81, 83.
SUJÁMA, a déwa, 176.
SUJAMPATI, the Sekra of the present sakwala, 176.
SUJATÁ, 97, 187.
SUJATÁ-SÁPASA, name of Gótama Bódhisat, 97.
Sujáta Játaka, quoted, 109.
SUJATÁ, daughter of Sénáni, a nobleman, 170.
SUKRA, (Venus) planet, 24.
SULU-ANÉPIDU, 307.
SUMANA, name of Mugalan in a former birth, 249.
SUMANA, a Budha, 97.

2 o

SUMANA, principal déwa of Samastakuta, 213.
Sumangala Wilásini, 532.
SUMANO, ascetic (sramana,) 68, 82, note.
Samantakuta wárnnanáwa, quoted, 214.
SUMÉDHA BRAHMANA, the name of Gótama Bódhisat in a former birth, 96.
SUMÉDHA, the mother of Dipankara, 26.
SUMÉDHA, a Budha, 97.
Sun, 20.
―― movement of the, 22.
SUNANDA, grass giver of Kondannya Budha, 97.
SUNANDA, father of Gotama Bódhisat, king of Puspawati, 96.
SUNANDA, queen of Kasyapa Budha, 99.
SUNANDA-ASANKYA, 95.
SUNÁPARANTAKA, a priest, 215, 259.
SUNÁPARANTAKA, a region.
SUPPIYA, an upásikáwa, 468.
SUPARNNAS, 182.
SUPRA-BUDHA, king of Kóli, a Sákya prince, father-in-law of Gótama, 63, 155.
―― punishment of, 351.
SUPRATISHTITA, a bathing place, 172.
SUPRIYÁ, daughter of Hastá, 183.
SURAMMA, a palace, 157.
Suriya Pirit, the sun's protection, 48.
SÚRYA (sun), formation of the, 66.
SURIYAWACHASÁ, daughter of the déwa Timbara, 299 ; the wife of the déwa Panchasikha, 300.
SURUCHI-BRAHMANA, name of Gótama Bódhisat, 97.
SURUCHI, a monarch, 132.
SURUCHI, queen of the Budha Kondannya, 97.
SURYA-PUTRA, the regent of the sun, 303.
Súryódgamana-sútrasanné, 14, 17.
SUSÍMA-TÁPASA, name of Gótama Bódhisat, 97.
Sútra-pitaka, 533.
SUWANA, lunar mansion, 24.
SÚYÁMA, a brahman, 151.
SWABHÁWA-SILA, 513.
SWÁMI, the ruler, 499.
SWARNNA-BHUMA, 92.

SWÁRTHIWAHANA, son of Kónágamana, 98.
SWÉTA-KUSHA, a disease (white leprosy), 137.
System of worlds, Sakwala, Dewalókas, Brahma-lókas, Rúpa brahma lókas, Arúpa brahma lókas, naraka, Lókántarika, Mahá Méru, Ajatákása, Wa'polowa, Jalapolowa, Maha-polowa, Wisayaksétra, Agnyá-sétra, Satwa-lóka, Awakása-lóka, San-skára lóka, Sala (Gal) polowa, Pas-polowa.

T.

Taking life, the crime of, 478.
TAKSÁLA, a collegiate city, 246.
TALA, measure, 31.
TAMBRAPARNNA, in Ceylon, 53.
TANHÁ, daughter of Mára, 183.
TANHANKARA, a Budha, 96.
TÁPA, a naraka, 27.
TAPASSU, a merchant becomes an upasaka, 186, 187.
TATÁGATA, 48, 91, 204, et pass.
TATRAMADYAS TOPÉKSHA, 524.
TAWUTISÁ, the déwa lóka of Sekra, 3, 11, 25, et pass.
Teacher, the, and scholar, 496.
TEJO-DHÁTU, fire, 415.
TEJO-KASINA, 485.
TELEKARNNIKA CHANDAPPRA JÓTI, a horse, 252.
TELESDHUTÁNGA, an ordinance, 259.
TEMÉ, a birth, 104.
THÁPANI QUESTIONS: seswatadrishti, ucchéda drishtirwada, ucchédrishti, séswata drishtiwada, amaráwikshépika-drishti, 490.
Theft, 482.
THINA, sleep, 434.
Things required of those who approached Budha, 388.
Things necessary to constitute the crime of taking life, 478.
Thought, sixteen different ways of production, 422.
Thúpa wansa, quoted, 366.
THUPÁRÁMA, 218.
Tigers, 17.
TILAKUNA, the three signs, 513.
TIMANDA, a fish, 13.
TIMBILI, drum, 175.
TIMI, a fish, 13.
TIMINGALA, a fish, 13, 309.
TIMIRIPINGALA, 13.

Tinduka Játaka, 116.
Tirókudha-sútra, 200, 322.
TIRTTAKAS, the 63 ; are put to shame, 300, et pass.
TIRTTÁKA, daughters of,
—— Awáwataka, 263.
—— Lalá, Patáchárá.
—— Sachá.
TISSA, a Budha, 97.
—— the disciple of Dipankara, 96.
—— principal disciple of Kásyapa, 99.
—— a priest, 261.
TISSAMETTEYYA, a brahman, 347.
TIYAGALLÁ, a rock, 17.
Transmigration, 79, et pass.
TRIKÚTA-PARWATA (rocks), 11, 45.
TRINA, caste of lions, 18.
TRISNÁWA, evil desire cleaving to existence, 449, 462, 514.
TRIWIDHADWÁRA, the three doors, 513.
TRIWIDHÁGNI, the threefold fire, 513.
TRIWIDHASAMPATTI, the threefold advantage, 513.
TRIWIDYÁWA, right understanding, 513.
Truths, the three, 288.
Truths, the four chief, 515, note.
TULÁ, a rási, white man, 23.
TUNBHAWA (TUNLÓKA), the three worlds, 26.
TUSI DÉWA-LÓKA, 474.
TUSITA, a déwa-lóka, 25, 127.

U.

UBHATO-WIBHANGA, 510.
UDACHA, disquietude, 433.
UDAYABHADDA, 133.
UDAYAGIRI, rock, 178, 191.
UDDAKA, an ascetic, 168, 188.
UDÉNA-DÉWÁLA, 343.
UDÉNIJA, country, 251.
UDHAYA, a brahman, 347.
UHÁ, a river, 328.
UHANA, combination, 431.
ULKÁMUKHA, son of Hastá, 133.
UNDU, a flower, 105.
UNDUWAP, a month, 23.
Universe, the periodical destruction and renovation of the, 28.
UNMAGAGANGA, name of the under-ground, 17.
Unprofitable conversation, 488.

Untruth, the first uttered among men, 131.
UPACHARA, a monarch, 131.
UPACHAYAN, aggregation, 418.
UPÁDÁNA, cleaving to existence, 409, 449.
UPAGHÁTA KARMA, 463.
UPAKAKA, an ajíwaka mendicant born in a brahma-lóka, 190.
UPÁLI, barber of the king, the history of, 238.
—— a grahapati, 274.
UPAPADYA-WÉDYA KARMA, 463.
UPAPIDAKA KARMA, 453.
UPÁSAKA, a lay devotee, 276, et pass.
UPASAMA, female disciple of Kakusanda, 98.
UPASAMPADÁ, an ordination, 84, 259, 354, 524.
UPÁSIKÁWAS, female lay disciples of Budha, 233.
UPASIWA, a brahman, 347.
UPASTHAMBA KARMA, 463.
UPASTHAYANA, the personal attendant (of Gótama), 96.
UPATISSA, a brahma village, 200.
UPITISSA, afterwards Seriyut, 200, et pass.
UPAWARTTANA, a garden of sal trees, 358.
UPÉKSHÁ, the power of, 524.
UPÉKSHA-PARÁMITA, virtue from equanimity, 104.
UPPHALA, formerly Krishnájiná, 127.
UPULWAN, a priestess, 63.
URDHAMUKHA, 7.
URULÁ, female disciple of Kásyapa, 99.
URUWEL KÁSYAPA, GAYÁ KÁSYAPA, NADI KÁSYAPA, three brothers, their history, 193, 196.
URUWELA FOREST, 168, 193.
URUWELÁ, female disciple of Kásyapa, 99.
USABHAKKHANDA ASANKYA, 95.
UTPALAWARNNA, a priestess, 485.
UTPHALAGANDHA, a priest, whose perfume was like the perfume of the lotus, 295.
UTRAPAL, lunar mansion, 24.
UTRAPALGUNA NEKATA, 21.
UTRAPUTUPÁ, lunar mansion, 24.
UTRASALA, lunar mansion, 24.
UTTARÁ, daughter of Púrnaka, 522.

INDEX.

UTTARA, disciple of Brahmáyu, 384.
UTTARA, disciple of Gótama Bódhisat, 99.
UTTARÁ, female disciple of Kónágamana, 99.
UTTARA, mother of Kónágamana, 98.
UTTARA, name of Gótama Bódhisat, 97.
—— the son of Kakusanda, 98.
UTTARAPANCHÁLA, a city, 131.
UTURU, a village, 341.
UTURUKURU, a continent, 194, 261, 466, et pass.
UTURUKURUDIWAYINA, 4, 14.

V.

VAISYÁS, (Waisyás) regarded by Budhists as merchants, 76, 83.
VAJRA PANI, 91.
Various orders of the sentient existence, 37.

W.

WACHIWINNYATTI, the faculty of speech, 418.
WÁDA, schism, 530.
WADHAKA, the executioner, 498.
WADHAMÁNA, a village near Danta, 480.
WADHÚRA, disciple of Kakusanda, 98.
WAGGULA PRIESTS, 310.
WAGGUMUDÁ, a river, 486.
WAISRÁWANA, a guardian déwa, 24.
WAISYÁS, caste of merchants, 68.
WAJIRÉNDRAYÁ, the cake giver of Kakusanda, 98.
WÁK (danda), speech, 274.
WÁKPRANIDHÁNA, 96.
WALLABHA, an expression of joy, 294.
WANGAHÁRA a country, 189.
WANKAGIRI, a rock, 119.
WANTÁSIKÁS PRÉTAS, 475.
WAP HAS, a month, 23.
WÁ-POLOWA, 3.
WAPPA, son of a brahman, 152.
War, a menacing about Budha's relics, 364.
WARA-KALPA, 97.
WARA-KALYÁNA, monarch, successor of Maha Sammata, 129.
WARA-MANDHÁTA, a monarch, 131.

WARARÓJA, monarch, successor of Maha Sammata, 129.
WÁRITRA-SÍLA, avoiding of all things forbidden by Gótama, 510.
Warnings, the five, 30, note.
WÁSABHAKHATTIKA, natural daughter of Maha-nama, 293.
WASANTA, the season of spring, 284.
WASAWARTTI-GHÓSÁ, Mára's drum, 175.
WASAWARTTI-MÁRA, a déwa, an evil spirit, 154, 176, 348, et pass.
—— his appearance to Gótama, 160.
WÁSETTHO, a brahman, 82, note.
WASS, a religious ordinance, 293, et pass.
WASTU, substance, 418.
WASTU-KÁMA, cleaving to existing objects, 462.
WATTAKALA, a village, 426.
WÁYOKASINA, a rite, 31, 33.
WÁYODHÁTU, wind, 415.
WÁYO-SANGWARTTA, destruction by wind, 34.
WÉBHÁRA, a rock, 495.
WÉDAGU, inward living principle, the, 452.
WÉDANÁ, sensation, 419.
WÉDANÁ-KHANDO, sensation, 418.
WÉDANÁNUPASSANÁ, 418.
Wédaná-parigrahana, 202.
WÉDANÓPÉKSHÁ, 524.
WÉDÉHA, a monarch, 133.
WEDUNNA, a rock twenty kelas from Kælani, (Kalyána), 214.
WÉHAPPALA, the tenth rúpa-brahma-lóka, 26, 33.
WELLÁLA, (Goy-wansa), the first caste among the Singhalese, 84.
WÉLUWANA, the garden of Bimsara, 198.
WÉMATIKA-SÍLA, 512.
WÉNA, a stringed instrument, 452.
WEPACHITTI, the chief of the asúrs, 48.
WERKSHAMÚLAKANGA, ordinance regarding the mode of living at the root of a tree, 338.
WESAK, a month, 23, 149.
WÉSAMUNA, the master of the revels, 52.
WESSÁ, 68.
WESSABHU, a Budha, 97.
WESSAMA, the first merchant according to the Singhalese legend, 77.

WESSANTARA, history of the king, 101.
WESSANTARA, the, birth of Bódhisat, 180.
WESSANTARA, a monarch, 133.
Wessantara Játaka, 118, 206.
WESSAWANO, a king of the Yakás, 46.
WESSO, 82, note.
WICHÁRA, investigation, 423.
WICHIKICHÁ, doubt, 433.
WIDARSANA, an ordinance, 289.
WIDARSANOPÉKSHÁ, 524.
WIDHÚRA, a nobleman, 75.
WIDÚDABHA, name of the son of the Kosol king, 294.
WIDYÁDHARAS, men performing wonders by the aid of mantras, 38.
WIDYÁMA-IRDHI, 523.
WIHÁRA, 53, 54, et pass.
WIJAYA BÁHU, son of the monarch Síha Báhu, 359.
WIJITÁ, daughter of Hastá, 133.
WIJITASÉNA, the son of the Budha Kondannya, 97, 99, 133.
WIJITÁWI-CHAKRAWARTTI, name of Gótama Bódhisat, 97.
WIJITÁWISAT, name of Gótama Bódhisat, 97.
WIJJA, a rock, 17.
WIKURWANA, (wikumbana,) the power to disappear from the sight of men, 519.
WIMANSIDHI-PÁDA, close investigation, 517.
WINATAKA, 12.
Winaya-pitaka, 239.
Winds, six different kinds of, in the body, 415.
WINYÁNA, what is the subject to consciousness, consciousness, 454, 519.
WINYÁNANCHÁYATANA, a rúpabrahma-lóka, 26.
WINYÁNA-KHANDO, faculties of consciousness, 34, 89.
WIPASSÍ, a Budha, 97.
WIPULA, a rock, 122.
WIRATI-SÍLA, 511.
WÍRAYA, persevering exertion, 424, 517.
WIRÚDHA, a guardian déwa, 24.
WIRÚPAKSHA, a guardian déwa, 24.
WÍRYA-PÁRAMITÁ, 109.
WÍRYOPÉKSHA, 524.
WISÁ, a nekata lunar mansion, 24, 149.
WISÁKHÁ, history of, 41, 53, 226.

WISÁKHÁ, queen of Amba, 133.
—— her family, 233.
—— daughter of Dhananja and Sumana, 226.
WISÁKHÁ, called Migára-Mátáwí, mother (chief) of the upásikáwas of Budha, 233.
———— mother of Kakusanda Budha, 98.
WISÁLA, city of, visited by pestilence, famine and sprites, 243.
WISAYÁ-SÉTRA, 2.
WISUDHI, the five, 429.
Wisudhi-margga, notions of the Burmese, as to its composition, 532.
Wisudhi-margga-sanné, 376, 392, 396, 457, 491, 506, 513, *described*, 530.
WISUDHI-SÍLA, 512.
WISWAKARMMA, the architect of the déwas, the wonder-worker of Sekra, 121, 154, 326.
WISWÁSA, faith, sincerity, 293.
WITARKA, attention, 423.
WIWARTTA-ASANKYA-KALPA, 5.
Wonders, the, thirty-two, at the time of the conception of Budha, 45.
Worlds, destruction of, 65.
World, the state of previous to the destruction. 34.
World, systems of the ancient nations, 12, note.
WRASHABA, a white bull, 23.
WRASHIKA, (rási) a black elk, 23.
WYÁGRAPURA, a city, (Kóli Dewudacha.
WYÁKARANA, the four kinds of questions belonging to the class, 490.
—— Ekansa,
—— Wibhajja,
—— Pratipuchhá,
—— Thápani.
WYÁPÁDA, wish to injure another.

Y.

YADÁSANNA, merit obtained when at the point of death, 507.
YADÁSANNA-KARMA, 197.
YÁGA, a sacrifice, 76.
YÁGAS, modes of sacrifice, an almsgiving, 281.
YAKA-ALAWAKA, overcome by Gótama Budha.

INDEX.

YAKÁS, the attendants of Waisrá-wana, 16, 17, 25, 31, 58, 219, et pass.
YAKADURÁ, the devil dancer, 46.
YALA, a measure, 225.
YAMA, a déwa-lóka, 25.
YAMUNA, a river, 17.
YASA, the son of Sujatá, 192.
YASÓDHARA, cake giver of Kondannya, 97.
YASÓDHARÁ-DÉWI, daughter of Supra Budha, the wife of Gótama, 155; her birth, 149, 208, 209; delivered of a prince, 159.
—— attains Nirwana, 353.
YASÓDHARÁ-DÉWI, formerly Madrí-déwí, 127.
YASÓDHARÁ-DÉWI, delivers a discourse on the seven kinds of wives, 498.
YATA-GIYA-DAWASA, the formula at the beginning of the "Játaka" in days of yore.
YATGARU KARMA, 463.
YOJANA, 11, note, et pass.
YON COUNTRY, 215.
YUGA, 7.
YUGANDHARA ROCKS, 11, 12, 15, 23.
YUWA-RAJA, secondary king, 129.